P9-ARZ-988

Fifty Years of Economic Measurement

Studies in Income and Wealth
Volume 54

National Bureau of Economic Research
Conference on Research in Income and Wealth

Fifty Years of Economic Measurement

The Jubilee of the Conference on Research in Income and Wealth

Edited by Ernst R. Berndt and Jack E. Triplett

The University of Chicago Press

Chicago and London

ERNST R. BERNDT is professor of applied economics at the Sloan School of Management, Massachusetts Institute of Technology, and a research associate of the NBER. JACK E. TRIPLETT is Chief Economist at the Bureau of Economic Analysis, U.S. Department of Commerce.

The University of Chicago Press, Chicago 60637
The University of Chicago Press, Ltd., London

Printed in the United States of America
99 98 97 96 95 94 93 92 91 90 5 4 3 2 1

Library of Congress Cataloging-in-Publication Data

Fifty years of economic measurement: the jubilee of the Conference on Research in Income and Wealth / edited by Ernst R. Berndt and Jack E. Triplett.
p. cm. — (Studies in income and wealth ; v. 54)
Contains part of the papers and discussion presented at the 50th Anniversary Conference of the Conference on Research in Income and Wealth held May 12–14, 1988, in Washington, D.C.
Includes bibliographical references and index.
ISBN 0-226-04384-3
1. Conference on Research in Income and Wealth—Congresses. 2. Income—Congresses. 3. Wealth—Congresses. 4. Saving and investment—Congresses. I. Berndt, Ernst R. II. Triplett, Jack E. III. Conference on Research in Income and Wealth. 50th Anniversary Conference (1988 : Washington, D.C.) IV. Series.
HC106.3.C714 vol. 54
[HC79.I5]
330 s—dc20
[330.1′6] 90-19371
CIP

♾ The paper used in this publication meets the minimum requirements of the American National Standard for Information Sciences—Permanence of Paper for Printed Library Materials, ANSI Z39.48-1984.

Since this volume is a record of conference proceedings, it has been exempted from the rules governing critical review of manuscripts by the Board of Directors of the National Bureau (resolution adopted 8 June 1948, as revised 21 November 1949 and 20 April 1968).

Contents

Prefatory Note

This volume contains part of the papers and discussion presented at the 50th Anniversary Conference in Washington, D.C., on 12–14 May 1988. Papers from the Jubilee Conference's "New Horizons in Data Sets" sessions, edited by Jack E. Triplett, were published in three issues of the *Survey of Current Business* (November 1988; March 1989; and May 1989).

Funds for the Conference on Research in Income and Wealth are provided to the National Bureau of Economic Research by grants from the Bureau of Economic Analysis, Statistics Canada, the Bureau of the Census, the Bureau of Labor Statistics, the Internal Revenue Service, and the National Science Foundation; we are indebted to them for their support. We also thank Ernst R. Berndt and Jack E. Triplett, who served as conference organizers and editors of this volume, and W. Erwin Diewert, who served on the conference organizing committee.

Random selection determined the order of the editors' names on the published volume.

Introduction

Ernst R. Berndt and Jack E. Triplett

This volume contains papers presented at a conference in May 1988 in Washington, D.C., commemorating the fiftieth anniversary of the founding of the Conference on Research in Income and Wealth (CRIW). As is apparent from Carol S. Carson's early history of the CRIW, the celebration itself was late. A proper observation of the actual anniversary date would have occurred a couple of years earlier. It is also true that the publication date for this anniversary volume prolongs the anniversary interval yet more, for despite the availability of modern computerized publication technology, the present editors have failed to duplicate Milton Friedman's editorial feat of bringing into publication the first three volumes of the Studies in Income and Wealth series in the same year in which each of those conferences was held. Future historians may determine whether this is evidence of a decline in efficiency, of increased consumption on the job, of substitution of capital (quality) for labor (quality), or of some as yet undetermined measurement error.

The call for papers emphasized assessments of broad topics in economic measurement, both conceptual and pragmatic. The organizers desired (and succeeded in obtaining) a mix of papers that, first, illustrate the range of measurement issues that economics as a science must confront and, second, mark major milestones of CRIW accomplishment. The papers concern prices and output (Griliches, Pieper, Triplett) and also the major productive inputs, capital (Hulten) and labor (Hamermesh). Measures of saving, the source of capital accumulation, are covered in one paper (Boskin); measuring productivity, the source of much of the growth in per capita income, is reviewed in another (Jorgenson). The use of economic data in economic policy analysis and in regulation are illustrated in a review of measures of tax burden (Atrostic and Nunns) and in an analysis of the data needed for environmental regulation (Russell and Smith); the adequacy of data for policy analysis is evaluated in a roundtable discussion (chapter 12) involving four distinguished policy analysts with extensive government experience in Washington and Ottawa.

Some of the papers present historical assessments (relevant to a fiftieth anniversary occasion). Others, consistent with our belief that the need for research on measurement in economics has in no way been diminished by the substantial progress that has occurred over 50 years, examine developing needs for data and work yet to be done in economic measurement. The reader can determine the quality and usefulness of the contents of this volume, but we are pleased that it contains both historical and forward-looking papers on economic measurement, as befits the jubilee celebrated in Washington in May 1988.

Perhaps the high point of the jubilee was a luncheon honoring individuals and institutions that participated in the first Income and Wealth conference held December 1936/January 1937. Remarks of six economists who attended that first meeting are contained in the edited transcript of the luncheon that is part of the present volume. Also attending the luncheon were thirteen other individuals whose writings appear in the first five volumes of Studies in Income and Wealth. One forms the conclusion that working in the area of economic measurement is conducive to longevity. Another conclusion is that, in the days when the CRIW had its beginning, economic measurement occupied some of the best minds in economics, as perusal of the distinguished careers of the honored guests at this special luncheon will prove. The transcript of the luncheon provides a unique tie to the past and an inspiration for the future.

1 The Conference on Research in Income and Wealth: The Early Years

Carol S. Carson

Since its formation in 1936, the Conference on Research in Income and Wealth has been an important force in the development of the national income field. In terms of the topics discussed and the people participating, the conference has changed as the field itself has changed. Yet, over the years, the papers and discussions presented at the conference and published in the volumes of the Studies in Income and Wealth series are evidence of a remarkable vigor.

The formation of the conference, which for several years had "national" in its title as a modifier of income and wealth, was responsive to the institutional needs of the National Bureau of Economic Research and the stage of development of the national income field. Simon Kuznets recounts that the need for a more systematic relation between the National Bureau and the universities was perceived. The Bureau, by its charter, was never attached to any particular university, yet it was obvious that it was supplying material for academic investigation (Kuznets 1969). In 1935 the National Bureau invited the economics departments of six universities to join with it in developing a program of cooperative research. The outgrowth was the formation of a Universities–National Bureau Committee to consider plans and procedures. This committee selected two fields that it believed could be cultivated through cooperation of numerous agencies and in which the National Bureau had special competence. Two conferences—one on research in national income and wealth, the other on price research—were organized.

A Conference on National Income and Wealth was called in January 1936, and it became a permanent body on its own initiative. At the time there were representatives from the economics departments of six universities (Chicago, Columbia, Harvard, Minnesota, Pennsylvania, and Wisconsin); the U.S. De-

Carol S. Carson is deputy director of the Bureau of Economic Analysis, U.S. Department of Commerce.

partments of Commerce (Bureau of Foreign and Domestic Commerce), Agriculture, Treasury, and Labor (Bureau of Labor Statistics); the National Resources Committee; the Board of Governors of the Federal Reserve System; the Central Statistical Board; the National Industrial Conference Board; Dun and Bradstreet; and the National Bureau of Economic Research.[1] The purposes of the conference were:

1. to exchange information among the various organizations and individuals carrying on or planning studies in the field, in order to prevent overlapping, to establish conditions for more intelligent division of work, and to facilitate cooperative activity;
2. to agree upon the most appropriate concepts, terminology, and methods of exposition;
3. to work out plans for research, calling attention to the particular segments of the field that demand more primary data or more analytical study;
4. to stimulate cooperative research in the field by initiating and sponsoring cooperative studies, and by using the facilities of the conference to assist in their prosecution (NBER 1937, xvii).

An executive committee was formed to plan conference meetings and carry out other administrative tasks. Simon Kuznets was the first chairman, and Milton Friedman was the first secretary. Topics were put on the program either because people already had projects underway or, in some cases, by assignment. Kuznets tried to plan the meetings about two years in advance, in the hope that the conference might precipitate completion of statistical work or some special application. It was also possible to adjust the agenda to accommodate a subject that members were anxious to discuss (Kuznets 1969).

The procedures for the early conference meetings established a tradition. Generally papers were circulated in advance; only summaries of the papers were presented at the actual meetings. Assigned discussants made comments, and remarks were received from the floor. Subsequent to the meeting, written comments could be submitted to the author, who had the opportunity to revise his paper. When the proceedings were published, as they usually were, these comments were also included.

Economic events were partly responsible for the keen interest in the subject of national income. Because the subject matter up to that time had been cultivated by people who had broken new ground, differences in approach, terminology, and rankings or priorities were not uncommon. The conference successfully combined people with academic and government affiliations and was thus able to cover a broad spectrum of topics.

The constructive force of the conference was especially felt in two areas

1. Shortly thereafter, representatives of the Census Bureau, the Brookings Institution, the Federal Deposit Insurance Corporation, the American Statistical Association, and the University of Cincinnati joined the conference.

during the early years. The first was terminology and concepts. Carl S. Shoup later commented: "The development of a common technical vocabulary has been one of the major achievements of the Conference" (Shoup 1948, 290). In accordance with the instructions of the conference, the Executive Committee in 1936 set up a committee on concepts and terminology, consisting of Morris A. Copeland, as chairman, Winfield W. Riefler, and Simon Kuznets. The task of the committee was "to prepare a report containing a clear exposition of the various terms, with the object of bringing about a better understanding of their significance and application and thereby helping to promote a greater uniformity of usage" (NBER 1936, 16).

The January 1937 meeting of the conference had before it several reports initiated by this committee. The papers included Morris A. Copeland's "Concepts of National Income," Solomon Fabricant's "On the Treatment of Corporate Savings in the Measurement of National Income," and Simon Kuznets's "Changing Inventory Valuations and Their Effect on Business Savings and on National Income Produced" (NBER 1937).

One of the terminological issues dealt with in these papers and in lengthy discussion at the meeting was the designation of the main income aggregate. In particular, conference participants debated the advisability of retaining the designations "national income produced" and "national income paid out" that had been used in *National Income, 1929–32* (U.S. Congress 1934). In that document, prepared under Simon Kuznets's direction by the U.S. Department of Commerce with the cooperation of the National Bureau, "national income produced" was used to refer to the net product of the national economy. The total of compensation in money or in kind for efforts in producing the net product was called "national income paid out." In general terms, the difference between national income produced and national income paid out is that the former includes saving by business establishments, but the latter does not. Kuznets later reported:

> It was concluded that the use of the two terms . . . as equally important concepts created confusion and led to misinterpretations; that the term "national income" should be reserved for the magnitude formerly called "national income produced" as being the most inclusive category and most consonant with the national income concept in economic writings; and that the magnitude formerly called "national income paid out," being a subdivision of national income, would be best described by a specific term." (Kuznets 1937, 4)

Kuznets, in his work for the National Bureau, immediately made the terminological change, calling his former "national income paid out" by the new name "aggregate income payments to individuals." In November 1938, when "Income in the United States, 1929–37" was released, the Department of Commerce still used the earlier designations. However, in defining "national income produced," it was parenthetically added that it "might better be termed merely the 'national income' because it is the most inclusive concept" (U.S. Department of Commerce 1938, 3). By June 1939, Robert Nathan's by-then annual article in the *Survey of Current Business* featured "national income" as the most inclusive concept (Nathan 1939). For a short while, "national income paid out" was called "income paid out," without "national" as a modifier, and then "total shares transferred by business enterprises." It was discontinued when "income payments to individuals," a forerunner of present-day "personal income," proved more useful as a measure of distributed income.

To be sure, agreement such as this was not reached in all cases. However, by 1939, when the third volume of the Studies in Income and Wealth series was published, the preface described the following accomplishments in dealing with conceptual and terminological issues:

> But they [the first two volumes] have served the function of laying bare the nature of and reasons for the divergencies, of setting forth the border areas where disagreement is sharp, and of making explicit the assumptions concerning them. We can now formulate, as we could not so clearly before, three major questions about the constitution and measurement of national income on which there is a fundamental division of opinion: first, whether capital gains and losses should be included in the income total; second, whether the net value product of illegal enterprises should be included in the income total; and third, how the services rendered by government should be valued. (NBER 1939, viii)

The preface of the third volume further noted that, while the papers of the first two volumes were devoted primarily to issues related to total national income and wealth, every paper of the third volume dealt with the division of a national total into meaningful constituents. In the third volume, three papers, by C. L. Merwin, Jr., Charles Stewart, and Enid Baird and Selma Fine, dealt with the division of the total among groups classified by size of income or of wealth holdings; a paper by R. W. Goldsmith dealt with the portion of income that is saved; a paper by Clark Warburton dealt with allocations among kinds of goods and services; and papers by R. R. Nathan and P. H. Wueller dealt with allocations of income by state.

The first Studies in Income and Wealth volumes were the proceedings from three consecutive annual meetings of the conference—in 1937, 1938, and 1939. Thereafter, the one-to-one correspondence between volumes and meetings did not hold for several years. The 1940 meeting of the conference was devoted primarily to discussion that seemed to be of "insufficient general interest to warrant publication" (NBER 1941, 1). The papers for the 1941 meeting centered around two themes—the uses of income estimates and the relation between the defense effort and national income. The first group included papers by Oscar C. Altman and Thomas C. Blaisdell, Jr., on uses of income estimates in measuring consumer welfare, planning public works, and analyzing fiscal and monetary policy; Eleanor L. Dulles on uses by the Social Security Board; Wroe Anderson on uses for market analysis; Louis H. Bean on uses in agricultural research and policy; and John C. Driver on use in estimating Federal tax revenues. The second group included papers by Gardner C. Means, Gerhard Colm, W. L. Crum, and Rollin F. Bennett. These papers, too, were not published, because it was recognized "that interest in the subject matter of some of the papers was restricted, and that some of the others were primarily of temporary . . . concern" (NBER 1941, 1). The fourth volume did not present the proceedings of a meeting; instead it represented the conference's efforts to stimulate and sponsor studies in the field of income and wealth measurement. As described in the foreword, in publishing *Outlay and Income in the United States, 1921–1938* by Harold Barger, the conference saw its role as "making available a stimulating and useful study . . . without endorsing the author's method in detail or underwriting his results" (Barger 1942, ix, x).

In the meantime, work on the second area in which the conference was an especially constructive force in the early years—preparation of distributions of income by size—was coming to fruition. The absence of data and studies on size distributions among consumer units, particularly on a consistent basis over time and by region, was generally seen as the biggest gap in the income field. The conference tried to remedy the situation in at least four ways.

First, Merwin's paper in the third volume of Studies in Income and Wealth reviewed the already-published distributions of income and wealth by size, concluding with some discussion of why they had been relatively inadequate. Second, advisory work in connection with the plans of the 1940 census led to the inclusion of income questions on the population schedule. Third, in 1938 the conference had initiated the preparation of a handbook of the more important recent studies of the distribution of personal income by size. A committee consisting of Milton Friedman, as chairman, Dorothy Brady, Clark Warburton, and C. Lowell Harris carried out the work, which resulted in the fifth volume of Studies in Income and Wealth (NBER 1943). The first part of that volume opened with a chapter on "The Why and How of Distributions of Income by Size" by Simon Kuznets. It then provided, as the work of the committee, a summary of the 16 most important U.S. studies on the distribution of income and a set of recommendations for the coordination of future research. Part 2 to volume 5 (mimeographed) presented the studies that were summarized in part 1. Fourth, close contact was also maintained with three state studies—for Wisconsin, Delaware, and Minnesota—of distribution of income by size in local areas (Kuznets 1940).

The conference's activities through its tenth anniversary in 1946 led to six more volumes of Studies in Income and Wealth. Two volumes—*Changes in Income Distribution during the Great Depression* by Horst Mendershausen and *Analysis of Wisconsin Income* by Frank A. Hanna, Joseph A. Pechman, and Sidney M. Lerner—were the further results of the conference's continuing support of work on size distributions. The four others—presenting the proceedings from the meetings in 1942, 1944, 1945, and 1946—reflected, as would be expected, strong interest in the problems of the war and postwar adjustment. However, they show a broadening scope. For example, they included papers on labor-force data, forecasting, and international comparisons and standardization of methods. With regard to the last, Edward F. Denison's report in the tenth volume, on the 1944 meeting of representatives of the estimating agencies of the United Kingdom, Canada, and the United States, is of particular interest. This meeting had been set up to discuss mutual conceptual and methodological problems and, to the extent possible, to bring about uniform terminology and treatments.

By the mid-1940s, Richard Stone, in referring economists and statisticians to work in the field, could say that the conference's publications "provide a mine of information on many topics, theoretical and practical" (Stone 1947, 96). This evaluation, coming from a contemporary who was already recognized as a world leader in the field, suggests the breadth and pervasiveness of the conference's influence during these early years.

References

Barger, Harold. 1942. *Outlay and Income in the United States, 1921–1938*. New York: National Bureau of Economic Research.

Kuznets, Simon. 1937. *National Income and Capital Formation, 1919–1935*. New York: National Bureau of Economic Research.

———. 1940. National and Regional Measures of Income. *Southern Economic Journal* 6 (January): 308–10.

———. 1969. Interview with author. Cambridge, Mass., October.

Nathan, Robert R. 1939. National Income in 1938 at 64 Billion Dollars. *Survey of Current Business* 19 (June): 10–16.

NBER. 1936. Bulletin no. 60 (June 30).

———. 1937. *Studies in Income and Wealth*, vol. 1. New York: National Bureau of Economic Research.

———. 1939. *Studies in Income and Wealth*, vol. 3. New York: National Bureau of Economic Research.

———. 1941. Preface. In the collection of papers for the May 1941 meeting of the Conference on Research in Income and Wealth. Mimeo.

———. 1943. *Income Size Distributions*. Studies in Income and Wealth, vol. 5, pt. 1. New York: National Bureau of Economic Research.

Shoup, Carl S. 1948. Development and Use of National Income Data. In *A Survey of Contemporary Economics*, vol. 1, ed. Howard S. Ellis. Homewood, Ill.: Irwin, for the American Economic Association.

Stone, Richard. 1947. Definitions and Measurement of the National Income and Related Totals. Appendix to *Measurement of National Income and Construction of Social Accounts*. Studies and Reports on Statistical Methods no. 7. Geneva: United Nations.

U.S. Congress. Senate. 1934. *National Income, 1929–32*. 73rd Cong., 2d sess. S. Doc. 124. (An article with the same title appeared in the February 1934 *Survey of Current Business*.)

U.S. Department of Commerce. Bureau of Foreign and Domestic Commerce. 1938. Income in the United States, 1929–37. Report prepared by Robert R. Nathan. Mimeograph.

2 Luncheon in Honor of Individuals and Institutions Participating in the First Income and Wealth Conference (December 1936–January 1937)

Roy Blough, Solomon Fabricant, Martin Feldstein, Milton Friedman, Robert R. Nathan, and Carl Sumner Shoup

Martin Feldstein

This fiftieth birthday party for the Conference on Research in Income and Wealth is an occasion to recognize and honor some of those who were present in the beginning and who helped to establish and put this organization on the very productive track that it has been on for these 50 years.

Let me begin by recognizing the honored guests here today who participated in the first Income and Wealth conference and whose work appears in Studies in Income and Wealth, volume 1.

The first is my friend Sol Fabricant, who indeed was there at the creation and contributed a paper to the first volume: "On the Treatment of Corporate Savings in the Measurement of National Income." Sol, of course, has had a lifetime attachment to the Conference on Research in Income and Wealth and to the National Bureau of Economic Research. He was the director of research at the NBER from 1953–65. He has been a member of the Board of Directors at the bureau ever since I have been associated with it. He is an emeritus research associate at the present time and continues to be an active participant in board meetings.

Next is Carl Shoup. I think of myself as a bit of a student of Carl Shoup's, although I never sat in his classroom. I had his big book on public finance on my shelf, I read through it, and I considered it a very critical part of my education as a public finance economist. His early participation in the Conference on Research in Income and Wealth shows how some of the issues that

Roy Blough is S. Sloan Colt Professor Emeritus of Banking and International Finance at Columbia University. Solomon Fabricant is the late professor emeritus at New York University and senior research staff emeritus for the National Bureau of Economic Research. Martin Feldstein is professor of economics at Harvard University and president of the National Bureau of Economic Research. Milton Friedman is a senior research fellow at the Hoover Institution at Stanford University. Robert R. Nathan is chair of Robert R. Nathan Associates, Inc. Carl Sumner Shoup is professor emeritus at Columbia University.

were being dealt with in the tax area were also being discussed at the same time in the national income measurement area. Indeed, the paper that he wrote for volume 1 was called "The Distinction Between 'Net' and 'Gross' in Income Taxation."

There was a young man at that first conference who was a discussant of Carl Shoup's paper, and he is here today also. He is known to us much more as a distinguished professor of economics at Columbia, and that is Roy Blough.

One of the great strengths of this organization has always been its ability to bring together people from the government and people from academia. The next person from the first income and wealth conference is an example, because Robert Nathan, at the time that he attended the first meeting as a member of the executive committee of the Conference on Research in Income and Wealth, was the director of the National Income Division of the Department of Commerce, having worked earlier with Simon Kuznets on the development of national income accounts. In the second conference he collaborated on a paper: "Problems in Estimating National Income Arising from Production by Government."

Simon Kuznets' personal devotion to measurement and to the understanding of the broad issues of income growth and capital formation made him the natural patron saint for the Conference on Research in Income and Wealth. Simon's early research assistant and the first secretary/editor of the conference, Milton Friedman, could not be with us, but his letter, reproduced below, describes his and Simon's roles in those early days.

Solomon Fabricant

There has been some talk at the conference and elsewhere about the aging of the population. I am amazed at the number of people that returned for this fiftieth reunion. I've been worrying about the hundredth anniversary of this outfit and how many people will be able to come after another 50 years. There is going to be a financial problem, Marty.

What happened at the first conference that might be mentioned to you people? Well a couple of things stick in my mind. One, which Martin mentioned, was that Milton Friedman was the first secretary of the conference and the first editor of the conference volume. I still remember him as a remarkably good editor, the best I have ever encountered. And I have been thinking over the years that if he had only stuck with that . . . [laughter] . . . if he had only stuck with that he might have amounted to something!

Another thing about the first conference was recalled to me by a story in the *Times* only a few weeks ago about the Pennzoil-Texaco problem. You remember Texaco had to pay several billion dollars to Pennzoil, and the story said that the Federal Reserve's computers couldn't handle the transfers because the computers were limited to $999,999,999.99—they could not handle a billion dollars. There is another very similar story that occurred in the 1930s. I was thumbing through Statistics of Income—thumbing through is not quite the word, I was working very hard on it—in the middle 1930s, and I took some first differences. The figures did not look right. I wrote to Edward White, who was then the chief statistician of the Internal Revenue Service, and asked him what was wrong. Well, he looked into it, which took some time in those days, and then wrote back and told me. All the figures were right, except the first two digits [laughter]. They were right down to the last penny—except the first digits. And the reason was very simple. The computer at that time—punch card equipment, rather—could not handle the number of digits that were involved in adding up the total net worth of all the corporations in the United States. So they had to make back-of-the-envelope calculations on the first two digits. They finally published a correction on it.

Well, I have got to admit that there has been a lot of progress in the Income and Wealth Conference. In the 1930s I remember having to argue with economists as to whether inventories were a part of the capital stock and whether the services of inventories ought to be included in measuring the services of capital. Their argument was: Inventories just sit there. They do not do anything, how could they provide services? And the same kind of question came up in connection with salaried employees. Salaried employees do not do anything, they are just Civil Service, they just sit there.

The National Bureau and the conference have been great educational institutions. Looking at it from another point of view, and my participation in them, they have been great adventures. So I want to express my thanks and appreciation for the good luck of being involved in all of this. Thank you.

Carl Shoup

Let me just reminisce briefly about the early days at the first conference. Certainly the Conference on Research in Income and Wealth did a great deal to inform public finance about the need to take into account national income in all its branches in designing public finance instruments and public finance policy. Of course, the data collected for use in tax policy come largely from national income definitions and we have to ask ourselves to what extent they are compatible; if not, what changes do we need to make? Beyond that, my own personal experience was that that first Conference on Research in National Income and Wealth propelled me into a sector of economic activity I probably would never have gotten into otherwise, and for better or worse led to the publication of a book, *Principles of National Income Analysis*. More to the point, I like to think that it informed a good deal of the work that I and my colleagues did and many of our tax reports.

The atmosphere at the early days, as I recall the first conference, was very, very congenial and encouraged a younger person to get into the intellectual fray and try to develop ideas. It was a permissive and stimulating atmosphere, which I always remember with very fond memory indeed. And, of course that goes back to, among other people, Simon Kuznets, and the sort of open, free, investigative atmosphere in the sense of research that prevailed there. I like to think, anyway, that public finance in the United States at least has been greatly influenced, and influenced for the better, by that early formation of the Conference on Research in Income and Wealth. Thank you.

Roy Blough

If I had not found the book [Studies in Income and Wealth, vol. 1] and found the article I discussed, I would not believe I was ever there!

I wish the Conference had come into existence about 10 years earlier. I was at Wisconsin and we had some wonderful statistics there, which later on were taken over by Joe Pechman and others. We could have done a lot more with them.

In fact, we did try to do something with them but socialism made it impossible. And I will tell you how that is. We got Hollarith machines in, in order to analyze the three-year averaging provision we had in the law. However, the Capitol had an electrical system which had been put in somewhat earlier, and was direct current. It fluctuated so widely that the Hollarith machines refused to behave, and our cross-classifications, which had all the good meat in them, were completely useless. So we could have used the conference, because an amateur like I was in those days was not really able to do much.

I had a piece in Studies in Income and Wealth, volume 1, and I had a piece in the second volume but I did not have anything after that because I went to the Treasury Department, and in one way I became less concerned with national income statistics and in another way I became more concerned with them. Anyway, I greatly appreciated the opportunity to be at the first conference. I owe it, I think, to Carl Shoup who was one of the first people to recognize that I was even alive in the economics profession and I have always appreciated that. And by the way, I appreciate the fact that, while I was there, I am still here! Thank you.

Robert R. Nathan

I really owe a tremendous debt of gratitude to Simon Kuznets because I had the privilege of being a student of his. Then when I decided to leave the University of Pennsylvania and came to Washington I walked into the Division of Economic Research and I saw Simon and said, "What are you doing here?" and he said, "What are you doing here?" Fortunately that afternoon he asked that I be assigned to him, and I was, and I worked on that first national income study and followed through with it for years.

What I regard as one of the great, great benefits of the national income work had to do with World War II's mobilization effort. As you remember, those of you that were around then, President Roosevelt had promised that he would never get the United States into the war, but in 1940 when I moved over to the Defense Advisory Commission, the main problem immediately was: What if we got into a war? So we did something that amounted to a full-employment national product, to see what the economy's requirements would be at full employment. One of the first bottlenecks we foresaw was the fact that we would have to expand our steel capacity. The steel industry said "You're crazy! Six years ago we were running at 15%–20% capacity, we're now at about 60%, and you're talking about expanding capacity." Well we did get an expansion, but that approach really helped.

Then in 1941 we never could get military requirements from the army and navy. And when we finally did, they said they would need 300,000 airplanes, 200,000 tanks or something, and before you knew it, the military ran to the Congress for unlimited appropriations, and they had probably 150 million tons of steel requirements scheduled instead of the 90 available. We were in a mess.

By that time Simon Kuznets had come down to Washington to work with us in the planning committee. I do not think many people recognized he was such a militant warrior, military oriented person. But he was magnificent. We did a little feasibility study, this study was geared to national income analysis. We gave this study to the War Production Board. Most of them were impressed, but they sent it over to the military. There was a general, very able but he thought all civilians were slightly cracked, and the military had the only real capability. Anyhow, he wrote a memo saying that he had reviewed this study, and he was unimpressed and therefore it should be kept from the eyes of thoughtful men [laughter]. In our reply, we went through and explained how you had to schedule things out, and we did it by years, and we explained all that to him again. I ended up by saying, "Your conclusion, that you are unimpressed, and therefore that it should be kept from the eyes of thoughtful men, is a non sequitur." If I could have been shot, I guess it legitimately could have been then.

The national income approach in the war mobilization effort—I think everyone who was involved there would agree—made a major contribution, because while Europe was hanging on by its fingernails it was American production and the promptness of that response to the victory program that made it possible that Britain was saved and the war ended. That was of major, major significance. So anybody interested in this field can look back on one very, very significant contribution right off the bat. Thanks.

Milton Friedman

The Conference on Research in Income and Wealth was a brainchild of Simon Kuznets. That explains my own connection with it. At the time of its first meeting, I was working as a research assistant to Simon Kuznets. We were working on the book that was later published under the title *Professional Incomes in the United States*. It in turn was an offshoot of Simon's work at the Department of Commerce in developing the original national income estimates. As part of that project, he had arranged for the collection of questionnaire data from lawyers, physicians, engineers, accountants, and other independent professionals to use as a basis for estimating their contributions to national income. Our joint project was to exploit that data for a broader purpose.

When he and others set up the conference, he asked me to serve as its secretary, which I did for some years, in particular editing volumes 1–3. At the time, the Keynesian revolution was in its infancy and national income accounting was in an early and highly transitional stage with many unresolved issues. All of the pioneers in that field participated in the Conference on Research in Income and Wealth. Needless to say, for a young man in his mid-twenties not long out of graduate school, my own participation proved an extremely stimulating and fascinating experience. Simon Kuznets's extraordinary tolerance and breadth of vision explains the wide range of persons who were involved in the work of the Conference, from highly statistical types at one extreme to highly theoretical types at the other extreme. Personally, I was a product of the University of Chicago, which gave me an extremely strong orientation toward theory, but also of Wesley Mitchell at Columbia and at the National Bureau, which emphasized a statistical and empirical orientation. As I recall it, what impressed me was the fruitfulness of combining the two strands of work, a view that I know Simon shared, although his orientation was far more statistical and empirical than my own.

As in any new venture, the early years are unquestionably the most exciting and productive. One of the most important developments instituted during those early years was emphasis on the distribution of income reflected in the various studies of Delaware and Wisconsin incomes as well as in a number of volumes of the conference proceedings.

My own involvement with the conference changed greatly when I left the National Bureau in 1940 to spend a year at the University of Wisconsin and then, when the war broke out, in government. As I recall it, I continued to participate in a desultory way in the activities of the Conference, even though my work turned in a very different direction. Yet I never again was as closely related to it as I was in its first three or four formative years.

It is impressive that it has continued to be a productive and important organization for enough years to justify a jubilee celebration. Clearly, the problems it deals with are not transitory and will not go away. New issues arise and new issues must be dealt with. More power to the conference.

Martin Feldstein

On an anniversary occasion like this it is important not just to look back but also to take a moment to look ahead, and so I will comment briefly on what I see as the future of the Conference on Research in Income and Wealth.

Even before I became actively involved with the National Bureau, I thought of the Conference on Research in Income and Wealth as one of the central activities of the National Bureau. I continue to believe that the Conference on Research in Income and Wealth is a very special part of the National Bureau's activities, in two unique ways.

Perhaps the single most important thing is that it is a partnership between economists in government and economists in the university. The early history of the conference, contained in this volume, makes it clear how at that time those two groups worked together. The Conference on Research in Income and Wealth continues to provide a unique forum for that kind of interaction within our profession, a unique opportunity to work together—government statisticians, government economists, academic economists—to improve economic statistics, to improve their conceptual and operational basis.

The subjects that have been discussed at the Conference on Research in Income and Wealth over the years are really central to what I think of as the mission of the National Bureau. Unfortunately that stands rather in contrast to much of the work of the economics profession today. As you all know, the Conference on Research in Income and Wealth focuses on improving economic measurement, not only measurement of income and wealth, strictly speaking, but also on the activities that contribute to the generation of income and wealth in the economy—improvements in the measurement of employment and unemployment, productivity, trade, and the like.

I think the need to improve our economic statistics in these areas is as important today as it was 50 years ago, although I agree with Sol Fabricant's comment that progress has been made. In the past 50 years we have seen a great many improvements, not only in our conceptual understanding but also in the availability of data and the availability of resources for the analysis of that data. Who could have imagined at those early Conference on Research in Income and Wealth meetings that now, 50 years later, we would have mountains of machine-readable data with the first two digits correct, that we would have computers that did not fail because of direct current, and that we would have these kinds of statistical tools in the hands of every graduate student.

Yet, I continue to think that there is as much need today for the work of the Conference on Research in Income and Wealth as there was 50 years ago—perhaps even more. The interests of the economics profession as a whole have strayed from the issues that impelled the Conference on Research in Income and Wealth in its original days. The profession has strayed from measurement and from serious empirical work to a greater emphasis on theory and to empirical studies that are often much more interesting methodologically than they are substantively. In addition to this shift within the profession, there have also been important changes in the economy itself. A more complex and a more sophisticated economy presents new challenges to economic measurement.

This is well illustrated by two measurement innovations that are among the principal research tools developed historically within the National Bureau. The most central of these is the National Income and Product Accounts. As you all know, that has been one of the seminal contributions of the National Bureau to the economics profession, to national policymaking, and was also the focus of much of the early work in the Conference on Research in Income and Wealth. But over the years, as the character of the economy's output has changed, I think we need to change and improve our measurement tools.

Consider services, for example—health care output, educational output, output of financial services. Services, as Victor Fuchs' book pointed out some years ago,[1] are an ever-increasing share of employment in the economy and now about two-thirds of all of the employment. How well do we actually measure the output in the service sector? If we do not do it very well, then what is the meaning of the GNP that we attribute to those sectors, or the productivity of the employees in those sectors? Or, what is the meaning of the measure of inflation that we use?

A second aspect is the quality of products. When economic growth meant largely more of the same products, it was relatively easy to think about measuring growth and inflation; now, so much of the year-to-year change is change in the quality of products, either improvements or, occasionally, deterioration. An increasingly affluent society wants better products—style and quality—not merely more products, and we see that when we talk as individuals about automobiles, or about hi-fi equipment, or about restaurants, or

1. Victor R. Fuchs, ed., *Production and Productivity in the Service Industries,* NBER Studies in Income and Wealth, vol. 34 (1969).

about clothing. How capable are we as a profession of measuring quality changes? Yet, allowing for quality change is clearly critical to the basic measurement of output, productivity, and inflation.

Another one of the major measurement tools that came out of the National Bureau is the flow of funds accounts. The FOF is a very useful tool for anybody concerned with financial market analysis. Today, there is a major new challenge to the flow of funds accounts, and that is the internationalization of our financial markets. Last year, as you know, we had about a $150 billion net capital inflow into the United States—that represented more than a third of all the net savings flow accumulated in the country. On a gross basis, the international capital flows were substantially larger. To undertake the analysis for which the flow of funds accounts were originally intended, we need to go beyond domestic flow of funds accounts to understand better interflows of funds in international markets.

I hope these two examples indicate why I think the kind of fundamental work of the Conference on Research in Income and Wealth deserves a bigger role in the profession and deserves a bigger role at the National Bureau. With this collaboration of academic economists and the talent in the government service, we can make real progress, and I think there is a need to do more of that. It is also very important for the Conference on Research in Income and Wealth to focus on these measurement issues. There is always the temptation to become another one of the dozens of conferences or projects that try to explain economic behavior, try to model the economy as a whole, try to analyze the effects of alternative government policies. Obviously those are very important activities and they are activities in which the National Bureau also plays a significant role, but I think the Conference on Income and Wealth is really unique and has a unique function. The conference provides the bedrock conceptual and quantitative work on which all further economic analysis must be based. I hope that we can continue and strengthen that tradition for the Conference on Research in Income and Wealth's second 50 years.

3 Productivity and Economic Growth

Dale W. Jorgenson

3.1 Introduction

The purpose of this chapter is to commemorate fifty years of research on economic measurement. I have chosen a theme—economic growth and its sources—that has played a highly significant and continuing role in the Conference on Research in Income and Wealth. Economic growth was a major professional concern of Simon Kuznets, the founder of the conference. During the last quarter of his life, Kuznets (1971) devoted much of his prodigious energy and talent to the study of economic growth. A sizable portion of the research on economic growth that I will review first appeared in the conference proceedings, Studies in Income and Wealth. Finally, growth is currently undergoing a dramatic resurgence in interest among economists. This interest is motivated in large part by practical concerns arising from the great slowdown in economic growth that occurred during the 1970s and has continued to the present.

Until very recently the study of sources of economic growth has been based on the notion of an aggregate production function. This concept is one of those masterful simplifications that make it possible to summarize a welter of detailed information within a single overarching framework. It is also a concept that seems tailor-made for the interpretation of data on output, input, and productivity of the type compiled in national product accounts. At the same time the concept of an aggregate production function is highly problematical, requiring very stringent assumptions on production patterns at the level of individual sectors of the economy. Intuitively speaking, the technology of each sector must contain a replica of the aggregate production function. It will be useful to spell out the assumptions underlying the aggregate production function and their implications in more detail below.

Dale W. Jorgenson is the Frederic Eaton Abbe Professor of Economics at Harvard University.

The origins of the concept of an aggregate production function can be clearly identified in the work of Paul H. Douglas and his associates. It is important to distinguish carefully between the notion of an aggregate production function and Douglas's more frequently cited contribution, the linear logarithmic or Cobb-Douglas functional form. Douglas did not make this distinction himself, but the existence of an aggregate production function is implied by the way he used the Cobb-Douglas function. Douglas introduced the aggregate production function in 1928 and pursued its empirical implementation with single-mindedness and determination until his election as U.S. senator from Illinois in 1948. He returned to the topic after his retirement from the Senate. His last contribution, published posthumously in 1976, appeared almost half a century after his initial paper. Douglas's body of empirical research is one of the major achievements in economic measurement of the first half of the twentieth century.

At first, Douglas and his collaborators worked in isolation, but their work gradually attracted the interest of other economists. The starting point for our discussion of economic growth is a notable but neglected article by the great Dutch economist, Jan Tinbergen, published in German in 1942.[1] Tinbergen's contribution is clearly recognizable as one of the earliest formulations of what we now call the neoclassical theory of economic growth. The supply side of the model was based on an aggregate production function. However, Tinbergen took a critical step beyond the conception employed by Douglas. He added a time trend to the function of capital and labor inputs, representing the level of "efficiency." Tinbergen's work languished in obscurity until the mid-1950s, when it was revived by Stefan Valavanis-Vail (1955). In the meantime, the notion of efficiency or total factor productivity was introduced independently by George J. Stigler (1947) and became the starting point for a major research program at the National Bureau of Economic Research.

The National Bureau program involved such pioneers of economic measurement as Moses Abramovitz and Solomon Fabricant and culminated in the epoch-making monograph by John W. Kendrick, *Productivity Trends in the United States,* published in 1961. Kendrick's work focused on the United States and employed an explicit system of national production accounts, including measures of output, input, and productivity for national aggregates and individual industries. The production account incorporated data on outputs from earlier studies by the National Bureau, especially the work of Kuznets (1961) on national product. The input side employed data from other research work at the National Bureau, including data on capital from Raymond Goldsmith's (1962) system of national wealth accounts. However, much of the data was generated by Kendrick himself. Kendrick's achievement is an important milestone in the progress of economic measurement during the second half of the twentieth century.

The contributions of Douglas and Tinbergen were integrated with the national product accounts generated by Kendrick (1956) in Robert Solow's frequently cited 1957 article, "Technical Change and the Aggregate Production Function." This article unified the economic theory of production, econometric methods for fitting production functions, and the generation of production accounts at the national level. Solow's work is solidly within the tradition of production modeling established by Douglas and extended by Tinbergen, but it goes beyond this tradition by generating index numbers appropriate to econometric modeling. Solow's approach was instrumental in the further extensions of Douglas's framework by Arrow, Chenery, Minhas, and Solow (1961), introducing the elasticity of substitution as a parameter to be estimated by econometric methods.

An excellent overview of research on sources of economic growth, including alternative data sources and methodologies, is provided by the Rees Report to the National Research Council (1979). Christensen, Cummings, and Jorgenson (1980) and Maddison (1987) have reviewed international comparisons of sources of economic growth among industrialized countries, while Kravis (1976) has surveyed international comparisons of productivity. Griliches (1984), Mansfield (1984), and Nelson (1981) have reviewed research on productivity at the level of the individual firm. Detailed surveys of the literature on productivity have been presented by Kennedy and Thirlwall (1972), Link (1987), and Nadiri (1970, 1972).

3.1.1 Sources of U.S. Economic Growth.

The conceptual framework developed by Kendrick, Solow, and other pioneers in the study of economic growth can be illustrated by the results presented in table 3.1. At the aggregate level, output is represented by the quantity of value added, which is expressed as a function of capital and labor inputs and the level of productivity. Growth rates for the period 1947–85 are given for output and the two inputs in the first column of table 3.1. Value added grows at the rate of 3.28% per year, while capital grows at 3.88% and labor input grows at 1.81%. The contributions of capital and labor inputs are obtained by weighting the corresponding growth rates by the shares of the inputs in value added. This produces the familiar allocation of growth to its sources: capital input is the most important source of growth in output by a substantial margin, accounting for 44.2% of economic growth during the period. Labor input accounts for 34.1% of growth. Capital and labor inputs together account for almost four-fifths of economic growth, while productivity accounts for only 21.6%.

The findings summarized in table 3.1 are not limited to the period as a whole. In the first panel of table 3.1 the growth of output is compared with the contributions of the two primary factor inputs and productivity growth for eight subperiods—1947–53, 1953–57, 1957–60, 1960–66, 1966–69, 1969–73, 1973–79, and 1979–85. The end points of the periods identified in table 3.1, except for the last period, are years in which a cyclical peak occurred. The growth rate presented for each subperiod is the average annual growth

Table 3.1 Aggregate Output, Inputs, and Productivity: Rates of Growth, 1947–85

Variable	1947–85	1947–53	1953–57	1957–60	1960–66	1966–69	1969–73	1973–79	1979–85
Value-added	.0328	.0529	.0214	.0238	.0472	.0360	.0306	.0212	.0222
Capital input	.0388	.0554	.0401	.0229	.0367	.0437	.0421	.0392	.0262
Labor input	.0181	.0251	.0037	.0124	.0248	.0226	.0128	.0219	.0146
Contribution of capital input	.0145	.0215	.0149	.0083	.0142	.0167	.0149	.0140	.0098
Contribution of labor input	.0112	.0153	.0022	.0077	.0151	.0140	.0082	.0139	.0089
Rate of productivity growth	.0071	.0160	.0043	.0078	.0179	.0053	.0074	−.0067	.0034
Contribution of capital quality	.0058	.0126	.0069	.0016	.0053	.0058	.0054	.0045	.0022
Contribution of capital stock	.0088	.0090	.0080	.0067	.0089	.0108	.0095	.0095	.0077
Contribution of labor quality	.0039	.0060	.0038	.0084	.0041	.0030	.0018	.0024	.0026
Contribution of hours worked	.0073	.0093	−.0016	−.0007	.0110	.0110	.0065	.0114	.0063
Rates of sectoral productivity growth	.0088	.0142	.0083	.0112	.0190	.0060	.0097	−.0012	.0029
Reallocation of value added	−.0019	.0007	−.0044	−.0021	−.0021	−.0007	−.0023	−.0053	.0006
Reallocation of capital input	.0005	.0003	.0013	.0005	.0009	.0001	.0006	−.0001	.0009
Reallocation of labor input	−.0003	.0009	−.0009	−.0019	.0001	−.0002	−.0005	−.0000	−.0010

rate between cyclical peaks. The contributions of capital and labor inputs are the predominant sources of U.S. economic growth for the period as a whole and all eight subperiods.

I have found that the contribution of capital input is the most significant source of output growth for the period 1947–85 as a whole. The contribution of capital input is also the most important source of growth for seven of the eight subperiods, while productivity growth is the most important source for only one, 1960–66. The contribution of capital input exceeds the contribution of labor input for seven subperiods, while the contribution of labor input is more important only for the period 1960–66. The contribution of labor input exceeds productivity growth for four of the eight subperiods.

In 1985 the output of the U.S. economy stood at almost three-and-a-half times the level of output in 1947. My overall conclusion is that the driving force behind the expansion of the U.S. economy between 1947 and 1985 has been the growth in capital and labor inputs. Growth in capital input is the most important source of growth in output, growth in labor input is the next most important source, and productivity growth is least important. This perspective focuses attention on the mobilization of capital and labor resources rather than advances in productivity.

The findings just summarized are consistent with a substantial body of research. For example, these findings coincide with those of Christensen and Jorgenson (1973a) for the United States for the period 1929–69 and the much earlier findings of Tinbergen (1942) for the period 1870–1914. Maddison (1987) gives similar results for six industrialized countries, including the United States, for the period 1913–84. However, these findings contrast sharply with those of Abramovitz, Kendrick, and Solow, which emphasize productivity as the predominant growth source. At this point it is useful to describe the steps required to go from these earlier findings to the results summarized in table 3.1.

The first step is to decompose the contributions of capital and labor inputs into the separate contributions of capital and labor quality and the contributions of capital stock and hours worked. Capital stock and hours worked are a natural focus for input measurement since capital input would be proportional to capital stock if capital inputs were homogeneous, while labor input would be proportional to hours worked if labor inputs were homogeneous. In fact, inputs are enormously heterogeneous, so that measurement of input aggregates involves compiling data on components of each input and weighting the growth rates of the components by the corresponding value shares. Capital and labor quality have growth rates equal to the differences between the growth rates of input measures that take account of heterogeneity and measures that ignore heterogeneity. In the Kendrick-Solow approach these components are ignored, since inputs are treated as homogeneous.

The results presented in table 3.1 reveal that the assumption of homogeneous capital and labor inputs is highly misleading. We find that growth in the quality of capital stock accounts for two-fifths of the growth of capital input during the period 1947–85. This quantitative relationship also characterizes the eight subperiods. For the period as a whole we find that the growth of labor quality accounts for more than one-third of the growth of labor input. The growth in hours worked actually falls below the growth in the quality of hours worked for the period 1953–60. For the period 1966–79 the contribution of hours worked accounts for almost two-thirds of the contribution of labor input. The relative proportions of growth in hours worked and labor quality are far from uniform. Although these proportions vary greatly from period to period, there is a decline in the relative importance of labor quality after 1960.

The development of measures of labor input reflecting heterogeneity is one of the many pathbreaking contributions of Edward F. Denison (1961, 1962b) to the analysis of sources of economic growth. Table 3.1 is based on an extension and revision of the measures of labor input presented by Jorgenson, Gollop, and Fraumeni (1987). Hours worked are cross-classified by age, sex, education, and employment status and weighted by wage rates.[2] A total of 160 types of labor input are distinguished at the aggregate level. Denison (1969, 1972) continues to adhere to capital stock as a measure of capital input. This approach ignores the heterogeneity among components of capital input reflected in the growth of capital quality in table 3.1. In this table, capital stocks are cross-classified by type of asset and legal form of organization and weighted by rental prices. At the aggregate level, a total of 169 components of capital input are measured separately. Assets of different ages are weighted in accord with profiles of relative efficiency constructed by Hulten and Wykoff (1981a).

The point has come where it is necessary to be more precise about the concept of an aggregate production function. In technical jargon the existence of an aggregate production function requires that the technology of each sector is separable in value added and that value added is a function of capital and labor inputs and the level of technology. Moreover, the sectoral value-added functions must be identical for all sectors, while the functions relating labor and capital inputs to their components must also be identical for all sectors. Finally, each component of these input aggregates must receive the same price in all sectors.

The assumptions just enumerated are well known to aggregation theorists and have achieved broader recognition as a consequence of the "reswitching controversy" initiated by Samuelson (1962). The lack of surface plausibility in this set of assumptions has not deterred economists from applying the concept of an aggregate production function in analyzing the sources of economic growth. The obvious question is, why? To attempt to answer this question we can decompose the rate of aggregate productivity growth into its sources at the level of 37 sectors of the U.S. economy. Fortunately, the data for production patterns in these sectors can be generated in a way that avoids the assumptions that underly the aggregate production model. This makes it possible to test the assumptions of the model and assess the importance of departures from these assumptions empirically.

Aggregate productivity growth can be represented as a weighted sum of sectoral productivity growth rates with weights given by ratios of the value of output in each sector to value added in all sectors. In addition, the aggregate productivity growth rate depends on reallocations of value added, capital input, and labor input among sectors. The growth rates of the reallocations are the differences between growth rates of aggregate indexes of value added, capital input, and labor input and the corresponding indexes obtained by weighting each of the components by prices specific to each sector. For example, the index of aggregate labor input involves weighting up the 160 components of labor input. The reallocation of labor input is the difference between this index and an index that separately weights the 5,920 types of labor input, cross-classified by the 37 sectors of the U.S. economy as well as the characteristics of labor input distinguished at the aggregate level.

Reallocations of value added, capital input, and labor input are measures of departures from the assumptions that underly the aggregate production model. Reallocations of value added incorporate differences in value-added functions among sectors and departures from the separability assumptions required for the existence of a value-added function in each sector. Reallocations of capital and labor inputs include differences in capital and labor aggregates among sectors, departures from separability assumptions required for the existence of these aggregates, and differences in prices of individual capital and labor inputs among sectors.

For the period 1947–85 as a whole the rate of aggregate productivity growth is somewhat lower than the weighted sum of sectoral productivity growth rates. The reallocations of value added, capital input, and labor input are small but not negligible, so that the model of production based on an aggregate production function provides a valuable and useful summary of the data. However, we find that the reallocations, especially the reallocation of value added, are very large for the periods 1953–57 and 1973–79. The contributions of the reallocations during the 1973–79 period contribute to a precipitous drop in the aggregate productivity growth rate.

I have already noted that the growth rate of output in the U.S. economy averaged 3.28% per year during the postwar period, 1947–85. During the subperiod 1973–79 the average growth rate is only 2.12%, a decline of 1.16%. The contribution of capital input declined by only 0.05% per year between the two periods, while the contribution of labor input actually increased by 0.27%. The decline in the rate of productivity growth was 1.38%, more than the decline in the growth rate of output. In the last panel of table 3.1 we can see that the weighted sum of sectoral productivity growth rates was negative for the period 1973–79 at 0.12% per year. The 1% decline in this sum is almost sufficient to account for the slowdown in U.S. economic growth. The decline in productivity growth at the sectoral level was augmented by a negative contribution of 0.53% per year from the reallocation of value added.

My conclusion from table 3.1 is that the aggregate production model used in analyzing economic growth by Denison, Kendrick, Kuznets, Maddison, Solow, Tinbergen, and a long list of others is appropriate for studying long-term growth trends. However, this model is highly inappropriate for analyzing the sources of growth over shorter periods. In fact, the aggregate production model has become a serious obstacle to understanding the causes of the slowdown in economic growth in the United States and other industrialized countries during the period 1973–79. There is a real danger that the analysis of economic growth will remain wrapped in the straitjacket of the aggregate production model. A disaggregated data set, like that presented in table 3.1, shows that the assumptions underlying this model are clearly inconsistent with the empirical evidence.

3.1.2 Sources of Sectoral Growth

The major accomplishment of recent research on the sources of U.S. economic growth is the integration of the growth of intermediate, capital, and labor inputs at the level of individual industrial sectors into an analysis of the sources of growth for the economy as a whole. This integration makes it possible to attribute U.S. economic growth to its sources at the level of individual industries. In table 3.1 the sources of U.S. economic growth are allocated among contributions of growth in capital and labor inputs, changes in productivity at the sectoral level, and intersectoral shifts of outputs and inputs.

The analysis of sources of growth at the industry level is based on the decomposition of the growth rate of sectoral output into the sum of the contributions of intermediate, capital, and labor inputs and the growth of productivity. The contribution of each input is the product of the value share of the input and its growth rate. In table 3.2 I compare the growth rate of output with the contributions of the three inputs and the growth of productivity for the period 1947–85. The sum of the contributions of intermediate, capital, and labor inputs is the predominant source of growth of output for 33 of the 37 sectors included in table 3.2.

Comparing the contribution of intermediate input with other sources of output growth, we find that this input is by far the most significant source of growth. The contribution of intermediate input exceeds productivity growth and the contributions of capital and labor inputs. If we focus attention on the contributions of capital and labor inputs alone, excluding intermediate input from consideration, we find that these two inputs are a more important source of growth than changes in productivity.

The findings presented in table 3.2 are based on the symmetrical treatment of intermediate, capital, and labor inputs.[3] To provide additional insight into

Table 3.2 Growth in Sectoral Output and Its Sources, 1947–85 (Average Annual Rates)

		Contributions to Growth in Output			
Industry	Rate of Output Growth	Intermediate Input	Capital Input	Labor Input	Rate of Productivity Growth
Agriculture, forestry & fisheries	.0192	.0068	.0014	−.0051	.0161
Metal mining	.0012	.0067	.0067	−.0071	−.0051
Coal mining	.0078	.0090	.0071	−.0098	.0015
Crude petroleum & natural gas	.0187	.0149	.0160	.0061	−.0182
Nonmetallic mineral mining	.0234	.0099	.0061	−.0003	.0077
Construction	.0308	.0182	.0028	.0086	.0012
Food & kindred products	.0228	.0160	.0010	.0001	.0057
Tobacco manufactures	.0033	.0065	.0017	−.0011	−.0039
Textile mill products	.0201	.0111	.0009	−.0022	.0103
Apparel & other textile products	.0245	.0106	.0012	.0010	.0118
Lumber & wood products	.0199	.0128	.0039	−.0014	.0046
Furniture & fixtures	.0299	.0150	.0024	.0046	.0078
Paper & allied products	.0318	.0189	.0049	.0034	.0047
Printing & publishing	.0299	.0185	.0040	.0070	.0004
Chemicals & allied products	.0457	.0217	.0080	.0041	.0119
Petroleum refining	.0288	.0169	.0021	.0010	.0088
Rubber & plastic products	.0453	.0272	.0015	.0083	.0084
Leather & leather products	−.0150	−.0118	.0005	−.0063	.0026
Stone, clay & glass products	.0252	.0142	.0040	.0030	.0040
Primary metals	.0032	.0038	.0010	−.0009	−.0007
Fabricated metal products	.0228	.0112	.0035	.0048	.0033
Machinery, except electrical	.0398	.0184	.0058	.0058	.0098
Electrical machinery	.0534	.0222	.0057	.0092	.0164
Motor vehicles	.0351	.0233	.0040	.0014	.0064
Other transportation equipment	.0441	.0273	.0039	.0105	.0024
Instruments	.0505	.0186	.0072	.0123	.0123
Miscellaneous manufacturing	.0204	.0090	.0023	−.0016	.0107
Transportation & warehousing	.0223	.0105	.0021	−.0006	.0103
Communication	.0637	.0113	.0223	.0083	.0218
Electric utilities	.0543	.0189	.0164	.0043	.0147
Gas utilities	.0398	.0285	.0075	.0017	.0020
Trade	.0354	.0113	.0074	.0062	.0104
Finance, insurance, & real estate	.0405	.0142	.0118	.0134	.0011
Other services	.0388	.0183	.0081	.0137	−.0013
Government enterprises	.0330	.0175	.0081	.0098	−.0025
Private households	.0489		.0494	−.0006	
Government, excluding government enterprises	.0316			.0316	

the sources of economic growth at the sectoral level, we can decompose the growth rate of intermediate input into growth of an unweighted index of intermediate input and growth in intermediate input quality. As before, we can decompose the growth of capital input into growth in capital stock and capital quality. Finally, we can decompose the growth of labor input into growth in hours worked and labor quality. In table 3.3 this decomposition is presented for 37 sectors for the period 1947–85.

We find that growth in quality is not an important component of growth in intermediate input. Inferences about the predominant role of intermediate input would be unaffected by the omission of changes in quality. Excluding intermediate input from consideration, however, we find that the relative importance of productivity growth and the contributions of capital and labor inputs would be reversed by using measures that omit changes in input quality. The incorporation of intermediate input is an important innovation in the methodology employed in generating the data presented in tables 3.2 and 3.3. The second major innovation is the measurement of changes in the quality of capital and labor inputs at the sectoral level.

The perspective on U.S. economic growth suggested by the results presented in tables 3.2 and 3 emphasizes the contribution of mobilization of resources within individual industries. The explanatory power of this perspective is overwhelming at the sectoral level. For 33 of the 37 industrial sectors included in tables 3.2 and 3.3, the contribution of intermediate, capital, and labor inputs is the predominant source of output growth. Changes in productivity account for the major portion of output growth in only four sectors.

3.1.3 Summary

The findings on the sources of U.S. economic growth summarized in tables 3.1, 3.2, and 3.3 have been generated by a truly massive empirical research effort. In section 3.2 I describe the sources and methods for construction of data on labor input. These data have incorporated all the annual detail on employment, weeks, hours worked, and labor compensation published in the decennial Census of Population and the Current Population Survey. Similarly, the data on capital input described in section 3.3 have incorporated all the available detail on investment in capital goods by industry and class of asset and on property compensation by legal form of organization from the U.S. national income and product accounts (NIPA). Finally, the data on intermediate input and output described in section 3.4 have incorporated all of the available annual data by industry from the U.S. national income and product accounts and the U.S. interindustry accounts.

The application of the theory of index numbers to the measurement of labor input requires weighting the components of labor input by wage rates. This was carried out at the aggregate level by Denison (1962b) and implemented for all industrial sectors of the U.S. economy by Gollop and Jorgenson (1980, 1983). Similarly, the measurement of capital as a factor of production involves weighting the components of capital input by rental rates. The conceptual basis for imputing rental prices for capital goods was established by Jorgenson (1963). These rental prices were employed in aggregate productivity measurement by Jorgenson and Griliches (1967). The rental price concept was further elaborated by Hall and Jorgenson (1967). This concept was implemented at the aggregate level by Christensen and Jorgenson (1969) and at the sectoral level by Fraumeni and Jorgenson (1980, 1986) and Gollop and Jorgenson (1980).

The model of capital as a factor of production originated by Walras (1954) was extended to encompass quality change for capital goods and relative efficiencies for capital goods of different vintages by Hall (1971). Hall's methodology generalizes the "hedonic technique" for measuring quality change of capital goods employed by Griliches (1961b). This methodology has been exploited by Hulten and Wykoff (1981b) in measuring depreciation of capital goods from vintage price data. Griliches (1964), Stone (1956), and Triplett (1983a, 1986) have discussed the rationale for incorporating quality-corrected price indexes into systems of national accounts.

The final step in developing the methodology for analyzing sources of economic growth is to aggregate over individual industrial sectors. This step is critical in integrating the analysis of sources of growth for individual industries into the analysis of growth for the economy as a whole. The methodology for aggregation over sectors originated by Domar (1961) has been generalized by Hulten (1978) and Jorgenson (1980). This methodology was implemented for the U.S. by Fraumeni and Jorgenson (1980, 1986) and underlies the data on aggregate productivity change presented in table 3.1. I describe sources and methods for construction of data on aggregate output, input, and productivity in section 3.5.

At a methodological level the integration of data generation and econometric modeling is an important achievement of recent research on the sources of economic growth. The extensive data development described in sections 3.2, 3.3, and 3.4 is firmly rooted in the economic theory of production. The conceptual basis for the measures of intermediate, capital, and labor inputs in Tables 3.1, 3.2, and 3.3 is provided by the theory of exact index numbers employed by Diewert (1976). Diewert showed that the index numbers utilized, for example, by Christensen and Jorgenson (1969) could be generated from the translog production function introduced by Christensen, Jorgenson, and Lau (1971, 1973).

The integration of the analysis of sources of economic growth with econometric modeling of producer behavior has suggested two alternative modeling strategies. The first is based on an aggregate production function, originally introduced by Cobb and Douglas (1928) and developed by Tinbergen (1942) in the form used for the analysis of sources of growth for the economy as a whole. A second strategy for modeling producer behavior is to disaggregate to the level of individual industrial sectors and replace the aggregate

Table 3.3 **Contributions of Input Quality to Growth in Sectoral Output: Rates of Growth, 1947–85**

	Average Annual Rates of Growth						
Industry	Quality of Intermediate Input	Unweighted Intermediate Input	Quality of Capital Stock	Capital Stock	Quality of Hours Worked	Hours Worked	Rate of Productivity Growth
Agriculture, forestry & fisheries	−.0004	.0071	.0023	−.0009	.0020	−.0071	.0161
Metal mining	−.0001	.0068	.0026	.0041	.0013	−.0083	−.0051
Coal mining	.0012	.0078	.0000	.0070	.0012	−.0110	.0015
Crude petroleum & natural gas	−.0010	.0159	.0007	.0152	.0013	.0048	−.0182
Nonmetallic mineral mining	.0000	.0099	.0001	.0060	.0011	−.0014	.0077
Construction	.0003	.0179	.0005	.0024	.0009	.0077	.0012
Food & kindred products	−.0005	.0165	.0002	.0007	.0005	−.0004	.0057
Tobacco manufactures	.0005	.0060	−.0001	.0017	.0006	−.0017	−.0039
Textile mill products	.0002	.0110	.0004	.0006	.0005	−.0027	.0103
Apparel & other textile products	.0008	.0098	.0002	.0010	.0005	.0004	.0118
Lumber & wood products	.0008	.0120	.0006	.0033	.0009	−.0023	.0046
Furniture & fixtures	.0000	.0150	.0003	.0021	.0008	.0038	.0078
Paper & allied products	.0000	.0189	.0014	.0034	.0012	.0022	.0047
Printing & publishing	.0001	.0184	.0012	.0028	.0014	.0056	.0004
Chemicals & allied products	−.0004	.0222	.0027	.0053	.0013	.0028	.0119
Petroleum refining	.0020	.0149	.0002	.0019	.0004	.0005	.0088

Rubber & plastic products	.0001	.0271	.0005	.0009	.0012	.0071	.0084
Leather & leather products	.0006	−.0124	−.0009	.0014	.0005	−.0068	.0026
Stone, clay & glass products	.0002	.0140	.0010	.0029	.0015	.0015	.0040
Primary metals	.0002	.0036	−.0009	.0020	.0008	−.0016	−.0007
Fabricated metal products	.0000	.0112	.0002	.0033	.0011	.0038	.0033
Machinery, except electrical	.0005	.0179	.0006	.0051	.0014	.0044	.0098
Electrical machinery	.0010	.0211	.0002	.0055	.0019	.0073	.0164
Motor vehicles	.0003	.0231	−.0008	.0048	.0007	.0007	.0064
Other transportation equipment	.0004	.0269	.0025	.0014	.0018	.0087	.0024
Instruments	.0000	.0186	.0004	.0068	.0021	.0102	.0123
Miscellaneous manufacturing	.0001	.0089	.0003	.0020	.0011	−.0026	.0107
Transportation & warehousing	.0004	.0102	.0025	−.0004	.0007	−.0014	.0103
Communication	.0001	.0112	.0039	.0184	.0018	.0065	.0218
Electric utilities	−.0009	.0198	.0022	.0142	.0008	.0035	.0147
Gas utilities	−.0025	.0311	.0015	.0060	.0007	.0011	.0020
Trade	.0003	.0111	.0025	.0049	.0016	.0046	.0104
Finance, insurance, & real estate	.0003	.0139	.0028	.0091	.0022	.0112	.0011
Other services	.0002	.0181	.0026	.0055	.0008	.0128	−.0013
Government enterprises	.0000	.0175	.0003	.0079	.0001	.0097	−.0025
Private households			.0121	.0373	−.0001	−.0005	
Government, excluding government enterprises					.0038	.0278	

production model by a general equilibrium model of production. Models of this type have been constructed for all U.S. industries by Berndt and Jorgenson (1973), Jorgenson and Fraumeni (1981), and Jorgenson (1984b).

The essential idea of the disaggregated approach is to model producer behavior through complete systems of demand functions for inputs into each industrial sector. This approach is a lineal descendant of the general equilibrium models of production introduced by Leontief (1951). By successive steps it is possible to relax the "fixed coefficients" assumption of input-output analysis by making the input-output coefficients functions of the input prices. This approach has the added advantage of relaxing the assumption of value added separability at the sectoral level. Finally, the approach makes it possible to endogenize the rate of productivity growth in each sector by making this growth rate a function of the input prices.

In section 3.6 I review the two modeling strategies outlined above and alternative strategies proposed in the econometric literature. The benefits of the radical simplifications that result from an aggregate production model must be weighed against the costs of departures from the highly restrictive assumptions that underly this model. The limitations of the aggregate production model can be illustrated by an analysis of the slowdown in U.S. economic growth since 1973. An econometric model of productivity growth for all U.S. industries is required for an explanation of the slowdown. In section 3.7 I conclude with a summary of the implications of recent studies of the sources of economic growth for future research on economic measurement.

3.2 Measuring Labor Input

The methodology for productivity measurement that underlies the data presented in tables 3.2 and 3.3 is based on a model of producer behavior. The point of departure for this model is a homogeneous production function $\{F^i\}$ for each of n industrial sectors:

$$Z_i = F^i(X_i, K_i, L_i, T), \quad (i = 1, 2, \ldots, n),$$

where T is time, $\{Z_i\}$ is output, and $\{X_i\}$, $\{K_i\}$, and $\{L_i\}$ are intermediate, capital, and labor inputs. We can define the shares of intermediate, capital, and labor inputs, say $\{v^i_X\}$, $\{v^k_K\}$, and $\{v^i_L\}$, in the value of output by:

$$v^i_X = \frac{P^i_X X_i}{q_i Z_i},$$

$$v^i_K = \frac{p^i_K K_i}{q_i Z_i},$$

$$v^i_L = \frac{p^i_L L_i}{q_i Z_i}, \quad (i = 1, 2, \ldots, n),$$

where $\{q_i\}$, $\{p_X^i\}$, $\{p_K^i\}$ and $\{p_L^i\}$ denote the prices of output and intermediate, capital, and labor inputs, respectively.

To analyze substitution among inputs I combine the production function for each sector with necessary conditions for producer equilibrium. These conditions are given by equalities between the shares of each input in the value of output and the elasticities of output with respect to that input:

$$v_X^i = \frac{\partial \ln Z_i}{\partial \ln X_i}(X_i, K_i, L_i, T),$$

$$v_K^i = \frac{\partial \ln Z_i}{\partial \ln K_i}(X_i, K_i, L_i, T),$$

$$v_L^i = \frac{\partial \ln Z_i}{\partial \ln L_i}(X_i, K_i, L_i, T), \quad (i = 1, 2, \ldots, n).$$

Under constant returns to scale, the elasticities and the value shares for all three inputs sum to unity, so that the value of output is equal to the value of the inputs.

Finally, we can define the rate of productivity growth, say $\{v_T^i\}$, for each sector, as the rate of growth of output with respect to time, holding intermediate, capital, and labor inputs constant:

$$v_T^i = \frac{\partial \ln Z_i}{\partial T}(X_i, K_i, L_i, T), \quad (i = 1, 2, \ldots, n).$$

It is important to note that this definition does not impose any restriction on substitution patterns among inputs. I employ the rate of productivity growth in analyzing changes in substitution possibilities over time.

3.2.1. Exact Index Numbers

The production function for each sector listed in tables 3.2 and 3.3 is defined in terms of output and intermediate, capital, and labor inputs. Each of the inputs is an aggregate that depends on the quantities of individual intermediate, capital, and labor inputs:

$$X_i = X_i(X_{1i}, X_{2i} \ldots X_{ni}),$$
$$K_i = K_i(K_{1i}, K_{2i} \ldots K_{pi}),$$
$$L_i = L_i(L_{1i}, L_{2i} \ldots L_{qi}), \quad (i = 1, 2, \ldots, n),$$

where $\{X_{ji}\}$ is the set of n intermediate inputs from the jth sector ($j = 1, 2, \ldots, n$), $\{K_{ki}\}$ the set of p capital inputs, and $\{L_{li}\}$ the set of q labor inputs. Here the production function is separable in intermediate, capital, and labor inputs.[4] If these inputs are each homogeneous in their components, we say that the production function is homothetically separable.[5] The aggregates for each sector are characterized by constant returns to scale.

The shares of the individual intermediate, capital, and labor inputs, say $\{v^i_{Xj}\}$, $\{v^i_{Kk}\}$, and $\{v^i_{Ll}\}$, can be defined in the values of the corresponding aggregates by:

$$v^i_{Xj} = \frac{p^i_{Xj} X_{ji}}{p^i_X X_i}, \quad (i, j = 1, 2, \ldots, n),$$

$$v^i_{Kk} = \frac{p^i_{Kk} K_{ki}}{p^i_K K_i}, \quad (i = 1, 2, \ldots, n; k = 1, 2, \ldots, p),$$

$$v^i_{Ll} = \frac{p^i_{Ll} L_{li}}{p^i_L L_i}, \quad (i = 1, 2, \ldots, n; l = 1, 2, \ldots, q),$$

where $\{p^i_{Xj}\}$, $\{p^i_{Kk}\}$, and $\{p^i_{Ll}\}$ are the prices of individual intermediate, capital, and labor inputs.

Necessary conditions for producer equilibrium are given by equalities between the shares of the individual inputs in the values of the corresponding aggregates and the elasticities of the aggregate with respect to the individual inputs:

$$v^i_{Xj} = \frac{\partial \ln X_i}{\partial \ln X_{ji}} (X_{1i}, X_{2i}, \ldots, X_{ni}),$$

$$v^i_{Kk} = \frac{\partial \ln K_i}{\partial \ln K_{ki}} (K_{1i}, K_{2i}, \ldots, K_{pi}),$$

$$v^i_{Ll} = \frac{\partial \ln L_i}{\partial \ln L_{li}} (L_{1i}, L_{2i}, \ldots, L_{qi}), \quad (i = 1, 2, \ldots, n).$$

Under constant returns to scale, the values of intermediate, capital, and labor inputs are equal to the sums of the values of their components.

The methodology that underlies the data presented in tables 3.2 and 3.3 is based on sectoral production functions of the translog form introduced by Christensen, Jorgenson, and Lau (1971, 1973).[6] Given translog production functions for all sectors, the corresponding price and quantity index numbers can be generated for all three inputs. The growth rate of each input between two periods is a weighted average of growth rates of its components. Weights are given by the average share of each component in the value of the input for the two periods. The corresponding price indexes are defined as ratios of the values of the inputs to the translog quantity indexes. Similarly, the translog index of productivity growth is the difference between the growth rate of output and a weighted average of growth rates of intermediate, capital, and labor inputs.[7]

The critical innovation in the methodology that underlies tables 3.2 and 3.3 is to distinguish among components of intermediate, capital, and labor inputs that differ in marginal productivity. For each sector intermediate input is represented as a function of deliveries from all other sectors. Capital input is broken down by class of asset and legal form of organization. Finally, labor input is broken down by characteristics of individual workers such as sex, age, education, and employment status.

3.2.2 Data Sources and Methods for Labor Input

A novel feature of the indexes of the quantity of labor input presented in tables 3.2 and 3.3 is that these indexes incorporate data from both establishment and household surveys. Estimates of employment, hours worked, and labor compensation for each industrial sector are controlled to totals based on establishment surveys that underlie the U.S. national income accounts. These totals are allocated among categories of the work force cross-classified by the characteristics of individual workers on the basis of household surveys. The resulting estimates of hours worked and average compensation per hour for each sector provide the basis for the indexes of labor input presented in table 3.2.

For each of the 37 sectors listed in table 3.2, prices and quantities of labor input are cross-classified by the two sexes, eight age groups, five educational groups, and two employment statuses—employee and self-employed. Annual data from 1947 to 1985 on hours worked and average labor compensation per hour are required for 160 components of the work force in each industry. For this purpose, employment, hours, weeks, and labor compensation within each sector are allocated on the basis of the available cross-classifications.[8] This methodology makes it possible to exploit all the published detail on labor input from the decennial Census of Population and the Current Population Survey.

The first step in developing sectoral measures of labor input is to construct employment matrices cross-classified by sex, age, education, and employment status for each year on the basis of household surveys from the Census of Population and the Current Population Survey. The resulting employment matrices are controlled to employment totals for each sector on the basis of establishment surveys from the U.S. national income and product accounts.[9] Hours worked by workers cross-classified by demographic characteristics are estimated on the basis of household surveys. The resulting estimates are controlled to totals for each industrial sector from the U.S. national accounts.[10] The third step in developing sectoral measures of labor input is to construct labor compensation matrices for each year on the basis of the Census of Population.[11] Control totals for annual labor compensation are taken from the U.S. national income accounts.

Average hourly compensation per person for employees is based on data on wage and salary income from the Census of Population. Differences in outlay on labor input per person reflect differences in marginal products among workers. However, the cost of labor input from the point of view of the producer also includes supplements. Differences in wage and salary income must be adjusted to incorporate employers' contributions to Social Security and unemployment compensation and other supplements to wages and salaries.

Earnings reported by the census for self-employed workers and income of unincorporated enterprises from the U.S. national income accounts include both labor and property income. Income from unincorporated enterprises can be divided between labor and property components, assuming that after tax rates of return are the same for corporate and noncorporate business. Labor compensation is distributed among the self-employed on the basis of wage differentials among employees in the corresponding industrial sector. To derive labor compensation per hour worked for each category of labor input, total labor compensation is divided by annual hours worked for each category.

The final step in constructing data on labor input for each of the 37 sectors is to combine price and quantity data, cross-classified by sex, age, education, and employment status, into price and quantity indexes of labor input. To construct an index of labor input for each sector, we express sectoral labor input, say $\{L_i\}$, as a translog function of its 160 individual components, say $\{L_{ji}\}$. The corresponding index of sectoral labor input is a translog quantity index of individual labor inputs:

$$\ln L_i(T) - \ln L_i(T-1) = \Sigma \bar{v}^i_{Ll} [\ln L_{li}(T) - \ln L_{li}(T-1)],$$

$$(i = 1, 2, \ldots, n),$$

where weights are given by average shares of each component in the value of sectoral labor compensation:

$$\bar{v}^i_{Ll} = \frac{1}{2}[v^i_{Ll}(T) + v^i_{Ll}(T-1)], \ (i = 1, 2, \ldots, n; \ l = 1, 2, \ldots, q),$$

and

$$v^i_{Ll} = \frac{p^i_{Ll} L_{li}}{\Sigma p^i_{Ll} L_{li}}, \quad (i = 1, 2, \ldots, n; \ l = 1, 2, \ldots, q).$$

The value shares are computed from data on hours worked $\{L_{li}\}$ and compensation per hour $\{p^i_{Ll}\}$ for each component of sectoral labor input, cross-classified by sex, age, education, and employment class of workers.

A measure of total hours worked for each sector can be derived by adding hours worked across all 160 categories of labor input within that sector. The quality of labor input is defined as the ratio of labor input to hours worked. Changes in the quality of hours worked represent the differences between changes in the translog quantity index of labor input and changes in an unweighted index of hours worked. Quantity indexes of labor input are presented in table 3.2 for 37 sectors. The corresponding indexes of labor input quality and hours worked are presented for each sector in table 3.3.

Translog index numbers for labor input were introduced for individual sectors of the U.S. economy by Gollop and Jorgenson (1980, 1983). The data on labor input that underly tables 3.2 and 3.3 are cross-classified by sex, age, education, employment status, and sector of employment for a total of 5,920 types of labor input. The growth of labor input can be decomposed to obtain the contributions to change in labor quality of all these characteristics.[12]

3.2.3 Alternative Sources and Methods

An overview of issues in the measurement of labor input is provided by the Rees Report (National Research Council 1979, esp. 122–28). Alternative quantity indexes of labor input and the corresponding price indexes are compared by Denison (1961), Kunze (1979), and Triplett (1983b). To provide additional perspective on the measurement of labor input, it is useful to compare the methodology and data sources that underly the indexes presented in tables 3.2 and 3.3, with those of the Bureau of Labor Statistics (BLS) (1983), Denison (1985), and Kendrick (1983a).[13] My comparative analysis covers both labor hours and compensation. I evaluate the alternative approaches in terms of the data sources and the requirements of the theory of producer behavior. Wherever possible, I test the assumptions implicit in the competing models.

My comparison begins with the measurement of hours. The BLS (1983, 66–68) measure of multifactor productivity employs the same data for hours as the traditional BLS (1971) measures of output per hour. About 85% of total hours are based on establishment surveys that collect information on hours paid rather than hours worked. Kendrick (1961a, 382, 496, 503, 515, 559; 1973, 156; 1983a, 56) and Kendrick and Grossman (1980, 25) present a strong case for an hours-worked series but use BLS (1971) establishment data on hours paid for some sectors. As evident from his earliest works, Denison (e.g., 1962b, 352) shares Kendrick's view that hours worked are more appropriate than hours paid.[14]

Both Denison and Kendrick attempt to measure hours worked on the basis of the hours-paid series published by BLS. The *BLS Handbook of Methods for Surveys and Studies* (1971) makes clear that separate hours estimates are developed for production and nonproduction workers only in the manufacturing sectors. According to the handbook (1971, 214–15), manufacturing production worker hours are taken directly from the data in the BLS area wage surveys and the study of *Employer Expenditures* (1963) published by BLS. For the nonmanufacturing industries the hours-paid series collected in the census employment survey program relate to nonsupervisory workers only. BLS assumes that these hours apply to all wage and salary workers. BLS does not provide estimates of hours paid for self-employed and unpaid family workers. For these groups, Denison and, for the most part, Kendrick use household survey data on hours worked.

There are important differences in the demographic mix of the supervisory and nonsupervisory occupations and in the average hours worked for different demographic groups. These differences make suspect the assumption that supervisory and nonsupervisory workers in each nonmanufacturing industry are paid for the same average number of hours per week. For example, according to the census (Bureau of the Census 1972, table 5), the 1970 female to male ratio was .87 in nonsupervisory occupations in the nonmanufacturing sector and only .22 in supervisory occupations. Furthermore, the census (1973a, table 45) data show that female nonsupervisory workers in 1970 worked 34.5 hours on average, while their male counterparts worked 41.5 hours.

Given that women work fewer weekly hours than men and are proportionately underrepresented in supervisory occupations, it is highly unlikely that supervisory laborers are paid for the same number of weekly hours as nonsupervisory laborers. A similar analysis could be based on age or education compositions; the evidence suggests that BLS estimates of annual hours paid are biased downward in the nonmanufacturing sectors. Shifts in the demographic composition of the supervisory and nonsupervisory occupational groups over time will bias estimates of productivity growth.

We next compare the Kendrick and Denison approaches to constructing indexes of labor input. Kendrick considers all workers within each industry to be homogeneous. He completely omits the influence of changing labor quality on his measure of each industry's labor input. Admittedly, Kendrick does distinguish between the hours worked by proprietors and unpaid family workers and those worked by wage and salary employees whenever the former group is a "significant fraction"; of the particular industry's labor force. Since Kendrick (1961a, 261; 1973, 12) decided not to weight labor hours from the two employment classes differently, he eliminates any potential effect of changing labor composition.

Kendrick does not attribute any significance to the differences among marginal products of various categories of workers. For Kendrick, the difference in the value of an hour's work by an electrical engineer and a truck driver should be attributed to differences in productivity rather than differences in labor input. Given Kendrick's definition, the appropriate index of labor input for each sector is an unweighted index of hours worked. By contrast, Denison posits that disaggregation by characteristics is essential in measuring labor input. In his view, however, any change in sector of employment does not reflect changes in labor input and should be captured by the measure of productivity growth.

Denison cross-classifies workers by demographic characteristics such as age, sex, and education in deriving indexes of labor input. He uses census data on earnings to construct weights for use in aggregating his education and sex-age hours series in his original *Sources of Economic Growth* (1962b) and his more recent work on productivity (1974, 1979, 1985). The principal problem with using census earnings data to measure marginal products is that reported earnings exclude all supplements to wages and salaries and include the return to capital invested by self-employed workers. Denison (e.g., 1979, 157–58) makes no adjustment to the census data to exclude returns to capital.

As Denison points out, earnings can be used in weighting the components of labor input only if the average earnings for workers cross-classified by education or by age and sex are proportional to the corresponding marginal products. Since supplements, particularly Social Security and unemployment insurance, are charged to employers, reported earnings do not reflect employers' relative labor outlays. If supplements are neglected, only those ratios of hourly earnings among groups of laborers with annual incomes below the lowest base for supplements will be unbiased estimates of relative wages as viewed by employers.

For example, if the average 35- to 64-year-old male has an annual income above the social security or unemployment insurance tax base, while the average 20- to 24-year-old female's earnings are below either base, then the relative valuation of an average hour's work by males and females based on earnings is clearly upward biased. Supplements add to the employers' outlay for both males and females but, in this example, supplements add proportionately more to the employers' outlay for females than for males. Based on 1969 earnings reported in the decennial *Census* (1973c, tables I and II), employed 35- to 64-year-old males had mean annual earnings ($10,008) well above either the Social Security ($7,800) or unemployment insurance ($3,000) tax bases in 1969. Females 18–24 years of age, however, had mean labor income of $2,960. Ratios of male (35–64 years old) to female (18–24 years old) hourly wage costs excluding supplements are upward biased estimates of relative labor costs incurred by employers.

The assumption of proportionality between earnings and labor outlay is valid only if the ratio of noncorporate property income to total earnings is constant across sex-age and education groups. If the representative 35- to 64-year-old male has a larger fraction of his earnings being generated from capital invested in noncorporate enterprises than does the representative 20- to 24-year-old female, then the earnings-based estimate for the relative valuation of an hour's work by males to an hour's work by females is upward biased. Data measuring the noncorporate property income of workers classified by demographic characteristics are unavailable. However, the reasonableness of Denison's assumption can be evaluated by comparing the distribution of employment in wage and salary versus self-employed activities across sex and age groups.

I refer to data published in the 1970 census to evaluate Denison's assumption. I construct ratios of self-employed persons to total employment in both wage and salary and self-employed activities. The ratios, reported in table 3.4, vary significantly across sex-age groups. For both males and females, the ratios generally increase with age; except for the two lowest age groups, the ratio for males is more than twice the ratio for females. The ratios for older males are considerably higher than the similar ratios for young females. The relevant ratio for 35- to 64-year-old males is .130; the corresponding ratio for 20- to 24-year-old females is .011. Compared to young females, older males

Table 3.4 Ratios of Self-employed Persons to Total Employment by Age and Sex, 1970[a]

Age	Male	Female
14–15 years	.044	.026
16–17 years	.016	.009
18–19 years	.014	.005
20–24 years	.029	.011
25–29 years	.052	.024
30–34 years	.078	.033
35–39 years	.101	.038
40–44 years	.114	.041
45–49 years	.124	.045
50–59 years	.154	.060
60–62 years	.166	.062
63–64 years	.183	.073
65–69 years	.243	.093
70–74 years	.300	.118
75 years and over	.336	.133

Source: Bureau of the Census (1973b), table 47.
[a]Total employed excludes unpaid family workers.

apparently allocate a greater proportion of their labor effort to self-employed activities.

We infer that earnings for a representative male include a higher percentage of returns to noncorporate capital than do the earnings for a representative female, even after controlling for age. In short, relative earnings are inadequate measures of relative marginal products. The wage and salary income of workers adjusted for supplements is a more appropriate starting point for a measure of labor compensation.

The final issue concerns changes in the pattern of hourly earnings and therefore weights for each labor category. Denison (1974, 1979, 1985) weights by sex-age and education categories but holds weights constant over various subperiods.[15] However, relative wages across industries and among demographic groups have shifted over time due to shifting demand conditions, altered production techniques, and the changing impact of constraints on labor supply. If relative hourly wages are the appropriate estimates of relative marginal products, the labor earnings weights must be allowed to change over time. If the weights are held constant, annual changes in marginal products are not reflected accurately. The resulting estimates of year-to-year productivity change are biased.

The discussion so far has focused on a comparison of data, assumptions, and measurement techniques. We close this section emphasizing an important conceptual difference distinguishing Kendrick's measures of sectoral labor input from the measures presented in tables 3.2 and 3.3. Kendrick (e.g., 1973, 146) purposefully defines any growth in sectoral output due to shifts in the demographic composition of the labor force as part of productivity change.

For Kendrick, any shift in labor's sex, age, and education mix that leads to greater levels of sectoral output reflects an advance in knowledge and is therefore part of productivity change. We evaluate Kendrick's definition of productivity change in terms of the theory of production in section 3.4.3, below.

The data on labor input presented in tables 3.2 and 3.3 incorporate changes in the composition of labor hours by sex, age, education, and employment status within each of the 37 sectors. The data on labor input in table 3.1 incorporate these shifts for the U.S. economy as a whole. Gollop and Jorgenson (1980) provide a detailed comparison between labor input indexes of this type and those of Kendrick for the period 1947–73. Quality change is an important component of the growth in labor input. This component accounts for much of the difference between Kendrick's measures of labor hours and the translog indexes of labor input given in tables 3.2 and 3.3.

3.3 Measuring Capital Input

The approach to the construction of the data on capital input presented in table 3.2 is strictly analogous to the approach outlined in section 3.2 for data on labor input. Capital services represent the quantity of capital input, just as labor services represent the quantity of labor input. Measures of capital services for depreciable assets are derived by representing capital stock at each point of time as a weighted sum of past investments. The weights correspond to the relative efficiencies of capital goods of different ages, so that the weighted components of capital stock have the same efficiency.

Rental rates for capital services provide the basis for property compensation, just as wage rates provide the basis for labor compensation. Information on rental transactions would be required in order to employ data sources for capital input that are analogous to those we have used for labor input. These data are not available in a readily accessible form, even for the substantial proportion of assets with active rental markets. However, rental values can be imputed on the basis of estimates of capital stocks and property compensation.

Data on rental prices for depreciable assets are generated by allocating property compensation for return to capital, depreciation, and taxes among assets. Depreciation is the decline in value of a capital good with age at a given point in time, so that estimates of depreciation depend on the relative efficiencies of capital goods of different ages. The estimates of capital input presented in table 3.1 incorporate the same data on relative efficiencies of capital goods into estimates of both capital stocks and rental prices.

3.3.1 Capital as a Factor of Production

The perpetual inventory method provides the theoretical framework for the measures of capital input presented in tables 3.1, 3.2, and 3.3.[16] The key innovation embodied in the quantity indexes of capital input presented in tables 3.1 and 3.2 is the rental price of capital input originated by Jorgenson (1963, 1965, 1967). This measure of the rental price was employed in the indexes of capital input introduced by Griliches and Jorgenson (1966) and Jorgenson and Griliches (1967).[17] The rental price concept was further developed by Hall and Jorgenson (1967, 1969, 1971). Their approach was employed by Christensen and Jorgenson (1969, 1970, 1973a, 1973b) to impute rental prices for capital goods that differ in depreciation pattern and tax treatment.[18]

We can refer to the capital goods acquired at different points of time as different vintages. Estimates of the relative efficiencies of capital goods of different ages are derived from a comprehensive study of acquisition prices of assets of different vintages by Hulten and Wykoff (1981a, 1981b, 1981c). We can outline the methodology employed by Hulten and Wykoff by first considering vintage price systems under geometric decline in efficiency with age. Under geometric decline in efficiency, both the rental price of capital services and the acquisition price of a capital asset decline geometrically with age. The rate of decline in efficiency can be estimated from a sample of prices of capital goods of different ages.

The econometric model for vintage price functions gives the price of acquisition of a capital good as a function of the age of the capital good and the time period of observation. This model can be generalized by introducing Box-Cox transformations of the prices of acquisition, the ages of capital goods, and the time period of observation.[19] A further generalization of the econometric model of vintage price functions has been proposed by Hall (1971). This generalization is appropriate for durable goods with a number of varieties that are perfect substitutes in production. Each variety is characterized by a number of attributes that affect relative efficiency. This "hedonic technique" for price measurement was originated by Court (1939) and Waugh (1929) and has been employed, for example, by Griliches (1961b) and studies in the volume edited by Griliches (1971b).[20]

As an illustration, Hall (1971) analyzes a sample of prices for half-ton pickup trucks with characteristics such as wheelbase, shipping weight, displacement, ratio of core to stroke, horsepower, torque, and tire width. Observations of these characteristics are analyzed for pickup trucks produced by Ford and Chevrolet in the United States for the period 1955–66. With perfect substitutability among pickup trucks of different ages, market equilibrium implies the existence of a vintage price function for trucks. This function gives the price of acquisition of a pickup truck as a function of age and the price of a new truck of the same type, expressed as a function of time. Hall estimates vintage price functions for each category of trucks from annual observations on the prices of used trucks.

Hulten and Wykoff (1981b) have implemented an econometric model of vintage price functions for eight categories of assets in the United States. In

1977, these categories included 55% of investment expenditures on producers' durable equipment and 42% of expenditures on nonresidential structures.[21] In the estimation of econometric models based on vintage price functions, the sample of used asset prices is "censored" by the retirement of assets from service. The price of acquisition for assets that have been retired from service is equal to zero. If only surviving assets are included in a sample of used asset prices, the sample is censored by excluding assets that have been retired. In order to correct the resulting bias in estimates of vintage price functions, Hulten and Wykoff (1981b) multiply the prices of surviving assets of each vintage by the probability of survival, expressed as a function of age.

Vintage price functions for commercial and industrial buildings are summarized in table 3.5. For each class of assets the rate of economic depreciation is tabulated as a function of the age of the asset. The natural logarithm of the price is regressed on age and time to obtain an average rate of depreciation, which Hulten and Wykoff refer to as the best geometric average (BGA). The square of the multiple correlation coefficient (R^2) is given as a measure of the goodness of fit of the geometric approximation to the fitted vintage price function for each asset. Vintage price functions are estimated with and without a correction for censored sample bias.

The first conclusion that emerges from the data presented in table 3.5 is that a correction for censored sample bias is extremely important in the estimation of vintage price functions. The Hulten-Wykoff study is the first to employ such a correction. The second conclusion reached by Hulten and Wykoff (1981b) is that "*a constant rate of depreciation can serve as a reasonable statistical approximation to the underlying Box-Cox rates even though the latter are not geometric*. This result, in turn, supports those who use the single

Table 3.5 **Rates of Economic Depreciation**

	With Censored Sample Correction		Without Censored Sample Correction	
Age	Commercial	Industrial	Commercial	Industrial
5	2.85	2.99	2.66	2.02
10	2.64	3.01	1.84	1.68
15	2.43	3.04	1.48	1.50
20	2.30	3.07	1.27	1.39
30	2.15	3.15	1.02	1.25
40	2.08	3.24	0.88	1.17
50	2.04	3.34	0.79	1.11
60	2.02	3.45	0.72	1.06
70	2.02	3.57	0.66	1.03
BGA	2.47	3.61	1.05	1.28
R^2	0.985	0.997	0.971	0.995

Source: Hulten and Wykoff (1981a), table 5, p. 387; commercial corresponds to office and industrial corresponds to factory.

parameter depreciation approach in calculating capital stocks using the perpetual inventory method" [italics in original.]. This finding has been corroborated by Hulten, Robertson, and Wykoff (1989).

Hulten, Robertson, and Wykoff (1989) have tested the stability of vintage price functions during the 1970s. After 1973 energy prices increased sharply and productivity growth rates declined dramatically at both aggregate and sectoral levels, as indicated by the data presented in table 3.1. Baily (1981) has attributed the slowdown in economic growth to the decline in relative efficiency of older capital goods, resulting from higher energy prices. Hulten, Robertson, and Wykoff (1989) find that the relative efficiency functions for nine types of producers' durable equipment were unaffected by higher energy prices: "While depreciation almost certainly varies from year to year in response to a variety of factors, we have found that a major event like the energy crises, which had the potential of significantly increasing the rate of obsolescence, did not in fact result in a systematic change in age-price profiles."[22]

In table 3.6 I present rates of economic depreciation derived by Jorgenson and Yun (1990) from the best geometric approximation approach of Hulten and Wykoff for all assets distinguished by the Bureau of Economic Analysis (BEA) in constructing the U.S. national income and product accounts. Hulten and Wykoff have compared the best geometric average rates with depreciation rates employed by BEA in constructing perpetual inventory estimates of capital stock. The Hulten-Wykoff rates for equipment average 0.133, while the BEA rates average 0.141, so that the two sets of rates are very similar. The Hulten-Wykoff rates for structures average 0.037, while the BEA rates average 0.060; these rates are substantially different.

Hulten and Wykoff (1981b) have summarized estimates of economic depreciation completed prior to their own study. The most common methodology for such studies is based on vintage price functions.[23] An alternative to the vintage price approach is to employ rental prices rather than asset prices in estimating patterns of decline in efficiency. This approach has been employed by Malpezzi, Ozanne, and Thibodeau (1987) to analyze rental price data on residential structures and Taubman and Rasche (1969) to study rental price data on commercial structures. While leases on residential property are frequently one year or less in duration, leases on commercial property are typically for much longer periods of time. Since the rental prices are constant over the period of the lease, estimates based on annual rental prices for commercial property are biased toward the "one-hoss shay" pattern found by Taubman and Rasche; Malpezzi, Ozanne, and Thibodeau find rental price profiles for residential property that decline with age.

A second alternative to the vintage price approach is to analyze investment for replacement purposes.[24] Coen (1980) compares the explanatory power of alternative patterns of decline in efficiency in a model of investment behavior that also includes the price of capital services. For equipment he finds that 11 of 21 two-digit manufacturing industries are characterized by geometric decline in efficiency, three by sum of the years' digits and seven by straight-

Table 3.6 **Economic Depreciation Rates: Business Assets**

Assets	Old Lifetime	Old Depreciation Rate	New Lifetime	New Depreciation Rate
1. Household furniture & fixtures	15	.1100	12	.1375
2. Other furniture	15	.1100	14	.1179
3. Fabricated metal products	18	.0917	18	.0917
4. Steam engines & turbines	21	.0786	32	.0516
5. Internal combustion engines	21	.0786	8	.2063
6. Farm tractors	8	.1633	9	.1452
7. Construction tractors	8	.1633	8	.1633
8. Agricultural machinery	17	.0971	14	.1179
9. Construction machinery	9	.1722	10	.1722
10. Mining & oilfield machinery	10	.1650	11	.1500
11. Metalworking machinery	16	.1225	16	.1225
12. Special industry machinery	16	.1031	16	.1031
13. General industrial	14	.1225	16	.1225
14. Office, computing	8	.2729	8	.2729
15. Service industry machinery	10	.1650	10	.1650
16. Communication equipment	14	.1179	15	.1100
17. Electrical transmission	14	.1179	33	.0500
18. Household appliances	14	.1179	10	.1651
19. Other electrical equipment	14	.1179	9	.1834
20. Trucks, buses, & truck trailers	9	.2537	9	.2537
21. Autos	10	.3333	10	.3333
22. Aircraft	16	.1833	16	.1833
23. Ships & boats	22	.0750	27	.0611
24. Railroad equipment	25	.0660	30	.0550
25. Scientific & engineering instruments	11	.1473	12	.1350
26. Photocopy & related equipment	11	.1473	9	.1800
27. Other nonresidential equipment	11	.1473	11	.1473
28. Industrial buildings	27	.0361	31	.0361
29. Mobile offices	36	.0247	16	.0556
30. Office buildings	36	.0247	36	.0247
31. Commercial warehouses	36	.0247	40	.0222
32. Other commercial buildings	36	.0247	34	.0262
33. Religious buildings	48	.0188	48	.0188
34. Educational buildings	48	.0188	48	.0188
35. Hospital & institutional buildings	48	.0233	48	.0233
36. Hotels & motels	40	.0247	32	.0247
37. Amusement & recreational	31	.0454	30	.0469
38. Other nonfarm buildings	31	.0454	38	.0370
39. Railroad structures	51	.0176	54	.0166
40. Telephone & telegraph structures	27	.0333	40	.0225
41. Electric light & power structures	30	.0300	40	.0225
42. Gas structures	30	.0300	40	.0225
43. Local transit	26	.0450	38	.0450
44. Petroleum pipelines	26	.0450	40	.0450
45. Farm structures	38	.0237	38	.0237
46. Petroleum & natural gas	16	.0563	16	.0563
47. Other mining exploration	16	.0563	16	.0563
48. Other nonresidential structures	31	.0290	40	.0225
49. Railroad replacement track	51	.0176	38	.0236
50. Nuclear fuel	—	—	6	.2500
51. Residential structures	—	.0130	—	.0130

Source: Jorgenson and Yun (1990), table 13B, p. 82.

line patterns. For structures he finds that 14 industries are characterized by geometric decline, five by straight-line, and two by one-hoss-shay patterns. Hulten and Wykoff (1981b) conclude that: "The weight of Coen's study is evidently on the side of the geometric and near-geometric forms of depreciation."

3.3.2 Data Sources and Methods for Capital Input

Data on capital input are unavailable for the government sector, excluding government enterprises, listed in table 3.2. For each of the 35 private industrial sectors listed in this table, prices and quantities of capital input are cross-classified by four asset classes—producers' durable equipment, nonresidential structures, inventories, and land—and three legal forms of organization—corporate and noncorporate business and nonprofit enterprises.

Data on producers' durable equipment can be further subdivided among the 27 categories listed in table 3.6, while data on nonresidential structures can be subdivided among 23 categories listed there. For the 35 private industrial sectors listed in table 3.2 annual data from 1947 to 1985 on capital stock and its rental price are required for an average of as many as 156 components of the capital stock. Households and institutions are treated as a separate sector with prices and quantities of capital input cross-classified by producers' and consumers' durable equipment, residential and nonresidential structures, and land.

The first step in developing sectoral measures of capital input is to construct estimates of capital stock by industry for each year from 1947 to 1985. Investment data from the Bureau of Economic Analysis (1987a) for producers' durable equipment and structures are distributed among industries on an establishment basis. Estimates of investment for all sectors are controlled to totals from the U.S. national product accounts. For residential structures investment data are taken directly from the U.S. national product accounts.[25] Investment goods prices from the U.S. national product accounts are employed to obtain estimates of investment in equipment and structures in constant prices.

Estimates of stocks of land by industry begin with estimates of the stock of land for the economy as a whole. Balance sheet data are employed to allocate land among industrial sectors and between corporate and noncorporate business within each sector with the exception of private households and nonprofit institutions. BEA has constructed estimates of inventory stocks in current and constant prices for all sectors. These estimates are consistent with data on inventory investment for the U.S. economy as a whole from the national product accounts. The data are broken down by legal form of organization within each industry.

The second step in developing sectoral measures of capital input is to construct estimates of prices of capital services from data on property compensation. For each asset the price of investment goods is a weighted sum of future rental prices, discounted by a factor that incorporates future rates of return. Weights are given by the relative efficiencies of capital goods of different ages. The same weights are used in constructing estimates of rental prices and capital stocks. For depreciable assets the weights decline with age; for nondepreciable assets the weights are constant.

Differences in the tax treatment of property compensation among legal forms of organization result in differences in rental prices of capital services. Estimates of the rental prices of capital services in the corporate sector include data on the corporate income tax. Data on property taxes for corporate business are also included. Property compensation for corporate business within each industrial sector must be allocated among equipment, structures, land, and inventories. Corporate property compensation is the sum of rental payments for capital services for all four classes of assets.

Similarly, data on property taxes for noncorporate business are included in estimates of the rental prices of capital services in the noncorporate sector. The noncorporate rate of return is set equal to the corporate rate of return after corporate taxes. This assumption makes it possible to allocate noncorporate income between labor and property compensation. Noncorporate property compensation is the sum of rental payments for capital services for all four classes of assets.

To derive prices of capital services for private households and nonprofit institutions, the rate of return on owner-occupied housing must be estimated. The rate of return for private households and nonprofit institutions is set equal to the corporate rate of return after corporate and personal taxes. Data on property taxes for private households are incorporated into estimates of the rental prices of capital services used in this sector. Property compensation for households and institutions is the sum of rental payments for all classes of assets.

The final step in constructing data on capital input for each of the 35 private industrial sectors is to combine price and quantity data, cross-classified by class of asset and legal form of organization, into price and quantity indexes of capital input. To construct an index of capital input for each industrial sector, I express sectoral capital input, say $\{K_i\}$, as a translog function of its 156 individual components, say $\{K_{ki}\}$. The corresponding index of sectoral capital input is a translog quantity index of individual capital inputs:

$$\ln K_i(T) - \ln K_i(T-1) = \Sigma \bar{v}^i_{Kk} [\ln K_{ki}(T) - \ln K_{ki}(T-1)], \quad (i = 1, 2, \ldots, n),$$

where weights are given by average shares of each component in the value of sectoral property compensation:

$$\bar{v}^i_{Kk} = \frac{1}{2} [v^i_{Kk}(T) + v^i_{Kk}(T-1), \quad (i = 1, 2, \ldots, n;\ k = 1, 2, \ldots, p),$$

and

$$v_{Kk}^{i} = \frac{p_{Kk}^{i} K_{ki}}{\Sigma p_{Kk}^{i} K_{ki}}, \quad (i = 1, 2, \ldots, n; k = 1, 2, \ldots, p).$$

The value shares are computed from data on capital services $\{K_{ki}\}$ and the rental price of capital services $\{p_{Kk}^{i}\}$, cross-classified by asset class and legal form of organization. An analogous approach is applied to data for private households and institutions.

A measure of capital stock for each sector can be derived by adding capital stocks across all categories of capital input within that sector. The quality of capital stock is defined as the ratio of capital input to capital stock. Changes in the quality of capital stock represent differences between changes in the translog quantity index of capital input and changes in an unweighted index of capital stock. Indexes of the quantity of capital input are presented in table 3.2 for 36 sectors. The corresponding indexes of capital quality and capital stock are presented in table 3.3.

The rental prices introduced by Christensen and Jorgenson (1969, 1970, 1973a, 1973b) were extended to the level of individual industrial sectors by Fraumeni and Jorgenson (1980) and Gollop and Jorgenson (1980). Fraumeni and Jorgenson (1986) have incorporated patterns of relative efficiencies based on the best geometric average (BGA) rates fitted by Hulten and Wykoff. The data on capital input that underly tables 3.2 and 3.3 incorporate differences in depreciation patterns by types of producers' durable equipment and nonresidential structures, differences in tax treatment by corporate and noncorporate business and nonprofit forms of organization, and differences in efficiency by age for an average of as many as 156 types of capital input for each of the 35 private industrial sectors. Additional types of capital input are distinguished for consumers' durable equipment and residential structures utilized by private households and institutions.

3.3.3 Alternative Sources and Methods

An overview of issues in the measurement of capital input is provided by the Rees Report National Research Council (1979, esp. 128–40). The treatment of capital as a factor of production became the central issue in an extended debate among Denison (1957, 1966, 1969, 1972), Griliches (1961a), Griliches and Jorgenson (1966), Hulten (chap. 4, in this volume), Jorgenson (1968, 1973a, 1980, 1989), Jorgenson and Griliches (1967, 1972a, 1972b), and Kendrick (1961b, 1968, 1973). The debate has been summarized and evaluated by Diewert (1980, 480), Katz (1988), Mohr (1988b, 1988c), and Norsworthy (1984a, 1984b). To provide additional perspective on the measurement of capital input I find it useful to compare the methodology and data sources that underly the indexes presented in tables 3.2 and 3.3 with those of BLS, Denison, and Kendrick.

Internal consistency of a measure of capital input requires that the same pattern of relative efficiency is employed in measuring both capital stock and the rental price of capital services. The decline in efficiency affects both the level of capital stock and the corresponding rental price. The estimates of capital stocks and rental prices that underly the data presented in tables 3.2 and 3.3 are based on geometrically declining relative efficiencies with the rates of decline presented in table 3.6. The same patterns of decline in efficiency are used for both capital stock and the rental price of each asset, so that the requirement for internal consistency of measures of capital input is met.

I next describe the methods and data sources employed by BLS, Denison, and Kendrick for estimating capital stocks. I then present their methods and sources for estimating rental prices of capital services and attempt to determine whether the resulting measures of capital input are internally consistent. Denison and Kendrick employ estimates of capital stock for equipment and structures from the BEA capital stock study. The methodology employed by BEA in constructing estimates of capital stock is described by the BEA (1987a), Gorman, Musgrave, Silverstein, and Comins (1985), Musgrave (1986), and Young and Musgrave (1980). These estimates are derived by the perpetual inventory method using investment data based on the U.S. national product accounts. BLS also utilizes the perpetual inventory method to derive estimates of capital stock for equipment and structures from investment data based on the U.S. national product accounts.

The perpetual inventory method for measuring capital input is employed in all four studies that we consider. In this method the sequence of relative efficiencies of capital goods of different ages $\{d(\tau)\}$ enables us to characterize capital stock at the end of each period, say $A(T)$, as a weighted sum of past investments:

$$A(T) = \sum_{\tau=0}^{\infty} d(\tau) I(T-\tau),$$

where $I(T - \tau)$ is investment in period $T - \tau$ and the weights are given by the sequence of relative efficiencies.

For each asset, the sequence of relative efficiencies of capital goods of different ages enables us to characterize the price of investment goods in each period, say $P_I(T)$, as a weighted sum of future rentals:

$$p_I(T) = \sum_{\tau=0}^{\infty} d(\tau) \prod_{S=1}^{\tau+1} \frac{1}{1 + r(T+S)} p_K(T+\tau+1),$$

where $p_K(T+\tau+1)$ is the rental price in period $T+\tau+1$ and the weights are given by the sequence of relative efficiencies $\{d(\tau)\}$. In this expression $r(T)$ is the rate of return on capital in period T and $\Pi_{S=1}^{\tau+1}\ 1/[1 + r(T+S)]$ is the discount factor in period T for future prices in period $T+\tau+1$.

Capital goods decline in efficiency at each point of time, generating needs for replacement of productive capacity. The proportion of an investment to be replaced at age τ, say $m(\tau)$, is equal to the decline in efficiency from age $\tau - 1$ to age τ:

$$m(\tau) = -[d(\tau) - d(\tau - 1)], \quad (\tau = 1, 2, \ldots, T).$$

I refer to these proportions as *mortality rates* for capital goods of different ages.

I define deprecation as the value that must be recovered in every period to keep wealth intact. Taking first differences of the expression for the price of investment goods in terms of future rental prices, we can express the depreciation on a capital good in period T, say $p_D(T)$, in terms of future rental prices and the mortality distribution $\{m(\tau)\}$:

$$p_D(T) = \sum_{\tau=1}^{\infty} m(\tau) \prod_{S=1}^{\tau} \frac{1}{1 + r(T+S)} p_K(T+\tau).$$

We begin our comparison of alternative measures of rental prices of capital services with a characterization of the rental price concept. In the absence of taxation the rental price of capital services at time T takes the form:

$$p_K(T) = p_I(T - 1)r(T) + p_D(T) - [p_I(T) - p_I(T - 1)],$$

where depreciation, $p_D(T)$, depends on the pattern of relative efficiencies. The value of the services of capital stock is the product of the rental price and the quantity of capital stock:

$$p_K(T)A(T - 1) = \{p_I(T - 1)r(T) + p_D(T) - [p_I(T) - p_I(T - 1)\} \cdot A(T - 1).$$

Finally, the value of capital services is equal to property compensation, so that we can solve for the rate of return, given data on property compensation:

$$r(T) = \frac{\text{Property compensation} - \{p_D(T) - [p_I(T) - p_I(T - 1)]\} \cdot A(T - 1)}{p_I(T - 1) \cdot A(T - 1)}.$$

The first and most important criterion for internal consistency of a measure of capital input is that the same patterns of relative efficiency must underlie both the estimates of capital stock $A(T)$ and the estimates of rental price $p_K(T)$ for each class of assets. Hulten and Wykoff (1981b) have shown that the BGA rates of depreciation provide an accurate description of the decline in the price of acquisition of capital goods with age. The Hulten-Wykoff geometric rates are utilized in compiling estimates of both capital stocks and rental prices for the indexes of capital input presented in tables 3.1 and 3.2.

BLS (1983, 57–59) also employs relative efficiency functions estimated by Hulten and Wykoff. However, BLS does not utilize the geometric relative efficiency functions fitted by Hulten and Wykoff. Instead, BLS has fitted a set of hyperbolic functions to the relative efficiency functions estimated by Hulten and Wykoff. Consistency is preserved between the resulting estimates of capital stocks and rental prices by implementing a system of vintage accounts for each class of assets. Implicitly, this set of accounts includes asset prices and quantities of investment goods of all ages at each point of time. BLS (1983, 57–59) shows that measures of capital input based on hyperbolic and geometric relative efficiency functions are very similar.

For each class of assets Denison's estimates of capital stock are based on a linearly declining pattern of relative efficiency. To derive the method of depreciation appropriate for linearly declining relative efficiencies, we first express depreciation for an asset of age V at time T, say $p_D(T, V)$, in the form:

$$\begin{aligned} p_D(T, V) &= \sum_{\tau=1}^{\infty} m(\tau+V) \prod_{S=1}^{\tau} \frac{1}{1 + r(T + S)} p_K(T+\tau), \\ &= \frac{1}{\theta L} \sum_{\tau=1}^{L-V-1} \prod_{S=1}^{\tau} \frac{1}{1 + r(T+S)} p_K(T+\tau) \\ &\quad + [1 - \frac{1}{\theta}(1 - \frac{1}{L})] \prod_{S=1}^{L-V} p_K(T+L-V). \end{aligned}$$

Assuming that the rates of return $\{r(T + S)\}$ and the prices of capital services $\{p_K(T+\tau)\}$ are constant, we obtain the following expression for depreciation on an asset of age V:

$$p_D(V) = \frac{1}{r\theta L} - \left[\frac{1}{r\theta L} - 1 + \frac{1}{\theta}\right]\left(\frac{1}{1+r}\right)^{L-V} p_K, \quad (V = 0, 1, \ldots, L-1).$$

Similarly, the value of a new asset is equal to the sum of depreciation over all ages:

$$\begin{aligned} p_I &= \sum_{V=0}^{L-1} p_D(V), \\ &= \frac{1}{r}\left(\frac{1}{\theta} - \left[\frac{1}{r\theta L} - 1 + \frac{1}{\theta}\right]\left[1 - \left(\frac{1}{1+r}\right)^{L}\right]\right)p_K, \end{aligned}$$

so that depreciation allowances appropriate for a linearly declining pattern of relative efficiency are given for each age by the formula:

$$\frac{p_D(V)}{p_I} = \frac{\frac{1}{\theta L} - r\left[\frac{1}{r\theta L} - 1 + \frac{1}{\theta}\right]\left(\frac{1}{1+r}\right)^{L-V}}{\frac{1}{\theta} - \left[\frac{1}{r\theta L} - 1 + \frac{1}{\theta}\right]\left[1 - \left(\frac{1}{1+r}\right)^{L}\right]}, \quad (V = 0, 1, \ldots, L-1).$$

The value of depreciation at time T for a linearly declining pattern of relative efficiency is the sum over assets of all ages:

$$\sum_{V=0}^{L-1} p_D(T, V)I(T-V-1) =$$

$$p_I(T) \sum_{V=0}^{L-1} \frac{\dfrac{1}{\theta L} - r\left[\dfrac{1}{r\theta L} - 1 + \dfrac{1}{\theta}\right]\left(\dfrac{1}{1+r}\right)^{L-V}}{\dfrac{1}{\theta} - \left[\dfrac{1}{r\theta L} - 1 + \dfrac{1}{\theta}\right]\left[1 - \left(\dfrac{1}{1+r}\right)^{L}\right]} I(T - V - 1).$$

Denison employs linearly declining relative efficiency in measuring capital stock; in fact, he employs three different weighted averages of the straight-line and "one-hoss shay" patterns.[26] For all three weighted averages Denison employs the straight-line method of depreciation. For linearly declining patterns of relative efficiency, depreciation allowances are increasing, constant, or decreasing with age for values of the parameter θ greater than, equal to, or less than $1 + (1/rL)$, respectively. For the straight-line pattern depreciation allowances are decreasing with age; for the one-hoss shay pattern depreciation allowances are increasing with age. Denison's assumption that depreciation allowances are constant is not appropriate for any of his methods of measuring capital stock, so that all three of the resulting measures of capital input are internally inconsistent.

Kendrick (1973, 27–29) employs capital stock estimates based on linearly declining relative efficiencies in allocating property compensation among assets on the basis of "net earnings." Kendrick's measure of net earnings is based on capital consumption allowances from the U.S. national income accounts as an estimate of depreciation. These estimates are based in turn on depreciation allowances for tax purposes and do not reflect a consistent valuation of assets over time or a consistent method of depreciation.

The method of depreciation appropriate for Kendrick's estimates of capital stock based on linearly declining relative efficiencies is the same as that we have given above for Denison with the parameter θ equal to unity:

$$\frac{p_D(V)}{p_I} = \frac{\dfrac{1}{L}\left[1 - \left(\dfrac{1}{1+r}\right)^{L-V}\right]}{1 - \dfrac{1}{rL}\left[1 - \left(\dfrac{1}{1+r}\right)^{L}\right]}, \quad (V = 0, 1, \ldots, L-1).$$

The value of depreciation at time T for linearly declining relative efficiencies is the sum over assets of all ages:

$$\sum_{V=0}^{L-1} p_D(T, V)I(T-V-1) = p_I(T) \sum_{V=0}^{L-1} \frac{\frac{1}{L}\left[1 - \left(\frac{1}{1+r}\right)^{L-V}\right]}{1 - \frac{1}{rL}\left[1 - \left(\frac{1}{1+r}\right)^{L}\right]} I(T - V - 1).$$

Kendrick (1973) also employs alternative capital stock estimates based on constant relative efficiencies in allocating property compensation among assets on the basis of "gross earnings." Constant relative efficiencies are also utilized by Kendrick and Grossman (1980, 26) and Kendrick (1983a, 56–57). The declining balance pattern of relative efficiencies employed by Kendrick is inappropriate for constant relative efficiencies. The correct method is given by the limit of the formula described above with θ going to positive infinity:

$$\frac{P_D(V)}{p_I} = \frac{r\left(\frac{1}{1+r}\right)^{L-V}}{1 - \left(\frac{1}{1+r}\right)^{L}}, \quad (V = 0, 1, \ldots, L-1).$$

The value of depreciation at time T for constant relative efficiencies is the sum:

$$\sum_{V=0}^{L-1} p_D(T, V)I(T - V - 1) = p_I(T) \sum_{V=0}^{L-1} \frac{r\left(\frac{1}{1+r}\right)^{L-V}}{1 - \left(\frac{1}{1+r}\right)^{L}} I(T - V - 1).$$

My conclusion is that neither of Kendrick's two measures of capital input is based on an internally consistent treatment of capital stocks and rental prices of capital services. In estimating capital stocks Kendrick uses straight-line and one-hoss shay patterns of relative efficiency. His weights based on gross earnings ignore differences among assets in rates of depreciation; his weights based on net earnings employ depreciation as calculated for tax purposes, so that neither the depreciation method nor the valuation of assets is consistent over time.

The estimates of capital service prices that underly the capital input indexes presented in table 3.2 incorporate differences in property tax rates among types of assets, differences in the tax treatment of corporate and noncorporate income due to the corporate income tax, and differences between equipment and structures due to variations in the tax formulas for depreciation and the investment tax credit for equipment. BLS (1983, 50) employs data on tax depreciation and the investment tax credit and differences in property tax rates among types of assets. However, corporate and noncorporate assets are assumed to have the same capital service prices, so that the effect of the corporate income tax is ignored. Denison and Kendrick ignore differences in property tax rates among types of assets, the effect of the corporate income tax, the tax treatment of depreciation, and the investment tax credit in allocating property compensation among assets.[27]

We have focused the discussion of capital input on the internal consistency of estimates of capital stocks and the corresponding rental prices. However, it is important to emphasize an important conceptual difference between Kendrick's measures of sectoral capital input and the measures we have presented in tables 3.2 and 3.3. Kendrick (e.g., 1973, 146) purposefully defines any growth in sectoral output due to shifts in the composition of the capital stock by class of asset or legal form of organization as part of productivity change. For Kendrick, any shift in the mix of capital by depreciation pattern or tax treatment that leads to greater levels of sectoral output reflects an advance in knowledge and is therefore part of productivity change. I evaluate Kendrick's definition of productivity change in section 3.4.3 below.

The data on capital input presented in tables 3.2 and 3.3 incorporate shifts in the composition of the capital stock by class of asset and legal form of organization within an industrial sector. The data on capital input in table 3.1 incorporate these shifts for the U.S. economy as a whole. Gollop and Jorgenson (1980) provide a detailed comparison between capital input indexes of this type and those of Kendrick for the period 1947–73. Quality change is an important component of the growth in capital input. This component accounts for much of the difference between Kendrick's estimates of capital stock and the translog indexes of capital input given in tables 3.2 and 3.3.

3.4 Measuring Output, Intermediate Input, and Productivity

An important innovation embodied in the data on productivity presented in table 3.2 is that intermediate, capital, and labor inputs are treated symmetrically at the sectoral level. The value of output at the sectoral level includes the value of intermediate input as well as the values of capital and labor inputs. All three inputs are employed in analyzing the sources of growth in sectoral output. The industry definitions employed in the U.S. national income accounts are used in measuring output. These definitions are based on establishments within each industry.

A more restrictive methodology for sectoral productivity measurement is based on the concept of value added. Output is represented as a function of intermediate input and value added; value added is represented in turn as a function of capital input, labor input, and time. In the value added approach intermediate input is not treated symmetrically with capital and labor inputs. The existence of the value added aggregate requires that time and capital and labor inputs are separable from intermediate input. Given the quantities of intermediate input and value added, output is independent of changes in technology.

The methodology for productivity measurement outlined in previous sections treats all three inputs symmetrically. The sectoral models of production do not require the existence of a value added aggregate in constructing an index of productivity growth. The value-added approach is based on more restrictive assumptions but requires precisely the same data. Both the restricted and unrestricted methodologies require prices and quantities of output and intermediate, capital, and labor inputs for full implementation.

3.4.1 Sectoral Output, Intermediate Input, and Productivity

I have employed a model of production based on a production function $\{F^i\}$ for each of the n sectors. The production function gives output $\{Z_i\}$ as a function of intermediate input $\{X_i\}$, capital input $\{K_i\}$, labor input $\{L_i\}$, and time T. We can specialize this model by introducing a value-added function $\{G^i\}$ for each sector, giving the quantity of value added, say $\{V_i\}$, as a function of capital input, labor input, and time:[28]

$$V_i = G^i(K_i, L_i, T), \quad (i = 1, 2, \ldots, n),$$

where

$$\begin{aligned} Z_i &= F^i(X_i, V_i), \\ &= F^i[X_i, G^i(K_i, L_i, T)], \quad (i = 1, 2, \ldots, n). \end{aligned}$$

I say that the production function is neutral with respect to intermediate input, since the substitution of intermediate input for value added is unaffected by changes in technology. If the value-added function is homogeneous of degree one in capital and labor inputs, we say that the production function is homothetically neutral. Homogeneity implies that proportional changes in capital and labor inputs result in proportional changes in value added, so that the value-added function is characterized by constant returns to scale. If the production function is homogeneous of degree one in intermediate, capital, and labor inputs, neutrality of the production function implies homothetic neutrality.

Denoting the price of value added by $\{p_V^i\}$, we can define the share of value added, say $\{v_V^i\}$, in the value of output by

$$v_V^i = \frac{p_V^i V_i}{q_i Z_i}, \quad (i = 1, 2, \ldots, n).$$

Necessary conditions for producer equilibrium include equalities between the share of value added and the elasticity of output with respect to value added:

$$v_V^i = \frac{\partial \ln Z_i}{\partial \ln V_i}(X_i, V_i), \quad (i = 1, 2, \ldots, n).$$

Under constant returns to scale the elasticities and the value shares for intermediate input and value added sum to unity, so that the value of output is equal to the sum of the values of intermediate input and value added. Necessary conditions for producer equilibrium also include equalities between the shares of capital and labor inputs in value added and the elasticities of the quantity of value added with respect to those inputs. Conditions for producer equilibrium imply that value added is equal to the sum of the values of capital and labor inputs.

In defining output Kendrick (1973, 17) considers whether or not to exclude the value of depreciation from the value of output. At the sectoral level, depreciation could be excluded along with the value of intermediate goods in the measurement of value added. Kendrick considers two measures of productivity, one based on value-added gross of depreciation and the other based on value-added net of depreciation. He associates the gross measure with gross capital stock as a measure of capital input and the net measure with net capital stock as a measure of capital input.

In section 3.3.3, above, I have shown that the selection of an appropriate concept of capital input depends on the relative efficiencies of capital goods of different vintages. Associated with each measure of capital input $A(T-1)$, there is a corresponding measure of depreciation $p_D(T)$. Gross capital stock, as defined by Kendrick, corresponds to the one-hoss shay pattern of decline in efficiency. I have given the corresponding measure of depreciation in section 3.3.3. There is no connection between gross capital stock as a measure of capital input and value added gross of depreciation as a measure of output. Similarly, there is no connection between net capital stock as a measure of capital input and value-added net of depreciation as a measure of output. For any pattern of decline in efficiency there are corresponding measures of depreciation and capital input. For any measure of depreciation, there are measures of value added both gross and net of depreciation.

Kendrick (1973, 18) indicates that he would have preferred to use a measure of output net of depreciation. Kendrick is able to implement an approach based on value-added net of depreciation only at the economy-wide level, where he uses net national product in place of gross national product as a measure of value added. To evaluate Kendrick's approach to the measurement of value-added net of depreciation we can decompose the value of capital input into the value of return to capital, evaluated at the own rate of return, and the value of depreciation:

$$p_K(T)A(T-1) = p_I(T-1)\left[r(T) - \frac{p_I(T) - p_I(T-1)}{p_I(T-1)}\right] A(T-1) + p_D(T)A(T-1).$$

As before, I have simplified this expression by ignoring the impact of taxation.

Value added $p_V(T)V(T)$ is the sum of the value of capital input

$p_K(T)A(T-1)$ and the value of labor input $p_L(T)L(T)$. Value-added net of depreciation is defined as the difference between value added and the value of depreciation:

$$p_V(T)V(T) - p_D(T)A(T-1) = p_I(T-1)\left[r(T) - \frac{p_I(T) - p_I(T-1)}{p_I(T-1)}\right] A(T-1) + p_L(T)L(T).$$

Capital stock $A(T-1)$ appears on both the left-hand side, where it is associated with depreciation, and on the right-hand side, where it is associated with the own rate of return on capital or, using Kendrick's terminology, the net earnings of capital.

Gross value added $\{V^i\}$ can be rationalized as a measure of output by imposing a separability assumption on the production function $\{F^i\}$ for each sector. This is done by introducing the value-added function $\{G^i\}$ for the sector. Intermediate input is separated from capital and labor inputs and changes in technology by the value added function. Gross value added is represented as a function of capital input, labor input, and time. If we were to attempt to represent net value added as a function of capital input, labor input, and time, net value added and the list of inputs would both involve the quantity of capital input.

By contrast with net value added, gross value added can be defined, implicitly, as a function of output and intermediate input. The corresponding definition of net value added would involve output, intermediate input, and capital input. I conclude that the quantity of net value added is not an appropriate point of departure for modeling producer behavior. At the economywide level only Kendrick's measure of productivity based on gross value added avoids including capital input in the definition of both output and input. Fortunately, only gross value added is used for Kendrick's sectoral aggregates of individual industries, so that his sectoral measures of productivity are free from this defect.

Kendrick and Grossman (1980, 22–25) and Kendrick (1983a, 56) have employed measures of output at the level of individual industries based on data from the BEA on gross product originating in each industrial sector. Both studies have dropped the concept of value added net of depreciation employed by Kendrick (1973). This important change in methodology has the advantage over the methodology employed in Kendrick's (1973) study that the problem of including capital input in both net value added and the list of inputs is entirely avoided.[29]

3.4.2 Data Sources and Methods for Output and Intermediate Input

Data on output in current and constant prices are available from the Office of Economic Growth of the Bureau of Labor Statistics (1987). In order to evaluate output from the point of view of the producing sector, excise and sales taxes must be subtracted and subsidies must be added to the value of output. The resulting price of output from the producers' point of view is equal to the ratio of the value of output in current prices to the value of output in constant prices.

Data on interindustry transactions published by BEA (1984 and various years) must be employed to disaggregate intermediate input by sector of origin. These data are based on industry definitions employed in the U.S. interindustry accounts. In order to bring measures of intermediate input into conformity with industry definitions from the U.S. national income accounts, interindustry transactions must be reallocated among sectors. This reallocation must take into account the reclassifications, redefinitions, and transfers employed in constructing the U.S. interindustry accounts, as discussed by Walderhaug (1973). To construct prices and quantities of intermediate input by sector of origin the value of intermediate input originating in each sector must be deflated by an index of purchasers' prices for the output of that sector. The indexes of producers' prices for the output of each sector are transformed to purchasers' prices by adding sales and excise taxes and subtracting subsidies.

The final step in constructing data on intermediate input for each of the 35 industrial sectors is to combine price and quantity data, classified by sector of origin, into price and quantity indexes of intermediate input. To construct an index of intermediate input for each industrial sector, I express sectoral intermediate input, say $\{X_i\}$, as a translog function of its n individual components, say $\{X_{ji}\}$. The corresponding index of sectoral intermediate input is a translog quantity index of individual intermediate inputs:

$$\ln X_i(T) - \ln X_i(T-1) = \Sigma \bar{v}_{Xj} [\ln X_{ji}(T) - \ln X_{ji}(T-1)], \quad (i = 1, 2, \ldots, n),$$

where weights are given by average shares of each component in the value of sectoral intermediate outlay:

$$\bar{v}^i_{Xj} = \frac{1}{2} [v^i_{Xj}(T) + v^i_{Xj}(T-1)], \quad (i, j = 1, 2, \ldots, n),$$

and

$$v^i_{Xj} = \frac{p^i_{Xj} X_{ji}}{\sum_j p^i_{Xj} X_{ji}}, \quad (i, j = 1, 2 \ldots n).$$

The value shares are computed from data on intermediate input $\{X_{ji}\}$ and the corresponding prices paid by the receiving sectors $\{p^i_{Xj}\}$ for each component of sectoral intermediate input.

An unweighted index of intermediate input for each sector is derived by adding across the intermediate inputs from all originating sectors. The quality of intermediate input is defined as the ratio of the translog quantity index to an unweighted index for each sector. Changes in the quality of intermediate input represent differences between changes in the translog quantity index and changes in the unweighted index. Indexes of the quantity of output and intermediate input are presented in table 3.2 for 35 sectors. The corresponding index of intermediate input quality and an unweighted index of intermediate input are presented in table 3.3 for each sector.

To allocate the growth of sectoral output among the contributions of intermediate, capital, and labor inputs and changes in productivity, I construct data on the rate of productivity growth. To construct on index of productivity for each industrial sector, I express sectoral output $\{X_i\}$ as a translog function of sectoral intermediate input $\{X_i\}$, capital input $\{K_i\}$, labor input $\{L_i\}$, and time T. The corresponding index of productivity is the translog index of the rate of productivity growth $\{\bar{v}_T^i\}$:

$$\begin{aligned}\bar{v}_T^i = {} & [\ln Z_i(T) - \ln Z_i(T-1)] - \bar{v}_X^i [\ln X_i(T) - \ln X_i(T-1)] \\ & - \bar{v}_K^i [\ln K_i(T) - \ln K_i(T-1)] - \bar{v}_L^i [\ln L_i(T) - \ln L_i(T-1)], \\ & (i = 1, 2 \ldots n),\end{aligned}$$

where weights are given by average shares of sectoral intermediate, capital, and labor inputs in the value of sectoral output:

$$\begin{aligned}\bar{v}_T^i &= \frac{1}{2}[v_T^i(T) + v_T^i(T-1)], \\ \bar{v}_X^i &= \frac{1}{2}[v_X^i(T) + v_X^i(T-1)], \\ \bar{v}_K^i &= \frac{1}{2}[v_K^i(T) + v_K^i(T-1)], \\ \bar{v}_L^i &= \frac{1}{2}[v_L^i(T) + v_L^i(T-1)], \quad (i = 1, 2, \ldots, n),\end{aligned}$$

and

$$\begin{aligned}v_X^i &= \frac{p_X^i X_i}{q_i X_i}, \\ v_K^i &= \frac{p_K^i K_i}{q_i Z_i}, \\ v_L^i &= \frac{p_L^i L_i}{q_i Z_i}, \quad (i = 1, 2, \ldots, n).\end{aligned}$$

The starting point for the construction of data on sectoral productivity growth is a sectoral production account in current prices. The fundamental accounting identity is that the value of output is equal to the value of input. The value of output excludes all sales and excise taxes and includes subsidies paid to producers. The value of input includes all taxes and supplements paid made by producers, as well as the compensation received by the suppliers of each input. Valuation from the producers' point of view is essential for the integration of data on output and input into measures of productivity growth at the sectoral level.

The concept of valuation from the point of view of the producer is used in the sectoral production accounts that underlie tables 3.2 and 3.3. This concept is intermediate between the national accounting concepts of valuation at market prices and valuation at factor cost. The value of output at market prices includes taxes paid by producers and excludes subsidies received by producers. The value of output at factor cost excludes these taxes and includes subsidies. Control totals for the values of output and intermediate, capital, and labor inputs are based on the U.S. national income accounts.

For the government sector, excluding government enterprises, output in tables 3.2 and 3.3 is defined as labor input; for private households, output is set equal to an index of capital and labor input. For these sectors productivity growth is zero by definition. Rates of productivity growth for the remaining 35 sectors are presented on an annual basis for the period 1947–85 in table 3.2.

3.4.3 Alternative Sources and Methods

An overview of issues in the measurement of intermediate input is provided by the Rees Report (National Research Council 1979, esp. 140–44). To provide additional perspective on the measurement of output, intermediate input, and productivity we find it useful to compare the methodology and data sources that underly the data presented in tables 3.2 and 3.3 with those of Kendrick and Leontief, who provide alternative estimates of sectoral productivity.[30] In table 3.2 intermediate input is treated symmetrically with capital input and labor input in measuring productivity growth at the sectoral level. The resulting measure of productivity is an index number constructed from data on prices and quantities of output, intermediate input, capital input, and labor input.

The first study of productivity for individual industrial sectors including intermediate input was that of Leontief (1953b). He compared interindustry transactions among 14 industries for the United States for 1919, 1929, and 1939 in constant prices of 1939. For each industry he tabulated relative changes in the ratios of intermediate inputs and labor input to output; the ratio of capital input to output was simply ignored. Relative changes between 1919 and 1929 and between 1929 and 1939 were weighted by averages of the quantities of inputs for each pair of years to obtain an index of productivity change for each sector. The weights were summed to the average value of input into each sector in constant prices of 1939, excluding capital input. If Leontief's weights had been applied to relative changes in the ratios of individual inputs to output, including capital input, he would have obtained the negative of the translog index of productivity growth presented in table 3.2.

Kendrick (1956, 1961a, 1973) advocates an approach to sectoral productivity measurement based on value added, where value added is defined as the sum of the value of capital input and the value of labor input. Kendrick's approach to productivity measurement is based on the model I have presented in section 3.4.1 above, with output represented as a function of intermediate input and the quantity of value added. The price and quantity of value added are index numbers constructed from data on prices and quantities of output and intermediate input. Value added is represented as a function of capital input, labor input, and time. The corresponding measure of productivity is an index number constructed from data on prices and quantities of value added, capital input, and labor input.

Kendrick combines value added functions for each sector with necessary conditions for producer equilibrium. The rate of productivity growth for value added is an appropriate measure of productivity, provided that output can be represented as a function of intermediate input and value added. In fact, Kendrick (1973, 17) does not use value added as a measure of output at the level of individual industries included in his study. He employs output in measuring productivity at the level of individual industries and simply ignores the growth of intermediate input. The resulting rates of productivity growth are measures of the rate of productivity growth for value added only if rates of growth of output and intermediate goods are identical.

To provide further perspective on Kendrick's approach, I represent the accounting identity between the value of output, say $\{q_i Z_i\}$, and the sum of the values of intermediate input $\{p_X^i X_i\}$, capital input $\{p_K^i K_i\}$, and labor input $\{p_L^i L_i\}$ in the form:

$$q_i X_i = p_X^i X_i + p_K^i K_i + p_L^i L_i, \quad (i = 1, 2, \ldots, n).$$

Value added, say $p_V^i V_i$, is defined as the difference between the value of output and the value of intermediate input:

$$\begin{aligned} p_V^i V_i &= q_i Z_i - p_X^i X_i, \\ &= p_K^i K_i + p^i L_i, \quad (i = 1, 2, \ldots, n), \end{aligned}$$

so that value added is equal to the sum of the values of capital and labor inputs. By employing output $\{q_i Z_i\}$ in place of value added $\{p_V^i V_i\}$ and setting the value of input equal to the sum of the values of capital and labor inputs, Kendrick has omitted on average more than half of the value of sectoral inputs.

The same problem arises in Kendrick's analysis of aggregates over individual industries. For these aggregates Kendrick (1973, 22) employs data from the Bureau of Economic Analysis on gross product originating. For approximately 50% of the business economy the data are based on output rather than value added, so that Kendrick's measures of productivity for aggregates over individual industries ignore the growth of intermediate input for half of the industries. The condition required for validity of his measures of productivity growth for aggregates is precisely the same as the condition we have given for individual industries: Rates of growth of output and intermediate inputs must be identical for all sectors.

We can test Kendrick's assumption directly, using the output and intermediate input data presented in tables 3.2 and 3.3. Table 3.7 presents the average annual rates of growth of output and intermediate input in each of 35 sectors over the 1947–69 period, the period analyzed by Kendrick (1973). The ratio

Table 3.7 Sectoral Intermediate Input and Output: Rates of Growth, 1947–69

Industry	Average Annual Rates of Growth		Ratio of Growth of Intermediate Input to Growth of Output
	Intermediate Input	Output	
Agriculture, forestry & fisheries	.0174	.0173	1.0023
Metal mining	.0419	.0153	2.7407
Coal mining	−.0113	−.0081	1.3881
Crude petroleum & natural gas	.0453	.0381	1.1885
Nonmetallic mineral mining	.0515	.0478	1.0775
Construction	.0383	.0422	.9084
Food & kindred products	.0214	.0253	.8482
Tobacco manufactures	.0042	.0075	.5567
Textile mill products	.0266	.0293	.9060
Apparel & other textile products	.0296	.0336	.8818
Lumber & wood products	.0242	.0191	1.2706
Furniture & fixtures	.0320	.0342	.9350
Paper & allied products	.0401	.0417	.9627
Printing & publishing	.0386	.0330	1.1691
Chemicals & allied products	.0461	.0625	.7382
Petroleum refining	.0314	.0406	.7722
Rubber & plastic products	.0538	.0549	.9804
Leather & leather products	−.0081	.0000	.0000
Stone, clay, & glass products	.0453	.0390	1.1598
Primary metals	.0305	.0218	1.3937
Fabricated metal products	.0332	.0337	.9866
Machinery, except electrical	.0418	.0359	1.1647
Electrical machinery	.0512	.0620	.8254
Motor vehicles	.0398	.0434	.9165
Other transportation equipment	.0837	.0765	1.0931
Instruments	.0398	.0506	.7864
Miscellaneous manufacturing	.0338	.0371	.9112
Transportation & warehousing	.0326	.0251	1.2998
Communication	.0560	.0701	.7984
Electric utilities	.0465	.0647	.7194
Gas utilities	.0964	.0787	1.2245
Trade	.0361	.0368	.9794
Finance, insurance, & real estate	.0553	.0471	1.1751
Other services	.0527	.0386	1.3663
Government enterprises	.0573	.0344	1.6663

of the average annual rate of growth of intermediate input to the corresponding growth rate of output is reported for each sector in the last column of table 3.7. Ratios greater than unity in table 3.7 suggest that Kendrick's measures of productivity growth are upward biased, while ratios less than unity imply downward biased measures. The data in table 3.7 illustrate that Kendrick's assumption is inappropriate and, more important, a significant source of bias. Even if one chooses to restrict the sectoral model of production by postulating the existence of a value-added aggregate, the growth rate of the quantity of value added cannot be measured by the growth rate of output alone.[31]

I have emphasized that Kendrick defines growth in sectoral output due to shifts in the demographic composition of the labor force and shifts in the composition of the capital stock by class of asset or legal form of organization as part of productivity change. However, Kendrick treats growth in sectoral output due to shifts in the composition of input between capital and labor inputs as growth in input rather than productivity change. To eliminate these shifts he weights capital and labor inputs by their marginal products, following the methodology originated by Tinbergen (1942).

It is inconsistent to weight capital and labor inputs by their marginal products without weighting the components of each input by the appropriate marginal products. The theory of production includes both the production function and the necessary conditions for producer equilibrium. These conditions involve the marginal products of capital and labor inputs. They also involve the marginal products of the components of each input. The inconsistency between Kendrick's aggregation of capital and labor inputs and his aggregation within each of these inputs gives rise to substantial biases.

To eliminate biases due to the effects of shifts in the composition of input among intermediate, capital, and labor inputs, these inputs must be weighted by their marginal products, as outlined in section 3.4.2 above. Finally, the components of intermediate input, like the components of capital and labor inputs, must be weighted by the corresponding marginal products. Intermediate inputs account for more than half of the value of inputs at the sectoral level. Omission of intermediate input is a very significant source of bias in Kendrick's measures of productivity growth, as demonstrated by the evidence presented in table 3.7.

In order to assess the biases that arise from using unweighted measures of intermediate, capital, and labor inputs, I have compiled measures of each input with appropriate weights for all components in table 3.2. In Table 3.3 I have compiled the corresponding unweighted measures together with ratios between the weighted and unweighted measures that we identify as indicators of input quality. Measures of input quality should be equal to unity for all sectors in all time periods in order to validate Kendrick's definition of productivity change. The data presented in table 3.3 show that Kendrick's definition is inappropriate and the source of very substantial bias in the measurement of productivity.

In section 3.1.2 I have pointed out that intermediate input is the most important source of growth in output at the sectoral level. In effect, Kendrick has set aside the task of measuring this source of sectoral growth by introducing the assumption that intermediate input and output grow at the same rate. This assumption is contradicted by the evidence presented in table 3.7. Similarly, Kendrick has assumed that capital and labor inputs do not change in quality at the sectoral level, setting aside the task of disaggregating these inputs by marginal productivity. This assumption is contradicted by the evidence presented in table 3.3. In this table capital input is disaggregated by an average of as many as 156 individual components in each sector, while labor input is disaggregated by 160 individual components in each sector.

The data on intermediate input, output, and productivity presented in tables 3.2 and 3.3 incorporate changes in the quality of intermediate, capital, and labor inputs. The data on capital and labor inputs in table 3.1 incorporate these changes for the U.S. economy as a whole. Gollop and Jorgenson (1980) provide a detailed comparison between productivity indexes of this type and those of Kendrick for the period 1947–73. Kendrick's indexes greatly exaggerate the role of productivity change as a source of growth at the sectoral level. Quality change is an important component of the growth of capital and labor inputs at both sectoral and aggregate levels. This component accounts for a substantial portion of the differences between Kendrick's estimates of productivity change and the translog indexes of productivity change given in tables 3.2 and 3.3. However, a sizable portion of these differences can be attributed to Kendrick's omission of intermediate input as a source of growth at the sectoral level.

3.5 Measuring Aggregate Output and Productivity

Following Solow (1957) and Tinbergen (1942), my aggregate model of production is based on a production function, say F, characterized by constant returns to scale:

$$V = F(K, L, T),$$

where T is time, V is value added, and K and L are capital and labor inputs. We can define the shares of capital and labor inputs, say v_K and v_L, in value added by:

$$v_K = \frac{p_K K}{p_V V},$$

$$v_L = \frac{p_L L}{p_V V},$$

where p_V, p_K, and p_L denote the prices of value added, capital input, and labor input, respectively.

Necessary conditions for producer equilibrium are given by equalities between the value shares of each input and the elasticity of output with respect to that input:

$$\nu_K = \frac{\partial \ln V}{\partial \ln K}(K, L, T),$$
$$\nu_L = \frac{\partial \ln V}{\partial \ln L}(K, L, T).$$

Under constant returns to scale, value added is equal to the value of capital and labor inputs. Finally, we can define the rate of productivity growth for the economy as a whole, say ν_T, as the growth rate of value added with respect to time, holding capital input and labor input constant:

$$\nu_T = \frac{\partial \ln V}{\partial T}(K, L. T).$$

The aggregate production function is defined in terms of value added, capital input, and labor input. The quantities of capital and labor inputs are functions of the quantities of their components:

$$K = K(K_1, K_2, \ldots, K_p),$$
$$L = L(L_1, L_2, \ldots, L_q).$$

We can define the shares of the components of capital and labor inputs, say $\{\nu_{Kk}\}$ and $\{\nu_{Ll}\}$, in the value of the corresponding aggregate by:

$$\nu_{Kk} = \frac{p_{Kk} K_k}{\Sigma\, p_{Kk} K_k}, \quad (k = 1, 2, \ldots, p),$$
$$\nu_{Ll} = \frac{p_{Ll} L_l}{\Sigma\, p_{Ll} L_l}, \quad (l = 1, 2, \ldots, q).$$

Necessary conditions for producer equilibrium are given by equalities between the value share of each component and the elasticity of the aggregate with respect to that component:

$$\nu_{Kk} = \frac{\partial \ln K}{\partial \ln K_k}(K_1, K_2 \ldots K_p), \quad (k = 1, 2, \ldots, p),$$
$$\nu_{Ll} = \frac{\partial \ln L}{\partial \ln L_l}(L_1, L_2 \ldots L_q), \quad (l = 1, 2, \ldots, q).$$

Under constant returns to scale, the value of each input is equal to the value of its components.

3.5.1. Aggregation over Sectors

We can also formulate a model of production for the economy as a whole by aggregating over models of production for individual industrial sectors.

The purpose of such a model is to integrate the analysis of sources of economic growth for individual industrial sectors presented in tables 3.2 and 3.3 with the analysis for the economy as a whole presented in table 3.1. For this purpose I adopt the restrictive assumption that a value-added function like that defined in section 3.4 above exists for all sectors. It is important to emphasized that this assumption is not used in constructing the data presented for individual industries in tables 3.2 and 3.3 However, this assumption is implicit in the analysis of sources of economic growth for the economy as a whole presented in table 3.1 and all studies at the aggregate level, beginning with Tinbergen (1942).

We can combine sectoral value added functions for all industrial sectors with market equilibrium conditions for each factor of production to obtain an aggregate model of production. Using this model of production, I allocate the growth of output among contributions of primary factor inputs and the rate of productivity growth in table 3.1. By combining sectoral and aggregate production models we can express the rate of aggregate productivity growth in terms of the rates of sectoral productivity growth and reallocations of value added, capital input, and labor input among sectors.

Aggregate value added V is the sum of quantities of value added $\{V_i\}$ in all industrial sectors. The aggregate model of production includes market equilibrium conditions that take the form of equalities between the supplies of each type of labor $\{L_i\}$ and the sums of demands for that type of labor by all sectors. Similarly, market equilibrium implies equalities between the supplies of each type of capital $\{K_k\}$ and the sums of demands for that type of capital by all sectors.[32] It is possible to distinguish among capital and labor inputs that differ in marginal productivity at the aggregate level as well as at the sectoral level. Deliveries to intermediate demand by all sectors are precisely offset by receipts of intermediate inputs, so that transactions in intermediate goods do not appear at the aggregate level.

The existence of an aggregate production function imposes very stringent requirements on the underlying sectoral models of production.[33] All sectoral value-added functions must be identical to the aggregate production function.[34] In addition, the functions giving capital and labor inputs for each sector in terms of their components must be identical to the corresponding functions at the aggregate level. In essence, the value-added function and the capital and labor input functions for each sector must be replicas of the aggregate functions. The reallocations of value added, capital input, and labor input among sectors presented in table 3.1 provide measures of departures from these assumptions.

Reallocations of value added incorporate differences in value-added functions among industries as well as departures from the separability assumptions required for the existence of a value-added function for each industrial sector. Similarly, reallocations of capital and labor inputs incorporate differences in these aggregates among sectors as well as departures from the separability assumptions required for the existence of the aggregates. If value added and all components of capital and labor inputs were to grow at the same rate for all industries, there would be no reallocations.

The methodology I have outlined for the economy as a whole can be implemented by considering specific forms for the aggregate production function and for capital and labor inputs as functions of their components. I take these functions to be translog in form, so that we can generate a translog index of the rate of productivity growth. The average rate of productivity growth is the difference between the growth rate of value added and a weighted average of growth rates of capital and labor inputs. Similarly, we can generate translog indexes of capital and labor inputs, giving the growth rate of each input as a weighted average of growth rates of its components.

The measures of aggregate output, input, and productivity presented in table 3.1 are derived by explicit aggregation over the industrial sectors listed in tables 3.2 and 3.3. The measure of aggregate productivity growth depends on sectoral productivity growth rates and on terms that reflect reallocations of value added, capital input, and labor input among sectors.[35] Sectoral productivity growth rates are weighted by ratios of the value of output in the corresponding sector to the sum of value added in all sectors.[36] This formula was originally proposed by Domar (1961) for a model with two producing sectors. Each sector is characterized by a Cobb-Douglas production function with output as a function of intermediate input from the other sector, capital input, labor input, and time as an indicator of the level of technology. A closely related approach to aggregate productivity measurement uses sectoral productivity growth rates based on value added rather than output.[37]

Domar's (1961) approach to aggregation over sectors has been extended by Hulten (1978) and Jorgenson (1980) to an arbitrary number of producing sectors without using the assumption that the sectoral production functions are linear logarithmic. Both Domar and Hulten assume that prices of intermediate inputs are the same for producing and receiving sectors and prices of capital and labor inputs are the same for all sectors. Jorgenson allows for differences in prices received and paid among sectors. Under the assumptions of Domar and Hulten the rate of productivity growth for the economy as a whole does not depend on the reallocations of value added, capital input, and labor input among sectors presented in the second panel of table 3.1.[38]

3.5.2. Data Sources and Methods for Aggregate Output and Productivity

The starting point for the measurement of aggregate productivity is a production account for the U.S. economy in current prices. The fundamental identity for the production account is that the value of output is equal to the value of input. The value of output and input is defined from the point of view of the producer. Revenue is measured as proceeds to the producing sector of the economy and outlay as expenditures of the sector. The role of an aggregate production account in a complete accounting system for the U.S. economy is discussed by Christensen and Jorgenson (1969, 1970, 1973a, 1973b) and Jorgenson (1980).[39]

The value of output for the U.S. economy as a whole is equal to the value of deliveries to final demand—personal consumption expenditures, gross private domestic investment, government purchases, and net exports—excluding indirect business taxes on output, excise and sales taxes, and including subsidies paid to producers. The value of input includes the value of primary factors of production—capital and labor inputs—including indirect business taxes on input, property taxes, and other taxes on property compensation.

The definition of aggregate output outlined above is intermediate between output at market prices and output at factor cost, as these terms are conventionally defined. The production account for the U.S. economy as a whole includes value added in the 37 sectors listed in table 3.2. These sectors include 35 industrial sectors, government, except for government enterprises, and private households and institutions.

As an accounting identity, the value of output is equal to the value of input from the point of view of the producing sector. The value of input includes income originating in business, households and institutions, and government, as defined in the U.S. national income and product accounts. The value of input also includes capital consumption allowances, business transfer payments, the statistical discrepancy, and certain indirect business taxes on property and property compensation. Finally, the value of input includes the imputed value of services of consumers' durables and durables held by institutions and net rent on institutional real estate.

The quantity of value added for each sector is derived by combining price and quantity data on output and intermediate input into price and quantity indexes of value added. To construct an index of value added for each industrial sector, I express sectoral output, say $\{Z_i\}$, as a translog function of sectoral intermediate input $\{X_i\}$ and sectoral value added $\{V_i\}$. The corresponding index of sectoral value added can be written in implicit form:

$$\begin{aligned} \ln Z_i(T) - \ln Z_i(T-1) = {} & \bar{v}_X^i[\ln X_i(T) - \ln X_i(T-1)] \\ & + \bar{v}_V^i[\ln V_i(T) - \ln V_i(T-1)], \\ & (i = 1, 2, \ldots, n), \end{aligned}$$

where the weights are given by the average value shares:

$$\bar{v}_X^i = \frac{1}{2}[v_X^i(T) + v_X^i(T-1)],$$

$$\bar{v}_V^i = \frac{1}{2}[v_V^i(T) + v_V^i(T-1)], \quad (i = 1, 2, \ldots, n).$$

and

$$v_X^i = \frac{p_X^i X_i}{q_i Z_i},$$

$$v_V^i = \frac{p_V^i V_i}{q_i X_i}, \quad (i = 1, 2, \ldots, n).$$

The growth rate of value added can be expressed in terms of growth rates of intermediate input and output and the average value shares:

$$\ln V_i(T) - \ln V_i(T-1) = \frac{1}{\bar{v}_V^i}[\ln Z_i(T) - \ln Z_i(T-1)] - \frac{\bar{v}_X^i}{\bar{v}_V^i}[\ln X_i(T) - \ln X_i(T-1)],$$

$$(i = 1, 2, \ldots, n).$$

The quantity of aggregate value added is the sum of quantities of value added in all industries. Finally, the price of aggregate value added is the ratio of value added to the quantity of value added for the economy as a whole.[40]

In section 3.2 I have described data on annual hours worked and labor compensation per hour, cross-classified by sex, age, education, and employment class of workers. The aggregate model of production includes equilibrium conditions between the supply of each type of labor and the sum of demands for that type of labor by all sectors. The value of each of the 160 labor inputs for the economy as a whole is equal to the sum of the values over all sectors. Labor compensation for the economy as a whole is controlled to labor compensation from the U.S. national income accounts.

Aggregate data on prices and quantities of labor input, cross-classified by sex, age, education, and employment class, but not by industry, underlie the indexes of labor input presented in table 3.1. For the economy as a whole, hours worked and labor compensation for each of 160 categories of the work force are added over all industries. Labor compensation is divided by annual hours worked to derive labor compensation per hour worked for each category. Finally, price and quantity data are combined into price and quantity indexes of aggregate labor input.

To construct an index of labor input for the economy as a whole, I express aggregate labor input L as a translog function of its 160 individual components $\{L_l\}$. The corresponding index of labor input takes the form

$$\ln L(T) - \ln L(T-1) = \Sigma \bar{v}_{Ll}[\ln L_l(T) - \ln L_l(T-1)],$$

where weights are given by the average shares of the individual components in the value of labor compensation:

$$\bar{v}_{Ll} = \frac{1}{2}[v_{Ll}(T) + v_{Ll}(T-1)], \quad (l = 1, 2, \ldots, q),$$

$$v_{Ll} = \frac{p_{Ll}L_l}{\Sigma pL_{Ll}L_l}, \quad (l = 1, 2, \ldots, q).$$

The value shares are computed from data on hours worked $\{L_l\}$ and compensation per hour $\{p_{Ll}\}$ for all components of labor input, cross-classified by sex, age, education, and employment class of workers. A measure of total hours worked for the economy as a whole can be obtained by adding hours worked across all categories of labor input. The quality of aggregate hours worked is defined, as before, as the ratio of labor input to hours worked. Indexes of the quantity of labor input and labor quality are presented for the economy as a whole in table 3.1.

In section 3.3 I have described data on capital stocks and rental prices, cross-classified by asset class and legal form of organization. The aggregate model of production includes market equilibrium conditions between the supply of each type of capital and the sum of demands for that type of capital by all sectors. The value of each of the capital inputs for the economy as a whole is equal to the sum of values over all sectors. Consistent with the treatment of labor compensation, property compensation for the economy as a whole is controlled to property compensation from the U.S. national income accounts.

Aggregate data on prices and quantities of capital input, cross-classified by asset class and legal form of organization, but not by industry, underlie the indexes of capital input presented in table 3.1. For the economy as a whole, capital stock and property compensation for each category are added over all industries. Property compensation is divided by capital stock to derive property compensation per unit of capital stock for each category. Finally, price and quantity data are combined into price and quantity indexes of aggregate capital input.

To construct an index of capital input for the economy as a whole, I express aggregate capital input K as a translog function of its individual components $\{K_k\}$. The corresponding index of capital input takes the form

$$\ln K(T) - \ln K(T-1) = \Sigma \bar{v}_{Kk} [\ln K_k(T) - \ln K_k(T-1)],$$

where weights are given by the average shares of individual components in the value of property compensation:

$$\bar{v}_{Kk} = \frac{1}{2} [v_{Kk}(T) + v_{Kk}(T-1)], \quad (k = 1, 2, \ldots, p),$$

and

$$v_{Kk} = \frac{p_{Kk}K_k}{\Sigma p_{Kk}K_k}, \quad (k = 1, 2, \ldots, p).$$

The value shares are computed from data on capital stocks $\{K_k\}$ and rental prices $\{p_{Kk}\}$ for all components of capital input, cross-classified by asset class and legal form of organization. A measure of capital stock for the economy as a whole can be obtained by adding capital stock across all categories of capital input. The quality of aggregate capital stock is defined, as before, as the ratio of capital input to capital stock. Indexes of the quantity of capital input and capital quality are presented for the economy as a whole in table 3.1.

3.5.3 Alternative Sources and Methods

To provide additional perspective on U.S. economic growth it is useful to compare the sources and methods that underly the analysis given in table 3.1 with those of other studies.[41] For the U.S. economy as a whole Christensen and Jorgenson (1969, 1970, 1973a, 1973b) have presented an analysis of sources of U.S. economic growth similar to that presented in the first panel of table 3.1. Their study covers the period 1929–69 for the private sector of the U.S. economy.

Christensen, Cummings, and Jorgenson (1978, 1980) have extended the estimates of Christensen and Jorgenson through 1973. Aggregate value added is defined from the producers' point of view, including the value of sales and excise taxes and including the value of subsidies; however, the quantity of value added is measured as an index of deliveries to final demand rather than the sum of quantities of value added over industrial sectors. The quantity of labor input is divided among categories of the labor force broken down by educational attainment, but not by sex, age, employment class, or occupation.

The empirical results of Christensen, Cummings, and Jorgenson (1980) for the period 1947–73 are very similar to those given in table 3.1. For this period their estimate of the average growth rate of value added for the private domestic sector of the U.S. economy is 4.00% per year; by comparison the estimate of the rate of growth for the U.S. economy given in table 3.1 is 3.79% per year. The two estimates are not precisely comparable since Christensen, Cummings, and Jorgenson do not include government sectors in their measure of aggregate output.

Christensen, Cummings, and Jorgenson estimate the average growth rate of capital input at 4.26% per year for the period 1947–73; the estimate for this period given in table 3.1 is 4.16% per year. These estimates are closely comparable, except that the estimates in table 3.1 include capital input for government enterprises. Christensen, Cummings, and Jorgenson estimate the average growth rate of labor input at 1.62% per year, while the estimate presented in table 3.1 is 1.80% per year. Finally their estimate of the rate of productivity growth is 1.34% per year, while the estimate given in table 3.1 is 1.11% per year. Again, the two estimates for labor input and the rate of productivity growth are not precisely comparable since the estimates given in table 3.1 include labor input for the government sectors.

Christensen, Cummings, and Jorgenson (1980) have presented estimates of aggregate productivity growth for Canada, France, Germany, Italy, Japan, Korea, the Netherlands, and the United Kingdom as well as for the United States. Their estimates cover various periods beginning after 1947 and ending in 1973; the estimates cover the period 1960–73 for all countries. Conrad and Jorgenson (1975) have developed data for Germany for the period 1950–73, Ezaki and Jorgenson (1973) have presented estimates for Japan for the period 1951–68 and Jorgenson and Nishimizu (1978) have given estimates for Japan for the period 1952–74. Christensen and Cummings (1981) have provided estimates for Korea for the period 1960–73.

Elias (1978) has developed data on a basis that is comparable with Christensen, Cummings, and Jorgenson (1980) for Argentina, Brazil, Chile, Columbia, Mexico, Peru, and Venezuela for the period 1940–74. Groes and Bjerregaard (1978) have developed comparable estimates for Denmark for the period 1950–72. On the basis of the close correspondence between the results for the U.S. economy as a whole given in table 3.1 and those of Christensen, Cummings, and Jorgenson, I conclude that it is appropriate to compare the aggregate results in the first panel of table 3.1 with those for the countries presented in their study and the other studies I have listed.[42]

BLS (1983) has employed private business product as a measure of value added in the U.S. economy as a whole. This measure is obtained from the gross national product by excluding output originating in general government, government enterprises, owner-occupied housing, rest of the world, households and institutions, and the statistical discrepancy. The resulting measure of value added is gross of depreciation. This has the important advantage of avoiding the confounding of measures of output and capital input that I have analyzed in section 3.4.1, above. I have summarized the differences between my methodology for measuring labor and capital inputs and that of BLS in sections 3.2.3 and 3.3.3.

Denison (1985) employs an approach to production based on value added at the economywide level. He uses national income as a measure of value added. This measure excludes capital consumption allowances and indirect business taxes. His measure of capital input is based on the net earnings of capital, also excluding business taxes. The prices and quantities of inputs and outputs employed in Denison's measure of productivity satisfy the accounting identity between the value of output and the value of input. However, the corresponding model of aggregate production involves net value added, so that output and inputs are confounded by including capital input in both categories, as I pointed out in section 3.4.1. I conclude that the quantity of net value added employed by Denison is not an appropriate starting point for modeling producer behavior at the aggregate level.[43]

The problem with net value added as a measure of output for the economy as a whole can be traced to the definition of capital consumption allowances introduced by Denison (1957, 238–55). This concept of depreciation is defined by Young and Musgrave (1980, 32), as follows: "Depreciation is the cost of the asset allocated over its service life in proportion to its estimated service at each date." Denison (1972, 104–5) refers to this method of allocation as the "capital input method." Within the framework for measuring capital input presented in section 3.3.1, above, Denison's concept of capital consumption allowances is based on allocating the cost of an asset over its lifetime in proportion to the relative efficiencies $\{d(\tau)\}$ of capital goods of different ages rather than in proportion to depreciation $p_D(T)$.

Young and Musgrave (1980, 33–37) contrast the Denison definition with the "discounted value definition" of depreciation $p_D(T)$ employed in the model of capital as a factor of production presented in section 3.3.1. Among the advantages for the "capital input method" claimed by Denison (1957, 240) and Young and Musgrave (1980, 33) is that this definition avoids discounting of future capital services. In fact, discounting can be avoided in the measurement of depreciation if and only if the decline in the efficiency of capital goods is geometric. In this case the relative efficiencies $\{d(\tau)\}$ decline with the age of an asset at a constant rate. Capital service prices $p_K(T)$ and investment goods prices $p_I(T)$ decline with age at the same rate, and depreciation $p_D(T)$ is proportional to the price of an investment good.

As I have pointed out in section 3.3.3, above, Denison's assumptions about the relative efficiencies of capital goods of different ages require discounting of future capital services to obtain an appropriate measure of depreciation. Denison's attempt to avoid discounting leads him to confuse the relative efficiencies $\{d(\tau)\}$ with decline in the value of an asset as a basis for measure depreciation $p_D(T)$. This leads, in turn, to an inconsistency between the assumptions about relative efficiencies utilized in measuring capital input $A(T-1)$ and the assumptions employed in measuring the rental price of capital input $p_K(T)$. This chain of inconsistencies and contradictions can be broken only by replacing the "capital input method" of measuring depreciation introduced by Denison (1957) with the "discounted value definition" presented in section 3.3.3. The "discounted value definition" is employed, for example, by Christensen, Cummings, and Jorgenson (1980) and BLS (1983).

Denison's (1974, 9) "capital input method" of depreciation leads him to draw an analogy between the consumption of intermediate goods and capital consumption allowances. Since the consumption of intermediate goods is eliminated in the course of aggregating over sectors, but capital consumption allowances are not eliminated by aggregation, this analogy is inappropriate and misleading. The price and quantity of capital input are index numbers obtained by weighting each component of capital input by its rental price. Rental prices depend on differences in depreciation among assets and differences in the tax treatment of the resulting property compensation. By suppressing these differences Denison greatly underestimates the contribution of capital input to economic growth. A comparison of the capital input measures of Denison (1967) with those of Christensen and Jorgenson (1969, 1970, 1973a, 1973b) is given by Jorgenson and Griliches (1972a). Jorgenson (1989) provides a detailed discussion of Denison's treatment of capital consumption allowances.

Maddison (1987) has recently constructed aggregate growth accounts for the period 1870–1984 for France, Germany, Japan, the Netherlands, the United Kingdom, and the United States. He has divided this period into the subperiod 1870–1913, almost the same as that considered by Tinbergen (1942), and the subperiods 1913–50, 1950–73, and 1973–84. For the period 1913–84 Maddison gives an analysis of the sources of growth in gross domestic product for all six countries, including hours worked, changes in labor quality, capital stock, and changes in capital quality. His analysis of the sources of growth for the period 1870–1913 includes only hours worked and capital stock, omitting changes in input quality.

Maddison draws on the work of Carré, Dubois, and Malinvaud (1975) for France. This study covers 1913 and the period 1949–66 on an annual basis and presents an analysis of sources of growth of gross domestic product that includes hours worked, quality of labor input, and capital stock. Maddison utilizes results from the study of Ohkawa and Rosovsky (1973) for Japan, which covers the period 1908–64 and analyzes the growth of gross domestic product. This analysis incorporates employment, quality of labor input, and capital stock. For the United Kingdom, Maddison employs the work of Matthews, Feinstein, and Odling-Smee (1982). This study covers the period 1856–1973 and gives an analysis of the sources of growth of gross domestic product, including hours worked, quality of labor input, and capital stock. For the United States, Maddison utilizes the work of Kendrick (1961a, 1973).

Although Maddison considers the measurement of the quality of capital input by introducing rental prices for individual capital inputs, he rejects this approach and assumes that the rate of growth of capital quality is 1.5% per year for the period 1913–84 for all six countries included in his study. This assumption is not based on empirical data, but Maddison modifies the assumption for the subperiods 1950–73 and 1973–84 by an adjustment for changes in the average age of capital goods that incorporates investment data. A more satisfactory approach to the long-term analysis of sources of U.S. economic growth has been presented by Abramovitz and David (1973a, 1973b) for the period 1800–1967. This analysis incorporates the results of Christensen and Jorgenson (1970) for the period 1929–67 and includes hours worked, quality of labor input, capital stock, and quality of capital input. For the period 1800–1927 the analysis is limited to hours worked and capital stock as sources of growth.

For the U.S. economy as a whole Kendrick (1961a, 1973), Kendrick and Sato (1963), Kendrick and Grossman (1980), and Kendrick (1983a) have employed an approach to the measurement of value added through summation over the growth rates of quantities of value added in all sectors with weights that change periodically. The corresponding estimates of the growth rates of capital and labor inputs are constructed by summing the corresponding quantities over all sectors with weights that depend on property and labor compensation by sector.[44]

Kendrick employs unweighted sums of capital stock and hours worked as measures of capital and labor inputs at the sectoral level. At the aggregate level he employs unweighted sums as a variant of his principal estimates. The differences between the weighted and unweighted measures of capital and labor inputs at the aggregate level are associated with differences in the prices of capital and labor inputs among industries. Since Kendrick's measures of capital and labor inputs at the sectoral level do not incorporate changes in the quality of these inputs, a substantial portion of the differences between his weighted and unweighted measures at the aggregate level is due to unmeasured differences in input quality at the sectoral level.

The measures of value added, capital input, and labor input presented in the first panel of table 3.1 are constructed from unweighted sums of value added, individual components of capital input, and individual components of labor input over all industries. An alternative measure of aggregate value added can be constructed by weighting value added in each industry by the price of value added in that industry. Similarly, alternative measures of aggregate capital and labor inputs can be constructed by weighting individual components of these inputs in each industry by the prices of these components in that industry.

Differences between growth rates of measures of output and input that reflect differences in prices of output and inputs among industries and measures that do not reflect these differences are presented in the second panel of table 3.1. These differences are the measures of reallocations of value added, capital input, and labor input among sectors. The rate of aggregate productivity growth can be represented as a weighted sum of sectoral productivity growth rates and the contributions of the reallocations. If the prices of value added, capital input, and labor input were the same for all industries, the contributions of reallocations to aggregate productivity growth would vanish.

I conclude that capital and labor inputs can be usefully classified by industry in decomposing the rate of aggregate productivity growth between reallocations of value added, capital input, and labor input among sectors and rates of productivity growth at the sectoral level.[45] For this decomposition measures of output and inputs with and without industry as a classification are required. It is important to note that this argument cannot be extended to other characteristics of labor input such as sex, age, education, and employment status. If there are differences in rates of remuneration of individual components of labor input differing in these characteristics, labor input must be broken down by characteristics at both aggregate and sectoral levels. Similarly, capital input must be broken down by type of asset and legal form of organization at both levels.

I have focused attention on the integration of sectoral measures of output, input, and productivity growth with the corresponding aggregate measures. To avoid including capital input in the measure of aggregate output and the aggregate inputs, as implied by Denison's (1962a, 1962b, 1967, 1974, 1979, 1985) measure of output, I present data in table 3.1 that utilize gross value added at the aggregate level. BLS (1983), Christensen, Cummings, and Jorgenson (1980), Kendrick (1984), and the studies utilized by Maddison (1987) also employ gross value added.[46] However, output in these studies is derived from aggregate production data rather than explicit aggregation over industrial sectors. The resulting measures of aggregate productivity growth are not integrated with corresponding sectoral measures, as in the second panel of table 3.1.

The existence of an aggregate production function implies that all sectoral value added functions are identical. If all sectors pay the same prices for primary factor inputs, the reallocations of value added, capital input, and labor input among sectors have no effect on aggregate output. The contributions of these reallocations can be regarded as measures of departures from the assumptions that underly the aggregate model of production. The data presented in table 3.1 make it possible to assess the significance of these departures. Over the period 1947–85 the reallocations are very small relative to the growth of capital and labor inputs and productivity growth. Over shorter periods, such as 1953–57 and 1973–79, these reallocations are large relative to aggregate productivity growth.[47]

The assumptions required to validate an aggregate model of production are obviously highly restrictive. The evidence presented in table 3.1 suggests that these assumptions are not seriously misleading over a time span as long as the period 1947–85 that we have considered. Similar evidence for other time periods is lacking. However, it seems plausible that an aggregate production model is an appropriate point of departure for studies of long-term growth like those of Abramovitz and David (1973a, 1973b) for the period 1800–1967, Christensen and Jorgenson (1973a) for the period 1929–69, Maddison (1987) for the period 1913–84, and Tinbergen (1942) for the period 1870–1914. For shorter periods an aggregate production model can be seriously misleading.

3.6 Econometric Modeling of Production

A key innovation in the methodology that underlies the indexes presented in tables 3.2 and 3.3 is the symmetric treatment of intermediate, capital, and labor inputs. Output can be represented as a function of all three inputs and time. Substitution possibilities among intermediate inputs and primary factor inputs can be incorporated explicitly. I have contrasted this approach with a more restrictive model based on the existence of a value-added aggregate within each sector. In this alternative approach output is represented as a function of intermediate input and the quantity of value added. Value added in turn is represented as a function of capital and labor inputs and time.

In section 3.5.1, above, I have pointed out that the existence of an aggregate production function requires the existence of sectoral value added functions. Furthermore, these value-added functions must be identical for all sectors. These highly restrictive assumptions are appropriate for studies of long-term growth, but can be seriously misleading for shorter periods. To explain important changes in rates of economic growth, such as the recent growth slowdown in industrialized countries, a disaggregated approach is required. It is important to emphasize that a disaggregated approach, based on models of production for individual industrial sectors, is far more costly than aggregate production modeling. However, such an approach is essential in overcoming the limitations of aggregate models of production.

An econometric model based on the symmetric treatment of intermediate, capital, and labor inputs makes it possible to dispense with the value-added approach employed by Kendrick and tested in table 3.7, above. The rate of sectoral productivity growth can be expressed as functions of the prices of all inputs and the level of technology. Models of production for all industrial sectors can be combined to form a general equilibrium model of production. Symmetric treatment of intermediate, capital, and labor inputs makes it possible to integrate the analysis of sources of economic growth with general equilibrium modeling.

3.6.1. Sectoral Production Modeling

General equilibrium modeling of production originated with the seminal work of Leontief (1951), beginning with the implementation of the static input-output model. Leontief (1953a) gave a further impetus to the development of general equilibrium modeling by introducing a dynamic input-output model. Empirical work associated with input-output analysis is based on estimating the unknown parameters of an interindustry model from a single interindustry transactions table. These estimates are based on a "fixed coefficients" assumption in modeling demands for all inputs. Under this assumption all inputs are proportional to output.

The first successful implementation of a general equilibrium model without the fixed coefficients assumptions of input-output analysis is due to Johansen (1976). Johansen retained the fixed coefficients assumption in modeling demands for intermediate goods. This form of the fixed coefficients assumption is tested in table 3.7, above. Johansen employed linear logarithmic or Cobb-Douglas production functions in modeling productivity growth and the substitution between capital and labor inputs within a value-added aggregate. Linear logarithmic production functions imply that relative shares of inputs in the value of output are fixed, so that the unknown parameters characterizing substitution between capital and labor inputs can be estimated from a single data point.

In modeling producer behavior Johansen employed econometric methods only in estimating constant rates of productivity growth. The essential features of Johansen's approach have been preserved in the general equilibrium models surveyed by Bergman (1990), Robinson (1989) and Shoven and Whalley (1984). The unknown parameters describing technology in these models are determined by "calibration" to a single data point. Data from a single interindustry transactions table are supplemented by a small number of parameters estimated econometrically. The obvious disadvantage of this approach is that arbitrary constraints on patterns of substitution are required in order to make calibration possible.

An alternative approach to modeling producer behavior for general equilibrium models is through complete systems of demand functions for inputs in each industrial sector. Each system gives quantities demanded as functions of prices of inputs and output. This approach to the modeling of producer behavior was originated by Berndt and Jorgenson (1973).[48] As in the descriptions of technology by Leontief and Johansen, production is characterized by constant returns to scale in each sector. Output is represented as a function of capital, labor, energy, and materials inputs and time as an indicator of the level of technology.[49]

Under constant returns to scale commodity prices can be expressed as functions of factor prices, utilizing the nonsubstitution theorem of Samuelson (1951). This greatly facilitates the solution of the econometric general equilibrium models constructed by Hudson and Jorgenson (1974) and Jorgenson and Wilcoxen (1990). The nonsubstitution theorem permits a substantial reduction in dimensionality of the space of prices to be determined by the model. The coefficients of the general equilibrium model can be determined endogenously, taking into account prices of primary factor inputs and levels of productivity.

The implementation of econometric models of producer behavior for general equilibrium analysis is very demanding in terms of data requirements. These models require the construction of a consistent time series of interindustry transactions tables. By comparison, the noneconometric approaches of Leontief and Johansen require only a single interindustry transactions table. Second, the implementation of systems of input demand functions requires econometric methods for the estimation of parameters in systems of nonlinear simultaneous equations.

Translog index numbers for intermediate, capital, and labor inputs and rates of productivity growth are employed in the analysis of sources of economic growth presented in tables 3.2 and 3.3. Translog production functions can be used in specifying econometric models for determining the distribution of the value of output among the productive inputs and the rate of productivity growth. In estimating the parameters of these models the quantity indexes of inputs, the corresponding price indexes, and indexes of productivity growth can be employed as data.

Jorgenson and Fraumeni (1981) and Jorgenson (1984b) have constructed econometric models of producer behavior based on the translog functional form for the 35 industrial sectors of the U.S. economy included in tables 3.2 and 3.3. Similar models for Japan have been constructed by Kuroda, Yoshioka, and Jorgenson (1984). Production models for all industrial sectors have been incorporated into an econometric general equilibrium model of the United States by Jorgenson and Wilcoxen (1990).[50] The econometric methodology for construction of sectoral models of production is discussed in detail by Jorgenson (1986a).

3.6.2. Aggregate Production Modeling

The traditional approach to modeling producer behavior at the aggregate level begins with the assumption that the production function is characterized by constant returns to scale. In addition, the production function is assumed to be additive in capital and labor inputs. Under these restrictions demand and supply functions can be derived explicitly from the production function and the necessary conditions for producer equilibrium. However, this approach has the disadvantage of imposing constraints on patterns of substitution—thereby frustrating the objective of determining these patterns empirically.

The traditional approach was originated by Cobb and Douglas (1928) and employed in empirical research by Douglas and his associates for almost two decades. These studies are summarized by Douglas (1948, 1967, 1976). The principal methodology employed in Douglas's research is based on the analysis of cross section data for manufacturing industries, treating individual industries rather than plants or firms as observations. The measure of output employed in these studies is based on the value-added model outlined in section 3.4.1 above.

The use of individual industries as observations requires the assumption that the value-added functions for all industries are identical, which is precisely the assumption required for the existence of an aggregate production function. Tinbergen (1942) was the first to formulate the aggregate production function with time as an indicator of the level of technology. This is the form of the production function employed in the analysis of sources of economic growth at the aggregate level.[51]

The limitations of the traditional approach were made strikingly apparent by Arrow, Chenery, Minhas, and Solow (1961; henceforward ACMS), who pointed out that the Cobb-Douglas production function imposes a priori restrictions on patterns of substitution among inputs. In particular, elasticities of substitution among all inputs must be equal to unity. The constant elasticity of substitution (CES) production function introduced by ACMS adds flexibility to the traditional approach by treating the elasticity of substitution between capital and labor as an unknown parameter to be estimated by econometric methods. However, the CES production function retains the assumptions of additivity and homogeneity and imposes very stringent limitations on patterns of substitution. McFadden (1963) and Uzawa (1962) have shown, essentially, that elasticities of substitution among all inputs must be the same.[52]

The translog index numbers for capital and labor inputs and the rate of productivity growth for the economy as a whole are employed in the analysis of the sources of economic growth presented in table 3.1. The translog production function can also be used in specifying an econometric model for determining the rate of productivity growth and the distribution of value added between the primary factor inputs. The quantity indexes of inputs, the corresponding price indexes, and the index of productivity growth can be employed as data in estimating the parameters of this econometric model.[53]

The benefits of an aggregate production model must be weighed against the costs of departures from the highly restrictive assumptions that underly the existence of an aggregate production function. Where these assumptions are inappropriate, the econometric approach to general equilibrium analysis outlined above can be employed in analyzing patterns of production for the economy as a whole. This approach is based on sectoral models of production rather than an aggregate production model. Sectoral models are also useful in decomposing aggregate economic growth into sectoral components.[54]

The results presented in table 3.1 show that an aggregate production model is appropriate for studies of long-term U.S. economic growth. However, an aggregate model can be misleading for relatively short time periods, such as the individual business cycles 1953–57 and 1973–79. For the period 1947–85 as a whole the rate of aggregate productivity growth is 0.71% per year, while the weighted sum of sectoral productivity growth rates of 0.88% per year. The difference between aggregate productivity growth and sectoral productivity growth provides a measure of departures from the stringent assumptions that underly the aggregate production model. This difference is not negligible, even for the period 1947–85.

Considering the second panel of table 3.1, we can decompose the decline in the aggregate productivity growth rate into the sum of sectoral productivity growth rates and the reallocations of value added, capital input, and labor input. The decline in sectoral productivity growth between the period 1947–85 and the subperiod 1973–79 was 1.00% per year. This decline is almost sufficient to account for the slowdown in U.S. economic growth. The precipitous fall in sectoral productivity growth was augmented at the aggregate level by a fall in the reallocation of value added of 0.34 percent. I conclude that the assumptions that underly the aggregate model of production failed to hold during the period 1973–79.

The decline in productivity growth at the level of individual industries can be identified as the main culprit in the slowdown of U.S. economic growth since 1973. To provide an explanation of this decline we must go behind the measurement of sectoral productivity growth rates to identify the determinants of productivity growth at the sectoral level. To illustrate the econometric approach to productivity growth we present a summary of the results of fitting an econometric model to detailed data on sectoral output and capital, labor, energy, and materials inputs for 35 industrial sectors of the U.S. economy.

Our econometric study is based on sectoral models of production for each 35 individual industries. Although production functions contain all the available information about producer behavior for each sector, we find it useful to express the sectoral models of production in an alternative and equivalent form. Under constant returns to scale we can introduce price functions for each industry.[55] The price function gives the price of output as a function of the prices of capital, labor, energy, and materials inputs and time, representing the level of technology. Price functions summarize the information about producer behavior contained in the production functions in a more convenient form.

Given the price function for each industry, we can express the shares of each of the four inputs in the industry—capital, labor, energy, and materials inputs—in the value of output as functions of the prices of inputs and the level of technology. We can add to the four equations for the value shares an equation that completes the model. This equation gives the sectoral rate of productivity growth as a function of the prices of the inputs and the level of technology. The equation determining the productivity growth rate is our econometric model of sectoral productivity growth.

Like any econometric model, the relationships determining the value shares of capital, labor, energy, and materials inputs and the rate of productivity growth involve unknown parameters that must be estimated. Included among these parameters are biases of productivity growth. For example, the bias of productivity growth for capital input gives the change in the share of capital input in the value of output in response to changes in technology.[56] It is said that productivity growth is capital using if the bias for capital input is positive. Similarly, it is said that productivity growth is capital saving if the bias for capital input is negative. The sum of the biases for all four inputs must be precisely zero since the changes in all four shares must sum to zero.

The biases of productivity growth appear as coefficients of time, representing the level of technology, in the four equations for the value shares of the four inputs. Our econometric model for each industrial sector of the U.S. economy also includes an equation that determines the rate of productivity growth. The biases appear with an opposite sign as coefficients of the prices in the equation for sectoral productivity growth. This feature of the econometric model makes it possible to use information about both changes in the value shares with the level of technology and changes in the rate of productivity growth with prices in estimating the biases of productivity growth.[57]

Capital-using productivity growth, associated with a positive bias of productivity growth for capital input, implies that an increase in the price of capital input diminishes the rate of productivity growth. Similarly, capital-saving productivity growth implies that productivity growth increases with the price of capital input. Ho and Jorgenson (1990) have fitted econometric models based on translog price functions to data for all 35 industrial sectors. Since our primary concern is with the determinants of sectoral productivity growth, I present a classification of industries by biases of productivity growth in table 3.8.

The pattern of productivity growth that occurs most frequently in table 3.8 is capital-using, labor-saving, energy-using, and materials-using productivity growth. This pattern occurs for 11 of the 35 industries. For this pattern the

Table 3.8 Classification of Industries by Biases of Productivity Growth

Pattern of Biases	Industries
Capital using, labor using, energy using, materials saving	textile mills; apparel; lumber & wood
Capital using, labor saving, energy using, materials using	agriculture; construction; food & kindred products; furniture & fixtures; paper & allied; printing & publishing; stone, clay, & glass; electrical machinery; miscellaneous manufacturing; transportation services; wholesale & retail trade
Capital using, labor saving, energy using, materials saving	nonmetallic mining; tobacco; leather; fabricated metal; machinery, except electrical; instruments; communications; services; government enterprises
Capital using, labor saving, energy saving, materials using	coal mining; petroleum & coal products
Capital saving, labor using, energy using, materials using	finance, insurance, & real estate
Capital saving, labor using, energy using, materials saving	motor vehicles
Capital saving, labor using, energy saving, materials using	metal mining
Capital saving, labor saving, energy using, materials using	oil & gas extraction; chemicals; rubber & miscellaneous plastics; transportation equipment & ordnance; electric utilities
Capital saving, labor saving, energy using, materials saving	primary metals; gas utilities

biases of productivity growth for capital, energy, and materials inputs are positive and the bias of productivity growth for labor input is negative. This pattern implies that increases in the prices of capital, energy, and materials inputs diminish the rate of productivity growth, while an increase in the price of labor input enhances productivity growth.

The most striking change in the relative prices of capital, labor, energy, and materials inputs that has taken place since 1973 is the substantial increase in the price of energy. Reversing historical trends toward lower real prices of energy in the U.S., the Arab oil embargo of late 1973 and early 1974 resulted in a dramatic increase in oil import prices. Real energy prices to final users increased by 23% in the U.S. during the period 1973–75, despite price controls on domestic petroleum and natural gas. In 1978 the Iranian revolution sent a second wave of oil import price increases through the U.S. economy. Real energy prices climbed by 34% over the following two-year period.[58]

I have now provided part of the solution of the problem of disappointing

U.S. economic growth since 1973. Higher energy prices are associated with a decline in sectoral productivity growth for 32 of the 35 industries included in table 3.8. The slowdown in sectoral productivity growth is more than sufficient to explain the decline in U.S. economic growth. It is important to emphasize that an econometric model of sectoral productivity growth is essential to solving the problem of the slowdown in U.S. economic growth since 1973. An aggregate model of production excludes energy and materials inputs by definition since deliveries to intermediate demand are offset by receipts of intermediate inputs.

Denison (1979, 1983, 1984, 1985) has attempted to analyze the slowdown in U.S. economic growth using an aggregate model of production and has pronounced the slowdown a "mystery." The results presented in the first panel of table 3.1 appear to bear out this conclusion. The decline in the rate of aggregate productivity growth is more than sufficient to account for the decline in the rate of growth of value added. However, the decline in economic growth is left unexplained in the absence of an econometric model to determine the rate of productivity growth. A model based on an aggregate production function would fail to establish the critical role of the increase in energy prices after 1973, since energy is excluded as an input at the aggregate level by assumption.

In section 3.5.1. above, I have pointed out that the existence of an aggregate production function requires sectoral value added functions that are the same for all sectors. In section 3.4.1 we have observed that the existence of a sectoral value-added function requires separability between the level of technology and intermediate input. Changes in technology have an impact on sectoral productivity growth only through their impact on value added. An econometric model of productivity growth based on a value-added function for each industry would also eliminate the role of energy prices by assumption. I conclude that the link between energy prices and productivity growth requires a sectoral model of production that treats inputs of energy and materials symmetrically with inputs of capital and labor.

The steps I have outlined—disaggregating the sources of economic growth to the sectoral level, decomposing sectoral output growth between productivity growth and the growth of capital, labor, energy, and materials inputs, and modeling the rate of growth of sectoral productivity growth rate econometrically—have been taken only recently. The results of Ho and Jorgenson (1990) have corroborated those of Jorgenson and Fraumeni (1981) and Jorgenson (1984b). Jorgenson (1984b) has further disaggregated energy between electricity and nonelectrical energy. Similar results have been obtained for the Japanese economy, which suffered a far more severe slowdown than the U.S. economy, by Kuroda, Yoshioka, and Jorgenson (1984).[59] Much additional research will be required to provide an exhaustive explanation of the slowdown of U.S. economic growth and the implications for the future growth of the economy.

3.6.3. Alternative Production Models

While the rate of productivity growth is endogenous in the econometric models I have outlined, these models must be carefully distinguished from models of induced technical change, such as those analyzed by Hicks (1963), Kennedy (1964), Samuelson (1965), von Weizsacker (1962), and many others. In those models the biases of productivity growth are endogenous and depend on relative prices. In the model that underlies the results presented in table 3.8 the biases are constant parameters that can be estimated econometrically. As Samuelson (1965) has pointed out, models of induced technical change require intertemporal optimization since technical change at any point of time affects future production possibilities.[60]

The simplest intertemporal model of production is based on capital as a factor of production. In the model presented in section 3.3, myopic decision rules can be derived by treating the price of capital input as a rental price of capital services. The rate of productivity growth at any point of time is a function of relative prices but does not affect future production possibilities. This greatly simplifies the intertemporal modeling of producer behavior and facilitates the construction of an econometric model. Given myopic decision rules for producers in each industrial sector, all of the implications of the economic theory of production can be described in terms of the sectoral production function or the sectoral price function.

A less restrictive intertemporal model of production generates costs of adjustment from changes in the level of capital input through investment. As the level of investment increases, the amount of marketable output produced from given input levels decreases. Marketable output and investment can be treated as joint outputs that are produced from capital and other inputs.[61] Models of producer behavior based on costs of adjustment can be implemented on the basis of myopic decision rules, provided that accumulated costs of adjustment can be observed. One approach to measuring these costs is to set them equal to the difference between the market value of the producing unit and the market value of its capital stock.[62]

As an alternative to myopic decision rules, expectations can be incorporated explicitly into dynamic models of producer behavior based on costs of adjustment. An objection to dynamic models of production based on static expectations is that current prices change from period to period, but expectations are based on unchanging future prices.[63] An alternative approach is to base the dynamic optimization on forecasts of future prices. Since these forecasts are subject to random errors, it is natural to require that the optimization process takes into account the uncertainty that accompanies forecasts of future prices.

Two alternative approaches to optimization under uncertainty have been proposed. Provided that the objective function for producers is quadratic and constraints are linear, optimization under uncertainty can be replaced by a corresponding optimization problem under certainty.[64] An alternative approach to optimization under uncertainty is to employ the information about expectations of future prices contained in current input levels. This approach has the advantage that it is not limited to quadratic objective functions and linear constraints.[65]

I have considered econometric models of production based on disembodied technical change. Changes in technology affect old and new vintages of capital goods symmetrically. An alternative approach is to embody changes in technology in new vintages of capital goods. The embodiment of technical change was originated by Solow (1957, 316–17).[66] The index numbers for productivity growth described in sections 3.4 and 3.5 are based on the residual between the growth of output and the growth of inputs. This residual can be interpreted as a measure of the rate of disembodied technical change. Measures of the rate of embodied technical change can also be constructed from data on the residual.[67]

Hall (1971) and Jorgenson and Griliches (1967) have identified embodied technical change with changes in the quality of capital goods. The line of research suggested by Solow's (1960) concept of embodied technical change involves substituting quality-corrected price indexes for existing price indexes of capital goods.[68] Changes in quality can be incorporated into price indexes for capital goods by means of the "hedonic technique" employed by Griliches (1961b) and studies in the volume edited by Griliches (1971b). For example, Cole, Chen, Barquin-Stolleman, Dulberger, Helvacian, and Hodge (1986) have recently developed quality corrections for computer price indexes employed in the U.S. national product accounts.[69]

At both sectoral and aggregate levels we have considered producer behavior under constant returns to scale. This methodology makes it possible to unify data generation, analysis of the sources of economic growth, and econometric modeling of production. The analysis of economic growth and the econometric modeling can be carried out independently. Both employ index numbers of output, inputs, and productivity. Under increasing returns to scale and competitive markets for output and all inputs, producer equilibrium is not defined by profit maximization, since no maximum of profits exists. The analysis of sources of economic growth and the modeling of producer behavior under increasing returns to scale cannot be carried out independently. The implementation of a model of producer behavior under increasing returns to scale requires an econometric approach.[70]

In regulated industries the price of output is set by regulatory authority. Given demand for output as a function of the regulated price, the level of output is exogenous to the producing unit. With output fixed from the point of view of the producer, necessary conditions for equilibrium can be derived from cost minimization. To illustrate the econometric modeling of economies of scale, we can briefly consider examples from the extensive literature on the U.S. electric power industry and the communications industry. An econometric model of electric power generation in the United States has been implemented by Christensen and Greene (1976). This model is based on translog cost functions for cross sections of individual electric utilities in 1955 and 1970. A key feature of the electric power industry in the United States is that individual firms are subject to price regulation. The regulatory authority sets the price for electric power. Electric utilities are required to supply the electric power that is demanded at the regulated price.

Christensen and Greene have employed translog cost functions fitted to data on individual utilities to characterize scale economies for individual firms. For both 1955 and 1970 the cost functions are U shaped with a minimum point occurring at very large levels of output. The cost function for 1970 is considerably below that for 1955, reflecting changes in technology.[71] Gollop and Roberts (1981) have employed translog cost functions for individual firms in analyzing annual data on eleven electric utilities in the United States for the period 1958–75. They use the results to decompose the growth of productivity between economies of scale and technical change. For the period as a whole economies of scale account for an average of 40% of productivity growth, while technical change accounts for the remaining 60%. Gollop and Roberts have provided a prototype for the analysis of sources of sectoral output growth in the electric generating industry.

A model with increasing returns to scale has been implemented for time-series data on Bell Canada, a regulated firm accounting for more than half of the output of the Canadian telecommunications industry, by Denny, Fuss, and Waverman (1981a). This model is based on cost minimization subject to regulatory pricing constraints. Bell Canada has multiple outputs consisting of different types of telecommunications services. Prices for these outputs are not proportional to marginal costs. Denny, Fuss, and Waverman provide an analysis of sources of growth of productivity for Bell Canada over the period 1952–76. Economies of scale account for 64% of productivity growth, technical change accounts for 20%, and nonmarginal cost pricing accounts for the remaining 16%.

Given the importance of economies of scale in the electric generating and communications industries, it is interesting to consider the implementation of a model for a whole industry, incorporating economies of scale. Such a model would require an econometric model for each firm, incorporating a panel of annual observations for all firms in the industry, similar to the panel constructed by Gollop and Roberts (1981) for 11 electric utilities.[72] To provide a decomposition of productivity growth for the industry between economies of scale and technical change the model would require an allocation of the growth of industry output among firms.

An important frontier in the econometric modeling of production lies in the disaggregation of sectoral production models to the level of the individual producing unit. For industries with significant economies of scale at this level, it is possible to supplement sectoral models of production with models based on panel data for individual firms and plants. This is already feasible for industries with well-documented production patterns at the level of the individual unit. At present, the required data are available only for regulated industries, such as electricity generation, communications, and transportation. However, the LRD project of the Bureau of the Census will provide a data source that may make it feasible to model production patterns for U.S. industry at the firm or plant level on a broader scale.[73]

The model of "learning by doing" proposed by Arrow (1962) provides an approach to modeling producer behavior with features similar in some respects to increasing returns to scale. This model has been employed in analyzing production from batch-type production processes, for example, in studies of the airframe industry summarized by Alchian (1963). Solow (1967) compares this model to models characterized by increasing returns to scale and provides additional references. Another alternative to the Christensen-Greene model for electric utilities has been developed by Fuss (1977, 1978). In Fuss's model the cost function is permitted to differ ex ante, before a plant is constructed, and ex post, after the plant is in place.[74] Fuss employs a generalized Leontief cost function introduced by Diewert (1971, 1973) with four input prices—structures, equipment, fuel, and labor. He models substitution among inputs and economies of scale for 79 steam generation plants for the period 1948–61.

It is worthwhile to consider the data requirements for development of a model of an industry incorporating differences between ex ante and ex post substitution possibilities. To simplify the discussion we can consider the special case of putty-clay technology with ex post "fixed coefficients." Such a model requires a panel of annual observations on individual establishments within an industry. The modeling of substitution possibilities at the establishment level requires estimates of lifetime costs for alternative technologies at the time of construction of each plant. The modeling of subsequent decisions about whether or not to retire the plant requires comparisons of the price of output and variable costs for each plant at every point of time.

We conclude that a wide variety of alternative production models are available for both aggregate and sectoral production modeling. The aggregate production model introduced by Cobb and Douglas (1928) and developed in Tinbergen (1942) in the form used in the studies of sources of economic growth cited in section 3.5, above, retains its usefulness in modeling long-term growth trends. However, the critical empirical evidence provided by the energy crisis of the 1970s has exposed important limitations of aggregate production modeling. These limitations cannot be overcome by introducing additional complexity at the aggregate level.

Sectoral production models are required to explain the slowdown in economic growth in the United States and other industrialized countries that took place after 1973. These models must incorporate inputs of energy and materials along with inputs of capital and labor. The "fixed coefficients" assumptions employed by Leontief and Johansen have been supplanted by econometric modeling of production at the sectoral level. This assumption is also implicit in the value-added models of production employed, for example, by Kendrick (1961a, 1973) and tested in table 3.7 above. The value-added model has also been supplanted at the sectoral level by a model that treats intermediate, capital, and labor inputs symmetrically.

The costs of assembling consistent time series of interindustry transactions tables and disaggregating measures of capital and labor inputs at the sectoral level are very substantial. These costs will continue to be a formidable obstacle to implementing econometric general equilibrium models of production. In addition, a great deal of further testing will be needed to establish the most appropriate specification for such models. However, this work will be essential in assimilating the important new evidence on patterns of production made available by the energy crisis of the 1970s and its aftermath. The new econometric tools that have been developed for modeling production will help to sustain the momentum in empirical research that has characterized the study of sources of economic growth ever since Tinbergen (1942).[75]

The analysis of sources of economic growth is an essential component of any study of economic growth. However, a theory of growth must also include an explanation of the growth in supplies of capital and labor inputs. In the neoclassical model of economic growth presented by Tinbergen (1942), saving generates growth in capital input and population growth generates growth in labor input. These features of the theory of economic growth have been retained in the neo-classical growth models developed by Solow (1956, 1970, 1988).

The theoretical underpinnings of an analysis of growth in factor supplies are to be found in the theory of consumer behavior. For example, the study of saving requires modeling saving-consumption decisions. Similarly, the analysis of labor supplies requires modeling demographic behavior and labor-leisure choices. A theory of economic growth must incorporate the sources of economic growth and the modeling of producer behavior. The analysis of growth of factor supplies and the modeling of consumer behavior are required to complete the theory.

Recent research on economic growth has given considerable emphasis to the analysis of sources of economic growth and the modeling of producer behavior. This has proved to be very fruitful, as suggested by the research I have summarized in this paper. However, the future agenda could usefully give greater attention to growth of factor supplies and the modeling of consumer behavior. This focus characterized the classic studies of economic growth by Goldsmith (1955, 1962), Kuznets (1961, 1971), Machlup (1962), and Schultz (1961).

3.7 Conclusion

In this paper I have used the sources of economic growth to illustrate the critical importance of interrelationships between national accounting and economic theory. The link between the two is the econometric modeling of production. The national accountant uses economic theories of production to generate systems of accounts and corresponding systems of price and quantity index numbers. Theories of production are used in determining what the accounts should include and exclude. The econometrician uses theories of production to generate systems of behavioral equations and the statistical methods employed in estimating the parameters of these equations.

The research activities I have mentioned can be carried out in isolation. Accounting systems and the associated systems of index numbers can be developed with no attempt to derive them from an underlying model of producer or consumer behavior. A purely statistical approach of this type can be compared, unfavorably in my view, with the economic approach pioneered by Simon Kuznets and embodied in modern systems of national accounts, like the U.S. NIPA or the United Nations system of national accounts.

Similarly, econometric studies can be conducted with no attention to accounting methods used in generating the underlying data. However, many of the most interesting problems in econometrics involve the characterization of higher order properties of technology and preferences. As examples, biases of technical change and elasticities of substitution are second-order properties of technology, since they depend on second-order derivatives of price and production functions. The lesson of decades of experience in modeling technology, dating back at least to Arrow, Chenery, Minhas, and Solow (1961), is that econometric estimates of these parameters are highly sensitive to methods of measurement. The best resolution of this problem is to generate accounting systems and econometric models within the same framework. This approach is articulated most fully in Diewert's elegant theory of exact index numbers.

Finally, theories of production can be generated in a form that abstracts from applications. For example, we can contrast the relatively general form of the theory of production presented in Hicks's (1946) *Value and Capital* with the more specific form of the theory presented by Hicks (1963) in *The Theory of Wages*. The concepts of the elasticity of substitution and the bias of technical change, introduced by Hicks (1963), have inspired a whole generation of econometric modelers of production. In section 3.6 I have shown that the bias of technical change is the key to understanding the slowdown in economic growth in industrialized countries since 1973. Clearly, the more specific form of the theory has proved to be better suited to applications.

My conclusion is that the most fruitful approach to research in economic measurement is one that combines national accounting, econometrics, and economic theory. This approach has emerged gradually in the successive volumes that report the proceedings of the Conference on Research in Income and Wealth. In the early days of the conference, econometrics was almost entirely absent, but economic theory and national accounting were by represented in the persons of Simon Kuznets and the other founders of the conference. This is not to say that every researcher has to play the role of national accountant, statistician, and economic theorist. Very few of us can combine such diverse talents in the way that Kuznets and many of the founders of the conference did.

We do not have to go all the way back to Adam Smith to appreciate the benefits of a division of labor. Accountants can design systems that are adapted to modeling, econometricians can develop models based on consistent systems of accounts and sound conceptualization, and theorists can choose a level of abstraction appropriate to applications in accounting and econometric modeling. It seems to me that these are the lessons that we, the current generation of participants in the Conference on Research in Income and Wealth, can derive from the experiences of our predecessors of the past half century.

In concluding this paper I would like to emphasize that our final objective remains economic measurement itself. I have used the sources of economic growth to illustrate how our measurements have become more precise and more comprehensive. The view of economic growth that is now coming into focus is very different from the picture based on Douglas's fateful abstraction of the aggregate production function. While this new perspective represents important scientific progress, additional challenges are constantly emerging, even in this much studied area. The research opportunities that have been created are more than sufficient to utilize the combined talents of a legion of national accountants, econometricians, and economic theorists for the next half century and beyond.

Notes

1. The first English-language reference to Tinbergen's article was by Valavanis-Vail (1955); an English translation appeared in Tinbergen's *Selected Papers* (1959). The article was also cited by Solow (1963a).

2. The initial version of the estimates of labor input presented in table 3.1 were published in Studies in Income and Wealth by Gollop and Jorgenson (1980, 1983). Denison (1985) has continued to publish more highly aggregated estimates of labor input growth. The Bureau of Labor Statistics has initiated a project to develop measures of labor input adjusted for changes in labor quality; see Waldorf, Kunze, Rosenblum, and Tannen (1986).

3. This approach can be contrasted with a more restrictive approach based on the existence of a value-added aggregate within each sector. The value-added approach is utilized by Kendrick (1956, 1961a, 1973, 1983a) and Kendrick and Grossman (1980).

These studies exclude intermediate input from consideration. The earlier study by Leontief (1953b) excluded capital input.

4. The concept of separability was introduced by Leontief (1947a, 1947b) and Sono (1961).

5. The concept of homothetic separability was originated by Shephard (1953, 1970). Lau (1969, 1978) has demonstrated that if the production function is homogeneous, separability implies homothetic separability.

6. The translog production function was first applied at the sectoral level by Berndt and Christensen (1973, 1974), using a value-added aggregate. The translog cost function incorporating intermediate input was applied at the sectoral level by Berndt and Jorgenson (1973) and Berndt and Wood (1975). Detailed references to sectoral production studies incorporating intermediate input are given by Jorgenson (1986a).

7. Translog quantity indexes were introduced by Irving Fisher (1922) and have been discussed by Christensen and Jorgenson (1969), Kloek (1966), Theil (1965), and Törnqvist (1936). These indexes were first derived from the translog production function by Diewert (1976). The corresponding index of productivity growth was introduced by Christensen and Jorgenson (1970). This index of productivity growth was first derived from the translog production function by Jorgenson and Nishimizu (1978). Earlier, Diewert (1976) had interpreted the ratio of translog indexes of output and input as an index of productivity. Samuelson and Swamy (1974) have provided a comprehensive survey of the economic theory of index numbers.

8. The allocations are based on the method of iterative proportional fitting discussed by Bishop, Fienberg, and Holland (1975, esp. 83–102, 188–91).

9. Establishment surveys count only persons actually at work during the survey week. By using establishment-based estimates of the number of jobs in each sector and assigning to absent workers the average annual hours worked by individuals with comparable characteristics, hours worked for each type of worker can be estimated on an annual basis.

10. Hours worked by workers cross-classified by demographic characteristics are estimated on the basis of household surveys. The resulting estimates are controlled to totals for each sector from the U.S. national accounts. Hours worked for each category of labor input is the product of employment, hours worked per week, and the number of weeks in the calendar year, 52. The concepts employed in these estimates of labor input reflect the conventions used in the Census of Population and the Current Population Survey.

11. These data provide estimates of average compensation per person rather than average compensation per job. To combine the data with estimates based on jobs from establishment surveys average compensation per person must be converted to average compensation per job. Matrices of weeks paid per year for each category of workers are required for this purpose. Labor compensation is the product of average compensation per person, the number of jobs per person, and the number of jobs. Estimates of average compensation per person and the number of weeks paid per year are based on household surveys, while estimates of the number of jobs are based on establishment surveys.

12. Chinloy (1980, 1981) provides such a decomposition for the U.S. economy as a whole, excluding sector of employment. Jorgenson, Gollop, and Fraumeni (1987) present a decomposition for all characteristics of individual workers, including sector of employment.

13. Domar (1962, 1963) has provided reviews of Kendrick (1961a); Abramovitz (1962) has reviewed Denison (1962b) and given a comparison with Kendrick (1961a).

14. In his subsequent works, Denison (1967, 1974, 1979, 1985) begins from an hours-paid series when constructing his hours estimates for wage and salary workers. He converts the average hours paid per job to average hours worked per job, using

unpublished BLS ratios of "hours at work" to "hours paid." These ratios, extrapolated from data for the year 1966, were developed by BLS for the 1952–74 period. Based on the trends in the 1952–74 series, Denison (1979, 155; 1985, 64) further extrapolates his hours-worked series back to 1947 and forward to 1982.

15. Denison (1974, 187) assumes that the sex-age earnings weights he creates for males and females from 1966 and 1967 data, respectively, and the education weights from 1959 data are constant over and thus representative of all postwar years. Denison (1979, 44–45, 158, 1985) constructs two sets of weights for both sex-age and education cohorts.

16. The model of capital input employed underlying the measures presented in table 3.1 was originated by Walras ([1877] 1954). The relationship between capital stock and rental prices was first analyzed by Hotelling (1925) and Haavelmo (1960) and has been further developed by Arrow (1964) and Hall (1968). Models of capital as a factor of production are discussed by Diewert (1980), Hulten (chap. 4, in this volume), and Jorgenson (1973a, 1989). Price and quantity indexes associated with capital as a factor of production are special cases of the index numbers proposed by Hicks (1946). Expositions of Hicks aggregation and references to the literature are given by Bruno (1978) and Diewert (1978, 1980, esp. 434–38).

17. These indexes of capital input have been discussed by Denison (1966, 1969).

18. The resulting indexes of capital input have been discussed by Denison (1972), Harper, Berndt, and Wood (1989), Jorgenson (1980), Jorgenson and Griliches (1972a, 1972b), Katz (1988), Mohr (1986, 1988b, 1988c), and Norsworthy (1984a, 1984b).

19. Hulten and Wykoff (1981b) employ Box-Cox transformations of all three variables and estimate separate parameters for each variable from a sample of capital goods prices.

20. The hedonic technique has been analyzed by Muellbauer (1975) and Rosen (1974). Surveys of the literature have been given by Deaton and Muellbauer (1980), Griliches (1971a, 1988a), and Triplett (1975, 1987).

21. Hulten and Wykoff have estimated vintage price functions for structures from a sample of 8,066 observations on market transactions in used structures. These data were collected by the Office of Industrial Economics of the U.S. Department of the Treasury in 1972 and published in *Business Building Statistics* (Office of Industrial Economics 1975). Hulten and Wykoff have estimated vintage price functions for equipment from prices of machine tools collected by Beidleman (1976) and prices of other types of equipment collected from used equipment dealers and auction reports of the U.S. General Services Administration.

22. The Baily hypothesis has also been discussed by Berndt, Mori, Sawa, and Wood (1990).

23. This methodology was first employed by Terborgh (1954). Detailed references to the literature are given by Hulten and Wykoff (1981b), Jorgenson (1989), and Mohr (1988a). Recent applications are presented by Hulten, Robertson, and Wykoff (1989) and Wykoff (1989).

24. This approach was originated by Meyer and Kuh (1957) and has been employed by Coen (1975, 1980), Eisner (1972), and Feldstein and Foot (1974).

25. Tenant-occupied housing is assigned to the finance, insurance, and real estate sector, while owner-occupied housing is assigned to the private household sector.

26. In *Sources of Economic Growth* (1962b, 97–98), Denison employs a measure of capital input for equipment and structures with relative efficiencies constant over the lifetime of the capital good, the one-hoss shay pattern of relative efficiency. In *Why Growth Rates Differ* (1967, 140–41), Denison uses a measure of capital input with relative efficiencies given by an unweighted average of the one-hoss shay and straight-line patterns:

$$d(\tau) = \begin{cases} 1 - \dfrac{\tau}{2L}, & (\tau = 0, 1 \ldots L-1), \\ 0, & (\tau = L, L+1 \ldots). \end{cases}$$

In *Accounting for United States Economic Growth, 1929 to 1969* (1974, 54–55) Denison introduces yet another relative efficiency pattern, based on a weight of one-fourth for straight-line patterns and three-fourths for one-hoss shay patterns:

$$d(\tau) = \begin{cases} 1 - \dfrac{\tau}{4L}, & (\tau = 0, 1 \ldots L-1), \\ 0, & (\tau = L, L+1 \ldots). \end{cases}$$

The corresponding measure of capital input is employed by Denison in *Accounting for Slower Economic Growth* (1979, 50–52) and *Trends in American Economic Growth, 1929–1982* (1985, 65).

For a linearly declining pattern of relative efficiency the mortality distribution can be represented in the form:

$$m(\tau) = \begin{cases} \dfrac{1}{\theta}L & (\tau = 1, 2 \ldots L-1), \\ 1 - \dfrac{1}{\theta}\left(1 - \dfrac{1}{L}\right) & (\tau = L), \\ 0 & (\tau = L+1, L+2 \ldots), \end{cases}$$

where θ is unity for straight-line replacement, positive infinity for one-hoss shay replacement, and two and four, respectively, for Denison's two averages of straight-line and one-hoss shay.

27. In *Sources of Economic Growth* (1962b) and *Why Growth Rates Differ* (1967, p. 10), Denison ignores differences in the tax treatment of corporate and noncorporate income. In *Accounting for United States Economic Growth, 1929 to 1969* (1974, 267–271) Denison employs separate estimates of corporate and noncorporate capital stock for the nonfarm business sector. He derives weights for these assets from data on corporate and noncorporate income by allocating noncorporate income between labor compensation of the self-employed and property compensation; however, his procedures ignore the effect of the corporate income tax. These procedures are also utilized in *Accounting for Slower Economic Growth* (1979, 171) and *Trends in American Economic Growth, 1929 to 1982* (1985, 56).

Kendrick (1973, 30) allocates noncorporate income between property compensation and the labor compensation of the self-employed. He assumes that the self-employed within each sector receive the same hourly compensation as employees. Kendrick does not separate corporate and noncorporate assets in measuring capital input. This approach is also employed by Kendrick and Grossman (1980, 26) and Kendrick (1983a, 56).

28. The model of production based on value added has been discussed by Arrow (1974), Bruno (1978), Diewert (1978, 1980), Sato (1976), and Sims (1969, 1977). Sato provides references to the literature.

29. de Leeuw (1989) and Denison (1989) have discussed the BEA (1987b) gross product originating data. Denison has proposed an alternative breakdown of aggregate productivity measures by end product.

30. Sectoral models of production have been implemented for the United States by Baily (1982), Fraumeni and Jorgenson (1980, 1986), Gollop and Jorgenson (1980, 1983), Gullickson and Harper (1987), Hall (1986, 1987, 1988), Kendrick (1956, 1961a, 1973, 1983a), Kendrick and Grossman (1980), Leontief (1953b), Massell

(1961), Star (1974), Thor, Sadler, and Grossman (1984), and Wolff (1985a). Sectoral models have been implemented for Germany by Conrad (1985), Conrad and Jorgenson (1985), and Frohn, Krengel, Kuhbier, Oppenlander, and Uhlmann (1973); for Japan by Ezaki (1978, 1985), Jorgenson, Kuroda, and Nishimizu (1987), Nishimizu and Hulten (1978), and Watanabe (1971); for Japan, Korea, Turkey, and Yugoslavia by Nishimizu and Robinson (1986); and for the United Kingdom by Armstrong (1974).

The studies of sectoral productivity for Germany by Conrad and Conrad and Jorgenson, for Japan by Jorgenson, Kuroda, and Nishimizu and for Japan, Korea, Turkey, and Yugoslavia by Nishimizu and Robinson are closely comparable in methodology to the study for the United States summarized in tables 3.2 and 3.3. Conrad and Jorgenson provide international comparisons among Germany, Japan, and the United States, including relative levels of productivity by sector in the three countries.

Thor, Sadler, and Grossman (1984) and Jorgenson, Kuroda, and Nishimizu (1987) provide international comparisons between Japan and the United States. The methodology of Thor, Sadler and Grossman is based on that of Kendrick and Grossman. Domar, Eddie, Herrick, Hohenberg, Intriligator, and Miyamoto (1964) provide international comparisons among Canada, Germany, Japan, the United Kingdom, and the United States for the period 1948–60 with separate estimates for as many as 11 sectors within each country. The methodology employed in this study is closely comparable to that of Kendrick (1956, 1961a). Englander and Mittelstadt (1988) have presented international comparisons among 20 OECD countries for the period 1960–86 for as many as 15 industrial sectors in each country. Their methodology is similar to that of Kendrick.

31. The data in table 3.7 also provide a test of Leontief's (1951, 1953a) "fixed coefficients" assumption in interindustry analysis. Under this assumption, all intermediate inputs are proportional to output, so that Leontief's (1936) approach to aggregation implies the existence of an intermediate input aggregate. The fixed coefficients assumption implies that ratios of growth of intermediate input to growth of output in table 3.7 must be equal to unity.

32. The derivation of a production possibility frontier from a multisectoral model of production was originated by Debreu (1951, 285) and has been discussed by Bergson (1961, 1975), Diewert (1980), Fisher (1982), Fisher and Shell (1972), Moorsteen (1961), and Weitzman (1983). Debreu's (1954, 52–54) definition of aggregate productivity growth has been discussed by Diewert (1976, 1980), Hulten (1973), Jorgenson and Griliches (1967), and Richter (1966).

33. The implications of aggregation over industrial sectors for the existence of an aggregate production function was a central issue in the "reswitching controversy" initiated by Samuelson (1962). This controversy has been summarized by Brown (1980) and Burmeister (1980a, 1980b), who provide extensive references to the literature.

34. This condition for the existence of an aggregate production function is due to Hall (1973) and has been discussed by Denny and Pinto (1978) and Lau (1978).

35. The relationship of aggregate and sectoral indexes of productivity growth was first discussed by Debreu (1954) and Leontief (1953b) under the assumption that prices paid for primary factors of production are the same for all sectors. The relationship between aggregate and sectoral productivity indexes under the assumption that prices of primary factors of production differ among sectors was first discussed by Kendrick (1956, 1961a) and Massell (1961).

36. This generalizes a formula originally proposed by Domar (1961), correcting the procedure introduced by Leontief (1953b). Domar's approach, like Leontief's, is based on the assumption that prices paid for primary factors of production are the same for all sectors. Leontief averages weighted relative changes in ratios of intermediate and

labor inputs to output over all sectors. Domar points out that the appropriate measure of aggregate productivity growth is a weighted sum rather than a weighted average. Leontief's approach fails to eliminate deliveries to intermediate demand in the process of aggregating over sectors.

Domar's approach has been discussed by Baumol and Wolff (1984), Diewert (1980), Gollop (1979, 1983), Hulten (1978), and Jorgenson (1980) and has been employed by Fraumeni and Jorgenson (1980, 1986), Nishimizu and Hulten (1978), and Wolff (1985a). One of the curiosities of the literature on productivity measurement is that Leontief's approach has been reintroduced by the Statistical Office of the United Nations (1968), Watanabe (1971), Star (1974), and Ezaki (1978, 1985). Watanabe advocates weights for sectoral productivity growth rates based on the ratio of the value of output in each sector to the sum of the values of outputs in all sectors. Ezaki and Star advocate the use of this same weighting system.

37. This approach was introduced by Kendrick (1956) and has been discussed by Bergson (1961, 1975), Domar (1961), Fisher (1982), Fisher and Shell (1972), Kendrick (1961a), Massell (1961), Moorsteen (1961), the Statistical Office of the United Nations (1968, 69, "Value Added and Primary Inputs: The Net System of Productivity Measurement"), and Weitzman (1983). This approach has been employed by Armstrong (1974), Frohn, Krengel, Kuhbier, Oppenlander, and Uhlmann (9173), Kendrick (1956, 1961a, 1973, 1983a), Kendrick and Grossman (1980), and Massell (1961).

38. Hulten's approach has been implemented for 10 sectors of the Japanese economy for the period 1955–71 by Nishimizu and Hulten (1978).

39. The data that underly tables 3.1 and 3.2 comprise a complete set of U.S. national production accounts for inputs as well as outputs at sectoral and aggregate levels. This system of accounts complements the existing U.S. national accounts for outputs presented by BEA (1986). These accounts can be integrated with the system of national accounts for income and expenditure, capital formation, and wealth outlined by Jorgenson (1980) and implemented by Fraumeni and Jorgenson (1980). The production accounts that underly tables 3.1 and 3.2 can also be combined with systems of national accounts such as those proposed by Eisner (1978, 1985, 1989), Kendrick (1976, 1979), and Ruggles and Ruggles (1970, 1973). Campbell and Peskin (1979) and Eisner (1988) have provided a useful summary and comparison among these accounting systems and give detailed references to the literature. Kendrick's accounting system has been discussed by Engerman and Rosen (1980). Finally, the production accounts can be combined with the system of accounts for the United States proposed by Ruggles and Ruggles (1982). This system integrates income and product accounts, flow of funds accounts, and balance sheets for assets and liabilities.

40. The existence of a value-added aggregate equal to the sum of the quantities of value added in all sectors is an implication of Hicks (1946) aggregation. Further details on Hicks aggregation are given by Bruno (1978) and Diewert (1978, 1980).

41. Models of aggregate production have been implemented for the United States by Abramovitz (1956), Abramovitz and David (1973a, 1973b), Baily (1981), BLS (1983), Christensen and Jorgenson (1969, 1970, 1973a, 1973b), Christensen, Cummings, and Jorgenson (1978, 1980, 1981), Denison (1962a, 1962b, 1967, 1974, 1979, 1985), Fabricant (1959), Jorgenson and Griliches (1967, 1972a, 1972b), Kendrick (1956, 1961a, 1973, 1983a), Kendrick and Grossman (1980), Knowles (1954, 1960), Mills (1952), Norsworthy and Harper (1981), Norsworthy, Harper, and Kunze (1979), Schmookler (1952), Solow (1957, 1960, 1962, 1963a), and Valavanis-Vail (1955).

42. Jorgenson and Nishimizu (1978) have developed methodology for measuring relative productivity levels between countries and have applied this methodology to bilateral comparisons between Japan and the United States during the period 1952–74. Caves, Christensen, and Diewert (1982a, 1982b) have developed methodology for

multilateral productivity comparisons. Denny and Fuss (1983) have presented an alternative approach. Christensen, Cummings, and Jorgenson (1981) have applied the methodology of Caves, Christensen, and Diewert in deriving estimates of relative levels of productivity for the nine countries analyzed by Christensen, Cummings, and Jorgenson (1978, 1980).

43. Denison (1985) has provided estimates of aggregate productivity for the U.S. economy covering the period 1929–82. Earlier, Denison (1967) presented comparable estimates at the aggregate level for Belgium, Denmark, France, Germany, the Netherlands, Norway, the United Kingdom, and the United States for the period 1950–62.

Correa (1970) has given estimates for Argentina, Brazil, Chile, Columbia, Ecuador, Honduras, Mexico, Peru, and Venezuela for the period 1950–62. Walters (1968, 1970) has provided estimates for Canada for the period 1950–67; Dholakis (1974) has presented estimates for India for the period 1948–69; for Japan Kanamori (1972) has given estimates for the period 1955–68 and Denison and Chung (1976) have given estimates for the period 1952–71; finally, Kim and Park (1985) have presented estimates for Korea for the period 1963–82. Bergson (1978) has provided estimates of aggregate productivity for the Soviet Union, France, Germany, Italy, and Japan for the period 1955–70. All of these estimates are closely comparable in methodology to Denison's estimates for the United States. Bergson (1987) has given estimates of relative productivity levels for Hungary, Poland, the Soviet Union, Yugoslavia, and France, Germany, Italy, Japan, Spain, the United Kingdom, and the United States for the year 1975, extending his earlier study of productivity trends.

Kuznets (1971) has compared Denison's productivity estimates with estimates derived from an analysis of long-term growth trends for Canada, France, Norway, the United Kingdom, and the United States.

44. Beckmann and Sato (1969) and Sato and Beckmann (1968) have compared aggregate productivity estimates for Germany, Japan, and the United States. These estimates are based on the methodology of Kendrick and Sato (1963) for the United States. Balassa and Bertrand (1970) have compared sources of economic growth for countries of Western and Eastern Europe, using methods similar to those of Kendrick. Kendrick (1983b) has provided aggregate productivity estimates for Canada, France, Germany, Italy, Japan, Sweden, the United Kingdom, and the United States for the period 1960–78. Kendrick (1984) has updated these estimates to 1979 and added Belgium to the list of countries.

45. The contribution of changes in the distribution of capital and labor inputs among sectors to productivity growth for the U.S. economy as a whole has been measured by Kendrick (1973) for 34 industry groups for the period 1948–66. The contribution of these changes to the rate of productivity growth for the U.S. manufacturing sector has been measured by Massell (1961) for 17 industry groups for the period 1946–57. Denison (1985) has measured the contribution of changes in the distribution of capital and labor inputs between farm and nonfarm sectors of the U.S. economy for the period 1929–82 and of labor input between self-employment and other employment within the nonfarm sector for the same period.

46. Norsworthy (1984b) compares the methodologies employed by Christensen, Cummings, and Jorgenson, Denison, and Kendrick. A detailed comparison of the empirical results of Christensen, Cummings, and Jorgenson (1980) with those of BLS, Denison, and Kendrick is presented by BLS (1983). As we have already pointed out, the concept of net value added used at the aggregate level in Kendrick's (1956, 1961a, 1973) early studies was abandoned by Kendrick and Grossman (1980) and Kendrick (1983a). Norsworthy concludes that Denison's (1985) concept of value added net of depreciation has been superseded by value added gross of depreciation as a starting point for studies of productivity at the aggregate level.

47. Gollop (1985) has surveyed the literature on the role of intersectoral shifts.

48. Bergman (1985), Johansen (1976), and Taylor (1975) provide detailed references to the literature on the approach to general equilibrium modeling originated by Johansen. The econometric approach to general equilibrium modeling, introduced by Hudson and Jorgenson (1974), is further discussed by Bergman (1990), Jorgenson (1982, 1984a, 1986a), and Jorgenson and Wilcoxen (1990).

49. An important issue in the modeling of producer behavior at the sectoral level is the existence of aggregate inputs, such as the capital, labor, energy, and materials inputs. The production function is required to be homothetically separable in the components of each of these aggregates in the approach of Berndt and Jorgenson. The methodology for testing homothetic separability was originated by Jorgenson and Lau (1975). This methodology has been discussed by Blackorby, Primont, and Russell (1977) and Denny and Fuss (1977). An alternative approach has been developed by Woodland (1978).

Berndt and Christensen (1973) and Norsworthy and Harper (1981) have tested the existence of aggregate capital input. Berndt and Christensen (1974) have tested the existence of aggregate labor input. Woodland (1978) has tested the existence of both capital and labor inputs. Berndt and Wood (1975) have tested the existence of the value-added aggregate discussed in section 3.4. The results of these tests are favorable to the existence of aggregates for capital input, but highly unfavorable to the existence of an aggregate for labor or an aggregate for value added like that employed in Kendrick's (1956, 1961a) studies of sectoral productivity growth.

50. Friede (1979) and Nakamura (1984) have constructed models of this type for Germany, while Longva and Olsen (1983) have constructed such a model for Norway.

51. Early studies of aggregate producer behavior, including those based on the Cobb-Douglas production function, have been surveyed by Heady and Dillon (1961) and Walters (1963). Samuelson (1979) discusses the impact of Douglas's research.

52. The implications of the results of McFadden and Uzawa have been discussed by Solow (1967). Econometric studies based on the CES production function have been surveyed by Griliches (1967), Jorgenson (1974), Kennedy and Thirlwall (1972), Nadiri (1970), and Nerlove (1967).

53. Aggregate models of producer behavior based on the translog functional form have been constructed for the United States by Christensen, Jorgenson, and Lau (1971, 1973) and Jorgenson and Yun (1986). Aggregate models for the United States have also been developed by Hall (1973), Burgess (1974), and Kohli (1981, 1983). Denny and Pinto (1978) have constructed an aggregate model of production for Canada. Conrad and Jorgenson (1977, 1978) have developed aggregate models for Germany.

54. Illustrations of this type of application are provided by the analysis of the impact of alternative energy policies on U.S. economic growth by Hudson and Jorgenson (1974) and the effects of environmental regulation on U.S. economic growth by Jorgenson and Wilcoxen (1990).

55. The price function was introduced by Samuelson (1953).

56. This definition of the bias of productivity growth is due to Hicks (1963). Alternative definitions of biases of productivity growth are compared by Binswanger (1978).

57. Further details on econometric modeling of sectoral productivity growth are given by Jorgenson (1986a).

58. Trends in energy prices since 1973 are discussed in greater detail by Jorgenson (1986b). Bruno (1984) has discussed the impact of higher raw materials prices after 1973. The bias of productivity growth for materials is positive for twenty of the 35 industries listed in table 3.8. For these industries an increase in the price of materials is associated with lower productivity growth.

59. Baily (1986), Baily and Chakrabarti (1988), Denison (1983), Griliches (1988b), Jorgenson (1988b), and Romer (1987) have discussed the slowdown in economic growth in the United States. A comparison of the slowdowns in Japan and the United States is presented by Jorgenson (1988a), Giersch and Wolter (1983) and Lindbeck (1983) have analyzed the slowdown in industrialized countries. Baily and Gordon (1988), Englander and Mittelstadt (1988), Maddison (1987), and Wolff (1985b) have provided surveys of the literature on the slowdown in productivity growth in industrialized countries.

60. Surveys of the literature on induced technical change are given by Binswanger (1978), Solow (1967), and Thirtle and Ruttan (1987).

61. Dynamic models of production based on costs of adjustment have been analyzed, e.g., by Lucas (1967) and Uzawa (1969).

62. This approach has been employed in models of investment behavior based on Tobin's (1969) *q* theory, such as those constructed by Hayashi (1982) and Summers (1981). The literature on econometric models of investment behavior based on Tobin's *q* theory has been surveyed by Chirinko (1988). Jorgenson (1973b) has discussed models of investment behavior based on costs of adjustment.

63. Dynamic models with static expectations have been employed by Denny, Fuss, and Waverman (1981b), Epstein and Denny (1980), and Morrison and Berndt (1981). Berndt and Fuss (1986) have surveyed the literature on dynamic models of production.

64. This approach has been developed in considerable detail by Hansen and Sargent (1980, 1981) and has been employed in modeling producer behavior by Epstein and Yatchew (1985), Meese (1980), and Sargent (1978).

65. Pindyck and Rotemberg (1983a, 1983b) have utilized this approach.

66. Models of producer behavior with embodied technical change were developed by Solow (1960, 1962, 1963a, 1964). Solow (1963a) provides a comparison of rates of embodied technical change between Germany and the United States and gives references to the literature. Barger (1969) presents estimates of rates of embodied and disembodied technical change for Denmark, France, Germany, Italy, the Netherlands, Norway, Sweden, the United Kingdom, and the United States for the period 1950–64.

67. Solow (1960, 1962) has pointed out that separate rates of embodied and disembodied technical change cannot be identified from the residual alone. This point has been elaborated by Denison (1964a, 1964b), Green (1966), Hall (1968), and Jorgenson (1966).

68. An overview of issues in the measurement of aggregate output, including the adjustment of price indexes for quality change, is presented in the Rees Report (National Research Council 1979, esp. 88–121). Highly preliminary estimates of the impact of these corrections on measures of productivity were presented by Jorgenson and Griliches (1967). Gordon (1990) has provided comprehensive quality corrections for price indexes of producers' durable equipment. Gordon's results have been discussed by Engerman and Rosen (1980).

69. Dulberger (1989) has presented econometric models of computer prices that underly the computer price indexes employed in the U.S. national accounts. Alternative models of computer prices are provided by Gordon (1989). Baily and Gordon (1988) and Triplett (1989) have surveyed the literature on computer price models. Denison (1989) has presented objections to the use of quality-corrected price indexes in the national accounts. Triplett (1990) and Young (1989) have discussed these objections in detail.

70. Econometric studies of economies of scale in the electric generating sector have been surveyed by Cowing and Smith (1978). A review of studies of economies of scale in transportation industries has been presented by Winston (1985). A review of such

studies in communications industries has been given by Fuss (1983). Econometric modeling of economies of scale in all three regulated industries has been surveyed by Jorgenson (1986a). Diewert (1981) reviews methods for measuring productivity in regulated industries. Studies of productivity in regulated industries are presented in the volume edited by Cowing and Stevenson (1981).

71. More recently, the Christensen-Greene data base has been extended by Greene (1983) to incorporate cross sections of individual electric utilities for 1955, 1960, 1965, 1970, and 1975. Greene is able to characterize economies of scale and technical change simultaneously.

72. Panel data sets have been constructed for the airline industry by Caves, Christensen, and Trethaway (1984) for the period 1970–81 and for the railroad industry by Caves, Christensen, Trethaway, and Windle (1985) for the period 1951–75. In these studies a distinction between economies of scale and economies of density is introduced. Economies of density are defined in terms of the elasticity of total cost with respect to output, holding points served, and other characteristics of output fixed. Economies of scale are defined as the elasticity of total cost with respect to output and points served. Economies of density are important in both airlines and railroads, but neither industry is characterized by economies of scale.

73. A description of the LRD program is provided by McGuckin and Pascoe (1988). Other data bases at the firm level are described by Griliches (1984).

74. A model of production with differences between ex ante and ex post substitution possibilities was introduced by Houthakker (1955–56). This model has been further developed by Johansen (1972) and Sato (1975) and has been discussed by Hildenbrand (1981) and Koopmans (1977). Recent applications are given by Bentzel (1978), Forsund and Hjalmarsson (1979, 1983, 1987) and Forsund and Jansen (1983). Fisher (1971), Fisher, Solow, and Kearl (1977), Liviatan (1966), and Solow (1963b) have analyzed the results of fitting "smooth" production functions to data generated from ex post fixed coefficients or putty-clay technology. A survey of the literature on putty-clay models and other alternatives to models based on production and cost functions is given by Solow (1967).

75. A detailed survey of econometric methods for modeling producer behavior is presented by Jorgenson (1986a).

References

Abramovitz, Moses. 1956. Resources and Output Trends in the United States since 1870. *American Economic Review* 46, no. 2 (May): 5–23.

———. 1962. Economic Growth in the United States (A Review Article). *American Economic Review* 52, no. 4 (September): 762–82.

Abramovitz, Moses, and Paul A. David. 1973a. Economic Growth in America: Historical Parables and Realities. *De Economist* 121, no. 3: 251–72.

———. 1973b. Reinterpreting Economic Growth: Parables and Realities. *American Economic Review* 63, no. 2 (May): 428–39.

Alchian, Armen. 1963. Reliability of Progress Curves in Airframe Production. *Econometrica* 31, no. 4 (October): 679–93.

Armstrong, Alan. 1974. *Structural Change in The British Economy, 1948–1968*. A Programme for Growth, 12. London: Chapman & Hall.

Arrow, Kenneth J. 1962. The Economic Implications of Learning by Doing. *Review of Economic Studies* 29(3), no. 86 (June): 155–73.

———. 1964. Optimal Capital Policy, the Cost of Capital, and Myopic Decision Rules. *Annals of the Institute of Statistical Mathematics* 16, nos. 1/2: 16–30.

———. 1974. The Measurement of Real Value Added. In *Nations and Households in Economic Growth,* ed. Paul A. David and Melvyn W. Reder, 3–20. New York: Academic Press.

Arrow, Kenneth J., Hollis B. Chenery, Bagicha S. Minhas, and Robert M. Solow. 1961. Capital-Labor Substitution and Economic Efficiency. *Review of Economics and Statistics* 63, no. 3 (August): 225–47.

Baily, Martin N. 1981. Productivity and the Services of Capital and Labor. *Brookings Papers on Economic Activity,* no. 1: 1–50.

———. 1982. The Productivity Slowdown by Industry. *Brookings Papers on Economic Activity,* no. 2, 423–54.

———. 1986. What Has Happened to Productivity Growth? *Science* (October): 443–51.

Baily, Martin N., and Alok K. Chakrabarti. 1988. *Innovation and the Productivity Crisis.* Washington, D.C.: Brookings.

Baily, Martin N., and Robert J. Gordon. 1988. Measurement Issues, the Productivity Slowdown, and the Explosion of Computer Power. *Brookings Papers on Economic Activity,* no. 2: 1–45.

Balassa, Bela, and Trent J. Bertrand. 1970. Growth Performance of Eastern European Economies and Comparable Western European Countries. *American Economic Review* 60, no. 2 (May): 314–20.

Barger, Harold. 1969. Growth in Developed Nations. *Review of Economics and Statistics* 51, no. 2 (May): 143–48.

Baumol, William J., and Edward N. Wolff. 1984. On Interindustry Differences in Absolute Productivity. *Journal of Political Economy* 92, no. 6 (December): 1017–34.

BEA. *See* Bureau of Economic Analysis.

Beckmann, Martin, and Ryuzo Sato. 1969. Aggregate Production Functions and Types of Technical Progress: A Statistical Analysis. *American Economic Review* 59, no. 1 (March): 88–101.

Beidleman, Carl R. 1976. Economic Depreciation in a Capital Goods Industry. *National Tax Journal* 29, no. 4 (December): 379–90.

Bentzel, Ragnar. 1978. A Vintage Model of Swedish Economic Growth from 1870 to 1975. In *The Importance of Technology and the Permanence of Structure in Industrial Growth,* ed. Bo Carlsson, Gunnar Eliasson, and Mohammed I. Nadiri, 13–50. Stockholm: Industrial Institute for Economic and Social Research.

Bergman, Lars. 1985. Extensions and Applications of the MSG-Model: A Brief Survey. In *Production, Multi-sectoral Growth and Planning,* ed. Finn R. Forsund, Michael Hoel, and Svein Longva, 127–61. Amsterdam: North-Holland.

———. 1990. The Development of Computable General Equilibrium Modeling. In *General Equilibrium Modeling and Economic Policy Analysis,* ed. Lars Bergman, Dale W. Jorgenson, and Erno Zalai, 3–30. Oxford: Basil Blackwell.

Bergson, Abram. 1961. *The Real National Income of the Soviet Union since 1928.* Cambridge, Mass.: Harvard University Press.

———. 1975. Index Numbers and the Computation of Factor Productivity. *Review of Income and Wealth,* ser. 21, no. 3 (September): 259–78.

———. 1978. *Productivity and the Social System—the USSR and the West.* Cambridge, Mass.: Harvard University Press.

———. 1987. Comparative Productivity: The USSR, Eastern Europe, and the West, *American Economic Review* 77, no. 3 (June): 342–57.

Berndt, Ernst R., and Laurits R. Christensen. 1973. The Translog Function and the

Substitution of Equipment, Structures, and Labor in U.S. Manufacturing, 1929–68. *Journal of Econometrics* 1, no. 1 (March): 81–113.

———. 1974. Testing for the Existence of a Consistent Aggregate Index of Labor Input. *American Economic Review* 64, no. 3 (June): 391–404.

Berndt, Ernst R., and Melvyn Fuss. 1986. Editor's introduction. *Journal of Econometrics* 33, nos. 1/2 (October/November): 1–5.

Berndt, Ernst R., and Dale W. Jorgenson. 1973. Production Structure. In *U.S. Energy Resources and Economic Growth,* ed. Dale W. Jorgenson and Hendrik S. Houthakker. Washington, D.C.: Energy Policy Project.

Berndt, Ernst R., Shunseke Mori, Takamitsu Sawa, and David O. Wood. 1990. Energy Price Shocks and Productivity Growth in the Japanese and U.S. Manufacturing Industries. In *Productivity Growth in Japan and the United States,* ed. Charles R. Hulten. NBER Studies in Income and Wealth, vol. 53. Chicago: University of Chicago Press.

Berndt, Ernst R., and David O. Wood. 1975. Technology, Prices, and the Derived Demand for Energy. *Review of Economics and Statistics* 56, no. 3 (August): 259–68.

Binswanger, Hans P. 1978. Issues in Modeling Induced Technical Change. In *Induced Innovation,* ed. Hans P. Binswanger and Vernon W. Ruttan, 128–63. Baltimore: Johns Hopkins University Press.

Bishop, Yvonne M. M., Steven E. Fienberg, and Paul W. Holland. 1975. *Discrete Multivariate Analysis*. Cambridge, Mass.: MIT Press.

Blackorby, Charles, Daniel Primont, and Robert R. Russell. 1977. On Testing Separability Restrictions with Flexible Functional Forms. *Journal of Econometrics* 5, no. 2 (March): 195–209.

BLS. *See* Bureau of Labor Statistics.

Brown, Murray. 1980. The Measurement of Capital Aggregates: A Postreswitching Problem. In *The Measurement of Capital,* ed. Dan Usher, 377–420. Chicago: University of Chicago Press.

Bruno, Michael. 1978. Duality, Intermediate Inputs, and Value Added. In *Production Economics: A Dual Approach to Theory and Applications,* ed. Melvyn Fuss and Daniel McFadden, 2: 3–16. Amsterdam: North-Holland.

———. 1984. Raw Materials, Profits, and the Productivity Slowdown. *Quarterly Journal of Economics* 99, no. 1 (February): 1–30.

Bureau of the Census. 1972. Census of Population: 1970, Occupation by Industry. Final Report PC(2)-7C. Washington, D.C.: U.S. Department of Commerce.

———. 1973a. Census of Population: 1970, Earnings by Occupation and Education. Final Report PC(2)-8B. Washington, D.C.: U.S. Department of Commerce.

———. 1973b. Census of Population: 1970, Industrial Characteristics. Final Report PC(2)-7B. Washington, D.C.: U.S. Department of Commerce.

———. 1973c. Census of Population: 1970, Occupational Characteristics. Final Report PC(2)-7A. Washington, D.C.: U.S. Department of Commerce.

———. 1985. Census of Population and Housing: 1980. One Percent Sample Computer Tape. U.S. Department of Commerce, Washington, D.C.

Bureau of Economic Analysis. 1984. The Input-Output Structure of the U.S. Economy, 1977. *Survey of Current Business* 64, no. 5 (May): 42–79.

———. 1986. *The National Income and Product Accounts of the United States, 1929–1982: Statistical Tables*. Washington, D.C.: U.S. Department of Commerce.

———. 1987a. *Fixed Reproducible Tangible Wealth in the United States, 1925–85*. Washington, D.C.: U.S. Government Printing Office.

———. 1987b. Gross National Product Originating by Industry for 14 Income Components. Computer Tape. U.S. Department of Commerce, Washington, D.C.

———. Various years. *Input-Output Transactions Tables*. Computer Tape. U.S. Department of Commerce, Washington, D.C.

Bureau of Labor Statistics, 1963, *Manufacturing Industries 1962: Employer Expenditures for Selected Supplementary Compensation Practices for Production and Related Workers*. Bulletin no. 1428. Washington, D.C.: Department of Labor.

———. 1971. *BLS Handbook of Methods for Surveys and Studies*. Bulletin no. 1711. Washington, D.C.: Department of Labor.

———. 1983. *Trends in Multifactor Productivity, 1948–81*, Bulletin no. 2178. Washington, D.C.: Department of Labor.

———. 1987. Time Series on Output, Prices, and Employment. Computer Tape. U.S. Department of Labor, Office of Economic Growth, Washington, D.C.

Burgess, David F. 1974. A Cost Minimization Approach to Import Demand Equations. *Review of Economics and Statistics* 56, no. 2 (May): 224–34.

Burmeister, Edwin. 1980a. *Capital Theory and Dynamics*. Cambridge: Cambridge University Press.

———. 1980b. Comment. In *The Measurement of Capital*, ed. Dan Usher, 421–31. Chicago: University of Chicago Press.

Campbell, Beth, and Janice Peskin. 1979. Expanding Economic Accounts and Measuring Economic Welfare: A Review of Proposals. Washington, D.C., Bureau of Economic Analysis, U.S. Department of Commerce, October.

Carré, J.-J., Paul Dubois, and Edmond Malinvaud. 1975. *French Economic Growth*. Stanford, Calif.: Stanford University Press.

Caves, Douglas W., Laurits R. Christensen, and W. Erwin Diewert. 1982a. The Economic Theory of Index Numbers and the Measurement of Input, Output, and Productivity. *Econometrica* 50, no. 6 (November): 1393–1414.

———. 1982b. Multilateral Comparisons of Output, Input, and Productivity Using Superlative Index Numbers. *Economic Journal* 92, no. 365 (March): 73–86.

Caves, Douglas W., Laurits R. Christensen, and Michael W. Trethaway. 1984. Economies of Density versus Economies of Scale: Why Trunk and Local Service Airline Costs Differ. *Rand Journal of Economics* 15, no. 4 (Winter): 471–89.

Caves, Douglas W., Laurits R. Christensen, Michael W. Trethaway, and Robert Windle. 1985. Network Effects and the Measurement of Returns to Scale and Density for U.S. Railroads. In *Analytical Studies in Transport Economics*, ed. Andrew F. Daughety, 97–120. Cambridge, Cambridge University Press.

Census of Population. *See* Bureau of the Census.

Chinloy, Peter T. 1980. Sources of Quality Change in Labor Input. *American Economic Review* 70, no. 1 (March): 108–19.

———. 1981. *Labor Productivity*. Cambridge, Mass.: Abt Books.

Chirinko, Robert S. 1988. Will "The" Neoclassical Theory of Investment Please Rise? In *The Impact of Taxation on Business Investment*, ed. Jack Mintz and Douglas Purvis, 107–67. Ottawa: John Deutsch Institute.

Christensen, Laurits R., and Dianne Cummings. 1981. Real Product, Real Factor Input, and Productivity in the Republic of Korea, 1960–73. *Journal of Development Economics* 8, no. 3 (June): 285–302.

Christensen, Laurits R., Dianne Cummings, and Dale W. Jorgenson. 1978. Productivity Growth, 1947–1973: An International Comparison. In *The Impact of International Trade and Investment on Employment*, ed. William Dewald, 211–33. Washington, D.C.: Government Printing Office.

———. 1980. Economic Growth, 1947–1973: An International Comparison. In *New Developments in Productivity Measurement*, ed. John W. Kendrick and Beatrice Vaccara, 17–131. Chicago: University of Chicago Press.

———. 1981. Relative Productivity Levels, 1947–1973. *European Economic Review* 16, no. 1 (May): 61–94.

Christensen, Laurits R., and William H. Greene. 1976. Economies of Scale in U.S. Electric Power Generation. *Journal of Political Economy* 84, no. 4 (August): 655–76.

Christensen, Laurits R., and Dale W. Jorgenson. 1969. The Measurement of U.S. Real Capital Input, 1929–1967. *Review of Income and Wealth,* ser. 15, no. 4 (December): 293–320.

———. 1970. U.S. Real Product and Real Factor Input, 1929–1967. *Review of Income and Wealth,* ser. 16, no. 1 (March): 19–50.

———. 1973a. Measuring the Performance of the Private Sector of the U.S. Economy, 1929–1969. In *Measuring Economic and Social Performance,* ed. Milton Moss, 233–38. New York: NBER.

———. 1973b. U.S. Income, Saving, and Wealth, 1929–1969. *Review of Income and Wealth,* ser. 19, no. 4 (December): 329–62.

Christensen, Laurits R., Dale W. Jorgenson, and Lawrence J. Lau. 1971. Conjugate Duality and the Transcendental Logarithmic Production Function. *Econometrica* 39, no. 4 (July): 255–56.

———. 1973. Transcendental Logarithmic Production Frontiers. *Review of Economics and Statistics* 55, no. 1 (February): 28–45.

Cobb, Charles W., and Paul H. Douglas. 1928. A Theory of Production. *American Economic Review* 18, no. 1 (March): 139–65.

Coen, Robert. 1975. Investment Behavior, the Measurement of Depreciation, and Tax Policy. *American Economic Review* 65, no. 1 (March): 59–74.

———. 1980. Depreciation, Profits, and Rates of Return in Manufacturing Industries. In *The Measurement of Capital,* ed. Dan Usher, 121–52. Chicago: University of Chicago Press.

Cole, Rosanne, Y. C. Chen, Joan A. Barquin-Stolleman, Ellen Dulberger, Nurhan Helvacian, and James H. Hodge. 1986. Quality-Adjusted Price Indexes for Computer Processors and Selected Peripheral Equipment. *Survey of Current Business* 66, no. 1 (January): 41–50.

Conrad, Klaus. 1985. *Produktivitatslucken nach Wirtschaftszweigen in internationalen Vergleich.* Berlin: Springer-Verlag.

Conrad, Klaus, and Dale W. Jorgenson. 1975. *Measuring Performance in the Private Economy of the Federal Republic of Germany, 1950–1973. Tübingen: J. C. B. Mohr.*

———. 1977. Tests of a Model of Production for the Federal Republic of Germany, 1950–1973. *European Economic Review* 10, no. 1 (October): 51–75.

———. 1978. The Structure of Technology: Nonjointness and Commodity Augmentation, Federal Republic of Germany, 1950–1973. *Empirical Economics* 3, no. 2: 91–113.

———. 1985. Sectoral Productivity Gaps between the United States, Japan, and Germany, 1960–1979. In *Probleme und Perspektiven der weltwirtschaftlichen Entwicklung,* ed. Herbert Giersch, 335–47. Berlin: Duncker & Humblot.

Correa, Hector. 1970. Sources of Economic Growth in Latin America. *Southern Economic Journal* 37, no. 1 (July): 17–31.

Court, Andrew T. 1939. Hedonic Price Indexes with Automotive Examples. In *The Dynamics of Automobile Demand,* 99–117. New York: General Motors Corporation.

Cowing, Thomas G., and V. Kerry Smith. 1978. The Estimation of a Production Technology: A Survey of Econometric Analyses of Steam Electric Generation. *Land Economics* 54, no. 2 (May): 158–68.

Cowing, Thomas G., and Rodney E. Stevenson, eds. 1981. *Productivity Measurement in Regulated Industries*. New York: Academic Press.

Deaton, Angus, and John Muellbauer. 1980. *Economics and Consumer Behavior.* Cambridge, Mass.: Cambridge University Press.

Debreu, Gerard. 1951. The Coefficient of Resource Utilization. *Econometrica* 19,no. 3 (July): 273–92.

———. 1954. Numerical Representations of Technological Change. *Metroeconomica* 6, no. 3 (August): 45–54.

de Leeuw, Frank. 1989. Gross Product by Industry: Comments on Recent Criticisms. *Survey of Current Business* 68, no. 7 (July): 132–33.

Denison, Edward F. 1957. Theoretical Aspects of Quality Change, Capital Consumption, and Net Capital Formation. In *Problems of Capital Formation,* 215–61. NBER Studies in Income and Wealth. Princeton, N.J.: Princeton University Press.

———. 1961. Measurement of Labor Input: Some Questions of Definition and the Adequacy of Data. In *Output, Input, and Productivity Measurement,* 347–72. NBER Studies in Income and Wealth. Princeton, N.J.: Princeton University Press.

———. 1962a. How to Raise the High-Employment Growth Rate by One Percentage Point. *American Economic Review* 52, no. 2 (May): 67–75.

———. 1962b. *Sources of Economic Growth in the United States and the Alternatives before Us*. New York: Committee for Economic Development.

———. 1964a. Capital Theory and the Rate of Return (Review Article). *American Economic Review* 54, no. 5 (September): 721–25.

———. 1964b. The Unimportance of the Embodied Question. *American Economic Review* 54, no. 5 (September): 721–25.

———. 1966. Discussion. *American Economic Review* 66, no. 2 (May): 76–78.

———. 1967. *Why Growth Rates Differ.* Washington, D.C.: Brookings.

———. 1969. Some Major Issues in Productivity Analysis: An Examination of Estimates by Jorgenson and Griliches. *Survey of Current Business* 49, no. 5, pt. 2 (May): 1–27.

———. 1972. Final Comments. *Survey of Current Business* 52, no. 5, pt. 2 (May): 95–110.

———. 1974. *Accounting for United States Economic Growth, 1929 to 1969,* Washington, D.C.: Brookings.

———. 1979. *Accounting for Slower Economic Growth.* Washington, D.C.: Brookings.

———. 1983. The Interruption of Productivity Growth in the United States. *Economic Journal* 93, no. 369 (March): 56–77.

———. 1984. Accounting for Slower Economic Growth: An Update. In *International Comparisons of Productivity and Causes of the Slowdown,* ed. John W. Kendrick, 1–45. Cambridge: Ballinger.

———. 1985. *Trends in American Economic Growth, 1929–1982*. Washington, D.C.: Brookings.

———. 1989. *Estimates of Productivity Change by Industry.* Washington, D.C.: Brookings.

Denison, Edward F., and William K. Chung. 1976. *How Japan's Economy Grew So Fast*. Washington, D.C.: Brookings.

Denny, Michael, and Melvyn Fuss. 1977. The Use of Approximation Analysis to Test for Separability and the Existence of Consistent Aggregates. *American Economic Review* 67, no. 3 (June): 404–18.

———. 1983. A General Approach to Intertemporal and Interspatial Productivity Comparisons. *Journal of Econometrics* 23, no. 3 (December): 315–30.

Denny, Michael, Melvyn Fuss, and Leonard Waverman. 1981a. The Measurement and

Interpretation of Total Factor Productivity in Regulated Industries, with an Application to Canadian Telecommunications. In *Productivity Measurement in Regulated Industries,* ed. Thomas G. Cowing and Rodney E. Stevenson, 179–218. New York: Academic Press.

———. 1981b. The Substitution Possibilities for Energy: Evidence from U.S. and Canadian Manufacturing Industries. In *Modeling and Measuring Natural Resource Substitution,* ed. Ernst R. Berndt and Barry C. Field, 230–58. Cambridge, Mass.: MIT Press.

Denny, Michael, and Cheryl Pinto. 1978. An Aggregate Model with Multi-Product Technologies. In *Production Economics: A Dual Approach to Theory and Applications,* ed. Melvyn Fuss and Daniel McFadden, 2: 17–52. Amsterdam: North-Holland.

Dholakis, Bankul H. 1974. *The Sources of Economic Growth in India.* New Delhi: Good Companions.

Diewert, W. Erwin. 1971. An Application of the Shephard Duality Theorem, A Generalized Leontief Production Function. *Journal of Political Economy* 79, no. 3 (May/June): 481–507.

———. 1973. Functional Forms for Profit and Transformation Functions. *Journal of Economic Theory* 6, no. 3 (June): 284–316.

———. 1976. Exact and Superlative Index Numbers. *Journal of Econometrics* 4, no. 2 (May): 115–46.

———. 1978. Hicks' Aggregation Theorem and the Existence of a Real Value-added Function. In *Production Economics: A Dual Approach to Theory and Applications,* ed. Melvyn Fuss and Daniel McFadden, 2: 17–52. Amsterdam: North-Holland.

———. 1980. Aggregation Problems in the Measurement of Capital. In *The Measurement of Capital,* ed. Dan Usher, 433–528. Chicago: University of Chicago Press.

———. 1981. The Theory of Total Factor Productivity Measurement in Regulated Industries. In *Productivity Mesaurement in Regulated Industries,* ed. Thomas G. Cowing and Rodney E. Stevenson, 17–44. New York: Academic Press.

Domar, Evsey. 1961. On the Measurement of Technological Change. *Economic Journal* 71, no. 284 (December): 709–29.

———. 1962. On Total Factor Productivity and All That. *Journal of Political Economy* 70, no. 6 (December): 597–606.

———. 1963. Total Productivity and the Quality of Capital. *Journal of Political Economy* 71, no. 6 (December): 586–88.

Domar, Evsey, Scott M. Eddie, Bruce H. Herrick, Paul M. Hohenberg, Michael D. Intriligator, and Michizo Miyamoto. 1964. Economic Growth and Productivity in the United States, Canada, United Kingdom, Germany, and Japan in the Post-war Period. *Review of Economics and Statistics* 46, no. 1 (February): 33–40.

Douglas, Paul H. 1948. Are There Laws of Production? *American Economic Review* 38, no. 1 (March): 1–41.

———. 1967. Comments on the Cobb-Douglas Production Function. In *The Theory and Empirical Analysis of Production,* ed. Murray Brown, 15–22. New York: Columbia University Press.

———. 1976. The Cobb-Douglas Production Function Once Again: Its History, Its Testing, and Some Empirical Values. *Journal of Political Economy* 84, no. 5 (October): 903–16.

Dulberger, Ellen. 1989. The Application of a Hedonic Model to a Quality-Adjusted Price Index for Computer Processors. In *Technology and Capital Formation,* ed. Dale W. Jorgenson and Ralph Landau, 37–76. Cambridge, Mass.: MIT Press.

Eisner, Robert. 1972. Components of Capital Expenditures: Replacement and Modernization. *Review of Economics and Statistics* 54, no. 3 (August): 297–305.

———. 1978. Total Incomes in the United States, 1959 and 1969. *Review of Income and Wealth,* ser. 24, no. 1 (March): 41–70.

———. 1985. The Total Incomes System of Accounts. *Survey of Current Business* 65, no. 1 (January): 24–48.

———. 1988. Extended Accounts for Income and Product. *Journal of Economic Literature* 26, no. 4 (December): 1611–84.

———. 1989. *The Total Incomes System of Accounts.* Chicago: University of Chicago Press.

Elias, Victor J. 1978. Sources of Economic Growth in Latin American Countries. *Review of Economics and Statistics* 60, no. 3 (August): 362–70.

Engerman, Stanley, and Sherwin Rosen. 1980. New Books on the Measurement of Capital. In *The Measurement of Capital,* ed. Dan Usher, 153–170. Chicago: University of Chicago Press.

Englander, A. Steven, and Axel Mittelstadt. 1988. Total Factor Productivity: Macroeconomic and Structural Aspects of the Slowdown. *OECD Economic Studies* 10 (Spring): 7–56.

Epstein, Larry G., and Michael Denny. 1980. Endogenous Capital Utilization in a Short-Run Production Model: Theory and an Empirical Application. *Journal of Econometrics* 12, no. 2 (February): 189–207.

Epstein, Larry G., and Adonis Yatchew. 1985. The Empirical Determination of Technology and Expectations: A Simplified Procedure. *Journal of Econometrics* 27, no. 2 (February): 235–58.

Ezaki, Mitsuo. 1978. Growth Accounting of Postwar Japan: The Input Side. *Economic Studies Quarterly* 29, no. 2 (June): 193–215.

———. 1985. Growth Accounting Based on Input-Output Tables. In *Input-Output Models,* ed. Shamsher Ali, 325–70. Tokyo: Institute of Developing Economies.

Ezaki, Mitsuo, and Dale W. Jorgenson. 1973. Measurement of Macroeconomic Performance in Japan, 1951–1968. In *Economic Growth: The Japanese Experience since the Meiji Era,* vol. 1, ed. Kazushi Ohkawa and Yujiro Hayami. Tokyo: Japan Economic Research Center.

Fabricant, Solomon. 1959. *Basic Facts of Productivity Change.* Occasional Paper no. 63. New York: NBER.

Feldstein, Martin S., and David K. Foot. 1974. The Other Half of Gross Investment: Replacement and Modernization Expenditures. *Review of Economics and Statistics* 56, no. 1 (February): 49–58.

Fisher, Franklin M. 1971. Aggregate Production Functions and the Explanation of Wages: A Simulation Experiment. *Review of Economics and Statistics* 53, no. 4 (November): 305–26.

———. 1982. On Perfect Aggregation in the National Output Deflator and Generalized Rybczynski Theorems. *International Economic Review* 23, no. 1 (February): 43–60.

Fisher, Franklin M., and Karl Shell. 1972. The Pure Theory of the National Output Deflator. In *The Economic Theory of Price Indexes,* 49–113. New York: Academic Press.

Fisher, Franklin M., Robert M. Solow, and James M. Kearl. 1977. Aggregate Production Functions: Some CES Experiments. *Review of Economic Studies* 44(2), no. 137 (June): 305–20.

Fisher, Irving. 1922. *The Making of Index Numbers.* Boston: Houghton-Mifflin.

Forsund, Finn R., and Lennart Hjalmarsson. 1979. Frontier Production Functions and Technical Progress: A Study of General Milk Processing Swedish Dairy Plants." *Econometrica* 47, no. 4 (July): 883–901.

———. 1983. Technical Progress and Structural Change in the Swedish Cement Industry 1955–1979. *Econometrica* 51, no. 5 (September): 1449–67.

———. 1987. *Analyses of Industrial Structure: A Putty-Clay Approach.* Stockholm: Almqvist & Wiksell International.

Forsund, Finn R., and Eilev S. Jansen. 1983. Technical Progress and Structural Change in the Norwegian Primary Aluminum Industry. *Scandinavian Journal of Economics* 85, no. 2: 113–26.

Fraumeni, Barbara M., and Dale W. Jorgenson. 1980. The Role of Capital in U.S. Economic Growth, 1948–1976. In *Capital Efficiency and Growth,* ed. George von Furstenberg, 9–25. Cambridge: Ballinger.

———. 1986. The Role of Capital in U.S. Economic Growth, 1948–1979. In *Measurement Issues and Behavior of Productivity Variables,* ed. Ali Dogramaci, 161–244. Boston: Martinus Nijhoff.

Friede, Gerhard. 1979. *Investigation of Producer Behavior in the Federal Republic of Germany Using the Translog Price Function.* Cambridge: Oelgeschlager, Gunn, & Hain.

Frohn, Joachim, Rolf Krengel, Peter Kuhbier, Karl H. Oppenlander, Luitpold Uhlmann. 1973. *Der Technische Fortschritt in der Industrie.* Berlin: Duncker & Humblot.

Fuss, Melvyn. 1977. The Structure of Technology over Time: A Model for Testing the "Putty-Clay" Hypothesis. *Econometrica* 45, no. 8 (November): 1797–1821.

———. 1978. Factor Substitution in Electricity Generation: A Test of the Putty-Clay Hypothesis. In *Production Economics: A Dual Approach to Theory and Applications,* ed. Melvyn Fuss and Daniel McFadden, 2:187–214. Amsterdam: North-Holland.

———. 1983. A Survey of Recent Results in the Analysis of Production Conditions in Telecommunications. In *Economic Analysis of Telecommunications,* ed. Leon Courville, Alain de Fontenay, and A. Rodney Dobell, 3–26. Amsterdam: North-Holland.

Giersch, Herbert, and Frank Wolter. 1983. Towards an Explanation of the Productivity Slowdown: An Acceleration—Deceleration Hypothesis. *Economic Journal* 93, no. 369 (March): 35–55.

Goldsmith, Raymond W. 1955. *A Study of Saving in the United States.* Princeton, N.J.: Princeton University Press.

———. 1962. *The National Wealth of the United States in the Postwar Period.* New York: NBER.

Gollop, Frank M. 1979. Accounting for Intermediate Input: The Link between Sectoral and Aggregate Measures of Productivity Growth. In *The Measurement and Interpretation of Productivity Growth,* 318–33. Washington, D.C.: National Academy of Sciences.

———. 1983. Growth Accounting in an Open Economy. In *Developments in Econometric Analyses of Productivity,* ed. Ali Dogramaci, 35–62. Boston: Kluwer-Nijhoff.

———. 1985. Analysis of the Productivity Slowdown: Evidence for a Sector-biased or Sector-neutral Industrial Strategy. In *Productivity Growth and U.S. Competitiveness,* ed. William J. Baumol and Kenneth McLennan, 160–86. New York: Oxford University Press.

Gollop, Frank M., and Dale W. Jorgenson. 1980. U.S. Productivity Growth by Industry, 1947–1973. In *New Developments in Productivity Measurement,* ed. John W. Kendrick and Beatrice Vaccara, 17–136. Chicago: University of Chicago Press.

———. 1983. Sectoral Measures of Labor Cost for the United States, 1948–1978. In *The Measurement of Labor Cost,* ed. Jack E. Triplett, 185–235, 503–20. Chicago: University of Chicago Press.

Gollop, Frank M., and Mark J. Roberts. 1981. The Sources of Economic Growth in the U.S. Electric Power Industry. In *Productivity Measurement in Regulated Industries,* ed. Thomas G. Cowing and Rodney E. Stevenson, 107–45. New York: Academic Press.

Gordon, Robert J. 1989. The Postwar Evolution of Computer Prices. In *Technology and Capital Formation,* ed. Dale W. Jorgenson and Ralph Landau, 77–126. Cambridge, Mass.: MIT Press.

———. 1990. *The Measurement of Durable Goods Prices.* Chicago: University of Chicago Press.

Gorman, John A., John C. Musgrave, Gerald Silverstein, and Kathy A. Comins. 1985. Fixed Private Capital in the United States. *Survey of Current Business* 65, no. 7 (July): 36–59.

Green, H. A. John. 1966. Embodied Progress, Investment, and Growth. *American Economic Review* 56, no. 1 (March): 138–51.

Greene, William H. 1983. Simultaneous Estimation of Factor Substitution, Economies of Scale, Productivity, and Non-Neutral Technical Change. In *Developments in Econometric Analyses of Productivity,* ed. Ali Dogramaci, 121–44. Boston: Kluwer-Nijhoff.

Griliches, Zvi. 1961a. Discussion. *American Economic Review* 51, no. 2 (May): 127–30.

———. 1961b. Hedonic Price Indexes for Automobiles: An Econometric Analysis of Quality Change. In *The Price Statistics of the Federal Government,* 137–96. New York: NBER.

———. 1964. Notes on the Measurement of Price and Quality Changes. In *Models of Income Determination,* 301–404. NBER Studies in Income and Wealth, vol. 28. Princeton, N.J.: Princeton University Press.

———. 1967. Production Functions in Manufacturing: Some Empirical Results. In *The Theory and Empirical Analysis of Production,* ed. Murray Brown, 275–322. New York: Columbia University Press.

———. 1971a. Hedonic Price Indexes Revisited. In *Price Indexes and Quality Change,* ed. Zvi Griliches, 3–15. Cambridge, Mass.: Harvard University Press.

———, ed. 1971b. *Price Indexes and Quality Change,* Cambridge, Mass.: Harvard University Press.

———. 1984. Introduction. In *R & D, Patents, and Productivity,* ed. Zvi Griliches, 1–20. Chicago: University of Chicago Press.

———. 1988a. Postscript on Hedonics. In *Technology, Education, and Productivity,* ed. Zvi Griliches, 119–22. Oxford: Basil Blackwell.

———. 1988b. Productivity Puzzles and R&D: Another Nonexplanation. *Journal of Economic Perspectives* 2, no. 4 (Fall): 9–21.

Griliches, Zvi, and Dale W. Jorgenson. 1966. Sources of Measured Productivity Change: Capital Input. *American Economic Review* 56, no. 2 (May): 50–61.

Groes, Nils, and Peter Bjerregaard. 1978. *Real Product, Real Factor Input and Productivity in Denmark.* Copenhagen: Institute of Economics, University of Copenhagen.

Gullickson, William, and Michael J. Harper. 1987. Multifactor Productivity in U.S. Manufacturing, 1949–83. *Monthly Labor Review* 110, no. 10 (October): 18–28.

Haavelmo, Trygve. 1960. *A Study in the Theory of Investment.* Chicago: University of Chicago Press.

Hall, Robert E. 1968. Technical Change and Capital from the Point of View of the Dual. *Review of Economic Studies* 35(1), no. 101 (January): 35–46.

———. 1971. The Measurement of Quality Changes from Vintage Price Data. In *Price Indexes and Quality Change,* ed. Zvi Griliches, 240–71. Cambridge, Mass.: Harvard University Press.

———. 1973. The Specification of Technology with Several Kinds of Output. *Journal of Political Economy* 81, no. 4 (July/August): 878–92.
———. 1986. Market Structure and Macroeconomic Fluctuations. *Brookings Papers on Economic Activity,* no. 2:285–322.
———. 1987. Productivity and the Business Cycle. Carnegie-Rochester Conference Series on Public Policy, vol. 28: 421–44.
———. 1988. The Relation between Price and Marginal Cost in U.S. Industry. *Journal of Political Economy* 96, no. 5 (October): 921–47.
Hall, Robert E., and Dale W. Jorgenson. 1967. Tax Policy and Investment Behavior. *American Economic Review* 57, no. 3 (June): 391–414.
———. 1969. Tax Policy and Investment Behavior: Reply and Further Results. *American Economic Review* 59, no. 3 (June): 388–401.
———. 1971. Applications of the Theory of Optimum Capital Accumulation. In *Tax Incentives and Capital Spending,* ed. Gary Fromm, 9–60. Amsterdam: North-Holland.
Hansen, Lars. P., and Thomas J. Sargent. 1980. Formulating and Estimating Linear Rational Expectations Models. *Journal of Economic Dynamics and Control* 2, no. 1 (February): 7–46.
———. 1981. Linear Rational Expectations Models for Dynamically Interrelated Variables. In *Rational Expectations and Econometric Practice,* ed. Robert E. Lucas and Thomas J. Sargent, 1:127–56. Minneapolis: University of Minnesota Press.
Harper, Michael J., Ernst R. Berndt, and David O. Wood. 1989. "Rates of Return and Capital Aggregation Using Alternative Rental Prices," In *Technology and Capital Formation,* ed. Dale W. Jorgenson and Ralph Landau, 331–72. Cambridge, Mass.: MIT Press.
Hayashi, Fumio. 1982. Tobin's Marginal q and Average q. *Econometrica* 50, no. 1 (January): 213–24.
Heady, Earl O., and John L. Dillon. 1961. *Agricultural Production Functions.* Ames: Iowa State University Press.
Hicks, John R. 1946. *Value and Capital,* 2d ed. Oxford: Oxford University Press. (1st ed., 1939)
———. 1963. *The Theory of Wages,* 2d ed. London: Macmillan. (1st ed., 1932)
Hildenbrand, Werner. 1981. Short-Run Production Functions Based on Microdata. *Econometrica* 49, no. 5 (September): 1095–1125.
Ho, Mun S., and Dale W. Jorgenson. 1990. Trade Policies and U.S. Economic Growth. Department of Economics, Harvard University, April. Typescript.
Hotelling, Harold. 1925. A General Mathematical Theory of Depreciation. *Journal of the American Statistical Association* 20, no. 151 (September): 340–53.
Houthakker, Hendrik S. 1955–56. The Pareto Distribution and the Cobb-Douglas Production Function in Activity Analysis. *Review of Economic Studies* 23(1), no. 60:27–31.
Hudson, Edward A., and Dale W. Jorgenson. 1974. U.S. Energy Policy and Economic Growth, 1975–2000. *Bell Journal of Economics and Management Science* 5, no. 2, (Autumn): 461–514.
Hulten, Charles R. 1973. Divisia Index Numbers. *Econometrica* 41, no. 6 (November): 1017–26.
———. 1978. Growth Accounting with Intermediate Inputs. *Review of Economic Studies* 45(3), no. 141 (October): 511–18.
Hulten, Charles R., James W. Robertson, and Frank C. Wykoff. 1989. Energy, Obsolescence, and the Productivity Slowdown. In *Technology and Capital Formation,* ed. Dale W. Jorgenson and Ralph Landau, 225–58. Cambridge, Mass.: MIT Press.
Hulten, Charles R., and Frank C. Wykoff. 1981a. Economic Depreciation and the

Taxation of Structures in United States Manufacturing Industries: An Empirical Analysis. In *The Measurement of Capital,* ed. Dan Usher, 83–120. Chicago: University of Chicago Press.

———. 1981b. The Estimation of Economic Depreciation Using Vintage Asset Prices: An Application of the Box-Cox Power Transformation. *Journal of Econometrics* 15, no. 3 (April): 367–96.

———. 1981c. The Measurement of Economic Depreciation. In *Depreciation, Inflation, and the Taxation of Income from Capital,* ed. Charles R. Hulten, 81–125. Washington, D.C.: Urban Institute Press.

Johansen, Leif. 1972. *Production Functions.* Amsterdam: North-Holland.

———. 1976. *A Multi-Sectoral Study of Economic Growth,* 2d ed. Amsterdam: North-Holland. (1st ed., 1960)

Jorgenson, Dale W. 1963. Capital Theory and Investment Behavior. *American Economic Review* 53, no. 2 (May): 247–59.

———. 1965. Anticipations and Investment Behavior. In *The Brookings Quarterly Econometric Model of the United States,* ed. James S. Duesenberry, Gary Fromm, Lawrence R. Klein, and Edwin Kuh, 35–92. Chicago: Rand McNally.

———. 1966. The Embodiment Hypothesis. *Journal of Political Economy* 74, no. 1 (February): 1–17.

———. 1967. The Theory of Investment Behavior. In *The Determinants of Investment Behavior,* ed. Robert Ferber, 129–56. New York: Columbia University press.

———. 1968. Industry Changes in Non-labor Costs: Comment. In *The Industrial Composition of Income and Product,* ed. John W. Kendrick, 176–84. New York: Columbia University Press.

———. 1973a. The Economic Theory of Replacement and Depreciation. In *Econometrics and Economic Theory,* ed. Willy Sellekaerts, 189–221. New York: Macmillan.

———. 1973b. Technology and Decision Rules in the Theory of Investment Behavior. *Quarterly Journal of Economics* 87, no. 4 (November): 523–43.

———. 1974. Investment and Production: A Review. In *Frontiers in Quantitative Economics,* ed. Michael D. Intriligator and David A. Kendrick, 2:341–66. Amsterdam: North-Holland.

———. 1980. Accounting for Capital. In *Capital, Efficiency and Growth,* ed. George von Furstenberg, 251–319. Cambridge: Ballinger.

———. 1982. Econometric and Process Analysis Models for the Analysis of Energy Policy. In *Perspectives on Resource Policy Modeling: Energy and Minerals,* ed. Rafi Amit and Mordecai Avriel, 9–62. Cambridge: Ballinger.

———. 1984a. Econometric Methods for Applied General Equilibrium Analysis. In *Applied General Equilibrium Analysis,* ed. Herbert E. Scarf and John B. Shoven, 139–203. Cambridge: Cambridge University Press.

———. 1984b. The Role of Energy in Productivity Growth, In *International Comparisons of Productivity and Causes of the Slowdown,* ed. John W. Kendrick, 270–323. Cambridge: Ballinger.

———. 1986a. Econometric Methods for Modeling Producer Behavior. In *Handbook of Econometrics,* ed Zvi Griliches and Michael D. Intriligator, 3:1841–1915. Amsterdam: North-Holland.

———. 1986b. The Great Transition: Energy and Economic Change. *Energy Journal* 7, no. 3: 1–13.

———. 1988a. Productivity and Economic Growth in Japan and the U.S. *American Economic Review* 78, no. 2 (May): 217–22.

———. 1988b. Productivity and Postwar U.S. Economic Growth. *Journal of Economic Perspectives* 2, no. 4 (Fall): 23–41.

———. 1989. Capital as a Factor of Production. In *Technology and Capital Formation,* ed. Dale W. Jorgenson and Ralph Landau, 1–36. Cambridge, Mass.: MIT Press.

Jorgenson, Dale W., and Barbara M. Fraumeni. 1981. Relative Prices and Technical Change. In *Modeling and Measuring Natural Resource Substitution,* ed. Ernst R. Berndt and Barry C. Field, 17–47. Cambridge, Mass.: MIT Press.

Jorgenson, Dale W., Frank M. Gollop, and Barbara M. Fraumeni. 1987. *Productivity and U.S. Economic Growth.* Cambridge, Mass.: Harvard University Press.

Jorgenson, Dale W., and Zvi Griliches. 1967. The Explanation of Productivity Change. *Review of Economic Studies* 34(3), no. 99 (July): 249–83.

———. 1972a. Issues of Growth Accounting: A Reply to Edward F. Denison. *Survey of Current Business* 52, no. 5, pt. 2 (May): 65–94.

———. 1972b. Issues in Growth Accounting, Final Reply. *Survey of Current Business* 52, no. 5, pt. 2 (May): 111.

Jorgenson, Dale W., Masahiro Kuroda, and Mieko Nishimizu. 1987. Japan-U.S. Industry-Level Productivity Comparisons, 1960–1979. *Journal of the Japanese and International Economies* 1, no. 1 (March): 1–30.

Jorgenson, Dale W., and Lawrence J. Lau. 1975. The Structure of Consumer Preferences. *Annals of Social and Economic Measurement* 4, no. 1 (January): 49–101.

Jorgenson, Dale W., and Mieko Nishimizu. 1978. U.S. and Japanese Economic Growth, 1952–1974: An International Comparison. *Economic Journal* 88, no. 352 (December): 707–26.

Jorgenson, Dale W., and Peter J. Wilcoxen. 1990. Environmental Regulation and U.S. Economic Growth. *Rand Journal of Economics* 21, no. 2 (Summer):314–40.

Jorgenson, Dale W., and Kun-Young Yun. 1986. The Efficiency of Capital Allocation. *Scandinavian Journal of Economics* 88, no. 1: 85–107.

———. 1990. *Tax Policy and the Cost of Capital.* New York: Oxford University Press.

Kanamori, Hisao. 1972. What Accounts for Japan's High Rate of Growth? *Review of Income and Wealth,* ser. 18, no. 2 (June): 155–72.

Katz, Arnold J. 1988. Conceptual Issues in the Measurement of Economic Depreciation, Capital Input, and the Net Capital Stock. Discussion Paper no. 30. Bureau of Economic Analysis, U.S. Department of Commerce, July.

Kendrick, John W. 1956. Productivity Trends: Capital and Labor. *Review of Economics and Statistics* 38, no. 3 (August): 248–57.

———. 1961a. *Productivity Trends in the United States.* Princeton, N.J.: Princeton University Press.

———. 1961b. Some Theoretical Aspects of Capital Measurement. *American Economic Review* 51, no. 2 (May): 102–11.

———. 1968. Industry Changes in Non-labor Costs. In *The Industrial Composition of Income and Product,* ed. John W. Kendrick. New York: Columbia University Press.

———. 1973. *Postwar Productivity Trends in the United States, 1948–1969.* New York: NBER.

———. 1976. *The Formation and Stocks of Total Capital.* New York: Columbia University Press.

———. 1979. Expanding Imputed Values in the National Income and Product Accounts. *Review of Income and Wealth,* ser. 25, no. 4 (December): 349–64.

———. 1983a. *Interindustry Differences in Productivity Growth.* Washington, D.C.: American Enterprise Institute.

———. 1983b. International Comparisons of Recent Productivity Trends. In *Energy, Productivity, and Economic Growth,* ed. Sam H. Shurr, Sidney Sonenblum, and David O. Wood, 71–120. Cambridge: Oelgeschlager, Gunn, & Hain.

———. 1984. International Comparisons of Productivity Trends. In *Measuring Productivity,* 95–140. Japan Productivity Center. New York: UNIPUB.
Kendrick, John W., and Elliot S. Grossman. 1980. *Productivity in the United States: Trends and Cycles*. Baltimore: Johns Hopkins University Press.
Kendrick, John W., and Ryuzo Sato. 1963. Factor Prices, Productivity, and Growth. *American Economic Review* 53, no. 5 (December): 974–1003.
Kennedy, Charles. 1964. Induced Bias in Innovation and the Theory of Distribution. *Economic Journal* 74, no. 298 (September): 541–47.
Kennedy, Charles, and A. P. Thirlwall. 1972. Technical Progress: A Survey. *Economic Journal* 82, no. 325 (March): 11–72.
Kim, Kwang S., and Joon K. Park. 1985. *Sources of Economic Growth in Korea: 1963–1982*. Seoul: Korea Development Institute.
Kloek, Tuun. 1966. *Indexcijfers: Enige methodologisch aspecten.* The Hague: Pasmans.
Knowles, James, 1954, *Potential Economic Growth of the United States during the Next Decade*. Joint Committee on the Economic Report, 83d Cong., 2d sess. Washington, D.C.: Government Printing Office.
———. 1960. *The Potential Economic Growth in the United States*. Study no. Paper 20. Joint Economic Committee, 86th Cong., 2d sess. Washington, D.C.: U.S. Government Printing Office.
Kohli, Ulrich R. 1981. Nonjointness and Factor Intensity in U.S. Production. *International Economic Review* 22, no. 1 (February): 3–18.
———. 1983. Non-joint Technologies. *Review of Economic Studies* 50(1), no. 160 (January): 209–19.
Koopmans, Tjalling C. 1977. Examples of Production Relations Based on Microdata. In *The Microeconomic Foundations of Macroeconomics,* ed. Geoffrey C. Harcourt, 144–71. London: Macmillan.
Kravis, Irving B. 1976. A Survey of International Comparisons of Productivity. *Economic Journal* 86, no. 341 (March): 1–44.
Kunze, Kent. 1979. Evaluation of Work-Force Composition Adjustment. In *Measurement and Interpretation of Productivity,* 334–62. National Research Council. Washington, D.C.: National Academy of Sciences.
Kuroda, Masahiro, Kanji Yoshioka, and Dale W. Jorgenson. 1984. Relative Price Changes and Biases of Technical Change in Japan. *Economic Studies Quarterly* 35, no. 2 (August): 116–38.
Kuznets, Simon. 1961. *Capital in the American Economy.* Princeton, N.J.: Princeton University Press.
———. 1971. *Economic Growth of Nations*. Cambridge, Mass.: Harvard University Press.
Lau, Lawrence J. 1969. Duality and the Structure of Utility Functions. *Journal of Economic Theory* 1, no. 4 (December): 374–96.
———. 1978. Applications of Profit Functions. In *Production Economics: A Dual Approach to Theory and Applications,* ed. Melvyn Fuss and Daniel McFadden, 1:133–216. Amsterdam: North-Holland.
Leontief, Wassily. 1936. Composite Commodities and the Problem of Index Numbers. *Econometrica* 4, no. 1 (January): 39–59.
———. 1947a. Introduction to a Theory of the Internal Structure of Functional Relationships. *Econometrica* 15, no. 4 (October): 361–73.
———. 1947b. A Note on the Interrelation of Subsets of Independent Variables of a Continuous Function with Continuous First Derivatives. *Bulletin of the American Mathematical Society* 53, no. 4 (April): 343–50.
———. 1951. *The Structure of the American Economy, 1919–1939,* 2d ed. New York: Oxford University Press. (1st ed., 1941.)

———. 1953a. Dynamic Analysis. In *Studies in the Structure of the American Economy,* ed. Wassily Leontief, 53–90. New York: Oxford University Press.

———. 1953b. Structural Change. In *Studies in the Structure of the American Economy,* ed. Wassily Leontief, 17–52. New York: Oxford University Press.

Lindbeck, Assar. 1983. The Recent Slowdown of Productivity Growth. *Economic Journal* 93, no. 369 (March): 13–34.

Link, Albert N. 1987. *Technological Change and Productivity Growth.* New York: Harwood Academic Publishers.

Liviatan, Nissan. 1966. The Concept of Capital in Professor Solow's Model. *Econometrica* 34, no. 1 (January): 220–24.

Longva, Svein, and Oystein Olsen. 1983. Producer Behaviour in the MSG Model. In *Analysis of Supply and Demand of Electricity in the Norwegian Economy,* ed. Olav Bjerkholt, Svein Longva, Oystein Olsen, and Steinar Strom, 52–83. Oslo: Central Statistical Bureau.

Lucas, Robert E. 1967. Adjustment Costs and the Theory of Supply. *Journal of Political Economy* 75, no. 4, pt. 1 (August): 321–34.

Machlup, Fritz. 1962. *The Production and Distribution of Knowledge in the United States.* Princeton, N.J.: Princeton University Press.

Maddison, Angus. 1987. Growth and Slowdown in Advanced Capitalist Economies: Techniques of Quantitative Assessment. *Journal of Economic Literature* 25, no. 2 (June): 649–98.

Malpezzi, S., L. Ozanne, and T. Thibodeau. 1987. Microeconomic Estimates of Housing Depreciation. *Land Economics* 63, no. 4 (November): 372–85.

Mansfield, Edwin. 1984. R & D and Innovation: Some Empirical Findings. In *R & D, Patents, and Productivity,* ed. Zvi Griliches, 127–48. Chicago: University of Chicago Press.

Massell, Benton F. 1961. A Disaggregated View of Technical Change. *Journal of Political Economy* 69, no. 6 (December): 547–57.

Matthews, Robin C. O., Charles H. Feinstein, and J. C. Odling-Smee. 1982. *British Economic Growth.* Stanford, Calif.: Stanford University Press.

McFadden, Daniel. 1963. Further Results on CES Production Functions. *Review of Economic Studies* 30(2), no. 83 (June): 73–83.

McGuckin, Robert H., and George A. Pascoe, Jr. 1988. The Longitudinal Research Database (LRD): Status and Research Possibilities. Discussion Paper CES 88-2. Center for Economic Studies, U.S. Bureau of the Census, July.

Meese, Richard. 1980. Dynamic Factor Demand Schedules for Labor and Capital under Rational Expectations. *Journal of Econometrics* 14, no. 1 (September): 141–58.

Meyer, John, and Edwin Kuh. 1957. *The Investment Decision.* Cambridge, Mass.: Harvard University Press.

Mills, Frederick C. 1952. *Productivity and Economic Progress.* Occasional Paper no. 38. New York: NBER.

Mohr, Michael F. 1986. The Theory and Measurement of the Rental Price of Capital in Industry-Specific Productivity Analysis. In *Measurement Issues and Behavior of Productivity Variables,* ed. Ali Dogramaci, 99–159. Boston: Kluwer-Nijhoff.

———. 1988a. Capital Depreciation and Related Issues: Definitions, Theory, and Measurement. Discussion Paper no. 28. Bureau of Economic Analysis, U.S. Department of Commerce, June.

———. 1988b. Capital Inputs and Capital Aggregation in Production. Discussion Paper no. 31. Bureau of Economic Analysis, U.S. Department of Commerce, August.

———. 1988c. The Rental Price of Capital: Two Views. Discussion Paper no. 34. Bureau of Economic Analysis, U.S. Department of Commerce, September.

Moorsteen, Richard H. 1961. On Measuring Productive Potential and Relative Efficiency. *Quarterly Journal of Economics* 75, no. 3 (August): 451–67.

Morrison, Catherine J., and Ernst R. Berndt. 1981. Short-run Labor Productivity in a Dynamic Model. *Journal of Econometrics* 16, no. 3 (August): 339–66.

Muellbauer, John. 1975. The Cost of Living and Taste and Quality Change. *Journal of Economic Theory* 10, no. 3 (June): 269–83.

Musgrave, John C. 1986. Fixed Reproducible Tangible Wealth in the United States. *Survey of Current Business* 66, no. 1 (January): 51–75.

Nadiri, Mohammed I. 1970. Some Approaches to the Theory and Measurement of Total Factor Productivity: A Survey. *Journal of Economic Literature* 8, no. 4 (December): 1137–78.

———. 1972. International Studies of Factor Inputs and Total Factor Productivity: A Brief Survey. *Review of Income and Wealth,* ser. 18, no. 2 (June): 129–54.

Nakamura, Shinichiro. 1984. *An Inter-industry Translog Model of Prices and Technical Change for the West German Economy.* Berlin: Springer-Verlag.

National Research Council. 1979. *Measurement and Interpretation of Productivity.* Washington, D.C.: National Academy of Sciences (Rees Report).

Nelson, Richard R. 1981. Research on Productivity Growth and Productivity Differences: Dead Ends and New Departures. *Journal of Economic Literature* 19, no. 3 (September): 1029–64.

Nerlove, Marc L. 1967. Recent Empirical Studies of the CES and Related Production Functions. In *The Theory and Empirical Analysis of Production,* ed. Murray Brown, 55–122. New York: Columbia University Press.

Nishimizu, Mieko, and Charles R. Hulten. 1978. The Sources of Japanese Economic Growth: 1955–1971. *Review of Economics and Statistics* 60, no. 3 (August): 351–61.

Nishimizu, Mieko, and Sherman Robinson. 1986. Productivity Growth in Manufacturing. In *Industrialization and Growth,* ed. Hollis B. Chenery, Sherman Robinson, and Moshe Syrquin, 283–308. New York: Oxford University Press.

Norsworthy, J. Randolph. 1984a. Capital Input Measurement: Options and Inaccuracies. In *Measuring Productivity,* 93–94. Japan Productivity Center. New York: UNIPUB.

———. 1984b. Growth Accounting and Productivity Measurement. *Review of Income and Wealth,* ser. 30, no. 3 (September): 309–29.

Norsworthy, J. Randolph, and Michael Harper. 1981. The Role of Capital Formation in the Recent Slowdown in Productivity Growth. In *Aggregate and Industry-Level Productivity Analyses,* ed. Ali Dogramaci and Nabil R. Adam, 122–48. Boston: Kluwer-Nijhoff.

Norsworthy, J. Randolph, Michael Harper, and Kent Kunze. 1979. The Slowdown in Productivity Growth: Analysis of Some Contributing Factors. *Brookings Papers on Econonmic Activity,* no. 2 (Fall): 387–421.

Office of Industrial Economics. 1975. *Business Building Statistics.* Washington, D.C.: Department of the Treasury.

Ohkawa, Kazushi, and Henry Rosovsky. 1973. *Japanese Economic Growth.* Stanford, Calif.: Stanford University Press.

Pindyck, Robert S., and Julio J. Rotemberg. 1983a. Dynamic Factor Demands and the Effects of Energy Price Shocks. *American Economic Review* 73, no. 5 (December): 1066–79.

———. 1983b. Dynamic Factor Demands under Rational Expectations. *Scandinavian Journal of Economics* 85, no. 2: 223–39.

Richter, Marcel K. 1966. Invariance Axioms and Economic Indexes. *Econometrica* 34, no. 4 (October): 239–55.

Robinson, Sherman. 1989. Multisectoral Models. In *Handbook of Development Economics,* ed. Hollis B. Chenery and T. N. Srinivasan, 2:885–947. Amsterdam: North-Holland.

Romer, Paul M. 1987. Crazy Explanations for the Productivity Slowdown. In *NBER Macroeconomics Annual 1987,* ed. Stanley Fischer, 163–201. Cambridge, Mass.: MIT Press.

Rosen, Sherwin. 1974. Hedonic Prices and Implicit Markets: Product Differentiation in Pure Competition. *Journal of Political Economy* 82, no. 1 (January–February): 34–55.

Ruggles, Nancy, and Richard Ruggles. 1970. *The Design of Economic Accounts.* New York: Columbia University Press.

———. 1973. A Proposal for a System of Economic and Social Accounts. In *The Measurement of Social and Economic Performance,* ed. Milton Moss. New York: Columbia University Press.

———. 1982. Integrated Economic Accounts for the United States, 1947–1980. *Survey of Current Business* 62, no. 5 (May): 1–53.

Samuelson, Paul A. 1951. Abstract of a Theorem Concerning Substitutability in Open Leontief Models. In *Activity Analysis of Production and Allocation,* ed. Tjalling C. Koopmans, 142–46. New York: Wiley.

———. 1953. Prices of Factors and Goods in General Equilibrium. *Review of Economic Studies* 21(1), no. 54:1–20.

———. 1962. Parable and Realism in Capital Theory: The Surrogate Production Function. *Review of Economic Studies* 29(3), no. 86 (June): 193–206.

———. 1965. A Theory of Induced Innovation along Kennedy-Weizsacker Lines. *Review of Economics and Statistics* 47, no. 4 (November): 343–56.

———. 1979. Paul Douglas's Measurement of Production Functions and Marginal Productivities. *Journal of Political Economy* 87, no. 5, pt. 1 (October):923–39.

Samuelson, Paul A., and Subramanian Swamy. 1974. Invariant Economic Index Numbers and Canonical Duality: Survey and Synthesis. *American Economic Review* 64, no. 4 (September): 566–93.

Sargent, Thomas J. 1978. Estimation of Dynamic Labor Demand Schedules under Rational Expectations. *Journal of Political Economy* 86, no. 6 (December): 1009–45.

Sato, Kazuo. 1975. *Production Functions and Aggregation.* Amsterdam: North-Holland.

———. 1976. The Meaning and Measurement of the Real Value Added Index. *Review of Economic Statistics* 58, no. 4 (November): 434–42.

Sato, Ryuzo, and Martin Beckmann. 1968. Neutral Inventions and Production Functions. *Review of Economic Studies* 35(1), no. 101 (January): 57–66.

Schmookler, Jacob. 1952. The Changing Efficiency of the American Economy, 1869–1938. *Review of Economics and Statistics* 39, no. 3 (August): 214–31.

Schultz, Theodore W. 1961. Investment in Human Capital. *American Economic Review* 41, no. 1 (March): 1–17.

Shephard, Ronald W. 1953. *Cost and Production Functions.* Princeton, N.J.: Princeton University Press.

———. 1970. *Theory of Cost and Production Functions.* Princeton, N.J.: Princeton University Press.

Shoven, John B., and John Whalley. 1984. Applied General-Equilibrium Models of Taxation and Trade. *Journal of Economic Literature* 22, no. 3 (September): 1007–51.

Sims, Christopher. 1969. Theoretical Basis for a Double-Deflated Index of Real Value Added. *Review of Economics and Statistics* 51, no. 4 (November): 470–71.

———. 1977. Remarks on Real Value Added. *Annals of Social and Economic Measurement* 6, no. 1 (Winter): 127–32.

Solow, Robert M. 1956. A Contribution to the Theory of Economic Growth. *Quarterly Journal of Economics* 70, no. 1 (February): 65–94.

———. 1957. Technical Change and the Aggregate Production Function. *Review of Economics and Statistics* 39, no. 3 (August): 312–20.

———. 1960. Investment and Technical Progress. In *Mathematical Methods in the Social Sciences, 1959,* ed. Kenneth J. Arrow, Samuel Karlin, and Patrick Suppes, 89–104. Stanford, Calif.: Stanford University Press.

———. 1962. Technical Progress, Capital Formation, and Economic Growth. *American Economic Review* 52, no. 2 (May): 76–86.

———. 1963a. *Capital Theory and the Rate of Return.* Amsterdam: North-Holland.

———. 1963b. Heterogeneous Capital and Smooth Production Functions: An Experimental Study. *Econometrica* 31, no. 4 (October): 623–45.

———. 1964. Capital, Labor, and Income in Manufacturing. In *The Behavior of Income Shares,* 101–28. Studies in Income and Wealth, vol. 0. Princeton, N.J.: Princeton University Press.

———. 1967. Some Recent Developments in the Theory of Production. In *The Theory and Empirical Analysis of Production,* ed. Murray Brown, 25–50. New York: Columbia University Press.

———. 1970. *Growth Theory.* Oxford: Oxford University Press.

———. 1988. Growth Theory and After. *Amercian Economic Review* 78, no. 3 (June): 307–17.

Sono, Masazo. 1961. The Effect of Price Changes on the Demand and Supply of Separable Goods. *International Economic Review* 2, no. 3 (September): 239–71.

Star, Spencer. 1974. Accounting for the Growth of Output. *American Economic Review* 64, no. 1 (March): 123–35.

Statistical Office of the United Nations. 1968. *A System of National Accounts,* Studies in Methods, ser. F, no. 2, rev. 3. New York: Department of Economic and Social Affairs, United Nations.

Stigler, George J. 1947. *Trends in Output and Employment.* New York: NBER.

Stone, Richard. 1956. *Quantity and Price Indexes in National Accounts.* Paris: Organization for European Economic Cooperation.

Summers, Lawrence H. 1981. Taxation and Corporate Investment: A q-Theory Approach. *Brookings Papers on Economic Activity,* no. 1: 67–127.

Taubman, Paul, and Robert Rasche. 1969. Economic and Tax Depreciation of Office Buildings. *National Tax Journal* 22, no. 3 (September): 334–46.

Taylor, Lance. 1975. Theoretical Foundations and Technical Implications. In *Economy-Wide Models and Development Planning,* ed. Charles K. Blitzer, Peter B. Clark, and Lance Taylor, 33–109. Oxford, Oxford University Press.

Terborgh, George. 1954. *Realistic Depreciation Policy.* Washington, D.C.: Machinery and Allied Products Institute.

Theil, Henri. 1965. The Information Approach to Demand Analysis. *Econometrica* 33, no. 1 (January): 67–87.

Thirtle, Colin G., and Vernon W. Ruttan. 1987. *The Role of Demand and Supply in the Generation and Diffusion of Technical Change.* New York: Harwood Academic Publishers.

Thor, Carl G., George E. Sadler, and Elliot S. Grossman. 1984. Comparison of Total Factor Productivity in Japan and the United States. In *Measuring Productivity,* 57–72. Japan Productivity Center. New York, UNIPUB.

Tinbergen, Jan. 1942. Zur Theorie der Langfristigen Wirtschaftsentwicklung. *Weltwirtschaftliches Archiv* 55, no. 1: 511–49.

———. 1959. *Selected Papers.* Amsterdam: North-Holland.

Tobin, James. 1969. A General Equilibrium Approach to Monetary Theory. *Journal of Money, Credit, and Banking* 1, no. 1 (February): 15–29.

Törnqvist, Leo. 1936. The Bank of Finland's Consumption Price Index. *Bank of Finland Monthly Bulletin,* no. 10:1–8.

Triplett, jack E. 1975. The Measurement of Inflation: A Survey of Research on the Accuracy of Price Indexes. In *Analysis of Inflation,* ed. Paul H. Earl, 19–82. Lexington, Mass.: Heath.

———. 1983a. Concepts of Quality in Input and Output Price Measures: A Resolution of the User-Value Resource-Cost Debate. In *The U.S. National Income and Product Accounts: Selected Topics,* ed. Murray F. Foss, 296–311. Chicago: University of Chicago Press.

———. 1983b. Introduction: An Essay on Labor Cost. In *The Measurement of Labor Cost,* ed. Jack E. Triplett, 1–60. Chicago: University of Chicago Press.

———. 1986. The Economic Interpretation of Hedonic Methods. *Survey of Current Business* 66, no. 1 (January): 36–40.

———. 1987. Hedonic Functions and Hedonic Indexes. In *The New Palgrave: A Dictionary of Economics,* ed. John Eatwell, Murray Milgate, and Peter Newman, 2:630–34. New York: Stockton.

———. 1989. Price and Technological Change in a Capital Good: Survey of Research on Computers. In *Technology and Capital Formation,* ed. Dale W. Jorgenson and Ralph Landau, 127–213. Cambridge, Mass.: MIT Press.

——— 1990. Two Views on Computer Prices. Discussion Paper no. 45. Bureau of Economic Analysis, U.S. Department of Commerce, February.

Uzawa, Hirofumi. 1962. Production Functions with Constant Elasticity of Substitution. *Review of Economic Studies* 29(4), no. 81 (October): 291–99.

———. 1969. Time Preference and the Penrose Effect in a Two-Class Model of Economic Growth. *Journal of Political Economy* 77, no. 4, pt. 2 (July/August): 628–52.

Valavanis-Vail, Stefan. 1955. An Econometric Model of Growth, U.S.A., 1869–1953. *American Economic Review* 45, no. 2 (May): 208–21.

von Weizsacker, C. Christian. 1962. A New Technical Progress Function. MIT, Department of Economics. Typescript.

Walderhaug, Albert J. 1973. The Composition of Value Added in the 1963 Input-Output Study. *Survey of Current Business* 53, no. 4 (April): 34–44.

Waldorf, William H., Kent Kunze, Larry S. Rosenblum, and Michael B. Tannen. 1986. New Measures of the Contribution of Education and Experience to U.S. Productivity Growth. U.S. Department of Labor, Washington, D.C.

Walras, Leon. 1954. *Elements of Pure Economics,* trans. William Jaffe, from the French Ed. Definitive, 1926. Homewood, Ill.: Irwin. (1st ed., 1877).

Walters, Alan A. 1963. Production and Cost Functions: An Econometric Survey. *Econometrica* 31, no. 1 (January–April): 1–66.

Walters, Dorothy. 1968. *Canadian Income Levels and Growth: An International Perspective.* Ottawa: Economic Council of Canada.

———. 1970. *Canadian Growth Revisited, 1950–1967.* Ottawa: Economic Council of Canada.

Watanabe, Tsunehiko. 1971. A Note on Measuring Sectoral Input Productivity. *Review of Income and Wealth,* ser. 17, no. 4 (December): 335–40.

Waugh, Frederick V. 1929. *Quality as a Determinant of Vegetable Prices.* New York: Columbia University Press.

Weitzman, Martin L. 1983. On the Meaning of Comparative Factor Productivity. In Padma *Marxism, Central Planning, and the Soviet Economy,* ed. Padma Desai, 166–70. Cambridge, Mass.: MIT Press.

Winston, Clifford. 1985. Conceptual Developments in the Economics of Transportation: An Interpretive Survey. *Journal of Economic Literature* 23, no. 1 (March): 57–94.

Wolff, Edward N. 1985a. Industrial Composition, Interindustry Effects, and the U.S. Productivity Slowdown. *Review of Economics and Statistics* 67, no. 2 (May): 268–77.

———. 1985b. The Magnitude and Causes of the Recent Productivity Slowdown in the United States: A Survey of Recent Studies. In *Productivity Growth and U.S. Competitiveness,* ed. William J. Baumol and Kenneth McLennan, 160–186. New York: Oxford University Press.

Woodland, Alan D. 1978. On Testing Weak Separability. *Journal of Econometrics* 8, no. 3 (December): 383–98.

Wykoff, Frank C. 1989. Economic Depreciation and the User Cost of Business-Leased Automobiles. In *Technology and Capital Formation,* ed. Dale W. Jorgenson and Ralph Landau, 259–92. Cambridge, Mass.: MIT Press.

Young, Allan. 1989. BEA's Measurement of Computer Output. *Survey of Current Business* 69, no. 7 (July): 108–15.

Young, Allan, and John C. Musgrave. 1980. Estimation of Capital Stock in the United States. In *The Measurement of Capital,* ed. Dan Usher, 23–58. Chicago: University of Chicago Press.

4 The Measurement of Capital

Charles R. Hulten

The measurement of capital is one of the nastiest jobs that economists have set to statisticians.

(Hicks 1981b, 204)

The theory of capital is one of the most difficult and contentious areas of economic theory. From Karl Marx to the Cambridge controversies, there has been an ongoing disagreement among economists as to what capital is and how it should be measured.[1] Economists have variously defined capital as congealed labor, as deferred consumption, as the "degree of round-a-boutness," as a stock of durable commodities, or as a flow of factor services. There is also disagreement about whether capital can be aggregated into a single measure, and, even within the relatively hospitable confines of neoclassical theory, exact aggregation is known to be problematic.

This presents the practical economist with something of a dilemma since many interesting economic problems require a measure of capital. How, for example, are we to understand the process of economic growth if we cannot agree on how to measure one of the potentially most important factors influencing that process? What can we say about such important issues as the productivity slowdown of the 1970s and why growth rates differ across countries? These issues are too important to ignore, and estimates of capital, income, and wealth, however imperfect, must somehow be developed in order to get on with the larger tasks at hand.

Charles R. Hulten is a professor of economics at the University of Maryland and research associate of the National Bureau of Economic Research.

The author would like to thank Dale Jorgenson, Frank Wykoff, Ingmar Prucha, and Robert M. Schwab for their valuable comments on earlier drafts of this chapter. Judy Xanthopoulos provided invaluable research assistance.

The Conference on Research in Income and Wealth and, more generally, the National Bureau of Economic Research have been at the forefront of the development process. Many of the 50-odd volumes of the Studies in Income and Wealth series are devoted, in whole or in part, to issues of capital measurement. These studies, by such pioneers as Kuznets, Goldsmith, Stigler, and Kendrick, have laid the conceptual foundation for many of the measurement procedures used today; they provide statistical series that are still in use. It is therefore fitting that the commemoration of the fiftieth anniversary of the conference should include an essay on the current state of the art of capital measurement.

I undertake this task with the recognition that the subject is too large to be easily encompassed by a single essay. I have therefore chosen to limit my focus largely to depreciable assets used in the business sector, although the discussion will sometimes stray across this boundary and many of the results discussed will be applicable to other sectors and other types of capital. I will also allocate the bulk of my space to a sketch of the *theory* of capital measurement. This choice reflects, in part, the historical objective of the conference in bringing together measurement theory and practice. However, it also reflects the too often ignored need for theoretical consistency in the construction of data as, for example, when capital stocks are estimated using one assumption about depreciation and estimates of capital income are based on another assumption.

The chapter is organized into two major parts. The first outlines the theory of capital measurement and is divided into six sections. The first three sections cover measurement and valuation of a single homogeneous type of capital, while the following section extends the analysis to the case of many capital goods. The final two sections deal with the issues of quality change and capacity utilization. The second part of the paper examines some practical issues in the measurement of capital. The scope and nature of existing estimates and procedures are reviewed, and then critiqued in light of the theory of the preceding sections.

4.1 Applied Capital Theory

Two aspects of capital (including human capital) differentiate it from a primary input like labor: capital is a produced means of production, and capital is durable.[2] The first aspect is the primary source of the Cambridge controversy in pure theory, but the latter causes much of the actual difficulty in measuring capital. Durability means that a capital good is productive for two or more time periods, and this, in turn, implies that a distinction must be made between the value of using or renting capital in any year and the value of owning the capital asset.

This distinction would not necessarily lead to a measurement problem if the capital services used in any given year were paid for in that year, that is, if all capital were rented. In this case, transactions in the rental market would fix the price and quantity of capital in each time period, much as data on the price and quantity of labor services are derived from labor-market transactions. But, unfortunately, much capital is utilized by its owner and the transfer of capital services between owner and user results in an implicit rent typically not observed by the statistician. Market data are thus inadequate for the task of directly estimating the price and quantity of capital services, and this has led to the development of indirect procedures for inferring the quantity of capital, like the perpetual inventory method, or to the acceptance of flawed measures, like book value. In this section, I begin by reviewing the strengths and weaknesses of these indirect methods, starting with the easiest case of a single (relatively) homogeneous type of capital and proceeding to more difficult cases later on.

4.1.1 The Single Homogeneous Good Case

We start by assuming that the statistician can observe the quantity of new capital added to the stock in each year, I_t, but not the amount of capital stock itself, K_t (we will ignore, for the moment, the distinction between stocks and flows). The problem is to infer the latter from the former, recognizing that part or all of past additions to the stock may have been retired from service and that the services yielded by older capital may be less productive. The problem, in essence, is to develop a reasonable procedure for adding up the individual I's into an estimate of K.

The perpetual inventory method is one attempt at solving this problem. In the perpetual inventory method, investment from all surviving vintages is weighted by a number, $\phi_{t-\nu}$, between zero and one to allow for the possibility that older capital is less productive than its newer counterparts, and the weighted investment series is then added up to form a total capital measure. The result may be expressed by the following equation:

$$(1) \qquad K_t = \phi_0 I_t + \phi_1 I_{t-1} + \ldots + \phi_T I_{t-T},$$

where $\phi_0 = 1$, and where $\nu = t - T$ is the date of the oldest surviving vintage.[3] Since one unit of vintage ν capital is treated as the equivalent of only $\phi_{t-\nu}$ units of new capital, the stock K_t has the natural interpretation as the number of units of new investment needed to equal the productive capacity of past investment ($I_t, I_{t-1}, I_{t-2}, \ldots, I_{t-T}$). Or, in other words, equation (1) defines the capital stock in *efficiency* units.[4]

It is evident from equation (1) that estimates of the efficiency weights $\phi_{t-\nu}$ are needed to complete the measurement of K given data on the I's. However, it is not evident how the ϕ's are determined or how they can be estimated. One possibility is to assume that the ϕ's are inherent in the nature of capital. For example, a block of dry ice (or a bar of soap) may shrink at a rate proportional to surface area, so that older blocks are proportionately smaller than new blocks. In this case, old and new capital can be thought of as differing by a constant ϕ and the aggregate K can be seen as a physically homogeneous entity. Much the same can be said of light bulbs, since older vintages shine as brightly as new ones (until they fail), and a homogeneous K can be formed by assigning ϕ a value of one for all surviving vintages and adding up past investment.

The efficiency sequence can be determined, in both examples, from the nature of the good itself—dry ice is homogeneous, and thus old and new units are prefect substitutes up to some constant ϕ. If the same were true of all capital, then the measurement problem would be reduced to determining the relative technological "size" of new and used capital. Unfortunately, most capital does not accommodate this kind of measurement because older machines are typically neither physically smaller nor dimmer than their newer counterparts. Nevertheless, such machines may be less efficient because of increased downtime, higher maintenance requirements, or reduced speed or accuracy, or they may embody less advanced technology than new machines.

The possiblity that older vintages of capital may be less productive suggests that the ϕ sequence might more usefully be defined in terms of the production process itself. The ϕ's could be thought of as relative marginal products, and the resulting K may be interpreted as the ability of the surviving vintages $(I_t, \ldots, I_{t-T})$ to produce output. This approach does not rule out the "dry ice" case of inherent productivity differences, but does allow for the possibility that relative efficiency is a matter of economic choice and that different technologies may imply different ϕ's for the same type of capital. Or, in other words, the capital aggregation depends on the nature of the technology and on market behavior.

This link between aggregate capital and the production function was developed by Leontief (1947a, 1947b), Solow (1960), and Fisher (1965). The basic issue involves the conditions under which different vintages of capital and technology can be collapsed into an aggregate production function defined with respect to an aggregate measure of capital. It is assumed that each vintage of capital can be combined with labor via its own production function to produce output

$$(2) \qquad Q_{t,v} = f^{v}(L_{t,v}, I_v) \quad v = t, t-1, t-2, \ldots, t-\mathrm{T},$$

where $Q_{t,v}$ is the output produced by capital of vintage v and $L_{t,v}$ is the homogeneous labor applied to that capital. The production functions are allowed to differ in order to incorporate the possibility of technical change, that is, old machines are installed with the technology prevailing in year v. Output from all vintages is assumed to be homogeneous and aggregate output is thus the sum of the $Q_{t,v}$, that is,

$$Q_t = \sum_{\nu} Q_{t,\nu} = \sum_{\nu} f^{\nu}(L_{t,\nu}, I_{\nu}). \tag{3}$$

The aggregation problem is to write (4) as

$$Q_t^* = F[L_t, K(I_t, \ldots, I_{t-T})], \tag{4}$$

where $L_t = \sum_{\nu} L_{t,\nu}$, Q_t^* is the maximum output that can be produced assuming labor is optimally allocated among vintages, and $K(\cdot)$ is independent of L. Necessary and sufficient conditions for this capital aggregation are given by the Leontief theorem, which states that the marginal rate of substitution between any pair of inputs within the aggregate must be independent of the inputs outside the capital aggregate:

$$\frac{\partial}{\partial L_t}\left[\frac{\partial Q^*/\partial I_{\nu}}{\partial Q^*/\partial I_{\xi}}\right] = 0 \quad \text{for all } \nu, \xi = t, \ldots, t-T, \tag{5}$$

or

$$\frac{\partial}{\partial L_t}\left[\frac{\partial f^{\nu}/\partial I_{\nu}}{\partial f^{\xi}/\partial I_{\xi}}\right] = 0 \quad \text{when } f_L^{\nu} = f_L^{\xi}; \quad \nu, \xi = t, \ldots, t-T. \tag{6}$$

Fisher (1965) shows that, under constant returns to scale, this condition requires that differences between vintages must be expressible as

$$f^{\nu}(L_{t,\nu}, I_{\nu}) = f(L_{t,\nu}, b_{t-\nu} I_{\nu}). \tag{7}$$

That is, the technology must be such that the difference between the productivity of old and new capital is a fixed constant depending only on vintage.[5] Or, as Hall (1971) puts it: "In vintage production functions with constant returns, the basic theorem of capital aggregation establishes that a capital aggregate exists if and only if the marginal product of capital of age τ at time t has the fixed ratio . . . to the marginal product of new capital at time t" (242). In our notation, this amounts to

$$\frac{\partial Q^*/\partial I_{\nu}}{\partial Q^*/\partial I_t} = \phi_{t-\nu}, \quad \nu = t, t-1, \ldots. \tag{8}$$

Thus, formal aggregation theory leads us back to the perpetual inventory method of capital aggregation. Old capital enters the production process as if it were equivalent to a smaller amount of new capital—as in the case of dry ice.

There is little reason to believe that real-world technologies exhibit the separability required by the Leontief conditions. Moreover, even if aggregation over vintages were possible, there is no guarantee that the aggregated production function (4) would be a valid representation of the technology of an entire industry or industrial sector. Further conditions are required for aggregation over establishments within an industry, for example, the Gorman conditions—and these are extremely restrictive.[6]

Capital aggregation must therefore be regarded as approximate, or as applying in exact form only under exceptional circumstances. Applied economists can either accept this unfortunate situation or try to work directly with a disaggregated form of their model. But as Fisher (1965) notes, "Estimation of the parameters of the production function using the various types of capital [i.e., vintages] is at best a nonlinear estimation problem of considerable magnitude, and may, in fact, be insoluble since it requires the *explicit* solution of the labor allocation problem in terms of parameters to be estimated and the quantities of the various capital goods" (263; emphasis added).

4.1.2 Asset Efficiency

The measurement of capital stocks using the perpetual inventory method requires an estimate of the efficiency sequence ($\phi_0, \phi_1, \ldots, \phi_T$). Unfortunately, this sequence is rarely observed directly, and indirect methods of inferring relative asset efficiency are necessary. One possibility is to exploit the assumed relationship between ϕ and relative marginal products developed in (8). This possibility is pursued in the following section. Another approach is to estimate the relative efficiency indirectly by assuming that the ϕ's follow some pattern that depends on an observable useful life T.

Several efficiency patterns have been discussed in the literature on estimating ϕ. Of these patterns, the one-hoss shay pattern commands the greatest intuitive appeal. Casual experience with commonly used assets suggests that most assets have pretty much the same level of efficiency regardless of their age—a one-year-old chair does the same job as a 20-year-old chair, and so on.[7] Thus, it is frequently assumed that ϕ takes the following form:

$$(9)\quad \phi_0 = \phi_1 = \ldots = \phi_{T-1} = 1, \quad \phi_{T+\tau} = 0 \quad \tau = 0, 1, 2, \ldots .$$

In the one-hoss shay form, assets retain full efficiency until they completely fall apart (hence the term "one-hoss shay," although "light bulb" efficiency decay would be equally apt). In this form, the efficiency sequence is completely characterized by the useful life T, and the measurement problem reduces to the problem of estimating T.

The straight-line efficiency pattern is the second commonly used form. Under straight line, the efficiency function takes the form

$$(10)\quad \begin{aligned} &\phi_0 = 1, \phi_1 = 1 - \frac{1}{T}, \phi_2 = 1 - \frac{2}{T} \ldots, \\ &\phi_{T-1} = 1 - \frac{T-1}{T}, \quad \phi_{T+\tau} = 0 \qquad \tau = 0, 1, 2, \ldots . \end{aligned}$$

In the straight-line form, efficiency decays in equal increments every year, that is,

(11) $$\phi_{\tau-1} - \phi_{\tau} = \frac{1}{T} \quad \tau = 1, \ldots, T-1.$$

As with the one-hoss shay form, T completely determines the efficiency pattern. The popularity of the straight-line pattern reflects the widely used convention, borrowed from *depreciation* accounting, that assets should be amortized in equal increments over a useful life.

Geometric decay is the third widely used pattern. In this form, productive capacity decays at a constant rate δ, that is,

(12) $$(\phi_{\tau-1} - \phi_{\tau})/\phi_{\tau-1} = \delta,$$

implying

(13) $$\phi_0 = 1, \phi_1 = (1-\delta), \phi_2 = (1-\delta)^2, \ldots, \phi_{\tau} = (1-\delta)^{\tau}, \ldots.$$

The geometric form is widely used in theoretical expositions of capital theory because of its simplicity. But, while it enjoys empirical support from studies of used capital prices, it is nevertheless regarded by some (e.g., Harper 1982) as empirically implausible because of the rapid loss of efficiency in the early years of asset life (e.g., 34% of an asset's productivity is lost over four years with a 10% rate of depreciation). Moreover, assets are (implausibly) never retired, so that the efficiency sequence is no longer a function of the useful life T. However, δ is frequently derived from published estimates of T using the double declining balance formula, $\delta = 2/T$, obtained from tax accounting, although other declining balance formulae are also used.[8]

We have thus far taken the date of retirement T to be the same for all assets in a given cohort (all assets put in place in a given year).[9] However, there is no reason for this to be true, and the theory is readily extended to allow for different retirement dates. A given cohort can be broken into components, or subcohorts, according to date of retirement and a separate T assigned to each. Each subcohort can then be characterized by its own efficiency sequence $\phi^{(i)}$, which depends among other things on the subcohort's useful life T_i. The contribution to total capital at time t made by a cohort of vintage ν is the sum over the subcohorts of that vintage

(14) $$\sum_i \phi^{(i)}_{t-\nu} I^{(i)}_{\nu}.$$

The stock of capital at time t is then equal to

(15) $$K_t = \sum_i \phi^{(i)}_0 I^{(i)}_t + \ldots + \sum_i \phi^{(i)}_{t-\nu} I^{(i)}_{\nu} + \ldots.$$

Letting $\omega^{(i)}_{\nu} = I^{(i)}_{\nu}/I_{\nu}$ be the weight of the ith subcohort in vintage ν investment, this can be written as

(16) $$K_t = \left(\sum_i \phi^{(i)}_0 \omega^{(i)}_t\right) I_t + \ldots + \left(\sum_i \phi^{(i)}_{t-\nu} \omega^{(i)}_{\nu}\right) I_{\nu} + \ldots.$$

When the subcohort weights ω are stationary over time, that is, independent of ν, (16) reduces to (1). In this case, the efficiency weight ϕ in (1) can be interpreted as the average efficiency of the investment in the cohort, and it thus captures both in-place loss of efficiency and efficiency loss due to retirement.

The average efficiency function of a cohort can be quite different from the individual efficiency functions $\phi^{(i)}$. Every $\phi^{(i)}$ can have the one-hoss shay form, while $\omega^{(i)}$ can be such that the average efficiency decline is geometric. This point has important consequences for the measurement of ϕ: as noted, the intuition that suggests that assets decay according to the one-hoss shay pattern is based on the observation of the individual $\phi^{(i)}$. But equation (16) implies that the extension of this intuition to an entire cohort of assets may involve a fallacy of composition in which each asset in the cohort follows one pattern but the cohort as a whole follows a different pattern.

Two final points should be noted before leaving the subject of efficiency functions. First, the early literature on capital measurement distinguished between net and gross capital stock. The net stock is defined as our (1) or (16) (we will largely ignore the distinction throughout the rest of this part of the paper). The gross stock is defined by

$$(17) \qquad K_t^G = I_t + I_{t-1} + \ldots + I_{t-T},$$

in the special case when all assets are assumed to be retired at the same point in time, or by the more general form

$$(18) \qquad K_t^G = \Omega_0 I_t + \Omega_1 I_{t-1} + \ldots + \Omega_T I_{t-T},$$

when retirements are distributed over time and Ω_τ is the (stationary) proportion of assets surviving to time τ.

Estimates of gross capital stock are commonly published along with estimates of the net stock (e.g., U.S. Department of Commerce 1987), and gross stocks are used in some analyses of productivity change.[10] However, it is clear from the separability condition of (18) that $\phi_{t-\nu}$ is defined with respect to relative marginal products, so it is the "net" measure of capital that is consistent with the production function $Q_t = F(L,K)$. That is,the net stock K_t, along with labor L_t, produces gross output Q_t, and the gross stock of capital is consistent with the production function only when the efficiency sequence is one-hoss shay, (9). But, in this case, net and gross stocks are the same, and the argument in favor of the gross capital stock is really an argument that the net stock *must* be one-hoss shay regardless of empirical evidence about the ϕ's.

Finally, it is important to emphasize a point made by Feldstein and Rothschild (1974): there are limitations to the use of any perpetual inventory method based on the procedures for estimating ϕ discussed in this section. For example, we have assumed that firms are not free to retire old capital as economic conditions dictate, maintenance and repair activities do not influence the ϕ's, and a higher rate of utilization does not cause asset efficiency to decline more rapidly. Each assumption is rather dubious, and a more complete model would recognize the endogeneity of $(\phi_0, \phi_1, \phi_2, \ldots)$ via these effects (albeit at the cost of vastly complicating the analysis).

4.1.3 Asset Valuation and Depreciation

The preceding sections have dealt with the problem of measuring the quantity of capital. We now turn to the corresponding problem of measuring the wealth associated with the physical quantity of capital K_t. While the value of an asset is clearly related to that asset's productivity, the exact nature of the relationship is far from obvious and is the source of much confusion in the literature on capital measurement.

In competitive equilibrium, the cost of producing an asset is equal to the value of owning the asset, which, in turn, is equal to the present value of the expected rents (user costs) generated over the life of the asset. For a newly produced asset, this relationship takes the form

$$P^I_{t,0} = \sum_{\tau=0}^{\infty} \frac{P^K_{t+\tau,\tau}}{(1+r)^{\tau+1}}, \tag{19}$$

where $P^I_{t,0}$ is the equilibrium purchase price of a new asset at time t, the term $P^K_{t+\tau,\tau}$ is the expected annual gross income generated by the asset when it is τ years old (in year $t + \tau$), and r is the nominal rate of interest at which the income flows are discounted (this is assumed constant for simplicity).[11]

The situation for vintage assets is analogous, except that the supply of vintage assets is inelastic over the range of prices in which vintage assets remain in service.[12] Thus, the equilibrium purchase price is

$$P^I_{t,s} = \sum_{\tau=0}^{\infty} \frac{P^K_{t+\tau,s+\tau}}{(1+r)^{\tau+1}}, \quad s = 1, 2, 3, \ldots, \tag{20}$$

where $s = t - v$ denotes asset age. This expression is a generalization of (19) and indicates that the value of an asset of any vintage is equal to the remaining value of the gross income, or rent, associated with the asset.

While equation (20) says nothing about asset efficiency, there is an indirect relationship arising from cost minimization. When rental markets exist for capital of all vintages, cost minimization implies that capital of each vintage will be rented up to the point that the value of its marginal product is equal to the rental price. Thus, the marginal rate of substitution between vintage v capital and new capital is equal to the corresponding ratio of the rental prices:

$$\frac{P^K_{t,s}}{P^K_{t,0}} = \frac{\partial Q/\partial I_v}{\partial Q/\partial I_t} = \phi_s, \quad s = 1, 2, \ldots, \tag{21}$$

where the second equality follows from (8). Equation (21) states that the relative efficiency parameter, ϕ_s, can be interpreted as a ratio of relative rental values as well as the ratio of relative productive efficiencies. Thus, there is the following symmetry between prices and quantities: $I_{v,s} = \phi_s I_{v,0}$ and $P^K_{t,s} = \phi_s P^K_{t,0}$.

This symmetry implies that the rental price of vintage v capital is ϕ_s times the rental price of new capital. The asset price, $P^I_{t,s}$, in (21) can therefore be written in terms of the relative efficiency sequence and the rental price of new assets:

(22) $$P^I_{t,s} = \sum_{\tau=0}^{\infty} \frac{\phi_{s+\tau} P^K_{t+\tau,0}}{(1+r)^{\tau+1}} \qquad s = 1, 2, \ldots .$$

This expression links asset valuation to asset efficiency. It has been derived in the case in which rental markets exist, but is also valid for the case in which capital is utilized by its owner. Indeed, (22) can be "solved" to obtain an expression of the implicit rent in terms of the other variables of (22).

(23) $$P^K_{t,s} = [r - \rho_{t,s} + (1+\rho_{t,s})\delta_{t,s}]P^I_{t,s}, \quad s = 0, 1, 2, \ldots ,$$

where

(24) $$\rho_{t,s} = \frac{P^I_{t+1,s+1}}{P^I_{t,s+1}} - 1,$$

is the expected "inflation" in the vintage asset price occurring between years t and $t + 1$, and

(25) $$\delta_{t,s} = -\left[\frac{P^I_{t,s+1}}{P^I_{t,s}} - 1\right],$$

is the rate of decline in the asset price with age s (or, more accurately, the decline in price as vintage v capital becomes like vintage $v - 1$ capital). Equation (23) thus has a straightforward interpretation: when assets are owner utilized, the equilibrium value of the implicit rental must cover the real opportunity cost of an investment of value $P^I_{t,s}$ as well as the loss in asset value as the asset ages. In practice, elaborations of this formula, based on Jorgenson (1963) and Hall and Jorgenson (1967), are used to impute a value of the rental price and thus the value of the marginal product of capital.

The term δ deserves attention in its own right, since it can be shown to be the rate of economic depreciation. Hicks (1946) defines income as the maximum amount that can be spent during a period while maintaining capital values intact; economic depreciation is then defined as the sum of money, in constant dollars, that needs to be set aside in order to maintain that capital value in real terms. In our notation, the Hicksian definition of depreciation is equivalent to $P^I_{t,s} - P^I_{t,s+1}$. This in turn implies that depreciation is equal to $\delta_{t,s}P^I_{t,s}$ by (25), which leads to the conclusion that the variable δ is the Hicksian rate of economic depreciation. When $\rho \neq 0$, a revaluation adjustment is necessary but essentially the same interpretation carries over.

Following Jorgenson (1973), equation (25) can also be used to link economic depreciation to changes in asset efficiency. Rearranging terms in (25) yields

$$\text{(26)} \qquad \delta_{t,s} P^{I}_{t,s} = P^{I}_{t,s} - P^{I}_{t,s+1} = \sum_{\tau=0}^{\infty} \frac{(\phi_{s+\tau} - \phi_{s+\tau+1})\, P^{K}_{t+\tau,0}}{(1+r)^{\tau+1}},$$

for an asset of age s. This expression states that Hicksian economic depreciation is the present value of the rental income loss due to the efficiency decay $\phi_{s+\tau} - \phi_{s+\tau+1}$ occurring in each year in the future ($\tau = 0, 1, 2, \ldots$). In other words, depreciation occurs because the efficiency pattern is shifted one year for every year the asset ages. It is the shift in the *entire* efficiency pattern that leads to a decline in asset value.

Equation (26) shows that economic depreciation (a price effect) and efficiency decay (a quantity effect) are not independent concepts. One cannot select an efficiency pattern independently of the depreciation pattern and maintain the assumption of competitive equilibrium at the same time. And, one cannot arbitrarily select a depreciation pattern independently from the observed path of vintage asset prices P^{I}_{s} (suggesting a strategy for measuring depreciation and efficiency). Thus, for example, the practice of using a straight-line efficiency pattern in the perpetual inventory equation in general commits the user to non-straight-line pattern of economic depreciation.[13]

This framework is useful for revealing what economic depreciation is, but it is also useful for revealing what it is *not*. Depreciation is not the replacement cost of the efficiency units used up in any year, that is, $\Sigma(\phi_{s} - \phi_{s+1})P^{I}_{t,0}$, because $P^{I}_{t,s}$ is not generally equal to $\phi_{s} P^{I}_{t,0}$ unless decay is geometric. This can be seen intuitively by considering a one-hoss shay asset with a 10-year useful life. The efficiency lost between years 8 and 9 is zero, by definition, so the cost of replacing the loss units is also zero. However, the decline in the price of the asset is certainly not zero, since the asset is almost at the point of retirement. As a result, Hicksian depreciation occurs because the efficiency pattern has shifted, despite the retention of asset efficiency.

A parallel confusion arises over the valuation of the capital stock. Recall that K defined in (1) can be thought of as the number of efficiency units embodied in the existing stock—that is, the amount of *new* capital that must be purchased in order to yield the same productive capacity as the existing vintages of capital. It is thus natural to think of the value of the stock as the cost of purchasing these equivalent efficiency units: $P^{I}_{t,0}K_{t}$. However, this is not the case. The value of the stock is the asset value of the separate pieces of the stock, that is, the amount that would be obtained from selling each piece of capital at its market price:

$$\text{(27)} \qquad V^{K}_{t} = \sum_{v} P^{I}_{t,s} I_{v}\,.$$

This is the wealth associated with the stock K_{t}. It is not the same as $P^{I}_{t,0}K_{t}$, except when depreciation follows the geometric pattern (again, because in general $P^I_{t,s} \neq \phi_s P^I_{t,0}$). Intuitively, if the stock is one-hoss shay, the value (as measured by $P^I_{t,0}K_t$) of a stock composed entirely of one-year-old assets is the same as the value of the identical number of nine-year-old assets. However, if this type of asset lasts only 10 years, the willingness to pay for the two stocks (as measured by [27]) can be vastly different.

One final valuation issue is of interest. The historical cost of acquiring capital is typically reported on the balance sheets of firms. This measure of capital stock is referred to as the "book value" of the capital stock and is equivalent to

$$(28) \qquad V^B_t = \sum_{\nu=t-A}^{t} \phi^A_s P^I_{\nu,0} I_\nu ,$$

where A is the accounting period over which the capital costs are amortized, and the sequence ϕ^A_s is the unamortized balance of the investment made s years ago when new assets cost P^I_ν,0. This book value differs from market value for several reasons: first, the accounting life A is not necessarily the same as the useful life T;[14] second, the depreciation method ϕ^A is typically based on the straight-line form and, thus, in general differs from the true pattern of economic depreciation; finally, and most important, inflation may cause the price of new assets to rise, so that $P^I_{\nu,0} \neq P^I_{t,0}$.

This analysis suggests that the book value of capital stock is generally not equal to the true value of the stock K_t. But, neither is the corresponding perpetual inventory estimate because the true values of the ϕ sequence are so hard to measure. While the perpetual inventory method avoids the historical cost valuation problem, book value estimates may nevertheless play an important role in assessing the reasonableness of the perpetual inventory method. Furthermore, perpetual inventory estimation is often impossible because of inadequate data on past investments (this is typically the case with data for individual companies), and book values then become the principal source of information about capital stocks.[15]

4.1.4 Heterogeneous Capital

A practical theory of capital measurement must be able to handle the multitude of capital goods that are present in the real world. Unfortunately, the extension of capital theory to the case of many goods involves at least as many difficulties and restrictive conditions as the single-good case. However, as before, practical theory proceeds under the assumption that even a restrictive theory offers a better guide to measurement than no theory at all.

Following the one good case, it is assumed that the technology is homothetically separable into a function of the N distinct types of capital flows used in production (I will continue to ignore the distinction between stocks and flows and assume that for each asset the one is proportional to the other):

$$(29) \qquad Q_t = F[L_t, K(K^1_t, \ldots, K^N_t)],$$

where each K^i is itself an aggregate over individual investment vintages (I assume, here, that the conditions for vintage aggregation discussed in sec. 4.1.1 are satisfied for each type of capital). A necessary condition is that the marginal rate of substitution *between* each type of capital be independent of the amount of labor used:

(30) $$\frac{\partial}{\partial L_t}\left[\frac{\partial Q/\partial K_t^i}{\partial Q/\partial K_t^j}\right] = 0, \quad i, j = 1, \ldots, N.$$

Under this restriction, the aggregator function $K(\cdot)$ determines the nature of the capital aggregate, and the measurement of aggregate capital thus becomes a matter of discovering the form of $K(\cdot)$. This can be done by direct estimation of $F(\cdot)$ and $K(\cdot)$, which obviates the need for constructing the capital aggregate, or by Divisia indexing procedures.

The Divisia index is constructed by weighting the growth rate of each type of capital by its share in total capital income, $S_t^i = P_t^{K_i} K_t^i \,/\, \Sigma\, P_t^{K_i} K_t^i$, and summing the result:[16]

(31) $$\frac{\dot{K}_t}{K_t} = \Sigma\, S_t^i \frac{\dot{K}_t^i}{K_t^i}.$$

This can be shown to be related to the logarithmic differential of the production function $F(\cdot)$ when rental prices are proportional to marginal products. As shown in Hulten (1973), the existence of a linearly homogeneous aggregator function $K(\cdot)$ allows this expression to be integrated to obtain the "level" of the aggregate capital in each year (with one time period arbitrarily normalized at one.)[17]

The Divisia index is formulated in continuous time and is therefore not generally applicable to economic data. In practice, a discrete approximation to (31) is used in which the continuous growth rates are replaced by the difference in natural logarithms, $\ln K_t^i - \ln K_{t-1}^i$, and the continuous shares by the arithmetic average $(\frac{1}{2})(S_t^i + S_{t-1}^i)$. The result is the discrete time Törnqvist-translog index of capital.[18] When rental prices are proportional to marginal products (e.g., under cost minimization) and when the production function has the homogeneous translog form, the Törnqvist-translot index of capital is exact (Diewert 1976).

This approach provides an internally consistent, but restrictive, procedure for aggregating capital. A problem arises, however, when the number of asset types N is very large. The Törnqvist-translog approach requires that a capital stock and a rental price be calculated for each type of capital, which in turn requires an investment series, asset prices, and efficiency sequences for each type of asset. This is a difficult requirement when the number of assets gets even moderately large, and it is impossible for the thousands (if not millions) of varieties of capital actually used in production.

The enormous variety of capital assets virtually insures that some types of capital will be treated as homogeneous even though they are not. Categories like "commercial buildings" and "machine tools" come to be regarded (out of necessity) as homogeneous for the purpose of measurement, despite the fact that they include quite diverse types of capital. In such cases, the quantity of the pseudohomogeneous good is found by adding up current dollar values of each component good and deflating the result to the price level prevailing in some base year. Data on current investment expenditures are relatively easy to obtain, but finding a plausible price index for the deflation process is another matter.

The price index problem is greatly simplified if individual asset prices move together (i.e., are proportional). In this case, the price *levels* differ only by a constant, so that units of quantity can, in principle, be redefined to make asset prices identical. This is the case in which the Hicks aggregation theorem applies and a capital stock can be calculated provided that the aggregate efficiency sequence is the same for each component of the aggregate.

The theory of hedonic prices provides another solution to the problem of excessive variety. In this framework, individual capital goods are viewed as bundles of characteristics rather than as discrete physical entities. For example, different types of personal computers may be classified with respect to speed, memory size, graphics capability, and so on. The "inputs" to the production function (1) are then the amount of each characteristic rather than the amount of each physical good. The hedonic approach is particularly useful when there are many varieties of capital embodying a few characteristics—that is, when there are many bands and/or options that can be reduced to far fewer characteristic dimensions.

Under certain conditions, hedonic techniques can be used to estimate the "prices" associated with different characteristics. These prices can be used to deflate the total dollar expenditure on a group of pseudohomogeneous capital goods or to deflate the components individually. But, while this is an appealing approach, it is greatly limited by the fact that capital goods are purchased as physical units and the prices of component characteristics are not directly observable. Furthermore, the shadow prices of the individual characteristic tend to be complicated functions of all other characteristics and not just parameters as with physical goods, so estimation is often difficult.

In the final analysis, the great diversity and variety of the capital stock virtually insures that simple adding-up procedures will occur at some level of disaggregation. Simple, and usually ad hoc, deflation procedures will inevitably be used for some portion of investment, and the use of more sophisticated translog and hedonic techniques may reduce aggregation bias but will not eliminate it. But, as Griliches (1971) has noted in his survey of hedonic methods, "half a loaf is better than none."

4.1.5 Embodied Technical Change

An important variant on the heterogeneity problem deserves attention in its own right: different vintages of capital may differ in quality because they embody different levels of technological efficiency. The practice of aggregating investment of different vintages as per the perpetual inventory method of equation (1) should take into account the improvement in technology since it is a measure of capital stock in efficiency units. The stock of computers, for example, should reflect the increases in computing power per machine of new assets entering the stock as well as the loss in power through decay and retirement of existing machines.

The Fisher aggregation result discussed in section 4.1.1 suggests a procedure for incorporating embodied technical change into the perpetual inventory calculation. The vintage production functions $f^{\nu}(L_{t,\nu}, I_{\nu})$, defined in 4.1.2, may differ because of differences in technology built into capital I_{ν} when it is new. According to equation (7), the Fisher aggregation condition requires that any difference in embodied technology be representable by a fixed coefficient, which, in turn, means that aggregation can take place when embodied technical change—that is, better capital—is equivalent to having more capital.

Analytically, the Fisher condition can be represented by a relative efficiency index ϕ that drifts upward over time as the technology embodied in new machines improves. A 10% improvement in technology will, for example, result in $\phi_{(t+1),0} = 1.1\ \phi_{t,0}$, implying that a new unit of investment would then count as 10% more capital than a unit of new capital in the preceding year. Assuming, for simplicity of exposition, that efficiency decays at a geometric rate δ, which is the same for all vintages, and letting b_{ν} denote the pure index of embodied technical progress, so that $\phi_{t,\nu} = b_{\nu}(1-\delta)^{t-\nu}$, the perpetual inventory equation can be written

$$(32)\qquad K_t = b_t I_t + (1-\delta)b_{t-1}I_{t-1} + \ldots + (1-\delta)^s\, b_{\nu}I_{\nu} + \ldots,$$

which is effectively the same as (1) except for the b_{ν}. Estimation of the b_{ν} would then produce the desired measure of capital, given δ.

The adjustment for embodied technical change can be obtained by multiplying the number of units of new investment in year t by the appropriate index b_{ν}. However, this solution supposes that an estimate of b_{ν} is available and, in general, that there is nothing in the translation of "better" into "more" that guarantees that the index of "more" is observable. Hall (1968, 1971) has shown that there is a fundamental indeterminacy in separating the effects of efficiency decay, embodied technical change, and disembodied technical change. The efficiency of an asset of vintage ν at time t is the product of all three effects: if efficiency declines at a constant rate, δ; new investment embodies technical improvements at a constant rate, γ; and overall disembodied technical change is occurring at a constant rate, λ; the efficiency index is given (in continuous time) by

$$(33)\qquad \phi_{t,\nu} = e^{-\delta s}e^{\gamma\nu}e^{\lambda t}.$$

Since $s = t-\nu$, this can also be written as

$$(33')\qquad \phi_{t,\nu} = e^{(\lambda+\gamma)t}e^{-(\gamma+\delta)s} = e^{\alpha t}e^{\beta s}.$$

Any number of combinations of (δ, γ, λ) can yield a given (α, β), and there is thus an identification problem.

This problem also occurs on the price side in identifying the separate effects of depreciation (the change in vintage asset price with respect to age, $t-\nu$), obsolescence (the change with respect to vintage, ν), and inflation (the change with respect to time, t). Assuming constant rates of growth, the price of a vintage ν asset at time t can be shown to equal

$$(34) \qquad P^{I}_{t,s} = e^{(\rho+\gamma)t}e^{-(\gamma+\delta)s}.$$

This implies that the trend in efficiency decay and obsolescence cannot be identified using data on used asset prices.

Hall suggests the following procedure to solve his identification problem: "As we have seen, if our framework is restricted to consideration of the *efficiency* of capital in use, the trend is ambiguous, and it would be senseless to try to estimate it. An alternative to this view is to suppose that embodied technical change, far from being a mystery, can be explained in terms of changes in the observed *characteristics* of capital goods. By characteristics, we mean size, weight, power, and other information of an engineering nature" (1971, 258; emphasis added). This approach brings us back to hedonics as a solution to the quality problem, but this time in response to quality change over time rather than asset diversity at any point in time. It is worth noting, here, that Hall's suggestion has been implemented for the computer component of equipment investment in the U.S. National Income and Product Accounts, and Gordon (1989) has extended this to 17 types of producers' durable equipment.[19]

The hedonic approach captures differences in quality that are revealed in price differentials. In competitive equilibrium, prices will tend to be driven into equality with marginal costs, implying that only those quality differences that are associated with cost differentials will be picked up by hedonic methods. This, in turn, implies that hedonic techniques will capture only part of the embodied change in the index ϕ. The use of hedonic prices to deflate investment expenditures is a complete solution to the embodiment problem only under restrictive assumptions.

4.1.6 Capital Stocks versus Capital Flows

Capital stock estimates are widely used in econometric and growth accounting analyses of production. However, the production function $Q = F(K, L)$ is conventionally interpreted as a relationship between the *flow* of output and the *flow* of input services. We have thus far ignored the distinction between capital stocks and flows and must now consider the problem of converting estimates of the latter into a flow equivalent.

The minimalist solution to this problem is to assume that capital flows are proportional to stocks, so that the one is a perfect surrogate for the other. In this case, capital utilization—defined as the ratio of the flow to the stock—is assumed to remain constant over time and, in particular, over the business cycle. However, while convenient, proportionality is clearly a dubious assumption, since published estimates of utilization tend to vary over the cycle.

An alternative approach is to multiply the estimated capital stock by an estimate of capital utilization. But, while this solves the problem of introducing variation in stock estimates over the business cycle, it merely converts the problem from one of measuring capital services (given the capital stock) to one of estimating utilization. If the flow of capital services cannot be measured, then estimation of the ratio of services to stock is also problematic. Ambiguity about the exact nature of capital services is at the center of the problem. What, exactly, is a capital "service"? Is a chair in "service" only when it is occupied? Or, does the availability of the chair for potential occupancy count for something too? If so, are potential services equivalent to actual services? And, how do we assess the decorative value of the chair if it adds to the office ambience? In the same vein, is an office building utilized only during business hours, or is it utilized all the time to keep out thieves and inclement weather?

In both cases, the services (whatever they are) cannot readily be observed because they are not easily defined. The measurement of such services, or of capital utilization, is thus problematic. An alternative approach is to dispense with the notion of capital service altogether and to analyze production from the standpoint of capital stocks alone. This is the approach taken in the recent literature on temporary equilibrium, in which the production function is interpreted as a relationship between the flow of output and a flow of variable labor input applied to a quasi-fixed stock of capital. Because the stock is taken as fixed in the short run, short-run fluctuations in demand can only be accommodated by changes in the amount of labor used in production. The capacity of the capital stock is defined with respect to the cost-minimizing level of output for the given amount of capital, and the optimal level of capacity occurs when actual output is at the cost-minimizing level. Capacity utilization, in this sense, is increased when more labor is applied to the fixed amount of capital.[20]

There are two concepts of rental price in the temporary equilibrium framework. The ex ante rental price is defined as the implicit (or possibly explicit) rent that is expected to be paid in each future period. The ex ante equilibrium condition is given by the analog of (19)

$$P^{I}_{t,0} = \sum_{\tau=0}^{\infty} \frac{P^{K}_{t+\tau,\tau}}{(1+r)^{\tau+1}}, \tag{35}$$

where the rental price, $P^{K}_{t+\tau,\tau}$ is now the expected cost in year $t+\tau$ given that demand is at its expected level, and r is now the rate of interest expected to prevail in future periods. The actual, or ex post, rental price, $Z^{K}_{t+\tau,\tau}$, is the gross quasi-rent realized from the capital stock when labor is adjusted to meet fluctuations in demand. It is the residual income accruing to the quasi-fixed stock (revenue less payments to all variable inputs):

$$(36)\qquad Z^K_{t+\tau,\tau} = (P^Q_{t+\tau} Q_{t+\tau,\tau} - P^L_{t+\tau} L_{t+\tau,\tau})/K_{t+\tau,\tau}.$$

If the expected value of $P^K_{t+\tau,\tau}$ is assumed to equal $Z^K_{t+\tau,\tau}$ then $Z^K_{t+\tau,\tau}$ can be substituted in (35). Furthermore, Berndt and Fuss (1986) show that it is the ex post $Z^K_{t+\tau,\tau}$ that equals the value of the realized marginal product of capital in each period. This implies that the ex post price is the appropriate concept for applications in which prices are used to estimate realized marginal products (e.g., in growth accounting analyses).[21]

Another approach to the capital service problem has developed along the lines of the Walras-Hicks-Malinvaud recursive method of production.[22] In this framework, the firm is viewed as using labor and capital stock to produce output *and* capital that is one year older. The firm is viewed as buying its stock at the beginning of the production period, using it to produce output, and then selling what is left of it at the end of the period. The objective of the firm is to maximize the difference between the cost of acquiring the capital plus the cost of labor on the one hand, and the revenue from selling output plus the proceeds from the sale of the used capital on the other. For the case in which capital is purchased when new:

$$(37)\qquad \pi^*_t = \frac{P^Q_t Q_t - P^I_{t+1,1}\phi_1 I_t}{(1+r)} - P^L_t L_t - P^I_{t,0} I_t.$$

The extension to capital of all vintages is straightforward. This expression is maximized subject to the constraint on technology, which now takes the implicit form $F(Q_t, \phi_1 I_t, I_t, L_t, t) = 0$. It is not obvious that this is the same problem as the maximization of profits, defined as the difference between revenue $P^Q Q$ and cost $P^L L + P^K I$, subject to $Q_t = F(I_t, L_t, t)$, but rearrangement of the terms in (37) and use of (23) reveals that the two are in fact equivalent. This implies that the optimal production plan can be viewed as emerging from a structure in which period-by-period capital costs are based on the implicit rent a firm must charge itself or on the implicit sale of capital by the firm to itself.

The conceptual equivalence of the two approaches does tend to conceal an interesting interpretation that can be given to the recursive framework. The technology $F(Q_t, \phi_v I_s, I_s, L_t, t) = 0$ can be defined with respect to the *stock* of the capital good and the issue of service flow left implicit. And, in this spirit, the amount of capital used up in production, $\phi_v - \phi_{v+1}$, can be made a choice variable of the firm, that is, the amount of depreciation is chosen as part of the overall production plan. The recursive model thus provides a natural framework for endogenizing the ϕ sequence, although it is not clear whether or not a measure of aggregate capital exists in this case, given the theoretical requirements of the Fisher conditions discussed at the outset.

The temporary equilibrium and recursive models of production fit more neatly into the category of "new developments" than into "accepted practice."

This may change in coming years, but it seems safe to say that these models have yet to have an impact on current national income and accounting practice, which relies on the more conventional measurement framework outlined above.

4.2 Practical Problems in the Measurement of Capital

The bits and pieces of theory presented in the preceding sections provide a practical framework for measuring capital stocks. The principal options are to look for a direct estimate of the capital stock, K_t, or to adjust book values for inflation, mergers, and accounting procedures, or to use the perpetual inventory method. This last option requires an estimate of the value of investment spending, $P^I I$, a quality-adjusted investment deflator, P^I, an efficiency sequence ϕ, and possibly a retirement distribution. Any of these procedures can be implemented at any level of industrial or asset detail for which the necessary data exists.

The discussion of section 4.1 reviews the conceptual difficulties with the various procedures. Statisticians involved in the actual estimation of capital stocks are, however, aware that the conceptual problems are only part of the problem. Dozens, if not hundreds, of "small" practical problems also cause headaches: Should estimates be assembled on a company or establishment basis? By industry of use or industry of ownership? Using data on investment expenditures or investment shipments? According to which industry and asset classification?

The various practical issues that must be addressed are too numerous and detailed to be dealt with in a relatively brief survey article. We will focus, instead, on three of the central problem areas of the perpetual inventory method: the estimation of investment in current dollars by industry and asset, the development of suitable investment-good deflators, and the estimation of efficiency sequences and retirement distributions. The following sections deal with these topics in turn, and a final assessment is offered in the conclusion.

4.2.1 Investment Data

Data on the current dollar value of U.S. investment are available from a variety of sources. The principal ones include: the U.S. National Income and Product Accounts (NIPA), the Bureau of Economic Analysis's (BEA) plant and equipment survey (P&E), and the investment data underlying the BEA capital stock studies (CSS). These data and others (like those from the input-output studies) are based on different classification systems and different degrees of coverage and must be interpreted accordingly. The NIPA equipment data, for example, are based on deliveries of investment goods, while the P&E and CSS data are largely based on investment expenditures. The P&E data, however, are collected on a company basis while the CSS data refer to establishments.

The choice between alternative investment series depends primarily on how the series will be used and not on inherent differences in data quality. Studies of the financial structure of firms or industries, for example, require company-based investment data since the decisions of interest are generally made at the company level of organization. Studies of productivity change, on the other hand, require establishment-level data since technology and production decisions are generally implemented at the establishment level within the company.[23] Similarly, studies of the distribution of wealth may require data on the *ownership* of capital, while studies of production require data on the *utilization* of capital. Leased capital should be attributed to the owner in the first type of study, but attributed to the user in the second.

There is thus no uniquely correct source of investment data. Furthermore, the choice among competing investment series depends on the desired level of asset and industry detail. There is a relative abundance of data for the economy as a whole, but the choice is far more limited at lower levels of aggregation. The BEA capital stock studies (Gorman et al. 1985; U.S. Department of Commerce 1987) provide the most extensive "official" investment data set for the United States: estimates of fixed nonresidential private investment (in current and constant dollars) are provided at the two-digit SIC industry level of detail; estimates are also provided for residential capital (by legal form of organization), durable goods owned by consumers (by type of good), fixed nonresidential government capital (by type of government and type of equipment and structure), and fixed nonresidential capital (by legal form of organization). The study also presents separate estimates of nonresidential capital for 22 types of producers' durable equipment and 14 types of nonresidential structures, and a cross-classification by two-digit industry and type of capital is available.

This impressive degree of detail requires data from many sources. Table A of the 1987 BEA study lists no fewer than 21 such sources. And, this covers only new nonresidential fixed investment. This multiplicity of sources is required in order to achieve the desired industry detail and to obtain sufficiently long investment series. The length of the investment series is an issue because, under the perpetual inventory method, the capital stocks at any point in time are the weighted sum of past investments. The investment series used in the perpetual inventory method must therefore span the years for which the efficiency weights are positive, or at least span the time period in which the weights are large enough to affect significantly the capital stock.

This problem can be illustrated by the case of geometric depreciation. With a constant rate of depreciation δ, the perpetual inventory equation (1) can be written as

$$(38) \quad K_t = I_t + (1-\delta)I_{t-1} + \ldots + (1-\delta)^{t-\nu}I_\nu + (1-\delta)^{t-\nu+1}K_{\nu-1}.$$

That is, the capital stock at time t is the efficiency-weighted sum of investment back to year ν, plus the remaining efficiency of the capital stock of time $\nu-1$. By making the investment series sufficiently long, that is, making ν sufficiently large, $(1-\delta)^{t-\nu+1}$ can be made arbitrarily small and the size of $K_{\nu-1}$ can then be ignored (i.e., assumed to be zero). Otherwise, a value for $K_{\nu-1}$— a "benchmark"—must be estimated.

The investment series presented in the BEA study are quite long. Investment data for various types of nonresidential structures are carried back to the period 1832–89, while the various producers' durable equipment series commence in the interval from 1877 to 1917. At a depreciation rate of 4% for structures, an investment made in 1832 had only 1% of its efficiency left by 1948. If equipment depreciates at a rate of 15% per year, only .5% of an investment made in 1900 remains in 1948. The BEA series are thus sufficiency long that the initial level of the capital stock can be set equal to zero, which is fortunate because there are no reliable benchmarks on which to base alternative estimates.

The need to combine data from different sources does, however, introduce additional errors into the estimates. Each different series must be adjusted to the classification of the data base as a whole (generally an establishment/industry-of-ownership/1972-two-digit-SIC basis). These adjustments, or "bridges," are a potential source of error because, for example, the bridges are frequently problematic.[24]

Still, it seems reasonable to conclude that this part of the capital measurement problem is in reasonably good shape, particularly in view of the difficulty of the problem of capital measurement and strides that have been made by the BEA in recent years. However, the same cannot be said of investment in other types of productive capital. There is no integrated wealth account that puts land, inventories, R&D investment, and investment in other intangibles on an equal footing with the BEA tangible fixed wealth estimates. Data on inventories can be obtained from the BEA (although the move to the full cost absorption method of accounting is a major problem), and estimates of R&D spending can be obtained from other sources, but there is no unified data base for productive capital as a whole, much less one that is linked to the financial claims against the income generated by productive assets.[25]

The availability of investment data at the firm level of detail is also a major problem. Firm-level data seldom produces sufficiently long times series on investment that the benchmark $K_{\nu-1}$ in (38) can be ignored. The perpetual inventory method is thus not feasible, and as previously noted, analysts are typically forced to adjust book value data in order to obtain estimates of capital stock.

4.2.2 Investment-Good Deflators

The perpetual inventory method requires an investment series expressed in constant dollars (or in physical units, but this is not normally a feasible option). Since data on capital formation typically originate from market transactions of investment goods, a price deflator is needed to convert market data in nominal dollars to a real (inflation adjusted) dollar basis. As we have seen in section 4.1, the process of deflation can introduce additional, and potentially serious, errors into the data.

Two potential sources of error have already been identified: the application of a single deflator to goods that are in fact heterogeneous and the adjustment for quality change. To this list can be added a host of practical problems in sample design. The range of issues is sufficiently large, and detailed, that it deserves (and has received) attention in its own right. A brief summary of the deflation procedures used in the BEA capital stock studies is given in the 1987 BEA publication cited above, and I will thus limit the discussion here to the two areas in which price deflation is widely thought to be a major problem: computers and nonresidential structures.

Investment in computers presents a particularly serious problem because of the phenomenal growth of computing power. According to our efficiency interpretation of the perpetual inventory capital stock, such advances in computing power must be counted as an increase in the quantity of capital rather than its price, and the deflator for computing equipment must therefore be adjusted for quality change. The study by Cole et al. (1986) provides a major step in this direction by estimating three types of hedonic price indexes for four categories of computing equipment (processors, disk drives, printers, and displays). They report a dramatic decrease in quality-adjusted price: for processors, the three hedonic methods yielded an average annual price change of −18.2% for the years 1972–84. With the 1982 index equal to 100, this implies a price decline from 888 in 1972 to 80 in 1984. The other categories of computing equipment showed similar price declines: −14% per year for disk drives, −13.2% for printers, and −7% for displays.

The hedonic methods yield much larger price declines than the more conventional "matched model" approach. The latter produced average annual percentage price declines of −8.5, −6.9, −3.5, and −1.3. The conventional approach thus portrays a very different, and probably inaccurate, picture of real investment in computing equipment. The hedonic approach seems preferable and has been adopted by the BEA (Cartwright 1986), which had previously assumed no change at all, and by Gordon (1989), who presents hedonic price estimates for a broad range of producers' durable equipment. The hedonic approach is, however, not free of theoretical and empirical problems (e.g., Denison 1989). For example, the three hedonic methods reported by Cole et al. (1986) yield rather different results in the case of processors (a range of −17.6% to −19.2% per year), disk drives (−12.6% to −16.9%), and printers (−10.4% to 15.5%). These are sizable differences considering that they represent compound rates of growth, and Cole et al. conclude: "Although there may be widespread agreement that the present procedure for deflating expenditures on computing equipment is inadequate, a completely satisfactory alternative is not readily devised" (1986, 49).

Nonresidential structures are another case in which price deflation is a major problem. Pieper (in this volume) provides a detailed analysis of this problem, and I will only note here that there are two major issues: the use of cost indexes rather than price indexes as deflators and the use of proxy indexes (an index derived from a different sector). The main conceptual difference between cost and prices indexes is the rate of productivity change in the construction industry. If construction wages and materials, and so on, grow at a rate of 5% a year, and the efficiency with which labor and materials are used grows at 2%, competition will cause prices to increase at only 3% a year. The use of a cost index as a deflator for construction is therefore justified only when productivity change is zero or a noncompetitive market structure causes productivity gains to be captured by the producers. Neither situation is particularly appealing as an a priori assumption about the construction industry. Furthermore, the use of proxy deflators is only justified when the proxy and target industries have identical price trends. This is also a problematic assumption about the construction industry, and it seems reasonable to conclude that major biases may be present in the deflation process.

4.2.3 Efficiency and Retirement Patterns and the Estimation of Capital Stocks

Deflated investment expenditures measure the amount of capital added to the existing stock. Since most fixed capital is produced and sold in markets, there is a data "trail" that can in principle be followed. The same cannot be said about deletions from the stock. The reduction in capital can occur through in-place declines in efficiency and through retirement. Neither presents a broad trail of market data that can be used to determine the magnitude of the deletions. As a result, imputational methods like those described in section 4.1.2 of this paper are necessary, and this aspect of the capital measurement problem is widely thought to be the most unsatisfactory.

The BEA capital stock studies follow a procedure based on the perpetual inventory equation (16). Implementation of this approach requires three ingredients: a mean useful life, a retirement distribution centered on that life, and an efficiency pattern $\phi^{(i)}$. In the BEA methodology, a useful life is estimated for the various types of structures and equipment included in the capital stock studies. These useful lives are derived from a variety of sources, including the 1942 edition of *Bulletin "F,"* (U.S. Department of the Treasury), data from regulatory agencies, and the (largely) unpublished studies conducted by the Office of Industrial Economics during the 1970s. Retirements are assumed to occur according to the Winfrey distributions developed in the 1930s: a modified Winfrey *S*-3 curve is used for nonresidential capital and residential structures and an *L*-2 curve is used for consumer durables. The nonresidential *S*-3 distribution is a truncated bell shaped curve in which retirement starts at 45% of mean life (T_{min}) and stops at 155% (T_{max}). The Winfrey distribution is used to determine the fraction of any year's investment I_t retired at the end of T_{min} years, $T_{min} + 1$ years, $T_{min} + 2$ years, . . . , T_{max} years. I_t is then allocated to subcohorts $I_t^{(i)}$ accordingly, and the $\phi^{(i)}$ for each subcohort is calculated under the assumption of one-hoss shay deterioration (eq. [9]). Given estimates of $\phi^{(i)}$ and $I_t^{(i)}$, an equation similar to (18) is used to estimate the capital stock.[26]

The Bureau of Labor Statistics has also developed estimates of capital stock for use in their multifactor productivity program. The BLS procedures for fixed nonresidential capital are similar to those of the BEA, with the major difference being the use of the Hulten-Wykoff (1981a, 1981b) depreciation studies to obtain data-based estimates of the efficiency function $\phi^{(i)}$. The Hulten-Wykoff studies present estimates of economic depreciation (including obsolescence) derived from vintage asset prices. In view of equation (34), the rate of depreciation (plus obsolescence) is equivalent to the rate of change of the vintage price $P^I_{t,s}$ with respect to s; thus, a panel sample of vintage prices for a range of t and s can be used to estimate the pattern of economic depreciation.[27] Hulten and Wykoff use this type of data for various categories of nonresidential structures, construction equipment, machine tools, and autos to test whether depreciation followed either of the three patterns described in section 4.1.2—one-hoss shay, straight line, or geometric. None of these forms was accepted by the data, but the estimated pattern was closest to the geometric form. A "best geometric approximation" was computed for each of the asset types in the study, and this was used to derive estimates of the rate of depreciation for the full range of the BEA fixed nonresidential capital assets.[28]

The studies of Fraumeni and Jorgenson (1986), Jorgenson, Gollop, and Fraumeni (1987), Boskin, Robinson, and Huber (1989), and Boskin, Robinson, and Roberts (1989) use the Hulten-Wykoff estimates of δ more or less directly. These studies accept the best geometric approximation and use the self-dual property of geometric depreciation to calculate capital stocks K_t and user costs $P^K_{t,0}$ using the same δ. This procedure assumes that the obsolescence component of s should be treated as a write-down of the physical stock. The BLS study (U.S. Department of Labor 1983), on the other hand, steers a middle course between these studies and the BEA capital stock studies. The BLS study assumes that the efficiency function has the beta, or hyperbolic, form (see n. 8):

$$(39) \qquad \phi_\tau = \frac{T-\tau}{T-\beta\tau}, \quad \tau = 0, 1, \ldots, T \quad \text{and} \quad -\infty < \tau \leq 1.$$

BLS constrained β to lie in the interval [0, 1], thereby constraining the efficiency function to lie between the straight-line and one-hoss shay forms. Using estimates of T obtained from the BEA, BLS found the value of β that provided the closest fit to the Hulten-Wykoff price depreciation patterns. It was determined that a beta value of 0.75 resulted in the best fit for structures and 0.50 for equipment.

A definitive appraisal of alternative methods is impossible without an independent benchmark.[29] However, any appraisal of these procedures would have to note that the Winfrey retirement studies are now a half-century old, and that it is unlikely that the three Winfrey distributions used by the BEA capture the diversity of retirement patterns present in the full range of residential and nonresidential capital. Furthermore, part of the useful life data is also dated—some of these lives are derived from the 1942 *Bulletin "F"*—and, while the OIE data are much more recent, they are largely inaccessible and therefore hard to evaluate. It should be noted, however, that both the OIE data and the *Bulletin "F"* data were assembled in order to administer the income tax code and were not developed explicitly for the purpose of measuring capital. Furthermore, the service lives used by the BEA and others are fixed for the entire period covered by the study; they do not vary over the business cycle as plants open and close nor do they change in response to obsolescence. This is potentially one of the most serious problems with the perpetual inventory method.[30]

Data on useful asset life and on retirement patterns are extremely scant, and there are few alternatives to current procedures (which do, by and large, make sensible use of the available information). Improvement in these areas must await future data development. On the other hand, the question of the appropriate efficiency pattern is the subject of active, and unresolved, debate. One view holds that the market price of used assets is a valuable source of information about the relative productivity of old and new assets and that the perpetual inventory method should incorporate this information. Opponents of this view argue that the use of vintage asset prices suffer from the"lemons" problem, in which only inferior, and hence nonrepresentative, assets enter resale markets. Thus, it is argued, the market price of used assets falls more rapidly than the true, or shadow, price of the nonlemon assets, which are rarely sold. According to this view, the rapid decline in the price of lemons explains why vintage price studies almost invariably find a near-geometric depreciation pattern. Therefore, since this pattern is intuitively implausible and supported only by biased data, the critics conclude that it should be rejected.

Proponents of the vintage price approach respond by arguing that the markets for used machine tools, construction equipment, and nonresidential buildings are typically dominated by specialists whose business is to know the quality of used assets. The asymmetrical information condition of the lemons model is thus not present (Hulten and Wykoff 1981b). And, while there are certainly problems with market data on vintage prices, most price data are flawed in some way or another.[31] The basic issue is whether or not market information should be ignored or discarded while one-hoss shay or constrained beta efficiency functions are adopted on the basis of largely subjective notions about asset deterioration.[32]

This issue will hopefully be resolved by further research on the characteristics of used asset markets, by using market data on capital rents, or perhaps by the econometric studies of endogenous depreciation described above in section 4.1. For now, it is one of the central problems of practical capital theory.

4.2.4 Conclusion

The measurement of economic variables almost always involves significant problems, but Sir John Hicks is certainly correct in his appraisal of the special difficulties encountered in the area of capital measurement. The theoretical problems are indeed "nasty," and the practical problems are even nastier. Despite the very substantial effort and ingenuity of economists and statisticians at the BEA, the BLS, the Census Bureau, and other agencies, much remains to be accomplished. And, in my judgment, real progress must await the development of new data sources.

Fortunately, such development is under way at the U.S. Treasury's Office of Depreciation Analysis and at Statistics Canada (see Koumanakos 1989). Both agencies are undertaking surveys of the retirement and depreciation practices of individual firms, and of the market prices of used assets. These studies hold the promise of clarifying the nature of used asset markets and will, it is hoped, generate information on the useful lives of a variety of industrial assets. But, even these valuable studies will leave us without a benchmark value for the capital stock. There is a critical need for such a benchmark in order to test the validity of alternative procedures and, more important, in order to "anchor" the perpetual inventory estimates of capital in nonbenchmark years. It therefore seems appropriate to end this survey with a renewed call for a national capital benchmark.

Notes

1. The literature on the theory of capital is enormous. In addition to standard references on the history of economic thought, summaries of the relevant issues may be found in Harcourt (1972), Diewert (1980), Burmeister (1980), and Hicks (1981a).

2. Whether or not a good is durable obviously depends on the length of the accounting period. A machine that lasts five years would not be considered a durable good if the accounting period is taken to be 10 years, and a bouquet of flowers would be durable relative to an accounting period of a few hours. Since capital is a produced means of production, it is useful to think of it as an intertemporal intermediate good that is distinguished from a normal intermediate good by an arbitrarily defined accounting period (see Hulten 1979).

3. I will generally adhere to the convention that t denotes the current year (or prime period) and ν denotes some year in the past. The variable $t-\nu$ is the age of the capital put in place in year ν (e.g., 1950) at year t (e.g., 1990), and T is the age of the oldest surviving asset. We will sometimes use the variable $s = t-\nu$ to denote asset age.

4. Aggregation in the case of nonconstant returns is also studied by Fisher (1965), but general results are hard to obtain. We will restrict our discussion to the "easy" case of constant returns and note that this is yet another restrictive condition under which aggregation is unambiguously possible.

5. It might also be noted that the Leontief theorem implies a restriction on the substitution possibilities between pairs of inputs. Berndt and Christensen (1973) show that (5) implies that the Allen elasticity of substitution between capital of vintage ν and

labor must equal the Allen elasticity of substitution between vintage ξ capital and labor. In other words, inputs within the aggregate must be equally good substitutes for inputs outside the aggregate.

6. See Diewert (1980) for an extensive discussion of the problems associated with the various types of aggregation, along with references to the relevant literature.

7. According to Jack Faucett Associates (1970) "This viewpoint can be defended on purely technological grounds: that with reasonable care and maintenance this is what capital goods do and there is nothing that can be done about it" (39).

8. The beta-decay, or hyperbolic, function developed by Jack Faucett Associates (1970), and used by Harper (1982) and the BLS (U.S. Department of Labor 1983), is also worthy of mention since it generalizes the three patterns discussed in the text. The beta-decay function is defined with respect to useful life T, the age of the asset τ, and a parameter β that determines the shape of the function:

$$\phi_\tau = \frac{T-\tau}{T-\beta\tau}, \quad \tau = 0, 1, \ldots, T \quad \text{and } -\infty < \beta \leq 1.$$

When $\beta = 1$ the function has the one-hoss shay form, and then $\beta = 0$ it has the straight-line form. Negative values of β can simulate geometric depreciation. The beta-decay approach thus adds flexibility to the derivation of an efficiency pattern from estimates of useful life, but the problem of determining the appropriate form (i.e., value of β) is still present. As noted in section 4.2.2, the "dual" of this problem has been addressed by using the Box-Cox flexible functional form applied to used asset prices (Hulten and Wykoff 1981a, 1981b).

9. A problem arises, however, in actually identifying this as retirement. Assets may be retained in stand-by pools after they have been removed from service in order to provide extra capacity when needed. Thus, ϕ may in some sense go to zero before the time T, when the asset is actually removed from the capital stock. To account for such circumstances, a more sophisticated model of the capital stock than the one offered in this review is necessary.

10. The BLS (U.S. Department of Labor 1983) provides a comparison of the assumptions about gross and net capital stock used in the studies of Denison (1979), Kendrick and Grossman (1980), and Jorgenson (1980).

11. The nature of expectations is obviously an important determinant of the present value of future income. A variety of assumptions have been employed in the literature on the investment price–rental price correspondence, most commonly static expectations and perfect foresight (see Harper, Berndt, and Wood 1989 for an elaboration of this point). It is also important to emphasize that capital is treated here as variable, and the adjustment costs are assumed to be zero.

12. The supply of vintage assets will depend, in part, on the retirement decision. An asset will presumably be removed from service if the remaining present value of the income from an asset falls below its scrap value.

13. Recall, here, the eq. (12) for geometric decay. This equation implies that $\delta(1-\delta)^{\tau+s}$ can be substituted for $\phi_{s+\tau} - \phi_{s+\tau+1}$ in (26). This, in turn, yields an expression for (25) in which economic depreciation is constant at the rate δ. In other words, when efficiency decay occurs at a constant rate, the investment good price decays at the *same* constant rate. Furthermore, Jorgenson (1973) notes that the geometric decay is ceteris paribus the only one in which both efficiency and investment prices decline according to the same pattern (see, however, Feldstein and Rothschild 1974 for qualifications of this result). Straight-line efficiency decay, for example, is not consistent with straight-line economic depreciation.

This property of geometric decay results in a simplified form of the rental eq. (23), and simplifies the perpetual inventory equation as well, since (1) can be written

$K_t = I_t + (1-\delta)K_{t-1}$. The same δ used in this computation can be used in the calculation of the rental price.

14. The accounting life A may be biased upward relative to the useful life T because managers may wish to understate depreciation costs in order to make current profits appear higher (the opposite is true for tax accounting, in which the incentive is to overstate depreciation cost). The short-run increase in accounting profit will, of course, be matched by an offsetting decrease sometime in the future, but the pressure on management to succeed now may make this consideration irrelevant. And, if the capital stock continues to grow, the decrease can be postponed, perhaps perpetually.

15. See Atkinson and Mairesse (1978) and Pakes and Griliches (1984) for a discussion of the methods that can be used to extract information from book value data.

16. Dots over variables denote a derivative with respect to time. The variable $\dot{K}_t/K_t$ is thus the rate of growth of K_t.

17. Equation (31) defines a growth rate and must be converted into a level index by line integration. Given the homotheticity of the aggregates, the separability condition (30) is both necessary and sufficient for path independent line integration and thus the existence of the level index.

18. The translog production function is due to Christensen, Jorgenson, and Lau (1973). However, the discrete approximation actually predates this paper (Törnqvist 1936; Theil 1960). Applications of this approximation to capital aggregation are developed in Christensen and Jorgenson (1969, 1970) and Jorgenson, Gollop, and Fraumeni (1987).

19. For a general discussion of the issues involved in linking price hedonics and technical change, with specific application to computers, see Triplett (1987, 1989). As an example of hedonic price deflation, consider the case in which the cost of a certain kind of personal computer is $2,000 in both 1987 and 1988, but the computer has doubled in computing power over this period. Then, the effective or equivalent cost of the 1988 computer is $1,000. If the $1,000 figure is used to deflate the cost of purchasing the computer in 1988 rather than the $2,000 figure, the improvement in quality ($b_{1988} = 2$) is built into the estimate of real investment, $b_{1988}I_{1988}$.

There has been an ongoing controversy over whether hedonic deflation is *ever* appropriate (see Triplett (1983) for a discussion of this debate). Denison (1989) argues against hedonic quality adjust on the grounds that advances in knowledge ought to be kept separate for increases in capital input, and quality adjustments have the effect of embedding technical advances in the measure of capital. However, Hulten (1989) shows how price-based estimates of quality change, such as those presented in Gordon (1990), can be "detached" from the quality-adjusted capital stock and exhibited as a separate contributor to output growth. Furthermore, it is shown that any attempt to ignore embodied technical change when it is present will suppress into the total factor productivity residual this "detachable" term that can be separately measured.

20. A related approach stresses the use of shift labor and the "work week" of capital as the framework for analyzing utilization (Betancourt and Clague 1981; and Foss 1981,1984).

21. The growth accounting papers by Jorgenson and Griliches (1967) and Christensen and Jorgenson (1969) develop the ex post user cost as a practical means of estimating the rate of return to capital and, thereby, of constructing a capital aggregate for use in the Divisia aggregation eq. (31). Berndt and Fuss (1986) were apparently the first to realize that this procedure results in a theoretically consistent correction for capital utilization (see also Hulten 1986).

22. This framework is described in Diewert (1977), and implemented in the endogenous depreciation models of Epstein and Denny (1980), Bischoff and Kokkelenberg (1987), and Kim (1988).

23. This is, indeed, the rationale for the company-establishment distinction. Com-

panies are legal entities of industrial organization while establishments are economic units which produce similar products. A company is frequently a collection of establishments as, e.g., a company which produces autos and washing machines.

24. The use of multiple data sources raises other questions of consistency. There are intrinsic differences in the way different series are constructed, and there is no a priori reason to expect that they give the same result. Seskin and Sullivan (1985), for example, compare the P&E investment data with the NIPA data at the aggregate level of detail (after expressing the P&E data on a NIPA basis) and find that the two series have somewhat different growth trends. The difference is not large, except in the early years of the comparison, but the difference does serve as a warning that combining data from differences sources may introduce internal inconsistencies into the data set.

25. For the extension of the accounting framework to include a longer list of capital goods and an integrated income and wealth account, see Christensen and Jorgenson (1973a, 1973b), Kendrick (1976), and Eisner (1985).

26. It is widely believed that BEA assumes straight-line depreciation in calculating capital stocks. The confusion arises over the distinction between depreciation and asset efficiency—i.e., between prices and quantities—noted in sec. 4.1 of this paper. BEA does indeed use the straight-line assumption in estimating wealth (its "net stocks"), but uses the one-hoss shay assumption in estimating the corresponding quantity of capital (its "gross stocks"). The two estimates are consistent, in the sense of sec. 4.1 under a zero rate of discount. For a more detailed discussion of the conceptual underpinnings of the BEA estimates, see Young and Musgrave (1980). A more detailed description and listing of the actual lives and retirement distributions is given in Gorman et al. (1985, 42–45) and in U.S. Department of Commerce (1987, xxi–xxiv).

27. Panel data on used assets prices must be adjusted for the retirement pattern of assets (the ω in [16]). Otherwise, vintage price data will reflect on the value of surviving assets and will therefore not reflect the average experience of the whole vintage. Hulten and Wykoff adjust for this problem by deflating observed vintage prices by an estimate of the probability of survival.

28. The procedure adopted by Hulten and Wykoff was based on the declining balance formula $\delta = X/T$, where δ is the rate of economic depreciation, T the useful life, and X a parameter defining the degree of the declining balance (e.g., $X = 2$ defines the double declining balance form). Estimates of T were available from BEA by asset category, but δ was available only for those assets studied by Hulten and Wykoff and others. Given estimates of δ and T for this more limited list, an estimate to X was obtained: 1.65 for equipment and .91 for structures. These values of X were then assumed to hold for all assets, and a value of δ was obtained for each T.

29. BEA has compared its estimates of historical-cost gross capital stock with IRS and census book values. Gorman (1987) reports that, in 1977, the BEA estimates for the corporate sector were 95% of the corresponding IRS estimate. These ratios showed substantial variation across major industry, ranging from 73% percent for mining to 121% for services. The comparison of the BEA estimates with census establishment data produced a ratio of 101%, with a variation of 93%–132% across major industries. These comparisons suggest a reasonable fit in the aggregate, but a less good fit at the industry level of aggregation (although this is partly due to a lack of data for insuring full compatibility). Furthermore, it should be noted that the comparisons are made using *gross* book value and not the net value that I have argued is the appropriate capital concept.

30. It is worth nothing, in this regard, that the recent study by Hulten, Robertson, and Wykoff (1989) found that depreciation rates derived from vintage asset prices showed a remarkable degree of stability over the period of the energy crisis. The rapid rise in energy prices in 1974, and again in 1979, could be expected to reduce the value of older energy-inefficient capital. The results of this study suggest that this did not

happen in any systematic way for the two classes of assets studied: machine tools and construction equipment. This finding is consistent with the earlier result by Hulten and Wykoff (1981a) that the depreciation pattern of structures was relatively stable over the period 1955–71. These findings suggest that depreciation rates are relatively constant over the business cycle and during periods of potential obsolescence, but they do not address the question of whether retirement patterns, and thus useful lives, vary over the cycle.

31. According to eq. 21, the relative efficiency of an s-year-old asset is equal, in equilibrium, to the rental price of an s-year-old asset relative to the rental price of a new asset. Thus, the efficiency pattern could also be estimated from data on market rental prices (see Taubman and Rasche 1969). However, this approach is also subject to the criticism that rental markets are thin, that rental prices differ by length of lease, and that tax considerations like "sales-lease-back" arrangements are important determinants of the rent (see the literature review in Hulten and Wykoff [1981b]).

32. Recall, here, the fallacy of composition that can arise when each component of an investment cohort is one-hoss shay but the retirement process is such that the whole cohort decays according to a geometric pattern. The vintage asset prices used in the Hulten-Wykoff studies were adjusted for the probability of retirement and thus correct for the cohort retirement effect.

References

Atkinson, Margaret, and Jacques Mairesse. 1978. Length of Life of Equipment in French Manufacturing Industries. *Annales de l'insee* 30–31:24–48.

Berndt, Ernst R., and Laurits R. Christensen. 1973. The Internal Structure of Functional Relationships: Separability, Substitution, and Aggregation. *Review of Economic Studies* 40: 403–10.

Berndt, Ernst R., and Melvyn A. Fuss. 1986. Productivity Measurement with Adjustments for Variations in Capacity Utilization, and Other Forms of Temporary Equilibrium. *Journal of Econometrics* 33:7–29.

Betancourt, Roger R., and Christopher K. Clague. 1981. *Capital Utilization: A Theoretical and Empirical Analysis*. New York: Cambridge University Press.

Bischoff, Charles W., and Edward C. Kokkelenberg. 1987. Capacity Utilization and Depreciation-in-Use. *Applied Economics* 19:995–1007.

Boskin, Michael J., Marc S. Robinson, and Alan M. Huber. 1989. Government Saving, Capital Formation, and Wealth in the United States, 1947–85. In *The Measurement of Saving, Investment, and Wealth,* ed. Robert E. Lipsey and Helen Stone Tice, 287–353. NBER Studies in Income and Wealth, vol. 52. Chicago: University of Chicago Press.

Boskin, Michael J., Marc S. Robinson, and John M. Roberts. 1989. New Estimates of Federal Government Tangible Capital and Net Investment. In *Technology and Capital Formation,* ed. D. W. Jorgenson and R. Landau, 451–483. Cambridge, Mass.: MIT Press.

Burmeister, Edwin. 1980. *Capital Theory and Dynamics*. Cambridge: Cambridge University Press.

Carson, Carol S. 1987. GNP: An Overview of Source Data and Estimating Methods. *Survey of Current Business* 67, no. 7 (July): 103–27.

Cartwright, David W. 1986. Improved Deflation of Purchases of Computers. *Survey of Current Business* 66, no. 3 (March): 7–9.

Christensen, Laurits R., and Dale W. Jorgenson. 1969. The Measurement of U.S. Real Capital Input, 1929–1967. *Review of Income and Wealth* 15 (December): 293–320.

———. 1970. U.S. Real Product and Real Factor Input, 1929–1969. *Review of Income and Wealth* 16 (March): 19–50.

———. 1973a. Measuring Performance in the Private Sector. In *The Measurement of Economic and Social Performance,* ed. Milton Moss, 233–351. NBER Studies in Income and Wealth, vol. 38. New York: Columbia University Press.

———. 1973b. U.S. Income, Saving, and Wealth, 1929–1969. *Review of Income and Wealth* 19 (December): 329–62.

Christensen, Laurits R., Dale W. Jorgenson, and Lawrence J. Lau. 1973. Transcendental Logarithmic Production Frontiers. *Review of Economics and Statistics* 55 (February): 28–45.

Cole, Rosanne, Y. C. Chen, J. A. Barquin-Stolleman, E. Dullberger, N. Helvacian, and J. H. Hodge. 1986. Quality-adjusted Price Indexes for Computer Processors and Selected Peripheral Equipment. *Survey of Current Business* 66, no. 1 (January): 41–50.

de Leeuw, Frank. 1979. Why Capacity Utilization Rates Differ. In *Measures of Capacity Utilization: Problems and Tasks,* 17–56. Board of Governors of the Federal Reserve System, Staff Studies no. 105. Washington, D.C.: Federal Reserve System.

Denison, Edward F. 1979. *Accounting for Slower Economic Growth: The United States in the 1970's.* Washington, D.C.: Brookings.

———. 1989. *The Sources of Economic Growth in the United States and the Alternatives before Us.* New York: Committee for Economic Development.

Diewert, W. Erwin. 1976. Exact and Superlative Index Numbers. *Journal of Econometrics* 4:115–45.

———. 1977. Walras' Theory of Capital Formation and the Existence of Temporary Equilibrium. In *Equilibrium and Disequilibrium in Economic Theory,* ed. G. Schwodiauer, 73–126. Dordecht: D. Reidel.

———. 1980. Aggregation Problems in the Measurement of Capital. In *The Measurement of Capital,* ed. Dan Usher, 433–524. NBER Studies in Income and Wealth, vol. 45. Chicago: University of Chicago Press.

Eisner, Robert. 1985. The Total System of National Accounts. *Survey of Current Business* 65, no. 1 (January): 24–48.

Epstein, L., and M. Denny. 1980. Endogenous Capital Utilization in a Short-Run Production Model (Theory and an Empirical Application). *Journal of Econometrics* 12:189–207.

Feldstein, Martin S., and Michael Rothschild. 1974. Towards an Economic Theory of Replacement Investment. *Econometrica* 42 (May): 393–423

Fisher, Franklin. 1965. Embodied Technical Change and the Existence of an Aggregate Capital Stock. *Review of Economic Studies* 32: 263–88.

Foss, Murray F. 1981. *Changes in the Workweek of Fixed Capital, U.S. Manufacturing, 1929 to 1976.* Washington, D.C.: American Enterprise Institute for Public Policy Research.

———. 1984. *Changing Utilization of Fixed Capital: An Element in Long Term Growth.* Washington, D.C.: American Enterprise Institute for Public Policy Research.

Fraumeni, Barbara M., and Dale W. Jorgenson. 1986. The Role of Capital in U.S. Economic Growth, 1948–1979. In *Measurement Issues and Behavior of Productivity Variables,* ed. Ali Dogramaci, 161–244. Boston: Martinus Nijhoff.

Goldsmith, Raymond W. 1962. *The National Wealth of the United States in the Postwar Period.* Princeton, N.J.: Princeton University Press.

Gordon, Robert J. 1989. The Postwar Evolution of Computer Prices, In *Technology and Capital Formation,* ed. Dale W. Jorgenson and Ralph Landau, 77–125. Cambridge, Mass.: MIT Press.

———. 1990. *The Measurement of Durable Goods Prices.* Chicago: University of Chicago Press.

Gorman, John A. 1987. *Comparison of BEA's Estimates of Gross Fixed Assets with IRS and Census Book Values.* Working Paper no. 15. Bureau of Economic Analysis, Washington, D.C. (March).

Gorman, John A., John C. Musgrave, Gerald Silverstein, and Kathy Comins. 1985. Fixed Private Capital in the United States. *Survey of Current Business* 65, no. 7 (July): 36–59.

Green, George R., and Marie P. Hertzberg. 1980. Revised Estimates of New Plant and Equipment Expenditures in the United States, 1947–1977. *Survey of Current Business* 60, no. 10 (October): 24–39.

Griliches, Zvi. 1971. Introduction to *Price Indexes and Quality Change: Studies in New Methods of Measurement,* ed. Zvi Griliches. Cambridge, Mass.: Harvard University Press.

Hall, Robert E. 1968. Technical Change and Capital from the Point of View of the Dual. *Review of Economic Studies* 35:34–46.

———. 1971. The Measurement of Quality Change from Vintage Price Data. In *Price Indexes and Quality Change,* ed. Zvi Griliches. Cambridge, Mass.: Harvard University Press.

Hall, Robert E., and Dale W. Jorgenson. 1967. Tax Policy and Investment Behavior. *American Economic Review* 57: 391–414.

Harcourt, G. C. 1972. *Some Cambridge Controversies in the Theory of Capital.* Cambridge: Cambridge University Press.

Harper, Michael J. 1982. *The Measurement of Productive Capital Stock, Capital Wealth, and Capital Services.* Working Paper no. 128. Bureau of Labor Statistics, Washington, D.C. (June).

Harper, Michael J., Ernst R. Berndt, and David O. Wood. 1989. Rates of Return and Capital Aggregation Using Alternative Rental Prices. In *Technology and Capital Formation,* ed. Dale W. Jorgenson and Ralph Landau, 331–372. Cambridge, Mass.: MIT Press.

Hicks, John. 1946. *Value and Capital.* London: Oxford University Press.

———. 1981a. *Capital and Growth.* New York: Oxford University Press.

———. 1981b. *Wealth and Welfare: Collected Essays in Economic Theory.* Cambridge, Mass.: Harvard University Press.

Hulten, Charles R. 1973. Divisia Index Numbers. *Econometrica* 41:1017–25.

———. 1979. On the "Importance" of Productivity Change. *American Economic Review* 69:126–36.

———. 1986. Productivity Change, Capacity Utilization and the Sources of Efficiency Growth. *Journal of Econometrics* 33:31–50.

———. 1989. The Embodiment Hypothesis Revisited. Paper presented at 1989 National Bureau of Economic Research Summer Institute. Typescript.

Hulten, Charles R., James W. Robertson, and Frank C. Wykoff. 1989. Energy, Obsolescence, and the Productivity Slowdown. In *Technology and Capital Formation,* ed. Dale Jorgenson and Ralph Landau. Cambridge, Mass.: MIT Press.

Hulten, Charles R., and Frank C. Wykoff. 1981a. The Estimation of Economic Depreciation Using Vintage Asset Prices. *Journal of Econometrics* 15:367–96.

———. 1981b. The Measurement of Economic Depreciation. In *Depreciation, Inflation, and the Taxation of Income From Capital,* ed. Charles R. Hulten. Washington, D.C.: Urban Institute.

Jack Faucett Associates. 1970. *Capital Stocks, Production Functions and Investment*

Functions for Selected Input-Output Sectors. BLS Report no. 355. U.S. Department of Labor, Bureau of Labor Statistics, Washington, D.C.

Jorgenson, Dale W. 1963. Capital Theory and Investment Behavior. *American Economic Review* 53, no. 2 (May): 247–59.

———. 1973. The Economic Theory of Replacement and Depreciation. In *Econometrics and Economic Theory,* ed. W. Sellykaerts. New York: Macmillan.

———. 1980. Accounting for Capital. In *Capital Efficiency and Growth,* ed. George von Furstenburg, 251–319. Cambridge: Ballinger.

Jorgenson, Dale W., Frank M. Gollop, and Barbara M. Fraumeni. 1987. *Productivity and U.S. Economic Growth*. Cambridge, Mass.: Harvard University Press.

Jorgenson, Dale W., and Zvi Griliches. 1967. The Explanation of Productivity Change. *Review of Economic Studies* 34 (July): 349–83.

Kendrick, John. 1961. *Productivity Trends in the United States*. New York: National Bureau of Economic Research.

———. 1976. *The Formation and Stocks of Total Capital*. New York: National Bureau of Economic Research.

Kendrick, John, and Elliot S. Grossman. 1980. *Productivity in the United States*. Baltimore: Johns Hopkins University Press.

Kim, Moshe. 1988. The Structure of Technology with Endogenous Capital Utilization. *International Economic Review* vol. 29 (February).

Koumanakos, P. 1989. The Capital Stock Survey Project. *Survey of Current Business* 69, no. 5 (May): 31–35.

Kuznets, S. 1962. *Capital in the American Economy,* Princeton, N.J.: Princeton University Press.

Leontief, W. W. 1947a. A Note on the Interrelation of Subsets of Independent Variables of a Continuous Function with Continuous First Derivatives. *Bulletin of the American Mathematical Society* 53: 343–50.

———. 1947b. Introduction to a Theory of the Internal Structure of Functional Relationships. *Econometrica* 15 (October): 361–73.

McKelvey, Michael J. 1981. Constant-Dollar Estimates of New Plant and Equipment Expenditures in the United States, 1947–80. *Survey of Current Business* 61, no. 9 (September): 26–41.

Malinvaud, E. 1953. Capital Accumulation and Efficient Allocation of Resources. *Econometrica* 21 (April): 233–68.

———. 1961. The Analogy between Atemporal and Intertemporal Theories of Resource Allocation. *Review of Economic Studies* 28 (June):143–60.

Pakes, Ariel, and Zvi Griliches. 1984. Estimating Distributed Lags in Short Panels with an Application to the Specification of Depreciation Patterns and Capital Stock Constructs. *Review of Economic Studies* 84: 244–62.

Seskin, Eugene P., and David F. Sullivan. 1985. Revised Estimates of New Plant and Equipment Expenditures in the United States, 1947–83. *Survey of Current Business* 65: 16–47.

Solow, Robert M. 1960. Investment and Technical Progress. In *Mathematical Methods in the Social Sciences, 1959,* ed. K. Arrow, S. Karlin, and P. Suppes. Stanford, Calif.: Stanford University Press.

Taubman, Paul, and Robert Rasche. 1969. Economic and Tax Depreciation of Office Buildings. *National Tax Journal* 22 (September): 334–46.

Theil, H. 1960. Best Linear Index Numbers of Prices and Quantities. *Econometrica* 28: 464–80.

Törnqvist, L. 1936. The Bank of Finland's Consumption Price Index. *Bank of Finland Monthly Bulletin* 10: 1–8.

Triplett, Jack E. 1983. Concepts of Quality in Input and Output Price Measures: A

Resolution of the User Value-Resource Cost Debate. In *The U.S. National Income and Product Accounts: Selected Topics,* ed. Murray F. Foss, 296–311. NBER Studies in Income and Wealth, vol. 47. Chicago: University of Chicago Press.

———. 1987. Hedonic Functions and Hedonic Indexes. In *The New Palgrave Dictionary of Economics,* ed. John Eatwell, Murray Milgate, and Peter Newman, 2:630–34. New York: Macmillan.

———. 1989. Price and Technological Change in a Capital Good: A Survey of Research on Computers. In *Technology and Capital Formation,* ed. Dale W. Jorgenson and Ralph Landau, 127–313. Cambridge, Mass.: MIT Press.

U.S. Department of Commerce, Bureau of Economic Analysis. 1974. Revised Deflators for New Construction, 1947–73. *Survey of Current Business* 54, no. 8 (August): 18–27.

———. 1987. *Fixed Reproducible Tangible Wealth in the United States, 1925–85.* Government Printing Office, Washington, D.C. (June).

U.S. Department of Labor, Bureau of Labor Statistics. 1983. *Trends in Multifactor Productivity, 1948–81.* Bulletin no. 2178. Government Printing Office, Washington, D.C. (September).

U.S. Department of the Treasury, Bureau of Internal Revenue. 1942. *Bulletin "F": Income Tax, Depreciation, and Obsolescence, Estimated Useful Lives and Depreciation Rates.* Government Printing Office, Washington, D.C. (rev. January).

Winfrey, Robley. 1935. *Statistical Analyses of Industrial Property Retirement.* Bulletin no. 125. Iowa State College, Iowa Engineering Experiment Station, Ames Iowa (December).

Young, Allan H., and John C. Musgrave. 1980. Estimation of Capital Stock in the United States. In *The Measurement of Capital.* ed. Dan Usher, 23–58. NBER Studies in Income and Wealth, vol. 45. Chicago: University of Chicago Press.

Comment Ernst R. Berndt

As a young economist just out of graduate school, I once had the privilege of listening to an exchange among three very wise men (given the age distribution of participants at this Conference on Research in Income and Wealth jubilee, you can understand why I refrain from calling them old, wise men)—Dale Jorgenson, Zvi Griliches, and Larry Lau. Based on his recently completed research that utilized sophisticated econometric estimation techniques, flexible functional forms, and the theoretical rigor provided by the notions of functional separability and consistent aggregation, Dale Jorgenson provocatively summarized his findings by saying something to the effect that "I do not believe value added exists." Looking toward Dale's bookshelf containing works by John Kendrick, Jack Faucett, Ed Denison, and others, Zvi Griliches scratched his beard and responded, "Of course value added exists. There's a whole set of value added measures on that bookshelf." And Larry Lau smiled. For me, this was heady stuff—measuring something that does not exist.

Ernst R. Berndt is professor of applied economics at the Massachusetts Institute of Technology and a research associate at the National Bureau of Economic Research.

Today, on the occasion of the fiftieth anniversary of the Conference on Research in Income and Wealth, (CRIW), I have a sense of déjà vu from that meeting in the old Harvard economics building at 1737 Cambridge Street, for I am obliged to present and discuss Chuck Hulten's paper on the measurement of capital input—How does one measure something that may not "exist"?

Now a wise man as well, Hulten begins his paper by acknowledging the tension between theory and practice when it comes to capital measurement, even opening with a celebrated quote from Sir John Hicks, "The measurement of capital is one of the nastiest jobs that economists have set to statisticians." In terms of theoretical criteria, there certainly is good reason to believe that the theoretical conditions required for a consistent aggregate measure of capital input to exist are not in fact satisfied. Dale Jorgenson's point—that value added does not exist—very likely carries over to capital input in the same way. But Zvi Griliches is also right. Come hell or high water, many of us will be using and/or producing measures of aggregate capital input, even if it does not "exist."

Appropriately, Hulten's paper reflects this ambiguity and tension—he seeks to inform us about how in practice we might best measure capital input, recognizing that compromises must be made and that approximation must be employed. Let me stress that this is not being intellectually dishonest—it is not an Easterner attempting to grapple with a mystical notion imported from California, nor for that matter is it Donald Regan groping with Nancy Reagan's astrology; in fact, how one measures capital is a very serious practical problem. Over the years, Hulten has thought about this issue from several vantages: as an academic theorist, as an econometrician measuring depreciation profiles, and as an employee of the government statistical establishment. It is fitting that he author this paper.

Before summarizing this paper, I believe it is useful to think of the purposes for which measures of capital input are employed. While there may be numerous others, three come to mind immediately. First, capital input measures have often been used to help explain and predict *investment* in producers' durable equipment and nonresidential structures. A rather simple and time-honored framework, for example, is that of the form

$$I_t = \lambda(K_t^* - K_t),$$

where current period net investment is a proportion λ (perhaps, λ_t) of the "gap" between "desired" or long-run equilibrium capital stock K_t^* and the actual beginning of time period capital stock K_t. Measures of capital stock, and of the estimated capital stock gap, are used to help explain net investment.

Second, capital input measures have been used by some to measure *productive capacity,* or potential output, say, y_t^*. In one well-known procedure, for example, the optimal capital-output ratio is $g = K_t/y_t^*$; given estimates of K_t and g (or, perhaps, g_t), potential or capacity output y_t^* is computed as $y_t^* = K_t/g$, and then actual output y_t is compared to capacity output y_t^* to obtain a measure of capacity utilization. In short, capital stock measures are often used to measure potential or capacity output, as well as capacity utilization.

Third, capital is but one of many inputs, and measures of capital input are required if one wants to measure *multifactor productivity growth* (MFP). Specifically, a common procedure for calculating MFP growth is

$$MFP_{growth} = \dot{y}/y - \dot{x}/x,$$

where $\dot{y}/y$ is growth in output and $\dot{x}/x$ is growth in aggregate input, which in turn is typically a share-weighted sum of growth in each of the X_i inputs, including capital, that is,

$$\dot{x}/x = \Sigma_i\, s_i\, (\dot{x}_i/x_i),$$

where s_i is the cost share and $\dot{x}_i/x_i$ is the rate of growth of the *i*th input. One point I will want to stress in my remarks here is that I believe the best way to measure and, especially, to weight capital input depends in large part on which of these three applications one has in mind. More on this later.

The first part of Hulten's paper provides an overview of applied capital theory and contains six sections. Hulten begins by noting that what makes capital measurement different is not just that capital is durable (for so, too, is labor input), but most transactions between the owner of capital and the user of capital input are implicit, and thus there is a paucity of data concerning explicit market prices and quantities for capital inputs. These measures must therefore instead be inferred.

In section 4.1.1, Hulten shows that even when capital goods are homogeneous in nature, they must be distinguished by vintage, and it must further be recognized that the differing vintages of surviving capital have varying marginal products. This leads to an aggregate capital stock over vintages, measured in efficiency units, computed as in the *perpetual inventory* relation,

$$K_t = \phi_0 I_t + \phi_1 I_{t-1} + \ldots + \phi_T I_{t-T},$$

where the efficiency weights are in the range $0 \leq \phi_t \leq 1$ and I_{t-T} is the oldest surviving vintage of capital, originally acquired as a new investment in time period $t - T$. This first section then concludes with a brief review of the separability assumptions required for the existence of an aggregate of homogenous capital over vintages.

In section 4.1.2, Hulten considers the ϕ_t weights in greater detail, weights that are necessary for computing K_t using the perpetual inventory method. Here he distinguishes three forms of decay: the "one-hoss shay" efficiency profile of, say, a light bulb, where

$$\phi_0 = \phi_1 = \ldots = \phi_{T-1} = 1, \phi_{t+\tau} = 0, \quad \tau = 0, 1, 2, \ldots,$$

from straight-line decay, where

$$\phi_0 = 1, \phi_1 = 1-(1/T), \phi_2 = 1-(2/T), \ldots, \quad \phi_{T-1} = 1 - (T-1)/T,$$

and

$$\phi_{T+\tau} = 0, \quad \tau = 0, 1, 2, \ldots,$$

and geometric or constant exponential decay, where

$$\phi_0 = 1, \phi_1 = (1-\delta), \phi_2 = (1-\delta)^2, \ldots, \phi_t = (1-\delta)^t,$$

where δ is the constant rate of physical deterioration.

Because it is so convenient analytically, the geometric form of decay is very widely used, but, as Hulten notes, geometric decay implies a very rapid loss of efficiency in the early years of the life of an asset, a decay so rapid that many think it implausible.

One remark worth making here is that although Hulten acknowledges that the asset life T may not be fixed, in practice T is measured by the mere passage of time and not by the cumulative hours the asset has been utilized over its life; unless one assumes constant utilization rates over time, T and cumulative utilization can differ. For example, following the fuel price shocks of 1973–74 and 1979–80, American car owners reduced considerably the total miles driven per year, from over 10,000 to a bit more than 9,000, that is, annual utilization rates fell. Since on average cars were still being scrapped after about 100,000 cumulative miles, the average lifetime T at which cars were scrapped *increased* as a result of the energy price shocks, even though total cumulative utilization at time of scrapping was essentially unaffected. I state this not only to highlight the fact that T may change and may be endogenous but, more important, to emphasize the distinction between lifetime measured as the passage of time versus lifetime measured as cumulative utilization. Incidentally, for several assets such as farm tractors and aircraft, data on cumulative utilization are available.

One very useful result that Hulten highlights is that because of varying vintage composition over time, the average efficiency function of an entire cohort can be quite different from the individual efficiency functions; while each asset in a stock cohort might, for example, follow the one-hoss shay form, the cohort as a whole can follow a rather different age-efficiency pattern. Some further analytical and simulation work on this topic seems warranted.

The other very useful discussion in this section is the one on net and gross capital stocks. This distinction is often confused in the literature, and Hulten's clear discussion is most welcome. It is worth noting, however, that the Ω weights of Hulten's equation (18) currently used by the BEA in forming their measure of gross capital are based on the Winfrey mortality distribution, originally published by Robert Winfrey at the Iowa Engineering Experiment Station in 1935. Although the July 1985 issue of the *Survey of Current Business* notes that these 1935 weights have been slightly revised, the Winfrey mortality distribution is critical to the practical construction of gross capital stocks. If one wants to assess this gross capital stock construction procedure, I believe one must confront the issue of how accurate are these mortality distribution tables today. Recall that the Winfrey distribution is even older than the Conference on Research in Income and Wealth.

The third section of Hulten's paper relates the value of an asset (the present value of its net quasi rents) to the age-efficiency profile, the ϕ_t's. This is a very important topic, and could involve a massive manuscript all by itself. Briefly, Hulten relates the value of an asset as it ages to its age-efficiency profile. The value implies a price—the asset price—whereas the latter, the age-efficiency profile, involves quantity flows. Although he and others have repeatedly pointed it out elsewhere, Hulten again stresses the frequently misunderstood point that only in the case of geometric decay does the age-price or the age-depreciation profile have the same shape as the age-efficiency profile. In particular, if deterioration is one-hoss shay, the age-price depreciation profile has a different shape; if deterioration is straight-line, then the age-price profile is not a straight line but instead is curvilinear.

There are many things that could be said here. Let me simply make three observations. The first is that Hulten himself has contributed significantly to deterioration-depreciation-efficiency profile measurement by using econometric techniques and estimating the shape of age-price profiles for various durable assets, based on used price data. I would like to see more of that research and, especially, see more of it embodied in our capital stock estimates.

Second, by stressing the fact that the value of an asset depends on the present value of its *expected* quasi rents, Hulten has brought us to the investment application of capital stock—one of the three applications I noted earlier. In this context, Hulten derives the one-period rental price of capital as, ignoring taxes for the moment, $P_K = (r + \delta)q_K - f(\dot{q}_K/q_K)$, where $f(\cdot)$ is the expected change in the asset price (expected capital gains). To me, this suggests that when measuring capital and capital rental prices for purposes of analyzing the investment decision, one must use ex ante expectations—both for interest or discount rates, and for capital gains. In particular, contrary to much literature, it does not make sense to use an ex post rate of return when doing ex ante investment analyses, unless one believes that all expectations are perfectly realized ex post.

Third, I do not think our applied community fully realizes just how precarious are the foundations to how one constructs a formula for the rental price of capital and, in particular, how one incorporates expectations. Though by far the most widely used, the seminal Hall-Jorgenson formula is but one of several different formulae that can be constructed, consistent with economic theory. On this matter, I recommend for useful reading the 1980 paper by W. Erwin Diewert, "Aggregation Problems in the Measurement of Capital," in the NBER volume edited by Dan Usher, and a 1989 empirical study by Mike Harper, David Wood, and me.

Let me next move on to section 4.1.4 of Hulten's paper, where he introduces heterogeneous capital, and then discusses aggregation. The aggregation that Hulten appears to consider here is that of aggregating heterogeneous capital stocks rather than heterogeneous capital service flows. Recall that in the late 1960s, Griliches, Denison, and Jorgenson were involved in a well-known debate that involved a number of measurement issues. One point stressed by Griliches and Jorgenson is that one should aggregate over flows, not stocks. Why? Since nonresidential structures, for example, are longer lived on average than producers' durable equipment, the amount of service flow derived per year from a $1 stock of equipment is larger than that from a $1 stock of structures. Since equipment investment has been growing more rapidly than that for structures, the aggregate of service flows has also been growing more rapidly than the aggregate equipment-structures stock. This change in the average "quality" of capital (as Griliches and Jorgenson called it) is important, both conceptually and empirically.

In the last section of the applied theory portion of this paper, Hulten considers several capital stock–capital service flow issues. To my taste, Hulten is a bit too willing to move from capacity to capital utilization. Going back to Cassell's work in 1937, one can define capacity utilization as the ratio of actual output to some capacity output (in Cassell's case, the output at which the short- and long-run average total cost curves are tangent). By contrast, capital utilization has been defined as the ratio of desired capital (given output quantity and input prices) to actual capital. As has been pointed out by, among others, Berndt and Fuss (1989), these two measures of utilization coincide only if there is but one fixed input (capital) and if production is characterized by constant returns to scale.

One point made by Hulten in this section is worth stressing, however. Specifically, if one wants to use a measure of capital to calculate actual multifactor productivity (MFP) growth (one of the three applications I mentioned earlier), then theory tells us quite clearly that we should weight the various traditionally measured capital inputs by their *realized* marginal products, not their *expected* marginal products. This means that in choosing capital service price weights, one should employ shadow values or ex post rates of return, and not the ex ante returns that are appropriate in the investment context. This illustrates the point I made earlier, that to some extent the appropriate measure of capital price and quantity depends on the particular application one has in mind.

Having considered these applied theory issues, in the second major portion of this paper Hulten briefly deals with practical problems in the measurement of capital. A number of important issues are addressed, including the importance of the so-called lemons problem. This is a very well-written discussion and will surely be of use to students using data on investment, investment good deflators, and capital stock constructs. Several issues not discussed here, however, include the following: How does one treat maintenance expenditures? Should they be expensed as primarily labor input or amortized as investment? If the latter, how should their age-efficiency pattern be formulated, over what lifetime? This could be particularly important in the construction of public sector capital stocks, such as those for highways and airports. Second, in terms of capital rental prices, which types of marginal or average tax rates should one employ? Does the choice depend on the application?

In summary, Hulten has written a very useful and readable paper on applied theory and practical issues in the measurement of capital. It is particularly appropriate for this conference, and it surely deserves a prominent place on the reading lists of our graduate courses in applied economics.

References

Berndt, Ernst R. and Melvyn A. Fuss. 1989. Economic Capacity Utilization and Productivity Measurement for Multiproduct Firms with Multiple Quasi-Fixed Inputs. NBER Working Paper no. 2932. Cambridge, Mass.: National Bureau of Economic Research, April.

Diewert, W. Erwin. 1980. Aggregation Problems in the Measurement of Capital. In *The Measurement of Capital,* ed. Dan Usher, 433–528. NBER Studies in Income and Wealth, vol. 45. Chicago: University of Chicago Press.

Harper, Michael J., Ernst R. Berndt, and David O. Wood. 1989. Rates of Return and Capital Aggregation Using Alternative Rental Prices. In *Technology and Capital Formation.* ed. Dale W. Jorgenson and Ralph Landau, pp. 331–72. Cambridge, Mass.: MIT Press.

5 Issues in the Measurement and Interpretation of Saving and Wealth

Michael J. Boskin

5.1 Introduction

The saving and wealth accumulation behavior of an economy reveal much about it, as they reflect preferences, incentives, institutions, and demographics. However, there are numerous measurement and interpretation issues surrounding data on, adjusted measures of, and empirical analyses about postwar U.S. saving and wealth. It is by now well known, and considered conventional wisdom, that the U.S. postwar saving rate is low by international standards and has fallen since the 1950s and 1960s. This "conventional wisdom" stems primarily from the traditional National Income and Product Account (NIPA) measures of gross and net private and national saving in the United States.

There are, however, other sources for measuring saving and reasons to believe the NIPA saving figures are the beginning, not the end, of the story. Serious conceptual and measurement issues, ranging from the comprehensiveness of the definition of saving to important details concerning deflators, as well as a host of other matters, remain unresolved. Since its inception, the Conference on Research on Income and Wealth has devoted a nontrivial fraction of its efforts to dealing with these and related issues, as have numerous other studies in the last decade, including some of my own, conducted by and for the National Bureau of Economic Research.

In the first three Conference on Research in Income and Wealth volumes, saving and wealth were prominent features. Issues I discuss below were discussed even then: the treatment of capital gains and losses in the NIPA, inflation and inventory valuation adjustments, real corporate profits. In volume 1,

Michael J. Boskin is professor of economics and director of the Center for Economic Policy Research at Stanford University, as well as a research associate with the National Bureau of Economic Research.

measuring national wealth, including valuation problems, government product; in volume 2, capital gains and alternative definitions of saving; in volume 3, alternative definitions and methods of measuring saving and its components. The talent mobilized to work on these issues in the 1930s was impressive, and included Simon Kuznets, Raymond Goldsmith, Milton Friedman, Gottfried Haberler, and Solomon Fabricant, among many others.

Since a complete review of that literature would constitute a lengthy paper itself, suffice it to say that a recent Conference on Research in Income and Wealth was devoted to issues in measuring saving and investment. The conference volume (Lipsey and Tice 1989) contains a large number of important, novel, and useful papers, many of which contain partial surveys of their respective subfields within the general area of study.

The most famous book ever written in economics, Adam Smith's *Wealth of Nations,* did not come by its title as a matter of coincidence. For 200 years, issues concerning the measurement of, positive analysis of, and normative prescriptions for increasing, national wealth have been an important component of the economics profession.

These concerns about the economic costs and benefits of saving also have an interesting and checkered history (see Klein 1986). Polonius's advice was, "Neither a borrower nor a lender be." Benjamin Franklin's quip that "a penny saved is a penny earned" is perhaps the most often-quoted schoolboy maxim concerning the benefits of thrift, but in the middle third of this century, it gave way to the Keynesian notion that spending might be insufficient to support full employment. Keynes and the postwar stagnationists were deeply concerned that insufficient spending would lead to chronic and massive unemployment, so they argued for policies designed to soak up excess saving. While it is not my purpose here to present my own or a summary of other views concerning this Keynesian proposition, suffice it to say that the force of that argument has been mitigated considerably by recent analytical and empirical research in economics, and that at best, it is a weak and temporary proposition.

It is obvious, however, that we could save too much. In order to save more, we must forgo current consumption. Therefore, individuals and societies must somehow balance the benefits of increased consumption in the future against the cost of forgone consumption opportunities today. To show how we have come full circle, the current chairman of the Federal Reserve Board, Allan Greenspan, has been calling for the federal government to run a budget surplus on average, primarily to compensate for what he regards as a chronically low saving rate.

That we save too little as a nation appears to be a widespread view among economists. Some refer to the apparent (usually measured by the NIPA saving figures) historical decline in the saving rate, as well as the better aggregate performance of the U.S. economy in the 1950s and 1960s than subsequently. Whether the low saving rate is a cause of the subsequent deterioration of the economy's performance or an effect thereof, or both, is generally left unspecified.

Others bemoan the low U.S. saving rate relative to other countries. It is clear that saving in the United States, as conventionally measured, is below that of other advanced economies. While I will discuss extended measures of saving that suggest that the traditional measures probably overstate this difference, it is still substantial. When I was a graduate student, it was common to argue that it was reasonable for the United States to have a much lower saving rate than other economies because we were so much richer than they, and they were saving rapidly to try to catch up and to finance the rebuilding of their infrastructure after the devastation from World War II (although the fact that this was still going on in the 1970s suggests convenient arguments die slowly). The rate of growth of GNP in many of these other economies exceeded that of the United States and our lower saving and investment rates were often singled out for a nontrivial share of the blame.

Recently, a new argument has claimed that the major problem with our low private and even lower national saving rate is that it falls substantially below our rate of net investment. The low investment rate is assumed to be one cause of slow productivity growth and is itself substantially below the investment rates of most other advanced economies. We appear to be unwilling to see the investment rate fall to the still lower rate of net national saving. This leads us to rely on historically large imports of foreign capital to finance a substantial fraction of our net investment and a modest fraction of our gross investment. If this continues for very long, it would imply an explosive growth of external debt and concomitant adjustment problems later on.

My own view of the relationship of domestic saving and investment is that they are indeed *eventually* linked. In the short and medium run, there is no necessary tie between domestic investment and saving, as capital is internationally quite mobile, at least over a modest fraction of the saving of any society. Eventually, however, an advanced economy such as the United States will need to finance its own domestic investment. This implies that, in the long run, domestic investment will be constrained by the available supply of private saving, an event that gives some force to the concern about an apparently low private-saving rate.

There is thus ample reason to be concerned about the measurement, interpretation, evolution, and analysis of saving and wealth in the postwar United States. Saving behavior may well be linked to our long-term growth as well as potentially to our short-run stability. As interesting as these analytical and empirical issues are (see Boskin 1988 and Bernheim 1987 for a discussion of some of these issues), my goal here is much more modest. Having raised these issues, I present a brief survey of some important issues in the definition and measurement of saving. I also present some selected recent results, identify some substantial progress made, and present some suggestions for future avenues of research. I do not have the time or space, nor is it my comparative advantage given the other participants and papers in this conference and previous conferences on income and wealth, to go into great technical detail concerning many of the issues raised. For that, the interested reader is referred to some references.

To this end, section 5.2 discusses definitions, measures, and sources of information concerning saving and wealth and their relationship to theories of saving and consumption. It briefly mentions some of the potential problems, such as sampling error, measurement error, and various data sources. After a brief discussion of the NIPA saving figures, the Federal Reserve Flow of Funds, household surveys, and the estate tax data, it turns to the definition of saving for an individual, a sector, and a nation. It discusses the Keynesian emphasis on short-run flows; the life cycle/permanent income view attempting to distinguish transitory and permanent components on the one hand, or the need to develop household age- or cohort-specific balance sheets combined with demographic information on the other; the Ricardian equivalence intergenerational altruism view that only aggregate resources matter for consumption and that the distribution of resources (conditional on the level) does not affect aggregate consumption and hence age-specific balance sheets would be beside the point.

Various well-known conceptual problems with the NIPA and the Flow of Funds are discussed, such as the failure of the NIPA to measure capital gains and losses, and so on. Issues such as the measurement and valuation of human wealth and changes therein, including the valuation of human and nonhuman wealth in a world of incomplete markets, appropriate deflators, inflation adjustment, cost-of-living indices, and so on, are discussed. A comparison of the traditional NIPA saving measures with those from the Federal Reserve Flow of Funds is presented, as are new, more comprehensive extentions of the NIPA saving data that incorporate net saving in government capital and consumer durables. These comparisons are interesting and informative, although I make no pretense of delving deeply into reasons for the differences (see Wilson et al. 1989 for a discussion thereof). They reveal a somewhat more complete story concerning the evolution of private and national saving and wealth than has heretofore been available. They suggest that more comprehensive measures of saving reveal substantially higher net saving rates in the United States than those found in the traditional NIPA estimates, but they reinforce the view that the saving rate, though higher, has fallen, as has the rate of wealth accumulation.

Section 5.3 discusses aggregation and disaggregation. Various theories of private behavior and the nature of credit markets suggest alternative views of the propriety of aggregating and disaggregating saving and wealth data by sector (household, business, government), by age, or other characteristics of households, by type of asset or liability, and so on. For example, what has come to be called Denison's law has led many people to suggest that gross private saving is the most appropriate variable to analyze for the economy, as households see through the corporate veil. I have elsewhere argued that both the gross and net numbers should be examined and that there is little stability in the net private saving rate. An asymmetric information model of the capital market which led to credit rationing would require a distinction between household saving and business saving, as the internal cost of funds to a firm would be less than external financing (see Stiglitz and Weiss 1981). Various assets and liabilities have different liquidity, risk, expected duration, and so on. These may also be important for analyzing the performance of the economy.

I also make a brief reference to my own work, with Lawrence Lau, that suggests the potential importance of taking extreme care in analyzing aggregation issues for U.S. saving.

Section 5.4 turns to some specific issues. First, I turn to consumer durables and present augmented NIPA figures, including durable purchases as saving and the rental flow from the stock of durables as consumption and income. I also mention government capital, including government tangible capital, government lending, government contingent and potential liabilities, and so on. Adjusted or augmented NIPA-type saving rates are also presented, including consumer durables and various components of government net capital formation. A comparison is made to Japan in order to highlight the potential importance such adjustments make in international comparisons of saving rates.

I also discuss education and human capital, pension and Social Security wealth, estimates of income and its components, revaluations of financial assets and liabilities due to interest rate changes or other factors, and inflation adjustment, as well as saving by Americans abroad.

For these items, I simply raise the issues surrounding them and, including them in an augmented, more comprehensive measure of saving, discuss their rough orders of magnitude and how they might affect the evolution of the saving rate in the United States and its comparisons with other countries.

Finally, in section 5.5 I conclude that we have come some distance to a better understanding of saving and wealth. I conclude that no single theory—Keynesian, permanent income, pure life cycle with no bequest motive or intergenerational altruism—is sufficient by itself to explain aggregate saving in the United States. While each of these models of saving behavior lend important insights and contain some elements of truth, none are sufficient by themselves, and all are strongly rejected in aggregate data.

We have also come a substantial way toward refining some of the adjustments to saving and wealth estimates that a more comprehensive definition of saving would entail, and the interpretation of these data depends heavily upon one's model of the economy. No one number will be the answer to all questions. For example, while many of the adjustments, such as that for consumer durables, would raise the U.S. private saving rate, there would also be a corresponding entry on the investment side, and that would do nothing to redress the shortfall of saving relative to domestic investment that necessitates capital imports. We may be somewhat less anxious about the rate that Americans are acquiring claims to assets, but other concerns remain. Capital gains and losses, such as those in the stock market, may partly explain swings in the traditional NIPA saving measures, both because consumption and saving are affected by changes in wealth and because of the institutional features of pension funds, the majority of which are of the defined-benefit type in the United States. This in turn implies that large swings in the stock market (and/or major changes in interest rates) will substantially change contributions to these pension funds and hence personal saving (Bernheim and Shoven 1988).

My penultimate conclusion is that the United States still has a low rate of saving (although not nearly so low as the traditional NIPA measure would reveal) and a low rate of wealth creation. We start from a high level of wealth but, on a per capita, or perhaps more important, per worker basis, the rate of wealth accumulation has slowed substantially. While saving in the United States takes on a somewhat different composition than saving in other countries, we are only beginning to understand not just how to measure it but also the implications thereof, and the policies and other factors that affect that composition. For all the advances made and the insights gained, there is still a substantial shortfall of national saving relative to domestic investment.

5.2 Definitions, Measures, Sources

The potential data on saving and wealth come from several, potentially complementary, sources. The three generic types of data used are the aggregate data from the National Income and Product Accounts (NIPA), the data from the Federal Reserve Flow of Funds, and household survey data. In addition, some information on wealth and its distribution has been derived from estate tax returns, usually federal but also state. The latter are particularly useful in dealing with a truncated sample of the upper tail of the wealth distribution. The relative advantages and disadvantages of household survey data with respect to the NIPA and Flow of Funds data have been discussed in detail in several other studies (see, e.g., Curtin, Juster, and Morgan 1989). Annual surveys chronically underestimate wealth and property income. While important advances have been made in attempting to aggregate up from household data, the quality, measurement error, sampling error, and other concerns are nontrivial. Further, to measure saving from household surveys, one would not generally be able to get an accurate measure of both income and total spending in order to get at saving by subtraction, and while surveys of saving behavior are more common in some other countries (e.g., the annual Family Saving Survey and Family Income and Expenditure Survey in Japan) than in the United States, there are several surveys in which it is possible to analyze data on the same households at two different points in time and thereby attempt to create balance sheets at those two points in time and to difference them to get a measure of saving or dissaving.

Another issue is the gray area between the business sector and the household sector in which substantial saving occurs—nonprofits, trusts, pensions, and other vehicles that may be either excluded from household surveys or in which individual responses may be subject to considerable error (e.g., accrued net saving in life insurance). Important recent data from the 1983 Survey of Consumer Finances, the 1984 Wealth Supplement to the Panel Study of Income Dynamics, and the 1984 Wealth Supplement to the Survey of Income and Program Participation are all fruitful data sources.

Numerous other household surveys contain substantial information on property income, and the question arises as to how to aggregate it to the presumably more accurate national control totals such as those in the National Income and Product Accounts, and then to capitalize them or to translate them into asset values. This is most easily done for interest-bearing assets of a fixed duration, and much more difficult to do for other types of assets and liabilities. Many of the recent studies of the dissaving behavior of the elderly (e.g., Hurd 1987; Bernheim 1984; Diamond and Hausman 1984; and others) attempt to make the best use possible of such household survey data. I shall say no more about this source of information other than that it is an important additional source that can be integrated with aggregate data on the one hand, and then disaggregated to provide details on distributions and characteristics that may be of great interest.

Before turning to NIPA and Flow of Funds saving estimates and the corresponding wealth estimates from the Flow of Funds, a few words concerning theories of saving and consumption and what sorts of data are consistent or inconsistent with them are in order.

The three leading theories of saving/consumption behavior are Keynesian (KN), life cycle/permanent income hypotheses (LCH/PIH), and intergenerational altruism (IGA). The Keynesian predilection to focus on short-run cash flows generally ignores capital gains and losses as components of income and focuses on the flow of saving out of current disposable income. In contrast, the permanent income hypothesis attempts to disentangle permanent from transitory components and has vastly different predictions concerning the response of saving to permanent and transitory components of income (including transitory components due to fiscal policy changes). It is important to note that the life-cycle hypothesis suggests that the marginal propensity to save depends upon age and that demographics are important. This leads immediately to going beyond aggregate saving data to attempt to analyze the effects of the age distribution of the population or resources on saving and suggests the calculation of age or cohort-specific balance sheets and saving rates may be quite useful in the analysis of trends in saving behavior and their responses to various policy experiments.

In sharp contrast to the LCH stands the strong implication of intergenerational altruism that aggregate consumption depends only on aggregate resources, not on their distribution across generations. Age-specific policies should have no impact on aggregate consumption and *national* saving, as private saving will adjust to public saving or dissaving. The potential usefulness of household balance sheets and age-specific saving rates for analyzing saving and its reaction to policy experiments is useful only in the context of testing Ricardian equivalence/intergenerational altruism. If one accepts the strong tenets of Ricardian equivalence, the usefulness of the data disaggregated by age disappears. In Boskin and Kotlikoff (1985), we build a finite approximation to an intergenerationally altruistic infinitely lived optimal consumption program and test whether the age distribution of resources affects consumption, given the aggregate level of resources. We reject this implication of Ricardian equivalence based on postwar U.S. time-series data. In Boskin and Lau (1988), we develop age- and cohort-specific balance sheets by combining Current Population Survey data on the age distribution of income with more usual aggregate variables. We estimate an economically important and statistically significant effect of the age distribution of human and nonhuman wealth on the share of aggregate wealth consumed. We also estimate a large, statistically significant generation effect: households headed by persons born since 1939 consume a larger share of their wealth than those born prior to 1939, at the same age. The strong implication of Ricardian equivalence is rejected.

Most aggregate time-series studies reject the simple Keynesian specification of consumption and suggest that there is tax discounting, or at least a large fraction of the population is forward looking and maximizing over a longer time horizon than the typical Keynesian short-run flows. For example, Hall and Mishkin (1982) conclude that about four-fifths of consumers could be modeled as if they are maximizing over a long time horizon, whereas one-fifth could not.

Studies of the dissaving behavior of the elderly have generally concluded that the strictest version of the LCH, an expected average propensity to consume over the lifetime of one, is inconsistent with the observed behavior, although Hurd (1987) presents data that are consistent with the LCH.

My own conclusion is that no single model of saving and consumption behavior is sufficient to explain aggregate saving fully. All of the theories are rejected in studies based on aggregate time-series data, and some are usually rejected in other studies. There appears to be substantial heterogeneity among consumers. This heterogeneity may be a function of age, income, and desired consumption profiles leading to liquidity constraints or a host of social, psychological, environmental, historical, and economic variables. I believe that there is now strong evidence that the age distribution of resources, given their aggregate level, affects aggregate consumption, and therefore there is some potential gain in attempting to integrate microeconomic (hopefully longitudinal) survey data on the distribution of resources by characteristics of households with aggregate data.

Saving is usually defined as forgoing current consumption and providing funds either directly or indirectly to capital markets to channel into productive investment, whether in tangible, financial, or human capital. It is a neat concept, but there are an inordinate number of difficulties in measuring it.

Let us start with the most basic definition that saving in period t, S_t, is equal to income minus consumption in that period, Y_t and C_t. Or,

$$(1) \qquad S_t = Y_t - C_t.$$

Hence, saving will equal investment ex post. From the Haig-Simon's definition of income,

$$(2) \qquad Y_t = C_t + (W_t - W_{t-1}) \, ,$$

income is the sum of consumption plus the change in net worth, the difference is the change in the value of assets and of liabilities. Therefore,

$$(3) \qquad S = W_t - W_{t-1} \, ,$$

or saving equals the change in net worth. The problem in measuring saving (and, when we integrate saving over a period of time, wealth) stem from difficulties in measuring Y, C, and W_t and W_{t-1}.

It is worth mentioning that so prominent an economist as Larry Klein (1986) has argued that "the importance of saving tends to be understated if we treat it as a mere residual." Klein emphasizes that households make genuine decisions about most asset and liability changes, whereas the residual concept was popularized from the Depression mentality as a typical representation of personal saving.

First, houschold saving in our national accounts is estimated as a residual, after subtracting consumer expenditures, taxes, and interest payments to business from estimated personal income. The measurement errors in these components (each of which is potentially quite large relative to net saving), will show up dollar for dollar in net saving. Suppose, heroically, that we have a good estimate of income. Then errors in the measurement of consumption that may be quite small relative to consumption translate into larger percentage errors in the measure of saving, which is much smaller. I consider this to be a problem, but much less of a problem than measuring income. Suppose we measure consumption properly, but mismeasure, say underestimate, income. Then in general, saving will be underestimated dollar for dollar. Again, I consider this to be an extremely important issue, perhaps the most important one. Numerous studies suggest that income is substantially underestimated in the national income accounts. The BEA makes an adjustment to personal income related, apparently, to IRS estimates of underreported adjusted gross income. While the range of estimates of this underestimation is substantial (see Feige 1983), I believe it is not trivial.

One extreme set of estimates based on a transactions methodology (Feige 1983) estimates that while unrecorded income was trivial in the 1950s and 1960s, by the late 1970s and early 1980s it amounted to 40% of the GNP. An unrecorded income which was primarily saved of even one-tenth this size would raise the net private saving rate by 80%, from 5% to 9% of the GNP. If net private saving runs about $250 billion per year, and gross private saving about $600 or $700 billion per year, an underestimate of income by a few percentage points will lead to a serious underestimate of saving. A related problem may be the understatement of the income earned and saving done abroad.

What are the likely reasons for underestimating income? A good discussion of some of these issues is presented in Holloway (1989); it includes where one draws the boundary in the GNP accounts (e.g., placing emphasis on market transactions with only a few imputations, excluding illegal activity, excluding capital gains, to which we will return below). Much has been made recently of the underground economy, and estimates of the size of the underground economy vary by two orders of magnitude (see Feige 1983). This includes illegal activity and activity that is deliberately unreported, usually for tax reasons, such as cash payments for services that go unreported. To the extent that personal income is seriously understated, we would expect the degree of underreporting to be positively correlated with marginal effective tax rates. Barro and Sahasakul (1983) estimate that the fraction of U.S. households subject to high marginal tax rates quadrupled between 1965 and 1980. While marginal tax rates have come down some since then, this suggests that by the late 1970s and early 1980s the underreporting of personal income had probably grown substantially.

But is personal income that underreported? Since consumption is two-thirds of income, and is estimated from transactions, some of the income that is unreported for tax purposes does show up in transactions, eventually working its way back into the income figures.

Still, the net degree of underreporting of personal income is a source of some concern, especially since there is reason to believe that it has grown substantially over precisely the period in which there is great concern about the fall in the saving rate. Finally, a word should be said about international comparisons. Since U.S. marginal tax rates are now much lower than those in most other advanced economies, we would expect the degree of underreporting and the underground economy to be somewhat less in the United States than in these countries. But this is only conjecture, for this will reflect social attitudes, the nature and resources devoted to tax enforcement, and so on, and on this I believe we have little evidence. In any event, I believe it is a fruitful area for future research. As already noted, the NIPA measure of saving excludes net capital gains or losses in its measure of saving, as in its measure of income.

A third problem is the treatment of expenditures on consumer durables as consumption rather than as saving. Finally, the treatment of government saving or dissaving in the U.S. NIPA is a rather mechanical reporting of the budgetary position, with no attempt to develop a separate capital account on the expenditure side for government units in reporting a surplus or deficit on current operating accounts (see Boskin 1982). The federal government's own budget suffers from this difficulty, but the Department of Commerce does attempt to estimate government capital stocks, investment, and depreciation. We will return to these two issues in section 5.4 below.

Let us turn to the NIPA saving figures for the United States. Table 5.1 presents estimates of gross and net national saving and their components in the United States, 1951–87. Net saving is decomposed into private saving, the state and local government surplus, and the federal government surplus. Private saving, in turn, is decomposed into personal and corporate saving. Numerous conjectures have been made concerning whether the appropriate rate to study is net or gross, private or total, or disaggregated personal and corporate saving. For example, David and Scadding (1974) find that the gross private saving rate at full employment is remarkably constant, reinforcing the finding of Denison (1958). They infer from this that households see through the corporate veil and that movements between personal and corporate saving reflect various factors such as changes in the relative tax advantages of the two forms of saving. However, they strongly reject the ultra-rationality argument that households see through the government veil, an argument associated with Martin Baily (1962) and Robert Barro (1974).

Recent theoretical work on credit markets (e.g., Stiglitz and Weiss 1981) suggests that maintaining the distinction between household and corporate saving may be quite important. Asymmetric information may lead to a situa-

able 5.1 U.S. Gross and Net Saving, 1951–87

	1951–60	1961–70	1971–80	1981	1982	1983	1984	1985	1986	1987
otal net saving:	7.1	7.8	7.0	5.7	2.0	2.0	4.1	2.3	1.8	1.9
Net private saving:	7.5	8.2	8.0	6.6	5.5	5.7	6.8	5.7	5.3	4.3
Personal saving	4.7	4.8	5.5	5.2	4.9	3.8	4.4	3.2	3.1	2.7
Corporate saving	2.8	3.4	2.4	1.4	.6	1.9	2.5	2.5	2.2	1.7
State & local government surplus	−.2	.1	.9	1.1	1.1	1.4	1.7	1.6	1.3	1.0
Federal government surplus	−.2	−.5	−1.8	−2.1	−4.6	−5.2	−4.5	−4.9	−4.8	−3.4
Memoranda: capital consumption	8.7	8.4	9.8	11.4	12.1	11.6	11.0	10.9	10.8	10.7
Gross private saving	16.2	16.6	17.8	18.0	17.6	17.4	17.9	16.6	16.1	15.0

urce: U.S. Department of Commerce, National Income and Product Accounts.
tes: Data are averages (except for 1981–87) of annual flow, as percentages of GNP.
tail may not add to totals because of rounding. 1987 figures are preliminary.

tion where the cost of internal funds is substantially below the cost of external funds, and therefore corporate cash flow may be an important separate determinant of business investment, a result consistent with investment equations in many large macroeconometric models. If this is the case, it may be important for some purposes not to aggregate private saving.

Further, focusing on gross saving and its apparent stability—although it has not been as stable through 1987—seems odd since virtually all theories are in terms of how households, firms, and even governments wish to form their *net* wealth position. In brief, any rationality hypothesis seems somewhat out of balance if it ignores the fact that depreciation is estimable. There is much less stability in the net private saving rate and in the net national saving rate than in the corresponding gross figures.

The most important items to note in table 5.1 are the levels of gross and net saving, which are low relative to that of other societies (see Blades and Sturm 1982) and the substantial decline in the net private saving rate, and especially the net national saving rate in the 1980s relative to the 1950s, 1960s, and 1970s. These data undoubtedly form the most important basis for concern over the level and trend in private and national saving in the United States.

As noted above in equation (3), saving can also be defined as the change in net worth. An alternative approach to measuring saving may be obtained from estimates of sectoral and national net worth through time. The Federal Reserve's year-end balance sheets for the U.S. economy provide just such a source of data. Recall that the NIPA saving and income measures exclude capital gains and losses. These are, in principle, captured by the Federal Reserve's balance sheets, which should also reflect some wealth accumulated in the underground economy. The Flow of Funds data have their own problems, both internally and relative to household surveys and the NIPAs (see, e.g., Curtin, Juster, and Morgan 1989; and Wilson et al. 1989). Among the more important are that bonds are carried at par (in recent years, the changes in the value of bonds will not necessarily net internally given the increase in foreign holdings), and the rudimentary treatment of the government sector in the Flow of Funds—in particular, as with the NIPA, there is no attempt to estimate changes in the value and the imputed income from government tangible capital. (I ignore the even thornier problem of contingent and potential liabilities and intangible capital discussed below.) The Flow of Funds balance sheets, however, do attempt to record the current value of all assets and liabilities in the economy, such as owner-occupied housing, consumer durables, inventories, and depreciable plant and equipment. In principle, the FOF not only includes traditional gains and losses, but revaluations of real assets caused by depreciation, obsolescence, or other sources. For business tangible capital, the estimates are of the replacement cost, not the current market value. Hence, when Tobin's q diverges systematically from one, the Flow of Funds data may over- or understate the value of tangible business capital.

Saving can now be defined as the change in net worth. Because of inflation, with the net worth data as year-end figures, we need to estimate saving in current dollars as

$$S_t = NW_t - P_t/P_{t-1} \cdot NW_{t-1},$$

where P_t is an index of prices. Because these are end-of-year data. I use the December consumer price index. There are numerous reasons why other indices might be more appropriate, but it is much more difficult to obtain them on a year-end basis rather than quarterly or as an average over the year.

The Flow of Funds also presents considerable disaggregation with respect to the sector (e.g., households, nonfinancial corporations, government units, etc.) and type of assets and liabilities. I present in table 5.2 the private, public, and national saving rates as a percentage of GNP from the period 1948–87. These data reveal some interesting differences relative to the data in table 5.1. While they are usually substantially higher, they vary quite a bit more, and, as they reflect changes in asset values, they are even negative on occasion (e.g., see national saving in 1982 and 1985). Table 5.3 presents estimates on a decade-by-decade average basis for private, public, and national saving. The net private saving rate in the 1950s is more than 150% as large as that reported in the NIPA. In the 1960s, it is somewhat larger, although it had fallen somewhat relative to the 1950s. The net private saving rate from the Flow of Funds rebounds in the 1970s and again is more than one and one-half times that of the corresponding data from NIPA. The data for the first half of the 1980s from the Flow of Funds reveals the tremendous fall in both the private saving rate and the national saving rate. As table 5.3 reveals, the public saving rate was about zero in the 1950s, 1960s, and 1970s, as traditionally measured budget deficits in the 1970s were offset by accumulation of financial assets by the public sector. The net national saving rates, therefore, are almost identical with the net private saving rates and, again, are much larger than the NIPA numbers. Net national saving has fallen tremendously in the 1980s, as both net private saving has fallen and the public sector has turned into a dissaver, even when one accounts for its accumulation of financial assets (although not of tangible assets).

Let us now turn our attention to measures of wealth and the rate of growth of wealth. Table 5.4 presents estimates, derived from the Flow of Funds, of private, public, and national net worth in billions of constant 1982 dollars, for the period 1948–87. Recall that the public sector data include only financial assets,not tangible assets. These data suggest that private real net worth has more than tripled in the period 1948–87 and that national real net worth has almost quadrupled in the same period. On a per capita basis, real net worth has about doubled.

Table 5.5 presents estimates of the rate of growth of net worth (i.e., the rate of change of net worth, both private and national). This reflects the rate of private and national saving in the numerator, including revaluations, and the preexisting level of net worth in the denominator. While there is substantial

Table 5.2 **Sectoral Saving Rates (% of GNP)**

Year	Private	Public	National
1948	15.5	5.0	20.5
1949	23.9	−3.8	20.1
1950	6.6	6.7	13.3
1951	9.8	4.8	14.6
1952	15.2	−1.2	13.9
1953	12.1	−1.9	10.2
1954	15.8	−2.8	13.0
1955	20.0	.0	20.0
1956	15.6	1.7	17.3
1957	6.4	.9	7.3
1958	9.3	−2.6	6.7
1959	10.3	−.6	9.7
1960	7.3	.5	7.7
1961	9.1	−1.5	7.5
1962	8.5	−.9	7.6
1963	5.5	.2	5.7
1964	13.2	−.6	12.6
1965	10.8	.3	11.1
1966	14.2	.6	14.8
1967	9.6	−1.2	8.4
1968	12.0	.0	12.0
1969	5.1	1.6	6.7
1970	2.5	.1	2.7
1971	14.0	−2.0	12.1
1972	16.4	−.4	16.0
1973	11.2	2.3	13.5
1974	12.5	2.1	14.6
1975	9.3	−3.3	6.0
1976	20.1	−1.8	18.3
1977	19.6	−.1	19.4
1978	20.3	.7	21.0
1979	2.5	2.1	4.7
1980	2.5	.3	2.8
1981	9.6	−.4	9.2
1982	−5.3	−3.9	−9.2
1983	11.1	−4.4	6.6
1984	7.2	−3.3	3.9
1985	1.6	−3.6	−2.0
1986	16.2	−4.7	11.5
1987	5.9	−2.6	3.3

Source: Author's calculations from *National Balance Sheets*, Board of Governors of the Federal Reserve System.

Table 5.3 **Sectoral Average Saving Rates (% of GNP)**

Years	Private	Public	National
1951–60	12.2	−.1	12.0
1961–70	9.0	−.1	8.9
1971–80	12.8	.0	12.8
1981–87	6.5	−3.3	3.2

Source: Author's calculations.

year-to-year variation in both the private and national growth rates of net worth, it is clear that the rate of growth of real net worth in the U.S. economy has slowed substantially in the period 1979–87 relative to any other extended subperiod since World War II.

Perhaps the most serious omission from these measures of net worth is that they reflect only nonhuman capital. The capitalized value of expected future earnings, human wealth, is not included. There have been many attempts to estimate measures of human wealth, and/or to incorporate them in analyses of consumption and saving behavior (see, e.g., Boskin and Lau 1988; Jorgenson and Fraumeni 1989). There are many difficulties in obtaining such estimates, including capitalization rates, the appropriate expected earnings process for forecasts, questions of differential risk, discounting, liquidity, bequeathability, and so on. Roughly speaking, about three-quarters of national income is a return to labor; ignoring all these differences would suggest that about three-quarters of total wealth would be human wealth. Of course, mortality, disability, and similar probabilities must be added to discount rates on future earnings; among other concerns, there is differential taxation of different sources and uses of income (although these have declined with the new tax law). Human wealth must be estimated in more indirect ways than many components of nonhuman wealth whose asset values can be determined via the market.

Finally, in discussing definitions, measures, and data needs, it is important to realize that the economy changes. The pace at which we want to augment or update measures of saving and wealth, or reclassify items, and so on, depends heavily upon the purpose in generating the data in the first place.

5.3 Aggregation and Disaggregation

Discussed above was the issue of whether to combine the household and corporate sectors following Denison's law, as enunciated and reconfirmed (as of that time) by David and Scadding (1974) or, at the other extreme, whether to separate household and business saving because of credit rationing. Additional distinctions might be drawn on the type of assets and liabilities, for example, their liquidity properties, fixed costs in shifting in and out of them, their duration, and so forth. I might also mention that a strong Ricardian

Table 5.4 **Net Worth in Billions of 1982 Dollars**

Year	Private	Public	National
1948	3,906.1	−831.2	3,074.9
1949	4,167.0	−873.0	3,294.1
1950	4,241.8	−797.2	3,444.7
1951	4,362.9	−738.2	3,624.7
1952	4,558.3	−754.2	3,804.1
1953	4,721.8	−779.7	3,942.1
1954	4,936.4	−817.9	4,118.5
1955	5,231.2	−817.3	4,413.9
1956	5,467.1	−791.1	4,676.0
1957	5,566.3	−777.2	4,789.1
1958	5,709.8	−817.8	4,892.0
1959	5,879.9	−828.4	5,052.0
1960	6,002.4	−820.3	5,182.1
1961	6,160.1	−846.9	5,313.3
1962	6,316.7	−862.8	5,454.0
1963	6,422.6	−859.8	5,562.8
1964	6,691.4	−872.0	5,819.4
1965	6,925.6	−865.7	6,059.9
1966	7,251.1	−851.5	6,399.6
1967	7,475.8	−878.8	6,596.9
1968	7,770.4	−879.6	6,890.8
1969	7,896.7	−838.6	7,058.1
1970	7,959.8	−835.4	7,124.4
1971	8,327.2	−886.8	7,440.4
1972	8,784.4	−897.5	7,886.9
1973	9,106.8	−832.7	8,274.1
1974	9,452.8	−774.0	8,678.8
1975	9,714.2	−867.8	8,846.4
1976	10,315.9	−922.6	9,393.3
1977	10,927.8	−926.4	10,001.4
1978	11,586.4	−902.6	10,683.8
1979	11,667.1	−834.9	10,832.3
1980	11,745.9	−827.1	10,918.7
1981	12,050.6	−839.5	11,211.1
1982	11,883.4	−962.9	10,920.5
1983	12,246.2	−1,108.5	11,137.6
1984	12,496.9	−1,223.9	11,273.1
1985	12,553.9	−1,352.9	11,201.1
1986	13,158.9	−1,528.0	11,630.9
1987	13,382.8	−1,626.1	11,756.7

Source: Author's calculations from *National Balance Sheets,* Board of Governors of Federal Reserve.

might aggregate all resources, ignoring their age distribution, and, depending upon the view of the substitutability of public and private capital, might even aggregate private and public saving, and focus only on national saving, as changes in public saving or dissaving might be exactly offset according to the theory by private saving.

Table 5.5 **Rate of Growth of Net Worth (percentage points)**

Year	Private	National
1948	4.2	7.1
1949	6.3	6.7
1950	1.8	4.4
1951	2.8	5.0
1952	4.3	4.7
1953	3.5	3.5
1954	4.3	4.3
1955	5.6	6.7
1956	4.3	5.6
1957	1.8	2.4
1958	2.5	2.1
1959	2.9	3.2
1960	2.0	2.5
1961	2.6	2.5
1962	2.5	2.6
1963	1.6	2.0
1964	4.0	4.4
1965	3.4	4.0
1966	4.5	5.3
1967	3.0	3.0
1968	3.8	4.3
1969	1.6	2.4
1970	.8	.9
1971	4.4	4.2
1972	5.2	5.7
1973	3.5	4.7
1974	3.7	4.7
1975	2.7	1.9
1976	5.8	5.8
1977	5.6	6.1
1978	5.7	6.4
1979	.7	1.4
1980	.7	.8
1981	2.5	2.6
1982	−1.4	−2.7
1983	3.0	1.9
1984	2.0	1.2
1985	.5	−.6
1986	4.6	3.7
1987	1.7	1.1

Source: Author's calculations.

The purpose of this section is to highlight two other issues of aggregation. First, within the household sector there have been tremendous changes in household formation, dissolution, the age structure of households, average household size, life expectancy, and household composition. Particularly when we begin to analyze consumer durables, the value of housing, and life-cycle or age-specific balance sheet data, it is important to keep these changes in mind. For example, Boskin and Lau (1988) document that slightly more than half of the average annual percentage increase in real consumption in the period 1950–80 was due to the growth in the number of households as opposed to the annual percentage increase in real consumption per household.

Thus, one might wish to decompose changes in the aggregate saving rate into the sum of the rates of change per household and the rate of change in the number of households. We know, for example, that in equation (1)

$$S_t = \sum_i \sum_j S_{ijt},$$

where we index households of type i, age j in year t. The households might differ by size, asset values, net worth, or access to credit markets, family composition, and so forth; age may be important for life cycle or other reasons. We know from survey data that some households are saving and others dissaving and that the aggregate saving rate is the sum of these household-specific saving rates. Probing a little deeper, changes in saving caused, for example, by changes in an exogenous (to the household) variable z, we note that the elasticity of aggregate saving with respect to z is a weighted average of the percentage changes of the saving of the different household types with respect to the given percentage change of the variable for them, with the weights being the share (possibly negative) of aggregate saving accounted for by that type or, mathematically,

$$\frac{d \ln S_t}{d \ln z_t} = \frac{\sum_i \sum_j N_{ijt} S_{ijt} \dfrac{d \ln S_{ijt}}{d \ln z_t}}{\sum_i \sum_j N_{ijt} S_{ijt}},$$

where N_{ijt} refers to the number of households of type i and age j in year t and S_{ijt} to the saving or dissaving of a household of type i, age j, in year t.

Thus, analyses of aggregate saving must come to grips with the problems of aggregation to the extent that households are heterogeneous (see Jorgenson, Lau, and Stoker 1982; and Boskin and Lau 1988). Quite apart from Lucas-type critiques, analyses of the effects of various variables on aggregate saving may be quite misleading if the shares of saving, or of income and wealth, held by households of different types and ages change through time. We know, for example, there have been tremendous changes in the age distribution of income in the United States (see, e.g., Boskin, Kotlikoff and Knetter 1985). Perhaps the most important aspect of this change has been the tremendous increase in the relative economic well-being of the elderly, which some theories of saving suggest should be dissaving during retirement.

5.4 Some Specific Issues

The NIPA treat expenditures on consumer durables as consumption rather than as saving. Many have argued (and I have generally been sympathetic to the argument) that it would be preferable to treat expenditures on consumer durables and the imputed rental flow of the durables as consumption (see David and Scadding 1974; Boskin, Robinson, and Huber 1989; Holloway 1989; and Hendershott and Peek 1989, among others). Recall that estimates of the value of consumer durables are included conceptually in the Flow of Funds estimates. Various issues arise in valuing the services of consumer durables (Katz 1983). In table 5.6 I present NIPA saving rates augmented to include consumer durables for a few years. Note that this adds about 5 percentage points to the NIPA estimate of gross saving. Of course, as mentioned in the introduction, it would also be included on the investment side and does nothing for the shortfall of our domestic saving relative to our investment. U.S. citizens invest much more in consumer durables than persons in other societies. This undoubtedly reflects a number of factors, including the size of homes. The difference is particularly important relative to Japan, where the durables adjustment closes the saving rate differential substantially (see table 5.6 for some comparisons with Japan, including durables adjust-

able 5.6 **Augmented Saving Rates, United States and Japan, Selected Years,[a]**

	Exclude Government Nonmilitary Investment (NIPA Basis)	Include Government Nonmilitary Investment in Fixed Reproducible Capital (OECD Basis)	Include Government Nonmilitary Investment in Fixed Reproducible Capital & Consumer Durables	All Government Investment & Consumer Durables
.S. Gross Saving Rates (Gross National Saving/GNP):				
1950	17.8	20.3	24.7	23.9
1960	15.0	18.3	21.9	22.9
1970	13.8	16.8	21.3	21.8
1980	16.4	18.1	23.2	24.0
1985	13.8	15.5	22.2	24.3
.S. Net Saving Rates (Net National Saving/NNP):				
1950	11.7	13.2	14.6	11.8
1960	8.2	10.6	10.9	11.1
1970	6.2	8.2	8.8	8.7
1980	7.7	8.5	8.7	9.2
1985	4.7	5.5	7.0	8.8
panese Net Saving Rates:				
1970	22.8	30.9	31.6	31.7
1975	14.7	22.6	23.1	23.2
1980	13.2	21.1	21.6	21.7
1984	14.4	19.8	20.2	20.4

urces: United States: Boskin, Robinson, and Huber (1989); Japan: Boskin and Roberts (1986).
NP and NNP augmented to include corresponding rental flows.

ments and also government capital). It might well be useful for the BEA to supplement (*not* replace) the current saving data with such estimates for durables.

Government tangible capital, as well as contingent and potential liabilities, are also of potential importance. Governments in all countries own, use, and provide services from capital. Differences in the rates of growth of public capital and differences in levels across societies can lead to misconceptions about aggregate national well-being and aggregate saving rates. Of course, government saving and investment do not pass the same kind of market tests as private saving and investment. In Boskin, Robinson, and Huber (1989), new estimates of government saving, capital formation, and wealth for the United States in the period 1947–85 are estimated. Table 5.6 includes estimates of NIPA saving figures augmented to include net government saving in the form of nonmilitary capital and total capital. Again, the saving rate rises several percentage points, but recall that government capital depreciates and that our ability to estimate that depreciation is subject to even more difficulties than our ability to estimate the depreciation of private tangible assets. The comparison with Japan is instructive, since, as a percentage of GNP, government military capital formation in the United States is substantially larger, but total government capital formation is substantially smaller, than in Japan.

Revaluations of assets and liabilities are presumably captured approximately by market values and represented in the Flow of Funds. Obviously, they do not do so precisely. Estimated revaluations of tangible capital for the NIPA estimates would be adjusted upward, reflecting generally positive real revaluations. These are caused by a variety of factors, but especially by the decline in investment goods prices relative to the overall price level. Revaluations of financial assets and liabilities other than general real interest rate changes should net internally as one household's capital gain is another's capital loss or, conversely, between the public and private sectors. Of course, a general mood of pessimism or optimism tending to change the rate at which future incomes are discounted could cause a substantial overall revaluation. Further, to the extent that there are foreign holdings by Americans and holdings of U.S. assets by foreigners, the real revaluations will not necessarily cancel for the United States as a whole. Indeed, the saving abroad by U.S. citizens is quite difficult to measure.

I noted in the introduction and in section 5.2 that the measurement of income was undoubtedly a major issue in the measurement of saving. Underreporting and measurement errors play a role and are likely to change systematically over time. The measurement of real income is even more difficult. Distortions caused by inflation create difficulties in computing changes in real corporate balance sheets, as well as other components of income. It is beyond the scope of this paper to go into detail here, but not only is the measurement of real income tremendously difficult and important (especially for corporate profits) but an appropriate real cost-of-living index would include the price of future consumption in it, and this obviously varies with the ex ante expected real net (of taxes) rate of return, which has varied over time.

Human capital, whether in education, health, nutrition, and so on, has been discussed very briefly above. Clearly, the United States spends a much larger fraction of its GNP on education than most other societies. This is especially true for higher education. Difficulties of comparability, however, abound. It is alleged, for example, that students in the United Kingdom or Japan are much further along when they finish high school than are U.S. students. A distinction between investment and consumption in educational expenditures is not easy to draw empirically. Estimates of the rate of return must rely on some estimate of the amount of such investment, and thus a certain amount of indirection is necessary in obtaining estimates. Despite improvements in correcting for sample selection bias, among other procedures, we are still some distance from estimating gross investment and saving in human capital. Some estimates (e.g., Kendrick 1976) place the amount of human capital investment at approximately the same level as nonhuman investment in the economy. Estimating *net* saving and investment in human capital is even more difficult. At what rate do knowledge and skill acquired in education, or on the job, depreciate or become obsolete? Clearly, unlike financial assets or tangible nonhuman capital, they cannot be bequeathed, although they may be an input into human investment in one's children. Again, I refer the interested reader to Jorgenson and Fraumeni (1989), and, perhaps just as important, Rosen's (1989) discussion, to gain a feel for some of the issues involved.

The appropriate treatment of private pensions in saving statistics is a subject of much dispute. Currently, for example, employer contributions of defined-benefit pension plans show up in the private saving statistics. Some have argued for a concept of pension wealth, that is, the expected present value of future pension payments. An analogous argument has been made for Social Security. It is not my purpose to review here the voluminous literature of the potential impact of Social Security wealth on real economic activity, such as saving choices, or the analogous literature on private or state and local and other government partially funded liabilities. At various points in history, currently unfunded liabilities have been large, subject to substantial variation depending upon assumed patterns of economic and demographic trends, and subject to enormous change through minor changes in the rules relating to benefit calculations or taxes. Further, Social Security has begun a systematic move away from pay-as-you-go finance toward building a historically large surplus.

How to define the expected obligations of the Social Security system, for example, is also open to much controversy. Under a closed group approach, the expected future taxes and benefits paid by particular cohorts—for example, all those alive or all those currently above a certain age, such as 18—would be calculated, discounted to the present, and compared. The difference between the expected present value of benefits and taxes would be the surplus or deficit. This concept, using current participants as a group, is adopted by Arthur Anderson & Co (1986). Such an estimate would add $100 billion or more per year to the federal government deficit. Likewise, to the extent there were accruing unfunded liabilities in state and local government or private pension funds, these would need to be netted out (to the extent that they were not netted explicitly or via market valuation of corporate equities in Flow of Funds or other data). Recall that the state and local surplus in recent years has been over 1% of GNP, but that much of it is in pension funds, whose simultaneously accruing liabilities are not included in the national saving statistics.

Under an open group concept, the expected present value of benefits and taxes paid over some time period, often taken to be 75-year actuarial projection period of the Social Security Administration, would be compared, with the difference being the surplus or deficit. Thus, taxes paid in the early working years of the currently unborn and benefits paid to persons during retirement who are not yet in the labor force would be counted. Social Security in the United States, as well as similar programs in most other advanced economies, has become so large and contains so many features, including insurance features, it may well affect private saving behavior. I believe the best we can do is provide some supplemental information to the traditional NIPA treatment of Social Security in the budget, simply netting the excess of taxes over outlays as positive government saving, currently offsetting the larger deficit in that part of the budget not including Social Security. The substantial unfunded liabilities I have dealt with elsewhere (see Boskin, Robinson, and Huber 1989).

I do not think it is sensible to include OASI contributions as part of personal saving, as suggested by Hendershott and Peek (1989). This would double the net private saving rate, but while it is true that some individuals believe that their contributions are a sort of saving, legally and by nature of the formulae in use at any point in time, there is no necessary relationship between an individual's marginal contribution and their own marginal returns. Of course, for the nation as whole, the aggregate saving is captured by the difference in the cash flow in the system plus (by no means easy to estimate) the change in expected real net accrued liabilities. For those interested in the relationship of marginal Social Security taxes paid and expected marginal benefits for households of different income levels, family type and ages, see Boskin, Kotlikoff, Puffert, and Shoven (1987).

I do not have the space to go into contingent liabilities by sector, such as those generated in the thrift industry or pension plans. The nature of deposit and pension insurance is to provide a put option and create a heads-I-win-tails-the-taxpayer-loses type situation, which may encourage excessive risk taking. I have dealt with these issues in the context of a more appropriate budgetary treatment elsewhere (Boskin, Barham, Cone, and Ozler 1987).

5.5 Conclusion

My conclusion is quite simple. We have come some way toward understanding, measuring, interpreting, and analyzing saving and wealth. While there is a substantial need for continued research into analyzing saving behavior and wealth accumulation, the following conclusions deserve emphasis.

1. While the United States has a saving rate that is low by historical and international standards, that saving rate is substantially higher when more comprehensive measures of saving are developed. While there are substantial difficulties in developing such augmented measures of national saving, various data sources and estimation methodologies all conclude that adjustments for net saving in durables, government capital, capital gains and losses, revaluations, and so on, are substantial.

2. The adjustments for durables and government capital are likely to narrow the saving-rate gap between the United States and Japan, and to a lesser extent between the United States and the European economies. This reduction in the saving-rate gap is much greater for gross saving than net saving.

3. No one saving-rate measure is the answer to all questions one might pose about saving and wealth accumulation. Often there will be offsetting tendencies by sector, asset type, and so on. A decrease in the traditional NIPA saving figures may reflect a rise in the stock market, which may decrease saving either because of direct adjustment on the part of households or mechanical adjustments due to the actuarial formulae for pension plans.

4. The reasonable, even permissible, level of aggregation, across types of households, ages of households, sectors of the economy, and types of assets and liabilities, depends heavily upon one's beliefs concerning an appropriate model of the economy (e.g., of credit markets in deciding whether to combine household and corporate saving, and of household behavior in deciding whether to analyze private saving and government saving separately from national saving).

5. Innumerable technical issues remain, ranging from appropriate deflators to valuation in nonmarket situations. While these often revolve around technical issues, they also involve components of saving and of wealth that can be large relative to the more traditional components, for example, Social Security, the contingent liabilities of the banking system, and so on. The remarkable change in the U.S. net international lending position in recent years suggests that the traditional argument that most capital gains and losses, and revaluations, will net internally is no longer accurate.

6. Perhaps the most important measurement issue for traditional saving estimates is improving the measures of personal income to include as much unrecorded income as plausible.

7. Supplementing the aggregate data with age-cohort-specific data may be of great value.

Many of these issues were addressed for the economy as a whole or for important subsectors of the economy, and important subsets of these issues, at the Conference on Research in Income and Wealth reported in Lipsey and Tice (1989). I have no doubt whatsoever that when future generations of economists celebrate subsequent major anniversaries of the Conference on Research in Income and Wealth, they will bear witness to considerable additional value added in measuring, interpreting, and analyzing saving and wealth.

References

Arthur Anderson & Co. 1986. *Sound Financial Reporting in the U.S. Government: A Prerequisite to Fiscal Responsibility.* Chicago.

Baily, M. J. 1962. *National Income and the Price Level.* New York: McGraw-Hill.

Barro, R. J. 1974. Are Government Bonds Net Wealth? *Journal of Political Economy* 82 (November/December): 1095–1117.

Barro, R. J., and C. Sahasakul. 1983. Measuring the Average Marginal Tax Rate from the Individual Income Tax. *Journal of Business* 56 (October):419–52.

Bernheim, B. D. 1984. Dissaving after Retirement. NBER Working Paper no. 1409. Cambridge, Mass.

———. 1987. Ricardian Equivalence: An Evaluation of Theory and Evidence," In *Macroeconomics Annual 1987.* ed. Stanley Fisher. *NBER* Cambridge, Mass.: MIT Press.

Bernheim, B. D., and J. B. Shoven. 1988. Pension Funding and Saving. In *Pensions in the U.S. Economy,* ed. Z. Bodie, J. B. Shoven, and D. A. Wise. Chicago: University of Chicago Press.

Blades, D. W., and P. Sturm. 1982. The Concept and Measurement of Savings: The United States and Other Industrialized Countries. In *Saving and Government Policy.* Federal Reserve Bank of Boston Conference Series no. 25.

Boskin, M. J. 1982. Federal Government Deficits: Myths and Realities. *American Economic Review* 72 (May): 296–303.

———. 1988. Concepts and Measures of Federal Deficits and Debt and Their Impact on Economic Activity. In *The Economics of Public Debt: Proceedings of a Conference Held by the International Economic Association,* ed. K. J. Arrow and M. J. Boskin. New York: St. Martins.

Boskin, M. J., B. Barham, K. Cone, and S. Ozler. 1987. The Federal Budget and Federal Insurance Programs. In *Modern Developments In Public Finance,* ed. M. Boskin. Oxford and New York: Basil Blackwell.

Boskin, M. J., and L. J. Kotlikoff. 1985. Public Debt and U.S. Savings: A New Test of the Neutrality Hypothesis. In Carnegie-Rochester Conference Series on Public Policy, *The "New Monetary Economics," Fiscal Issues and Unemployment,* ed. K. Brunner and A. H. Meltzer, 23:55–86.

Boskin, M. J., L. J. Kotlikoff, and M. Knetter. 1985. Changes in the Age Distribution of Income in the United States, 1968–1984. NBER Working Paper no. 1766. Cambridge, Mass.

Boskin, M. J., L. J. Kotlikoff, D. J. Puffert, and J. B. Shoven. 1987. Social Security: A Financial Appraisal across and within Generations. *National Tax Journal* 40 (March):19–34.

Boskin, M. J., and L. J. Lau. 1988. An Analysis of Postwar U.S. Consumption and Savings Behavior. Mimeograph. Stanford University.

Boskin, M. J., and J. M. Roberts. 1986. A Closer Look at Saving Rates in the United States and Japan. American Enterprise Institute Working Paper no. 9. Washington, D.C.

Boskin, M. J., M. S. Robinson, and A. M. Huber. 1989. Government Saving, Capital Formation, and Wealth in the United States, 1947–1985. In *The Measurement of Saving, Investment, and Wealth,* ed. R. E. Lipsey and Helen Stone Tice, 287–353. Chicago: University of Chicago Press.

Curtin, R. T., F. T. Juster, and J. N. Morgan. 1989. Survey Estimates of Wealth: An Assessment of Quality. In *The Measurement of Saving, Investment, and Wealth,* ed. R. E. Lipsey and H. S. Tice, 473–548. Chicago: University of Chicago Press.

David, P. A., and J. Scadding. 1974. Private Saving: Ultrarationality, Aggregation, and "Denison's Law." *Journal of Political Economy* 82 (March/April): 225–49.

Denison, E. F. 1958. A Note on Private Saving. *Review of Economics and Statistics* 40 (August): 261–67.

Diamond, P. A., and J. A. Hausman. 1984. Individual Retirement and Savings Behavior. *Journal of Public Economics* 23 (February/March): 81–114.

Feige, E. L. 1983. The Meaning of the "Underground Economy" and the Full Compliance Deficit. In *Studies in Contemporary Economics: The Economics of the Shadow Economy,* ed. W. Gaertner and A. Wenig. Berlin: Springer-Verlag.

Hall, R. E., and F. S. Mishkin. 1982. The Sensitivity of Consumption to Transitory Income: Estimates from Panel Data on Households. *Econometrica* 50 (March): 461–81.

Hendershott P., and J. Peek. 1989. Aggregate U.S. Private Saving: Conceptual Measures. In *The Measurement of Saving, Investment and Wealth,* ed. R. E. Lipsey and H. S. Tice, 185–223. Chicago: University of Chicago Press.

Holloway, T. M. 1989. Present NIPA Saving Measures: Their Characteristics and Limitations. In *The Measurement of Saving, Investment and Wealth,* ed. R. E. Lipsey and H. S. Tice, 21–93. Chicago: University of Chicago Press.

Hurd, M. 1987. Savings of the Elderly and Desired Bequests. *American Economic Review* 77 (June): 298–312.

Jorgenson, D. W., and B. M. Fraumeni. 1989. The Accumulation of Human and Nonhuman Capital, 1948–84. In *The Measurement of Saving, Investment, and Wealth,* ed. R. E. Lipsey and H. S. Tice, 227–82. Chicago: University of Chicago Press.

Jorgenson, D. W., L. J. Lau, and T. M. Stoker. 1982. The Transcendental Logarithmic Model of Aggregate Consumer Behavior. *Advances in Econometrics* 1:97–238.

Katz, A. J. 1983. Valuing the Services of Consumer Durables. *Review of Income and Wealth* 29 (December): 405–27.

Kendrick, J. W. 1976. *The Formation and Stocks of Total Capital.* New York: National Bureau of Economic Research.

Klein, L. 1986. International Aspects of Saving. In *Savings and Capital Formation: The Policy Options,* ed. G. F. Adams and S. M. Wachter. Lexington, Mass.: Lexington Books.

Lipsey, R. E. and H. S. Tice, eds. 1989. *The Measurement of Saving, Investment, and Wealth.* Chicago: University of Chicago Press.

Rosen, S. 1989. Comment. In *The Measurement of Saving, Investment, and Wealth,* ed. R. E. Lipsey and H. S. Tice, 282–85. Chicago: University of Chicago Press.

Stiglitz, J. E., and A. Weiss. 1981. Credit Rationing in Markets with Imperfect Information. *American Economic Review* 71 (June): 393–410.

Wilson, J. F., J. J. Freund, F. O. Yohn, Jr., and W. Lederer. 1989. Measuring Household Saving: Recent Experience from the Flow-of-Funds Perspective. In *The Measurement of Saving, Investment, and Wealth,* ed. R. E. Lipsey and H. S. Tice, 101–45. Chicago: University of Chicago Press.

6 Hedonic Price Indexes and the Measurement of Capital and Productivity: Some Historical Reflections

Zvi Griliches

6.1 Introduction: History

More than thirty years have passed since I stumbled onto the topic of "hedonic" price indexes. More than twenty years have passed since Dale Jorgenson and I pointed to "quality change" problems as a major potential "explanation" of productivity growth as it was then being measured. It may be opportune, therefore, on this festive occasion to reminisce a bit about from where and how far we have come and also how much still remains to be done in this, as in many other, areas of empirical research.

Before I get very far, however, I should first enter a disclaimer. There was nothing particularly original about my first hedonic price indexes paper (Griliches 1961). The notion that one might use regression techniques to relate the prices of different "models" or versions of a commodity to differences in their characteristics, "qualities," and discover thereby the relative valuation of such qualities is reasonably obvious and has been rediscovered a number of times by many people. The earliest references I know of today come primarily from agricultural economics: Fred Waugh's Columbia thesis on vegetable prices (Waugh 1928, 1929) and Vail's (1932) work on mixed fertilizer prices. At the time, in the late 1950s, when I went looking for references to buttress my own regressions, I was pointed first to Stone's (1956) analysis of liquor prices and Court's (1939) explicit use of the hedonic label for his automobile price regressions. At the theoretical level the issues had been discussed by Hofsten (1952), Houthakker (1951–52), Adelman (1960), and others. It was clear to me then, and I think it is also clearly stated in the 1961 paper, that the idea

Zvi Griliches is Paul M. Warburg Professor of Economics, Harvard University, and director of the Productivity Program at the National Bureau of Economic Research.

The author is indebted to the National Science Foundation for its support of this work over the last thirty years. A significant portion of this paper has been adopted from the Introduction to the collection of my early papers (Griliches 1988b).

itself was not particularly original. What was impressive about that paper is that it took the idea seriously, did a lot of work with it, and showed that something interesting can indeed be accomplished this way. Showing that something interesting is actually doable had a significant impact on the subsequent literature, generating much new work in this style and also quite a bit of theoretical controversy and elaboration. But I am running ahead of my story.

There were two influences, two lines of research that led me to work on this problem. In my thesis on hybrid corn (Griliches 1956, 1957b) I had studied the diffusion of an innovation as it was affected by various economic forces. Central to that work was the concept of a diffusion curve or path, I had used the logistic for this purpose, in which "time" is essentially exogenous (as it was also to be in the concurrent and subsequent theories of technological change). The model specified an adjustment path to the new equilibrium, but the equilibrium level itself, the "ceiling" level for the new technology, was fixed and unchanging over time (though I allowed it to differ cross-sectionally). I was not entirely happy with such a formulation and had already explored in an appendix to my thesis an alternative model that made the rate of adoption a direct function of profitability with improvements in the "quality" of the technology (rising relative yields of hybrid vs. open pollinated corn) and the fall in its price as its major driving forces. The arrival of partial-adjustment distributed-lag models at Chicago via Cagan (1956) and Theil (who had brought Koyck's 1954 model to Nerlove's and my attention) led me to try them as an alternative framework for the analysis of technical change in my work on the demand for fertilizer in agriculture (Griliches 1958a). That work interpreted the growth in fertilizer use as a lagged response to the continued decline in its real price. For that I needed, however, a reasonable price series, and I was not satisfied with the official USDA price index on this topic. The "quality" of the fertilizers used was changing rapidly, the use of nitrogen was increasing relative to the other components, and the official price series were not capturing it adequately. An alternative was available to me in the form of a series of "total plant nutrients used" and an estimate of the average price per plant nutrient unit could be derived from it and the total fertilizer expenditure series. But that series gave equal weight to each of the three major plant nutrients (nitrogen N, phosphoric acid P, and potash K), which looked wrong to me. It was then that I ran my first hedonic regression, though I did not know its name at that point [in 1957], relating the prices of different mixed fertilizers to their "formula" (the mix of their ingredients) to derive better weights for the construction of a total "constant quality" fertilizer quantity and price series. This regression, which yielded 3.5, 2, and 1 as the approximate "correct" weights for the three major plant nutrients (N, P, and K, respectively) instead of the equal weights implicit in the total plant nutrients concept, is buried in a footnote in the final published version (Griliches 1958a, 599). I had not realized yet what was going to sprout from it in the future.

The other line of work that merged with it was the direct measurement of "technological change" using output over input indexes. This line was based on earlier work in agriculture by Barton and Cooper (1948), was summarized for me by Schultz (1953), and had been pursued at Chicago by Ruttan (1954, 1957), before the topic was transformed by Solow's (1957) elegant reformulation and its subsequent elaboration by Jorgenson and Griliches (1967). Similar work had been done in industry by Schmookler (1952) and Abramovitz (1956), among others. The stylized facts that had emerged were quite clear. The lion's share of the observed growth in output was attributable to "technical change" or, more correctly, to the "residual."

Having come to this problem with a background in econometrics, I had used Schultz's numbers to estimate the social returns to public investments in agricultural research (Griliches 1958b), I found the spectacle of economic models yielding large residuals rather uncomfortable, even when we fudged the issue by renaming them as "technical change" and then claiming credit for their "measurement." My interest in specification analysis (Griliches 1957a) led me to a series of questions about the model used to compute such residuals and also, especially, about the ingredients, the data, used in the model's implementation. This led me to a research program that focused on the various components of such computations and alternatives to them: the measurement of the services of capital equipment items and the issues of deflation, quality change, and the measurement of a relevant depreciation concept; the measurement of labor input and the contribution of education to its changing quality; the role of "left-out" variables (inputs) such as public and private investments in R&D; and formula misspecification issues, especially economies of scale and other sources of disequilibria, which led me to a continued involvement with production function estimation. This program of research, which was announced, implicitly, in "Measuring Inputs in Agriculture" (Griliches 1960) and found its fullest expression in my two papers on agricultural productivity (Griliches 1963, 1964a), served me rather well in subsequent years and to this date. It was in certain aspects rather similar to the task pursued by Denison (1962) at about the same time, except that I put more emphasis on its econometric aspects, on the explicit testing of the various proposed adjustments, and the "sources of growth" attributions.

It was in this context, when I turned to the examination how the various capital measures were being constructed and especially deflated, that I escalated my incipient efforts in agriculture into a more general staff report for the Stigler Committee (NBER 1961), resurrecting thereby the "hedonic regression" approach to the measurement of quality change problem. This paper appeared at a rather opportune moment, just as data, computer resources, econometric training and sophistication, and general interest in this range of topics were all expanding, and a whole literature developed in its wake, influencing the measurement of real estate prices, wage equations, environmental amenities, and other aspects of "qualitative differences." This literature has become too vast for one person to survey it. I tried to do so earlier on in its development in the introduction to the volume of essays on this topic (Griliches 1971). More recent surveys can be found in Triplett (1975, 1987), Berndt (1983), and Bartik and Smith (1987). Here I can only indicate what I consider to be a few of the highlights of this literature.

6.2 Hedonics Revisited

There are three major issues that tend to be addressed, in different proportions, in the hedonic literature. There is a range of theoretical questions: How should different "qualities," characteristics, of commodities (outputs or inputs) be modeled, entered into utility or cost functions, and translated into demand and supply functions and the resulting market outcomes? Can one give a theoretically consistent interpretation to "quality adjusted" price indexes, and can one derive valid restrictions from the theory that the empirical price-characteristics regressions should satisfy? There is also a wide range of empirical problems. What are the salient characteristics of a particular commodity? Under what conditions should one expect their market valuation to remain constant? How should the regression framework be expanded, what variables should be added to it, so as to keep the resulting estimates "stable" in face of changing circumstances? And there is also a whole host of econometric methodology issues associated with the attempt to estimate a relationship that can be thought of as being the result of an interaction of both demand and supply forces, and with the use of detailed microdata, often in the form of an unbalanced panel of data for a fixed number of manufacturers, but a different and changing number of "models" (commodity versions).

The theoretical literature tends to focus either on the demand side (Lancaster 1966, 1971; Muellbauer 1974; and Berndt 1983, among others) or the supply side (see, e.g., Ohta, 1975) with very few (Rosen 1974 being a notable exemption) attempting a full general equilibrium discussion (see also Epple 1987 for a recent discussion). There is much finger pointing at the restrictive assumptions required to establish the "existence" and meaning of hedonic "quality" or price indexes (see, e.g., Muellbauer 1974; and Lucas 1975). While useful, I feel that this literature has misunderstood the original purpose of the hedonic suggestion. It is easy to show that, except for unique circumstances and under very stringent assumptions, it is not possible to devise a perfect price index for *any* commodity classification. With finite amounts of data, different procedures will yield (hopefully not very) different answers, and even "good" formulae, such as Divisia-type indexes, cannot be given a satisfactory theoretical interpretation except in very limiting and unrealistic circumstances. Most of the objections to attempts to construct a price index of automobiles from the consideration of their various attributes apply with the same force to the construction of a motor-vehicles price index out of the prices of cars, trucks, and motorcycles.

My own point of view is that what the hedonic approach tries to do is to estimate aspects of the budget constraint facing consumers, allowing thereby the estimation of "missing" prices when quality changes. It is not in the business of estimating utility or cost functions per se, though it can also be very useful for these purposes (see Cardell 1977; McFadden 1978; and Trajtenberg 1983 for examples.) What is being estimated is actually the locus of intersections of the demand curves of different consumers with varying tastes and the supply functions of different producers with possibly varying technologies of production. One is unlikely, therefore, to be able to recover the underlying utility and cost functions from such data alone, except in very special circumstances. Nor can theoretical derivations at the individual level really provide substantive constraints on the estimation of such "market" relations. (See the detailed discussion of many of these issues, in the context of estimating the value of urban amenities, in Bartik and Smith 1987.) Hence my preference for the "estimation of missing prices" interpretation of this approach. Accepting that, one still faces the usual index number problems and ambiguities but at least one is back to the "previous case." In this my views are close to those articulated by Triplett (1983a, 1986). The following passage from Ohta and Griliches represents them reasonably well:

> Despite the theoretical proofs to the contrary, the Consumer Price Index (CPI) "exists" and is even of some use. It is thus of some value to attempt to improve it even if perfection is unattainable. What the hedonic approach attempted was to provide a tool for estimating "missing" prices, prices of particular bundles not observed in the original or later periods. It did not pretend to dispose of the question of whether various observed differentials are demand or supply determined, how the observed variety of models in the market is generated, and whether the resulting indexes have an unambiguous welfare interpretation. Its goals were modest. It offered the tool of econometrics, with all of its attendant problems, as a help to the solution of the first two issues, the detection of the relevant characteristics of a commodity and the estimation of their marginal market valuation.
>
> Because of its focus on price explanation and its purpose of "predicting" the price of unobserved variants of a commodity in particular periods, the hedonic hypothesis can be viewed as asserting the existence of a reduced-form relationship between prices and the various characteristics of the commodity. That relationship need not be "stable" over time, but changes that occur should have some rhyme and reason to them, otherwise one would suspect that the observed results are a fluke and cannot be used in the extrapolation necessary for the derivation of missing prices. . . .
>
> To accomplish even such limited goals, one requires much prior information on the commodity in question (econometrics is not a very good tool when wielded blindly), lots of good data, and a detailed analysis of the robustness of one's conclusions relative to the many possible alternative specifications of the model. (1976, 326)

The theoretical developments have been useful, however, in elucidating under what conditions one might expect the hedonic price functions to be stable or shift and which variables might be important in explaining such shifts across markets and time. My own work in this area has had more of a methodological-empirical flavor to it though there were also nonnegligible attempts to formulate and clarify the theory underlying such measurement techniques in Adelman and Griliches (1961), Griliches (1964b), and in Ohta and Griliches (1976, 1986). The last two papers represent also my efforts to pursue additional empirical work in this area. In the 1976 paper with Ohta we extended the earlier approach to the analysis of used automobile prices and investigated differences between performance and specification characteristics and pricing differences between manufacturers of different makes of automobiles. The 1986 paper focuses on the role of gasoline price changes in shifting the hedonic price relationships for cars, extends the theory to incorporate operating costs components, and shows that allowing for such price changes leaves the "extended" hedonic function effectively unchanged, permitting one to maintain the stability of tastes hypothesis in this market. See also Gordon (1983) and Kahn (1986) for related work.

The major recent "success" of hedonic methods has been their acceptance by the official statistical agencies after many years of resistance. Hedonic methods had been used for a long time by the Bureau of the Census to compute its index of single family houses, and much experimental work was carried on at the Bureau of Labor Statistics, but it was not until January 1986, when the *Survey of Current Business* announced a revision of the U.S. National Income Accounts that incorporated a new price index for computers based on the hedonic methodology, that one could feel that they had received the official imprimatur. This index is described and discussed in Cole et al. (1986) and Triplett (1986); see also Gordon (1989) for alternative computations. It would be interesting to speculate why it has taken so long for these methods to penetrate into the "official" circles. This is not, of course, the first use of such methods by the statistical agencies. The Bureau of the Census has used hedonic methods for years in the construction of its residential housing price indexes and there has been significant experimental work with these methods at the BLS, by Gavett, Early and Sinclair, Triplett, and others. But the recent computer price indexes revision is the first time an agency has embraced these methods publicly in a significant way.

It is easy to forget how vehement the opposition was. One needs to go back to the 1962 and 1965 exchanges between Gilbert, Denison, Jaszi and myself to recapture the flavor of some of these arguments (see Griliches 1962 and 1964b and the associated comments). The objections could be caricatured as either saying that it could not be done, or it should not be done, or it was already being done by the standard conventional methods. The fact that it is difficult to do, that an actual empirical implementation calls for much judgment on the part of the analyst and hence exposes him to the charge of subjectivity, is still the most telling objection today. The fact that the standard procedures also involve much judgment and "ad-hockery" is usually well hidden behind the official facade of the statistical establishment. Hedonic methods are difficult. They require more data and more analysis and judgment. Their virtue is that they use more data and that they expose some of these judgments to the final user of the results, providing an implicit warning of their tenuousness. Here, as everywhere else in economics, there is no free lunch.

The notion that one should stick only to "cost" based quality differentials was preposterous at the time and has been largely given up by its proponents. The difference between "resource" use and "utility" based quality adjustments was first stated by Fisher and Shell (1972) and further clarified by Triplett (1983a) in his debate with Gordon (1983). It is now well understood that both concepts make sense in different circumstances and that both are interesting and useful, especially when they do not coincide.

The notion that the statistical agencies were already doing all this under the guise of "linking" was largely wishful thinking, though matters have improved greatly over the years. The problem was not that a detailed "all models" Divisia index would not come close to a hedonic regression result. It might even be superior to it. It was just that it was not being done, in part because the detailed data were not being collected and new products and new varieties of older products were not showing up in the indexes until it was much too late. The hedonic approach was one way of implementing what they should have been doing in the first place. It was also more willing to carry the "linking" idea further, across models that differed significantly in more than one dimension. It could not solve the really new product problem, that is, the appearance of a product whose uses and dimensions had no precedent or anticipation. But it was willing to push comparisons much further than they had been pushed before, not giving up as easily in the face of a changing world. Buried within the hedonic idea was already the germ of Becker's (1965) "household production function" and the notion that one should look at the relevant activity as a whole, at its "ultimate" product in terms of utility or productivity, and not just at the individual components. In this sense, there remains still much to be done in this area. I do not think that we have actually been daring enough. We have not yet produced a decent price index of "health" nor have we done the simpler task of tracing through the relevant history of the price of computation, from the days of the abacus, through the electric desk calculators of my student days (who remembers still the Marchants, Monroes, and Friedens of yore?) the electronic mainframes of our youth, and the PC revolution of recent years. I think that it is doable and I believe that it is worth doing, whether we use the results to revise the National Income and Product Accounts or not.

6.3 Capital Measurement

The work on hedonic price indexes connected to my more general interest in the measurement of capital for the analysis of productivity change. A rather complete statement of my original position on this matter can be found in the Yehuda Grunfeld Memorial volume paper (Griliches 1963). This was to be refined later in joint work with Jorgenson (Griliches and Jorgenson 1966; Jorgenson and Griliches 1967). The difficulty with the available capital measures then, was, and to a great extent is still now, in my view, the fact that they were being overdeflated and overdepreciated, that items with different expected lives were being added together in a wrong way, and that no allowance was being made for changes in the utilization of such capital. The overdeflation issue was already alluded to in the discussion above; it was fed by the strong suspicion that the various available machinery and durable equipment price indexes did not take quality change into account adequately, if at all. This issue connects also to the "embodied" technical change idea (Solow 1960) and the literature that flowed from it. My view on overdepreciation remains controversial (see Miller 1983). I turned early to the evidence of used machinery markets to point out that the official depreciation numbers were too high, that they were leading to an underestimate of actual capital accumulation in agriculture, but I also argued that the observed depreciation rates in secondhand markets contain a large obsolescence component that is induced by the rising quality of new machines. This depreciation is a valid subtraction from thc present value of a machine in current prices but it is not the right concept to be used in the construction of a constant quality notion of the flow of services from the existing capital stock in "constant prices." The fact that new machines are better does not imply that the "real" flow of services available from the old machines has declined, either potentially or actually. The point is illustrated visually in figure 6.1, taken from the original 1963 paper that plots the information on different performance concepts for farm tractors as a function of their age. These data and my subsequent attempts to explore some of these issues econometrically (see esp. Pakes and Griliches 1984) all throw doubt on the current practice of assuming that the services of physical capital deteriorate at a rapid and fixed rate, independent of their age. But the available data on types of machinery in place and their actual age structure have been rather sparse, and there has been less progress in this direction than I think is desirable or perhaps even possible.

6.4 Explanation of Technological Change

Several strands of this work came together in "The Explanation of Productivity Change" (Jorgenson and Griliches 1967) in an attempt at a more complete accounting of the sources of economic growth. Given its twentieth anniversary in 1987, it may be worthwhile to review some of the issues raised there.

In 1967 we argued that a "correct" index number framework and the "right" measurement of inputs would reduce greatly the role of the residual ("advances in knowledge," total factor productivity, disembodied technical

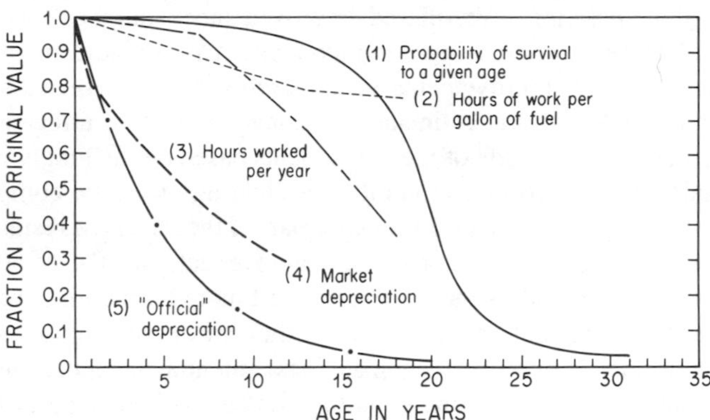

Fig. 6.1 The aging of tractors

change, and/or other such terms) in accounting for the observed growth in output. It brought together Jorgenson's work on Divisia indexes, on the correct measurement of cost of capital, and on the right aggregation procedures for it, with my own earlier work on the measurement of capital prices and quality change and the contribution of education to productivity growth (Griliches 1960, 1963, 1964a). It produced the startling conclusion, already foreshadowed in my agricultural productivity papers, that an adjustment of conventional inputs for measurement and aggregation error may eliminate much of the mystery that was associated with the original findings of large unexplained components in the growth of national and sectoral outputs. It did this with a "Look Ma! No hands!" attitude, using neither additional outside variables, such as R&D, or allowing for economies of scale or other disequilibria. This did indeed attract attention and also criticism. The most penetrating criticism came from Denison (1969) which led to an exchange between us in the May 1972 issue of the *Survey of Current Business*.

Denison found a number of minor errors and one major one in our computations. By trying to adjust for changing utilization rates we used data on energy consumption of electric motors in manufacturing, a direct measure of capital equipment utilization in manufacturing (borrowed to a large extent from Foss 1963), but extrapolated it also to nonequipment components of capital in manufacturing and to all capital outside of manufacturing, including residential structures. There was also the uneasy issue of integrating a utilization adjustment within what was otherwise a pure equilibrium story. Once we conceded most of the utilization adjustment, our "explanation" of productivity growth shrank from 94% to 43% and with it also our claim to "do it all" (without mirrors).

I still believe, however, that we were right in our basic idea that productivity growth should be "explained" rather than just measured and that errors of measurement and concept have a major role in this. But we did not go far enough in that direction. We offered improved index number formulae, a better reweighting of capital input components, a major adjustment of the employment data for improvements in the quality of labor, revisions in investment price indexes, and estimates of changes in capital utilization. The potential orders of magnitude of the adjustments based on the first two contributions, index number formulae and the reweighting of capital components, are not large enough to account for a major part of the observed residual. The labor quality adjustment was not really controversial, but the capital price indexes and utilization adjustments deserve a bit more discussion. We argued for the idea that technical change could be thought of, in a sense, as being "embodied" in factor inputs, in new machines, and human capital, and that a better measurement of these inputs via the nontautological route of hedonic index numbers for both capital and labor could account for most of what was being interpreted as a residual. It became clear, however, that without extending our framework further to allow for R&D and other externalities, increasing returns to scale and other disequilibria, we were unlikely to approach a full "explanation" of productivity change (see the last paragraphs of Jorgenson and Griliches 1972).

It may appear that adjusting a particular input for mismeasured quality change would not have much of an effect on productivity growth measurement since one would need also to adjust the output figures for the corresponding industry. But as long as the share of this industry in final output is less than the elasticity of output with respect to this input, the two adjustments will not cancel themselves out. Since the share of investment in output is significantly lower than reasonable estimates of the share of capital in total factor costs, adjusting capital for mismeasurement of its prices does lead to a net reduction in the computed residual. Empirically it is clear that even without considering any of the potential externalities associated with new capital, there are enough questions about the official price indexes in these areas to make further work on this topic a high priority.

The utilization adjustment fit uneasily within the rather strict competitive equilibrium framework of Jorgenson and Griliches (1967). The analogy was made to labor hours, calling for the parallel concept of machine hours as the relevant notion of capital services. We had also in mind the model of a continuous process plant where output is more or less proportional to hours of operation. Since we were interested primarily in "productivity" change as a measure of "technical" change, a change that is due to changes in techniques of production, fluctuations in "utilization," whether a plant worked one shift or two, 10 months or 12, were not really relevant for this purpose. But while labor unemployment was happening offstage as far as business productivity accounts were concerned, capital "underemployment" was difficult to reconcile with the maximizing behavior with perfect foresight implicit in our framework.

There are two somewhat separate "utilization" issues. Productivity as measured is strongly procyclical. Measured inputs, especially capital and labor services, fluctuate less than reported output. The resulting fluctuations in "productivity" do not make sense if we want to interpret them as a measure of the growth in the level of technology or the state of economically valuable knowledge of an economy. The U.S. economy did not "forget" 4% of its technology between 1974 and 1975. Nor was there a similar deterioration in the skill of its labor force. (National welfare did go down as the result of OPEC-induced worldwide rise in energy prices, but that is a separate story.)

What is wrong with the productivity numbers in this case is that we do not measure accurately the actual amounts of labor or machine hours used rather than just paid for. Since both capital and labor are bought or hired in anticipation of a certain level of activity and on long-term contracts, actual factor payments do not reflect their respective marginal products except in the case of perfect foresight and only in the long run. Underutilization of factors of production is the result of unanticipated shifts in demand and various rigidities built into the economic system due to longer term explicit and implicit contracts (and other market imperfections) between worker and employer and seller and buyer. If our interest is primarily on the "technological" interpretation of productivity measures, we must either ignore such shorter run fluctuations or somehow adjust for them. This was the rationale behind our original use of energy consumed by electric motors (per installed horsepower) as a utilization adjustment.

We used energy consumption as a proxy for the unobserved variation in machine hours and not on its own behalf as an important intermediate input. Used in the latter fashion it is a produced input which would cancel out at the aggregate level (as was pointed out in 1969 by Denison in his comment on our paper). Alternatively, one could adjust the weight (share) of capital services in one's total input index to reflect the fact that underutilization of the existing stock of resources should reduce significantly the shadow price of using them. (This is the approach suggested in Berndt and Fuss 1986). Unfortunately, it is difficult to use the observed factor returns for these purposes, both because prices do not fall rapidly enough in the face of unanticipated demand shocks and because of a variety of longer run contractual factor payments arrangement that break the link between factor rewards and their current productivity.

This reflects, in a sense, the failure of the assumption of perfect competition that is the basis for much of the standard productivity accounts. The actual world we live in is full of short-run rigidities, transaction costs, immalleable capital, and immobile resources, resulting in the pervasive presence of quasi rents and short-term capital gains and losses. While I do not believe that such discrepancies from "perfect" competition actually imply the presence of a significant market power in most industries (as argued, for example, by Hall 1986), they do make productivity accounting even more difficult.

The other aspect of utilization is the longer run trend in shift work, the length of the workweek, and changes in hours of operation per day by plants, stores, and service establishments. Consider, for example, a decline in overtime or night-shift premia due, say, to a decline in union power. This would reduce the price of a certain type of capital service and expand its use. If capital is not measured in machine hours, we would show a rise in productivity even though there has been no "technological" change in methods of production. I would prefer not to include such changes in the definition of productivity since I interpret them as movements along (or toward) a stable production possibilities frontier. But there did occur an organizational change that allowed us to get more "flow," more hours per day or year, from a given stock of equipment or other resources. One way to look at this is to think of two types of activities: output production that rents machine and labor hours and the supply of capital services (and also effective labor hours) from the existing resource levels. A decline in overtime premia would be similar to a decline in the tariff on a certain kind of imported input. It would lead to an improvement in "efficiency" but not necessarily to a "technical" change.

It is still my belief that we need to adjust our data for such capacity utilization fluctuations for a better understanding of "technical" change, the issue that brought us to the analysis of such data in the first place. A consistent framework for such an adjustment will require, however, the introduction of adjustment costs and ex post errors into the productivity measurement framework. (See Morrison 1985 and the literature cited therein for recent developments in this area.) It is not clear, however, whether one can separate longer run developments in the utilization of capital from changes in technology and the organization of society. Much of capital is employed outside continuous process manufacturing and there the connection between its utilization and productivity is much looser. The rising cost of human time and the desire for variety and flexibility have led to much investment in what might be called "standby" capacity with rather low utilization rates. The hi-fi system in my home is operating only at a fraction of its potential capacity. Much inventory is held in many businesses to economize on other aspects of labor activity. Nor is it clear that an extension of store hours with a resulting decline in productivity per square-foot-hour of store space is necessarily a bad thing. Thus it is difficult to see how one could separate long-run trends in utilization from changes in production and consumption technologies. It is, however, a topic worth studying and a potentially important contributor to "explanations" of apparent swings in the statistics on measured productivity.

Whether we include or exclude such changes from our "productivity" concept will affect our ability to "account" for them. But that is not the important issue. We do want to measure them, because we do want to understand what happened, to "explain" productivity. The rest is semantics.

Many of these problems arise because we do not disaggregate adequately and do not describe the production process in adequate detail. A model that would distinguish between the use of capital and labor at different times of the day and year and does not assume that their shadow prices are constant between different "hours" or over time would be capable of handling these kind of shifts. We do not have the data to implement such a program, but it underscores the message of our original paper: much of what passes for productivity change in conventional data is the result of aggregation errors, the wrong measurement of input quantities, and the use of wrong weights to combine them into "total factor input" indexes.

Something more should be said about the rather vague notions of "explanation" and "accounting." National Income and Product accounts and associated index numbers are economic constructs, based on an implicit model of the economy and a variety of more or less persuasive logical and empirical arguments. They are not well adapted to "hypothesis testing" or debates about causality. In proposing a better measure of, say, labor, we rely on the evidence of market wage differentials. By bringing in more evidence on this topic we are not just reducing the "residual" tautologically. But the fact that it goes down as the result of such an adjustment does not make it right either. A different kind of evidence is required to provide a more persuasive justification for such adjustments. That is why I turned early on to the use of production functions for econometric testing. Without moving in such a direction one tends to run into various paradoxes. For example, capital growth accelerated in the 1970s in many industries without a comparable increase in the growth of output. In the index-number sense of growth accounting, capital "explained" a larger fraction of the growth of output, and we did, indeed, have a smaller residual. But in spite of this "accounting" the mystery only deepened.

The "econometric" approach to growth accounting involves one in the estimation of production functions. This allows one to test or validate a particular way of measuring an input or adjusting it for quality change; to estimate and test the role of left-out public good inputs such as R&D and other externality generating activities; to estimate economies of scale; and to check on the possibility of disequilibria and estimate the deviation of "true" output elasticities from their respective factor shares. Production function estimation raises many problems of its own, including issues of aggregation and errors of measurement and simultaneity, but it is one of the few ways available to us for checking the validity of the suggested attributions of productivity growth to its various "sources."

My work on agricultural productivity (Griliches 1963, 1964a), which used production function estimation as its main organizing device, left me with the conviction that education, investment in research, and economies of scale (both at the level of the firm and at the level of the market) were the important sources of productivity growth in the long run. Since in the paper with Jorgenson we had not allowed for the two latter sources of growth, I was not too surprised or disheartened when it turned out that we could not really explain all of aggregate productivity change by formula and labor- and capital-quality adjustments alone. It was clear, however, that one would need more and better data to make such additional adjustments more reliable and convincing. I turned, therefore, to trying to amass more data and more evidence on these topics, especially the measurement of the contribution of education (Griliches 1977) and the role of R&D (Griliches 1980, 1986).

Even though we now have more data, more advanced econometric technology, and better computer resources, the overall state of this field has not advanced all that much in the last 20 years. We are really not much closer to an "explanation" of the observed changes in the various productivity indexes. A tremendous effort was launched by Jorgenson and his co-workers (Christensen, Fraumeni, Gollop, Nishimizu, and others) to improve and systematize the relevant data sources, to produce and analyze a consistent set of industry-level total factor productivity accounts, to extend and generalize our original labor-quality adjustments, and to extend all of this also to international comparisons of productivity. In the process, however, rather than pursuing the possibly hopeless quest for a complete "explanation" of productivity growth, they chose to focus instead on developing more precise and detailed productivity measures at various levels of aggregation and devising statistical models for their analysis. Denison (1974, 1979), in parallel, was pursuing his quest for a more complete accounting of the sources of growth, putting together as many reasonable scraps of information as were available, but not embedding them in a clear theoretical framework or an econometrically testable setting. The incompleteness of both approaches and the unsatisfactory state of this field as a whole was revealed by the sharp and prolonged slowdown in the growth of measured productivity, which began in the mid-seventies. Despite the best attempts of these and other researchers, it has not been possible to account for this slowdown within the standard growth accounting framework without concluding that the "residual" had changed, that the underlying total factor productivity growth rate fell sometime in the late 1960s or early 1970s (see Denison 1984; Griliches 1980a and 1988a; Kendrick 1983; and many others).

I do not believe, however, that this slowdown can be interpreted to imply that the underlying rate of technical change has slowed down, that we have exhausted our technological frontiers. In my opinion, it was caused by misguided macro policies induced by the oil price shocks and the subsequent inflation and the fears thereof. Without allowing for errors in capital accumulation (which continued initially at a rather high rate, in spite of the sharp declines in aggregate demand) and widespread underutilization of capacity, it is not possible to interpret the conventional productivity statistics. Surely "knowledge" did not retreat. Moreover, I do not believe that one can use statistics from such periods to infer anything about longer term technological trends. If we are not close to our production possibilities frontier, we cannot tell what is happening to it and whether the underlying growth rate of an economy's "potential" has slowed down or not. We need a better articulated theoretical framework, one that would allow for long-term factor substitution and short-term rigidities and errors, before we shall be able to understand better what has happened to us recently. We also need better data, especially on output and input prices and various aspects of labor and capital utilization.

References

Abramovitz, Moses. 1956. *Resource and Output Trends in the U.S. since 1870*. NBER Occasional Paper no. 52. New York: NBER.

Adelman, Irma. 1960. On an Index of Quality Change. Paper given at the meeting of the American Statistical Association. Stanford, Calif., August.

Adelman, Irma, and Zvi Griliches. 1961. On an Index of Quality Change. *Journal of the American Statistical Association* 56:535–48.

Bartik, Timothy J., and V. Kerry Smith. 1987. Urban Amenities and Public Policy. In *Handbook of Regional and Urban Economics,* ed. E. S. Mills, vol. 2, chap. 31, 505–52. Amsterdam: Elsevier.

Barton, G. T., and M. B. Cooper. 1948. Relation of Agricultural Production to Inputs. *Review of Economics and Statistics* 30 (May): 117–26.

Becker, Gary S. 1965. A Theory of the Allocation of Time. *Economic Journal* 75(299):493–517.

Berndt, Ernst R. 1983. Quality Adjustment, Hedonics, and Modern Empirical Demand Analysis. In *Price Level Measurement,* ed. W. E. Diewert and C. Montemarquette. Ottawa: Statistics Canada.

Berndt, Ernst, and Melvin Fuss. 1986. Productivity Measurement with Adjustments for Variations in Capacity Utilization and Other Forms of Temporary Equilibrium. *Journal of Econometrics* 33(1/2):7–29.

Cagan, Phillip. 1956. The Monetary Dynamics of Hyperinflation. In *Studies in the Quantity Theory of Money,* ed. M. Friedman, 25–117. Chicago: University of Chicago Press.

Cardell, Nicholas Scott. 1977. Methodology for Predicting the Demand for New Electricity Using Goods. Charles River Associates Report no. 244. Cambridge, Mass.

Cole, R., Y. C. Chen, J. A. Barquin-Stolleman, E. Dulberger, N. Helvacian, and J. H. Hodge. 1986. Quality Adjusted Price Indexes for Computer Processors and Selected Peripheral Equipment. *Survey of Current Business* 66(1):41–50.

Court, Andrew T. 1939. Hedonic Price Indexes with Automotive Examples. In *The Dynamics of Automotive Demand,* 99–117. New York: General Motors.

Denison, Edward F. 1962. *The Sources of Economic Growth in the U.S. and the Alternatives Before Us*. Supplementary Paper no. 13, Committee for Economic Development. New York.

———. 1969. Some Major Issues in Productivity Analysis: An Examination of Estimates by Jorgenson and Griliches. *Survey of Current Business* 49, no. 5, pt. 2, 1–27.

———. 1974. *Accounting for United States Economic Growth, 1929–1969,* Washington, D.C.: Brookings.

———. 1979. *Accounting for Slower Economic Growth*. Washington, D.C.: Brookings.

———. 1984. Accounting for Slower Economic Growth: An Update. In *International Comparisons of Productivity and Causes of the Slowdown,* ed. J. W. Kendrick, 1–46 Cambridge, Mass.: Ballinger.

Epple, Dennis. 1987. Hedonic Prices and Implicit Markets: Estimating Demand and

Supply Functions for Differentiated Products. *Journal of Political Economy* 95(1):59–80.

Fisher, Franklin M., and Karl Shell. 1972. *The Economic Theory of Price Indices.* New York: Academic Press.

Foss, Murray. 1963. The Utilization of Capital Equipment. *Survey of Current Business* 43(6):8–16.

Gordon, Robert J. 1983. Energy Efficiency, User-Cost Charge, and the Measurement of Durable Goods Prices. In *The U.S. National Income and Product Accounts,* ed. M. F. Foss, 205–68. NBER Studies in Income and Wealth, vol. 47. Chicago: University of Chicago Press.

———. 1989. The Postwar Evolution of Computer Prices. In *Technology and Capital Formation,* ed. D. W. Jorgenson and R. Landau, 77–125. Cambridge, Mass.: MIT Press.

Griliches, Zvi. 1956. Hybrid Corn: An Exploration in the Economics of Technological Change. Ph.D. thesis. University of Chicago.

———. 1957a. Specification Bias in Estimates of Production Functions. *Journal of Farm Economics* 39, no. 1 (February): 8–20.

———. 1957b. Hybrid Corn: An Exploration in the Economics of Technological Change. *Econometrica* 25, no. 4 (October): 501–22.

———. 1958a. The Demand For Fertilizer: An Econometric Interpretation of a Technical Change. *Journal of Farm Economics* 40(3):591–606.

———. 1958b. Research Cost and Social Returns: Hybrid Corn and Related Innovations. *Journal of Political Economy* 66, no. 5 (October):419–31.

———. 1960. Measuring Inputs in Agriculture: A Critical Survey. *Journal of Farm Economics,* Proceedings Issue, vol. 17, no. 5 (December): 1411–33.

———. 1961. Hedonic Price Indexes for Automobiles: An Econometric Analysis of Quality Change. In *The Price Statistics of the Federal Government,* 173–96. NBER Staff Report no. 3, General Series no. 73. New York: NBER.

———. 1962. Quality Change and Index Numbers: A Critique. *Monthly Labor Review* (May):542–44.

———. 1963. The Sources of Measured Productivity Growth: U.S. Agriculture, 1940–1960. *Journal of Political Economy* 72, no. 4 (August): 331–46.

———. 1964a. Research Expenditures, Education, and the Aggregate Agricultural Production Function. *American Economic Review* 54, no. 6 (December): 961–74.

———. 1964b. Notes on the Measurement of Price and Quality Changes. In *Models of Income Determination,* 381–418. NBER Studies in Income and Wealth, vol. 28. Princeton: Princeton University Press.

———, ed. 1971. *Price Indexes and Quality Change*. Cambridge, Mass.: Harvard University Press.

———. 1977. Estimating the Returns to Schooling: Some Econometric Problems. *Econometrica* 45(1):1–22.

———. 1980a. R&D and the Productivity Slowdown. *American Economic Review* 70(2):343–48.

———. 1980b. Returns to Research and Development Expenditures in the Private Sector. In *New Developments in Productivity Measurement,* ed. J. W. Kendrick and B. Vaccara, 419–54. NBER Studies in Income and Wealth, vol. 44. Chicago: University of Chicago Press.

———. 1986. Productivity, R&D, and Basic Research at the Firm Level in the 1970s. *American Economic Review* 76(1):141–154.

———. 1988a. Productivity Puzzles and R&D: Another Non-Explanation. *Journal of Economic Perspectives* 2, no. 4 (Fall): 9–21.

———. 1988b. *Technology, Education and Productivity: Early Papers with Notes to Subsequent Literature*. New York and Oxford: Basil Blackwell.

Griliches, Zvi, and Dale Jorgenson. 1966. Sources of Measured Productivity Change: Capital Input. *American Economic Review* 56, no. 2 (May): 50–61.

Hall, Robert E. 1986. Market Structure and Macroeconomic Fluctuations. *Brookings Papers on Economic Activity* 2:285–322.

Hofsten, Erland von. 1952. *Price Indexes and Quality Changes*. Stockholm: Boklorlaget Forum AB.

Houthakker, Hendrik H. 1951–52. Compensated Changes in Quantities and Qualities Consumer. *Review of Economic Studies* 19:155–64.

Jorgenson, Dale, and Zvi Griliches. 1967. The Explanation of Productivity Change. *Review of Economic Studies* 34, no. 3 (July): 249–83.

———. 1972. Issues in Growth Accounting: A Reply to Denison. In *The Measurement of Productivity,* special issue of *Survey of Current Business* 52, no. 5, pt. 2 (May): 31–111.

Kahn, James A. 1986. Gasoline Prices and the Used Automobile Market: A Rational Expectations Asset Price Approach. *Quarterly Journal of Economics* 101(2): 323–40.

Kendrick, John W. 1983. International Comparisons of Recent Productivity Trends. In *Energy, Productivity, and Economic Growth,* ed. S. H. Shurr. Cambridge, Mass.: Delgeschlager.

Koyck, L. M. 1954. *Distributed Lags and Investment Analysis*. Amsterdam: North Holland.

Lancaster, Kelvin. 1966. A New Approach to Consumer Theory. *Journal of Political Economy* 74: 132–57.

———. 1971. *Consumer Demand: A New Approach*. New York: Columbia University Press.

Lucas, Robert E. B. 1975. Hedonic Price Functions. *Economic Inquiry* 13(2):157–78.

McFadden, Daniel. 1978. Modelling the Choice of Residential Location. In *Spatial Interation Theory and Residential Location,* ed. A. Karlquist et al., 75–96. Amsterdam: North Holland.

Miller, Edward M. 1983. Capital Aggregation in the Presence of Obsolescence-Inducing Technical Change. *Review of Income and Wealth* 29(23):283–96.

Morrison, Catherine J. 1985. On the Economic Interpretation and Measurement of Optimal Capacity Utilization with Anticipatory Expectations. *Review of Economic Studies* 52:295–310.

Muellbauer, John. 1974. Household Production Theory, Quality and the "Hedonic Technique." *American Economic Review* 64(6):977–94.

National Bureau of Economic Research. 1961. *The Price Statistics of the Federal Government*. General Series no. 73. New York: NBER.

Ohta, Makoto. 1975. Production Technologies in the U.S. Boiler and Turbo Generator Industries and Hedonic Indexes For Their Products: A Cost Function Approach. *Journal of Political Economy* 83(1):1–26.

Ohta, Makoto, and Zvi Griliches. 1976. Automobile Prices Revisited: Extensions of the Hedonic Hypothesis. In *Household Production and Consumption,* ed. N. Terleckyj, 325–90. NBER Studies in Income and Wealth, vol. 40. New York: Columbia University Press.

———. 1986. Automobile Prices and Quality Change: Did the Gasoline Price Increases Change Consumer Tastes in the U.S.? *Journal of Business and Economic Statistics* 4(2):187–98.

Pakes, Ariel, and Zvi Griliches. 1984. Estimating Distributed Lags in Short Panels with an Application to the Specification of Depreciation Patterns and Capital Stock Constructs. *Review of Economic Studies*. 51(2):243–62.

Rosen, Sherwin. 1974. Hedonic Price and Implicit Markets: Product Differentiation in Pure Competition. *Journal of Political Economy* 82(1):34–55.

Ruttan, Vernon W. 1954. *Technological Progress in the Meatpacking Industry, 1919–47*. USDA Marketing Research Report no. 59. Washington: Government Printing Office.

———. 1957. Agricultural and Non-agricultural Growth in Output per Unit of Input. *Journal of Farm Economics* 39 (December): 1566–76.

Schmookler, Jacob. 1952. The Changing Efficiency of the American Economy, 1869–1938. *Review of Economics and Statistics* 34 (August): 214–31.

Schultz, Theodore W. 1953. *The Economic Organization of Agriculture*. New York: McGraw Hill.

Solow, Robert M. 1957. Technical Change and the Aggregate Production Function. *Review of Economics and Statistics* 39(3):312–20.

———. 1960. Investment and Technical Progress. In *Mathematical Methods in the Social Sciences,* ed. K. Arrow et al. Stanford, Calif.: Stanford University Press.

Stone, Richard. 1956. "Quantity and Price Indexes in National Accounts." Paris: Organization for European Economic Cooperation.

Trajtenberg, Manuel. 1983. Dynamics and Welfare Analysis of Product Innovations. Ph.D. thesis. Harvard University.

Triplett, Jack E. 1975. The Measurement of Inflation: A Survey of Research on the Accuracy of Price Indexes. In *Analysis of Inflation,* ed. Paul H. Earl, 19–82.

———. 1983a. Concept of Quality in Input and Output Price Measures: A Resolution of the User-Value Resources-Cost Debate. In *The U.S. National Income and Product Accounts,* ed. M. F. Foss. NBER Studies in Income and Wealth, vol. 47. Chicago: University of Chicago Press.

———. 1983b. Introduction: An Essay on Labor Cost. In *The Measurement of Labor Cost,* ed. J. E. Triplett. NBER Studies in Income and Wealth, vol. 48. Chicago: University of Chicago Press.

———. 1986. The Economic Interpretation of Hedonic Methods. *Survey of Current Business* 86(1):36–40.

———. 1987. Hedonic Functions and Hedonic Indexes. In *The New Palgrave: A Dictionary of Economics,* ed. J. Eatwell, M. Milgate, and P. Newman, 630–34. London: Macmillan.

Vail, E. E. 1932. Retail Prices of Fertilizer Materials and Mixed Fertilizers. *AES Bulletin 545*. Ithaca, N.Y.: Cornell University.

Waugh, F. V. 1928. Quality Factors Influencing Vegetable Prices. *Journal of Farm Economics* 10:185–96.

———. 1929. *Quality as a Determinant of Vegetable Prices*. New York: Columbia University Press.

Comment Robert E. Lipsey

These historical reflections on hedonic price indexes grossly understate Zvi Griliches' contribution. As he mentions, his contribution was not original. However, even though there had been some earlier instances, the fact is that the idea was totally dead before he revived it, although it offered some hope

Robert E. Lipsey is professor of economics, Queens College, and the Graduate School and University Center, the City University of New York. He is also an NBER research associate and the director of the New York office of the National Bureau of Economic Research.

to problems that appeared completely intractable. Although the earliest examples cited go back to 1929 and 1932 and Andrew Court's ingenious paper on automobiles prices was published in 1939, von Hofsten wrote a whole book about *Price Indexes and Quality Changes* in 1952 without mentioning hedonic indexes or Court's work. Richard Stone (1956) did calculate a hedonic price index, referred to Court's study of automobile prices, and endorsed the idea of pricing the characteristics of a product, but his advocacy, perhaps because this was only one of many topics considered in his book, had little impact. I recall that when I studied the literature on price indexes in the early 1950s before beginning my work on export and import price indexes, I was not pointed toward Court's work in any of my reading. When I did come across it accidentally, I was astonished and fascinated, but I did not think of actually using such an unconventional method. What Griliches did was to be enterprising enough to take this idea seriously, bring the methods and the analysis up to date, and start a whole new branch of research on price and quantity measurement. He was not the inventor, but he certainly was the crucial entrepreneur.

One of the points in Griliches' paper is that the hedonic method gives us a method of estimating "missing" prices: prices that have not been observed. The prices may be missing either because we failed to observe them when the transactions took place, as in the case of a new product that escaped the notice of price collectors in its early stages. Or they may be missing because they were unobservable, as, for example, if no transactions took place.

In our international price studies (Kravis and Lipsey 1971), Irving Kravis and I came across an interesting example of the use of the hedonic method to estimate a missing price on the part of noneconomists who seemed to be unaware of the economic literature. The engineering staff of an aircraft company was faced with the task of estimating the price the company would have to pay for engines, not yet in production and with specifications outside the range of existing engines, for a proposed new aircraft. The method they used was to run a multiple regression relating prices of existing aircraft engines to various characteristics such as thrust, the main influence, and many other characteristics in a number of different equation forms. This calculation was performed in 1962, very shortly after the time Griliches published his first paper on hedonic price indexes. They were speaking hedonics without knowing it. It would be interesting to know if this was a common practice among engineers.

The hedonic method also offers a solution to another problem that has proved extremely difficult in price collection. The producers of price data have been urged for many years to move toward the use of transactions prices in place of list prices, and the Price Statistics Review Committee urged the BLS to try to collect prices from buyers rather than, or in addition to, sellers. However, in most types of complex products such as machinery, that objective conflicts with the standard procedure of pricing the same specification in period after period, because no two purchases are of products with exactly the same combination of specifications or exactly the same terms of sale. The choice is between getting fictitious prices for a consistent specification or collecting actual transaction prices and somehow adjusting them for inconsistent specifications to some consistent basis. The first use of that solution that I know of, and one that did use a hedonic analysis on actual transaction prices, was by Dean and de Podwin (1961).

An alternative method, which was described in an article about the electrical equipment conspiracy cases of the early 1960s (Kuhlman 1967), was to derive the prices of characteristics from the companies' price lists and, given the characteristics of each individual transaction, to calculate the amount "off-book" that it involved. The combination of an index of list prices over time, based on specification pricing from the price lists, with changes in the percentage "off-book," gives an estimate of the movement of transaction prices. The chief drawback of the method, in comparison to hedonic price measurement, is that the relative values of the product characteristics are determined by the seller in his list price formulation, rather than by the consumers in the market. But the method does permit its user to make use of actual transaction prices in a way that is not possible if the usual specification pricing is used.

On another topic, I am skeptical about the usefulness of the estimation of production functions as a way of organizing the study of productivity growth. At the necessary level of aggregation, they are fictions far removed from what I would think of as genuine production functions for very specific products or processes. I can see their value for estimating economies of scale, but I am not at all sure that they are particularly suited to judging the contribution of R&D and other "externality-generating activities," such as health, education, public safety, and so on. It seems to me that the production function technology inevitably tends to emphasize direct inputs over indirect inputs.

There is a broader question that is raised by the use of the production function idea for measuring productivity. That is, whether we want to confine our interest to inputs and outputs that go through the business or "production" sector and ignore those outside it. We could, presumably, increase our output per unit of measured input by forcing low productivity labor and capital out of production, for example, by raising wages and imposing taxes on the use of capital goods. Ideally, perfect quality adjustments for labor and capital inputs would break the illusion of productivity growth, but that does not seem to be a likely outcome.

If we want to know about the efficiency of the society as a whole, rather than that of a narrowly defined "production sector," and that is, surely, at least one of the things we want, we should count the inputs and outputs outside the production sector. We should consider the input of time by consumers in shopping, commuting, banking, and so forth, and the difference, as Griliches mentions, between the value of input according to the time of day or the day of the week. A withdrawal from a bank on a holiday or a weekend must have some different value and different cost to the parties from that of a withdrawal during banking hours. In particular, as we become more interested in the output and productivity of the service sector, and if we are skeptical about the official measures, as I am, we will be compelled to think more seriously about the meaning of output and input in service industries and about the relationships between service industry inputs and outputs and inputs and outputs in the home. I suspect that there is more to be learned about the mysteries in recent productivity developments along these lines than in pursuing that picture of the continuous process plant producing a single output from labor and capital inputs.

References

Court, Andrew T. 1939. Hedonic Price Indexes with Automotive Examples. In *The Dynamics of Automotive Demand,* ed. Charles F. Roos 99–117. New York: General Motors.

Dean, Charles R., and Horace J. de Podwin. 1961. Product Variation and Price Indexes: A Case Study of Electrical Apparatus. In *1961 Proceedings of the Business and Economic Statistics Section*. American Statistical Association.

Hofsten, Erland von. 1952. *Price Indexes and Quality Changes*. Stockholm: Bokforlaget Forum AB.

Kravis, Irving B., and Robert E. Lipsey. 1971. *Price Competitiveness in World Trade*. New York: National Bureau of Economic Research.

Kuhlman, John M. 1967. Theoretical Issues in the Estimation of Damages in a Private Antitrust Action. *Southern Economic Journal* (April).

Stone, Richard. 1956. Quantity and Price Indexes in National Accounts. Paris: Organization for European Economic Corporation.

7 Hedonic Methods in Statistical Agency Environments: An Intellectual Biopsy

Jack E. Triplett

The Price Statistics Review Committee (1961)—usually referred to as the Stigler Committee after its chairman, George Stigler—recommended that statistical agencies explore hedonic methods, which the committee felt would provide a "more objective" way for dealing with quality change than traditional Bureau of Labor Statistics (BLS) methods. A major hedonic study by Zvi Griliches (1961), was among the staff papers published with the Stigler Committee Report. Griliches' study is—by far—the most often cited portion of the report, and it may fairly be said to have set off the entire modern literature on hedonic functions and hedonic indexes.

The term "hedonic methods" encompasses *any* use in an economic measurement of a "hedonic function,"

$$P = h(c). \tag{1}$$

In this paper I adopt the convention that capital letters designate "goods" variables and lower-case ones refer to characteristics: in (1), P is accordingly a cross section of goods prices—one P_{ijt} for each jth "variety" or "model" of the ith good or service (e.g., the prices of different models of automobiles) available at time t, and the matrix c has a row of "characteristics" for each of the same models.[1]

The first employment of hedonic methods in any official U.S. government price statistic occurred in the Census Bureau's "Price Index of New One-

Jack E. Triplett is chief economist of the Bureau of Economic Analysis, U.S. Department of Commerce.

Valuable comments were received from B. K. Atrostic, Ernst R. Berndt, and Ellen Dulberger, and from members of the 1987 National Bureau of Economic Research Summer Institute, where an earlier version was presented. Views expressed are those of the author and do not represent official positions of either the Bureau of Economic Analysis or the U.S. Department of Commerce.

Family Houses Sold," which was introduced in 1968 with data commencing in 1963. This index was adopted for the construction components of the National Income and Product Accounts (*Survey of Current Business* 54, no. 8 [August 1974]: 18–27). In fact, the single-family house price index is used as a proxy in deflating a variety of construction activities in addition to houses (see U.S. Department of Commerce 1987; and Pieper, in this volume).

The second employment of hedonic methods in a U.S. price index occurred nearly 20 years later. The BEA-IBM computer equipment price indexes (covering four different products) were introduced into the National Income and Product Accounts in the benchmark revision announced in December 1985 (see Cole et al. 1986; Cartwright 1986). Though a substantial amount of research on hedonic methods took place within the BLS or under its sponsorship from the mid-1960s on,[2] the first BLS use in an official price index came in 1988, when an adjustment for aging, estimated with a hedonic function, was put into consumer price index (CPI) housing components (U.S. Department of Labor 1988).[3]

To put it succinctly, hardly any use has been made of hedonic methods in U.S. government price indexes. The same statement holds for price indexes of other countries.[4] Why has this been the case? It is especially remarkable that the once-controversial cost-of-living (COL) index concept has been embraced in the BLS, while hedonic methods have found little role in the price statistics for which they were developed.

The following sections review reasons why statistical agencies have resisted hedonic methods. The list of factors impeding the adoption of hedonic methods is inherently speculative, in that it is based on my perception of how statistical agency operating units viewed hedonic methods as a practical device for use in constructing price indexes. The list is not derived from official agency positions or other documented sources, and the positions I outline may not necessarily all have been held by any agency manager. In particular, these positions should not necessarily be attributed to present managers.

I should note at the outset that I am not entirely unsympathetic to most of the positions I am reporting, even when I disagree with them. In each case, I review how these operating perceptions meshed, or did not mesh, with problems or findings that were present in the research literature. Many concerns of operating mangers had parallels, 15 or so years ago, in the research literature. Most of the points I discuss have now, however, been resolved and are no longer valid reasons for resistance to the use of hedonic methods.

I am also aware that some readers may regard these points simply as "excuses." Perception, or perhaps interpretation, varies with the eye of the beholder. One of the difficulties in the interaction between analytic (read "academically oriented") economists and statistical agency managers is a kind of "two different worlds" syndrome. What one thinks a fatal shortcoming, the other regards as an excuse; and what the second judges vital, the first deems trivial. Nevertheless, there is more parallelism than has usually been appreciated between the hedonic research literature and the concerns of statistical agency managers—or at least that was so 10–15 years ago. This review is intended to promote some communication, as well as to precipitate a current reassessment.

7.1 Hedonic Methods Had No Theory

The statement that statistical agency managers were reluctant to adopt a technique because it lacked theory may seem surprising. However, directly in the research institutions and indirectly in statistical agencies, hedonic methods and research were questioned for theoretical reasons.

Griliches's (1961) revival of hedonic methods arrived when economists were showing increased or heightened interest in index number theory and in more rigorous application of theory to empirical work. Nearly every graduate reading list in the 1960s contained Koopman's (1947) classic "Measurement without Theory," and the 1960s and early 1970s research ethos held that empirical relationships should be derived from theory. For a consumption price measure, this view translated into the demand that the hedonic function and hedonic indexes should be derivable from the utility function (by analogy to deriving empirical demand functions from utility functions and to deriving the form of the COL index from the consumption cost function—see the examples in Christensen and Manser 1976). Hedonic indexes were widely believed within the profession to be empirical constructions that lacked any relation to economic theory.[5]

Within the BLS, theoretical concerns took a parallel but particularized form—the view that hedonic measures could be given no conceptual interpretation within a Laspeyres-formula price index. In the 1960s the CPI was still thought of within the BLS as a separate concept from a COL index. Once the COL index was adopted as the conceptual basis for the CPI, the internal statistical agency concern matched exactly the one in the research literature (though it was not necessarily voiced in the same language).

7.1.1 Filling the Theoretical Gap

By the mid-1970s, however, the gap in theory was well on its way to being filled.[6] The theoretical relation of the hedonic function to utility and production functions was established by Rosen (1974). To outline Rosen's contribution, we first assume that the characteristics of goods, rather than the goods themselves, are the true arguments of the utility function (true inputs to the production function). This is an implication of the "hedonic hypothesis" that heterogeneous goods are aggregations of characteristics. Thus we have

$$Q = Q(c, Z) \tag{2}$$

where Q is utility (scalar output), Z is a vector of other, homogeneous goods (productive inputs), and for expositional simplicity we specify only one heterogeneous good in the system with characteristics (c). It is convenient to suppose that (2) can be written:

(2a) $$Q = Q(q(c), Z),$$

where $q(\cdot)$ is an aggregator over the characteristics (c) that are embodied in the heterogeneous good. A parallel development of the theory on the producer side makes the production of a heterogeneous good the joint output of the set of characteristics it contains.

The economic behavior of buyers and sellers of heterogeneous goods can be described by sets of demand and supply functions for characteristics. These demand and supply functions are derived from the optimization of buyer's and seller's objective functions over characteristics. On the demand side, for example, $q(\cdot)$, above, carries information about preferences (using technology) and the hedonic function—$h(\cdot)$ from equation (1)—provides information about the characteristics price surface.

Rosen (1974) showed that if there are n competitive buyers, with dispersion in tastes (using technologies), the hedonic function, $h(\cdot)$, will trace out an envelope to the set of preferences (using technologies), described by the n aggregator functions, $q_1(\cdot), \ldots, q_n(\cdot)$. As with any envelope, the form of $h(\cdot)$ is thus independent of the form of $q(\cdot)$—except for special cases—and is determined on the demand side by the distribution of buyers across characteristics space. A parallel condition exists on the seller side.

As a consequence, the form of the hedonic function, $h(\cdot)$, is, in the general case, purely an empirical matter.[7] In particular, and despite many statements to the contrary that have appeared over many years, nothing in the theory rules out the semilogarithmic form, which has frequently emerged as "best" in functional form tests in the hedonic literature (Griliches 1971). The hedonic function represents a *price* surface in characteristics space, and empirically it can take on any of a large number of functional forms. It is not analogous to (say) a demand (or supply) function that is derived from a utility (production) function—nor is the hedonic function a reduced-form function of normal demand and supply functions (as is so often, but erroneously, stated in recent literature).

Understanding hedonic *indexes* required extending index number theory into characteristic space (that is, reformulating price index theory using the characteristics of goods as quantities, rather than just the numbers of goods themselves, and the characteristics prices or costs, instead of goods prices). The main reference for this extension is Triplett (1983). A summary follows.

It is well known that a COL index (input cost index) shows the minimum change in cost between two periods that leaves living standards (output) unchanged—that is, the ratio of costs of optimal points on the same indifference curve (production isoquant) under two input price regimes (see Pollak 1983). Such an index is often termed an "exact" index.

For the separable function (2a), an exact "subindex" (Pollak 1975; Blackorby and Russell 1978) can be computed that involves only the characteristics of the heterogeneous good. A subindex might be a price index for, say, automobiles, which would be computed as the ratio of the costs, under two characteristics price regimes, of two constant utility (constant output, where autos are investment goods) collections of auto characteristics (Triplett 1983, 1987). The subindex is a "constant quality" or "equivalent quality" price index because the two collections of characteristics implied by it are equivalent in utility (equivalent in producing output).

The hedonic price index can be thought of as an approximation to the exact characteristics subindex, provided conditions necessary for the exact subindex are met—that is, the utility (production) function can be written as (2a). A parallel exact characteristics price index can be developed on the output side (Triplett 1983), and again the hedonic index provides an approximation.

In view of some confusion that exists in the hedonic literature, one should note that in the general case the hedonic index is not an exact (characteristics) subindex. When the hedonic index is taken from the hedonic function (the "dummy variable" method—see below), the functional form of the hedonic index depends solely on the form of the hedonic function, which is in general independent of the form of both using and producing technologies (see above). The exact (characteristics) index, on the other hand, requires information on the utility (production) function and incorporates the effects of substitution among characteristics as relative characteristics prices change.[8] A similar statement can be made for the output price index case. Special cases exist for which the hedonic index and the exact characteristics subindex for inputs—or the hedonic index and the exact output price index—coincide, but these cases are ignored here.

A recent statement of these developments in the conceptual foundations for hedonic functions and hedonic indexes is Triplett (1987); see also the "Summary of the Theory" section in Triplett (1989). I do not mean to imply there are no unresolved problems. However, by the mid- to late 1970s, to say that hedonic methods had "no theory" was no longer correct.

7.1.2 Empirical Consequences of the Theoretical Gap

Historically, the no-theory perception inhibited empirical research on hedonic methods, both inside statistical agencies and outside them. In academic circles, such work was thought, in some sense, not "respectable," and in fact little hedonic price index research appeared in the journals, particularly after about 1973 or so.[9] With that attitude in the profession at large, one did not find good graduate students in the 1970s choosing dissertation topics on the subject, and, accordingly, there was no stock of such researchers from which to recruit for work inside statistical agencies. The contrast between the availability of complementary research outside statistical agencies for empirical estimation of COL indexes and the absence of it in the case of quality change and hedonic methods is striking.

The perception that hedonic methods had no theoretical foundation also, I am convinced, lowered the quality of the hedonic research that was done: it was all too easy to rationalize a hedonic function whose variables had little or no relation to the technology being investigated, on the grounds that all one wanted was a maximum R^2. That, in my opinion, resulted in a large quantity of poor work.

One should not, however, overemphasize the negative effects of the "no theory" perception. It is always valuable to straighten out theoretical issues. Theoretical thinking about hedonic functions in the late 1960s and early 1970s contained too many theoretical "proofs" that were not, and "impossibility theorems" that were irrelevant. In its present stage of development, the theory of hedonic functions provides a useful guide to empirical research—an implication of the theory, for example, is that the arguments of hedonic functions are technical or engineering variables. Theory also provides guidance on the search for functional form and on the appropriate construction of hedonic indexes.

7.2 The Perception That Hedonic Methods Required That Price Index Calculation Procedures Be Changed

In most early hedonic research, price indexes were calculated by the "dummy variable method"—a time dummy variable, or a series of them, inserted into a "pooled" cross-section regression (that is, eq. [1], with two or more periods of data) estimates the price change that is *not* accounted for by changing characteristics. This remained the dominant approach in the research literature even though, as Griliches (1971,7) remarked, the dummy variable method was "not well articulated with the rest of the index number literature."

Within statistical agencies the perception formed that adopting hedonic methods meant estimating the price index from a regression, as opposed to the traditional calculation of matched-models, matched-outlets price relatives. Indeed, within statistical agencies, the hedonic technique was usually referred to as *the* "regression method," and hedonic indexes as "regression indexes," or indexes computed by "the regression method."

This statistical agency perception was always quite wrong. Griliches (1961), for example, used his automobile hedonic functions in several ways to calculate price indexes; his were not exclusively dummy variable price index estimates. The Census Bureau's price index for new single family houses is not a dummy variable index; it is a price index for characteristics.[10] Triplett (1971) discusses in a general way how to integrate hedonic methods into traditional BLS price index procedures, and Triplett and McDonald (1977) demonstrated empirically how to use a hedonic function within existing producer price index (PPI) methodology to make quality adjustments to the price quotes gathered for the PPI (Early and Sinclair 1983 followed the Triplett-McDonald procedure). The IBM-BEA computer equipment price indexes (Cole et al.

1986) use the hedonic function to impute prices for "missing" computers—those observed in one period but not in another—within an index that is calculated by computing price relatives for matched models and (because they are used as deflators in the National Income and Product Accounts, or NIPAs) a Paasche price index formula.[11] All these calculations fit the definition of hedonic methods (see above), they can all be described as hedonic indexes, and all fit comfortably within established statistical agency procedures for producing price indexes.

It is thus a little puzzling that the perception lingered on so long that hedonic methods required altering index calculation procedures. Hedonic methods affect only the way quality change is evaluated.

Actually, though, the reverse side of the same perceptual shortcoming applied outside statistical agencies. There was far too little concern given in the research literature to the form of the hedonic price index—that is, to the way one goes from the estimated hedonic function to the hedonic price index.

Most researchers constructed a hedonic price index by the dummy variable method and compared the results with some relevant published statistical agency index (and sometimes with some that were not relevant). They called the difference between the two the "effect of quality change." Few considered that the difference, or part of it, might also have been attributable to the fact that the implicit index formula for calculating the (dummy variable) hedonic index differed from the one used by the statistical agency. Equally few researchers considered the robustness of hedonic indexes to variations in the way the hedonic function was employed to create a "quality adjusted" index—despite the good example set by Griliches (1961, 1964). Statistical agency managers were more aware of these points (and even might have overemphasized them) and were accordingly less impressed with the evidence presented by researchers than were many of those researchers themselves.

Thus, statistical agency reservations about dummy variable hedonic indexes had parallels in attitudes of researchers outside statistical agencies. Both groups were wrong in their own ways. The idea that adopting hedonic methods forces a change in calculation procedures has no validity. Quantification of the empirical effects of alternative ways of using hedonic methods, however, is a research topic that has been neglected. Indeed, it is peculiar that, with all of the focus on index number formulas that occurred in the index number literature, the question of index number form was almost entirely ignored when researchers turned to quality change.

7.3 The Perception That Hedonic Indexes Were More Sensitive to Arbitrary Research Procedures Than Were Traditional Approaches

This very widespread perception within statistical agencies drew on some of the evidence from research studies, yet the conclusion is unsupportable.

The lack of robustness in some of the empirical hedonic indexes that have appeared in the economics literature made agency managers very nervous indeed. Cases exist in which different hedonic price indexes were submitted by the same researcher from the same data, using the same dummy variable method, with outcomes that were quite far apart. The suspicion arose that other investigators got similar dispersions and might not have published them. Also, initial, usually unpublished, trials within some statistical agencies obtained unsatisfactory results, including poor fits, wrong signs, and implausible indexes.

On this score, statistical agency managers perceived correctly that empirical hedonic indexes sometimes lacked sufficient robustness to be reliable. Many of the published hedonic studies simply were not very good. Some foundered because researchers did not have access to good quality data. Their cross sections of prices were usually published list prices, with some unknown sets of errors with respect to transactions prices that were probably (from the evidence) correlated with the explanatory variables. Researchers often paid little attention to the selection of explanatory variables and too uncritically accepted published (in trade journals and the like) values on the explanatory variables they chose, without checking the accuracy of published information (against, e.g., manufacturers' information). Even a cursory review of the hedonic literature suggests the need for much more care in the choice of variables to serve as characteristics and the need for more effort on the part of economic researchers to understand the technology of production and use of the product (in order to choose appropriate variables). Moreover, researchers often failed to present the effect of some of their data decisions on their price indexes.

Put another way, research methods for producing valid hedonic functions were not written down anywhere in the literature (and still are not). Perhaps the best examples of such methodological discussion, combining technological knowledge of the product and the economics of hedonic functions, is in the literature on computer hedonic functions (see Fisher et al. 1983; Cole et al. 1986; Dulberger 1989; Flamm 1987; and Triplett 1989).

A related point is that researchers have often presented or used hedonic index variances in inappropriate or irrelevant ways. One usually sees in research studies, for example, a test of the null hypothesis that quality-adjusted (hedonic) indexes do not differ from zero, a test that is obviously not invariant to the true rate of inflation. Because the hedonic technique is a mechanism for adjusting for quality change, it is more appropriate to test the null hypothesis that the hedonic index does not differ from an index, computed from the same data, that has no quality adjustment—in other words, to test the statistical significance of the hedonic quality adjustments, not the statistical significance of the measured rate of inflation. When researchers noted with satisfaction that their hedonic indexes were "significant," they were usually reporting only that the rate of inflation was positive, no matter how measured; the actual "hedonic" part of a good many hedonic studies lacked statistical significance.

It is not surprising that poor hedonic studies tarnished the reputation of the method: poor research can sometimes be as influential as good. Yet, the conclusion that hedonic methods were more arbitrary than conventional approaches to quality change cannot follow from one-sided evaluation of the poorer of the hedonic studies.

For one thing, the robustness of conventional methods for compiling price indexes is not known because there is little or no information on the subject. Consider a possible robustness test of the conventional method: one could assemble alternative teams of BLS commodity specialists, give each team the same information on examples of quality change, and ask them to reach independent judgments about how the examples should be treated in the indexes. I predict that the teams would sometimes reach different outcomes and that the outcomes would, in many cases, produce perceptible effects on the indexes. There is thus a stochastic element to the conventional quality-adjustment process, in the sense that repeated trials yield different outcomes. Those outcomes could be used to produce a quasi-variance estimate for this part of the price index calculation procedure. Though I have no idea whether this variance component would be larger than the comparable variance one gets in a hedonic index, a comparison of the two would prove quite interesting and should be carried out by some statistical agency.

Second, the usefulness of hedonic methods should, of course, be judged on the potential of the best hedonic studies, not on the poorer of them. Though statistical agency managers perceived correctly the inadequacies in a good many published hedonic studies, the better studies show that hedonic methods have great potential for improving measurement.

7.4 Hedonic Functions Need Large Cross Sections of Transactions Prices

This topic reflects another anomaly in the research literature: there has always been much—valid—concern that price quotations gathered for the wholesale price index (WPI), the PPI, and other price indexes might represent list rather than transactions prices. Yet, researchers on quality change were too frequently content to produce a hedonic price index that was nothing more than a quality-adjusted list price series. In this case, statistical agency managers were correct in perceiving the potential error of such approaches, and many outside researchers were too cavalier (Zvi Griliches was, always, an exception; see Griliches 1961).

It is true that on certain assumptions one might form quality *adjustments* from cross sections of list prices and apply them to transactions price quotes obtained for the indexes (this was the approach of Triplett and McDonald 1977). But one never knows the size of biases that ensue when the assumptions do not hold.

Production use of hedonic methods does require cross sections of transactions prices, gathered at least periodically, and such data have seldom been available, even in government price programs. Lack of the required data inhibited use of hedonic methods.

Gathering cross sections of transactions prices, even on a periodic basis, would be both expensive and burdensome to respondents. On the other hand, collecting cross-section information to improve quality adjustment in the price indexes has never received managerial consideration in the BLS, at least since an unsuccessful effort in the mid-1960s.

7.5 The Perception That Automobiles Were the Test Case

Automobiles were the subject in much of the early exploratory work on hedonic price indexes. For a number of reasons they were a poor test case.

A great amount of effort has gone into adjusting government automobile price indexes for quality changes in "new models." The BLS staff faced many problems for which available procedures were recognized as inadequate. However, existing hedonic functions for automobiles contained little potential for resolving the measurement problems that have arisen in automobile price indexes since at least the mid-1960s. It was perhaps therefore too easy—and certainly incorrect—for agency managers to decide that the auto studies proved that hedonic methods were not useful. Because the relation between hedonic measures and the adjustments that were actually performed in the auto indexes is not well understood, and because that relation is important in determining the potential of hedonic methods to improve the indexes, it is worth considering quality change and the automobile indexes in more detail.

7.5.1 Cost-based Quality Adjustments in Automobiles

Since the early 1960s, quality change in automobiles has been handled in BLS price indexes (both the CPI and the PPI are handled similarly) by obtaining production cost information from manufacturers. For example, cost-based quality adjustments for 1988 model cars accounted for 54% of the recorded $400 increase in average auto prices collected for the PPI at new model introduction in October 1987 (table 7.1). This production cost method was instituted (perhaps expanded is a better word) in response to the Stigler committee's judgment that BLS methods for treating quality change were inadequate.

A three-step sequence occurs in the use of manufacturer's cost information. (*a*) For each car included in the indexes, a detailed list of engineering and specification changes is obtained from the manufacturer at the beginning of the model year. (*b*) Information (obtained from the manufacturers and other sources) about each of these changes is used by BLS staff to determine whether each of the changes is to be treated as a quality change. At various times, a set of internal "guidelines" have spelled out the principles governing this stage, but the guidelines are general rules, not specific ones, and in most

Table 7.1 **Values of Cost-based Quality Adjustments in Sample of Automobiles in Producer Price Index, Model Years 1967–88**

	Manufacturer's Level			Retail Level		
Automobile Model Year	Average Value of Quality Change	Of Which, Value of Mandatory Changes[a]	Average Price Increase	Average Value of Quality Change	Of Which, Value of Mandatory Changes[a]	Average Price Increase[b]
1988	$214.94	n.a.	$399.01	$245.56	$65.42	$458.66
1987	37.89	n.a.	694.29	47.13	1.92	776.38
1986[c]	154.55	n.a.	616.86	186.50	27.42	745.52
1985[d]	125.52	n.a.	232.50	151.45	20.02	268.20
1984	91.87	n.a.	183.65	110.08	46.80	221.70
1983	107.66	n.a.	215.55	128.04	64.65	263.92
1982	104.70	n.a.	463.61	126.32	84.68	562.54
1981[d]	438.39	n.a.	664.57	530.85	470.94	536.14
1980	195.19	n.a.	n.a.	241.51	131.33	365.85
1979	37.00	n.a.	n.a.	46.35	17.85	300.30
1978[d]	40.88	n.a.	n.a.	50.12	9.99	424.49
1977[d]	47.05	n.a.	n.a.	59.19	21.21	322.30
1976	12.00	n.a.	n.a.	15.60	21.00	198
1975	102.30[e]	n.a.	n.a.	129.90[e]	147.20[e]	386
1974	91.30	n.a.	n.a.	117.90	109.00	n.a.
1973	95.40	n.a.	n.a.	123.80	113.30[f]	n.a.
1972	n.a.	n.a.	n.a.	20	9.00[f]	19
1971	n.a.	n.a.	n.a.	25[e]	29[e]	220
1970	n.a.	n.a.	n.a.	46	13	107
1969	n.a.	n.a.	n.a.	1	14	41
1968	40.05	$40.75	87.54	57.00[g]	58.00[h]	n.a.
1967	n.a.	n.a.	n.a.	55[i]	—	55

Sources: Annual Bureau of Labor Statistics press releases on quality change in new model automobiles, 1966–87.
Note: n.a. = not available.
[a]cost of changes to meet federal smog, safety, and fuel-efficiency standards.
[b]In most, if not all, cases, average change in manufacturer's suggested retail (list) price.
[c]Calculating procedure changed: under the former system, the five values in the 1986 row are $150.11, $402.68, $181.22, $27.42, and $482.03.
[d]One or more cars in the sample were downsized in this year. In most cases values for these cars are excluded from the quality-change data.
[e]Includes an additional quality adjustment made after new-model introduction, and reported in a subsequent press release.
[f]Includes "voluntarily added" equipment in anticipation of future increases in standards.
[g]Estimated by the author by assuming the −$0.70 manufacturer's value for nonmandatory quality change (col. 2 less col. 1) would amount to −$1.00, retail.
[h]Reported in a subsequent note; press release gave manufacturer-level values for this year.
[i]Press release does not give a value, but rather states that the quality adjustment was equal to "practically all" of the price increase.

cases the final decision about whether a particular engineering change is or is not a quality change rests on staff judgment. As an example, at one point a company's substitution of a digital clock for an analog clock was judged by BLS staff as a styling change, not a quality change, so any price differential associated with the new clock was allowed to pass forward into the indexes. (*c*) *After* the determination in (*b*), the production cost of each of the accepted changes is used to adjust new car prices.

In the early years of the process, the full value claimed by manufacturers became the quality adjustment, but by the early 1970s, if not before, manufacturers' claims were often not fully allowed by the BLS staff.[12] In a number of cases, model changes in autos have been regarded as too extreme to apply the cost procedures. An example was the so-called downsizing that occurred on some domestic cars beginning with the 1977 model year, where the new models were smaller externally, but offered the same or more interior capacity (refer to table 7.1, n. *d* above). In these cases other quality-adjustment methods were substituted (usually, imputing the price change, after cost-based quality adjustments, from another car that was less fundamentally changed).

Engineering changes that occur from one model year to the next, even on cars that are not substantially changed, are complex, perplexing, and multitudinous. They were often hard for a staff without engineering expertise to evaluate, and sometimes were not easy for the manufacturer to fit into price index objectives. In one example, an inexperienced auto company executive had great difficulty locating for BLS staff a brace that was added one year to reduce transmission vibration and also spent some effort searching for the "roll center," which the company claimed it had altered for the new model year (the roll center is an imaginary point—the center of the arc described by the body of the car as it leans into a corner). Some early attempts to obtain evaluations from government agencies involved in automobile regulation failed.

Moreover, it is clear that the cost data provided by manufacturers are frequently not the relevant costs, even for a "resource cost" adjustment (see below). There are thus many reasons for dissatisfaction with cost-based quality adjustments.

7.5.2 Technical Change and Automobile Hedonic Functions

If one were to evaluate most of the automobile quality changes for which the BLS has made a quality adjustment over the past 25 years, using any automobile hedonic function that has appeared in the literature, one would conclude that the individual changes were frequently too small to justify an adjustment. That is, most of those changes in specifications, when introduced as variables into a hedonic function, would have insignificant coefficients. Yet, in total those changes have involved substantial adjustments to car prices, amounting to several hundred dollars in some of the last 20 years (see table 7.1). It is doubtful that one wants to accept conclusions from the hedonic function that these cases should have been ignored. If "quality" encompasses a very large number of characteristics, or the product is complex in its use, the hedonic function suffers from missing variable bias.

The biggest problem with cost-based adjustment, however, centers on the appropriate treatment of mandatory antipollution and safety equipment and, in the second half of the 1970s, engineering changes that were necessary to meet federal fuel economy regulations. These mandatory changes account for a large share of the cost-based adjustments (see table 7.1).

Hedonic studies provided no information to adjust for mandatory changes. In part, the hedonic measures might have been right and the BLS wrong. It is certainly easy to argue that mandatory air pollution devices, for example, should have been treated as a tax on transportation rather than as an improvement in the quality of transportation services that automobiles render to consumers and to business users. Similarly, the right way for improved fuel efficiency to enter a COL index is through a reduction in gasoline consumption, and not by reducing the price of cars by an amount equal to the "cost" of manufacturing fuel-efficient engines.

In summary, the automobile hedonic functions in the *existing* literature did not provide BLS managers with any information at all on the most difficult of their problems.

7.5.3 The Automobile May Be too Complicated for Hedonic Studies

What one might call the 1960s hedonic technology (which really does not differ from Court's initial study in the 1930s) defined automobiles as functions of size and, especially, weight (Griliches 1961; Triplett 1969; Dhrymes 1971). The weight of the car is obviously a proxy for a large number of other characteristics. It has the undeniable advantage that most items of equipment (an air conditioner, say, or a tape deck, or better insulation against noise and vibration) have a weight penalty. Weight can serve as a proxy for a very large number of separate characteristics that could not feasibly be entered into a single regression.

The difficulty is that weight is an unreliable proxy, precisely because weight for its own sake is undesirable (as Court noted in his original paper in 1939). Periodic engineering innovations have reduced the ratio of weight to the characteristics that are truly desired. Automobile hedonic functions based on weight give biased price indexes.

It is not all that hard to improve on the 1960s hedonic technology. Instead of taking weight and the external size of a car, one can specify a hedonic function that is defined on the auto's internal passenger- and luggage-carrying volume, plus a small number of other characteristics. The "fit" for such a function is as satisfactory as for the 1960s version hedonic functions. Measures of cornering, braking, acceleration, ride quality, and even quietness are available from various test programs, and more careful modeling of the automobile as a consumer product (or as an investment good providing input services to production) might yield more believable results that have so far appeared in the literature.

However, the bane of automobile hedonic functions in the past has been the degree of multicollinearity among explanatory variables. Multicollinearity, because it leads to the exclusion of important characteristics, assures that changes in the omitted characteristics can swamp the effect of the included ones, without providing a clear signal to the investigator. One might not care to argue that, from an engineering standpoint, the automobile is more complicated than, say, a computer or an airplane; however, the way automobile characteristics enter the utility function—what the automobile does for its user—is in fact very complicated indeed, and very hard to model, and for this reason the appropriate set of variables is hard to determine. It is in this sense that automobiles may have been the wrong place to start because more credible results can be obtained from hedonic studies on other products.

7.6 The Perception That Hedonic Methods Measured User Value, Not Resource Cost

Actually, I doubt that this factor significantly inhibited the adoption of hedonic methods. It has, however, often been so perceived, and because so much ink has been spilled over the user-value, resource-cost controversy one can hardly review hedonic methods without discussing this set of issues.

Andrew Court himself was probably the originator of the resource-cost, user-value debate. He selected the name "hedonic" because of his belief that his new indexes measured value to the user: "Hedonic price comparisons are those which recognize the potential contribution of any commodity, a motor car in this instance, to the welfare and happiness of its purchasers and the community" (Court 1939, 107).

The view that hedonic indexes carried a user-value interpretation has lingered on through the years. It was adopted by the Stigler Committee, for whom the user-value interpretation was a desirable property (because under this interpretation use of hedonic methods in the CPI would move it in the direction of a COL index). Others who favored the use of hedonic methods have accepted the same interpretation.

The view that hedonic methods represented uniquely user-value measures was also held by some professional critics, who argued that resource cost, not user value, was the appropriate criterion to use for quality adjustments in price indexes for the national accounts. Denison (1957), Jaszi (1964), and Gilbert (1961) were among the economists who took this position.

I emphasize that both proponents and opponents of hedonic methods in the 1960s shared the common view that they represented a user-value approach to measuring quality change. Historically, proponents of hedonic methods almost invariably advocated a user-value quality standard; opponents have favored the resource-cost standard. The resource-cost, user-value debate was spirited and even acrimonious at times, and has often been interpreted as aligning statistical agencies on one side and academic users on the other.

7.6.1 Statistical Agency Positions

There is, however, no evidence that the equation of hedonic methods with user value had any effect whatever on the willingness of statistical agencies to adopt hedonic methods. Under the federal government's decentralized system for producing economic statistics, the BLS has responsibility for price indexes. During the entire period under discussion, the BLS accepted value to the user as the appropriate quality criterion for the CPI and—at least up to 1978—for the WPI as well.[13] Thus, if it were true that hedonic methods measured user value, then the technique fit the BLS's own view of what was conceptually appropriate for its price measures. In my association with the BLS (which began on an intermittent basis in 1968), I never on any occasion heard "hedonic methods equals user value" raised as an objection to their use in BLS price indexes.

When the Census Bureau's new single-family house price index was announced in 1968, it was described as a response to the Stigler Committee's criticism of construction price statistics (Musgrave 1969). So far as I have been able to determine, the user-value, resource-cost controversy was never an issue in the development of the single-family house index, nor was it a reason that the Census hedonic index program was never extended, as originally promised, to other construction activities.[14]

Finally, whenever a hedonic index has become available, and has proven superior to the alternatives, the Bureau of Economic Analysis has used it in the NIPAs. For example, the article that describes the introduction of the Census new house price index for NIPA construction deflation (*Survey of Current Business* 54, no. 8 [August 1974]: 18–27), refers to hedonic methods as measuring "the current price that the purchaser implicitly pays for each of [the] characteristics . . ."; this language is consistent with the then-prevailing user-value interpretation of hedonic methods. Concerns of a conceptual nature, if there were any at the time, appear to have been sublimated to the pragmatic need for improved data.[15]

It is certainly true that a vigorous debate over the proper treatment of quality change in economic statistics was carried on between (roughly) the mid-1960s and the mid-1970s. It is also true that some of the participants in the theoretical debate were identified with statistical agencies. There is little evidence, however, that the theoretical debate had much to do with agencies' willingness to adopt hedonic methods. My belief is that the factors discussed elsewhere in this article were far more important.[16]

7.6.2 The Resolution of the User-Value, Resources-Cost Debate

That this particular conceptual debate has not been a major factor in the adoption of hedonic methods is ironic. Our current understanding of hedonic methods shows that the identification of hedonic measures uniquely with user-value measures is incorrect; they provide, in most cases, approximations to both user-value and resource-cost concepts of quality change. Moreover, resource-cost and user-value concepts are not competitive (in the sense that if the one is right, the other must always be wrong); rather, each of the two concepts corresponds to a particular use of the data. User value is conceptually correct for quality change in a COL index (and thus for the CPI) or for a measure of investment or of productive inputs or their prices. Resource cost is the conceptually correct quality change concept for measures of output or for output price indexes (e.g., the revised PPI is notionally an output price index).

One important theoretical result is Rosen (1974), as noted above, who showed that in the competitive case the hedonic function provides estimates of the incremental acquisition cost of, and also revenues from, characteristics. Accordingly, implicit hedonic "prices" can serve as approximations either to user-value or to resource-cost valuations, an interpretation that is analogous to our normal interpretation of prices of goods. Jaszi (1964) had already noted that the effects of differing mixes of characteristics on the price of the product (he used as an example the proportion in a coffee-chickory mix) would be determined in equilibrium according to the costs of the separate components. Though Jaszi used his example to argue that hedonic methods should give the same measure as conventional approaches, his example also implies that economic forces assure that production cost will be reflected in the coefficients for hedonic function variables. From this, one can make the further argument that in competitive equilibrium hedonic prices will reflect both marginal production costs and incremental user values, so that the interpretation of a hedonic price is similar to the interpretation of any other price under competitive conditions. Thus, the presumption shared by both sides in the user-value, resource-cost debate (that hedonic methods provided uniquely user-side measures) was misconceived.

That the mid–twentieth century debate about the interpretation of hedonic prices parallels mid–nineteenth century debates about the theory of value suggests how difficult it is for economists to shift their mental gears from goods to characteristics. Marshall's two scissors blades cut in characteristics space in exactly the same interdependent mode of operation as they have long been known to function in goods space.

The question of which of the two criteria—user value or resource cost—was theoretically or conceptually *correct* was central to the controversy and was a more difficult issue to resolve. Fisher and Shell (1972) were the first to show that different index number measurements (they considered output price indexes and consumer COL indexes) imply alternative theoretical treatments of quality change, and that the theoretically appropriate treatments of quality change for these two indexes correspond, respectively, to "resource-cost" and "user-value" measures. Triplett (1983) derives this same result for cases where "quality change" is identified with characteristics of goods—and therefore with empirical hedonic methods; the conclusions are that the resource cost of a characteristic is the appropriate quality adjustment for the output price index, and its user value is the quality adjustment for the COL index or input cost index.

Intuitively, these conclusions are appealing. The output price index is defined on a fixed value of a transformation function. The position of a transformation function, technology constant, depends on resources employed in production; accordingly, "constant quality" for this index implies holding resources constant, or a resource-cost criterion.

On the other hand, the COL index is defined on a fixed indifference curve, and the analogous input-cost index is defined on a fixed (user) production isoquant. For these two "input" price indexes, "constant quality" implies holding utility or output constant, or a user-value criterion (an extended discussion is contained in Triplett 1983).

The debate on this subject sometimes generated more heat than light because (*a*) it was not recognized that there were, in effect, two different questions and accordingly two correct answers, not one; and (*b*) as already noted, there was an inappropriate linking, on both sides of the debate, of hedonic indexes with the user-value criterion. It was thus thought, incorrectly, that use of hedonic methods in an economic measurement implied accepting one of the two theoretical positions over the other one.[17]

7.7 The Position That Traditional Methods Should Yield the Same Measurement as Hedonic Methods

I list this one toward the end because it is a relatively recent line of reasoning. In equilibrium, the argument goes, the quality-corrected prices of all varieties ought to be equal (that is, the "quality ratio" should always equal the price ratio of any two varieties); therefore, price movements of varieties or models that have not been changed (matched models) can stand for those models in which quality change has been observed. Traditional "linking" (described below), sometimes termed a "matched models" index—more appropriately, a "matched models only" index—will always give the correct answer and hedonic methods are unnecessary (see also Jaszi 1964).

Linking, as a quality-adjustment method, takes the following form. Suppose that a particular variety or model of the *i*th good, call it Y_{i1}, is selected for pricing accordingly to probability procedures in one of the indexes. Suppose further that Y_{i1} disappears from the outlet from which prices are being collected and is replaced in the second period by a second variety or model, Y_{i2}. In most realistic situations, we have only the price of variety Y_{i1} in period 1 (P_{i11}) and the price of variety Y_{i2} in period 2 (P_{i22}). "Linking" introduces the new price into the index in such a way that the unadjusted price ratio P_{i22}/P_{i11} does not determine the movement of the index.

For historical reasons that seem lost in the mist of time, the procedures differ in the CPI and the PPI. The CPI linking procedure imputes price movements in other (unchanged) varieties—in this example, designated *j*—to the variety that changed; the implicit "quality adjustment" is

$$(3) \qquad A_1 = P_{i22} / P_{i11} - \Sigma_j W_j (P_{ij2} / P_{ij1}), \quad j \neq 1,2,$$

where the weight, W_j, is the sampling weight for observation *j*—or just $1/(n - 1)$, ignoring sampling considerations.

The PPI follows the old WPI procedure, in which the entire price change P_{i22} / P_{i11} is attributed to quality change. It is thus assumed that no price change took place in the item whose quality changed. The PPI procedure implies that the quality adjustment is

$$(4) \qquad A_2 = P_{i22}/P_{i11},$$

so that the quality-adjusted price change for this observation is unity.

In either case, the error that quality change puts into the index occurs when price change for new models (i.e., the quality-corrected price ratio for variety *i*2 compared with *i*1) differs from what is implied by the adjustment—or, what is the same thing, when the true quality change, A_T, differs from A_1 (in the CPI) or A_2 (in the PPI). Matched-models-only price changes may be biased because only price comparisons for models that can be "matched" exactly in the two periods are accepted for the index, and the implicit quality adjustments the procedure produces for unmatched varieties does not yield their true price change.

Note that the matched-models-only index is biased by quality change *even if* the statistical agency detects and "links out" correctly every example of quality change that takes place. Moreover, the "tighter" or more narrowly drawn the product specification, the larger the number of price observations that will be rejected for failing the exact-match test and, accordingly, the larger the bias from this source. Note also that the direction of bias is unknown: the sign of the bias depends on the sign of $(A_1 - A_T)$—or the sign of $(A_2 - A_T)$, in the PPI case—and *not* on the sign of A_T. Though quality may be improving (A_T positive), the adjustment implied by equations (3) and (4) may be too large, biasing the index downward.

Whether "linking" invariably works—that is, whether the bias from matched-model-only pricing is small—is an empirical issue, on which there is relatively little evidence. The most careful comparison of hedonic and traditional matched-model linking methods is contained in Dulberger (1989).

Dulberger computed hedonic price indexes for computer processors, using three different methods. As indicated in table 7.2, the three hedonic indexes, though not identical, indicate that computer prices fell about 90% over this interval.[18] A traditional matched-model or linked price index, computed from the same data, fell by two-thirds (67%), considerably less than the price decline recorded by the hedonic computer indexes. This is thus strong evidence that hedonic and linking methods will not always produce the same answers.

Table 7.2 **Alternative Estimates Compiled from the Same Data, Price Change for Computers (1972–84 percent change)**

Hedonic Indexes			
Time Dummy[a]	Characteristics Price[b]	Composite (Imputation)[c]	Matched-Model[d]
−92.2	−89.8	−90.3	−66.6

Source: Dulberger (1989), table 8.
[a]Computed from coefficients of time dummy variables inserted in a multiyear hedonic regression (similar to eq. [1] in the text).
[b]Computed from coefficients of the characteristics in a hedonic regression similar to eq. [1] in the text.
[c]Computed from prices of matched models, where "missing" prices (for "new" or "discontinued" models, present in one year but not the other) were imputed from the hedonic function.
[d]Chained index of matched models, no use of hedonic function ("new" models introduced by linking).

On the other hand, the position that *in equilibrium* the two approaches should yield the same measurement is not refuted by Dulberger's research. Her hedonic regression contains a device for testing for equilibrium—defined in her case as failure to reject the hypothesis that the price/performance ratio of "old" computer models had been bid down to equal that of newer computers that embodied the latest technology. When this price/performance definition of equilibrium obtained for computer processors, hedonic and matched-model computer indexes tended to coincide. When the equilibrium hypothesis was rejected, the price movements recorded by the matched-models index often differed greatly from those of the hedonic indexes.

Some reservations about the result should be recorded. The research used list prices. Discounts on older machines are probably more prevalent than on newly introduced ones, so that, even on Dulberger's definition, a smaller disequilibrium would have been measured had transactions prices for computer processors been available; accordingly, smaller differences between hedonic and matched-model methods might have been recorded had computer transactions prices been employed in Dulberger's research.

In a second study, on semiconductors, Dulberger (1988) reports a similar finding (see table 7.3). In this case, the PPI index (produced with conventional methods) moved, approximately, with a measure of the unadjusted average price per chip. Careful matching on a single characteristic of the chip (kilobits) gave an index—the right-hand column of table 7.3—that declined much more than the average price per chip. Note also (see table 7.3) that the differences are *very* large: The price index that controls for kilobits drops *eight to nine times* as much as the PPI index between 1975 and 1982. Though this study was not, strictly speaking, a hedonic one, average price per kilobit can be thought of as approximating a crude one-variable hedonic function, so the results are suggestive.

Table 7.3 **Alternative Price Indexes for MOS Memory Semiconductors (Shipments of U.S. Manufacturers)**

		Dataquest		
Selected Years	Published Producer Price Index (BLS 11784221)	Average Price/ Chip[a]	Average Price/ Kilobit[a]	Laspeyres Matched Models[a]
1975	212.1	313.5	1,846.2	1,662.5
1978	168.8	147.5	579.5	452.5
1980	129.7	213.9	371.4	344.2
1982	100.0	100.0	100.0	100.0
1985	73.4	80.1	22.8	30.2
1986	61.7	89.4	12.7	23.3
1987	62.8	111.2	11.4	23.2

Source: Dulberger (1988).
[a]Weights are U.S. value shares from Dataquest.

The computer and semiconductor empirical studies demonstrate the danger in relying on equilibrium assumptions in measuring prices, especially for technologically dynamic products.[19] The "traditionalist" or "equilibrium" position amounts to stating that the differences recorded in tables 7.2 and 7.3 should not exist; since they do exist empirically, the traditionalist position does not provide a compelling argument for rejecting hedonic methods.

7.8 Hedonic Methods Give Price Indexes That Fall "Too Fast"

One hears this position more frequently from index users than from price index producers, but it demands consideration here. Government price indexes that are not accepted as meeting user needs are deficient, no matter what their producers believe of them.

Most often cited as "falls too fast" examples are the IBM-BEA computer price indexes (Cole et al. 1986; Cartwright 1986), which are hedonic indexes and show almost unprecedented declines (see table 7.4). Such price behavior is not a recent phenomenon: Research studies on computer equipment show comparable price declines going back to the birth of the electronic computer.[20]

When shipments data are deflated with indexes that drop so far and so fast as do the hedonic computer price indexes, the resulting quantity measures grow very rapidly indeed. Some business economists have reportedly argued that when government "real" quantity data for producer durable equipment are compared with various business records, computer growth in the government data seems high relative to that of other equipment. Note, however, that price indexes for other "high tech" equipment are produced with conventional methods: distortion in the deflated quantity data could arise from upward biases in the conventional indexes as well as from downward bias in the computer hedonic indexes.

A similar assessment comes from compilers of the Federal Reserve Board's Industrial Production Index. The IBM-BEA computer indexes were not used in the IPI because would they allegedly create output growth in computers that is "too large."

Denison (1989) points out that the IBM-BEA computer price indexes create productivity growth in computers that is far larger than in other producer durables. Had computers behaved as other producer durables (that is, had their prices risen) or had their price indexes been compiled as have those for other capital equipment (e.g., the matched-model computer price index in table 7.2), the recent divergence between productivity rates in manufacturing and nonmanufacturing would have been diminished—the manufacturing productivity rate would be lower because output growth would have been lowered.

I do not know any independent data with which to test the view that computer price indexes decline too fast—or that real output or productivity in computers rises too rapidly—when hedonic indexes are employed. The nearly 30 studies reviewed in Triplett (1989) include some conducted by computer scientists and engineering technologists whose objective was to measure the rate of the computer's technical advance, not to produce price indexes. Authors of the computer science studies (which give results consistent with the

Table 7.4 **"Fixed-Weight" NIPA Price Index for Computers[a] (1982 weights, 1982 = 100)**

Year	Index
1972	566.2
1973	567.1
1974	498.0
1975	448.3
1976	414.4
1977	308.3
1978	186.0
1979	158.5
1980	123.6
1981	108.3
1982	100.0
1983	83.9
1984	70.0
1985	55.7
1986	47.9
1987	41.9
1988:III	36.2(p)

Source: Bureau of Economic Analysis.
[a]"Computers" includes processors and major items of peripheral equipment (see Cartwright 1986) combined with 1982 shipments weights.

economic ones)[21] did not seem to find their results implausible. To cite the very evidence being disputed, even if originating from a technological discipline, is not, of course, compelling.

All the critical positions noted above depend, in some degree, on the idea that the computer indexes are suspect because "nothing else" shows similar behavior. If one uses, for example, conventional measures of computer industry inputs and the BEA-IBM price indexes to deflate the industry's output, then productivity in computer manufacturing is very great indeed.

On the other hand, semiconductor inputs are clearly a major source of technical change in computers. If the PPI semiconductor indexes are replaced by measures like those of table 7.4, the effect is to reallocate part of the measured productivity improvement from computers to semiconductors (because real input measures to computers grow more rapidly when a falling semiconductor price index is used for deflation). It is far from clear that this reconstructed picture is implausible.

Though the use of "quality-corrected" computer price and output measures along with other data that are poorly or inadequately measured may introduce some distortions in the allocation of productivity across industries, it seems doubtful that a better picture would emerge if all the data were consistent but wrong. Additional research on computer prices, output, and productivity would be of considerable interest.[22]

7.9 Conclusions

The adoption of hedonic methods has been impeded by conceptual issues, by doubts about the validity of hedonic indexes (especially when they differ greatly from conventional measures), and by the lack of cross sections of transactions prices needed as dependent variables. Conceptual issues have mostly been resolved, and should no longer pose any barrier. Most of the old validity issues have likewise been disposed of, though some remain unresolved. The data problem remains formidable, but of course a data-gathering exercise is well within the jurisdiction of statistical agencies and could be undertaken if they were convinced that hedonic methods would improve price indexes.

Notes

1. There is no standard terminology in economics for heterogeneity in goods and services. I use "variety" and "model" interchangeably as synonyms. The term "model" is customary for durable goods; a "model" should be understood as, say, a Buick Regal four-door sedan with a specified range of accessories, options, and appointments. Any deviation from the detailed specification is a "new model." For nondurables and ser-

vices, "variety" seems a more natural term than "model"; if a box of Kellogg's Corn Flakes contains 17 ounces where it formerly held 18, it is a different "variety." A similar definition applies to services, where, however, it is sometimes difficult to observe the specification of what is being sold. For purposes of this article, a "good" (or a "service") is defined as a set of models or varieties that "fit" a common hedonic function. "Characteristics" are defined in Triplett (1983).

2. The earliest serious BLS hedonic study appears to be the unpublished work of Gavett (1967). Triplett (1971) was commissioned by the BLS. Gillingham (1975) was a dissertation funded by BLS. Other examples of hedonic research in the 1970s may be found in the list of BLS working papers.

3. Also, Dryden, Reut, and Slater (c. 1987) report that a "regression model" (presumably, a hedonic model was meant) on CPI data for a number of products was used to estimate international price comparisons.

4. However, Cahill (1988) cites a number of regression-based quality adjustments in Canadian price indexes that could be termed hedonic.

5. So far as I know, this "no-theory" position appeared exclusively in oral and workshop presentations and not in any published place, but by the early 1970s such challenges were commonly encountered. The earliest published works on the theory of hedonic indexes (Muellbauer 1974; Lucas 1975) tended to support the no-theory charge because they concluded—incorrectly, I believe—that existing empirical work was inconsistent with theoretical requirements. Later work (see below) has now clarified these issues.

6. The following paragraphs are condensed from the "Summary of the Theory" section in Triplett (1989). A more formal treatment is Triplett (1987). The major basic sources are, as noted, Rosen (1974) and Triplett (1983).

7. Functional form is thus appropriately determined with normal econometric procedures. I have argued elsewhere (Triplett 1989), however, that for theoretical reasons researchers should explore a richer range of functional forms than the limited number that have appeared in most empirical hedonic work to date, and that in some circumstances the functional form question demands being treated as a frontier estimation problem.

8. Thus, estimating an exact characteristics price index requires estimating the hedonic function *and* the utility or production function (properly, the indirect utility function or the production cost function, or else demand functions derived from those functions). The formidable econometric problems in such a task are explored in Epple (1987).

9. An explosion of research using hedonic methods occurred in labor economics ("hedonic wage studies") and in urban economics (the extensive literature on valuing air quality and urban amenities), much of which acknowledged the guidance of Rosen (1974) and, to an extent, the example of Thaler and Rosen (1976).

10. That is, the census housing measure is an index of the hedonic prices of square feet, bathrooms (and so forth), where weights are the average number of square feet, average number of bathrooms (and so forth), in houses constructed in the base period (Laspeyres form) or the current period (Paasche form). Another way of stating it is that the index measures (in its Laspeyres form) the change in the price of a house with (mean) base-period characteristics.

11. The study also compared dummy variable and characteristics price indexes computed from the same data. See Cole et al. (1986) and Dulberger (1989) and also the review of calculation methods for hedonic indexes in Triplett (1989).

12. At one time, e.g., comparison of claims by different manufacturers for the same change or sequence of changes required by federal air-pollution and safety legislation led to a "low ball" rule: the maximum adjustment allowed on any manufacturer's cars was the lowest cost reported by any manufacturer. As federal requirements became

more stringent, however, a wider range of engineering alternatives for meeting the standards developed, so the changes introduced by one company might bear little relation to what was done by another, and the rule was abandoned.

13. For example, the 7 October 1968 BLS press release that provided the data for 1969 model cars used for table 7.1 states: "Quality in an automobile is measured in terms of safety, reliability, performance, durability, economy of operation, carrying capacity, maneuverability, comfort and convenience." Similarly, the internal BLS "guidelines" for adjusting automobiles for quality change (version of 25 July 1980) states: "The basic concept of quality in an automobile or truck is the utility to the user. It is usually thought of in terms of reliability, durability, convenience, safety, economy, speed, acceleration, carrying capacity, maneuverability, comfort, appearance, prestige, etc." This matter is made somewhat cloudy by the fact that the BLS published documentation for its price indexes sometimes used language that was inconsistent with its "quality guidelines" (which were internal working documents).

14. For reasons that are not entirely clear at this writing, exploratory Census Bureau hedonic functions on multifamily dwellings have not produced usable results (Pollock 1987).

15. One of the criteria listed in the article is that "the indexes should measure construction with fixed specifications." Hedonic measures are listed as a variant of the fixed-specification method, a position I believe is correct: the variables in the hedonic function serve as the specification for what is being priced. The (Laspeyres version) Census house price index can be interpreted as the price through time of a house having the mean specification of those built in the base year.

16. It should be noted (see also n. 13 above) that examination of agency documentation can sometimes produce confusing or contradictory passages on the treatment of quality change, and it would be easy to quote selectively from agency documents to challenge the interpretation I have set forth above. For anyone who wishes to pursue this matter for intellectual reasons, I would note that the whole resource-cost, user-value debate was a confused one. Neither the theory of quality change for different economic measurements, nor the theory of hedonic functions and hedonic indexes, was well worked out. Hindsight, from the vantage of a better understanding of the theory, shows error as well as insight on both sides of the debate. See also n. 17 below.

17. An example of the difference of positions on this issue is contained in the report of the Panel to Review Productivity Statistics (1979). Because the report's chapters were authored by different panel members, who ascribed to one or the other of the positions outlined in the text, its chapter on measuring output endorses a user-value quality concept (incorrect for this case), while its chapter on measuring inputs endorses resource-cost for capital (incorrect) and user-value (marginal productivity) for labor inputs (correct).

18. The "composite" estimate in table 7.2 was introduced as a deflator for computer processors in the NIPAs in December 1985. In the composite, price relatives for matched models are used whenever they are available, but when a price is available in one period but "missing" in the other, the missing price is imputed from a computer hedonic function. Indexes for three other items of computer equipment, also calculated by the composite-imputation method, are included in the "computers" category of Producers' Durable Equipment. See Cole et al. (1986) and Cartwright (1986).

19. Fisher, McGowan, and Greenwood remark that "the computer market . . . has never been close to long-run equilibrium in its entire existence" (1983, 149).

20. Some 30 studies are reviewed in Triplett (1989), which presents price indexes for computer processors and peripheral equipment that go back into the 1950s. The computer processor price index, which was compiled by combining "best practice" research studies, declined from 1,320 in 1953 to 14.8 in 1972 (1965 = 100), a decline comparable with that of the post-1972 index in table 7.4.

21. The technical change studies in the computer science literature were readily converted into price indexes since the technological investigators measured performance per dollar, and economists want price indexes to measure the inverse—cost per unit of performance.

22. Rapidly falling computer price indexes also create large changes in relative prices; substantial substitution toward relatively cheaper computer equipment can be observed in investment aggregates such as office machinery, or Producers' Durable Equipment. When these aggregates are combined with fixed-weight index numbers (of price or quantity), the "substitution bias" associated with such index number formulas can be substantial. It appears that some users who have expressed dissatisfaction with the behavior of the computer measures are really upset about the behavior of fixed-weight aggregates that employ the computer data. I am exploring the fixed-weight bias issue in investment categories of GNP, in work to appear elsewhere (using the Time-series Generalized Fisher Ideal, or TGFI, index number that first appeared in the final section of Triplett 1989).

References

Blackorby, Charles, and R. Robert Russell. 1978. Indices and Subindices of the Cost of Living and the Standard of Living. *International Economic Review* 19 (February): 229–40.

Cahill, Leonard. 1988. Quality Change Adjustment Manual. Ottawa: Statistics Canada, Prices Division.

Cartwright, David W. 1986. Improved Deflation of Purchases of Computers. *Survey of Current Business* 66 (March): 7–9.

Christensen, Laurits R., and Marilyn E. Manser. 1976. Cost-of-Living Indexes and Price Indexes for U.S. Meat and Produce. In *Household Production and Consumption,* ed. Nestor E. Terleckyj, 399–446. NBER Studies in Income and Wealth, vol. 40. New York: National Bureau of Economic Research.

Cole, Rosanne, Y. C. Chen, Joan A. Barquin-Stolleman, Ellen Dulberger, Nurhan Helvacian, and James H. Hodge. 1986. Quality-adjusted Price Indexes for Computer Processors and Selected Peripheral Equipment. *Survey of Current Business* 66 (January): 41–50.

Court, Andrew T. 1939. Hedonic Price Indexes with Automotive Examples. In *The Dynamics of Automobile Demand,* 99–117. New York: General Motors.

Denison, Edward F. 1957. Theoretical Aspects of Quality Change, Capital Consumption, and Net Capital Formation. In *Problems of Capital Formation: Concepts, Measurement and Controlling Factors.* NBER Studies in Income and Wealth, vol. 19. Princeton, N.J.: Princeton University Press.

———. 1989. *Estimates of Productivity Change by Industry: An Evaluation and An Alternative.* Washington, D.C.: Brookings.

Dhrymes, Phoebus J. 1971. Price and Quality Changes in Consumer Capital Goods: An Empirical Study. In *Price Indexes and Quality Change: Studies in New Methods of Measurement,* ed. Zvi Griliches. Cambridge, Mass.: Harvard University Press.

Dryden, John, Katrina Reut, and Barbara Slater. c. 1987. Bilateral Comparison of Purchasing Power Parity between the United States and Canada. Ottawa: Statistics Canada.

Dulberger, Ellen. 1988. Price Index for MOS Memories. Presentation at the National Bureau of Economic Research Summer Workshop, Cambridge, Mass., July.

———. 1989. "The Application of an Hedonic Model to a Quality Adjusted Price Index for Computer Processors." In *Technology and Capital Formation,* ed. Dale W. Jorgenson and Ralph Landau. Cambridge, Mass.: MIT Press.

Early, John F., and James H. Sinclair. 1983. Quality Adjustment in the Producer Price Indexes. In *The U.S. National Income and Product Accounts: Selected Topics,* ed. Murray F. Foss, 107–45. NBER Studies in Income and Wealth, vol. 47. Chicago: University of Chicago Press.

Epple, Dennis. 1987. Hedonic Prices and Implicit Markets: Estimating Demand and Supply Functions for Differentiated Products. *Journal of Political Economy* 95 (February): 59–80

Fisher, Franklin M., John J. McGowan, and Joen E. Greenwood. 1983. *Folded, Spindled, and Mutilated: Economic Analysis and U.S. v. IBM.* Cambridge, Mass.: MIT Press.

Fisher, Franklin M., and Karl Shell. 1972. *The Economic Theory of Price Indices: Two Essays on the Effects of Taste, Quality, and Technological Change.* New York: Academic Press. (Essay 1 also published in Zvi Griliches, ed., [1971], below.)

Flamm, Kenneth. 1987. *Targeting the Computer.* Washington, D.C.: Brookings.

Gavett, Thomas W. 1967. Research on Quality Adjustments in Price Indexes, Part III: Experiments in Multivariate Analysis of Quality Change. Bureau of Labor Statistics memorandum (Office of Prices and Living Conditions). Washington, D.C.

Gilbert, Milton. 1961. Quality Changes and Index Numbers. *Economic Development and Cultural Change* 9 (April): 287–94.

Gillingham, Robert F. 1975. Place to Place Rent Comparisons. *Annals of Economic and Social Measurement* 4 (Winter): 153–73.

Griliches, Zvi. 1961. Hedonic Price Indexes for Automobiles: An Econometric Analysis of Quality Change. In *The Price Statistics of the Federal Government,* 173–96. (See Price Statistics Review Committee [1961] below.)

———. 1964. Notes on the Measurement of Price and Quality Changes. In *Models of Income Determination,* 381–418. NBER Studies in Income and Wealth, vol. 28. Princeton, N.J.: Princeton University Press.

———, ed. 1971. *Price Indexes and Quality Change: Studies in New Methods of Measurement.* Cambridge, Mass.: Harvard University Press.

Jaszi, George. 1964. Comment. In *Models of Income Determination,* 404–9. NBER Studies in Income and Wealth, vol. 28. Princeton, N.J.: Princeton University Press.

Koopmans, Tjalling. 1947. Measurement without Theory. *Review of Economics and Statistics* 29 (August): 161–72.

Lucas, R. E. B. 1975. Hedonic Price Functions. *Economic Inquiry* 13 (June): 157–78.

Muellbauer, John. 1974. Household Production Theory, Quality, and the "Hedonic Technique." *American Economic Review* 64 (December): 977–94.

Musgrave, John. 1969. The Measurement of Price Changes in Construction. *Journal of the American Statistical Association* 64 (September): 771–86.

Panel to Review Productivity Statistics. 1979. *Measurement and Interpretation of Productivity.* Washington, D.C.: National Academy of Sciences.

Pollak, Robert A. 1975. Subindexes in the Cost of Living Index. *International Economic Review* 16 (February): 135–50.

———. 1983. The Theory of the Cost-of-Living Index. In *Price Level Measurement: Proceedings from a Conference Sponsored by Statistics Canada,* ed. W. E. Diewert and C. Montmarquette, 87–161. Ottawa: Minister of Supply and Services.

Pollock, Jesse. 1987. Research into a Cost Index for Multiunit Residential Construction. Presentation to the American Statistical Association Census Advisory Committee, October.

Price Statistics Review Committee. 1961. *The Price Statistics of the Federal Govern-*

ment. U.S. Congress, Joint Economic Committee. *Government Price Statistics, Hearings*, pt. 1. 87th Cong., 1st sess. (Also published as National Bureau of Economic Research, General series no. 73.)

Rosen, Sherwin. 1974. Hedonic Prices and Implicit Markets: Product Differentiation in Pure Competition. *Journal of Political Economy* 82 (January–February): 34–55.

Thaler, Richard, and Sherwin Rosen. 1976. The Value of Saving a Life: Evidence from the Labor Market. In *Household Production and Consumption*, ed. Nestor E. Terleckyj, 265–97. NBER Studies in Income and Wealth, vol. 40. New York: National Bureau of Economic Research.

Triplett, Jack E. 1969. Automobiles and Hedonic Quality Measurement. *Journal of Political Economy* 77 (May–June): 408–17.

———. 1971. The Theory of Hedonic Quality Measurement and Its Use in Price Indexes. BLS Staff Paper no. 6. Washington, D.C.: U.S. Bureau of Labor Statistics.

———. 1983. Concepts of Quality in Input and Output Price Measures: A Resolution of the User Value–Resource Cost Debate. In *The U.S. National Income and Product Accounts: Selected Topics*, ed. Murray F. Foss, 269–311. NBER Studies in Income and Wealth, vol. 47. Chicago: University of Chicago Press.

———. 1987. Hedonic Functions and Hedonic Indexes. In *The New Palgrave: A Dictionary of Economics*, ed. John Eatwell, Murray Milgate, and Peter Newman, 2:630–34. London: Macmillan.

———. 1989. Price and Technological Change in a Capital Good: A Survey of Research on Computers. In *Technology and Capital Formation*, ed. Dale W. Jorgenson and Ralph Landau. Cambridge, Mass.: MIT Press.

Triplett, Jack E., and Richard J. McDonald. 1977. Assessing the Quality Error in Output Measures: The Case of Refrigerators. *Review of Income and Wealth* 23 (June): 137–56.

U.S. Department of Commerce, Bureau of Economic Analysis. 1987. GNP: An Overview of Source Data and Estimating Methods. Methodology Paper Series MP-4. Washington, D.C.: U.S. Government Printing Office, September.

U.S. Department of Labor, Bureau of Labor Statistics. 1988. *CPI Detailed Report*. January.

Comment W. Erwin Diewert

Triplett has a nice discussion of recent methods for adjusting for quality change that have been used by the Bureau of Labor Statistics. In keeping with the historical nature of this conference, I shall briefly review the ancient literature on methods for quality adjustment.

Some of the early researchers on price measurement were aware of the problem of quality change, but the pace and direction of the change did not seem large enough to warrant an explicit treatment.[1]

W. Erwin Diewert is professor of economics at the University of British Columbia and a research associate of the National Bureau of Economic Research.

The author is indebted to R. C. Allen, B. M. Balk, and J. E. Triplett for valuable historical references and discussions over the years. This research was supported by the SSHRC of Canada and by the Summer Institute of the National Bureau of Economic Research Program on Productivity. Neither institution is to be held responsible for any opinions expressed by the author.

However, by the latter part of the nineteenth century, Sidgwick (1883) realized that not only were improvements in the quality of goods leading to a bias in price comparisons, but also the growth of international and interregional trade (due primarily to transportation improvements) led to the systematic introduction of "entirely new kinds of things" and this too led to a bias in price comparisons. As the following quotation indicates, Sidgwick thought that utility theory would play a role in eliminating these biases: "Here again there seems to be no means of attaining more than a rough and approximate solution of the problem proposed; and to reach even this we have to abandon the prima facie exact method of comparing prices, and to substitute the essentially looser procedure of comparing amounts of utility or satisfaction" (1883, 68). Unfortunately, the mathematical apparatus of consumer theory was not sufficiently developed at that time to enable Sidgwick to make any specific progress on the new-good problem.

In a brilliant paper, Marshall (1887) not only proposed the tabular standard, the chain system, and the Edgeworth-Marshall index number formula, he also made the first real progress on the appropriate treatment of new goods, as the following quotation indicates:

> This brings us to consider the great problem of how to modify our unit so as to allow for the invention of new commodities. The difficulty is insuperable, if we compare two distant periods without access to the detailed statistics of intermediate times, but it can be got over fairly well by systematic statistics. A new commodity almost always appears at first at something like a scarcity price, and its gradual fall in price can be made to enter year by year into readjustments of the unit of purchasing power, and to represent fairly well the increased power of satisfying our wants which we derive from the new commodity. (1887, 373)

As the above quotation indicates, Marshall was well aware of the product cycle and he felt that the early introduction of new commodities into the consumer price index in the context of the chain system would capture *most* of the benefits due to the introduction of new commodities. As we shall see later, not quite *all* of the benefits are captured using Marshall's suggested method, since his method incorrectly ignores the new good in the first period that it makes its appearance.

Marshall (1887, 373–74) also realized that improvements in transportation led to the general availability of location-specific goods, such as fish at the seaside or strawberries at a farm. Marshall correctly felt that these "old" goods that suddenly became available at many locations should be regarded as "new" goods and treated in the same way as a genuinely new good. His words on this important observation are worth quoting:

> This class of consideration is of much more importance than at first sight appears; for a great part of modern agriculture and transport industries are devoted to increasing the periods of time during which different kinds of food are available. Neglect of this has, in my opinion, vitiated the statistics

> of the purchasing power of many in medieval times with regard to nearly all kinds of foods except corn; even the well-to-do would hardly get so simple a thing as fresh meat in winter. (374).

Marshall's suggested treatment of the new-good problem was acknowledged and adopted by many authors including Irving Fisher (1911, 204) and Pigou (1912, 47). Divisia (1926, 45), working from his independent perspective, also suggested the use of the chain method as a means of dealing with the new-good problem.

The next important contributor to the discussion of new goods in price measurement was Keynes (1930, 94), who described in some detail one of the most common methods for dealing with the new-good problem: simply ignore any new or disappearing goods in the two time periods under consideration and calculate the price index on the basis of the goods that are common to the two situations. The corresponding quantity index was to be obtained residually by deflating the relevant value ratio by this narrowly based price index. Keynes called this method the *highest common factor method.* This method would be identical to Marshall's chain method if the two time periods were chosen to be adjacent ones. However Keynes (1930, 105–6) advocated his method in the context of a fixed-base system of index numbers, and he specifically rejected the chain method for three reasons: (1) each time a new product is introduced, a chain index does not take into account the benefits of the expanded choice set, and thus over long periods of time, the chain price index will be biased upward and the corresponding quantity index will be biased downward; (2) the chain index fails Walsh's multiperiod identity test (see Diewert 1988, eq. [13]), and (3) the chain method was statistically laborious.

Keynes's last objection to the chain method is no longer relevant in this age of computers. Moreover, Keynes was unable to offer any positive alternative to the chain method for comparing situations separated by long periods of time, as the following quotation indicates: "We cannot hope to find a ratio of equivalent substitution for gladiators against cinemas, or for the conveniences of being able to buy motor cars against the conveniences of being able to buy slaves" (Keynes 1930, 96).

However, Keynes's first objection to the chain method (which was later echoed by Pigou [1932, 72]) was certainly valid (as was his second objection).[2] A satisfactory theoretical solution to Keynes's first objection did not occur until Hicks adapted the analytical apparatus of consumer theory to the problem.

When new consumer goods make their appearance for the first time, say in period 2, their prices and quantities can be observed. In period 1, the quantities of the new goods are all obviously zero, but what are the corresponding prices? Hicks (1940, 114) provided a theoretical solution:

> They are those prices which, in the one situation, would *just* make the demands for these commodities (from the whole community) equal to zero. These prices cannot be estimated, but we can observe that between the two

situations the demands for these commodities will have increased from zero to certain positive quantities; and hence it is reasonable to suppose that the "prices" of these commodities will usually have fallen relatively to other prices. This principle is sufficient to give us a fairly good way of dealing with the case of new goods.

Of course, in the context of the producer price index, the appropriate period-1 shadow prices for the new goods are those prices that just induce each period-2 producer of the new goods to produce zero quantities in period 1.

Hicks's basic idea was used extensively by Hofsten (1952, 95–97) who dealt not only with new goods but also adapted the Hicksian methodology to deal with disappearing goods as well. Hofsten (1952, 47–50) also presents a nice discussion of various methods that have been used to adjust for quality change, similar to Triplett's (in this volume) discussion of quality-change measurement techniques.

Franklin Fisher and Karl Shell (1972, 22–26) laid out the formal algebra for constructing the first period Hicksian "demand reservation prices" defined in the above quotation by Hicks. Diewert (1980, 498, 501) used the Hicksian framework to examine the bias in the Fisher price index P_F (defined by using vector notation):

$$P_F(p^1,p^2,q^1,q^2) \equiv [p^2 \cdot q^1 \; p^2 \cdot q^2 / p^1 \cdot q^1 \; p^1 \cdot q^2]^{1/2}. \tag{1}$$

Diewert calculated P_F when the reservation prices were incorrectly set equal to zero and compared this index to the Fisher price index that simply ignored the existence of the new goods in the two periods under consideration (which is Marshall's method).[3] Diewert (1980, 501–3) also made some suggestions for estimating the appropriate Hicksian reservation prices in an econometric framework.

Is the new-good bias large or small? One can only answer this question in the context of the price measurement procedures used by individual statistical agencies. In Diewert (1987, 779), some simple hypothetical examples were given that showed that traditional fixed-base procedures could generate much higher measures of price increase than would be generated using the chain method.[4] However, what is needed is empirical evidence.

Numerical computation of alternative methods based on detailed firm data on individual prices and quantities where new goods are carefully distinguished would cast light on the size of the new-good bias. Another line of empirical work that would be of interest would be to collect industry price and quantity data on various major new goods (e.g., microwave ovens, video recorders, home computers, satellite dishes, etc.) and then attempt to rework the relevant price indexes in the light of this extra data.

Notes

1. Thus Lowe (1823, app. 87) states: "In regard to the quality of our manufactures, we must speak with more hesitation, and can hardly decide whether the balance be in

favour of the present or of a former age; for if our fabrics are now much more neat and convenient, they are in a considerable degree less durable."

2. Pigou (1932, 71) also has a nice criticism of Keynes's highest common factor method, which was later repeated by Hofsten (1952, 59). Pigou also criticized Fisher's (1922, 308–12) later preference for the fixed-base method.

3. The second index has a smaller bias than the first index.

4. Since 1978, the U.S. Bureau of Labor Statistics has used a probability sampling approach in the consumer price index that probably reduces some of this fixed-weight bias, but the bias is not eliminated.

References

Diewert, W. E. 1980. Aggregation Problems in the Measurement of Capital. In *The Measurement of Capital,* ed. Dan Usher, 433–528. NBER Studies in Income and Wealth, vol. 45. Chicago: University of Chicago Press.

———. 1987. Index Numbers. In *The New Palgrave: A Dictionary of Economics,* ed. J. Eatwell, M. Milgate and P. Newman 2:767–80. London: Macmillan.

———. 1988. The Early History of Price Index Research. NBER Discussion Paper no. 2713. Cambridge, Mass.: National Bureau of Economic Research.

Divisia, F. 1926. *L'indice monétaire et la theorie de la monnaie*. Paris: Société anonyme du Recueil Sirey.

Fisher, I. 1911. *The Purchasing Power of Money.* London: Macmillan.

———. 1922. *The Making of Index Numbers*. Boston: Houghton Mifflin.

Fisher, F. M., and K. Shell. 1972. *The Economic Theory of Price Indices*. New York: Academic Press.

Hicks, J. R. 1940. The Valuation of the Social Income. *Econometrica* 7:108–24.

Hofsten, E. von. 1952. *Price Indexes and Quality Change*. London: Allen & Unwin.

Keynes, J. M. 1930. *Treatise on Money,* vol. 1. London: Macmillan.

Lowe, J. 1823. *The Present State of England in Regard to Agriculture, Trade and Finance,* 2d ed. London: Longman, Hurst, Rees, Orme & Brown.

Marshall, A. 1887. Remedies for Fluctuations of General Prices. *Contemporary Review* 51:355–75.

Pigou, A. C. 1912. *Wealth and Welfare*. London: Macmillan.

———. 1932. *The Economics of Welfare,* 4th ed. London: Macmillan.

Sidgwick, H. 1883. *The Principles of Political Economy.* London: Macmillan.

8 The Measurement of Construction Prices: Retrospect and Prospect

Paul E. Pieper

The deflation of construction expenditures is both one of the most difficult and one of the most important areas of national income accounting. Accurate deflation is essential for a number of issues, including measuring construction productivity and measuring the real capital stock. However, developing accurate structures deflators is very difficult due to the heterogeneity of most structures. This difficulty has in the past been compounded by a lack of resources devoted to construction deflation.

As the title suggests, this paper takes both a retrospective view of past construction deflation methods and a look forward at possible ways of improving the existing deflators. Section 8.1 reviews the development of the Bureau of Economic Analysis' (BEA) construction deflators. The section discusses both the improvements that have been made over the past 40 years and the weaknesses that still remain. Section 8.2 reviews the academic literature on construction deflation. This section evaluates and updates the work of a number of earlier authors and examines whether the BEA has overdeflated construction output. The final section discusses the strengths and weaknesses of different deflation methods.

8.1 The Development of the Department of Commerce Construction Deflators

The problem of construction deflation stems from the extreme heterogeneity of structures. Because most structures are unique, most construction deflators do not price a complete prototype structure. Instead, inputs or intermedi-

Paul Pieper is an associate professor of economics at the University of Illinois at Chicago.

The author wishes to thank Ed Coleman of the Bureau of Economic Analysis and Stan Seymour of Statistics Canada for their help on this chapter. All views expressed in the chapter are the author's alone.

ate units of output are deflated. The term "cost index" will be used here to refer to a weighted average of input prices.[1] Most cost indexes are simple averages of materials prices and wage rates although a few attempt to measure overhead costs and profit. The main problem with cost indexes is that they assume the same relationship between inputs and output over time, or, in other words, they assume constant productivity. Cost indexes will thus be biased upward if productivity is increasing. A few cost indexes attempt to adjust labor costs for productivity, but the adjustment is usually arbitrary or subjective.[2]

Other construction deflators attempt to price intermediate units of output termed components. Components may refer to a specified quantity of materials in place or some physical attribute such as square feet. While each structure may be unique, it is assumed that they are composed of a number of homogeneous components. The term "component-price index" is used in the construction literature to refer to an average of the price of one or more components. This paper will use the more succinct term "price index" to refer to indexes that price some form of construction output rather than construction inputs.

The Department of Commerce first published a deflator for new construction expenditures in September 1946.[3] The deflator was an expenditure-weighted average of 12 indexes, all but two of which were cost indexes instead of price indexes. The two exceptions were the Bureau of Public Roads' highway price index and the Interstate Commerce Commission's (ICC) railroad price index. Both indexes measured the price of specified quantities of materials in place, such as cubic yards of concrete or pounds of steel. The prices were based on contractors' bids for these items in newly awarded contracts and reflected not just materials costs but all construction costs. Since the two indexes together had only about a 10% weight, an implicit deflator for new construction (hereafter termed the composite) was still essentially an average of wage rates and materials prices.[4] From the beginning, the Commerce Department recognized the limitations of such an index. It admitted that its constant dollar estimates of new construction would "provide only crude indicators of physical change" (U.S. Department of Commerce, Office of Domestic Commerce 1947, 25).

Though well aware of its defects, the Department of Commerce did not make a single change in the composite for the first 17 years of its existence. Construction deflation did not receive widespread attention until the NBER's Price Statistics Review Committee (also known as the Stigler committee after its chairman, George Stigler) issued its report in 1961. The report was highly critical of the composite, terming it "defective in almost every possible way" (NBER 1961, 87). Its primary criticism was that the composite relied almost entirely on cost indexes that assumed no change in construction productivity. The Stigler committee was also very critical of the methodology of the cost indexes. For example, it stated that the indexes were unrepresentative of the expenditures they were used to deflate, both in terms of geographic coverage and in terms of the inputs priced. Other problems included a failure to use transaction prices and inaccurate and outdated weights. No fewer than eight of the 10 cost indexes used weights based on the 1910–14 period. Finally, most of the indexes were compiled by private firms that were either unwilling or unable to provide detailed descriptions of their methodology.

The Stigler committee recommended "a radical expansion and reorientation" of research in construction deflation (NBER 1961, 29). It suggested in particular developing a residential deflator based on the price per square foot of various categories of new homes. Following this suggestion, the Census Bureau began collecting data on single-family homes in 1963. Its subsequent experiments with a hedonic price index lead to the creation of the census single-family homes price index (hereafter termed census index). The census index replaced the Boeckh cost index as the BEA's deflator for residential construction in 1968, for the period from 1963 onward.

The census regressed the sales price of new single-family homes against eight housing characteristics: square feet of floor space, number of bathrooms and stories, metropolitan and regional location, and presence of a garage, basement and central air conditioning.[5] A Laspeyres price index was then formed by multiplying the regression coefficients by the base-year averages of the characteristics. The BEA initially adjusted the index for land costs using Federal Housing Authority (FHA) site-to-value data. Land costs were estimated by the survey respondent beginning in 1969.

The BEA made two other deflation changes during the sixties. The ICC railroad index ceased publication in 1967. Until the introduction of the census index a year later, this left the Bureau of Public Roads index as the sole price index in the composite. The other change was the introduction of the AT&T cost index for telephone construction in 1963.

The Stigler report set in motion a long review of the existing construction deflators, which finally culminated in a major revision of the deflators in 1974. Six cost indexes, all but one privately compiled, were dropped from the composite. Three indexes were added, including two that were, in part, price indexes. The Federal Energy Regulatory Commission (FERC) pipeline index and the Bureau of Reclamation index, used in deflating conservation and development expenditures, were hybrid indexes, part price index and part cost index. For example, the Bureau of Reclamation index is an average of a number of individual indexes, some of which measure the price of excavation and structural concrete in place, but others that are simple averages of wage rates and materials prices.

The most problematic area for deflation was probably nonresidential buildings. The revised construction deflators included four indexes that were at least in part price indexes: the Bureau of Public Roads, Bureau of Reclamation, FERC, and census indexes. The first three indexes were based on the nonbuilding sector, while the census index represented the residential sector.

Lacking an available price measure for nonresidential buildings, the BEA took an unweighted average of the census, Turner construction company, and Bureau of Public Roads structures indexes. The Turner index measures the cost of office construction, while the Bureau of Public Roads structures index is a subindex of the Bureau of Public Roads index measuring the price of highway structures such as bridges and overpasses. Since the Turner index was the only cost index of the three, this procedure greatly increased the percentage of construction deflated by price indexes. The obvious drawback to this method was that the Turner index was also the only one of the three indexes that was actually based on the nonresidential building sector.

The 1974 revisions form the basis for much of the present BEA deflation methodology. However, the BEA has made a number of modifications over the past 14 years, including the net addition of two indexes. A new deflator for military construction was first published in 1983 (Sachs and Ziemer 1983). The military deflator is based on a variety of physical measures of output, most commonly square feet in the case of buildings and materials in place in the case of nonbuilding construction. The second addition was the consumer price index for maintenance and repair expenditures, which was given a 50% weight in the deflator for residential additions and alterations. On the other hand, the AT&T cost index for telephone construction was discontinued in 1983 after the breakup of AT&T. It was replaced by the Engineering News-Record index, a very simple cost index.

Nonresidential buildings continue to be a problematic area for deflation. Because of the volatility of the highway structures index during the seventies and early eighties, the BEA removed it from the private nonresidential building deflator during the 1985 benchmark revisions. Presently, private nonresidential buildings are deflated by an average of the census and Turner indexes, while public buildings use various combinations of the census, Turner, and highway structures indexes. The BEA also changed the form of the census index from a Laspeyres index to a Paasche index.

Table 8.1 summarizes a few main characteristics of the BEA deflation methodology. The table compares three different composite construction deflators, each of which represents a major phase in the development of the BEA's methodology. BEA I is based on the deflation methodology at the time of the Stigler committee's report in 1961. BEA II represents the methodology of the 1974 revisions, while BEA III refers to the present (1988) method of deflation. Since 1961 there has been a large increase in the use of price indexes. There are presently six total or partial price indexes in use compared to only two in 1961. The present price indexes also have a disproportionate weight, deflating about two-thirds of new construction versus only 11% under BEA I. This percentage is down slightly from 1974, largely due to the increased weight of the Turner cost index in the nonresidential building deflator. Since most of the price indexes are also government compiled, there has been

Table 8.1 Selected Characteristics of the BEA Composite Construction Deflators, 1982 Expenditure Weights

	BEA I	BEA II	BEA III
1. Number of component indexes	12	9	11
2. Number of price indexes[a]	2	4	6
3. Number of government compiled indexes	3	5	7
4. Percentage of construction deflated by prices indexes:			
Residential	.0	100.0	100.0
Nonresidential buildings	.0	66.7	49.5
Nonresidential nonbuilding	38.2	44.7	42.9
Total construction	10.9	72.7	66.4
5. Percentage of construction deflated by government-compiled indexes:			
Residential	1.9	100.0	100.0
Nonresidential buildings	.0	66.7	49.5
Nonresidential nonbuilding	43.5	66.4	63.2
Total construction	13.2	78.9	72.2
6. Percentage of construction deflated by proxy indexes:			
Residential	53.0	55.4	32.6
Nonresidential buildings	68.5	89.9	85.3
Nonresidential nonbuilding	31.8	30.3	33.8
Total construction	52.3	59.7	51.0
7. Percentage of construction deflated by both price and nonproxy indexes:			
Residential	.0	45.6	67.4
Nonresidential buildings	.0	.0	.0
Nonresidential nonbuilding	37.3	25.8	29.1
Total construction	10.7	24.3	33.4

Source: See appendix.
Note: The headings BEA I, BEA II and BEA III refer to the BEA's deflation methodology in the years 1961, 1974, and 1988, respectively.
[a]Includes hybrid indexes

a similar rise in the percentage of construction deflated by government compiled indexes.

On the other hand, the BEA has made little progress in reducing the use of "proxy" indexes. The term proxy index is used here to refer to an index based on a different sector of construction than the one it is used to deflate. An example is the use of the census single-family homes index to deflate nonresidential buildings. In order to quantify this, construction was divided into 19 sectors corresponding roughly to the breakdown in the national income and product accounts. About half of all new construction is deflated by indexes based on other sectors, or nearly the same percentage as in 1961. The main sectors lacking their own deflators are multiunit residential construction and most types of nonresidential buildings.

A more stringent criteria for evaluating the construction deflators is the percentage of construction deflated by both a price index and a nonproxy index. Only about one-third of new construction meets both criteria, consisting mostly of single family homes and highways. Seen in this light, progress in construction deflation has been quite limited over the past 40 years. One problem is that some of the BEA's present price indexes represent small construction sectors such as petroleum pipelines, military and conservation and development. Little or nothing is known of price movements in the important nonresidential building, public utility, and multiunit residential sectors.

Table 8.2 lists the individual indexes used to deflate construction. The main feature is the very large weight of the census index in the BEA II and BEA III deflators. Altogether about one-half of new construction is presently deflated by the census index, including multiunit residential and half of nonresidential

Table 8.2 1982 Weights of the BEA Construction Deflators

	BEA I	BEA II	BEA III
Cost indexes	89.1	23.9	30.7
1. U.S. Department of Agriculture	2.2	.0	.0
2. American Appraisal	17.4	.0	.0
3. Associated General Contractors	4.0	.0	.0
4. AT&T	.0	2.9	.0
5. Boeckh	36.4	.0	.0
6. *Engineering News-Record*	4.0	.0	2.9
7. Environmental Protection Agency	.0	2.8	2.8
8. Fuller	9.6	.0	.0
9. Handy-Whitman	7.5	6.0	6.9
Buildings	.8	.6	.6
Electric utility	5.5	5.4	6.3
Gas utility	1.2	.0	.0
10. Turner Construction Co.	7.9	12.2	18.0
Combined cost and price indexes	.0	5.9	5.3
1. Bureau of Reclamation	.0	3.9	3.3
2. Federal Energy Regulatory Commission Pipeline	.0	2.0	2.0
Price indexes	10.9	70.2	64.0
1. BEA Military	.0	.0	1.0
2. Census Single-Family Homes	.0	49.3	46.4
3. CPI Maintenance and Repair	.0	.0	8.1
4. Federal Highway Administration	6.8	20.9	8.5
Composite	.0	11.9	1.0
Structures	6.8	8.9	7.5
5. ICC Railroad	4.1	.0	.0

Source: See appendix.

Table 8.3 Annual Rates of Change of BEA Composite Deflators, 1963–1982, 1982 Expenditure Weights

	1963–82	1963–72	1972–82
1. Total construction			
BEA I	7.2	6.0	8.3
BEA II	7.0	4.9	9.0
BEA III	7.0	4.9	9.0
2. Residential construction			
BEA I	7.2	6.2	8.2
BEA II	6.9	4.1	9.5
BEA III	7.0	4.4	9.4
3. Nonresidential buildings			
BEA I	7.3	6.2	8.2
BEA II	7.1	5.6	8.5
BEA III	7.1	5.3	8.7
4. Nonbuilding construction			
BEA I	7.2	5.6	8.6
BEA II	7.0	4.9	8.9
BEA III	7.1	5.1	8.9

Source: See appendix.

buildings. Next to the census, the two most important indexes are the Turner and Federal Highway Administration (formerly Bureau of Public Roads, abbreviated here FHWA), which together have about a 25% weight. These two indexes and the two Handy-Whitman indexes are the only indexes that have been used continuously since the introduction of the composite in 1946.

Table 8.3 calculates rates of change of fixed weight construction deflators using the three methodologies. The 1963–82 period was chosen for comparison because the endpoints are BEA benchmark years and, more important, because it is the only period in which most of the component indexes overlap.[6] Despite using different methods, the three composites show remarkably similar rates of increase in all construction sectors over the 1963–82 period. This similarity is surprising given that BEA I is heavily dependent on cost indexes while BEA II and BEA III are based mostly on price indexes. All other things equal, a cost index will increase faster than a price index if productivity growth is positive. Thus the BEA's use of cost indexes has been heavily criticized in the past for imparting an upward bias to the composite. However the increased use of price indexes in the BEA II and BEA III composites has not appreciably lowered the measured rate of construction inflation.

The similarity of the three deflators over the 1963–82 period masks major differences over the two subperiods. Although BEA I increases faster than the other two deflators in the 1963–72 period, it actually increases 1% per year slower in the 1972–82 period. The BEA I deflator, therefore, shows only a two-percentage-point increase in inflation between the two subperiods compared to the four-percentage-point increase in the BEA II and BEA III deflators. That the BEA III deflator could increase significantly faster than a cost index could be taken as evidence of an upward bias in the BEA deflator in the seventies but it would also be consistent with an actual decrease in construction productivity.

Although most critics of the BEA construction deflators have been concerned with their ability to measure the long-run trend of prices, for some purposes the ability to accurately measure short-run price movements is equally or more important. There are several reasons for believing that cost indexes will understate the change in construction inflation over the business cycle. For one, cost indexes usually do not measure the contractor's profit. Since profits are procyclical, this will understate the extent of cyclical fluctuations in prices. Second, cost indexes by definition fail to fully account for productivity. Gordon (1968) has presented evidence that construction productivity is countercyclical, falling during expansions and rising during slumps. Therefore construction prices will tend to increase faster than costs during expansions and slower during contractions.

In addition, many cost indexes do not use actual transaction costs but use instead union wage scales, list prices of materials, or other types of quoted prices. For example, the American Appraisal cost index for industrial buildings, used in the BEA I composite, made "no allowance for the extreme costs resulting from overtime wages, premiums on materials or sacrifice prices and omissions of overhead costs and profits during depression periods" (U.S. Department of Commerce, Office of Business Economics 1956, 210). These are of course some of the same reasons why construction prices fluctuate. The use of nontransactions prices will therefore give the indexes an artificial stability.

For the reasons outlined above, cost indexes will generally be insensitive to changes in competitive conditions. In order to quantify this, construction inflation ($\dot{P}$) was regressed against lagged inflation and the gap between actual and trend real construction activity (GAP):

(1) $$\dot{P}_t = b_0 + b_1\dot{P}_{t-1} + b_2\,\mathrm{GAP}_t,$$

The trend level of construction activity was determined as the predicted value of a regression of the log of construction employment against a time trend.[7]

Equation (1) can be thought of as a Phillips curve for the construction industry. The main coefficient of interest is, of course b_2, which measures the response of prices to the level of construction activity. This coefficient should be positive and, if the preceding arguments are correct, higher for price indexes than cost indexes. Results of regressions of the three composites are shown in table 8.4. The gap coefficient for the BEA I composite is smaller than the other composites, reflecting the early composite's heavy use of cost indexes. However the difference is statistically significant only between the BEA I and BEA II composites and only at the 10% level. To put the point estimates in perspective, construction employment is about 10% below its trend level in a major recession such as in 1982. This would reduce the inflation rate as measured by the BEA I composite by about 2%, versus 4.9% for the BEA II measure.

Lines 4–8 of table 8.4 compare the behavior of individual indexes. The main feature is the high sensitivity of the FHWA structures index, which is undoubtedly due to the index's use of bid prices.[8] The gap coefficient of the Turner cost index is also statistically significant, which may be partly due to Turner's subjective adjustment of the index for competitive conditions. On the other hand, the gap coefficient of the American Appraisal index is close to zero, reflecting its use of list prices. The census index has a larger gap coefficient than the Boeckh cost index but the difference is not statistically significant. However the census index probably understates the change in prices over the business cycle because it ignores buyer incentives that effectively act as price reductions. Buyer incentives such as below-market financing were both common and of significant size during the 1981–82 recession. The census index increased by 2% during 1982 but the true rate of price change was probably negative.

Table 8.4 **Rates of Construction Inflation and the Output Gap**
$$\dot{P}_t = b_0 + b_1 \dot{P}_{t-1} + b_2 \text{GAP}_t, \quad t = 1965\text{–}82^a$$

		Regression Coefficients				Tests of Equality of b_2 Coefficient[b]	
Equation	Index	b_0	b_1	b_2	$\hat{R}^2$	Equations	f-Statistic
Total construction:							
1.	BEA I	3.846	.476	.203	.577	(1),(2)	3.43
		(1.145)	(.150)	(.066)			
2.	BEA II	4.714	.318	.489	.456	(2),(3)	.63
		(1.527)	(.177)	(.140)			
3.	BEA III	3.444	.507	.354	.561	(3),(1)	1.61
		(1.258)	(.154)	(.098)			
Single-family homes							
4.	Boeckh	3.415	.560	.011	.311	(4),(5)	2.39
		(1.532)	(.210)	(.073)			
5.	Census	2.941	.588	.147	.483	—	—
		(1.368)	(.167)	(.077)			
Nonresidential structures							
6.	American appraisal[c]	5.355	.262	.058	.014	(6),(7)	2.96
		(1.834)	(.255)	(.123)			
7.	Turner	4.286	.396	.371	.349	(7),(8)	6.48
		(1.552)	(.190)	(.134)			
8.	FHWA structures	8.654	−.160	1.471	.374	(8),(6)	10.87
		(2.854)	(.195)	(.411)			

[a]Ordinary least squares; standard errors are shown in parentheses.
[b]Tests the equality of coefficient b_2 between the equations listed. Critical values are $F_{.10} = 2.63$, $F_{.05} = 4.17$, and $F_{.01} = 7.56$.
[c]Regression for the 1965–81 period. $\dot{P}$ = percentage change in the construction price index. The composite indexes are calculated using fixed 1982 expenditure weights. GAP = difference between actual and trend construction activity as a percentage of trend.

In conclusion, there are some significant differences in the short-run movements of cost and price indexes. Given that two-thirds of new construction is still deflated by either cost or proxy indexes, the BEA deflators still probably understate the true extent of cyclical price fluctuations.

8.2 Alternative Construction Deflators

The Stigler committee's report in 1961 coincided with an increased interest in construction deflation among academic economists. Interest in construction deflation was prompted in large part by research in the process of economic growth and by growth accounting models in particular. Pinpointing the sources of economic growth required accurate measures of real capital, which in turn lead researchers such as Gordon (1961) and Kendrick (1961) to question the existing construction deflators. By the early sixties, the deficiencies of the commerce deflators were well known, but there were as yet no alternative deflators available.

Responding to the demands of researchers, the BEA in 1966 published an alternative deflator for private nonresidential construction, which it termed "constant cost 2" (Grose, Rottenberg, and Wasson 1966). The constant-cost-2 deflator was a weighted average of five indexes, with by far the largest weight given to the Bureau of Reclamation index. Component indexes of the Bureau of Reclamation index were used to deflate several types of construction, including buildings and electric and gas utilities. The constant-cost-2 deflator also included the AT&T cost index, the Turner cost index and the FHWA index, and a small weight for the ICC railroad index.

The constant-cost-2 deflator was probably only a marginal improvement over the BEA I composite. It relied heavily on the Bureau of Reclamation index, which was only partly a price index and often distantly related to the expenditures it deflated. About two-thirds of the Bureau of Reclamation index is constructed of cost measures such as union wage scales and materials and equipment prices. In addition, the AT&T and Turner indexes were also cost indexes. Altogether only about one-third of the constant-cost-2 index was based on construction price indexes. Owing to the lack of suitable alternatives, the index was still used in a number of growth studies, including Jorgenson and Griliches' (1967) well-known study of long-run productivity growth.

Dacy (1964, 1965) proposed an entirely different method of deflating construction. Dacy simply assumed that real construction output was proportional to real construction materials:

$$\frac{C}{P^c} = \frac{M}{P^m}, \tag{2}$$

where C and M are indexes of nominal construction and nominal materials, P^c is a construction price index and P^m is a materials price index. Equation (2) may be rewritten in a form similar to the one used by Dacy:

(3) $$P^c = P^m/b,$$

where b is an index of the share of nominal materials in nominal construction. The Dacy index therefore required only a price index for materials and an estimate of the share of materials in construction. The construction price index would equal the materials price index if there was no change in the materials share. An increasing share of materials in construction output would indicate that the price of materials is increasing faster than the price of other inputs. Hence in this case the construction price index would be lower than the materials price index.

There are two major problems with Dacy's method, one practical and one theoretical. Despite its simple appearance, the Dacy index is surprisingly difficult to estimate. The main problem is estimating the materials' share of output. Present data on materials production does not distinguish between construction and nonconstruction usage and is thus not comparable to the construction expenditure series. Alternatively, one could calculate the materials' share of output as one minus the value-added share. But here again the value-added and expenditure series are not comparable since the latter series also includes force account construction.

The second problem is more fundamental. Dacy's method is equivalent to assuming a fixed proportions Leontief technology in which there is no possibility of substitution between materials and other factors of production. In practice, contractors may substitute for on-site labor and capital by using prefabricated materials or by switching to more materials-intensive types of construction. Increased use of prefabricated materials would not represent a proportional increase in output, as assumed by Dacy, but would instead represent less on-site production. A long-term trend toward prefabrication would thus bias Dacy's index downward. This bias is small if the elasticity of substitution between materials and on-site factors is low, but increases exponentially as the elasticity approaches minus one.[9] On the other hand, Dacy's index would be biased upward if the relative price of materials rose. This seems to be the likely case after 1973, when materials prices increased rapidly but construction wage inflation was moderate.[10]

Gordon (1968) created an alternative construction deflator using a modified version of the Dacy index, the FHWA index, and a third index that he called the component-price hybrid (CPH).[11] To construct the CPH index, Gordon first averaged the ICC, FHWA, and Bureau of Reclamation indexes of the price of structural steel and structural concrete in place. He then compared these prices indexes to cost indexes for the same items and applied this ratio to the entire building sector. Algebraically, this may be written as:

(4) $$\text{CPH} = CI^c\,(P^{ss}/CI^{sc} + P^{ss}/CI^{ss})\,/\,2,$$

where CI is a cost index, P is a price index for materials in place, and the superscripts c, sc, and ss refer to all building construction, structural concrete, and structural steel, respectively. Gordon averaged the CPH and Dacy indexes to form a deflator for buildings. His nonbuilding deflator was an average of the Dacy and FHWA indexes.

The CPH was probably the most interesting feature of Gordon's index. The ratio of the price indexes for steel and concrete to their cost indexes will reflect changes in productivity, profit margins, and any other factors that cause price and cost indexes to differ. Thus the CPH assumes that productivity in steel and concrete construction is the same as for construction as a whole. One possible bias that Gordon suggests is that "concrete and steel may have been unusually suitable for mechanization, and efficiency improvements may have been less rapid in other components" (Gordon 1968, 422). Still, Gordon's method seems preferable to the assumption of no productivity change made by most of the indexes in the BEA I composite.

After a long hiatus, construction deflation has recently received renewed attention. This interest was motivated by the large unexplained fall in construction productivity during the late sixties and seventies. Allen (1985) estimated that about half of the construction productivity decline was due to an overdeflation of construction output. Allen accepted the BEA's use of the census index to deflate residential construction but made two adjustments to the nonresidential deflator. First, he replaced the nonresidential building deflator with a price per square foot index. Allen also used the urban portion of the FHWA index to deflate highways on the assumption that the rural portion was biased upward due to the decline in interstate highway construction. Allen deflated the remainder of the nonbuilding sector by an average of the urban highway price index and the building price per square foot index.

A crucial assumption of Allen's index is that square feet is a good proxy for output.[12] The price per square foot index is almost certainly biased upward since, as Allen notes, "there is no adjustment for likely increases in amenities or improved design" (Allen 1985, 668). In addition, building mechanical and electrical systems have become more sophisticated over time. A square foot index seems particularly unsuited for institutional buildings since these buildings have a very high concentration of amenities.

In earlier work (Pieper 1989a) I also used a price per square foot index to deflate nonresidential buildings, but one based on the more homogeneous category of office buildings. Residential construction was deflated with an index that removed the very largest category of homes, those over 2,400 square feet. This category of houses is the most amenity intensive and therefore the least suitable for a square foot based index such as the census. For the post-1973 period, we used a simple price per square foot index of homes less than 2,400 square feet. This is likely to be upward biased because it again does not adjust for other quality improvements. For example, houses have become more energy efficient and are more likely to include extras such as appliances and landscaping.[13]

We also adjusted the FHWA index for the size of highway contracts. The average size of high contracts has fallen in half in real terms since 1972, reflecting a decline in large interstate projects and a shift from new construction to reconstruction and repair projects. The effect of this shift was estimated from a 1981 cross-section regression of highway construction prices. The nonbuilding index was then an average of the adjusted FHWA index and the bid price components of the Bureau of Reclamation index.

Table 8.5 summarizes the methodology of the deflators while table 8.6 lists their rates of growth over the 1963–82 period. The BEA constant-cost-2 and Allen indexes increase at about the same rate as the BEA index. However this does not really provide support for the BEA composite since the constant-cost-2 deflator is based mainly on cost indexes, while a major portion of the Allen index, the building price per square foot index, is almost certainly biased upward. Indeed, nonresidential building square footage costs increased 2.6% faster per year than the BEA deflator in the 1947–63 period (Otelsberg 1972), which is a much faster relative rate of increase than after 1963.

Table 8.5 **Summary of the Alternative Construction Deflators**

Index	Description
1. BEA constant cost 2	
Nonresidential buildings	Unweighted average of the Turner and AT&T building cost indexes, FHWA composite, and BR indexes for power plants and pumping plants.
Nonbuilding	Weighted average of the FHWA, BR, AT&T, and ICC indexes, with heaviest weight on the BR index.
2. Dacy	Assumed real construction output was proportional to real construction materials usage.
3. Gordon	
Buildings	Unweighted average of Dacy's index and the "component price hybrid," an index based on the bid price components of the FHWA and BR indexes.
Nonbuilding	Unweighted average of Dacy's index and the FHWA index.
4. Allen	
Residential	Census index.
Nonresidential buildings	Index of the price per square foot of all nonresidentical buildings.
Highways	FHWA urban highway construction price index.
Other nonbuilding	Average of the nonresidential price per square foot index and urban portion of the FHWA index.
5. Pieper	
Residential	Price index of houses less than 2,400 square feet.
Nonresidential buildings	Index of the price per square foot of commercial buildings.
Nonbuilding	Average of the bid price components of the BR index and the FHWA index adjusted for contract size.

Note: Abbreviations used: BR = Bureau of Reclamation construction price index; FHWA = Federal Highway Administration highway construction price index; ICC = Interstate Commerce Commission railroad construction price index

On the other hand, the other three alternative indexes increase between 0.5% and 0.8% less per year than the BEA index. The Dacy index is probably downward biased in the 1963–72 period when the relative price of materials was decreasing but upward biased after 1972 when the opposite was true. The Gordon index indicates no bias in the 1963–72 period but an upward bias of almost 1% per year in the 1972–82 period. As mentioned previously, the Gordon index would be biased downward if concrete and steel productivity has increased more (or decreased less) than average construction productivity. However, a potentially much larger upward bias is that the FHWA index, a major input to the Gordon index, is upward biased due to the completion of the interstate highway system. Pieper's index is likely to be very conservative since it assumes no quality change per square foot in either office buildings or single family homes.

In conclusion, the preponderance of evidence indicates an overdeflation of new construction of at least 0.5% per year between 1963 and 1982. While a

Table 8.6 Annual Rates of Change of Alternative Construction Deflators, 1963–82

	1963–82	1963–72	1972–82
1. Total Construction:			
BEA	7.0	4.9	9.0
BEA constant cost 2[a]	7.1	5.5	8.6
Dacy[b]	6.2	3.6	8.5
Gordon	6.5	4.8	8.2
Allen	7.3	4.3	10.0
Pieper	6.3	4.2	8.2
2. Residential construction:			
BEA	7.0	4.4	9.4
Gordon	6.5	4.8	8.1
Allen	6.9	4.1	9.5
Pieper	6.5	4.2	8.7
3. Nonresidential buildings:			
BEA	7.0	5.3	8.6
BEA constant cost 2	7.3	5.7	8.6
Gordon	6.5	4.8	8.1
Allen	7.8	4.1	11.4
Pieper	6.2	3.9	8.3
4. Nonbuilding construction:			
BEA	7.1	4.9	9.0
BEA constant cost 2	6.9	5.0	8.6
Gordon	6.6	4.6	8.4
Allen	7.0	4.8	9.0
Pieper	6.1	4.4	7.6

Source: See appendix.
[a]Deflator for private nonresidential construction only.
[b]Not available separately by type of construction.

0.5% annual overdeflation may appear to be modest, if true, it would have major consequences. Construction productivity growth would be understated by roughly twice this amount because of the BEA's double deflation technique for measuring real construction value added. Investment would also be understated. Relative to 1963, gross private domestic investment would be larger by about 1% of GNP, which would substantially weaken the conventional argument that there was an investment slowdown in the seventies.

8.3 Improving the Construction Deflators

Most construction price indexes price intermediate units of output termed components. The price indexes can be divided into three types according to their method of pricing components. This section discusses the strengths and weaknesses of each method and speculates about their most promising applications. The section ends with some comments about cost indexes.

8.3.1 Bid Prices

In many types of heavy construction, contractors bid separately on each item specified in the contract. It is then relatively straightforward to construct a price index by averaging winning bids on the most important components. When individual components are not bid on separately, the contract bid price can still in principle be used to form a price index if there is some output measure available such as square feet. The main difficulty with bid price indexes is identifying a relatively homogeneous physical measure. Where heterogeneity occurs, the price index will be biased when quality change occurs within the component categories.

The FHWA index is usually considered a successful application of the bid-price method. However, a closer examination of this index reveals that its components are far from homogeneous. The FHWA publishes average bid prices by state for each of its six components. Since there are anywhere from five to 150 contracts per state, much of the price variation on individual projects has already been removed. Yet the average state prices still vary enormously, certainly by more than can be attributed to regional cost differences. For example, in 1981, average state excavation prices ranged from $0.78 to $15.71 per cubic yard (U.S. Department of Transportation, Federal Highway Administration 1982). The standard deviation of average state prices for the most homogeneous components, bituminous concrete, and reinforcing steel, is still about two times greater than the standard deviation of state construction costs.[14]

The BEA military price index attempts to solve the heterogeneity problem by first grouping construction into a number of narrowly defined categories based upon Department of Defense "performance specifications." For example, barracks are categorized by the number of bathrooms and permissible noise transmission levels. The category is then deflated by a price per square foot index. A similar procedure may be possible for some types of nonresidential buildings if they can be narrowly categorized. However, in general the potential use of bid prices seems somewhat limited due to the lack of homogeneous measures of construction.

8.3.2 Hedonic Price Indexes

Hedonic price indexes may be considered a type of component pricing where the component prices are estimated from a cross-section regression. The successful development of the census index lead to the hope that the construction deflation problem could be solved through the widespread use of the hedonic technique. However, census experiments with a hedonic price index for the multiunit residential sector have been largely unsuccessful (Pollock 1984) and little work has been done for other types of construction.[15]

In practice hedonic price indexes usually include only physical characteristics such as size and ignore quality characteristics such as design, materials and construction quality, and building amenities. It is therefore not surprising that hedonic indexes for buildings often differ little from price per square foot indexes. Figure 8.1 plots the annual percentage change in the census index and the percentage change in the price per square foot of new houses. With the exception of 1972 and 1973, the two series move virtually in tandem. The mean absolute difference between the annual census inflation rate and the per-

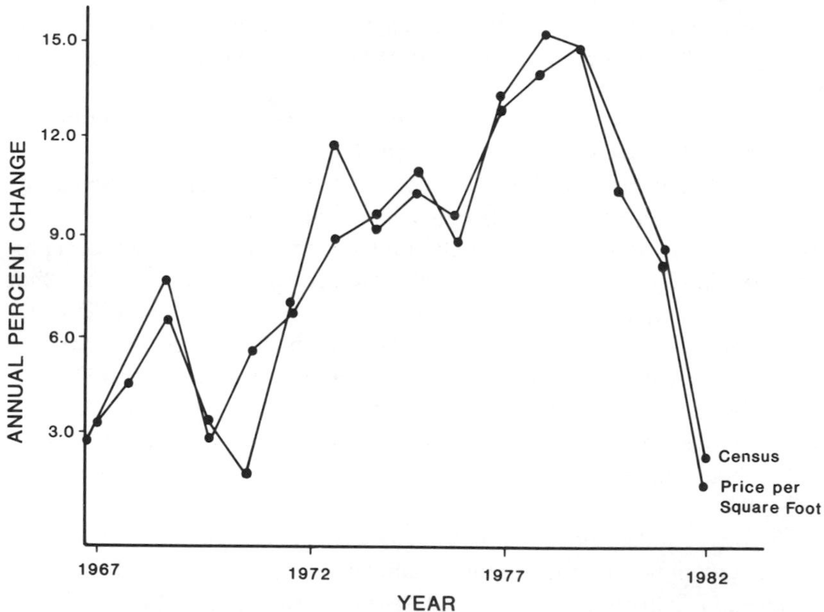

Fig. 8.1 Annual rates of change of the census index and an index of the price per square foot of single-family homes, 1967–82

centage change in the price per square foot is only 0.8%, while the mean difference is 0.3%.

The main weakness of hedonic price indexes is therefore the difficulty of quantifying many construction characteristics. For example, building design and the quality of materials are two very important factors which are extremely difficult to quantify. One of the problems with the experimental multiunit residential index is that only three characteristics (region, square feet, and number of bathrooms) were quantified. In addition, square feet appears to be a more homogeneous measure for houses than for apartments and nonresidential buildings.[16] Therefore the success of the census index may not be easily repeated for other types of buildings. Finally, hedonic price indexes require a significant number of observations, which can be a problem for smaller construction sectors. Lack of observations was a problem even in the relatively large multiunit residential sector for quarterly time periods.

One promising area for the hedonic technique may be highway construction. As shown earlier, the units priced by the FHWA index are not very homogeneous. Quantifiable characteristics such as the division of construction between interstate and noninterstate, rural and urban, and new and reconstruction projects may be able to explain some of the price variability. In addition, the FHWA awards over 2,000 large (greater than $500,000) contracts a year, so lack of observations would not be a problem.

8.3.3 Estimation Indexes

This method uses estimates from contractors, cost engineers, or other types of "informed judgment." A typical estimation index would survey firms and ask them to estimate the cost of constructing a hypothetical project with fixed specifications. The respondent may be asked to price the entire project or the project may be divided into components, with each respondent estimating only the price of a particular component.

Although deflation by estimation indexes is rare, there are a few precedents. The FHA 70-cities index, which forms half of the BEA's residential deflator for the 1947–63 period, was based on a survey of single-family home contractors. The FERC has received courtesy bids on a hypothetical pipeline project from three companies since 1972. This information is given a small subjective weight in the FERC index.

Statistics Canada uses the estimation approach to construct a price index for nonresidential buildings. In contrast to the FERC and FHA 70-cities indexes, which priced the entire structure, Statistics Canada uses a disaggregated approach, dividing a building into its component operations. Statistics Canada first selects prototype models of five types of nonresidential buildings: an office, warehouse, small shopping center, light industrial building and high school.[17] The construction of each building is divided into five main categories: architectural, structural, mechanical and electrical trades and the general contractor's overhead and profit. Representative items for each category are priced, mostly on the basis of surveys of subcontractors. The architectural and structural items generally refer to a specified quantity of materials in place and thus reflect all construction costs. The mechanical and electrical trades are deflated using more of a cost-based approach. In these trades, materials are deflated by conventional materials price indexes while labor costs are deflated by wages adjusted for productivity on the basis of a subcontractor survey. Roughly 100 different items are priced for each building type.

The obvious advantage of estimation indexes is that they can control for construction heterogeneity by keeping the specifications fixed over time. Their main weakness is that they are based on hypothetical prices rather than on actual transaction prices. Contractors submitting hypothetical bids know they will not be required to construct the project in question. They also do not have the normal incentive of bidding as low as possible in order to win the contract. Under these conditions, they may bid differently than they would on an actual project.

There is some evidence that construction estimates are insensitive to changes in competitive conditions. Both the Federal Highway Administration and the Bureau of Reclamation have engineers estimate the cost of a project before its contract is awarded. The engineer's estimate, therefore provides a measure of informed judgment that is likely to be similar to that provided by a survey of contractors. The actual contract cost varies from 76% to 111% of the engineer's estimate over the 1977–86 period. What is most striking about this ratio is its procyclical behavior. Actual bid prices fall much more in recessions than the estimates and rise more rapidly in expansions. This can be clearly seen in figure 8.2, which plots the ratio of the low bid to the engineer's estimate against the ratio of actual to trend construction employment. The simple correlation coefficient between the employment ratio and the low bid ratio is 0.76 for the Federal Highway Administration and 0.72 for the Bureau of Reclamation.

Engineers' estimates thus tend to be more "sticky" than actual prices and may thus measure short-run price movements poorly. To quantify this, the FHWA index was compared to a highway price index based on the engineer's estimates.[18] The mean absolute difference between the semiannual percentage change in these two indexes, expressed at an annual rate, was 4.4%. This compares to a mean absolute percentage change in the FHWA index of 9.2%. There are a few cases where the discrepancy between the two indexes is very large, such as in the second half of 1980, when the estimated prices rose by 15% but actual prices fell slightly. On the other hand, the FHWA index is unusually sensitive to competitive conditions because it is based on auction prices. It may thus exaggerate the insensitivity of estimation indexes.

The Stigler committee considered the problems with construction estimates so severe that it recommended that they be used "only as a last resort" (NBER 1961, 90). However, this is probably too harsh a judgment. Since the specifications of a hypothetical project are held fixed over time, an estimation index

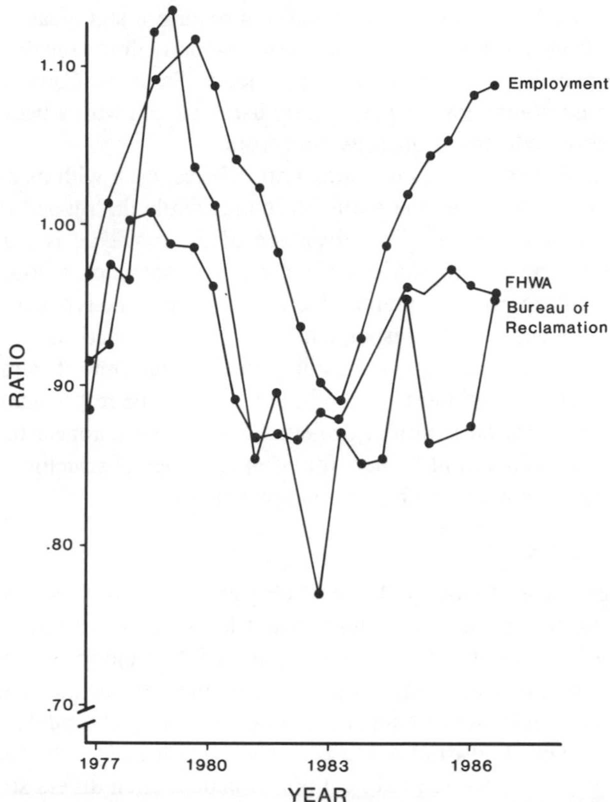

Fig. 8.2 Ratio of low bid to engineer's estimate, FHWA, and BR indexes, and ratio of actual to trend construction employment

controls for construction heterogeneity, and thus quality change, better than other methods. Its weaknesses in measuring short-run price movements must then be balanced against its strength in measuring the long-run trend. This type of deflation would seem especially appropriate for very heterogeneous types of construction such as institutional buildings and utilities. Furthermore, the problem of price stickiness may be reduced by carefully questioning the estimators. Statistics Canada's index for overhead and profit is very volatile, and, as a result, its overall index appears to be more sensitive to changes in competitive conditions than conventional construction price indexes.

A few other comments on estimation indexes are in order. First, there is no obvious method of weighting the responses when several contractors are surveyed. If the project was real, then only the low estimate would be relevant. However, since the project is hypothetical, the low estimate may be a statistical outlier that should be ignored. The FERC therefore uses an average of its courtesy bids while Statistics Canada makes a judgmental decision on which estimate to use. Second, estimation indexes require a significant amount of cooperation from contractors since it takes time and effort to make a realistic estimate, especially on more complex projects. Statistics Canada has been able to increase contractor cooperation by using people with a background in the construction industry as quantity surveyors.

Finally, there are two types of estimation indexes, each with its own advantages. The first type prices the entire structure, while the second type prices the structure's components. The advantage of the first type is that the estimated price will reflect the services of the general contractor, whose functions are very difficult to price separately. However, since some types of structures are very heterogeneous, the respondent may have no practical experience in pricing the structure in question. Dividing the structure into its simpler component operations would increase the likelihood that the respondent has actually performed work on a similar project. Thus it would appear that the disaggregated approach would be best for complex types of structures while the aggregate approach would be best for simpler structures.

8.3.4 Cost Indexes

Cost indexes are obviously the least desirable method of deflation. However, cost indexes are also the simplest and least expensive indexes to construct and will be continued to be used by the BEA in the foreseeable future. This section simply makes the point that cost indexes for the same type of construction can differ widely depending upon their weights and data sources.

A large number of cost indexes use cost data published by the *Engineering News-Record* (ENR), a trade publication. This data often differs significantly from government estimates for the same items. For example, ENR publishes a construction cost index that is a weighted average of union wage rates and the price of lumber, steel, and cement. This index is presently used by the BEA to deflate telephone construction. As a comparison, a cost index with identical weights for the same items was constructed using the Bureau of Labor Statistics (BLS) producer price indexes and a BLS index of union wages.[19] Despite their identical methods, the BLS index increases about 0.7% less per year between 1963 and 1982. The main source of the discrepancy is the ENR wage measure, which increases 1.3% faster per year than the BLS measure. On the other hand, ENR materials prices increased 0.5% per year less than the BLS producer price indexes. However, the materials price indexes differ greatly among the 20 individual cities for which ENR publishes data. For example, ENR estimates the increase in lumber prices between 1967 and 1982 as 61% in Chicago but 250% in Cleveland. Such large differences hardly instill much confidence in the reliability of the ENR data.

The EPA sewer construction cost index is also based on ENR data. The EPA index is actually an average of two indexes, one representing sewer lines and the other sewage treatment plants. Table 8.7 calculates cost indexes for both types of construction using the same weights as the EPA but with BLS

Table 8.7 **Cost Indexes for Sewer Construction**

Index	1982 Index Level (1967 = 100)	Annual Rate of Growth, 1967–82
1. EPA sewer lines construction cost index	341.7	8.5
2. BLS sewer lines cost index—EPA weights:		
a. Based on industry wages	338.4	8.5
b. Based on union wages	330.5	8.3
3. BLS sewer lines cost index—BLS weights:		
a. Based on industry wages	309.7	7.8
b. Based on union wages	317.6	8.0
4. EPA sewage treatment plant construction cost index	348.9	8.7
5. BLS sewer plant cost index—EPA weights:		
a. Based on industry wages	314.3	7.9
b. Based on union wages	305.9	7.7
6. BLS sewer plant cost index—BLS weights:		
a. Based on industry wages	302.4	7.7
b. Based on union wages	310.4	7.8

Source: See appendix.
Note: Lines 2 and 4 calculate the EPA cost index with BLS data used in place of *ENR* data. Lines 3 and 6 do the same except the data is weighted by a BLS study of sewer construction.

price and wage data. Because unionized construction declined during the seventies, a union wage index may overstate the increase in labor costs. Therefore table 8.7 uses two wage series, one based on union wages and one based on average construction industry wages. The substitution of BLS data for ENR data has little effect on the sewer line index but it lowers the rate of increase of the treatment plant index by about 1% per year over the 1967–82 interval.

The EPA index weights the different inputs based on a study of sewer construction during the 1956–62 period. A more recent study was undertaken by the BLS in 1971 as part of its series on materials and labor requirements in construction. Lines 3 and 6 of table 8.7 recalculate a sewer cost index using BLS data weighted by the BLS 1971 study. Both sewer indexes increase significantly less than the EPA index over the 1967–82 period. A closer inspection of the EPA index weights reveals a few anomalies. For example, the sewer line index gives structural steel an enormous weight of 50% in the materials portion of the index. The reason for the large weight is that EPA used structural steel as a proxy for the price of construction equipment. Since the relative price of steel rose during this period, this contributed to the fast rise of the EPA index.

Given that cost indexes for the same type of construction may differ significantly, it should go without saying that if cost indexes must be used for deflation, then they should at least have recent weights and reliable data sources. The presumption here is in favor of public data sources over private data sources such as ENR. The former, but not the latter, must pass some level of statistical standards before they are published. However cost indexes frequently use private data sources. No less than five of the indexes in the present BEA composite use some ENR data: the EPA, FERC, Bureau of Rcclamation, and Handy-Whitman indexes and the ENR index itself.

8.5 Conclusion

The BEA still relies heavily on cost indexes and proxy indexes to deflate construction output. Price indexes are available for only two major construction sectors, single-family homes and highways. Partly as a consequence, it seems likely that the BEA deflator for new construction has a significant upward bias in the 1963–82 period.

This paper will close with two general observations. First, progress in construction deflation has been made in the past when there has been interaction between government statisticians and the academic profession. The harsh criticisms of the commerce indexes by the Stigler committee and other academics in the sixties lead to a demand for better statistics, which spurred changes in deflation by the BEA. Similarly the profession's lack of interest in the area in the past decade has abetted an inactivity by government. Second, there is probably no single best method for deflating construction. Each method has its strengths and weaknesses, the relative amounts of which will vary by the type of construction. With a few minor exceptions, the estimation approach has not been used in the past because it is not based on transaction prices. However, given the heterogeneity of many types of construction, it appears that some type of estimation indexes are necessary if reliance on cost and proxy indexes is to be reduced.

Appendix

Sources and Methods for Selected Tables and Figures

Tables 8.1 and 8.2

The sources for the three deflation methodologies are the NBER (1961), U.S. Department of Commerce, Bureau of Economic Analysis (1974), and my conversations with BEA staff members. Published accounts of recent BEA deflation changes may also be found in the July issues of the *Survey of Current Business*. The value of new construction expenditures, rounded to the nearest $100 million, may be found in table 5.4 of the U.S. Department of Commerce, Bureau of Economic Analysis (1986). I have used an unpublished version of table 5.4 that shows construction expenditures in millions of dollars. The hybrid Bureau of Reclamation and FERC indexes are weighted by their price index percentage, 32% and 65%, respectively, when calculating the percentage of construction expenditures deflated by price indexes. The percentage of construction deflated by proxy indexes is calculated by dividing construction into the following 19 sectors, corresponding roughly to the breakdown in table 5.4 of the national income accounts: single-unit residential, multiunit residential, additions, alterations and replacements, industrial, office, other commercial, institutional and other buildings, telephone, railroad, electric utilities, gas, petroleum pipelines, nonresidential farm, highways, military, conservation and development, sewer, water, and other private and public. The CPI maintenance and repair index is assumed to be representative of the additions, alterations, and replacements sector.

Table 8.3

The methodology for the three composites and the source of the expenditure weights are listed above. The individual indexes that constitute the composite are taken from a variety of sources. The following indexes are taken from the July/August 1983 issue of *Construction Review:* American Appraisal, Boeckh, Engineering News-Record, FHWA, Bureau of Reclamation, Turner, Handy-Whitman buildings and electric power, AT&T, and FERC. The census and BEA military price indexes are from lines 25 and 39 of table 7.12 of U.S. Department of Commerce, Bureau of Economic Analysis (1986). The CPI maintenance and repair is from U.S. Council of Economic Advisers (1986, table B-56), the Fuller index is from *Engineering News-Record* (various issues), and the EPA index is from the U.S. Environmental Protection Agency (1983). Four of the BEA I component indexes are not available for the entire 1963–82 period. The ICC, Associated General Contractors, and U.S. Department of Agriculture indexes were discontinued in 1967, 1971, and 1973, respectively. The Handy-Whitman gas index, while still compiled, is not publicly available after 1974. Values for these four indexes until their date of discontinuance are taken from *Historical Statistics of the United States* and *Statistical Abstract of the United States.* The ICC railroad and telephone indexes are extrapolated from their date of discontinuance to 1982 by the FHWA and AT&T indexes, respectively. The Handy-Whitman gas index is extrapolated by an average of the Handy-Whitman building and electric utility indexes. The other two indexes are extrapolated by cost indexes using a methodology as close as possible to that of the original indexes. The Department of Agriculture index is extrapolated by an average of the producer price index for construction materials (U.S. Council of Economic Advisers 1986, table B-60) and an index of wages for farm labor (table B-96), using weights of 78% and 22%. The Associated General Contractors index is extrapolated by the cost of five types of materials and two types of labor, using weights found in the U.S. Department of Commerce, Bureau of the Census (1964) and cost indexes published in the July/August 1983 issue of *Construction Review.* The above extrapolations will have very little effect on the overall composite because the four indexes together have a weight of only about 10%.

Table 8.4

The BEA composites are fixed weight deflators using 1982 expenditure weights. Sources for the indexes used in table 8.4 are listed in the appendix description of table 8.3. The gap variable is defined as the difference between actual and trend construction employment as a percent of trend. Trend construction employment is calculated as the predicted value of a 1963–82 regression of the log of construction employment (U.S. Council of Economic Advisers 1986, table B-40) against a time trend. A weighted least squares procedure, with weights based on the regression standard errors, is used when testing for the equality of coefficient b_2 between regressions.

Table 8.6

BEA: The BEA index is a fixed-weight price index using 1982 expenditure weights. The index refers to the present published deflator, which is a combination of different deflation methods that have been linked together in the past. It will thus differ slightly from the BEA III composite which uses one method continuously throughout the 1963–82 period. The source for expenditures and prices by type of construction is *The National Income and Product Accounts of the United States, 1929–1982,* tables 5.4 and 7.12. The BEA's published price index for all structures includes the following nonconstruction items: brokers commissions, mining exploration, shafts and wells, and mobile homes. The structures price index will thus differ from the index for total construction shown in table 8.6, which excludes these items.

BEA constant cost 2. The methodology of the BEA constant-cost-2 index is described in U.S. Department of Commerce, Bureau of Economic Analysis (1971). The source of the individual components of the Bureau of Reclamation index is the U.S. Department of Interior (1984). The sources for the other indexes are listed under the description for table 8.3

Dacy. The Dacy index is calculated using the producer price index for construction materials (U.S. Council of Economic Advisers 1986, table B-60). The share of materials is calculated as materials costs divided by the cost of materials plus labor. Data are from the 1967, 1972, and 1982 Census of Construction, U.S. Summary, table B-1 (U.S. Department of Commerce, Bureau of the Census 1985). The materials share is extrapolated back to 1963 on the basis of the percentage of intermediate inputs in total new construction in the 1963 and 1967 input-output tables.

Gordon. Gordon's version of the Dacy index uses the same sources listed above. The only difference between the two versions is that Gordon calculated the material's share as materials cost divided by output. The price of structural steel in place is from the Federal Highway Administration (1983). The price of structural concrete in place is an average of prices from U.S. Department of Transportation, Federal Highway Administration (1983) and the Bureau of Reclamation (unpublished information from the Construction Support

Branch). The Gordon CPH index originally also used the ICC index and the Bureau of Reclamation index for steel bridges. The former has been discontinued while the latter is not used here because it is in fact a materials price index. The cost index for steel and concrete in place is formed by averaging wages for highway construction (U.S. Department of Labor, BLS 1985) and producer price indexes for ready-mix concrete (*Construction Review* [July/August 1983]) and structural steel (PPI code 1013–0245). The steel and concrete cost indexes use 1963 materials and labor weights for highway construction (U.S. Department of Transportation, Federal Highway Administration 1975). The cost index for all construction is a weighted average of the producer price index for construction materials and the average hourly earnings of construction workers (U.S. Council of Economic Advisers 1986, table B-41). Labor and material weights are from the 1967 Census of Construction, U.S. Summary, table B-1.

Allen. The urban highway price index for the years 1968–82 is published in the Federal Highway Administration (1983). The urban price index is not available before 1968 and is therefore extrapolated back to 1963 by the FHWA composite index. The source for nonresidential building square feet and contract value is the *Statistical Abstract of the United States*. The residential price index is from table 7.12, line 25 of the *National Income and Product Accounts of the United States, 1929–82*.

Pieper. The census index used nine dummy variables to characterize house size in the 1963–73 period. The residential price index for these years is calculated by simply excluding the dummy variable for houses over 2,400 square feet, reweighting the remaining size categories to sum to one and then using the census Laspeyres index formulation. The regression coefficients are unpublished information provided by the Bureau of Census, construction statistics division. Index weights are published in U.S. Department of Commerce, Bureau of Census, *Price Index of New One-Family Houses Sold,* 1973. Average sales prices for houses in six different square foot categories are published in the Bureau of the Census, *Characteristics of New Housing,* table 22. The residential index for 1973 onward is a weighted average (using number of houses as weights) of sales price indexes for the five size categories under 2,400 square feet. Finally, the residential index is adjusted for land costs by applying the ratio of the census index excluding land to the index including land. The price per square foot of contracts for new office buildings in the 1963–68 period is from Musgrave (1969). This index is extended to 1971 using an index for commercial buildings found in Otelsberg (1972). Contract value and square feet for office building contracts is published in the November issue of *Architectural Record* for 1971 onward. The price per square foot values refer to new contracts and not construction in place. A price index for construction in place is calculated by taking a three-year moving average of the index for new contracts, using weights of 31%, 56%, and 13%. These weights are based on a F. W. Dodge study of progress patterns (U.S. Department of Commerce, Bureau of the Census, 1970). The bid price components of the Bureau of Reclamation index are unpublished data from the Construction Support Branch of the Bureau of Reclamation. The adjusted FHWA index is calculated as

$$\ln P^* = \ln P - .2 \ln \text{size}, \tag{1}$$

where P^* is the adjusted index, P is the FHWA composite, and size is average real contract size. The coefficient of .2 is based on a 1981 cross-section regression (Pieper 1989a). Average contract size is from the U.S. Department of Transportation, Federal Highway Administration's "Bid Opening Report."

Table 8.7

The source for the methodology of the EPA index is the Federal Water Pollution Control Administration (1967). The EPA indexes price labor and 10 types of materials. Lines 2 and 5 price the same items but use BLS producer price indexes and BLS wage series. The BLS union wage index is from *Construction Review,* table E-3. Because the series ended in 1981, it was extrapolated to 1982 using average construction industry wages. The industry wage series is the average hourly earnings for construction workers (U.S. Council of Economic Advisers 1986, table B-41). Lines 3 and 6 show cost indexes for sewer construction using the above-mentioned BLS wages series and producer price indexes for 27 types of materials with weights taken from U.S. Department of Labor, Bureau of Labor Statistics (1979). (Details of the items priced are available from the author on request.)

Figure 8.1

The census price index including land is from the U.S. Department of Commerce, Bureau of the Census, *Price Index of New One-Family Houses Sold.* The price per square foot index is calculated as the average sales price of new one-family houses sold divided by average square feet. Both series are taken from the Bureau of the Census, *Characteristics of New Housing.*

Figure 8.2

The source of the ratio of bid to engineer's estimate is the U.S. Department of Transportation, Federal Highway Administration, "Bid Opening Report," and the U.S. Department of the Interior, Bureau of Reclamation, "Construction Cost Trends." See appendix description of table 8.4 above for a discussion of the ratio of trend to actual employment.

Notes

1. The term input-cost index is also used in the construction literature to refer to an average of input prices. However, I use the term cost index because the term input-cost

is also used in the price index literature to convey a different meaning, namely the cost change of inputs required to produce some constant level of output.

2. For example, the American Appraisal index made an adjustment based on a survey of contractors on the productivity of workers in a few specific crafts. The AT&T outside plant index simply assumed 2% productivity growth in the 1967–81 period. The reason that arbitrary or subjective methods are used is that cost indexes do not measure output and thus cannot measure productivity changes directly.

3. The Commerce Department had previously published an average of six cost indexes but had not used them as deflators.

4. The term composite is used here to refer to a deflator for total new construction based on BEA methodology. The Census Bureau also publishes a composite construction price index but it differs in a few respects from the BEA measure.

5. The Census Bureau originally entered floor space in the regression by using dummy variables for nine different size categories. Beginning in 1974, floor space was entered as a continuous variable. The census also added two other variables, fireplaces and lot size, to the regression in 1974.

6. A major part of the BEA II and BEA III composites, the census index, is only available beginning in 1963. Two important components of the BEA I composite, the American Appraisal and Fuller indexes, were discontinued in the early eighties.

7. I use total construction employment to measure activity in the residential and nonresidential sectors. It would be desirable to have a measure of economic activity for each of the sectors but construction employment by sector is only available beginning in 1972.

8. See Foss (1961) for an earlier discussion of the sensitivity of the FHWA index.

9. This assumes an inelastic rate of substitution between materials and on-site factors of production. The Dacy index would be downward biased if the rate of substitution between materials and on-site factors is elastic. See Pieper (1984) for details.

10. The increase in the cost of on-site factors is not observable since it should be adjusted for productivity, an unknown. However, the increase in hourly construction wages between 1973 and 1982 was 81%, well below the 115% increase in materials prices. It seems unlikely that productivity decreases could account for the difference.

11. Dacy measured the materials share as materials divided by materials plus wages. He thus ignored non-labor components of value added. Gordon measured the parameter b as the materials share of nominal construction output.

12. See Pieper (1989b) for a critique of Allen's adjustments.

13. Unfortunately only a limited amount of information on housing amenities is available but the evidence strongly suggests increasing quality. The share of new houses with dishwashers increased by 58 percentage points between 1963 and 1982, while the share with stoves and refrigerators increased by about 10 percentage points in the same period. Real production of wood kitchen cabinets increased three times faster than real expenditures on new housing in the 1967–80 period. This suggests higher quality kitchens. Houses are also much more likely to include a full second bathroom rather than a half bathroom. As for energy efficiency, the percentage of new homes with double-glazed windows increased from 25% in 1974 to 54% in 1982. Eighty-four percent of all new houses built after 1975 have wall insulation, compared with 54% of those built between 1950 and 1969. The source for these figures is Pieper (1984), chap. 3.

14. The standard deviation of the state bid-price means for bituminous concrete and reinforcing steel is about 20% of the mean of the state means (Pieper 1989a, 314). Cost indexes reported by Allen (1984) for 27 states and regions indicate a standard deviation of construction costs equal to 8.2% of the state means.

15. Hedonic price indexes for nonresidential buildings have been estimated by Allen (1984) and Shriver and Bowlby (1985).

16. Otelsberg (1972) reports that the standard deviation of the price per square foot of apartments and most types of nonresidential buildings is between 50% and 80% of the mean. In contrast, data from *Characteristics of New Housing* (U.S. Department of Commerce, Bureau of the Census 1982) indicate standard deviation of the price per square foot of single family homes of about 25% of the mean.

17. The models are based on actual buildings constructed. The weights of the different items are based on an analysis of the blueprints and bid documents. The material in this paragraph is drawn primarily from the author's phone conversations with D. S. Seymour of Statistics Canada.

18. The estimation index was calculated as the actual FHWA index divided by an index of the ratio of the engineer's estimate to the low bid.

19. The weights of the ENR index are given by the U.S. Department of Commerce Office of Business Economics (1956), para. 210. The source for both the materials prices and union wage rates is *Construction Review,* tables E-2 and E-3. The union wage rate series ends in 1981. It was extrapolated to 1982 on the basis of average hourly earnings of construction workers (U.S. Council of Economic Advisers 1986, table B-41).

References

Allen, Steven G. 1984. Unionized Construction Workers Are More Productive. *Quarterly Journal of Economics* 67 (May): 251–74.

———. 1985. Why Construction Productivity Is Declining. *Review of Economics and Statistics* 67 (November): 661–69.

Dacy, Douglas. 1964. A Price and Productivity Index for a Nonhomogeneous Product. *Journal of the American Statistical Association* 59 (June): 469–85.

———. 1965. Productivity and Price Trends in Construction since 1947. *Review of Economics and Statistics* 47 (November): 406–11.

Federal Water Pollution Control Administration. 1967. Sewer and Sewage Treatment Plant Construction Cost Index. Washington, D.C.: Government Printing Office.

Foss, Murray. 1961. How Rigid are Construction Costs during Recessions? *The Journal of Business* 34 (July): 374–83.

Gordon, Robert A. 1961. Differential Changes in the Prices of Consumers' and Capital Goods. *American Economic Review* 51 (December): 937–47.

Gordon, Robert J. 1968. A New View of Real Investment in Structures, 1919–1966. *Review of Economics and Statistics* 50 (November): 417–28.

Grose, L., I. Rottenberg, and R. C. Wasson. 1966. New Estimates of Fixed Business Capital in the United States, 1925–65. *Survey of Current Business* 46 (December): 34–40.

Jorgenson, Dale, and Zvi Griliches. 1967. The Explanation of Productivity Change. *The Review of Economic Studies* 34 (July): 249–84.

Kendrick, John W. 1961. *Productivity Trends in the United States*. Princeton, N.J.: Princeton University Press, for the National Bureau of Economic Research.

Musgrave, John C. 1969. Trends in Valuation per Square Foot of Building Floor Area, 1956–68. *Construction Review* 15 (November): 4–12.

National Bureau of Economic Research (NBER). 1961. *The Price Statistics of the Federal Government*. New York: NBER.

Otelsberg, Jonah. 1972. Trends in Valuation per Square Foot of Building Floor Area, 1947–71. *Construction Review* 18 (August): 4–11.

Pieper, Paul. 1984. The Measurement of Real Investment in Structures and the Construction Productivity Decline. Ph.D. diss., Northwestern University.

———. 1989a. Construction Price Statistics Revisited. In *Technology and Capital*, ed. Dale Jorgenson and Ralph Landau. *Formation*. Cambridge, Mass: MIT Press.

———. 1989b. Why Construction Productivity Is Declining: Comment. *The Review of Economics and Statistics* 71 (August): 543–46.

Pollock, Jesse. 1984. Research into a Cost Index for Multiunit Residential Construction. Bureau of the Census, Washington, D.C. Typescript.

Sachs, Abner, and Richard C. Ziemer. 1983. Implicit Deflators for Military Construction. *Survey of Current Business* 63 (November): 14–18.

Shriver, William R., and Roger L. Bowlby. 1985. Changes in Productivity and Composition of Output in Building Construction, 1972–1982. *Review of Economics and Statistics* 67 (May): 318–22.

Statistics Canada. 1978. Output Price Indexes of Non-residential Construction. *Construction Price Statistics* 5 (August): 5–31.

U.S. Council of Economic Advisers. 1986. *Economic Report of the President*. Washington, D.C.: Government Printing Office.

U.S. Department of Commerce, Bureau of Economic Analysis. 1971. *Fixed Nonresidential Business Capital in the United States, 1925–1970*. Springfield, Va.: National Technical Information Services.

———. 1974. Revised Deflators for New Construction, 1947–73. *Survey of Current Business* 54 (August): 18–27.

———. 1986. *The National Income and Product Accounts of the United States, 1929–82*. Washington, D.C.: Government Printing Office.

U.S. Department of Commerce, Bureau of the Census. 1964, 1970. *Value of New Construction Put in Place*. Construction Report Series C30–61 and C30–1970–12. Washington, D.C.: Government Printing Office.

———. 1973, 1983. *Price Index of New One-Family Houses Sold*. Construction Reports Series C27. Washington, D.C.: Government Printing Office.

———. 1973–82. *Characteristics of New Housing*. Construction Reports Series C25. Washington, D.C.: Government Printing Office.

———. 1975. *Historical Statistics of the United States*. Washington, D.C.: Government Printing Office.

———. Various issues. *Statistical Abstract of the United States*. Washington, D.C.: Governing Printing Office.

———. 1985. 1982 *Census of Construction Industries*. Washington, D.C.: Government Printing Office.

U.S. Department of Commerce, Bureau of Industrial Economics. Various issues. *Construction Review*. Washington, D.C.: Government Printing Office.

U.S. Department of Commerce, Office of Business Economics. 1956. *Business Statistics 1955*. Washington, D.C.: Government Printing Office.

U.S. Department of Commerce, Office of Domestic Commerce. 1947. *Construction and Construction Materials Industry Report*. Washington, D.C.: Government Printing Office.

U.S. Department of the Interior, Bureau of Reclamation. 1977–87. Construction Cost Trends. Denver: Bureau of Reclamation.

U.S. Department of Labor, Bureau of Labor Statistics. 1979. *Labor and Materials Requirements for Sewer Works Construction*. Bulletin 2003. Washington, D.C.: Government Printing Office.

———. 1985. *Employment and Earnings, United States, 1909–84*. Bulletin 1312–12. Washington, D.C.: Government Printing Office.

U.S. Department of Transportation, Federal Highway Administration. 1975. *Highway Statistics*. Washington, D.C.: Government Printing Office.

———. Various issues. Bid Opening Report. Washington, D.C.: Federal Highway Administration.
———. 1981–82. Price Trends for Federal-Aid Highway Construction. Washington, D.C.: Government Printing Office.
U.S. Environmental Protection Agency, Office of Water Program Operations. 1983 (4th Qtr). Construction Cost Indexes. Washington, D.C.: U.S. Environmental Protection Agency.

Comment Robert P. Parker

In "The Measurement of Construction Prices: Retrospect and Prospect," Paul Pieper reviews the past 40 years of development of the price indexes used by the Bureau of Economic Analysis (BEA) to prepare the constant-dollar structures (construction) components of GNP.

Pieper traces these developments, and the impact on them by academicians and by the staff of the Department of Commerce, and draws two major conclusions: "Progress in construction deflation has made in the past when there has been interaction between government statisticians and the academic profession"; and, "There is probably no single best method for deflating construction." It is difficult to quarrel with such general statements.

Pieper reviews four major types of price indexes available for the preparation of the constant-dollar construction estimates of GNP, evaluates their relative merits, and suggests some future directions for improvement. On indexes based on unit prices, such as price per square foot, Pieper sees very limited applications because it is difficult to identify a relative homogeneous physical measure. He indicates that the present Federal Highway Administration (FHWA) price index is defective because it treats all highway projects as homogeneous. On the use of hedonic price indexes, he is optimistic that they can be used for types of structures for which construction characteristics can be quantified and where there are a sufficiently large number of observations. He suggests that an effort be made to estimate a hedonic index for highway construction, using the detailed FHWA's data base. For contractor estimates, or the pricing of hypothetical structures, he seems to be favorably disposed if the work can be done properly. He observes, however, that previous efforts, except for those of Statistics Canada, have had too many shortcomings. Finally, he indicates that cost indexes are the least desirable type for deflation and expresses concern about the quality of the privately prepared cost data

Robert P. Parker is associate director for National Economic Accounts at the Bureau of Economic Analysis, U.S. Department of Commerce.

The views expressed are those of the author and do not necessarily reflect the opinions of the Bureau of Economic Analysis or any other members of its staff.

that are used to prepare many cost indexes. Later, I will review each of these types of price indexes and indicate how I think BEA should distribute its resources among them.

Pieper reviews developments at the Commerce Department, concluding that there has been little progress since 1946 when the department first published the Commerce Composite Construction Index. The only major steps forward, according to Pieper, were the development at the Census Bureau of the hedonic index for the sales price of single-family homes and the development at BEA of price indexes for military construction. The other changes appear to be minor improvements as BEA shifted from one proxy index to another with only slightly improved estimates. In addition, Pieper's analysis of differences over time of the various indexes shows that these changes had little quantitative impact. Pieper, however, does not discuss why there has been so little progress or why so many major deficiencies remain unresolved. He merely implies that the lack of progress reflects the slowdown in the interaction between those of us at Commerce and academic economists. I do not share this interpretation. BEA welcomes constructive criticism or new ideas from any source. Unfortunately, during the period covered in this paper, such help was minimal. In the 1960s, Dacy and Gordon each made thoughtful suggestions, but BEA reviewed them and concluded that they were no better than the measures used at that time. More recently, Allen and Pieper have suggested changes, but again nothing that one would consider a major improvement. Pieper also notes that the NBER's review of price statistics in 1961, which identified the problems with the indexes in use, did not result in proposals for an improvement program.

Pieper's observations on the sources of progress, or the lack thereof, are, in my opinion, incomplete. For example, he neglects to discuss the lack of support for improvements from interested parties in the private sector. The construction industry apparently lacks strong trade associations with an interest in statistical issues and influence in the U.S. Congress. There have been several studies on declining productivity in the construction industries that blamed part of the decline on the lack of adequate price indexes, but they failed to arouse any private-sector support for improvement. Such support for improved statistics usually is crucial to obtaining additional resources from Congress. For example, private-sector support appears to have been a major factor behind recent increases in funding for programs to improve the availability of statistics on services. The story of services also points to the need for some current policy issue within the government to rally support for the improved statistics. Services statistics became important because of international trade issues and issues relating to changes in the industrial composition of the domestic economy.

Pieper also did not recognize that BEA, which prepares the constant-dollar structures estimates, generally does not collect the source data it uses; that is, it is not the primary price statistics agency for the federal government and, in this regard, is limited in both resources and technical expertise to collect and compile price indexes. Pieper also does not acknowledge that the Office of Management and Budget (OMB), through its responsibilities in approving new surveys and in coordinating statistical policy in the federal government, is a major player in the development of federal statistics. Despite identification by BEA and others that these statistics were a major problem, OMB has not made improvement of construction price statistics a major goal; it could have done so either by establishing an interagency effort to resolve the problem or by initiating funding for improvements. In summary, by looking only at the Department of Commerce, Pieper has neglected several of the groups whose responsibility for improved construction price indexes is as great if not greater than that of academics or BEA.

Now let us turn from the past and look at the work that is underway at BEA and the Census Bureau on construction prices and what work is likely in the future. The Census Bureau, as Pieper reports, is developing a hedonic price index for multifamily housing. Early efforts have been hampered by the use of only a small number of characteristics; fortunately, other data items are available in the material already collected by the Census Bureau so that other alternatives can be tested. BEA is currently engaged in two major efforts, neither of which are discussed by Pieper. One effort involves working with the FHWA's highway cost indexes to compile price data on a put-in-place basis. The second effort is a comprehensive study of the quality of private construction cost/price indexes—including indexes that BEA has not previously worked with. This study will enable BEA to evaluate each of these indexes and to determine both their relative and absolute quality for use as price indexes in GNP. The results of this study may lead to some changes in price indexes used in deflation. As I have indicated, however, they are unlikely to be considered as major improvements as it appears that the private indexes all have at least one serious shortcoming.

After these efforts are completed, I would recommend that BEA look seriously at the contractor-estimates approach. This approach would consist of two elements. First, BEA would contract for the preparation of detailed specifications for several types of structures; the work would be done by private architectural or engineering firms or some similarly qualified group in another government agency. Second, a group of professional cost estimators with appropriate geographic distributions, again under contract, would price these structures at least once a year. This information would be used by BEA to compile price indexes for various types of structures to replace the currently used indexes for nonresidential buildings, both private and public. In addition, these same specifications would be used by BEA to develop cost indexes using various government price indexes. The cost indexes would serve both to cross-check the contractor estimates and to extrapolate them in the current period.

Although these efforts conflict with previous judgments about both of these approaches, they should be tried again. Contractor estimates prepared by professional cost estimators should provide very accurate information, especially if estimators are paid for their services. The use of hypothetical building specifications also seems reasonable, provided they are updated to take into account changes in technology. Pieper expresses several concerns about the contractor-estimate approach—it does not use transaction prices, it does not recognize competitive conditions, it does not use representative weighting, and it usually is based on poor responses. I believe that these concerns can be taken care of with a well-run program, just as Statistics Canada has been successful with a similar program.

As for continuing work on cost indexes, properly estimated cost indexes can be viewed as providing an upper boundary on price changes because there seems to be general agreement that cost indexes overstate true price increases as they fail to recognize changes in productivity or decreases in price resulting from competitive conditions. Another virtue of having well-constructed cost indexes is that they can serve as a means of testing the validity of price indexes derived using other approaches.

Pieper and others criticize cost indexes and construction estimates because of their insensitivity to short-run developments. Although such criticisms are likely to be valid for monthly or quarterly indexes, they are not likely to be valid when the indexes are estimated annually. Introduction of accurate annual price indexes should be BEA's major goal for improving construction prices. Finally, there seems little or no recognition by the critics of cost indexes that for "own-use" construction—that is, buildings where the owner is the builder—there is no difference between cost and price. This situation is very likely to be the case for a substantial part of industrial buildings.

The programs I have described will cost money, although BEA may be able to get some free assistance from private trade associations and government agencies in obtaining the detailed specifications for certain types of structures. The Business Roundtable, for example, for many years has expressed concerns about the government's construction statistics, and the National Bureau of Standards has a unit devoted to issues of building technology. The results of these programs, of course, will not be perfect, but I think their use will significantly improve the accuracy of the estimate of constant-dollar structures expenditures in GNP. Pieper's paper has been very useful to our ongoing evaluation of alternatives to improve construction prices. We look forward to his continued interest in this area and hope he can interest some of his academic colleagues to do likewise.

9 Data Difficulties in Labor Economics

Daniel S. Hamermesh

9.1 Introduction

In the fifty years of the existence of the Conference on Research in Income and Wealth, labor economics has become a leader among subspecialties in economics in linking empirical work and theory, in acquiring large amounts of data, and in making strides in analyzing those data. Despite this distinction there are substantial imbalances in data resources in this area and in the progress in understanding labor-market phenomena that the available data have made possible. Also, areas in which we think that our knowledge has been furthered by recent studies are in fact less advanced than we believe because of problems with data. Finally, the ability to generalize our findings is in many cases limited by difficulties involving the interaction of the sets of data used and the nature of the problems under study.

In section 9.2 I present a general framework for analyzing the appropriateness of a variety of data sets to the purposes for which they are used. This approach is narrower than that of Griliches (1986), who laid special emphasis on problems of measurement error. The view implicit here is, though, both broader and different from that of Stafford (1986). He concentrated on the few major longitudinal household data sets and developed an almost Schumpeterian theory of how newly available sources of data both are called forth by and, in turn, advance theory and inform policy. Most of his attention was focused on the use of these data sets in analyzing issues in labor supply. I pay attention to labor supply in section 9.3; the bulk of the paper considers, however, three other major areas of interest to labor economists in light of this discussion of the appropriateness of data sets.

Daniel S. Hamermesh is professor of economics at Michigan State University and a research associate of the National Bureau of Economic Research.

The author is deeply indebted to Jeff Biddle for many helpful suggestions and to Steve Allen, Paul Chen, Zvi Griliches, Harry Holzer, Nick Kiefer, John Pencavel, Sherwin Rosen, Jack Triplett, and Steven Woodbury for useful comments.

Much of the discussion is of labor demand, including issues of employment adjustment, "the elasticity of labor demand," and problems of labor-labor substitution that have been addressed by very few sets of data. Of particular note in this regard are the KLEM (capital, labor, energy, and materials) data on U.S. manufacturing assembled by Berndt, Fuss, and Waverman (1979) and others. Since much of our knowledge comes from these aggregate data (see Hamermesh 1986), it is essential to analyze how well they meet the criteria presented in section 9.2. Much of the rest of what we have learned recently comes from the estimation of complex production technologies applied to data from household surveys. In section 9.4 I examine the usefulness of these studies according to the criteria I set out.

Sections 9.5, 9.6, and 9.7 present shorter discussions of labor market–wide phenomena, of trade union behavior, and of the desirability of international comparisons. In the 1940s and early 1950s, labor economists engaged in massive studies of specific local labor markets. With the exception of Rees and Shultz (1970), this type of work ceased by 1955. Today's research on labor markets must be deductive from data on samples of workers in many markets. How well suited is today's approach to analyzing how a labor market operates, as compared to the approach of nearly two generations ago? Is there a possible compromise that can meet the objections to which each might be subject under the consideration of the appropriateness of data sets? In the past ten years interest has burgeoned in analyzing what, if anything, unions attempt to maximize. Much of the work has been on one particular set of data (Dertouzos and Pencavel 1981). How representative are these data? Are the available data resources sufficient to allow us to draw any general inferences about what unions seek to do? The cultural imperialism of American empirical economics should not blind us to the possibility that the structure that describes a relationship in the United States may not be representative of some (any?) other economies. Thus it is worth considering under what circumstances the consideration of descriptions of behavior for several economies is more or less important in generalizing about behavior.

Based on the general framework for analyzing the appropriateness of data sets and its specific applications to these central issues in labor economics, I draw conclusions about the types of additional data that should be collected. Because the issues are to some extent overlapping, it should be possible to address the lacunae in the data jointly rather than treating data problems in each area separately.

9.2 A Framework for Evaluating Data Describing Workers and Employment

The general linear model describing the structure of an economic relationship at a time that the researcher wishes to characterize (usually the present) can be written as

(1) $$y_t = bx_t + e_t,$$

where y is the outcome variable, x is a vector of independent variables, b is a vector of parameters describing the structure of the relationship, t is time, and e is a disturbance term. The relationship that is estimated is not this at all, but is instead

(2) $$Y_{IT} = b_{IT}X_{IT} + e_{IT},$$

where the subscript I indexes the units chosen to represent the economic relationship, and T indicates the time(s) at which they were observed. I assume throughout that (2) is estimated by best-practice technique. Thus the assumption of a linear model is merely for expositional simplicity, and the discussion applies to more complex models too. Thus $\hat{b}_{IT}$ is an unbiased estimate of b_{IT} for the particular set of data $\{Y_{IT}, X_{IT}\}$ chosen to represent the relationship between y and x, so that $E(\hat{b}_{IT}/b_{IT}) = b_{IT}$.

While I assume that $\hat{b}_{IT}$ has all the nice statistical properties we desire, it can be viewed as the best estimate of only one of a large number of vectors of parameters b_{IT} based upon possible sets of data $\{Y_{IT}, X_{IT}\}$ chosen. Essentially there is a distribution of parameter vectors b_{IT} corresponding to the distribution of the data sets. The question of interest is whether

(3) $$E(b_{IT}|\{Y_{IT}, X_{IT}\}) = b,$$

where the unsubscripted b is the true value of the parameter describing the relationship of interest to the researcher. Four questions are relevant in analyzing whether (3) holds: (1) Does the particular set of variables $\{Y, X\}$ that is chosen represent the true variables $\{y, x\}$ well? This is essentially a question of measurement and specification error. Both random measurement errors and systematic errors of measurement are likely to be important problems in labor-related data. They have, though, been well covered in the econometric literature, and I pay them relatively little attention in the discussion hereafter. (2) Is the sample that underlies the set of subunits $\{I\}$ that is used to estimate (2) representative of the population to whom the theoretical relationship (1) is supposed to apply? This goes far beyond the narrow econometric issue of sample selection bias that has received so much attention from labor economists and econometricians. (3) Is the set of time periods $\{T\}$ likely to allow the researcher to draw correct inferences about the relationship between y and x that holds at time t for the typical unit (perhaps different from the representative unit in $\{I\}$)? The issue here is one of structural change. (4) Are the intervals between units in the sets $\{I\}$ and $\{T\}$ appropriate for the relationship between y and x that is being studied? This is an issue of appropriate aggregation.

Consider the second question: Is the set $\{I\}$ typical of all the units in the economy whose economic behavior we are trying to describe by (1)? If the analysis of (2) for the data set indexed by $\{I, T\}$ is to be more than an econometric case study, $\{I\}$ should cover a broad set of subunits in the economy or cover a few typical subunits. If we are confident that the data set meets all of these worries, can it be used to draw inferences about the relationship in (1) in other economies during the time period under study?

The third question should be answered on two levels. The simpler, and more frequently discussed one, is that of structural change: What do the $\hat{b}_{IT}$ tell us about the structural relationship between y and x today, or has that relation changed so drastically that the estimation of (2) has become economic history that sheds little light on today's economy? The answer to this question depends on how rapidly structural change occurs in the particular relationship and on how far in time we are removed from the observations in the set $\{T\}$. The more complex issue is a combination of structural change and misspecification: Is the relationship between Y and X no longer the same as in (2) because of the growth in importance of additional factors, denoted by Z? If data were collected on the Z, and if nothing else made the data set $\{I,T\}$ unrepresentative for current purposes, it would be a simple matter to respecify and reestimate (2) and use it to draw inferences about today's structure. If, however, data on Z were not *or could not* have been collected, there is no hope of resurrecting (2) to analyze behavior today.

The length of "the short run" varies with the problem under study. The intervals in the set $\{T\}$ should be such as to make it possible for the estimates of (2) to inform us about the speed with which equilibrium is reestablished after the system underlying (1) is shocked. Also, while we often view cross-section data as allowing us to infer equilibrium relationships, that assumption is not necessarily valid. A time series of sufficiently long T can be useful in allowing the inference of the structure of the equilibria that arise after a shock. The problem here is to use the level of temporal disaggregation appropriate to the question under study. Another difficulty arises if the units in $\{I\}$ are too large to prevent us from assuming that all underlying relationships are linear, and thus that estimation over aggregated data yields unbiased results. Are they small enough so that decision makers' nonlinear responses can be detected, or are they so highly aggregated that nonlinearities and discontinuities are all smoothed out? The problem here is that of appropriate spatial disaggregation.

This discussion is couched in terms of estimation (of the true underlying parameter vector b characterizing the relationship of interest). Clearly, though, labor economists are interested in hypothesis testing as well as in estimation. A discussion similar to that above could be developed to deal with the structuring of data appropriate to hypothesis testing. The main difference would be that, in addition to the four problems discussed above, problems that produce the equivalent of the bias term in a mean squared error based on a comparison of $\hat{b}_{IT}$ and b, we would also have to consider the statistical distributions of the $\hat{b}_{IT}$ and of the set of b_{IT} that might arise from the entire range of choices of I and T used to estimate the relationship. The problems we consider here to analyze data appropriate to estimation are a subset of those necessary to analyze data appropriate to hypothesis testing.

9.3 Labor Supply—Synergy among Data, Estimation, and Theory

During the past twenty-five years the study of labor supply has been a central focus of labor economics. We have learned something about important phenomena; major threads of microeconomic theory that had not been used in empirical work have been explicitly employed in estimation; and these applications have generated important advances in econometric theory that have been used elsewhere in economics. The data are representative of the underlying populations being studied; there is no reason to assume the results are irrelevant today because of intervening structural changes; and there is no major problem of excessive aggregation of decision-making units in what are chiefly sets of data that have households as the units of observation.

The important explorations in labor supply occurred along with a flowering of data collection. Carefully constructed cross-section sets of household data became available during the 1960s; and the computer technology, both hardware and software, to analyze them was developed simultaneously. By the mid-1970s the major longitudinal household data sets, the National Longitudinal Surveys and the Panel Study of Income Dynamics, began to be used to study labor supply. It is impossible to believe that the development of these sources of information "forestall[ed] the demise of empirical economics," as implied by the title of Stafford's (1986) essay, or even to prove that causality ran from the development of these data to advances in theory and econometrics. It is difficult enough to prove causality in well-specified econometric models dealing with hypotheses that are grounded in economic theory. One should not expect in this case to demonstrate something that historians of science have debated and about which philosophers of science have prescribed for generations. One must believe, though, that we would know a lot less, and labor economists' fascination with problems of labor supply would be less intense, if these data sources had not been constructed and the resources devoted to them had instead gone into data more readily usable in other areas of labor economics or in other subfields of economics.

I believe there have been three major advances in the empirical study of labor supply: (1) The estimation of income and substitution effects; (2) the growth in our understanding of labor-force dynamics; and (3) the recognition of the life-cycle nature of labor supply. Obviously there have been advances in understanding other supply-related phenomena, such as household production, population, and the demand for education. None of these, though, is as central to labor supply as these three main thrusts; and in none of the other areas are the links among theory, econometrics, and data so well articulated.

The first advance, spurred by Mincer (1962), led to a flowering of research using various household surveys, particularly the Survey of Economic Opportunity, that eventually gave empirical meaning to the basic results of the theory of consumer demand. It allowed better predictions about the response of labor supply to changes in the parameters of incomc-support programs and more careful inferences and predictions about patterns of labor supply in a growing economy. Without microdata neither of these achievements could have been attained with the same precision. As a result of the research of the 1960s our knowledge is fairly secure about the *relative* magnitudes of labor-supply elasticities of different demographic groups, and some consensus limits have been placed on the range of the absolute magnitudes of these parameters.

The second advance taught us that for many groups there is substantial mobility into and out of the labor force. The work of Heckman and Willis (1977) and others demonstrated that it is as wrong to view a 65% participation rate as reflecting participation by 65% of the population all year long as it is to view it as reflecting part-year participation by the entire population. Without longitudinal data this demonstration could not have been made. The discovery affected the course of advances in theoretical econometrics, for it generated an interest in developing econometric techniques and borrowing techniques pioneered by sociologists to analyze the determinants of mover-stayer distinctions. These techniques have been used extensively in other areas of labor economics and have been applied to other subfields of economics as well. Thus, for example, the distinction between unemployment spells and unemployment duration (e.g., Clark and Summers 1982) and issues in the burden of unemployment could not have been analyzed without longitudinal data.

The final major advance saw labor economists putting empirical meat on the bones of life-cycle theory by analyzing intertemporal substitution using longitudinal data (e.g., MaCurdy 1981; and many others). Obviously this advance was spurred by developments in macroeconomic theory; but without the microeconometric analysis by labor economists, helped along by the general implausibility of the assertion that intertemporal substitution could be very large, we would not be fairly secure in our knowledge of its relative unimportance of affecting labor supply.

The development of information useful for research in labor supply and, more generally, in studying labor-force dynamics, has proceeded from aggregated Census of Population data, to micro cross-section data on households, to longitudinal surveys of individuals and households. These developments are no longer confined to the United States. Indeed, some of the most interesting efforts in collecting these sorts of data are being made elsewhere, particularly in Australia and Sweden.

One must ask, though, where this continuing concentration of resources on collecting longitudinal household data is leading us. As a brief foray into this question I extended Stafford's (1986, table 7.1) work categorizing published studies on labor supply in six major journals. Table 9.1 presents the results of this analysis.[1] It provides some indication that professional interest in labor

Table 9.1 **Articles in Major Journals: Labor Supply Subject, by Year, 1965–87**

	1965–69	1970–74	1975–79	1980–83	1984–87
Population size and structure	7	14	19	10	5
Household production	0	11	8	8	4
Labor supply of men	2	5	7	6	6
Labor supply of women	0	3	9	6	4
Labor supply of others and income support disincentives of UI, NIT, taxes, or other	2	7	16	15	8
Retirement	0	1	4	1	4
Educational demand	3	11	9	2	2
Migration	13	9	14	4	5
Total	27	61	86	52	38

Sources: Cols. 1–4 from Stafford (1986); col. 5, author's tabulation.

supply has been slipping since the late 1970s. The only growth areas in the mid-1980s were studies of retirement and migration. Interest in retirement was probably spurred by concern about an increasingly important general economic problem and by the creation of the Longitudinal Retirement History Survey. Interest in migration stemmed from concern about policy; there was no sudden availability of data that made it possible to examine the issue. Studies in the mainstream areas of labor supply, particularly in the effects on labor supply of government programs, have been of decreasing interest.

It is, of course, impossible to identify the causes of the reduced interest in the central areas of the study of labor supply. I would argue, though, that at least in part it stems from the lack of new advances in the kinds (not the quantities) of data that are available for this purpose. The rich lode of the feedback relationship between data development and the expansion of knowledge about labor supply is now yielding decidedly diminishing returns.

Clearly there are many areas that have not been well explored and many questions that can be answered with better data. We could take the position of Wagner, the dull student in *Faust,* "zwar weiss ich viel, doch moecht ich alles wissen."[2] The collection of panels that follow a cohort from school through middle age, for example, will enable us to distinguish better between the economic determinants of labor-force behavior and background effects, and between transitory economic effects and those stemming from life-cycle behavior. Additional studies of life-cycle behavior that tie labor supply to liquidity and labor-market constraints will undoubtedly be made. The potential for acquiring knowledge appears limited, though. It is not clear that the efforts of the 1970s and 1980s (since the studies in Cain and Watts [1973] that represent the initial phase of the first major achievement I discussed above) at refining our knowledge of labor-supply elasticities (or their component income and substitution effects) have done anything to narrow the agreed-upon range of estimates. There is nothing on the horizon or even imaginable that seems likely to provide the kind of spur to research in this area that it received from the development of new sets of data between 1965 and the late 1970s.

9.4 Labor Demand—a Case of Underdevelopment

Unlike the study of labor supply, in which the creation of large data sets led to tremendous strides in linking theory to empirical analysis, those of us who study labor demand have been less fortunate. The many interesting questions on the demand side have as important implications for policy as those more widely studied supply questions. Thus issues of the demand for older workers, the impacts of technical change and international competition on the distribution of employment, and the effects of mergers and acquisitions on job creation should be motivating research on the demand for labor in much the same way that interest in income maintenance programs spurred much of the research on labor supply in the 1960s and 1970s. That this has not happened—that we have made less progress in answering questions about labor demand—is largely the result of the failure to invest in the kinds of data that would allow us to obtain answers, a failure that continues today.

The questions and previous studies designed to answer them fall into two categories: those involving employment dynamics and those concerned with factor substitution. Let us consider the first group. One set of questions involves the analysis of paths of employment adjustment in response to exogenous shocks. Subsumed here is the attempt to discover the nature of the costs of adjusting employment that presumably generate observed adjustment paths. The analysis of how firms adjust employment leads to questions about how labor productivity (most simply, the output-total hours ratio) changes cyclically. These are inputs into the analysis of cost-based inflationary pressures, so that this aspect of the study of labor demand becomes a crucial macroeconomic issue. Similarly central to macroeconomics are the implications that adjustment paths have for the path of unemployment.

The study of employment adjustment should not be restricted to firms that are assumed to be infinitely lived. Rather, it should enable us to understand the economic process by which output shocks generate a continuing opening and closing of different work sites that in turn produces changes in employment. The analogy to the growth in the study of labor-force dynamics, including the study of gross flows data in the Current Population Survey (CPS), should be clear.

How well do existing studies of employment dynamics meet the criteria of appropriate aggregation, representativeness, and current structure? One broad group of studies (most recently, Morrison 1986) uses annual data on a set of factor inputs aggregated over a large number of establishments in manufacturing to analyze demand dynamics in the context of a model allowing for substitution among all pairs of inputs. (In Morrison's and many others' studies these are the KLEM data.) This strand of the literature has severe problems under two of our criteria. Almost all the available evidence (see Hamermesh 1988 for a survey) suggests that employment responds to shocks fairly rapidly. This means that annual data are inherently incapable of telling us much about the underlying path of employment adjustment: the data are too highly aggregated temporally. They are also too highly aggregated spatially. If there is any nonlinearity in the adjustment process at the microlevel, the use of aggregate data will in general fail to identify it. Aggregation should be done over the relationships estimated as characterizing the microunits, not over the microdata in a way that requires assumptions of linearity in those relationships. Since many reasonable structures of adjustment costs generate nonlinearities, this set of studies will not help much in identifying what generates the path of employment adjustment. Because the data cover only manufacturing, it is also hard to claim that the results do well on the criterion of representativeness.

Another group of studies (beginning with Nadiri and Rosen 1969 and extended by Sargent 1978) uses aggregate employment data to model how firms' expectations about product demand affect paths of employment. These allow the researcher to distinguish adjustment costs from changes in expectations; and their use of monthly or quarterly data does provide the appropriate temporal disaggregation. However, because the data cover all manufacturing employment, they suffer from excessive spatial aggregation while at the same time perhaps being unrepresentative of the entire economy.

These are not criticisms of the intellectual value of these series of studies. We do now understand more about how to model factor adjustment and how to extricate lags arising from adjustment costs from those produced by shifts in expectations. What these studies have not done is tell us much about the nature of adjustment at the plant level for the typical plant, since nonlinear adjustment may mean there is no "typical" plant, or much about the true structure of adjustment in the aggregate. Because many of them use annual data, they cannot inform us about the path of the response to exogenous demand shocks.

None of the empirical models estimated in either strand of this literature makes a serious attempt to infer anything about the level or structure of the costs that face firms when they change employment. The assumption is usually made that adjustment costs can be approximated by a quadratic, which in turn generates standard linear decision rules that are easily modeled as distributed lags. Although she offers no formal modeling of adjustment costs, Houseman (1988) does estimate lag structures for employment-output relations in basic steel production using monthly time-series data for the United States, France, and Germany. The data are not ideal, as they do not allow estimating microrelationships, but they are much closer to the ideal than even two-digit SIC data. The monthly observations guarantee that there is no problem of temporal overaggregation. The only difficulties with the results are their lack of a theoretical basis, possibly severe structural changes that have occurred and the industry's possible failure to be representative. Slightly different problems are presented by Mairesse and Dormont (1985), who use data for the same three countries based on observations of a representative group of individual (manufacturing) plants. The difficulty here is that the observations are only annual, so that no serious attempt at inferring the size or structure of adjustment costs is possible.

Two other studies are based more soundly in micro theory, but each has problems of its own that prevent us from concluding that we know much about adjustment costs. Nickell (1979) estimates standard employment-output relations on quarterly time series covering U.K. manufacturing, but he does search for structural changes induced by changes in legislation that he believes have affected the costs of hiring and dismissing workers. The difficulty here is one of spatial overaggregation, perhaps coupled with too much temporal aggregation as well. Hamermesh (1989) uses monthly plant-level data. While the results do test explicitly for alternative structures of adjustment costs that generate different paths of employment demand, the coverage of the data may not be representative, and the time series are very short.

Recently there has been a recognition in empirical studies of labor demand that plants are not infinitely lived. Dunne, Roberts, and Samuelson (1989) have assembled and performed simple statistical analyses of a file of all manufacturing plants present in any of the five Censuses of Manufactures between 1963 and 1982. The data provide the most detailed available picture of the totals of gross flows of plants into and out of existence and of the concomitant flows of employment opportunities. This is a gargantuan and praiseworthy undertaking. Nonetheless, we should recognize that what they have achieved is still not up to a level that will provide the basis for analyzing the determinants of plant closings and openings at the microlevel. The plants are observed only quinquennially. Decomposing employment changes over an observation period this long induces positive and negative biases in the estimated fraction of net employment change that is accounted for by births and deaths of plants: positive, because month-to-month or even yearly fluctuations in net employment are missed; negative, because short-lived establishments' births and deaths go unnoticed. Still more important is that this very high degree of temporal aggregation prevents one from inferring anything about the short- or even intermediate-run causes of employment change. (The absence of output or factor-price data for each plant also renders this impossible.) The restriction to manufacturing makes the data increasingly unrepresentative.

Jacobson (1986) and Leonard (1987) assembled similar sets of longitudinal data that have the advantages of covering all private nonfarm establishments and of being available annually. This mitigates some of the problems of temporal overaggregation. (Spatial aggregation is obviously not a problem.) The only difficulties are that the data are available starting only recently; each data set covers only one state, Pennsylvania and Wisconsin, respectively; and output data are not available (though payroll and, by calculation, earnings data are in Jacobson's data). Thus far these data have also been used only to decompose aggregate net changes in employment into births, deaths, and expansions/contractions of plants.

The interesting questions in factor substitution have to do with the effects of imposed changes in factor prices on the quantity of labor employed and with the effects of changes in the supply of labor on wage rates. These questions are of interest at the aggregate level and for various disaggregations of the work force. In the former case the crucial issue is the aggregate elasticity of labor demand; in the latter case it is one of substitution among workers of different types. In both cases, though, the question can be discussed by analyzing how firms' employment of different groups of workers responds to exogenous changes in their wage rates.

Research on labor-demand elasticities and labor-labor substitution can be divided into pure time-series studies and cross-section or pooled time-series, cross-section varieties. The former group consists mostly of analyses of annual aggregate data in which labor is treated as homogeneous or is disaggregated into production and nonproduction workers. (Berndt and Christensen 1974 was the first, McElroy 1987 the most recent strand of this literature.) As noted above, the underlying data suffer from problems of representativeness. Though their high degree of temporal aggregation is not a severe problem for measuring labor-demand elasticities, the aggregation of all workers into at most two groups limits their applicability to questions of labor-labor substitution. Their excessive spatial aggregation poses especially severe problems. The relationships that are estimated involve nonlinear transformations of the underlying data. There is no reason to assume that the aggregation of these relations for the underlying establishments would produce the same estimates as the aggregate data. Without simulation studies of the effects of aggregation of the establishment data (ignoring issues of aggregation of labor into one or two homogeneous groups), we cannot be sure how much is learned about the essentially microeconomic question being asked. Similar problems exist in the vast set of time-series analyses based on data aggregated over all establishments within an industry (see Hamermesh 1986).

Recently there have been a few efforts to answer questions about factor substitution using pooled time-series, cross-section data based on establishments. Barbour, Berger, and Garen (1987) examine four years of quarterly observations on nearly 1,000 coal mines in Kentucky; Hart and Wilson (1988) use five annual observations on nearly 50 metal-working establishments in the United Kingdom. Both data sets allow the authors to infer labor-demand elasticities (for homogeneous labor) at the appropriate levels of spatial and temporal disaggregation. The only difficulties with the data used in these commendable studies are that they are clearly unrepresentative of anything other than their particular industries and locales, and their coverage of very short time periods makes it unlikely that they capture (average out) any short-term fluctuations in the *b*, the parameters describing the structure of the underlying economic relationship.

The estimation of labor-demand elasticities using cross-section data has been a growth industry since the late 1970s. Unfortunately, these studies, all of which estimate flexible approximations to cost or production functions, have been based on data from widely available household surveys rather than on establishment data. Thus some of the work (e.g., Grant and Hamermesh 1981; Grossman 1982) uses Census of Population data aggregated to the standard metropolitan statistical area (SMSA) level and linked to data on the capital stock by SMSA. Another (Berger 1983) uses time series of CPS data for states in a similar manner.

The main problem in this set of studies is the general inappropriateness of household data for the purpose of estimating demand relationships, basically a problem of potentially severe unrepresentativeness. Essentially each worker in the household survey represents the establishment that employs him or her; many plants have none, while others have several representatives in the survey. There is no reason to expect biases due to this unusual sampling procedure, but it is hardly designed to minimize sampling error in data used to describe the behavior of plants. The spatial aggregation (to the SMSA level) is also excessive, due to the nonlinearity of the relationships that we noted above in discussing time-series estimates on aggregated data. The only virtue of these studies is that they do allow the authors to draw inferences about substitution among groups of workers, as they disaggregate the work force into a substantial number of potentially interesting categories.

An alternative approach, exemplified by Borjas (1986), avoids the spatial aggregation in the studies cited above by using individuals' wages from the Census of Population as dependent variables in a generalized Leontief model of production. The major problem with the other studies is not obviated here, though: the household data used are representative of employers' demand for the individuals, but they are likely to have very large errors in their role of measuring firms' behavior.

Two studies (Sosin and Fairchild 1984; and Allen 1986) use plant-level data to estimate production relationships. Those studies satisfy all the criteria of appropriate spatial disaggregation required to estimate the relevant parameters, assuming we believe the cross-section data reflect equilibria. (Temporal disaggregation is not a major problem in this area.) The data are representative of the structures (several industries in Latin America, and school and office building construction in the United States, both in the early 1970s), though clearly not of all industry or of other economies. These studies should be models of how appropriate data can be assembled and used to estimate parameters describing a particular production technology.

Unlike the study of labor supply, which was rejuvenated by the development of large longitudinal household surveys, no similar advance has occurred in data on establishments that might produce a renascence in the study of labor demand. We do have the Longitudinal Research Database (LRD) on establishments, an annual establishment-based file constructed from the same sources that generate the published data in the *Annual Survey of Manufactures*. Though this set of data does overcome problems of spatial aggregation, annual observations are too infrequent to capture many of the labor-demand phenomena of interest. Also, the restriction to manufacturing plants means the data suffer from serious problems of unrepresentativeness. Also available are the Employment Opportunity Pilot Project (EOPP) data, a panel with two observations on each of a large number of establishments in 28 sites. The difficulties with this set of data are that it is no longer an on-going data collection effort, the sites are not representative, and only limited information is provided on sales in the participating establishments.

What is needed is a quarterly, or even better, a monthly longitudinal survey of an appropriately stratified sample of establishments that is representative of all private nonfarm business. This survey should be establishment based, should replace defunct establishments with appropriate substitutes, and should be benchmarked at regular intervals to available censuses of business, manufactures, mining, and so on. Given the frequency of observations that is required, only a small sample is feasible, but with careful sampling this can be reasonably representative. The survey should contain data on total employment and on employment disaggregated into several meaningful skill categories, on hours worked by each group of workers, on the payroll for each type of worker, on other labor costs (to allow the very much needed study of the effects of nonwage costs on labor demand) and on total sales and production. These latter two series are especially important if the empirical study of labor demand at the appropriate microlevel is to have any basis in microeconomic theory.

The data collection effort I am proposing is mostly an extension and rationalization of what already exists. The monthly BLS-790 data that form the published series on disaggregated weekly earnings, hours, establishment-based employment, and so on, cover a much larger sample than is needed for this proposed survey. The OSHA sampling frame is similar and has the virtue of mandatory reporting requirements that the BLS-790 data set lacks. What the survey requires is expanding one of these or some other existing sampling frame, requiring mandatory sampling if possible, to obtain information on nonwage labor costs and output/sales, to include a more meaningful disaggregation of skills, to reduce the sample size tremendously while enhancing its representativeness, and to develop a means of building an appropriately constructed longitudinal format in which to handle the data files. The additional data to be collected—nonwage labor costs—are already collected through the mechanisms that produce the employment cost index (ECI). It should be possible to use the procedures that generate the inputs into the ECI in constructing the proposed longitudinal file. The only new information is that on output and sales, and the new skill classifications, and, at least for manufacturing establishments, all but the skill classifications are already collected on an annual basis.

The collection of data on a quarterly or monthly basis would enable us to characterize adjustment paths more satisfactorily. Its basis in establishments would also provide most of the information that would allow us to obviate the more important difficulties with the data underlying studies of labor-labor substitution. The only additional requirement on this proposed data set is that employment in each establishment (and hours and payroll too) be disaggregated by various cuts of the labor force. At the very least, disaggregation by sex, race, three age groups, and several skill categories would be useful in answering questions most relevant to issues of policy involving the distribution of job creation and the effects on wages of changes in relative supplies of workers in different demographic groups.

Strides in constructing complex models for inferring the nature of error structures in factor adjustment and the nature of the technology of factor substitution have neither been matched nor motivated by similar strides in the collection of data appropriate to the estimation. We are piling more theoretical and econometric structure upon the same sets of unsuitable data. Until we create the kind of data set outlined here, the situation is likely to become worse.

9.5 Labor-Market Studies—Can the Past Be Recaptured?

During the late 1940s two major studies of local labor markets were undertaken, Reynolds (1951) for New Haven, and Myers and Shultz (1951) for Nashua, New Hampshire. (Segal 1986 presents an excellent discussion and evaluation of these studies' lasting importance.) While not the first studies of entire labor markets, these did carry the genre to its peak. Similar work, which advanced the literature by using more complex methods of analyzing the data, was carried out by Rees and Shultz (1970) in the early 1960s for the Chicago labor market. The general approach of these studies was to combine household and establishment data. In each case questions were asked of employers in a number of plants and of substantial numbers of workers in those plants. In essence the studies can be described as cross-section combined establishment-household surveys. This combined approach has not been repeated.[3] We have been relegated to using increasingly complex sets of household data and fairly paltry sets of establishment data.

Is their absence a loss? That is, did we learn anything from the labor-market studies, and are there questions of interest today that could be answered better if we had data like those collected in the labor-market studies? One set of analyses that was novel at the time was of the role of spatial differences in wage rates among workers with similar characteristics in identical jobs at different plants (stressed especially by Rees and Shultz 1970). To some extent this information is now duplicated with journey-to-work information from the Censuses of Population, though the level of occupational detail is not so great as in the labor-market studies. Nonetheless, the studies were the first to stress the importance of distance and the relative locations of workers and jobs in producing large wage differences among otherwise identical workers.

The labor-market studies were ahead of their time in their focus on how job vacancies are filled, on how workers search for jobs, and on wage structures. It is true, particularly in the two studies from the late 1940s, that much of the research is based on the attitudinal questions that we economists abhor. In those same studies, though, there is much discussion of the role of unemployment insurance benefits in job search; of reports on how workers acquire knowledge about alternative jobs when they become unemployed; and of the nature of jobs, including trade-offs between wages and job characteristics, that affect workers' search behavior. Even the best empirical studies of job search of the last 20 years based on large household data sets (e.g., Holzer 1987) could have proceeded better using data from the labor-market studies of the 1940s if the same theoretical issues had been posed and the statistical techniques now in use had been widespread then.

The labor-market studies meet most of the criteria in section 9.2 fairly well. Their particular distinction is the appropriateness of the level of aggregation—to individual firms and households. In some ways they fail on the criterion of representativeness, in that the labor markets studied are not representative of anything but themselves. In another sense, though, the data are quite representative: they provide the best possible way of describing the inherently market phenomena that the authors were trying to examine and that still interest us today. Obviously the industrial structures of the local labor markets have changed over forty years (consider Nashua [Myers and Shultz 1951] in particular). Whether this means that the labor-market facts that these studies demonstrated remain valid is unclear, but their approach to thinking about labor markets is surely still useful.

The kinds of data collected in the labor-market studies would provide much better answers to some of the questions about which labor economists are most concerned today. Consider first the notion of efficiency wages, the idea that there are substantial wage differentials that arise from firms' attempts to elicit effort from workers. Much of the "evidence" on this consists of demonstrating the existence of unexplained wage differentials in household data across narrowly defined industries (e.g., Krueger and Summers 1988). While the concept was not addressed in today's terms, the role of efficiency wages and unemployment as a discipline device was recognized in the labor-market studies, "The change from a balanced to a loose local labor market unquestionably brought with it a tightening up of plant discipline" (Myers and Shultz 1951, 144).

Analyzing the combined establishment-household data using today's techniques and concepts could shed far more light on the importance of efficiency wages. (Beginning efforts in this direction were made by Osberg, Apostle, and Clairmont 1986; and Groshen 1986.) For example, with wage data on individuals in the same specific occupations one could easily measure the importance of firm-specific effects. This would provide two substantial advances over current studies of wage differentials, in that it would allow us to examine wages within very detailed occupations at the level of individual establishments. Longitudinal data from labor-market studies would also allow one to examine how occupation-specific wage differences across plants affect turnover, a manifestation of worker dissatisfaction and the obverse side of the extra effort that efficiency wages are alleged to elicit.

The second area of current research is on the relative roles of job-matching and on-the-job training in producing observed patterns of wage growth with job tenure (see Abraham and Farber 1987). The question is whether wage growth results from firm-specific training or whether it just reflects sorting of workers so that more senior workers are those who have remained with the employers with whom they are well matched. The kinds of data produced in the old labor-market studies would not add much to this discussion because of their limitation to single cross sections. If such data were collected longitudinally, though, these questions could be answered as definitively as is possible in empirical work. With combined longitudinal establishment-household data we could follow workers in specific jobs as output and productivity vary in the plants where they work. That would enable us to observe more closely the effects of actual investments in training (if any) that are taking place and contributing to wage growth. Similarly, examining the detailed characteristics of job vacancies in relation to the characteristics of current and new workers would allow us to study the matching hypothesis directly rather than infer it from complicated modelling of the error structures of wage equations.

A revival of the kinds of data collection that underlay the labor-market studies would yield very high returns in instructing us about how labor markets function. One method is to replicate the early studies in specific labor markets using modern sampling techniques and collecting data that we now obtain in household and establishment surveys. An approach that will probably yield more information at lower cost would combine the longitudinal establishment survey proposed in section 9.4 with a linked survey of substantial samples of individuals employed in the establishments. This approach has the virtue of increasing spatial representativeness and providing the desired combined longitudinal establishment-household data. Still another method, though one that will not provide the monthly or quarterly data that are necessary for some purposes, is to use the establishment data underlying the Area Wage Surveys as a starting place for the construction of the kinds of data needed for the purposes of this section. This approach to data collection will also allow for the easy acquisition of detailed product- and labor-market characteristics that would be useful both for the specific topics discussed above and for other market-based issues.

9.6 Union Goals

For many years economists and industrial relations specialists have discussed what unions try to maximize. Developing the pioneering work of Dunlop (1944), economists have recently specified models designed to allow the estimation of the parameters of "union utility functions" on microdata. In simple models particular forms of these functions are combined with loglinear labor-demand equations to infer the parameters. More complex models test whether the union's marginal rate of substitution between employment and wages equals the slope of the labor-demand curve, or whether unions and employers move off the demand curve to a Pareto-superior point on the contract curve.

The main strand of research (Dertouzos and Pencavel 1981; Pencavel 1984; Brown and Ashenfelter 1986; MaCurdy and Pencavel 1986) is entirely based on pooled annual time-series, cross-section data describing wages and employment in locals of the International Typographical Union (ITU). The studies proceed from the simple labor-demand model to various tests of whether the bargain is constrained by demand. The second strand, Farber (1978) for the United States, and Carruth and Oswald (1985) for the United Kingdom, uses annual time series on mine workers to estimate the degree of relative risk aversion in union utility functions.

The authors are very aware of problems with specifying a single utility function for the union. Pencavel in particular argues that the ITU is well suited to finessing the problem of internal union decision-making, because (he argues) the workers are homogeneous and the union is very democratic. (Thus he implies that the median and average voters are identical.) No one would make these claims about miners' unions in the United States or the United Kingdom, so that one wonders whether the idea of estimating a union utility function makes sense for them. A similar problem exists with Eberts and Stone's (1986) cross section of teachers in New York state school districts.

The difficulty in all these studies, but particularly in the strand of work by Pencavel and his colleagues, is the limitation to what is essentially one small and remarkably atypical (see Lipset, Trow, and Coleman 1956) segment of the union sector. Here is a case where tremendous resources have been devoted to building and testing ever more complex models on what is essentially the same set of data. Assuming the model is relevant beyond the ITU, it is difficult to believe that additional effort at collecting a new set of data on another union would not add more to our understanding of what unions do than introducing yet more complexities to the basic model.

9.7 Is There a Need for Validation Using International Data?

In the discussion in section 9.2 I set out as the desideratum the acquisition of data that will provide the best estimates of the vector of structural parameters *b* describing the underlying economic relationship. Do these parameters describe behavior generally, or are we only concerned with characterizing agents' actions in one particular economy? If the former we must be especially careful to consider whether, even if our data meet all the criteria for appropriateness that I have laid out, the results they generate can be used to draw inferences that apply beyond this country's borders. The issue is basically one of representativeness of the data, except that too often we think that the universe we are trying to represent is the economy of the particular country where we reside. The obverse question involves the uses to which studies of other countries' labor markets can be put by American economists. These are basically (1) To provide additional laboratories for the estimation of parameters describing economic behavior generally and (2) to provide contrasts to our own labor market.

Whether such generalization is possible depends to a large extent on whether (1) there are sufficient similarities in consumers' tastes across countries that we should expect similar behavioral responses to various stimuli; (2) markets are sufficiently interconnected and technology diffuses sufficiently rapidly that competition eliminates much of the international differences in behavior that would otherwise arise; and (3) the institutions that regulate behavior are sufficiently similar so that the similar behavior inherent in economic agents is not altered by nonmarket forces. Since technology flows more freely across borders than does labor, these considerations suggest that generalizing about supply behavior from studies on data characterizing only one economy is likely to be more risky than drawing inferences about labor demand. Institutional differences do inhibit generalization; they also provide opportunities to predict the effects of altering domestic institutions and to obtain data that allow for independent replication of estimates of their impacts (assuming international differences in tastes and technology are not too great).

Killingsworth's (1983) monumental study of labor supply summarizes a vast array of research and (among other contributions) tries to determine the reasons for the disturbingly wide range of estimates of supply parameters. While different estimation techniques, data sets, and measurement difficulties undoubtedly contribute to the problem, one wonders how much of the range results from underlying differences among the different populations being sampled. Although, as I noted in section 9.4, the data are not very satisfactory, we have obtained a number of stylized facts about labor demand (see Hamermesh 1986). Given the sorry quality of the data, even the minimal knowledge we have obtained about labor-demand behavior generally would not be possible without the accretion of demand studies from several economies.

In the area of predicting the effects of institutional change American economists can learn much from studies of other economies. An excellent example is in inferring the effects of imposing comparable worth, where comparative studies (e.g., Gregory, Daly, and Ho, 1986) can tell us at least as much as generalizations based on the existing structure of the domestic labor market. In other cases our institutions are similar to those of other countries, but our federal system imposes such uniformity that it is difficult to have much confidence about estimates of labor-market effects. A particularly good example is the evaluation of the employment and labor-force effects of the federal minimum wage (Mincer 1976). A study for Canada (Swidinsky 1980), where provincial laws produce greater cross-section variation in effective minimum wages, substantially increases one's confidence in the results obtained for the United States.

The answer to the titular question of this section—whether we should validate our work on data from countries beyond the United States—is a resounding yes. We will never be able to make universally applicable statements about all aspects of labor-market behavior; but with more attention to studies that use data from countries other than the United States, we will at least avoid the embarrassing ethnocentricity that often characterizes our attempt to generalize empirical results. At the same time, such attention will improve our understanding of the domestic labor market.

9.8 What Is to Be Done?[4]

Doing applied economics properly is an art—and the data used in practicing this art must meet the criteria of appropriate aggregation, representativeness and current structure. Too often we empirically oriented labor economists have the lazy person's habit of tailoring our methods of analysis, and sometimes even the basic questions we ask, to fit the available data. In the case of analyzing labor supply, where the available data are representative, offer the appropriate degree of disaggregation and capture current structures well, this is an excellent approach. In other cases it is not. Studies of labor-demand phenomena and of the interaction of supply and demand in the labor market have been based on data that are often inappropriately disaggregated, unrepresentative, or uncharacteristic of current structures. Indeed, the tremendous resources devoted to collecting data that are best suited for analyzing labor supply, and the consequent availability of those data, have reduced incentives to collect data that are more suitable for these other questions.

This is not a condemnation of recent empirical research on issues other than labor supply. We have learned a lot; but what we can possibly learn about these issues is severely limited by the lack of appropriate data. Rather than rely on inappropriate data, those of us interested in empirical research in labor economics outside the narrow and decreasingly fertile area of labor supply must adopt some of the sociologists' willingness to generate new sets of data (though, one would hope, without abandoning our willingness to construct models to organize the analysis of those data). Also, given the limited resources available for collecting data, we must urge public officials responsible for funding data collection to get out of the rut of concentrating on ever-larger and ever-longer sets of household data and redirect resources toward the kinds of data that are more likely to yield new basic insights into the operation of labor markets. The individual data-collection efforts implied by such a redirection of public and private activities cannot take place without expending large amounts of time and money. If coupled with some curtailing of the increasing tendency to spend energy and budget resources on accumulating additional longer household-based longitudinal studies, they need not add to the share of public resources devoted to the collection of data in labor-related areas.

The major area toward which resources should be shifted is the collection of longitudinal, monthly or quarterly, establishment data to which household data on workers in the sampled establishments are linked. This data set should contain the information now collected by the BLS in its immense monthly surveys of establishments as well as information on output and sales. The sample of establishments need not be large, but it must be representative of the entire economy, not merely the over-studied manufacturing sector. Simultaneous sampling of panels of workers in these establishments that provides information like that now available in the NLS and the PSID, or even in the CPS supplements, should also be undertaken. In ten years we would thus have in hand at little extra cost a tool that would allow us to understand increasingly important phenomena that have been heretofore either relatively neglected or studied using inappropriate data.

Without the kind of endeavor proposed here the only progress possible in these areas of research and public policy will come through the continued efforts of individuals who collect small, usually unrepresentative, and incomplete sets of establishment-household data. This catch-as-catch-can approach has been and can continue to be important. It is unlikely to provide sufficient additional knowledge to save the study of labor economics from increasingly sterile empirical work using the existing massive sets of household data and from the growth of "labor theory" that is increasingly detached from the analysis of empirical phenomena.

Notes

1. The six journals are the *American Economic Review, Econometrica, Journal of Political Economy, Quarterly Journal of Economics, Review of Economics and Statistics,* and *International Economic Review.* I tried to follow the same sets of exclusions as Stafford (1986).

2. Johann Wolfgang Goethe, *Faust:* "To be sure [we] know a lot, but would like to know everything" (Pt. 1, scene 1).

3. The EOPP data set does combine establishments and households. However, employers are asked questions only about the characteristics of their most recent hire, so that very little is made of the combined nature of the data.

4. Apologies to V. I. Lenin.

References

Abraham, Katharine, and Henry Farber. 1987. Job Duration, Seniority and Earnings. *American Economic Review* 77:278–97.

Allen, Steve. 1986. Union Work Rules and Efficiency in the Building Trades. *Journal of Labor Economics* 4:212–42.

Barbour, James, Mark Berger, and John Garen. 1987. The Short-Run Demand for Labor in the Coal Industry. University of Kentucky. Typescript.

Berger, Mark. 1983. Changes in Labor Force Composition and Male Earnings: A Production Approach. *Journal of Human Resources* 17:177–96.

Berndt, Ernst, and Laurits Christensen. 1974. Testing for the Existence of a Consistent Aggregate Index of Labor Inputs. *American Economic Review* 64:391–404.

Berndt, Ernst, Melvyn Fuss, and Leonard Waverman. 1979. A Dynamic Model of Cost Adjustment and Interrelated Factor Demands. Discussion paper no. 79-30. University of British Columbia.

Borjas, George. 1986. The Demographic Determinants of the Demand for Black Labor. In *The Black Youth Employment Crisis,* ed. Richard Freeman and Harry Holzer. Chicago: University of Chicago Press.

Brown, James, and Orley Ashenfelter. 1986. Testing the Efficiency of Employment Contracts. *Journal of Political Economy* 94:S40–S87.

Cain, Glen, and Harold Watts. 1973. *Income Maintenance and Labor Supply.* Chicago: Markham.

Carruth, A. A., and A. J. Oswald. 1985. Miners' Wages in Post-war Britain: An Application of a Model of Trade Union Behavior. *Economic Journal* 95:1003–20.

Clark, Kim, and Lawrence Summers. 1982. The Dynamics of Youth Unemployment. In *The Youth Labor Market Problem,* ed. Richard Freeman and David Wise. Chicago: University of Chicago Press.

Dertouzos, James, and John Pencavel. 1981. Wage and Employment Determination under Trade Unionism: The International Typographical Union. *Journal of Political Economy* 89:1162–81.

Dunlop, John. 1944. *Wage Determination under Trade Unionism.* New York: Macmillan.

Dunne, Timothy, Mark Roberts, and Lawrence Samuelson. 1989. Plant Turnover and Gross Employment Flows. *Journal of Labor Economics* 7:48–71.

Eberts, Randall, and Joe Stone. 1986. On the Contract Curve: A Test of Alternative Models of Collective Bargaining. *Journal of Labor Economics* 4:66–81.

Farber, Henry. 1978. Individual Preferences and Union Wage Determination: The Case of the United Mine Workers. *Journal of Political Economy* 86:923–42.

Grant, James, and Daniel Hamermesh. 1981. Labor Market Competition among Youths, White Women and Others. *Review of Economics and Statistics* 63:354–60.

Gregory, Robert, A. Daly, and V. Ho. 1986. A Tale of Two Countries: Equal Pay for

Women in Australia and Britain. Discussion paper no. 147. Centre for Economic Policy Research, Australian National University.

Griliches, Zvi. 1986. Economic Data Issues. In *Handbook of Econometrics,* ed. Zvi Griliches and Michael Intriligator. Amsterdam: North-Holland.

Groshen, Erica. 1986. Sources of Wage Dispersion: How Much Do Employers Matter? Ph.D. diss., Harvard University.

Grossman, Jean. 1982. The Substitutability of Natives and Immigrants in Production. *Review of Economics and Statistics* 64 (1982): 596–603.

Hamermesh, Daniel. 1986. The Demand for Labor in the Long Run. In *Handbook of Labor Economics,* ed. Orley Ashenfelter and Richard Layard. Amsterdam: North-Holland.

———. 1988. The Demand for Workers and Hours and the Effects of Job Security Policies. In *Employment, Unemployment and Labor Utilization,* ed. Robert Hart. London: Unwin Hyman.

———. 1989. Labor Demand and the Structure of Adjustment Costs. *American Economic Review* 79:674–89.

Hart, Robert, and Nicholas Wilson. 1988. The Demand for Workers and Hours: Micro Evidence from the UK Metal Working Industry. In *Employment, Unemployment, and Labor Utilization,* ed. Robert Hart. London: Unwin Hyman.

Heckman, James, and Robert Willis. 1977. A Beta-logistic Model for the Analysis of Sequential Labor Force Participation by Married Women. *Journal of Political Economy* 85:27–58.

Holzer, Harry. 1987. Informal Job Search and Black Youth Unemployment. *American Economic Review* 77:446–52.

Houseman, Susan. 1988. Shorter Working Time and Job Security: Labor Adjustment in the European Steel Industry. In *Employment, Unemployment and Labor Utilization,* ed. Robert Hart. London: Unwin Hyman.

Jacobson, Louis. 1986. Job Creation and Destruction in Pennsylvania, 1975–85. W. E. Upjohn Institute, Kalamazoo, Mich. Typescript.

Killingsworth, Mark. 1983. *Labor Supply.* Cambridge: Cambridge University Press.

Krueger, Alan, and Lawrence Summers. 1988. Efficiency Wages and the Wage Structure. *Econometrica* 56:259–94.

Leonard, Jonathan. 1987. In the Wrong Place at the Wrong Time: The Extent of Frictional and Structural Unemployment. In *Unemployment and the Structure of Labor Markets,* ed. Kevin Lang and Jonathan Leonard. New York: Basil Blackwell.

Lipset, Seymour, Martin Trow, and James Coleman. 1956. *Union Democracy: The Internal Politics of the International Typographical Union.* Glencoe, Ill.: Free Press.

MaCurdy, Thomas. 1981. An Empirical Model of Labor Supply in a Life-Cycle Setting. *Journal of Political Economy* 89:1059–85.

MaCurdy, Thomas, and John Pencavel. 1986. Testing between Competing Models of Wage and Employment Determination in Unionized Markets. *Journal of Political Economy* 94:S3–S39.

Mairesse, Jacques, and Brigitte Dormont. 1985. Labor and Investment Demand at the Firm Level: A Comparison of French, German and U.S. Manufacturing, 1970–79. *European Economic Review* 28:201–31.

McElroy, Marjorie. 1987. Additive General Error Models for Production, Cost and Derived Demand or Share Systems. *Journal of Political Economy* 95:737–57.

Mincer, Jacob. 1962. Labor Force Participation of Married Women. In *Aspects of Labor Economics,* ed. H. Gregg Lewis. Princeton, N.J.: Princeton University Press.

———. 1976. Unemployment Effects of Minimum Wages. *Journal of Political Economy* 84:S87–S104.

Morrison, Catherine. 1986. Structural Models of Dynamic Factor Demands with Nonstatic Expectations. *International Economic Review* 27:365–86.

Myers, Charles, and George Shultz. 1951. *The Dynamics of a Labor Market*. New York: Prentice-Hall.
Nadiri, M. I., and Sherwin Rosen. 1969. Interrelated Factor Demand Functions. *American Economic Review* 59:457–71.
Nickell, Steven. 1979. Unemployment and the Structure of Labor Costs. *Journal of Monetary Economics* 11:187–222.
Osberg, Lars, Richard Apostle, and Don Clairmont. 1986. The Incidence and Duration of Individual Unemployment: Supply Side or Demand Side? *Cambridge Journal of Economics* 10:13–33.
Pencavel, John. 1984. The Trade-off between Wages and Employment in Trade Union Objectives. *Quarterly Journal of Economics* 99:215–32.
Rees, Albert, and George Shultz. 1970. *Workers and Wages in an Urban Labor Market*. Chicago: University of Chicago Press.
Reynolds, Lloyd. 1951. *The Structure of Labor Markets*. New York: Harper & Bros.
Sargent, Thomas. 1978. Estimation of Dynamic Labor Demand Schedules under Rational Expectations. *Journal of Political Economy* 86:1009–45.
Segal, Martin. 1986. Post-institutionalism in Labor Economics: The Forties and Fifties Revisited. *Industrial and Labor Relations Review* 39:388–403.
Sosin, Kim, and Loretta Fairchild. 1984. Nonhomotheticity and Technological Bias in Production. *Review of Economics and Statistics* 66:44–50.
Stafford, Frank. 1986. Forestalling the Demise of Empirical Economics: The Role of Microdata in Labor Economics Research. In *Handbook of Labor Economics*, ed. Orley Ashenfelter and Richard Layard. Amsterdam: North-Holland.
Swidinsky, Robert. 1980. Minimum Wages and Teenage Unemployment. *Canadian Journal of Economics* 13:158–71.

Comment Sherwin Rosen

Hamermesh's paper reflects on how new data can improve our understanding of several problems in labor economics. He reaches two main conclusions. First, highly disaggregated (monthly firm or even establishment) time-series data are necessary to make further progress on the demand side of labor markets. Second, labor-market surveys of the kind done by Reynolds, Rees, and Shultz in the 1950s and 1960s are the next logical step in the evolution of empirical labor economics. I disagree with the first conclusion, not because such data will be without interest, but rather because they will not solve the main difficulty with existing work. I agree with the thrust of the second conclusion (though not those particular survey instruments) because matched firm and worker samples hold promise for resolving empirical problems with existing theories and for advancing concepts and models to incorporate broader and more complex forms of behavior.

Modern labor economics has forged some of the closest connections between data and theory in all of applied economics. It is difficult to even imag-

Sherwin Rosen is the Edwin A. and Betty L. Bergman Professor of Economics at the University of Chicago and a research associate of the National Bureau of Economic Research.

ine the field without the existence of the one-in-one-thousand 1960 census tape and the early computers used to process those numbers. The gradual emergence of panel data expanded the range of questions that could be examined. These more demanding questions stimulated development of more sophisticated theories and statistical methods to deal with them. It is perhaps worth reminding ourselves from time to time that progress in any branch of empirical economics must involve such interactions between data and theory. Constructing models and organizing our thoughts about a problem is greatly influenced by available data and existing empirical regularities. A good model illuminates the main trends and facts these data reveal, but it is limited and must flounder at some level of empirical detail. Failures of this kind are, however, most interesting if they suggest how an expanded conception of the problem might remedy the situation and incorporate a broader class of phenomena.

Hamermesh points to the problem of labor supply as central to the field of labor economics and suggests that progress in this area has been so large that not much more can be expected from it. Now much has been learned about labor-supply behavior, but few would argue that we are anywhere close to full understanding. If there are diminishing returns, it is probably because the year-to-year changes in labor hours worked by individuals in panel data are poorly explained by current theories. The fact is that it has been very difficult to find wage and other pure, unilateral labor-supply price effects in the time-series behavior of individuals, at least at business cycles frequencies where recent interest in the subject came from. Is this because the data are inadequate for the theory or, as seems likely to me, is it the theory that needs overhauling to account for the data? Evidently more attention must be focused on the conceptual issues of joint decisions concerning hours and layoffs by both firms and workers.

The bulk of Hamermesh's paper is devoted to questions of labor demand. I am skeptical that monthly panels of establishments and firms will greatly advance our knowledge of this subject for the following reasons. First, is the unfortunate statistical constraint of measurement error that reduces the signal-to-noise ratio to intolerable proportions in very disaggregated data. For instance, problems of estimating meaningful capital stocks at the firm or establishment level are well known. And firms differ greatly in the qualities of their outputs and inputs. None of that fits neatly into our models but is more or less averaged away in more aggregate data.

Second, technological differences across firms and productivity change over time are very important for understanding detailed micro behavior, but are basically nuisance issues from the point of view of labor-demand elasticity questions. Their immense importance at this level of disaggregation reduces one's ability to study the primary question. To be sure, technical change affects factor demand studies at any level of aggregation, but industry-level data renders this problem less important. And more pragmatically, the great hope for disaggregation expressed by many economists in the 1950s and 1960s has not exactly been fulfilled in the intervening years. That situation is not going to change any time soon.

Third, there are compelling conceptual reasons to be wary of highly disaggregated firm-level data for these questions. The most useful concept of labor demand by far is the *market or industry demand.* That is why the standard theory is built upon constant-returns-to-scale production functions at the industry (aggregate) level. This is a wonderful finesse of such complicated issues as the size distributions of firms, the extensive margin, and firm-specific rents that do not have to be explicitly considered for a market concept of factor demand. Furthermore, looking only at the firm ignores scale effects—the tendency for the industry to contract or expand through output demand efforts in response to variations in output prices provoked by factor price changes. This important part of the problem is best studied at the industry level even if data are perfect.

Fourth, I doubt if monthly establishment data will contribute much toward understanding the dynamics of factor demand. Monthly data are ideal for studying seasonal variations, and those are important for some industries such as fishing and construction. But what can they tell us about the longer term movements associated with business cycles that motivate much of the interest in this subject? Quarterly data are better for that purpose. However, even quarterly data do not show much sensitivity of factor demand to quarter-to-quarter movements in factor prices, as Nadiri and I showed in an early NBER study.[1] While methodological improvements in our methods have been proposed, no convincing explanation for this finding has been found. So if substitution effects cannot be found in quarterly data, how in the world will seasonally dominated monthly data improve the situation?

Neoclassical theory of labor supply and demand works quite well on a longer time frame and in cross sections. However, the empirical finding that wages do not matter much for explaining quarter-to-quarter variations in either supply or demand calls for both new data and some new conceptions of these problems. Many of us think that the conception somehow lies in the economics of contracts suggested by the long-term relations observed between workers and employers. This makes me very enthusiastic about Hamermesh's proposal for renewed interest in matched worker-firm surveys because having matched data is the only way in which the marriage aspects of labor-market exchange can be thoroughly studied. This is bound to yield many interesting results whether or not the economic theory of contracts proves useful. Existing matched records from different administrative sources (e.g., SSA, CPS, and IRS) do not provide nearly enough information for this.

Two important barriers must be overcome in this endeavor. First, we must

1. M. Ishaq Nadiri and Sherwin Rosen, *A Disequilibrium Model of Demand for Factors of Production,* General Series no. 99. (New York: National Bureau of Economic Research, 1973.)

convince decision makers at the appropriate statistical agencies that the effort will be worthwhile. This must include mechanisms for preserving confidentiality of firm records. Second, serious thought and resources must be put into designing the survey instrument, pretesting it, and implementing it statistically. The fact is that economists such as Hamermesh and myself who are interested in using such data are not well equipped to carry out these important production matters. However, if we keep waiting for someone else to do all of that hard work we are likely to be waiting for an awfully long time.

10 Demands for Data and Analysis Induced by Environmental Policy

Clifford S. Russell and V. Kerry Smith

10.1 Introduction

Economic analysis of environmental policies is, if not uniquely, at least unusually difficult. Resolution of these difficulties requires substantial investment in data collection and model construction, only some of which is directly economic. Some of the reasons for the difficulties of environmental benefit-cost analysis are well known, appearing in intermediate and even elementary microeconomic and policy analysis texts (Baumol and Oates 1975; Fisher 1981). Thus, even the average economics undergraduate major can be expected to appreciate that there is a problem finding demand functions for many services of the natural environment because they are public goods. At more advanced levels, they will learn about such thorny technical issues in implementing proposed solutions to this problem. Those interested in policy learn about the conflicting maze of environmental legislation, including problems of overlapping jurisdiction, differences in burdens of proof, and, most significantly, disagreements between laws over what role, if any, economic analysis should play.

But neither the technical economic matters nor the special policy problems, challenging though they may be, provide the principal explanation for our assertion that the benefit-cost analysis of environmental policy may well be uniquely difficult. Rather, that assertion is based on the central place in such

Clifford S. Russell is a professor of economics at Vanderbilt University and the director of the Vanderbilt Institute for Public Policy Studies. V. Kerry Smith is a university distinguished professor of economics at North Carolina State University and a university fellow in the Quality of the Environment Division, Resources for the Future.

Partial support for this research was provided through U.S. Environmental Protection Agency Cooperative Agreement CR812564. The authors thank Ernie Berndt, Tom Tietenberg, Peter Caulkins, Bill Desvousges, and Paul Portney for their suggestions on research related to this paper.

analyses of the complex relationship between policy implementation choices on the one hand and the relevant natural systems (especially atmosphere, water bodies, soil and resident plant communities, and ground water) on the other.[1]

To set the stage for a more careful examination of this assertion, let us consider the nature of the system of environmental regulation and the origin of the complications in which we are especially interested. Figure 10.1 combines an overview of the linkage between policy choice and resulting benefits, with indications of the complications arising at each stage in the linkage. In the next three sections we shall examine in turn each of the links in the figure. In section 10.2, we shall describe some of the problems implied by the way standard setting is constrained and practiced, and by the necessity of choosing an accompanying implementation plan. In section 10.3, we concentrate on the central role of knowledge of natural systems interacting with choice of implementation system. In section 10.4, we come to some of the more obviously and traditionally economic issues connected with valuing environmental services.

The final section of the paper brings together the analysis of sections 10.2–10.4 with a brief assessment of key emerging policy issues to produce our version of a catalog of data-gathering strategies likely to be most relevant and valuable for analyzing future decisions on the allocation and management of environmental resources.

While our approach to identifying data needs builds from specific examples of current policy issues, the questions raised are general ones. Thus, we do not attempt to catalog what we consider to be the most important environmental policy issues in the late 1980s and then base an evaluation of data requirements on them. Instead we argue that the interactions between the statutes defining the character of environmental policy and the role of natural systems for economic agents' behavior affect the problems that would appear on any list that might be composed. Thus, regardless of whether one believes global warming or indoor air pollution is among the most pressing environmental questions, economic analysts will need to incorporate what is known about a form of these interactions in developing their analyses.

10.2 Choosing Standards and Implementation Plans

Table 10.1 (adapted from U.S. Environmental Protection Agency [EPA] 1987a) summarizes the major criteria to be considered by the administrator of EPA in deciding on standards under a variety of legislative mandates. Two features of this table are especially striking. First, the criteria used to choose standards frequently focus on a subset of the information that would be part of a full benefit-cost analysis. For example, under the Clean Air Act the primary standards for criteria air pollutants are to be based on human health effects but cannot include compliance costs in the process of defining the stan-

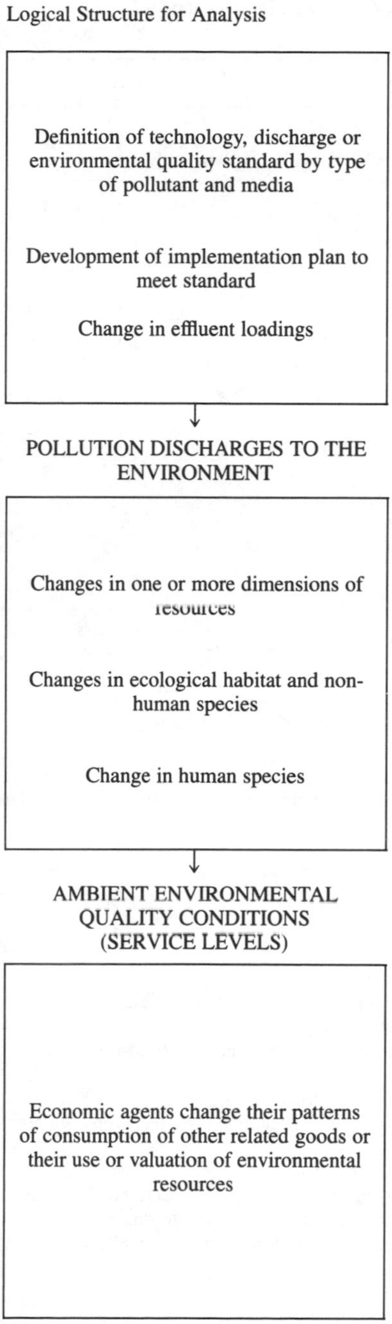

Logical Structure for Analysis	Rationale for the Logical Structure
Definition of technology, discharge or environmental quality standard by type of pollutant and media Development of implementation plan to meet standard Change in effluent loadings	The institutional structure governing the definition and implementation of environmental policy is complex. As a result of multiple, overlapping statutes defined by both environmental media (e.g., Clean Air Act and Clean Water Act) and the types of residuals generated (e.g., Resource Conservation and Recovery Act, Comprehensive Environmental Response, Compensation and Liability Act, etc.), policies must be responsive to multiple objectives. Moreover, they can involve the definition of standards in a format inconsistent with available environmental data or in generic terms that require considerable judgment to implement, enforce, or evaluate.
↓ POLLUTION DISCHARGES TO THE ENVIRONMENT	
Changes in one or more dimensions of resources Changes in ecological habitat and nonhuman species Change in human species	The services of environmental resources are produced within a complex physical system where the effects of different patterns and types of uses depend on temporal aspects of those uses. In particular, the pattern of environmental quality corresponding to a chosen standard is influenced by the implementation program to be used to attain the standard.
↓ AMBIENT ENVIRONMENTAL QUALITY CONDITIONS (SERVICE LEVELS)	
Economic agents change their patterns of consumption of other related goods or their use or valuation of environmental resources	The services of environmental resources exchange outside markets, and therefore, the information normally present from market exchanges is not available. Indeed, as part of their ordinary consumption choices, individuals may not have been required to consider changes comparable to those envisioned in any specific policy analysis. Information on the quality and character of these services can be quite technical, involve subtle measurement problems, and is unlikely to be generated through the informal processes individuals use to learn about other commodities they consume.

Fig. 10.1 Schematic description of issues in using economic analysis for environmental policies

Table 10.1 Components of Economic Analysis Identified in EPA's Enabling Legislation

	Benefits			Costs		
Economic Legislation/Regulation	Human Health	Other[b] Effects	Welfare[c]	Compliance	Cost Effective	Impacts
Clean Air Act:						
Primary NAAQS[a]	x	x				
Secondary NAAQS			x			
Hazardous air pollutants	x					
New source performance	*	x	*	**	**	**
Motor vehicle emissions[d]	x	x	x	x	x	x
Fuel standards[d]	x	x	x	x		
Aircraft emissions	x	x	x	x		x
Clean Water Act:						
Private treatment		e	***	x	x	x
Public treatment		e				
Safe Drinking Water Act:						
Maximum contaminant level goals	x					
Maximum contaminant levels				x		x
Toxic Substances Act	x	x	x	x	x	x
Resource Conservation and Recovery Act	x		x			
CERCLA (SARA):						
Reportable quantities	x		x			
National contingency		x			x	
Federal Insecticide, Fungicide and Rodenticide Act:						
Data requirements			x			
Minor uses	x	x	x	x	x	x
Atomic Energy Act						
Radioactive waste	x	x	x			
Uranium mill tailings	x	x	x	x	x	x

Source: Adapted from U.S. EPA (1987a), table 3-1, p. 3-2.

Note: *includes non-air-quality health and environmental impacts. **statute refers only to cost. ***includes non-water-quality environmental impacts only.

[a]NAAQS designates the National Ambient Air Quality Standards and relates to the criteria air pollutants.

[b]"Other Effects" refer to nonhealth effects on humans and firms.

[c]"Welfare Effects" refer to visibility and aesthetics, effects on nonhuman species, crops, sodding, materials damage.

[d]The type of analysis here depends on the grounds for control.

[e]There is some question about whether any benefit information may be considered. One school of thought is that national aggregate benefit estimates might be allowed into this process. Such estimates would here reflect especially recreation as a pathway for accrual of benefits to society.

dard.[2] In contrast, under the Clean Water Act, the definition of one type of technology-based standard, best conventional treatment (BCT), can be based on costs (in comparison with the marginal costs of secondary treatment at municipal waste treatment facilities) but not on the specific benefits to be realized at individual water bodies.

Second, the mandates involve significant areas of overlap where different regulatory analyses are intended to influence the same types of pollutants in the ambient environment, for example, primary standards for criteria air pollutants and New Source Performance Standards defined on the basis of the effects new discharge sources would have on the concentrations of these pollutants.

One important implication is that economic analysis (in this case, benefit-cost analysis) usually involves an evaluation of the net effect of standards chosen on some basis other than economic efficiency. Another is that standards set under one provision of one law may well overlap in their effects with those set under another provision or law. This raises difficulties for the definition of benefits—at least whenever marginal benefits are nonlinear—because of the interdependence of baselines.

Other serious problems introduced by the standard setting operation can be considered in a few specific examples. Setting an environmental standard of either the discharge or ambient sort requires that the regulator must (Richmond 1983):

1. identify the pollutant to be regulated;
2. select the form of the standard (i.e., a technology to achieve an emissions rate or an ambient concentration);
3. choose the concentration or discharge amount that will be the average target;
4. pick the averaging time over which the target is to be met (an hour, a day, a week, a year, etc.);
5. define the exceedance rate(s) of interest (e.g., a weekly average standard might be paired with a daily upper limit);
6. define what constitutes a violation, taking account of the statistical error structure displayed by the monitoring equipment and other relevant sources of uncertainty (such as measurements made across a sample of different applications of a technology where the standard is technology based).

Thus, evaluating the net benefits of an environmental standard is a complicated business (Portney 1984; Smith 1984). Not only do we need information on the effects of average (or peak, as applicable) exposures to particular pollutants (or ecological effects of average concentrations), we also should be able to evaluate alternative patterns of allowed exceedance. In practice we are fortunate if we have the data from which to estimate dose-response functions over *any* range and averaging time.

The case of the particulate matter (PM) ambient air quality standards permits us to see some of the troubles that can arise even within this limited context. The benefit-cost analysis done for PM was the most expensive of those discussed in the EPA report cited above (U.S. EPA 1987a; see our n. 1). It seems reasonable to assume that the quality of the analysis reflects these expenditures.

The first and largest problem in analyzing PM benefits was that the available laboratory evidence on the health effects of airborne particulates did not match up with the available ambient measurements. Laboratory toxicology suggested that particles smaller than 10 microns across were responsible for whatever health damage was observed. Since preventing health damage was the mandated basis of the standard, the ambient standard had to be written in terms of these small particles. Ambient measurements, with a few isolated exceptions, had for years been done in terms of total suspended particulates (TSP). As a consequence, epidemiological studies aimed at finding health effects associated with airborne particulars inevitably labored under an imposed errors-in-variables problem.

More fundamentally, however, analyzing the total net benefits of the 10-micron PM standard required that the relation between TSP and the distribution of particles by size, both before and after a standard, be understood. In addition, the analysis does not end with health because other benefits could be identified that depended on other sizes of particulate matter. In fact, the PM study conducted by EPA (and subcontractors) involved separate assessments of the health benefits (including mortality and morbidity effects), the household benefits from reduced soiling and materials damages, and the benefits to the manufacturing sector from reduced soiling and materials damage. The first two relied on judgmental appraisals (see MathTech 1982) of the "best" estimates of dose-response relationships and the last two involved the development of new models linking consumer expenditures (on commodities related to household cleaning) and sectoral cost functions to measures of particulate concentrations.

The importance of the institutional setting in combination with the technical and natural systems also can be seen in the cost estimates for the PM standard. Developing these estimates required a specification of how states would formulate their state implementation plans (SIPs), the degree of compliance with the plans, and the resulting estimated levels of particulate emissions. Emissions then had to be translated into estimates of the ambient concentrations of particulates. Of course, uniform ambient air quality standards do not imply uniform levels of actual air quality, a point we return to in section 10.3. The changes in air quality from a specified baseline defined spatially will depend on how the assumed SIP describes the process (the set of discharge reductions) used to meet the standard in each air quality control region.

To stress the analytically arbitrary nature of the institutional context, we report an example drawn from Liroff (1986). When states decide how to

Table 10.2 **Average Emission Reductions of Volatile Organic Compounds Predicted to be Required to Meet Ozone NAAQS in Selected Ohio Cities**

City	Technique 1[a] (%)	Technique 2[b] (%)	Technique Selected
Cleveland	87	50	1
Akron	35	18	2
Toledo	47	25	2
Columbus	43	25	2
Canton	22	10	2
Youngstown	64	44	2
Dayton	61	40	2
Cincinnati	40	50	1

Source: Adapted from Pacific Environmental Services, Study of the 1979 State Implementation Plan Submittals (Elmhurst, Ill.: Report prepared for U.S. National Commissioner on Air Quality [December 1980], 7–12) and published in Liroff (1986).
[a]Known as "EKMA."
[b]Known as "rollback."

achieve the National Ambient Air Quality Standard (NAAQS) for a pollutant, they may have a choice among different average levels of emission reduction depending on which mathematical model of the local atmospheric system they choose to use to predict ambient concentrations. Table 10.2, based on Liroff's table 2.2, shows the choice facing Ohio in designing its implementation plan for ground-level ozone. The two alternative models lead to alternative patterns of predicted ambient concentrations, though both would show no violation at any monitoring site. Thus, the predicted net benefits of the ozone NAAQS in Ohio (and generally in any state) will depend on the choice of modeling technique, not just on the average level of the standard. Of course, it is possible that either or both models may be wrong. Neither pattern of reductions might in fact result in meeting the NAAQS.

We now shift our focus and turn to natural system information and modeling and the implications of how we handle such matters for our estimates of the benefits of environmental standards.

10.3 Bringing in the Natural World

The evaluation of environmental policies inevitably involves economists with the systems that make up the ambient environment. If a policy mandates a reduction in polluted waste water discharge from industrial and publicly owned sources, the streams, rivers, lakes, and ponds that constitute the receiving waters translate the discharge reduction into ambient quality improvements that are valued by individuals. If we turn this notion around—if public policy involves mandated upper limits for concentrations of pollutants in the ambient atmosphere, the transportation, dilution, and transformation processes at work in that atmosphere must have a key role in determining how much discharge reduction has to be accomplished to meet the standard.

While this seems intuitively clear, the importance of knowledge of those processes is greater than these observations suggest. There are two reasons for this. One is ubiquitous; the other is found to be central to some situations and not to others. The ubiquitous influence is *space,* the differential location of pollution sources and pollution receptors in the two-dimensional plane.[3] Additional complication is introduced by the nonlinearity of most environmental processes.

Consider the role of location. In the simple situation, a policy is represented graphically or mathematically by a single marginal benefit (or damage) and a single marginal cost function. These may have as arguments either ambient pollutant concentrations or pollution discharged. The optimum policy is defined by the usual MB = MC condition. The addition of spatial detail merely replicates this condition at each location. That is, efficient policies equate the marginal benefits to the marginal costs of realizing a given level of ambient quality at each location. In conventional Pareto efficiency terms this corresponds to equality of the relevant sum (for that location and its residents) of the marginal rates of substitution for environmental quality (in relation to a numeraire) to the corresponding shadow price describing the real costs of attaining it. The natural system is implicit in the definition of the real marginal costs. When perfect mixing of all pollution discharges produces uniform concentrations of pollutants everywhere in the ambient environment—as is roughly true for some air pollutants under certain physical and meteorological conditions—the simple model offers a reasonably good approximation.

But in the largest number of cases, it does not. For a mandated policy of emission reductions, even if that policy involves equal percentage reductions at all sources, the amount of ambient quality improvement will, in general, be different at every point in the relevant environmental medium. If the policy to be evaluated involves mandated ambient quality standards, the situation is even more at odds with the simple model. Not only will the concentration in the standard characterize only a few points in the environment after the policy is implemented, but which points those are and by how much the quality at every other point is better than the standard will, in general, depend on exactly how the standard is implemented.

Both environmental quality levels and, more important, improvements in quality attributable to a policy are different at every point in the environment. Moreover, every point is usually characterized by different levels of human "use." Thus, for example, some points in the atmosphere coincide with dense residential population, some with sparse; some coincide with industrial plants, some with office buildings, some with vacant space. Similarly, along a river some segments will have heavy recreational use (or prospectively have such use) because of conditions of access, bank type, current, and temperature. Other segments may be unattractive to recreationists for reasons having nothing to do with the level of pollution at that location.

Therefore, the estimates of benefits of proposed (or actual) environmental management policies are intrinsically dependent on the accuracy of our knowledge of the natural world processes, upon the detail required for the spatial resolution, and on the implementation plan assumed in the analysis.[4] The net benefits of a given policy, $\bar{P}$, can be written in fairly general terms as follows:

$$
\begin{aligned}
(1)\quad NB(\bar{P}) = {} & B_1\{f_{11}[D_1(\bar{P})] + f_{21}[D_2(\bar{P})] + \dots + f_{n1}[D_n(\bar{P})]\} \\
& + B_2\{f_{12}[D_1(\bar{P})] + f_{22}[D_2(\bar{P})] + \dots + f_{n2}[D_n(\bar{P})]\} \\
& + B_m\{f_{1m}[D_1(\bar{P})] + f_{2m}[D_2(\bar{P})] + \dots + f_{nm}[D_n(\bar{P})]\} \\
& - C_1(X_1 - D_1(\bar{P})) - C_2(X_2 - D_2(\bar{P})) - \dots \\
& - C_n(X_n - D_n(\bar{P})),
\end{aligned}
$$

where there are m points (call them receptor locations) at which we agree to measure ambient quality and infer benefits, and n sources of pollution. The functions $f_{ij}[D^i(\bar{P})]$ represent the environmental transformation of discharge level $D_i(\bar{P})$ into a contribution to ambient quality at point j. Writing D_i as a function of $\bar{P}$, the policy, we can emphasize the point that (in most cases) pollution management policies operate through affecting discharges of pollutants. The $C_i(\cdot)$ functions describe the costs to source i of reducing emissions by $X_i - D_i(\bar{P})$, with X_i the uncontrolled emissions of that source.

In general, the benefit functions $[B_j(\cdot)]$ are different for every j because of the factors mentioned above. Thus, every discharge level is a function of the policy choice, and the ambient quality at every receptor location can, in principle, be a different function of every discharge level. For example, if $\bar{P}$ consists of a required 50% reduction of prepolicy discharge at every source, that defines the vector $\{D_1(\bar{P}), \dots, D_n(\bar{P})\}$.[5] These discharges are transformed by the functions $f_{ij}(D_i)$ into ambient pollution (or quality levels; and the resulting quality at each receptor location is valued using the functions $B_k(\ )$. If, on the other hand, the policy $\bar{P}$ requires an upper limit on ambient pollution at any receptor location, call it S_k, analytical implementation implies finding a vector of discharges satisfying the requirement. This will depend on the functions $f_{ij}(D_i)$, for we are solving a problem of the following form:

$$\text{find } D_i(\bar{P}) \text{ such that } \forall_j \sum_i f_{ij}[D_i(\bar{P})] \leq S_k.$$

This is different than the description in textbooks because the policy is not defined to meet an efficiency criterion. We simply use (1) to evaluate how its implications relate to the net benefits realized with some baseline or status quo position. There may be no such vector. More often, since $n > m$, there will be an infinite number. The benefits flowing from the choice S_k will depend on which vector $D(\bar{P})$ is evaluated. This is because every such vector will, in general, produce a different pattern of ambient quality across receptor locations. Further, in this general formulation, there is no presumption that quality better than the standard is valued at zero.[6]

To illustrate what happens if we ignore the natural system, we offer one very simple and two not-so-simple examples. First, consider a hypothetical region with two sources of air pollution and three receptors or agreed-on monitoring locations. The sources are, in fact, linked to the receptors by an atmospheric system that can be characterized by a matrix of transfer coefficients, *T*, as follows:

	Receptor		
Source	I	II	III
A	2	1	.5
B	1	2	2

Ambient quality, Q, is determined on the basis of source discharge as:[7]

$$Q = DT, \quad \text{where } D = (D_A, D_B). \tag{2}$$

The benefits of discharge reductions are assumed obtainable, as damages avoided, from a quadratic damage function.

$$G_i(Q) = Q_i^2 \quad \text{for each receptor } i^8. \tag{3}$$

If initial discharges are $D_{AO} = 4$, $D_{BO} = 2$, the base or initial quality levels are:[9]

$$(Q_{io}) = (10, 8, 6), \tag{4}$$

with resulting damages

$$\sum_{i=\mathrm{I}}^{\mathrm{III}} G_i = 200. \tag{5}$$

The effect of what we might call environmental ignorance is illustrated by considering three different methods of evaluating the benefits of setting increasingly stiff ambient quality standards, S_j:

(i) We know nothing about the environment (in particular, we do not know T), so we simply work from the regional average concentration before the standard is set and assume that the standard is the average concentration after it is set. Let us denote this approach to estimating benefits as method (i), designated B^1. Then

$$B_j^1 = 3\left[G\left(\frac{\Sigma Q_{io}}{3}\right) - G(S_j)\right], \tag{6}$$

where j indexes the severity of the standard.

(ii) We still know nothing about the atmospheric system (T) but disaggregate benefits. In this formulation, benefits are calculated only for receptors where the initial quality level is worse than the standard. Moreover, it assumes that at every such point, after the imposition of the standard, quality just equals the standard. This is method (ii) (B^2), given by (7):

$$B_j^2 = \sum_i G(Q_{io}) - G(S_j), \tag{7}$$

for all i such that $Q_{io} > S_j$.

(iii) We know and use T. Implementation policy is a "rollback" rule from base period discharges. That is, with particular standard, S_j, the rollback rule specifies that each discharge is reduced by the proportion R_j, given by:

$$R_j = \frac{\max\,(Q_{io}) - S_j}{\max_i(Q_{io})}, \tag{8}$$

so that benefits are

$$B_j^3 = \sum_i [G(Q_{io}) - G\,(Q(R_{ij}))], \tag{9}$$

where

$$Q(R_{ij}) = (1-R_j)\,(D_{AO}, D_{BO})[T]. \tag{10}$$

Each of these methods provides a definition of the aggregate benefit function and with it describes our knowledge of the environment. Table 10.3 summarizes the aggregate benefits under the three definitions and four levels of ambient quality standard: 8, 6, 4, and 2. Both total and marginal benefits are

Table 10.3 Aggregate and Marginal Benefits: The Two Source–Three Receptor Example

		Aggregate Total Benefits by Standard				Aggregate Marginal Benefits by Standard			
Method	Definition	8	6	4	2	8	6	4	2
B^1	Average initial regional concept of quality relative to standard	0	84	144	180	0	42	30	18
B^2	Actual initial quality relative to standard	36	92	152	188	18	28	30	18
B^3	Actual initial quality relative to actual quality as determined for rollback implementation	72	128	168	192	36	28	20	12

shown, with the latter defined as the difference between the benefit at standard $S_j + 2$ and at S_j divided by two.

At those standards with small improvements over the baseline quality, the three measures exhibit the least agreement for both total and marginal benefits. Methods (i) and (ii) ignore benefits produced by improvements beyond the standard required by the control actions necessary to meet the standards at the binding receptor.[10] As the standard is tightened they exhibit closer correspondence. This is not surprising because as the standard is tightened toward zero pollution, the variation around the average ambient level is reduced. Thus, the difference between the standard and the quality level at any particular nonbinding receptor is reduced, and with it the sources for the differences between B^1, B^2, and B^3 diminish.

The marginal benefits calculated ignoring the natural system are an especially unreliable guide to optimal policy choice. These results are not simply artifacts of our example. Two more realistic cases illustrate the peril of ignorance of the natural world's systems. The first is based on the data developed for the Baltimore, Maryland, region in the paper by Oates, Portney, and McGartland (1989), using their air quality results (for total suspended particulates) and translating them into versions of our surrogate benefit measures. The primary difference is that method (iii) reflects a least-cost rather than a rollback scheme for implementation. So we refer to it as method (iii′) (see app. A for data and methods). Table 10.4 contains a summary of the results

Table 10.4 **Surrogate Benefits of Reductions in Total Suspended Particulates for Baltimore by Level of Ignorance and Standard (millions per year)**

	Level of Standard (ug/m³)						
	115	110	105	100	95	90	85
Method (i):							
Total	0	0	0	0	0	0	0
›thod (i) (modified):[a]							
Total	12.3	23.6	34.5	45.2	55.1	64.5	73.6
Marginal	12.3	11.3	10.9	10.7	9.9	9.4	9.1
Method (ii):							
Total	2.6	6.0	9.7	15.4	21.2	28.2	35.2
Marginal	2.6	3.4	3.7	5.7	5.8	7.0	7.0
Method (iii′):							
Total	7.7	19.7	27.7	34.9	46.2	59.1	73.7
Marginal	7.7	12.0	8.0	7.2	11.3	12.9	14.6
Marginal benefits[b]	7.2	12.9	9.1	8.5	13.2	15.1	16.4

Source: See the appendix for a description of the data and method.

[a]The modification consists of comparing initial average concentration to projected average concentrations for each standard, where the projection depended on the percentage change in the standard.

[b]Taken from Oates, Portney, and McGartland (1989); amounts given are in millions of 1980 dollars.

for total and marginal (surrogate) benefits for each estimation approach or level of knowledge. The marginal benefits calculated by Oates et al. (1989) are shown at the bottom of the table.

Thus, in a much more realistic example, the methods that ignore the natural environment produce problematic estimates of marginal and total benefits. Method (i) shows no benefits because the base case average TSP concentration is already below all the standards considered. Method (ii) produces substantial underestimation of both marginal and total benefits. It ignores improvements at receptors that have quality better than the standard before it is imposed.

Modified method (i) depends on simple reduction of the average TSP concentration for the region for each standard level by the same percentage as that standard represents a reduction of the baseline standard that McGartland et al. (1988) use in their benefit calculations: 120 micrograms per cubic meter (120 ug/m^3). It produces total benefit numbers roughly similar to those obtained in method (iii), the method reflecting best available knowledge of the environment. But this apparent improvement does not extend to marginal benefits. The actual pattern obtained via method (iii) shows an early peak at 100 ug/m^3, followed by a dip and, then, subsequent increases. Indeed, marginal benefits are still increasing at the strictest standard shown.[11]

Of course, one might criticize this example as well, noting that we are not working with a "real" damage function. Our last example does just that, using data on water quality changes, as measured by dissolved oxygen, generated by a complex and quite realistic model of the Delaware River estuary; a mapping of dissolved oxygen (DO) into sustainable recreation types from a second source; and an annual per capita willingness to pay for the availability of water-based recreation by type from a third source. (The details of the data and calculations are set out in the appendix.) The results for total and marginal benefit estimates are given in table 10.5.

Table 10.5 **Surrogate Benefits of Improvements in Water Quality in the Delaware Estuary by Level of Ignorance of Standard**

	Water Quality Standard (ppm of Dissolved Oxygen)	
	3.5	5.0
Method (i):		
Total	0	420.2
Marginal	0	420.2
Method (ii):		
Total	184.5	510.6
Marginal	184.5	326.1
Method (iii):		
Total	372.7	581.4
Marginal	372.7	208.7

The patterns of marginal benefits once again display the largest effects from ignorance of the natural world. Method (i) implies there would be no benefits of going from the baseline situation to a standard of at least 3.5 parts per million (ppm) of DO for every reach of the river. But the marginal benefit of tightening the standard from 3.5 ppm to 5.0 ppm of DO is 420.2. Under method (ii)—reach-by-reach disaggregation, but assuming benefits only for reaches that are initially worse than the standard—the marginal benefit of the 3.5 ppm standard is 184.5 and that of the 5.0 ppm standard is 326.1. This pattern is almost exactly the reverse of that observed when complete knowledge is used in method (iii). In this case, the marginal benefits associated with the lower standard are 372.7, while those associated with the next improvement to 5.0 ppm are 208.7. Thus, even though the total benefits estimated to be associated with the tougher standard are roughly similar for methods (ii) and (iii), the marginal benefit patterns are very different.

The results of these examples may be so obvious that their applicability seems doubtful. Who would ever use methods such as (i) or (ii)? The answer—and this is the key to our later recommendations—is just about everyone. An examination of the invaluable compilation of benefit estimates published by Freeman (1982) reveals that every one of the reported air pollution benefit studies uses a version of B^1 or B^2, with most relying on a method very like method (i). The water pollution benefit studies he summarizes all use a version of B^2 in which full attainment of the most ambitious standards (or ambient quality goals) of the Clean Water Act (CWA) is assumed.

As important as pointing out the prevalence of benefit estimates based on ignorance of natural systems is, an attempt to understand why this is the case also merits consideration. In the case of water pollution control benefits, the answer is generally that insufficient resources have been invested in the research needed to reduce our ignorance. Translating the technology-based discharge standard definitions of the CWA into actual discharges from tens of thousands of point sources of water pollution is hard enough. But then translating such changes in discharges, were they available, into changes in water quality indicators that in turn can be valued by individuals, involves data gathering, modeling, and basic conceptual research efforts beyond what the sponsors of such research have been willing to pay.[12] Finally, the data on valuation that is available generally is in the form of step functions unsuited to the valuation of benefits of small improvements in quality, especially at reasonably clean receptor locations.

For air pollution benefits, the state of the art of emission inventories and air quality modeling has for some time been capable of supporting the sort of disaggregated, location-specific benefit estimates obtained by Oates et al. (1989) for Baltimore. When national total benefit estimates have been the object of the exercise, however, it apparently has been too daunting a task to manage the necessarily massive data banks and atmospheric models.

Finally, before we turn to the next concern of this paper, the valuation of

Table 10.6 **Marginal Benefits of Reductions in Total Suspended Particulates for Baltimore by Implementation Method and Standard (millions of 1980 dollars)**

	Level of Standard (ug/m³)						
Implementation Method	115	110	105	100	95	90	85
Command and control	2.2	10.5	9.7	11.5	7.5	10.0	6.5
Least cost	7.2	12.9	9.0	8.5	13.2	15.1	16.4

Source: Oates, Portney, and McGartland (1989), table 1.

environmental quality changes, we should consider the effects of implementation plans on benefits. This is the primary focus of Oates et al. (1989). While their paper actually is addressed to the relevance of benefit estimates for the choice between regulatory approaches ("command and control" vs. use of economic incentives), their results provide a fine illustration of the point that for any given level of environmental knowledge, estimates of benefits will depend on the method of implementation—the pattern of discharges—assumed.

Thus, in table 10.6 we reproduce their marginal benefit estimates for the command and control and "least cost" implementation approaches. In this case, neither set of estimates can be characterized as "wrong." Both reflect the best environmental information available. Nonetheless, they are very different. Thus, the statement that a particular standard yields particular benefits has meaning only when an implementation method is explicitly assumed.

The same standard, treated as an upper bound on a pollutant's allowable concentrations, can imply an infinite number of aggregate marginal benefit patterns because these benefits will depend on how the standard is implemented and on what the natural system implies this implementation plan will yield as the ambient concentrations for each receptor location. In most theoretical treatments of these issues, this problem is avoided by simplifying assumption. The benefits are taken to be measured at a single, representative point in the environment. The costs of improving quality at that point are assumed to reflect the environmental transformations implicitly.

10.4 Evaluation Benefits: Learning from Past Research and Identifying New Initiatives[13]

The statutory guidelines creating the demand for valuation measures for environmental resources and the time horizons written into the statutes make it impossible to develop new benefit-cost studies for each decision. This has led to growing interest in the methods used to transfer valuation (or demand) estimates derived in one situation to a new one. Both the Oates et al. (1989) study of air quality in Baltimore and our own analysis of water quality in the

Delaware River used valuation estimates derived from one or more studies in the literature (see the Appendix). For the most part, these were derived from judgmental reviews of the literature and propose a best estimate (or a range of values).

Because the services of environmental resources exchange outside markets, the methods used to estimate consumers' values for them have developed along two lines. The first focuses on observable behavior that can be linked by assumptions to the resource of interest. Methods relying on this strategy have usually been labeled the indirect approaches. They include: the travel cost recreation-demand models, hedonic price functions (property value and wage rate), hedonic travel cost functions, damage-averting cost models, and factor productivity (or reverse value-added) methods. In each case, an individual's (or a firm's) actions are assumed to be partially motivated by a desire to obtain the service of an environmental resource (or to avoid the detrimental effects of pollution to that resource). Using models based on these actions, researchers attempt to estimate the marginal value of changes in the quantity or the quality of the nonmarketed resource.

The second group of methods relies on survey techniques that ask respondents how they would value (contingent valuation) or change their behavior (contingent behavior) in response to a postulated, hypothetical change in the services of an environmental resource.[14] This method assumes that an individual's response to a hypothetical situation provides an authentic description of how he (or she) would respond to an actual change.

The purpose of this section is to suggest that efforts to summarize and evaluate benefit estimates offer another kind of opportunity—to evaluate what we have learned about the values of environmental resources; to examine the sensitivity of these estimates to the modeling decisions required to develop them; and, based on these two appraisals, to identify new data and analyses required to resolve the uncertainties leading to the disparities in valuation estimates. The required analyses treat the results from past studies as data to "test" whether differences in the estimates (across studies) reflect systematic variations in the resources being valued or in the assumptions and the methods underlying them.

While this approach appears to be a new one for evaluating empirical research in economics, it is not new to other social and health sciences.[15] "Meta-analysis" describes a research method that seeks to provide systematic summaries of the findings from empirical evaluations of educational or social programs. Du Mouchel and Harris (1983), for example, proposed a similar strategy for the transfer of risk assessment models from animal to human populations.

Our objective is broadly similar. However, we seek to evaluate whether there are systematic influences on the values estimated for specific types of environmental resources and whether these influences can be distinguished from the assumptions and features of the methods. Ideally, such an analysis would be undertaken within a single empirical study in which consistency in data sources, reporting conventions, and statistical modeling criteria could be maintained across the resources and models studied. Unfortunately, this was not possible. Consequently, we summarize the results of a pilot study conducted by Smith and Kaoru (1990) that uses the existing literature as the basis for an examination of the determinants of valuation estimates for recreation resources. The focus on value estimates is deliberate because, regardless of the original objective of the research, benefit estimates have been the single most important policy use of the outputs this type of research.

Equation (1) defines the basic model. To use it, we maintain that the valuation estimate relevant for our example, the real consumer surplus, RCS, per unit of use of a site is a function of four types of variables: the type of recreation site, X_S; the assumptions inherent in the model specification, X_A; the form of the demand model, X_D; and the estimator used, X_E.

$$\text{(11)} \qquad \text{RCS}_i = \alpha_0 + \alpha_S X_{Si} + \alpha_A X_{Ai} + \alpha_D X_{Di} + \alpha_E X_{Ei} + e_i,$$

where X_{ji} and α_j, $j = S, A, D, E$ are conformably dimensioned vectors and e_i is the stochastic error for the ith estimate.

Smith and Kaoru (1987, 1988) have reviewed over 200 published and unpublished travel cost demand models prepared over the period 1970–86 and developed a data set summarizing the valuation estimates, features of the resources involved in these demand studies, and characteristics of the models involved. The results reported here are based on 77 studies. They yield 734 observations for the consumer surplus per unit of use. The individual observations vary by recreation sites, demand specification, modeling assumptions, and estimator used.

There was enormous variability in the information reported across studies. Often the objective of the research was something other than estimating the values for a recreational facility. It may have been testing a specific hypothesis, with the results reported confined to the specifics of the hypothesis test. Smith and Kaoru did not attempt to contact individual authors to supplement (or check) what was reported in the individual papers. Rather their data set relies exclusively on the information reported within these limitations. Table 10.7 defines some of the variables that could be consistently defined across the studies in each class of variable.

To interpret the results obtained from statistical analyses of valuation estimates across different studies, we must formulate specific hypotheses concerning how and in what dimensions these estimates might be sensitive to modeling judgments. A beginning step in this process can be found in past literature reviews (i.e., Ward and Loomis 1986; Smith and Desvousges 1986; Bockstael et al. 1987), as well as in what seem to be established conventions in developing travel cost demand models. A few such protocols would include:

Table 10.7 Description of Variables for Analysis

Name	Definition
RCS (real consumer surplus)	Marshallian consumer surplus estimated per unit of use, as measured by each study (i.e., per day or per trip) deflated by consumer price index (base = 1967)
Surtype	Qualitative variable for measure of site use = 1 for per trip measure, 0 for per day measure
Recreation site variable	Lake, river, coastal area of wetlands, forest or mountain area, developed or state park, national park with or without wilderness significance are the designations; variables are unity if satisfying designation, 0 otherwise
Substitute price	Qualitative variable = 1 if substitute price term was included in the demand specification, 0 otherwise
Opportunity cost type no. 1	Qualitative variable for measure used to estimate opportunity cost of travel time = 1 if an average wage rate was used
Opportunity cost type no. 2	Qualitative variable for the second type of opportunity costs of travel time measure = 1 if income per hour used (omitted category was predicted individual specific wage)
Fraction of wage	Fraction of wage rate used to estimate opportunity cost of travel time
Specific site	Qualitative variable for use of a state or regional travel cost model describing demand for a set of sites = 1, 0 otherwise
Demand specifications	Linear, log-linear and semilog (dep) are qualitative variables describing the specification of functional form for demand (semi-log in logs of independent variables was the omitted cateogory).
Estimators used	OLS, GLS, and ML-TRUNC are qualitative variables for estimators used, omitted categories correspond to estimators with limited representation in studies including the simultaneous equation estimators.

1. Use trips as the quantity measure where possible and attempt to segment the sample when it is known that the length of stay per trip is different.
2. Take account through sample segmentation of differences that might arise from use during different seasons or during different time periods when there may be different time or resource constraints.
3. Treat travel time as an element affecting the cost of a trip.
4. Include vehicle-related costs and the costs attributed to travel time as well as any entrance fees or site usage costs (i.e., parking costs, lift fees for skiing, etc.) in the unit cost estimated for a trip.
5. Use substitute prices to measure effects of substitute sites rather than an index of substitution; complete systems of demand functions are unnecessary if the objective is to measure demand for one of the sites.

6. Reflect quality features of the site in the demand models.
7. Recognize that heteroscedasticity is likely to be an issue with zone data and that selection effects can be important with individual data.
8. Avoid the problems posed by cost allocation issues that can arise with multiple destination trips by segmenting the sample according to the distance traveled to the site.
9. Substitute sensitivity analysis for strict adherence to one particular functional form of the demand function.

Equally important, areas exist for which there are either insufficient data or the absence of a clear consensus. These are:

1. the measurement of the opportunity cost of travel time; simple scaling of the wage rate was not found to be consistent with several of the demand studies based on individual data, yet explicit recognition of multiple prices for recreation time is generally beyond the information set available in most current studies; to date no compromise has been proposed to deal with this problem;
2. the treatment of the attributes of a site's services; and
3. the definition of a recreation site for modeling demand, especially where there are many comparable sites within a small geographic area or where there is one large "site" that extends over a wide area.

What has been missing in past assessments is some gauge of how important the decisions might be in influencing the valuation estimates that result.

From the perspective of being able to transfer valuation estimates, we would prefer that the empirical estimates of equation (11) be consistent with a maintained hypothesis that $\alpha_A = \alpha_D = \alpha_E = 0$. That is, judgmental modeling assumptions contribute to the variability in benefit estimates but do *not* impose systematic influences on the size of the benefits estimated. Of course, to the extent this is not our conclusion, then we believe the process has identified areas where further research, modeling, and data collection may be warranted.

Table 10.8 provides some descriptive statistics from the Smith-Kaoru data on the features of the studies, classified by the type of site involved. It reports the number of estimates for each type of resource, the mean and range in real consumer surplus (per unit of use) estimates, the proportion of the studies based on individual (as compared with origin zone) data, and the range of years represented in the studies. It is clear that there are exceptionally wide variations in the consumer surplus per unit of use—from under \$1 to over \$100 in five of the seven cases. Two of these have estimates over \$200. These differences could represent dramatic differences in the character of the resources in each group, in the models used, or in the characteristics of the recreationists in each sample.

Table 10.9 reports the ordinary least squares (OLS) estimates for five models which consider whether the variations in real consumer surplus across

Table 10.8 A Comparison of Travel Cost Demand Results by Type of Resource

Type of Resource	No. of Estimates	Real Consumer Surplus[a]			
		Mean	Range	PI[b]	Years[c]
River	257	$17.05	$.29–$120.70	.61	1966–83
Lake	483	16.85	.09–219.80	.55	1968–83
Forests	114	31.36	.80–129.90	.59	1968–84
National parks	12	44.01	23.48–120.70	.50	1980–83
Wetlands	9	45.86	17.45–120.70	.78	1980–83
State parks	107	42.49	.67–327.20	.07	1972–83
Coastal areas	28	35.49	.67–160.80	.61	1972–84

Source: Smith and Kaoru (1990).
[a]Real consumer surplus deflates the nominal estimates by the consumer price index (base 1967).
[b]This variable designates the proportion of the studies based on samples of individual recreationists' trip-taking decisions compared with origin zone aggregate rates of use.
[c]The range of years in which the data used in these studies were collected. Thus, this variable designates the range of years across the studies in each category in which behavior was observed.

Table 10.9 The Determinants of Real Consumer Surplus per Unit of Use

Independent Variables	Models				
	1	2	3	4	5
Intercept	23.72	16.07	20.30	27.03	18.75
	(5.62)	(2.08)	(6.19)	(3.68)	(0.58)
			[3.92]	[3.64]	[1.04]
Surtype	7.99	−4.13	−9.97	15.38	19.88
	(2.76)	(−1.45)	(−2.72)	(2.97)	(3.74)
			[−1.36]	[2.34]	[3.55]
Type of site (X_S):					
Lake	−11.70			−18.69	−20.32
	(−3.18)			(−3.24)	(−3.52)
				[−2.36]	[−2.48]
River	−5.57			−14.29	−19.03
	(−1.93)			(−2.99)	(−2.19)
				[−1.95]	[−1.75]
Forest	−.45			−18.45	−25.99
	(−.93)			(−2.36)	(−3.01)
				[−1.93]	[−2.49]
State park	19.93			24.95	22.37
	(4.44)			(3.47)	(3.44)
				[3.27]	[3.19]
National park	2.54			.56	−3.77
	(0.20)			(.04)	(−.23)
				[.08]	[−.13]
Model assumption (X_A):					
Substitute price			−18.73		−13.71
			(−3.27)		(−2.12)
			[−4.58]		[−1.80]

Table 10.9 ***(Continued)***

Independent Variables	Models 1	2	3	4	5
Opportunity cost of type no. 1			−14.97		−16.49
			(−2.10)		(−2.11)
			[−2.09]		[−2.48]
Opportunity cost of type no. 2			3.95		−15.86
			(1.02)		(−3.30)
			[.45]		[−2.87]
Fraction of wage			37.24		48.59
			(8.56)		(9.76)
			[3.83]		[6.94]
Specific site/regional TC model			22.23		24.21
			(4.10)		(3.85)
			[3.35]		[2.77]
Model specification (X_D)					
Linear		2.35			−2.87
		(.31)			(−.27)
					[−.31]
Log-linear		14.63			23.37
		(1.89)			(2.37)
					[2.88]
Semilog (dep)		11.26			16.89
		(1.52)			(1.86)
					[2.97]
Estimator (X_E):					
OLS					−14.45
					(−.48)
					[−.84]
GLS					−8.58
					(−.28)
					[−.54]
ML-TRUNC					−67.38
					(−2.15)
					[−3.43]
R^2	.11	.03	.25	.15	.42
n	722	722	399	399	399

Source: Smith and Kaoru (1990).
Note: The numbers in parentheses below the estimated parameters are the ratios of the coefficients to their estimated standard errors. The numbers in brackets are the Newey-West (1987) variant of the White (1980) consistent covariance estimates for the standard errors in calculating these ratios. Small sample properties of the White estimate are discussed by Chesher and Jewitt (1987) and MacKinnon and White (1985). While these studies raise questions with the approach for dealing with heteroscedasticity, it has not been evaluated in this more general case.

studies can be "explained" by the classes of variables hypothesized in equation (11). Models 1 and 2 in the table contain the least variables, with 1 considering only qualitative variables describing the types of recreation site and 2 variables describing the model specification. The remaining three models introduce groups of variables to illustrate the sensitivity of the estimates to the model specification, as well as to the reductions in sample size implied by these more detailed formulations. These reductions arise from the incomplete information available in the papers used to construct the Smith-Kaoru data base. Model 5 is their preferred specification.

The numbers in parentheses below the estimated coefficients are the *t*-ratios calculated with the OLS standard errors. Those in brackets below models 3–5 are the *t*-ratios using the standard errors estimated from the Newey-West (1987) proposed adaptation of the White (1980) consistent covariance matrix. They are reported to gauge whether the panel nature of these data might have influenced any judgments on the importance of variables describing the sites or the modeling decisions.

The Smith-Kaoru data set is a panel because there are a number of cases of multiple consumer surplus estimates reported from a single study. These can reflect different models estimated with data for a common recreation site, different sites and associated data, or both. Given this diversity in the source of multiple observations per study, the model does not readily conform to either a simple fixed or a random effects model. Newey and West's (1987) covariance estimator allows for a generalized form of autocorrelation and heteroscedasticity. As such, it provides a convenient gauge of the potential effects of the stochastic assumptions maintained in estimating the determinants of the real consumer surplus.

Several conclusions emerge from this statistical summary of the literature. The results clearly support the basic approach to reviewing empirical literature. The models' estimates indicate that the type of resource, the modeling assumptions, specification of the demand function, and estimator can influence the resulting real consumer surplus estimates.

For the most part, individual variables had effects consistent with a priori expectations. Nonetheless, there is at least one important aspect of the variable definitions that should be recognized. Our site classification variable is not a class of mutually exclusive categories. Some sites fall in multiple categories. For example, a state park with a lake would imply unitary values for both of these variables. The estimated coefficients must also be interpreted relative to an omitted category (coastal sites and wetlands), because all sites fell within at least one of these definitions. Thus the differential a state park with a lake would imply in per unit consumer surplus over coastal areas is about $2.00. Nearly all the variables describing modeling decisions were found to be statistically significant factors in describing the variation in real consumer surplus.

Examples of these results, that are on the one hand consistent with intuition yet also disturbing from the perspective of developing benefit estimates that are readily transferred, include the effects of the treatment of substitute price measures; the value of the opportunity costs of time; the specifications used to capture the effects of multiple sites (e.g., the regional travel cost model); the demand specification (notably the double-log form); and estimator used to account for the truncation effects present with site-intercept surveys.

Overall these findings emphasize the sources of ambiguity in demand modeling described earlier. While the Smith-Kaoru findings represent a beginning and should be interpreted cautiously, some specific areas can be targeted despite this qualification. More careful consideration is warranted of why the treatment of time costs and the selection of an estimator are so important to these valuation estimates. In the first case, the sensitivity reflects the fact that we do not know how the constraints to an individual's time affect his recreation decisions or how an individual's implicit values on time vary with the nature of his choices. Data can be sought on both issues.

Similarly, the importance of the choice of estimator probably reflects the difficult subsidiary issues involved in deciding how to deal with the sampling (Shaw 1988) and selection (Smith 1988) effects associated with intercept surveys. An effort to improve the situation through data collection would involve returning to the early population surveys (i.e., samples designed to be representative of all households, not just users) that elicited information on households' recreation choices. These surveys originally were sponsored by the Bureau of Outdoor Recreation (see Cicchetti, Seneca, and Davidson 1969). However, any new surveys would require information on the sites individuals use and their patterns of use to overcome the problems that arise in the on-site surveys. (The early BOR surveys did *not* collect this type of information.) Understanding the "market" for a recreation site lies at the heart of evaluating why substitute prices and the qualitative variable for regional travel cost models were important.

We know very little of how individuals learn about and subsequently define (for choice purposes) the recreation opportunities available to them. Decisions on the use of "local" recreation sites versus more distant "national" sites will most certainly be made with different time horizons and constraints. How are these decisions to be distinguished and can they be modeled separately? Progress in modeling recreation decisions requires answers.

The empirical models also identify an important role for the functional form selected to describe demand. The recreational demand literature has seen increasing criticism of the use of arbitrary specifications selected largely for convenience or based on some fitting criteria. Several recent studies have argued that behavioral derivations of demand models would be preferable. That is, they suggest models should begin with specific utility functions and derive estimating equations by assuming optimizing behavior and by specifying the budget and time constraints assumed to face individuals. Of course, analytical tractability constrains how these efforts can proceed.

We believe that there is not an obvious answer to the question of imposing prior theory versus using approximations. In a genuine sense, all applications are approximations. What is important is whether the way they are undertaken affects the findings in important ways. The Smith-Kaoru results indicate that greater efforts are needed in developing more robust specifications. Both enhanced data and theory will be required to meet this need.

10.5 Recommendations for Data and Analytical Development

When compared with the effort and experience devoted to the conventional topics considered under the auspices of the Conference on Income and Wealth, the record of empirical analyses of public policies for the management of environmental resources is quite limited. While there has been rapid progress in the last two decades, our ability to deliver estimates of individuals' values for a wide array of environmental resources and, a fortiori, for changes in specific aspects of resource quality lags significantly behind the expectations of current environmental statutes and the projected needs for coming to grips with emerging policy issues. We have tried to describe the sources of these demands and the clear interaction between the needs for economic *and* noneconomic information.

In what follows we propose to use three themes to organize our proposals for new data developments in support of empirical research in environmental economics: learning about natural systems, learning what we know, and responding to emerging policies. As we noted at the outset, our objective is to consider first the generic problems extending over multiple problems that require data and, second, broad classes of environmental problems that seem likely to be important policy issues in the near future. The policy orientation is deliberate. Resources for addressing data and modeling needs are scarce, and we need to consider their net returns here just as in other allocation decisions.[16]

10.5.1 Learning about Natural Systems

As we have stressed at several points, analysis of the benefits (or damages) of proposed or actual changes in the use of natural resources inevitably depends on our abilities to trace the effect of the changed use through to a change in the valuation by consumers of a resource service. This implies that we must be able to (*a*) characterize the current state of the relevant system(s); (*b*) identify a mechanism by which the change in use affects the system; (*c*) model how the change has affected (for ex post damage assessment) or will affect (for ex ante regulatory analysis) the ambient quality of the system in terms relevant to consumer valuation.

In many cases, our knowledge is deficient in every one of these categories. For example, we have a great deal of data on water quality but are generally short of information that systematically covers all the water bodies that our activities affect and that our regulations are designed to protect or enhance. Further, the available information usually covers items relevant to scientists' search for understanding of aquatic biological or chemical processes rather than those that can be related to consumer valuation (David 1971). Even so, to a large extent our abilities to model aquatic processes are inadequate. The models often do not accept as inputs discharges or give as outputs indicators of use or of resulting ambient quality relevant to policy evaluation needs.

The great need here is for data-gathering and model-building efforts to reflect the demands of policy analysis. Identifying the need is a great deal easier than meeting it, for the required interaction has all the difficulties of interdisciplinary research plus those of interstate and interagency jurisdictional disputes. Leadership from U.S. EPA and the Council of Environmental Quality is clearly needed.

10.5.2 Learning What We Know

Over a decade ago, in closing his overview of the state of the art in benefit estimation, Freeman (1979) observed that economists could advise the EPA administrator how to measure benefits from a particular pollution control policy. All that was needed were the data and learning that accompany implementation. The intervening decade has seen some positive investments in both data collection and in empirical modeling. However, we cannot be overly sanguine about what has been accomplished. For the most part, the efforts have been very specialized—relying on existing data on consumer behavior or developing special purpose contingent valuation surveys to estimate how individuals would value (or respond to) changes in very specific resources. This process has made it clear that under currently shrinking budgets (or even with modestly expanding resources), we cannot possibly estimate the values for all the resources of current interest.

The notion of evaluating the conditions for transferring estimates from one resource to another is a relative new one. It has been an important part of the practice of developing the information benefit-cost evaluations involving nonmarketed resources. Freeman (1984) distinguished top-down and bottom-up transfers, where the former attempts to allocate an aggregate benefit for a change in all of one type of resource (e.g., the share of the national benefits from a water quality improvement attributed to one site), and the latter refers to using microestimates for the household and a specific resource in other contexts and aggregating. Naughton, Parsons, and Desvousges (1991) recently considered the generic issues in performing benefit transfers at the microlevel using the pulp and paper industry. Their results suggest that a transfer-based strategy for policy analyses is desirable but may require restructuring the design of future benefit estimation studies for environmental resources.

Another possibility proposed by Mitchell and Carson (1986) involves using survey methods to obtain estimates for national improvements in an environmental resource from individual households. These estimates would then be attributed to individual areas based on the amount of the resources present in the area. The example these authors used involved water quality improvements, and comparison of their approach with the results from a separate contingent valuation indicated a fairly close correspondence between the estimates derived from a specific survey and those from their national survey adjusted with their proposed proportioning method. At this stage, however, the literature is very preliminary. There has been no attempt to develop how the tasks involved in deriving transferable models are related to the factors (i.e., household and resource characteristics) affecting the variation in benefit estimates across resources and user groups.

First, we must learn what we know from experiences to date, and then we must proceed to identify what we need to learn. There is a long tradition in resource economics involving attempts to develop consensus practices in benefit-cost analysis and even specifying benchmark valuation estimates for resource services most closely aligned with water resource projects. These attempts were traditionally associated with the Water Resources Council. Our suggestion here is that we should extend these efforts to the valuation estimates for all environmental resources and thereby move beyond a judgment-based, single value for each type of resource service.

By treating the existing set of estimates for changes in the quantities or qualities of environmental resources as data, it is possible to develop a systematic appraisal of whether the state of the art has advanced to the point where we can associate variations in estimates with differences in the procedures used or with features of the resources (or consumers) involved. This process should identify the areas with greatest uncertainty.

The experience with the Smith-Kaoru pilot study of travel cost demand studies suggests that a more systematic approach, contacting authors to fill in missing details, is essential if a reasonably adequate data base is to be developed in areas in which there has been less research activity. Such efforts would also promote the development of statistical methods for dealing with the unique features of "panel" data sets composed from existing empirical studies.

10.5.3 Emerging Policy Needs

We have classified our views of the emerging policy needs into four categories and now consider each in turn.

1. Environmental Risk

This is one of the most difficult areas for current uses of economic analysis, especially because it appears that individuals' responses to a wide range of environmental risks do not conform to our conventional characterization of rational behavior. A recent EPA publication (see U.S. EPA 1987a) has highlighted just how dramatically inconsistent are public concerns and the rankings of environmental risks based on expert opinion (U.S. EPA 1987b). A comprehensive program of data acquisition and research is needed to determine how and why households value reductions in these types of risks more highly than other sources that often have greater likelihoods of serious effects.

This type of analysis will be important to the design of information programs associated with pollutants EPA does not currently regulate, such as radon, and to the development of labeling standards for products for which they do have responsibility. It is also likely to play a central role in defining "clean" for Superfund sites, in establishing priorities for policy initiatives involving monitoring the underground storage tanks, and in devising new policies associated with more stringent drinking water standards.

2. Air Quality

Acid deposition is hardly "emerging" as an issue; rather the reverse. But that is not because the scientific questions have been answered and the problems have been solved. Indeed, there is still debate in the scientific literature over the relative contribution of different compounds and source locations to observed low pH precipitation, fog, and dry acidic deposition. Under these circumstances, benefit estimation linked to a discharge-reduction policy cannot proceed to meaningful results. So a clear need is for further research into long-run atmospheric transport and chemical transformation processes, with the ultimate aim of allowing predictions of the form: If we reduce sulfur dioxide (SO_2) discharges in this region by this much, average pH of precipitation in this other region will increase by this much.

Even then we shall still be several steps from successful benefit estimation for a policy of SO_2 reduction. It must be possible to extend predictive natural system models to such issues as the link between average annual (or season-specific) precipitation, pH, and soil quality to vegetation health and growth, and to aquatic ecological system functions. For example, if we reduce SO_2 discharge in the Middle West, will New England and New York lakes and ponds have better fish populations (more and larger fish of more highly valued species)?

Only with those tools in hand will it be possible for economists to produce meaningful benefit estimates for the sorts of policies that are regularly debated in the Congress. To prepare for that day, the problems of benefit (or damage) function transfer must be addressed in this problem setting. In particular, it is necessary to consider how best to use the results of national studies on the one hand (e.g., Vaughan and Russell 1982) and local studies on the other (e.g., Smith and Desvousges 1986) to value *regional* effects.

A second air quality issue with even larger potential economic implications is ground-level ozone and particularly the value of trying to attain the currently mandated National Ambient Air Quality Standards for that secondary pollutant.[17] Here it is necessary to improve our knowledge of (a) the sources and actual levels of the precursor pollutants (especially volatile organic compounds [VOCS]), of ground-level ozone in urban and rural areas; (b) the morbidity effects of different levels of ozone; (c) the effects of ozone on vegetation and a variety of materials such as paints, plastics, and synthetic rubbers. Our estimates of the damages attributable to days of sickness of various types and severities must be refined. Moreover, theoretically consistent but practically implementable ways of measuring the value of damage to materials providing services to households, businesses, and governments must be developed.

3. Water Quality

One of the key policy initiatives in water quality will be associated with the national estuarine program. For point sources of waterborne pollution, the first round of effluent guidelines will be in place with over 30 regulations promulgated. All should be in place by the early 1990s. The future here is best characterized as one requiring extensions in the ability of economic valuation to realize greater degrees of resolution in valuing small changes in pollutants.

Present methods and data would not permit such evaluations. Clearly an improved understanding of the linkage between the technical dimensions of water quality and individuals' perceptions of and corresponding valuations for that quality will be necessary (David 1971).

Nonpoint sources, especially agricultural runoff of pesticides and fertilizers to surface waters, represent the largest unregulated source of water pollutants. Presently, EPA does not have authority to regulate these sources. However, recent opportunities to coordinate the selection of areas for the Department of Agriculture's Conservation Reserve Program, based on the effects of pollutants on water resources, expose a new area for economic valuation. Can we set priorities for the selection of lands for inclusion in this system based on their contributions to nonpoint source pollution? To answer this question we need both economic and noneconomic data. Agriculture has been wiling to pay premia over normal reserve payments for withholding lands that might otherwise contribute to impairing significant environmental resources.

4. Stock Pollutants and Global Climate Change

This last area is fundamentally different than the first three emerging issues we discussed in that the policy time horizon is long-term and extends over several decades. While not a new issue (Revelle 1985 suggested that it was identified over 100 years ago), it has achieved a more prominent role on the policy agenda with the Global Climate Protection Act of 1987. This legislation assigns to EPA the responsibility of summarizing the scientific understanding of the greenhouse effect (i.e., the role of the accumulation of carbon dioxide, chlorofluorocarbons, methane, and other trace gases in the upper atmosphere in increasing the average surface temperatures on earth) and in enumerating the policies available for stabilizing these concentrations.

As in our other examples, a key need in this area is for greater understanding of the natural system. In this case it is the link between these atmospheric gases and the extent and timing of any global warming, as well as of the implications of that global warming for regional weather patterns. This issue raises some distinct methodological needs because of the extent of scientific uncertainty over these questions, the time horizon for the potential climatic changes, and the irreversibility of the process.

The requirements for economic information depend, in part, on the progress made in improving our understanding of the natural system. As this proceeds, there is a clear need to understand the processes by which economic activities adapt and the institutions that facilitate such adjustment. Historical and cross-cultural analyses may well offer the only means for developing such insights. Equally important, there is a fundamental need to describe the inherent uncertainties in a way that is genuinely informative for policy. While not unique to this problem, this issue of communicating the inherent uncertainties remains one of the most significant problems facing economists involved in environmental policy.

Finally, in evaluating these data and modeling needs as compared with other data priorities, it is important to recognize that in contrast to positive uses of economic analysis where a lack of data may prevent decisions from being made, this is *not* the case in normative applications. *Decisions are made regardless of whether the economic information is available.* In some cases they are very bad ones. Consequently, here new data developments represent opportunities to improve the quality of decisions and the resource allocations affected by them.

Appendix

Calculating Surrogate Benefits Based on the Baltimore and Delaware River Environmental Quality Projections

Air Quality Surrogate Benefits

Oates, Portney, and McGartland (1989) reproduce their atmospheric model's projected patterns of total suspended particulate concentrations for 23 receptor locations in Baltimore for two alternative implementation approaches. We used and reproduce their table 2 here as table 10A.1. (We ignore their results for 83 micrograms/m^3, ug/m^3.) We follow them in taking the pattern associated with the 120 ug/m^3 standard as our base situation.

While Oates et al. (1989) describe the basis for their damage, and hence benefit estimates, they did not provide the functions they used. However, it turns out that a surrogate function that reproduces the pattern of their margi-

Table 10A.1 **TSP Concentrations by Receptor: Least-Cost Case**

Receptor Location	120	115	110	105	100	95	90	85
1	67.8	67.4	66.2	66.0	65.3	63.7	61.6	59.3
2	64.6	63.7	62.2	61.8	60.9	58.7	55.5	51.7
3	56.2	56.0	55.5	55.5	55.3	54.6	53.7	52.5
4	85.4	83.9	81.2	78.7	76.8	73.7	70.9	68.1[a]
5	94.3	92.5	89.0	86.2	83.8	80.5	76.9[a]	73.5[a]
6	107.2	102.6	99.7	97.9[a]	95.0[a]	90.7[a]	85.7[a]	80.8[a]
7	116.3	113.8[a]	107.8[a]	104.3[a]	100.0[a]	95.5[a]	90.0[a]	85.0[a]
8	93.3	88.7	86.1	84.4	81.6	75.6	69.9[a]	63.5[a]
9	119.7	115.3[a]	110.4[a]	105.5[a]	100.0[a]	95.2[a]	89.5[a]	84.7[a]
10	52.4	51.6	49.1	47.5	46.0	43.4	40.9	38.2
11	80.2	78.4	77.4	72.0	70.1	68.8	65.7	63.5
12	102.8	101.1	91.9	88.6	84.3[a]	79.7[a]	74.5[a]	69.2[a]
13	61.6	60.8	58.9	57.5	56.0	53.9	51.4	49.2
14	53.3	52.8	51.8	51.2	50.6	49.4	48.1	46.4
15	120.0	114.9[a]	110.4[a]	101.0[a]	99.6[a]	93.0[a]	79.5[a]	53.3[a]
16	56.4	56.4	55.3	55.1	54.3	52.9	52.2	50.9
17	72.4	69.9	66.5	65.1	63.5	59.4	53.1	43.3
18	84.9	84.0	74.9	74.2	73.0	66.4	62.5	55.9
19	51.6	51.4	50.8	50.5	50.1	49.3	48.3	47.3
20	67.3	66.1	64.4	63.3	62.1	60.0	57.5	54.4
21	64.0	63.6	61.2	60.8	60.0	57.1	55.0	52.0
22	64.6	64.3	62.0	61.8	59.7	56.5	55.4	53.1
23	105.3	102.8	98.9	97.7[a]	95.1[a]	90.4[a]	83.8[a]	74.1[a]
Unweighted averages of receptor TSP levels:								
	80.1	78.3	75.3	73.3	71.4	68.2	64.4	59.6
Population-weighted averages of receptor TSP levels:								
	77.4	75.7	72.9	70.9	69.0	66.2	62.9	59.3

Source: Oates, Portney, and McGartland (1989).
[a]Concentration reflected in the calculation of benefits using method (ii).

nal benefits is easy to find. We used a simple quadratic damage surrogate. That is:

(A1) $$G_i = \text{damage at receptor } i = [\text{TSP ppm}]^2 \times 10^3 \text{ (in millions)}.$$

Benefits of increasingly strict standards are then simply

(A2) $$B_i = G_i\,(120) - G_i(j) \quad \text{for } j < 120 \text{ ug/m}^3.$$

We reproduce here, as table 10A.2, a sample calculation of the damages and benefits for six receptor locations, one standard, and three methods. Inspection of table 10A.1 reveals immediately that method (i) yields an estimate

Table 10A.2 **Examples of Surrogate Damage and Benefit Calculations by Method**

		Method (i) (Modified)		Method (ii)		Method (iii′)	
Receptor	Damages at Base Level	Damages at 110	Benefits	Damages at 110	Benefits	Damages at 110	Benefits
2	4.2			4.2	0	3.9	0.3
7	13.5			12.1	1.4	11.6	1.9
10	2.7			2.7	0	2.4	0.3
12	10.6			10.6	0	8.4	2.2
15	14.4			12.1	2.3	12.1	2.3
18	7.2			7.2	0	5.6	1.6
For average level:	6.4	5.4	1.03 × 23				
Total			23.6		6.0		19.7
Marginal			11.4		3.4		12.0

Note: For modified method (i), base average surrogate damages = damages at the base average concentration, 80.1. Damages at the 110 standard = damages calculated for an average concentration of 80.1 × 110/120 = 73.4. Total damages for every standard are obtained by multiplying the damage associated with the average by 23 (receptors).

of zero benefits for all standards, since the initial average quality is already better than the strictest standard to be examined.

Water Quality Benefits

Water quality benefits are based on predicted water quality improvements in the Delaware estuary published in Spofford, Russell, and Kelley (1976). The quality indicator used is dissolved oxygen (DO) and the base levels are interpolated from their figure 2 reproduced here as figure 10A.1. Improvements associated with alternative standards are taken from table C-3 in the source. Their run, using a 3.0 ppm standard, is used here as a surrogate for a 3.5 ppm standard because in all but one reach, better than 3.5 ppm is attained under it. The predicted levels of DO for that standard and for a run with a 5.0 ppm standard are set out in table 10A.3. The implementation plan implicit in these runs is the least-cost arrangement of discharge reductions.

To calculate benefits, dissolved oxygen is translated into sustainable recreation activities using the table of equivalents developed by Vaughan (1981) and displayed here schematically as table 10A.4. Then the three alternative methods of benefit calculation were applied as summarized in table 10A.5, where the per capita per day values of the alternative sustainable activity measures of quality are drawn from (Smith and Desvousges 1986).

What we have not done is to associate numbers of people with particular receptor locations along the river. ("Receptor location" is usually called "reach" in the water pollution field. It means a stretch of river within which ambient quality is assumed the same.) This is difficult to do in any case without a study to measure the recreational suitability as determined by nonwater

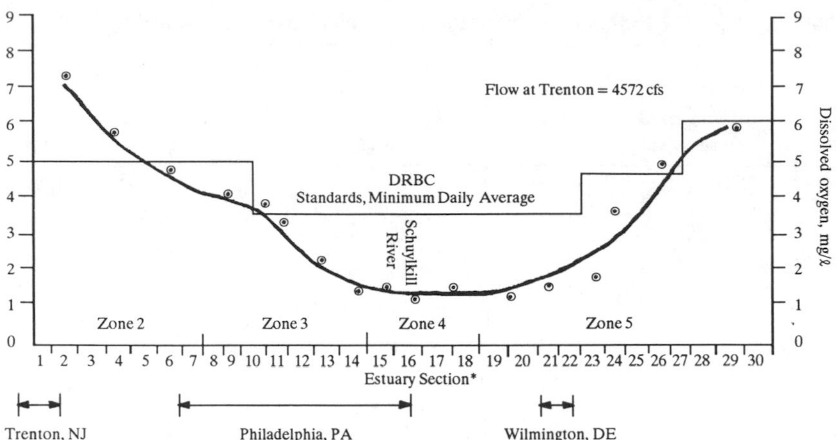

Fig. 10A.1 Delaware Estuary dissolved oxygen profile: July to September 1968
Source: Delaware River Basin Commission, "Final Progress Report: Delaware Estuary and Bay Water Quality Sampling and Mathematical Modeling Project," May 1970, figure 12.
Notes: *Delaware River Basin Commission sections. Note that these section designations differ from the ones in the RFF Study. "—": predicted by the DRBC's Delaware Estuary Model. " ⊙ ": mean of measurements for the three-month period (July, August, September 1968).

quality characteristics. But it is even more difficult to do within a massive urbanized agglomeration such as that which surrounds the Delaware estuary from Wilmington, Delaware, to Trenton, New Jersey. The figures in table 10.5 are therefore simply the sums of the relevant per capita benefits over all the reaches. These figures exaggerate the penalty for ignorance of the environment to the extent that more individuals could easily travel to and recreate on the middle reaches. They are the most heavily polluted, and therefore benefits associated with their cleanup show up in methods (i) and (ii), while any benefits associated with further cleanup of the most upstream and most downstream reaches tend to be ignored in those methods.

Note that the use of Vaughan's equivalence in essence begs an important question: Do we have an environmental quality indicator that is connectable both to discharges and to valued human uses of the environment? Dissolved oxygen is only one of the elements of a vector of water quality characteristics that determine how a body of water can be used. It may be the key element for fish populations but is certainly much less important in determining whether water is "boatable" (that is to say, pleasant to boat on) or swimable (where bacterial counts or turbidity are much more important).

Notes

1. To say that the analysis is difficult (and expensive) is not to say that it is of dubious value. The U.S. Environmental Protection Agency's (1987a) review of its use

Table 10A.3 **Base Case and Predicted Levels of Dissolved Oxygen: Two Alternative Standards Applied to the Delaware Estuary (ppm)**

Reach	Base Situation	3.5 ppm Standard	5.0 ppm Standard
1	8.3	8.6	8.6
2	7.0	7.7	7.7
3	5.6	6.6	6.9
4	4.9	6.0	6.3
5	4.6	5.7	5.9
6	4.4	5.9	6.0
7	3.8	5.9	5.9
8	2.7	5.8	5.9
9	1.8	6.1	6.4
10	1.3	5.3	6.8
11	1.2	3.6	5.3
12	1.2	3.7	6.1
13	1.3	3.6	5.7
14	1.5	4.0	5.7
15	1.8	4.5	6.1
16	2.3	5.2	6.4
17	2.8	3.0[a]	5.0
18	3.5	3.7	5.1
19	4.2	4.8	5.7
20	5.0	5.8	6.1
21	5.8	6.2	6.2
22	6.6	6.6	6.6
Average	3.7	Standard 3.5	Standard 5.0

Source: Spofford, Russell, and Kelley (1976).
[a]The standard actually imposed by Spofford, Russell, and Kelley (1976) was 3.0 ppm. But 3.5 is a lower bound for boatable quality water in the Vaughan scale, so we treat this run as though the standard were 3.5 for purposes of method (ii) calculations.

Table 10A.4 **Water Quality, Recreational Activities, and Associated Willingness to Pay**

DO ppm	Sustainable Activity[a]	Shorthand	Associated Annual Marginal Willingness to Pay per Person ($)[b]
7.0	Swimable (plus fishing and boating)	S	35.4
6.5			
6.0			
5.5	Game fishable (plus boating)	G	19.1
5.0			
4.5	Boatable	B	20.5
4.0			
3.5			
	Unacceptable for boating	U	0

[a]*Source*: Vaughan (1981).
[b]*Source*: Smith and Desvousges (1986).

Table 10A.5 **Calculating Surrogate Benefits for Dissolved Oxygen Improvements in the Delaware Estuary by Method**

A. Method (i)

Base Case Average:	3.7 ppm (B)	
3.5 ppm Standard:	3.5 ppm (B)	Benefit = 0 × 22 = 0
5.0 ppm Standard:	5.0 ppm (G)	Benefit = \$19.1 × 22 = 420.6

B.

	Methods (ii) and (iii)	Marginal Benefits Method (ii)		Marginal Benefits Method (iii)	
Reach	Base Case Sustainable Use	3.5 Standard	5.0 Standard	3.5 Standard	5.0 Standard
1	S	—	—	—	—
2	S	—	—	—	—
3	G	—	—	S (35.4)	—
4	B	—	G (19.1)	G (19.1)	—
5	B	—	G (19.1)	G (19.1)	—
6	B	—	G (19.1)	G (19.1)	—
7	B	—	G (19.1)	G (19.1)	—
8	U	B (20.5)	G (19.1)	G (39.6)	—
9	U	B (20.5)	G (19.1)	G (39.6)	—
10	U	B (20.5)	G (19.1)	G (39.6)	S (35.4)
11	U	B (20.5)	G (19.1)	B (20.5)	G (19.1)
12	U	B (20.5)	G (19.1)	B (20.5)	G (19.1)
13	U	B (20.5)	G (19.1)	B (20.5)	G (19.1)
14	U	B (20.5)	G (19.1)	B (20.5)	G (19.1)
15	U	B (20.5)	G (19.1)	B (20.5)	G (19.1)
16	U	B (20.5)	G (19.1)	G (39.6)	—
17	U	U	G (39.6)	U	G (39.6)
18	B	—	G (19.1)	—	G (19.1)
19	B	—	G (19.1)	—	G (19.1)
20	G	—	—	—	—
21	G	—	—	—	—
22	S	—	—	—	—
Totals		184.5	326.1	372.7	208.7

Note: A dash (—) indicates no improvement in sustainable recreational use over the next lower standard or over the base case as appropriate. S = swimable; G = game fishable; B = boatable; U = unacceptable for boating.

of benefit-cost (B-C) analysis concludes that for three regulatory decisions, B-C analysis identified improvements with potential benefits of over \$10 billion (lead in automotive fuels, \$6.7 billion; used lubricating oil, \$3.6 billion; and premanufacturing review of toxic substances, \$.04 billion). Further, EPA estimates the costs of all regulatory impact analyses (RIAs) done under the terms of President Reagan's Executive Order 12291 as less than \$10 million. Therefore, the return to analytical investment appears to be over 1,000 to 1 in the aggregate.

Several cautions are in order in interpreting this conclusion. Most fundamentally, our argument in this paper, if one accepts it, must inevitably throw some doubt on these benefit estimates. Second, we cannot necessarily project such a return ratio in the future because it is likely that the biggest and easiest targets have already been attacked. And finally, we should include a grain of salt because the self-interest of those preparing the report was consistent with finding large returns.

2. This statutory requirement has not prevented benefit cost information from being included in the RIAs prepared for cases involving the primary standards. The proposed standard subjected to analysis is health based. It is too early to know whether the final standard that emerges after OMB review can be argued to have been affected by the benefit-cost findings.

3. Location is, of course, three dimensional, and altitude can make a big difference in some situations; but the points we make are only reinforced by considering a third dimension, while exposition is much simpler for two.

4. This last point is stressed by Oates, Portney, and McGartland (1989). We shall return to it below.

5. Our discussion assumes that producers will in fact comply with the regulations in question. Making sure this is even roughly the case requires investment in monitoring and enforcement. These costs should be counted as costs of the policy, and their amount and how they are used will help determine the realized level of benefits. It is also true that choices open in the design of implementation systems can affect monitoring and enforcement costs and thus also indirectly affect benefits by that route. We ignore these added complications, though they open up an entirely new and largely unexplored source of demand for data and analysis.

6. Reasonably straightforward theoretical expositions are available that include differential location. See, e.g., Førsund (1972), Tietenberg (1978), and Siebert (1985).

7. The matrix T may be thought of as representing the steady-state solution to a set of differential equations that reflects the transportation of pollution by average winds characterized by velocities and directions, and the diffusion of the pollution particles due to random motion in the plume. If the units of discharge are, say (average) tons per day, the units of the elements of T could be (average) micrograms per cubic meter.

8. For simplicity, it is assumed that the same damage relation applies at each receptor location, though as just stressed, we would expect the damages for a given pollutant concentration to differ across the various points in the regional space.

9. Here we calculate $\{Q\}$ on the basis of D_O and T, but for the argument that follows, it is important to note that baseline ambient quality is actually realized and therefore can be measured. Thus, there is no inconsistency in assuming knowledge of $\{Q\}$ and ignorance of T. As a practical matter, however, we may very well be ignorant of $\{Q\}$ in any but the loosest, one might say anecdotal, sense. See, e.g., Russell, Vaughan, and Feng (1983). To be useful, our knowledge of ambient quality conditions must be reflected in measurements that are (1) meaningful in terms of their links with or effects on human valuation of environmental services, and (2) connectable to pollution discharges that will have to be altered to change ambient quality. We return to this matter of baseline quality in the final section.

10. The actual patterns of ambient quality produced by the rollback implementation method under the baseline and the alternative standards are:

Receptor	Base	S_8	S_4	S_u	S_2
I	10	8.0	6.0	4.0	2.0
II	8	6.4[a]	4.8	3.2	1.6
III	6	4.8[a]	3.6[a]	1.6	1.2

Superscript "a" indicates a quality level not reflected at all in benefit calculation (ii).

11. It should be emphasized that there is no reason to expect a mathematically desirable—or even smooth—pattern for marginal benefits. The complex relation among standard, discharge reduction amounts and location required under a given implemen-

tation method, and resulting pattern of ambient quality changes, can produce virtually any pattern of marginal benefits.

12. For a description of efforts to use natural world models in water quality benefit estimation, although some of the threshold aspects of the B^2 method are still used, see Vaughan and Russell (1982).

13. This section is based on research undertaken by Yoshiaki Kaoru and Smith and is reported in more detail in Smith and Kaoru (1990).

14. See Mitchell and Carson (1989) for an overview of the issues involved in using these methods.

15. This approach is not completely new to economics. Berndt's (1976) early attempt to reconcile the diverse estimates of elasticities of substitution between capital and labor is similar to our objectives. However, in his case, the focus was on the assumptions inherent in the estimation models and their likely implications for the estimates. Somewhat more closely aligned is the Hazilla-Kopp (1986) summary of their findings on the sensitivity of the characterization of substitution possibilities across different modeling decisions made with the 36 different manufacturing sectors they analyzed. In this case, the analysis parallels what we propose, but their objective was to summarize their own findings, rather than detect sources of differences across studies conducted by different individuals.

16. Thanks are due to Tom Tietenberg for suggesting that we make this point more explicit.

17. Ozone is "secondary" because it is formed in the atmosphere from chemical reactions involving sunlight and certain "primary" or discharged pollutants, especially volatile organic compounds such as gasoline, solvents, and oxides of nitrogen.

References

Baumol, William J., and Wallace E. Oates. 1975. *The Theory of Environmental Policy.* Englewood Cliffs, N.J.: Prentice Hall.

Berndt, Ernst R. 1976. Reconciling Alternative Estimates of the Elasticity of Substitution. *Review of Economics and Statistics* 58 (February): 59–69.

Bockstael, Nancy E., W. Michael Hanemann, and Ivar E. Strand, Jr. 1987. *Measuring the Benefits of Water Quality Improvements Using Recreation Demand Models,* vol. 2. University of Maryland, Department of Agricultural and Resource Economics.

Chesher, Andrew, and Ian Jewitt. 1987. The Bias of a Heteroskedasticity Consistent Covariance Matrix Estimator. *Econometrica* 55 (September): 1217–22.

Cicchetti, Charles J., Joseph J. Seneca, and Paul Davidson. 1969. *The Demand and Supply of Outdoor Recreation.* New Brunswick, N.J.: Rutgers University, Bureau of Economic Research.

David, Elizabeth L. 1971. Public Perception of Water Quality. *Water Resources Research* 7 (June): 453–57.

Du Mouchel, William, and Jeffery E. Harris. 1983. Bayes Methods for Combining the Results of Cancer Studies in Humans and Other Species. *Journal of the American Statistical Association* 78 (June): 293–308.

Fisher, Anthony C. 1981. *Resource and Environmental Economics.* Cambridge: Cambridge University Press.

Førsund, Finn R. 1972. Allocation in Space and Environmental Pollution. *Swedish Journal of Economics* 74:19–34.

Freeman, A. Myrick, III. 1979. *The Benefits of Environmental Improvement: Theory and Practice.* Baltimore: Johns Hopkins University Press.

———. 1983. *Air and Water Pollution Control: A Benefit-Cost Assessment.* New York: Wiley.

———. 1984. On the Tactics of Benefit Estimation under Executive Order 12291. In *Environmental Policy Under Reagan's Executive Order,* ed. V. Kerry Smith. Chapel Hill: University of North Carolina Press.

Hazilla, Michael, and Raymond J. Kopp. 1986. Systematic Effects of Capital Service Price Definition on Perceptions of Input Substitution. *Journal of Business and Economic Statistics* 4 (April): 209–24.

Liroff, Richard. 1986. *Reforming Air Pollution Regulation.* Washington, D.C.: Conservation Foundation.

MacKinnon, James G., and Halbert White. 1985. Some Heteroskedasticity Consistent Covariance Matrix Estimators with Improved Finite Sample Properties. *Journal of Econometrics* 29:305–25.

Math-Tech, Inc. 1982. *Benefits Analysis of Alternative Secondary National Ambient Air Quality Standards for Sulfur Dioxide and Total Suspended Particulates,* vol. 2. Report to the U.S. Environmental Protection Agency. Research Triangle Park, N.C.: Office of Air Quality Planning and Standards, EPA, August.

Mitchell, Robert Cameron, and Richard T. Carson. 1986. The Use of the Contingent Valuation Data for Benefit/Cost Analysis in Water Pollution Control. Report to U.S. Environmental Protection Agency, Resources for the Future, September.

———. 1989. *Using Surveys to Value Public Goods: The Contingent Valuation Method.* Washington, D.C.: Resources for the Future.

Naughton, Michael C., George R. Parsons, and William H. Desvousges. 1991. Benefits Transfer: Conceptual Problems in Estimating Water Quality Benefits Using Existing Studies. *Water Resources Research,* forthcoming.

Newey, Whitney K., and Kenneth D. West. 1987. A Simple, Positive Semi-definite, Heteroscedasticity and Autocorrelation Consistent Covariance Matrix. *Econometrica* 55 (May): 703–8.

Oates, Wallace E., Paul R. Portney, and Albert M. McGartland. 1989. The *Net* Benefits of Incentive-based Regulation: A Case Study of Environmental Standard Setting. *American Economic Review* 79, no. 5 (December): 1233–42.

Portney, Paul R. 1984. The Benefits and Costs of Regulatory Analysis. In V. Kerry Smith, editor, *Environmental Policy Under Reagan's Executive Order: The Role of Benefit-Cost Analysis,* ed. V. Kerry Smith. Chapel Hill: University of North Carolina Press.

Revelle, Roger. 1985. The Scientific History of Carbon Dioxide. In *The Carbon Cycle and Atmospheric CO_2: Natural Variations Archean to Present,* ed. E. T. Sundquist and W. S. Broecker. Washington, D.C.: American Geophysical Union.

Richmond, Harvey. 1983. Criteria for Specifying Alternative Primary Standards. Memorandum. Ambient Standards Branch, U.S. Environmental Protection Agency, May 3.

Russell, Clifford, William J. Vaughan, and Therese Feng. 1983. The Potential for Application in Benefit Measurement. In *Marine Ecosystem Modeling,* ed. K. W. Turgeon. Washington, D.C.: U.S. Department of Commerce, National Oceanic and Atmospheric Agency.

Shaw, Daigee. 1988. On-Site Samples Regression: Problems of Non-negative Integers, Truncation and Endogenous Stratification. *Journal of Econometrics* 37 (February): 221–24.

Siebert, Horst. 1985. Spatial Aspects of Environmental Economics. In *Handbook of Natural Resource and Energy Economics,* ed. A. V. Kneese and James L. Sweeney. New York: North Holland.

Smith, V. Kerry. 1988. Selection and Recreation Demand. *American Journal of Agricultural Economics* 70 (February): 29–36.

———, ed. 1984. *Environmental Policy under Reagan's Executive Order: The Role of Benefit-Cost Analysis*. Chapel Hill: University of North Carolina Press.

Smith, V. Kerry, and William H. Desvousges. 1986.; *Measuring Water Quality Benefits*. Boston: Kluwer Nijhoff.

Smith, V. Kerry, and Yoshiaki Kaoru. 1987. Recreation Benefits Transfer Project. Third Quarterly Report to U.S. Environmental Protection Agency, July 17.

———. 1990. Signals or Noise? Explaining the Variation in Recreation Benefit Estimates. *American Journal of Agricultural Economics* (May): 420–33.

Spofford, W. O., Jr., C. S. Russell and R. A. Kelley. 1976. *Environmental Quality Management: An Application to the Lower Delaware Valley.* Washington, D.C.: Resources for the Future.

Tietenberg, Thomas H. 1978. Spatially Differentiated Air Pollutant Emission Charges: An Economic and Legal Analysis. *Land Economics* 54:265–77.

U.S. Environmental Protection Agency. 1987a. *EPA's Use of Benefit-Cost Analysis: 1981–1986*. Washington, D.C.: Office of Policy Planning and Evaluation.

———. 1987b. *Unfinished Business: A Comparative Assessment of Environmental Problems*. Washington, D.C.: U.S. Environmental Protection Agency, February.

Vaughan, William J. 1981. The Water Quality Ladder. Appendix 2 In *An Experiment in Determining Willingness to Pay for National Water Quality Improvements,* by Robert Cameron Mitchell and Richard T. Carson. Draft report to U.S. Environmental Protection Agency, Washington, D.C., Resources for the Future.

Vaughan, William J., and Clifford S. Russell. 1982. *Freshwater Recreational Fishing*. Washington, D.C.: Resources for the Future.

Ward, Frank A., and John B. Loomis. 1986. The Travel Cost Demand Model as an Environmental Policy Assessment Tool: A Review of Literature. *Western Journal of Agricultural Economics* 2 (December): 164–78.

White, Halbert. 1980. A Heteroskedasticity-Consistent Covariance Matrix Estimator and a Direct Test for Heteroskedasticity. *Econometrica* 48:817–83.

Comment Thomas H. Tietenberg

This is a pioneering paper in the field. Very few authors have taken on the awesome responsibility of assessing the state of the art in data availability for supporting environmental policy. Pioneering papers written by top-notch scholars, such as Russell and Smith, are exciting for the new insights they offer and the possibilities for further research that they uncover. They are also a bit frustrating because they serve to open our eyes to how far we are from complete understanding of the most rational course of action for the future.

In investigating data needs for environmental policy, economists are confronted with problems above and beyond those faced by those collecting data for more conventional purposes. Not only are data on natural systems essential, a point made with appropriate force and clarity in the Russell-Smith paper, but also substantial and vocal opposition inevitably arises whenever the idea of putting a price tag on certain aspects of the environment is discussed.

Thomas H. Tietenberg is Christian A. Johnson Distinguished Teaching Professor of economics at Colby College.

The very idea of monetizing our relationship with nature debases that relationship in the eyes of many activists in the area. The fact that much, if not most, of the environmental legislation specifically excludes benefit information from the standard-setting process reveals that this is no backwater view held by a few. In short, we continuously find it necessary to defend vigorously the objective of data collection, not merely to devote more time to thinking up better data to collect.

There is much to admire in this paper and I shall single out some areas for special attention. It represents an inductive approach to setting priorities; Russell and Smith review what has been done as a means of identifying the holes. By drawing upon their considerable experience in empirical environmental policy analysis, the authors are able to isolate some areas where the data needs are apparent. Their conclusions are reasonable and helpful.

Yet I could not help feeling that a deductive approach, perhaps as a complement to their analysis rather than as a substitute, would have been helpful. Such an approach would have set some broad goals for data collection and modeling and then sought to derive priorities from these goals. Motivated by this feeling that a deductive approach has merit and could generate some insights that would be overlooked by an inductive approach, let me briefly explore this idea.

A very simple economics of information model provides the framework for my critique. Information is a scarce commodity and increasing its supply is expensive. Efficient management of information is a corollary to the efficient design of environmental policy. Efficiency is achieved when the value of the marginal dollar spent on data collection and model building is equal to the marginal cost.

The first point suggested by this model is not likely to be a popular one with this audience. *It is not obvious that economists can in general be counted upon to recommend an amount of data collection that would conform to the efficiency condition.* At this kind of conference economists have an understandable bias toward calling for more and better data and being somewhat less sensitive to the costs of this commodity than would be normal for other commodities. Our ability to make unique contributions to policy debates frequently hinges crucially on our ability to back up our arguments with empirical results. Add the realization that we do not directly pay the bill for the requested data makes the urge for more data almost irresistable. To their credit Russell and Smith have not fallen into this trap. At least they have not completely fallen into this trap.

I would like to share with you a few other implications of applying this simple economics of information model to the problem at hand—deducing the needs for improving the data available to assist in creasing more efficient environmental policy. In many, but not all, cases these insights support the conclusions reached in the Russell-Smith paper.

Where should resources be committed first? Recognizing the existence of a budget constraint, what principles should be used to prioritize data collection expenditures? Russell and Smith focus most of their paper on the need for better data collection to support improved benefit estimates to be used in standard setting. In the beginning of their paper they do not really distinguish between data needs for setting *discharge* standards and data needs for setting *ambient* standards.

The economics of information model suggests that *data collected to support the setting of ambient air quality standards probably produces a higher value than data collected in support of setting discharge standards*. The value of additional data is largely determined by its contribution to improved policy. Since the EPA's Emissions Trading Program creates a pressure toward cost-effective air-pollutant discharge standards even when the decisions of the regulatory authority are based on limited or poor information, better data contributes little to this particular standard-setting process.

Why this particular regulatory program has such a remarkable capacity to produce more cost-effective outcomes in the face of limited information is not difficult to understand. Setting standards for each discharge point where air pollutants are emitted is a very difficult task for the regulator. Ideally control costs would play a role in setting these standards, but as a practical matter this is rarely done. The regulatory simply do not possess the requisite amount of information. To compensate for this lack of information, under the Emissions Trading Program the EPA allows various sources to trade control responsibility among themselves, as long as air quality is improved (or at least not degraded) by the trade. Mechanically this is accomplished by certifying any emission reduction that exceeds legal requirements as an "emission reduction credit." This credit then becomes completely transferable and can be used to satisfy the legal requirements at another, presumably more expensive to control, discharge point.

The power of this approach is derived from the fact that individual polluters have very good information on the menu of control options at their disposal, but the regulators do not. This system provides the incentive for those who have the information to use it in socially productive ways, eliminating the need to transfer that information from plant managers to regulators. As is well known, there is every reason to believe that any transferred information would be biased anyway, since regulatory outcomes would be based on it. In the Emissions Trading Program the responsibility for choosing the best outcome was transferred to those with the best knowledge as an alternative to generating more data for the regulators.

While this is a powerful argument against devoting large amounts of resources to better define *discharge* standards, it does not apply to the process for setting *ambient* standards. Since no corresponding market-type process exists for assuring the desirability of the ambient standards, data collection and modeling efforts aimed at improving ambient standards are likely to have a much higher payoff, in terms of improved outcomes, than efforts directed at improving discharge standards.

Not all ambient standards are equally deserving of enhanced data collection efforts. While it is not my intention to lay out before you which ones are the most deserving (the fact that I do not know probably has something to do with my reluctance), a few of the variables that would enter that analysis can be identified, and merely identifying them raises some interesting questions.

For ambient standards the benefits are a function of the magnitude of the individual damage inflicted upon each exposed human, tree, structure, and so on, multiplied by the number of those exposed. Given the sheer number of people and geographic areas exposed, does this imply that the global pollutants (such as those responsible for the destruction of the ozone shield or for global warming) should receive special attention in our data gathering efforts? Historically they have not.

One possible response might be that the effects of global pollutants are likely to occur so far into the future that the present value of more data collection is small at any reasonable discount rate. Is the use of the present value criterion ethically justified in this circumstance where current decisions are likely to have irreversible impacts on the earth's climate? I believe it is not.

The desire for better risk management does not always translate into large expenditures designed to provide better data availability to regulators, especially for employment and product-related risks. An alternative approach is to use the court system to generate information directly for consumers so that they can evaluate the risks they face as an alternative to direct regulation of that risk. For example, the courts have recently made clear to asbestos suppliers that corporate awareness of a risk associated with their products triggers a duty to warn those exposed to it. Failure to respect this duty usually results in the firm being forced to bear the liability for the resulting damage, whereas firms providing adequate warning can escape liability as long as they are not otherwise negligent.

Appropriately applied tort law remedies trigger new data for consumers without the unnecessary intermediate step of supplying more data for regulators. While analysts will still need to contribute to the development of a consistent research methodology for use by the courts in measuring damages, this is a rather different role than deriving national benefit estimates to be used in defining the level of "acceptable" risk. And it implies a rather different data-gathering strategy as well.

Two of the contributions of this paper that I found particularly stimulating dealt usefully and realistically with the problem of constructing reasonable policy in the face of limited data and very short deadlines for the analysis. The first was the rather extended analysis of the accuracy of traditional and widely used rules of thumb in benefit estimation. This is an important issue precisely because it recognizes that information is a scarce commodity. To the extent that simple rules of thumb, which require little informational input, are "in the ballpark," their use may be a preferred solution to gathering all of the costly information necessary to provide a full-blown evaluation. Unfortunately the Russell-Smith results are primarily negative; simple rules of thumb seem to do rather poorly.

The second noteworthy contribution reported on the Smith-Kaoru attempt to determine the degree to which existing estimates can be transferred to new valuation problems. The ability to transfer estimates would facilitate maximizing the value of the limited amount of data allowed by permitting its use for many purposes. Here the preliminary results are mixed. On the one hand their results suggest that estimates cannot be transferred from one recreation site to another by simply noting the differences in site attributes as isolated by hedonic price approaches. On the other hand, the fact that those areas were analytical judgments seem to exert a systematic influence can be isolated at least provides a point of departure for beginning to eliminate those influences.

Since the process that governs the effects of environmental policy is so complex (and therefore the data needed to completely document what is going on would be so expensive to collect), the Russell-Smith admonition that we should pay much more attention to getting the most out of any data that we do collect makes a great deal of sense. Studies designed as an integral piece in a larger research puzzle have rather different characteristics than studies designed to shed light on a single, geographically isolated policy concern; not all urgent policy issues have an equal claim on scarce data-collection dollars. The Russell-Smith recommendation for establishing protocols for research procedures to facilitate the transfer of estimates from one setting to another would be a very good start, providing we can be clear about what are the right protocols.

The large cost of these studies has implications not only for the standardization of research methodology, but also for public-sector research funding. Orchestrated research depends upon orchestrated funding. Since orchestrated finding is more difficult than independent funding, this will impose an additional public-sector burden, especially since the statutory responsibility for controlling environmental problems falls on so many different agencies. However, if the resulting information can be synthesized to produce insights that are more than the simple sum of the conclusions of the individual studies, the results would have a much wider applicability and the expenditures would be easier to justify.

In summary, the environmental and natural resource research community has its work cut out for it in the future. The data needed for "full-information" support of environmental policy is sufficiently costly that it is unreasonable for us to simply expect that all desired data will be forthcoming. Realizing this, it is incumbent upon us to set priorities for data collection, to use the available information more effectively, and, where appropriate, to use innovative means to manage risk, such as involving the court system or artificial markets, as an alternative to transferring a great deal of information to regulators. Russell and Smith have made some very useful contributions in this paper to this emerging field of inquiry. I have tried to complement their analysis by suggesting further considerations for setting priorities and constructing reasonable policy in a very limited information world. Much more remains to be done.

11 Measuring Tax Burden: A Historical Perspective

B. K. Atrostic and James R. Nunns

11.1 Introduction

11.1.1 Overview

Measures of tax burden are indicators of how well tax policy meets one of its primary goals, equitably raising the revenues needed to run government. Equity has two aspects. The first, vertical equity, concerns the way taxes are distributed among taxpayers with different abilities to pay. The second, horizontal equity, concerns the way taxes are distributed among taxpayers with the same ability to pay. Tax burden measures thus answer broad economic and social questions about the effect of tax policy on the distribution of income and wealth.

The history of these measures incorporates the histories of economic and world affairs, major tax and economic policy legislation, intellectual and social movements, and data and technological innovation in the fifty years since the first meeting of the Conference on Research in Income and Wealth. This paper reviews the effect of these measures on federal tax policy in a historical and statistical context.

The variety of tax burden measures over this period reflect advances in economic and measurement theory, changing policy concerns, new data sources,

B. K. Atrostic is a Financial Economist with the Office of Tax Analysis, U.S. Department of the Treasury. James R. Nunns is Director, Individual Taxation, Office of Tax Analysis, U.S. Department of the Treasury.

Views expressed in this paper are solely those of the authors and in no way reflect opinions of the Department of the Treasury. All errors and omissions are the sole responsibility of the authors. The authors particularly wish to thank Margaret Acton, whose knowledge of the history and the files of the Office of Tax Analysis and its predecessor offices was invaluable. Ray McFadden provided valuable research assistance. Carolyn Greene provided valuable support in preparing the manuscript and tables.

and external social and economic forces. Advances in the theory and measurement of income, wealth, and taxes generated corresponding changes in the analytical and computational methodologies used to measure tax burden. Throughout the history of empirical tax burden measurement in the United States, changing policy concerns focused attention on different distributional questions. The changing focuses provided the impetus for new analytical techniques. New data sources, together with these techniques, in their turn suggested new views of tax burden and new directions for tax reforms. The major social and economic forces of the last fifty years as well as advances in economic theory and data development influenced evaluations of tax burden measures. The timeline in table 11.1 indicates overlaps among these developments.

The focus throughout this paper is the interrelation among tax burden measures, the development of tax policy, and the policy implications and uses of advances in data, economic theory, and measurement. Each of these topics is treated fully elsewhere. The structure of the U.S. tax system and of the general process of tax policy formulation are discussed in Blough (1952) and Pechman (1987). Summaries and syntheses of tax incidence theory are given in Mieszkowski (1969), Whalley (1984), Musgrave (1985), and Kotlikoff and Summers (1987). Shoup (1972) assesses the state of quantitative work on tax incidence and tax burden in light of fifty years of effort by the National Bureau of Economic Research to improve quantitative research in economics. Reviews and assessments of some tax burden measures are given in Musgrave and Thin (1948), Atkinson (1980), Devarajan, Fullerton, and Musgrave (1980), Auerbach and Rosen (1980), and Kiefer (1984).

11.1.2 Tax Burden Defined

Definitions of a tax, of ability to pay, and of the burden of taxes are necessary prerequisites to measuring tax burden. A tax is a compulsory payment to the government from which the taxpayer receives no direct benefit. This definition distinguishes user charges and commercial receipts from government enterprises (e.g., state-owned liquor stores) from taxes. All three are government receipts, but only the tax component is included in tax burden studies. The inclusion of income, sales, and excise taxes generates little controversy. The appropriate treatment of property taxes and other taxes that are tied to benefits, such as the payroll taxes for Social Security and unemployment insurance, are less clear-cut. In the case of payroll taxes, individuals receive direct benefits when they qualify for the insurance payments but receive these payments at a time removed from the time the taxes were paid. Most tax burden studies include property and benefit taxes in their measures of total taxes paid.

Ability to pay is generally measured by income. The Haig-Simons income definition, a broad-based concept of net accretions to economic power (or consumption plus change in net worth), is the most common theoretical income concept (see Musgrave 1985). The actual income measures used in tax

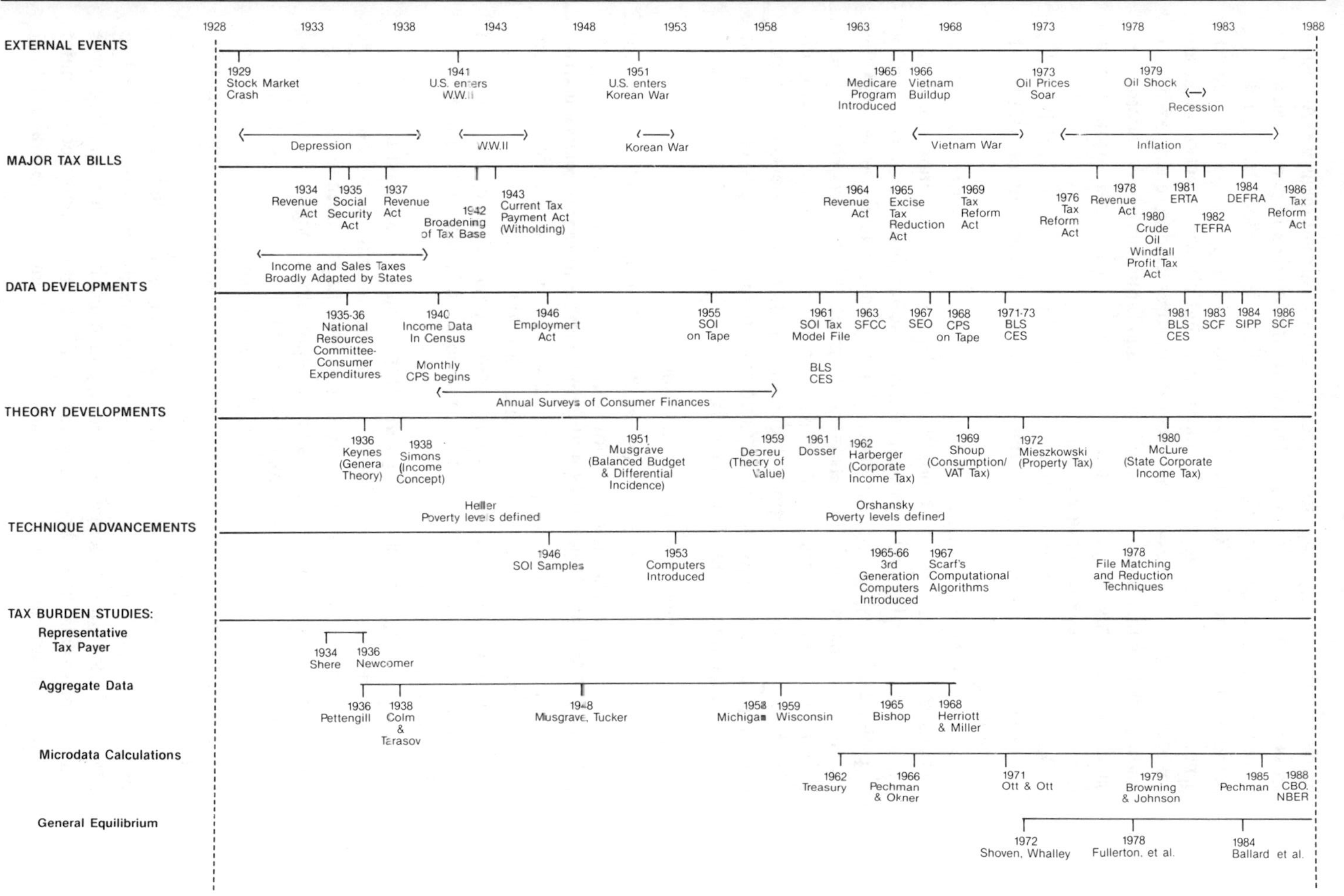
1928
1933
1938
1943
1948
1953
1958
1963
1968
1973
1978
1983
1988
EXTERNAL EVENTS
1929 Stock Market Crash
1941 U.S. enters W.W.II
1951 U.S. enters Korean War
1965 Medicare Program Introduced
1966 Vietnam Buildup
1973 Oil Prices Soar
1979 Oil Shock
Recession
Depression
W.W.II
Korean War
Vietnam War
Inflation
MAJOR TAX BILLS
1934 Revenue Act
1935 Social Security Act
1937 Revenue Act
1942 Broadening of Tax Base
1943 Current Tax Payment Act (Witholding)
1964 Revenue Act
1965 Excise Tax Reduction Act
1969 Tax Reform Act
1976 Tax Reform Act
1978 Revenue Act
1980 Crude Oil Windfall Profit Tax Act
1981 ERTA
1982 TEFRA
1984 DEFRA
1986 Tax Reform Act
Income and Sales Taxes Broadly Adapted by States
DATA DEVELOPMENTS
1935-36 National Resources Committee-Consumer Expenditures
1940 Income Data In Census
Monthly CPS begins
1946 Employment Act
1955 SOI on Tape
1961 SOI Tax Model File
BLS CES
1963 SFCC
1967 SEO
1968 CPS on Tape
1971-73 BLS CES
1981 BLS CES
1983 SCF
1984 SIPP
1986 SCF
Annual Surveys of Consumer Finances
THEORY DEVELOPMENTS
1936 Keynes (Genera Theory)
1938 Simons (Income Concept)
1951 Musgrave (Balanced Budget & Differential Incidence)
1959 Debreu (Theory of Value)
1961 Dosser
1962 Harberger (Corporate Income Tax)
1969 Shoup (Consumption/ VAT Tax)
1972 Mieszkowski (Property Tax)
1980 McLure (State Corporate Income Tax)
Heller Poverty levels defined
Orshansky Poverty levels defined
TECHNIQUE ADVANCEMENTS
1946 SOI Samples
1953 Computers Introduced
1965-66 3rd Generation Computers Introduced
1967 Scarf's Computational Algorithms
1978 File Matching and Reduction Techniques
TAX BURDEN STUDIES:
Representative Tax Payer
1934 Shere
1936 Newcomer
Aggregate Data
1936 Pettengill
1938 Colm & Tarasov
1948 Musgrave, Tucker
1958 Michigan
1959 Wisconsin
1965 Bishop
1968 Herriott & Miller
Microdata Calculations
1962 Treasury
1966 Pechman & Okner
1971 Ott & Ott
1979 Browning & Johnson
1985 Pechman
1988 CBO, NBER
General Equilibrium
1972 Shoven, Whalley
1978 Fullerton, et al.
1984 Ballard et al.

burden studies usually differ from a complete Haig-Simons measure. Adjusted gross income (AGI) is widely used in tax burden studies in part because it is readily available in *Statistics of Income* publications. Defined by the relevant sections of the Internal Revenue Code, AGI generally omits many components of income, such as transfer payments, and allows deductions that are not costs of doing business. Other income measures used in recent tax burden studies, such as modified economic income and family economic income, expand adjusted gross income to approximate more nearly Haig-Simons measures that are independent of current tax laws.

Definitions and measures of income and wealth are given in NBER (1937) and (1943), National Resources Committee (1938), Goldsmith et. al. (1954), and Smith (1975).

Payment of taxes, through lower factor incomes or higher product prices, reduces a taxpayer's real income. Tax burden measures attempt to quantify this decrease in utility and to evaluate the decrease against a measure of ability to pay. Taxes may impose an excess burden on the taxpayer beyond the amount of tax payments if they also induce distortions in the economic system by altering relative prices. Taxation also imposes administrative and compliance costs. With the exception of general equilibrium models, tax burden studies use taxes paid as the tax measure and attempt neither to calculate the excess burden nor to count administrative and compliance costs.

11.1.3 Approaches to Measuring Tax Burden

Tax burden studies of the 1930s are the earliest U.S. studies to include measures of taxes at all levels of government. These studies commonly present results in terms of the tax liability and income of representative taxpayers. A typical category of representative taxpayer would be married taxpayers with no dependents whose income is under $5,000 annually. This form of tax burden measure continues to be widely used in policy debates because it can be focused on particular aspects of a tax proposal and because it is most accessible to nonspecialists.

Aggregate data studies calculate the proportion of taxes paid by each income class and also the proportion of taxes to income within each class. These measures, first calculated in the early 1940s, have largely been replaced.

Current tax policy analysis relies on disaggregated general equilibrium and microdata measures, although representative taxpayer studies continue as a third strain. Both of the newer approaches make use of advances in the frequency and availability of detailed economic data from the federal statistical system.

Microdata models depend on the large amount of survey and administrative record information on individuals that became available starting in the late 1950s and the 1960s together with computer capabilities for handling large and complex data files. Applied general equilibrium models became more useful for policy analysis as computational algorithms became available that permitted larger and more realistic models than the original analytical two-by-two models.

As analytical capabilities have grown, so too have the demands of policymakers in the number, frequency, and detail of desired analyses of the distributional consequences of specific tax proposals as well as for overviews of the entire tax structure. Microdata simulation models are the major tool that Congress and the Treasury use in examining these detailed policy questions. Constraints on the ability of these models to answer policy questions, however, continue. One constraint is the lack of sufficiently detailed data on taxes, income, wealth, and consumption for the analyses now required. In general, these data are not collected together in the same survey. Methodologies for statistical linkages between surveys continue to be topics of professional disagreement. The concerns Morgenstern (1963) raised about the false precision economists attribute to data derived from surveys and to estimates based on a series of data sources that are themselves estimates also apply to estimates of tax burden. Few statistics are presented with measures of overall reliability of the estimates. Another constraint is the practical capacities of available computer systems in providing multiple simulations, at the desired level of detail, on a daily basis during legislative consideration of tax measures.

11.1.4 Organization of the Paper

The second section of this paper provides the historical, statistical, and theoretical background to the approaches that formed tax policy over the last half century. The four major approaches to measuring tax burden, representative taxpayers, aggregate data, microdata, and applied general equilibrium, are discussed in detail in sections 11.3–11.6. The microdata model currently used at the Department of the Treasury in analyzing tax legislation is described in greater detail in section 11.7 to highlight continuing policy needs for improved capabilities for measuring income and tax burden.

11.2 Background

11.2.1 Historical Background

Assessments of the extent and distribution of tax burdens became important once income taxes became important sources of federal, state, and local revenues. Prior to the initiation of the modern federal income tax in 1913, most federal revenues came from customs duties and excise taxes. For many years after 1913, only a small number of relatively well-to-do individuals paid income tax, and subsequent legislation continued to exempt lower-income persons while raising a growing proportion of federal revenues. The four Revenue Acts of the 1920s (1921, 1924, 1926, and 1928), for example, raised personal exemptions. By the beginning of the Depression, federal personal and corporate income taxes had grown in importance and constituted about

60% of federal revenues although relatively few persons were federal taxpayers. During the 1930s, both the sources of government revenues and their shares of gross national product (GNP) changed. Income and sales taxes were broadly adopted by states. At the same time, the federal government increased its revenue demands to try to bring the budget into balance during the Depression and to finance reform and relief programs. Federal excise taxes, understood at the time to be regressive, accounted for growing proportions of revenues. By 1934, just prior to the period covered by this paper, excise taxes had grown to 61% of federal revenues and had grown in absolute terms from $1.0 billion in 1930 to $2.2 billion in 1934. The changing sources of government revenues and the growing share of taxes relative to GNP since 1929 are given in table 11.2.

The major external events of the last fifty years that affected federal tax policy are well known. The timeline of table 11.1 above gives an overview of these events and of the developments in economic theory and measurement that gave rise to new measures of tax burden. After the Depression of the 1930s came an upturn caused by a combination of the prewar military buildup and relief spending. World War II was followed by a brief bout of high inflation and by small economic downturns. Another military buildup and inflation accompanied the Korean War, followed by two downturns in the 1950s and another in 1960. The subsequent and lengthy economic expansion included the Vietnam War buildup of the late 1960s and its accompanying inflation. The 1970s brought two oil price shocks, two recessions, and continuing inflation. The deepest of the postwar recessions in 1981–82 preceded a long-awaited downturn in inflation and the current sustained expansion.

Tax policy kept pace throughout this period with the changing role of government in the economy and with changing economic circumstances. The Revenue Acts of the Roosevelt administration reviewed and somewhat reformed federal tax laws during the 1930s to accord more closely to principles of ability to pay, reduction of tax avoidance, closure of loopholes, and simplification of tax administration. The Social Security Act of 1935 established two new tax and benefit systems, Social Security and the federal-state unemployment compensation systems. Both systems were funded by payroll taxes.

At the outset of the Second World War, the need to finance a rapid military buildup and restrain growing consumer demand required estimates of the tax burden and its distribution to influence policy direction. Income tax rates could be increased selectively to staunch an increase in demand, if the income classes that consumed the items that would be in shortest supply could be identified. Selective increases in excise taxes could also slow demand.

Testimony on the Revenue Revision of 1941 by the chief of staff of the Joint Committee on Internal Revenue Taxation expressed concern about inflation arising from full employment. "The tax base should be broadened to curtail private consumption by either general or specific consumption taxes" (U.S. Cong. House Committee on Ways and Means 1941, 82). In the same series of hearings, the administrator of the Office of Price Administration and Civilian Supply argued for taxes that would imply "positive encouragement of defense production and the discouragement of civilian consumptions of those commodities and services which compete with military demands" (642). Selective excise tax increases were endorsed along with an increase in individual income tax rates in the lower and middle income brackets (646). At the same time, policymakers were concerned that war financing not worsen inequities in the current distribution of tax burden or impose economic hardship on low-income taxpayers (e.g., Blum 1965, 318). Their concerns were reflected in the continuing series of Treasury tax burden studies (e.g., Shere 1934; U.S. Department of the Treasury 1937, 1940, 1947a, and 1947b) and in the continuing discussion of tax burden in decision making (e.g., U.S. Congress, House Committee on Ways and Means 1942; U.S. Congress, House 1942; U.S. Congress, Senate 1942; U.S. Department of the Treasury 1942).

The Revenue Act of 1942 dramatically increased the proportion of the population that would pay income tax by lowering exemptions. (The number of taxable individual income tax returns increased from 4 million in 1939 to 43 million in 1945.) Collecting the income tax through the existing estimated tax payment system created difficulties for the new taxpayers. The Current Tax Payment Act of 1943 initiated wage withholding at the source, beginning in 1944, to ease collection and also to move income from the taxpayer to the government more quickly.

The massive unemployment of the Depression raised concerns about whether the full employment during World War II would be followed by repeating either the Depression or the post-World War I inflation. One consequence of those concerns, and a clear statement of the policy influence of Keynesian principles, was the enactment of the Employment Act of 1946 in February 1946. The first of a three-part declaration of policy made it "the continuing policy and responsibility of the Federal Government to use all practicable means . . . to foster and promote useful employment opportunities . . . and promote full employment and production, and increased real income" (U.S. Congress, JEC 1981, 1). Another consequence of those concerns was the delay in tax reductions for individuals. The Revenue Act of 1945, recognizing the length of the adjustment to peacetime and the pent-up demand, kept the wartime structure of personal income and excise taxes in place. The Revenue Act of 1946 reduced income taxes somewhat by lowering tax rates and raising personal exemptions.

By the 1950s, Korean War requirements for increased defense spending and curtailed consumption raised concerns about setting off another streak of inflation in the process. As with World War II financing, an increase in income taxes was recommended. Tax burden became an important policy consideration because existing statutory federal income tax rates were high, reflecting the tax structure of World War II. Surtax rates reached 50% at an income of $16,000 and rose to a maximum of 91% in 1950. The administration's

Table 11.2 **Federal, State, and Local Taxes Relative to GNP, 1929–88**

Calendar Year	Taxes as a % of GNP: Federal: Personal	Federal: Corporate	Federal: Indirect Business Taxes	Federal: Social Insurance	Federal: Total	State and Local	Total	GNP ($ billions)	Nominal Taxes ($ billions): Federal: Personal	Federal: Corporate	Federal: Indirect Business Taxes	Federal: Social Insurance	Total Federal Taxes	State and Local	Total taxes
1929	1.3	1.2	1.2	.2	3.8	7.3	11.1	103.9	1.3	1.2	1.2	.2	3.9	7.6	11.5
1930	1.2	.8	1.1	.2	3.3	8.6	11.9	91.1	1.1	.7	1.0	.2	3.0	7.8	10.8
1931	.8	.5	1.2	.3	2.7	10.1	12.8	76.4	.6	.4	.9	.2	2.1	7.7	9.8
1932	.5	.5	1.5	.3	2.9	12.5	15.4	58.5	.3	.3	.9	.2	1.7	7.3	9.0
1933	.9	.9	2.9	.4	5.0	12.9	17.9	56.0	.5	.5	1.6	.2	2.8	7.2	10.0
1934	.9	.9	3.4	.3	5.5	13.1	18.6	65.6	.6	.6	2.2	.2	3.6	8.6	12.2
1935	1.1	1.1	3.0	.3	5.5	12.5	18.0	72.8	.8	.8	2.2	.2	4.0	9.1	13.1
1936	1.3	1.6	2.8	.5	6.1	10.3	16.5	83.1	1.1	1.3	2.3	.4	5.1	8.6	13.7
1937	1.9	1.4	2.6	1.8	7.7	10.0	17.6	91.3	1.7	1.3	2.4	1.6	7.0	9.1	16.1
1938	1.9	1.1	2.6	2.1	7.6	10.9	18.5	85.4	1.6	.9	2.2	1.8	6.5	9.3	15.8
1939	1.3	1.4	2.5	2.1	7.3	10.5	17.9	91.3	1.2	1.3	2.3	1.9	6.7	9.6	16.3
1940	1.4	2.6	2.6	2.1	8.7	10.0	18.6	100.4	1.4	2.6	2.6	2.1	8.7	10.0	18.7
1941	1.6	5.8	2.9	2.1	12.4	8.3	20.6	125.5	2.0	7.3	3.6	2.6	15.5	10.4	25.9
1942	3.0	7.0	2.5	2.0	14.5	6.7	21.1	159.0	4.7	11.1	4.0	3.2	23.0	10.6	33.6
1943	8.6	7.1	2.5	2.2	20.3	5.7	26.0	192.7	16.5	13.6	4.9	4.2	39.2	10.9	50.1
1944	8.3	5.9	2.9	2.3	19.4	5.3	24.7	211.4	17.5	12.5	6.2	4.9	41.1	11.1	52.2
1945	9.1	4.8	3.3	2.8	20.0	5.4	25.4	213.4	19.4	10.2	7.1	5.9	42.6	11.6	54.2
1946	8.1	4.0	3.7	3.3	19.2	6.1	25.3	212.4	17.2	8.6	7.8	7.1	40.7	13.0	53.7
1947	8.3	4.5	3.3	2.6	18.8	6.5	25.3	235.2	19.6	10.7	7.8	6.1	44.2	15.4	59.6
1948	7.3	4.5	3.1	2.0	16.8	6.8	23.6	261.6	19.0	11.8	8.0	5.2	44.0	17.7	61.7
1949	6.2	3.7	3.1	2.2	15.1	7.5	22.6	260.4	16.1	9.6	8.0	5.6	39.3	19.5	58.8
1950	6.3	6.0	3.1	2.2	17.5	7.4	24.9	288.3	18.1	17.2	8.9	6.3	50.5	21.3	71.8
1951	7.8	6.5	2.8	2.2	19.4	7.0	26.4	333.4	26.1	21.7	9.4	7.5	64.7	23.4	88.1
1952	8.8	5.3	2.9	2.2	19.3	7.2	26.5	351.6	31.0	18.6	10.3	7.8	67.7	25.4	93.1
1953	8.7	5.2	2.9	2.1	18.9	7.4	26.3	371.6	32.2	19.5	10.9	7.8	70.4	27.4	97.8
1954	7.8	4.5	2.6	2.3	17.3	7.8	25.0	372.5	29.0	16.9	9.7	8.7	64.3	29.0	93.3

1957	8.3	4.5	2.6	2.9	18.3	8.5	26.8	451.0	37.4	20.4	11.8	12.9	82.5	38.5	121.0
1958	8.1	3.9	2.5	2.9	17.4	9.2	26.6	456.8	36.8	18.0	11.5	13.1	79.4	42.0	121.4
1959	8.0	4.5	2.5	3.2	18.3	9.4	27.7	495.8	39.9	22.5	12.5	15.7	90.6	46.6	137.2
1960	8.5	4.2	2.6	3.6	18.8	9.7	28.5	515.3	43.6	21.4	13.4	18.5	96.9	50.0	146.9
1961	8.4	4.0	2.5	3.6	18.5	10.1	28.7	533.8	44.7	21.5	13.6	19.2	99.0	54.1	153.1
1962	8.5	3.9	2.5	3.7	18.7	10.2	28.9	574.6	48.6	22.5	14.6	21.5	107.2	58.6	165.8
1963	8.5	4.1	2.5	4.0	19.0	10.4	29.5	606.9	51.5	24.6	15.2	24.3	115.6	63.4	179.0
1964	7.5	4.0	2.5	3.9	17.9	10.7	28.6	649.8	48.6	26.1	16.1	25.4	116.2	69.8	186.0
1965	7.6	4.1	2.3	3.8	17.8	10.7	28.5	705.1	53.9	28.9	16.4	26.6	125.8	75.5	201.3
1966	8.0	4.1	2.0	4.5	18.6	11.0	29.6	772.0	61.7	31.4	15.5	34.9	143.5	85.2	228.7
1967	8.3	3.7	2.0	4.8	18.7	11.5	30.2	816.4	67.5	30.0	16.2	38.9	152.6	94.1	246.7
1968	8.9	4.0	2.0	4.8	19.8	12.1	31.9	892.7	79.7	36.1	17.9	43.2	176.9	107.9	284.8
1969	9.9	3.7	2.0	5.1	20.7	12.5	33.3	963.9	95.1	36.1	18.9	49.6	199.7	120.8	320.5
1970	9.1	3.0	1.9	5.2	19.2	13.4	32.6	1,015.5	92.6	30.6	19.2	52.9	195.3	135.8	331.1
1971	8.2	3.0	1.8	5.3	18.4	13.9	32.3	1,102.7	90.3	33.5	20.3	58.7	202.8	153.6	356.4
1972	8.9	3.0	1.6	5.6	19.1	14.8	33.9	1,212.8	108.2	36.6	19.9	67.5	232.2	179.3	411.5
1973	8.4	3.2	1.6	6.2	19.4	14.4	33.8	1,359.3	114.7	43.3	21.1	84.6	263.7	196.4	460.1
1974	8.9	3.1	1.5	6.5	20.0	14.5	34.4	1,472.8	131.3	45.1	21.6	95.9	293.9	213.1	507.0
1975	7.9	2.7	1.5	6.4	18.4	15.0	33.4	1,593.4	125.9	43.6	23.8	101.6	294.9	239.6	534.5
1976	8.3	3.1	1.3	6.5	19.1	15.2	34.2	1,782.8	147.3	54.6	23.3	115.0	340.2	270.1	610.3
1977	8.5	3.1	1.3	6.4	19.3	15.1	34.4	1,990.5	169.8	61.6	25.0	127.7	384.1	300.1	684.2
1978	8.7	3.2	1.2	6.5	19.6	14.7	34.3	2,249.7	194.9	71.4	28.0	147.0	441.3	330.3	771.6
1979	9.2	3.0	1.2	6.8	20.1	14.2	34.3	2,508.2	231.0	74.4	29.3	170.3	505.0	355.3	860.3
1980	9.4	2.6	1.4	6.8	20.3	14.3	34.5	2,732.0	257.9	70.3	38.8	186.8	553.8	390.0	943.8
1981	9.8	2.2	1.8	7.2	21.0	13.9	34.9	3,052.6	298.9	65.7	56.2	218.8	639.6	425.6	1,065.2
1982	9.6	1.5	1.5	7.4	20.1	14.2	34.3	3,166.0	304.5	49.0	48.1	233.7	635.3	449.4	1,084.7
1983	8.6	1.8	1.5	7.4	19.4	14.3	33.7	3,405.7	294.5	61.3	51.6	252.5	659.9	487.6	1,147.5
1984	8.2	2.0	1.5	7.5	19.2	14.3	33.6	3,772.2	310.3	75.2	55.7	284.7	725.9	540.4	1,266.3
1985	8.6	1.9	1.4	7.7	19.7	14.5	34.1	4,010.3	346.6	76.1	55.2	310.6	788.5	579.7	1,368.2
1986	8.6	2.0	1.2	7.8	19.5	14.6	34.1	4,235.0	363.0	83.7	50.9	329.8	827.4	618.8	1,446.2
1987	9.0	2.4	1.2	7.8	20.4	14.6	35.0	4,488.5	403.7	109.4	54.1	348.4	915.6	651.1	1,566.7
1988[a]	8.2	2.8	1.2	8.1	20.2	14.5	34.7	4,830.0	397.0	133.4	56.2	389.0	975.6	700.3	1,676.0

Source: U.S. Department of Commerce. Bureau of Economic Analysis. 1988. National Income and Product Accounts of the United States, 1929–1982. Statistical Tables, 1986; and *Survey of Current Business* (May).

[a]denotes estimate.

proposal would have raised these rates to 54% and 95% respectively (U.S. Congress, Senate 1951). The existing structure had provoked enough public displeasure over the preceding 15 years that at least 25 states adopted resolutions calling for a constitutional amendment to cap effective rates at 25% on income, estate, and gift taxes (U.S. Congress, JCER and Select Committee on Small Business 1952). A series of tax burden studies entered the debate on several Revenue Acts (Musgrave et al. 1951; Tucker 1951; U.S. Congress, JCER 1951; Colm and Wald 1952). The Revenue Act of 1951 nevertheless raised tax rates, but not to the full extent of the administration proposal.

The tax burden studies of the early 1950s generated heated debate among economists. At the same time, objections to conflicting assumptions in statistical computations of the tax burden opened further avenues of debate (Prest 1955). The return to a peacetime economy in the mid-1950s, together with two recessions in that decade, continued to place tax policy among the leading economic policy tools and tax burden, therefore, among the leading policy questions. A major review of federal income tax provisions was conducted in a series of congressional hearings in 1959. The published report of those hearings dedicated a quarter of its 2,400 printed pages to the individual income tax and its distributive consequences (U.S. Congress, House Committee on Ways and Means 1959). The postwar Internal Revenue Code, however, remained largely unaltered through a major recodification in 1954, apart from surtaxes imposed permanently during the Korean War.

By 1963, the level and structure of taxes were perceived to be sufficient impediments to full employment and economic growth that President Kennedy's State of the Union Address deemed "a substantial reduction and revision in Federal income taxes" to be "the most urgent task confronting the Congress in 1963." The Revenue Act of 1964 embodied some of the reforms in the President's Tax Message of 1963 by lowering tax rates across the board and lowering overall tax liabilities. It also set the tax-free income level (by adjusting the personal exemption and the standard deduction) to correspond to the official poverty level so that the poor would be exempt from federal income tax. The Excise Tax Reduction Act of 1965 continued reforms by repealing many excise taxes and lowering excise tax rates raised during the Korean War. A Vietnam War financing surtax applied from 1968 to 1970.

Inflation adjustments were reflected in the changes of the Revenue Act of 1969, which instituted a schedule to raise personal exemptions and standard deductions over the following several years. The Tax Reform Act of 1976 raised deductions, increased the capital gains rate, increased the minimum tax rate, and lowered the minimum tax exemption. Tax acts of the late 1970s adjusted exemptions and widened tax brackets in response to inflation-induced bracket creep. The Crude Oil Windfall Profit Tax, essentially an oil profits surtax, was enacted in 1980. The Economic Recovery Tax Act of 1981 (ERTA) lowered tax rates, introduced inflation indexing, and lowered the maximum rates on capital gains. Both the Tax Equity and Fiscal Responsibility Act (TEFRA) in 1982 and the Deficit Reduction Act (DEFRA) in 1984 responded to growing federal deficits by raising additional revenues. Most recently, the Tax Reform Act of 1986 broadened the tax base, lowered tax rates, and raised tax thresholds above the poverty level for most taxpayers while maintaining revenue neutrality.

11.2.2 Statistical and Theoretical Background

The heavy data demands of tax burden measures confronted the same scarcity of data as did other policy needs in the 1930s. The integral link between measures of income and wealth and tax burden are clearly shown in the proceedings of the first Conference on Research in National Income and Wealth (NBER 1937). The treatment of tax revenues in the measurement of income, tax incidence, and distinctions between taxable income and national income were discussed in papers and comments by Shoup, Blough, Colm, and Newcomer. One major data gap, for tax burden measurement as well as for other social and economic policy development, was an estimate of the distribution of income. A review of data sources for constructing a size distribution of income noted serious gaps, including "No continuous source yields a distribution by size of either family or individual income for the United States. . . . In the absence of complete coverage, a good sample would meet the chief needs. That we are far from such a goal is obvious" (NBER 1943, p. 84). Income tax–return data themselves were a crucial component of estimates of the upper tail of that distribution whose other major component was a 1935–36 survey of consumer purchases (see Baird and Fine 1939).

In response to the absence of vital data, among other reasons, the Office of Statistical Standards was established in the Bureau of the Budget in 1939. Congressional concern over data needed for policy analysis was reflected in debate preceding the Employment Act of 1946 and in its provisions. To help effect its goals, the act required the president to submit a semiannual economic report to Congress. The act also established the Council of Economic Advisers to the President, whose responsibilities included assisting in the preparation of the President's Economic Report, and the Joint Committee on the Economic Report (now the Joint Economic Committee) whose responsibilities included advising Congress with respect to the President's Economic Report, in part by submitting its own reviews of the report. One thread of the debate on the passage of this act was the lack of timely and detailed data on employment, expenditures, and prices. The Joint Committee on the Economic Report (JCER) quickly set up the Subcommittee on Economic Statistics in 1947 to review the existence and timeliness of economic data necessary to make and evaluate federal economic policy. One of the subcommittee's first acts was to issue a brief report on statistical gaps in 1948 (U.S. Congress JCER 1948). Efforts at filling the gaps noted in the subcommittee report on statistical gaps were detailed in subsequent Economic Reports of the President. The Subcommittee on Economic Statistics itself continued to hold hearings and publish detailed reports (see, e.g., U.S. Congress, JCER 1954).

The National Income and Product Accounts (NIPA—themselves dependent on growing data availability), new consumer budget and finances studies, the addition of income data to the 1940 decennial census, and the Statistics of Income program contributed some of the basic data necessary for calculating measures of tax burden. By the 1950s, exclusions from taxable income such as fringe benefits had grown in importance. Data on income, consumption, and taxes of individuals, rather than aggregates by income class, were required to examine concerns that these exclusions were distributed unevenly among taxpayers with similar incomes.

Filling the data gaps was a slow process, however, and the lack of data became a recurring theme of both researchers attempting to measure tax burden and policy users of those measures. Neither the data themselves nor the technology to access and link large samples of individual records were available until the mid-1960s. The first item listed in the Subcommittee on Economic Statistics' 1948 report on statistical gaps was data on individual income, expenditure, and savings patterns, data required to analyze "the effect of possible [postwar] tax reductions on consumer demand and savings" (U.S. Congress, JCER 1948, 20). Income data were collected in the decennial census for the first time in 1940. The 1936 Survey of Consumer Purchases remained the most recent large-scale national survey of income, expenditures, and savings until the results of the 1950–51 expenditure survey became available in the mid-1950s. The postwar expenditure studies available for tax policy decision making during the Korean War were limited to certain income groups and narrow areas in any single year. Annual Surveys of Consumer Finances, while national in scope, were based on samples too small to permit detailed analysis at subnational levels and did not collect asset data.

Rapid advances in computer technology accompanied by declining prices for given levels of computer performance (Triplett 1989) made computers increasingly available and affordable research tools. The advent of the computer age in the mid-1950s coincided with growing concerns about horizontal equity within the tax system (see Colm and Wald 1952), and provided the first practical means of addressing this question. But implementing that tool took several years. The first tax burden calculations based on the Statistics of Income microdata were run on these early machines in the early 1960s. While the studies were now possible, they were time consuming and costly.

Third-generation computing technology introduced in 1965 provided much-improved price/performance ratios compared to the earlier technologies. At the same time, new large-scale surveys (such as the Survey of Economic Opportunity [SEO]) were undertaken, and both these and existing surveys (such as the Current Population Survey [CPS]) became available as public-use computer tapes in the late 1960s. Increased computer performance characteristics such as speed and memory size began to make research using these large surveys feasible, whether the surveys were used alone or in research linking information among multiple surveys. The first estimates of horizontal equity in a tax burden study, Pechman and Okner (1974), required both the SEO and the CPS and advanced computer technology. Continuing increases in computer performance make large-scale microsimulation models inexpensive and fast enough for daily use in the making of tax policy.

Advances in statistical techniques and theory reduced the resources needed to make statistical matches between individual records in multiple microdata files. The development of efficient computational algorithms (Scarf 1967) made applied multisector general equilibrium models practical for research.

Tax burden measurement depends as well on prevailing economic theory. Keynes's General Theory, introduced in 1936, contributed new ideas for government fiscal policy that were soon adopted. The preferred public finance definition of income against which tax burden should be measured had been discussed by Haig in the 1920s but received new attention in Simon's restatements in 1938 and 1950.

A general proof of the existence of competitive equilibrium was first provided by Debreu in 1959. Shortly thereafter, Harberger (1962) presented a theory of corporate tax incidence in a general equilibrium setting. The role of economic growth and dynamic principles generally in the context of tax incidence were first stated by Dosser (1961). A separate strain of general-equilibrium models that considered the dynamics of the adjustments between general equilibria followed from Dosser's work.

Tax incidence theory determines how the burden of a tax should be allocated among economic units; the burden may fall on units other than those specified in tax statutes. Incidence therefore is an integral theoretical component of any tax burden measure. Continuing developments in incidence theory brought corresponding changes in tax burden measures. One important advance was the distinction, drawn by Musgrave in 1951, between two alternative ways of thinking about the joint effect of the taxes imposed by the government and the spending financed by them: balanced-budget incidence and differential incidence. Balanced-budget incidence combines the effect on taxpayers of taxation and of government spending on goods and services financed by that taxation. Differential incidence holds government expenditures constant, and compares one tax structure with another yielding equal revenues. The comparison tax structure is typically a flat-rate income tax or a lump-sum tax.

The incidence of value-added and expenditure or consumption taxes was analyzed by Shoup (1969). A revision of the standard view of the incidence of the property tax was introduced by Mieszkowski (1972), and revisited recently (Mieszkowski and Zodrow 1984). McLure (1980) provided a theory of the incidence of the state corporate income tax. Dynamic concerns, including tax incidence over the life cycle and during the course of adjustment between two equilibria, have received increasing attention (Hall 1968; Feldstein 1974; Kotlikoff and Summers 1979). As recent surveys of this literature show (Musgrave 1985; Kotlikoff and Summers 1987), incidence theory continues to evolve, and the theory of the incidence of many taxes is far from settled.

11.3 Representative Taxpayer Studies

11.3.1 Summary

Representative taxpayer studies draw together data on the income, consumption patterns, and tax payments of categories of taxpayers. The categories are chosen either for their generality (e.g., the employed head of a family whose spouse is not employed outside the home, with an average number of dependent children), or their specificity (e.g., the class of taxpayer widely believed to be unfairly benefited or harmed by patterns of taxation). Representative taxpayer burden measures may compare only one kind of tax payment or all taxes at all levels of government across different categories of representative taxpayers. The tax measures may be rate schedules, actual dollars paid (on average or at the break point of a tax bracket), or taxes as a percentage of income. The earliest empirical tax burden studies that include the full range of federal, state, and local taxes examine the tax liabilities of representative taxpayers. Such a study (Shere 1934) appears first to have been conducted as part of a U.K. Treasury Department review of the federal tax system in 1934 at the beginning of Morganthau's era as Secretary of the Treasury (Blum 1959; Shoup 1972). The methodology in that study is similar to Newcomer's (1937a), whose work is the earliest published modern tax burden study to include taxes at all levels. Prior U.S. analyses typically explored instead the circumstances of hypothetical taxpayers, although attempts at empirical measures had been made in Great Britain since 1756 (Newcomer 1937a), and a study of all central government taxes in the United Kingdom had recently been completed (Report of the Committee on National Debt and Taxation [U.S. Parliament 1927], known as the Colwyn Commission Report). Studies in the United States lagged behind in part because income and excise taxes played a relatively lesser role in U.S. revenues until the Depression and in part because the necessary data simply did not exist.

Although the representative taxpayer is the oldest form of empirical tax burden measure and has numerous drawbacks, it has not been completely replaced by more recent methodologies. To the contrary, studies of the tax burden of representative taxpayers continue to the present, most recently entering the debate preceding and following the Tax Reform Act of 1986. Reasons why this form persists despite its drawbacks are straightforward. For both policymakers and their constituents, examples of the tax burden (however measured) of representative taxpayers have obvious intuitive appeal. Moreover, for tax provisions that are believed or intended to affect one group more than another, these comparisons can be focused on the specific provisions (subject always to caveats about the effects of alternative income definitions and incidence assumptions).

11.3.2 Data

The early representative taxpayer studies comment on the scarcity of the necessary income, wealth, and consumption data. Shere (in 1934) and Newcomer (in 1937) rely primarily on income data from the Statistics of Income, the National Resources Committee, the National Industrial and Conference Board, and the study by Loven, Moulten, and Warburton. State tax and property ownership data were readily available only for states for which tax burden studies existed (New York, for Shere and Newcomer and Illinois, as well, for Newcomer). Expenditure data, such as it was, came from small-scale surveys, typically conducted by the Bureau of Labor Statistics (BLS). Shere notes, "The chief deficiency in our present study is the lack of a Census of Consumption, by classes of people on basis of age, occupation, size of income, etc" (1934, R-3). Both Shere and Newcomer depend on expenditure distributions for subsets of the population based on surveys as much as 15 years old "because of the lack of statistical information" (Shere 1934, R-3). Absent data, they relied on assumptions about likely distributions of consumption and expenditure across income classes.

11.3.3 Assumptions and Results

The studies by Shere (1934) and Newcomer (1937) share similar, although not identical, methodologies and reach similar conclusions about the tax structure of the mid-1930s. The following characterization of the structure and conclusions of this class of tax burden study is based on Newcomer's study. Reflecting the diversity in the theory of tax incidence and tax shifting, tax burdens are calculated under alternative sets of incidence assumptions. For most taxes, the incidence assumptions are stable. Personal income taxes generally are assumed to be borne by the payer, business net income and capital stock taxes are borne by stockholders or owners, stock transfer taxes are borne by the taxpayer, and mortgage taxes are born by the individual who mortgages the property. Alternative assumptions are made for land taxes, payroll taxes, and a category consisting of taxes on improvements, gross receipts, commodities, motor vehicles, and motor fuels. In the alternatives, these taxes are shifted to the final consumer, or shifted in various proportions between the taxpayer and the final consumer (and the seller or employer, for receipts and payroll taxes). The resulting tax burdens are calculated for a family of four in each income class, both in dollars and as a percentage of income. Portions of representative summary tables from Newcomer's study are reproduced in table 11.3. Federal and state taxes (in the example given, for the state of New York only) and incomes are shown separately for families in 10 income classes under five sets of incidence assumptions. Taxes also are shown as a percentage of income.

Based on detailed, tax-by-tax analyses, Newcomer concludes that the tax system "as a whole is regressive for those income groups not subject to income and death taxes. The regressive elements appear to be more numerous . . . than the progressive elements at the lower end of the income scale," while the system is "progressive for the income groups subject to income and death taxes," which were the five upper-income groups (1937b, 41).

Part A of table 11.3 reports estimates of total tax burden, including federal,

Table 11.3

A. Total Tax Burden, Federal, State, and Local, Based on Assumptions in Series I (in % of income)

	A	B	C	D	E	F	G	H	I	J
Federal and New York total	12.0	10.9	9.8	18.6	17.2	20.8	23.9	31.6	44.3	84.5
Direct	7.4	6.5	5.3	11.7	10.7	10.4	18.0	11.0	23.7	55.6
Shifted	4.6	4.4	4.5	6.9	6.5	10.4	5.9	20.6	20.6	28.9
Federal total	1.6	1.4	1.3	3.1	2.6	5.9	5.2	16.9	27.0	66.1
Direct	.2	.2	.4	.5	.4	.9	3.7	3.9	14.0	46.6
Shifted	1.4	1.2	.9	2.6	2.2	5.0	1.5	13.0	13.0	19.5
State and local total	10.4	9.5	8.5	15.5	14.6	14.9	18.7	14.7	17.3	18.4
Direct	7.2	6.3	5.0	11.2	10.3	9.5	14.3	7.1	9.6	9.0
Shifted	3.2	3.2	3.5	4.3	4.3	5.4	4.4	7.6	7.7	9.4

B. Potential Incomes under Different Assumptions of Series I–V (in $)

	A	B	C	D	E	F	G	H	I	J
Series:										
I and V	500	1,000	2,000	972	1,944	5,106	4,864	23,591	116,023	1,319,015
II and III	527	1,033	2,047	972	1,944	5,151	5,095	25,119	119,663	1,382,718
IV	551	1,068	2,106	986	1,972	5,217	5,266	25,315	121,620	1,397,586

C. Total Tax Burden, Federal, State, and Local, Based on Assumptions in Series I, II, III, IV, and V (in $)

	A	B	C	D	E	F	G	H	I	J
Federal:										
Series I	8	14	25	30	50	300	254	3,999	31,308	872,315
Series II	6	9	17	17	30	264	221	3,919	31,085	871,578
Series III	6	9	17	17	30	264	221	3,919	31,085	871,578
Series IV	6	9	17	17	30	264	221	3,919	31,085	871,578
Series V	8	14	25	30	50	300	328	5,138	46,236	1,110,215
State and Local:										
Series I	52	95	170	151	284	761	910	3,460	20,123	242,282
Series II	73	109	181	133	246	703	1,025	3,760	21,577	284,044
Series III	73	109	181	133	246	703	1,025	3,760	21,577	284,044
Series IV	99	154	260	157	294	825	1,246	4,156	24,534	308,909
Series V	52	95	170	151	284	761	915	3,676	23,736	329,336
All:										
Series I	60	109	195	181	334	1,061	1,164	7,459	51,431	1,114,597
Series II	79	118	198	150	276	967	1,246	7,679	52,662	1,155,622
Series III	79	118	198	150	276	967	1,246	7,679	52,662	1,155,622
Series IV	105	163	277	174	324	1,089	1,467	8,075	55,619	1,180,487
Series V	60	109	195	181	334	1,061	1,243	8,814	69,972	1,439,551

Source: Reproduced from Newcomer (1937b, 28–29).
Note: Column headings A–J refer to income classes. Series I–V assumptions are sets of alternative tax incidence assumptions.

state, and local taxes, for New York families in various income classes, under one of the five sets of incidence assumptions. Total tax burden declines from 12.0% of income for the lowest income families to 10.9% and 9.8% for the next two income classes. After rising to 18.6% for the fourth income class, tax burden drops to 17.2% in the fifth class before becoming strictly progressive (from 20.8% to 84.5%) in the upper five classes. Neither the federal nor the combined state and local tax burden is progressive in the lower income classes, but the federal burden is clearly progressive for higher incomes. The pattern of tax burden for state and local taxes is less clear-cut, declining from 10.4% for the lowest income class to 8.5% for the third, then fluctuating between 14.6% and 18.7% over the upper seven income classes.

11.3.4 Policy Uses

Both varieties of representative taxpayer studies entered directly into tax policy formation in the mid-1930s and continue their influence to the present, as examples from the earlier and current eras illustrate. The report of the House of Representatives on its version of the Revenue Bill of 1934 addressed the combined effects of proposed changes in tax rates on earned and dividend income on single and married taxpayers with various levels and sources of net income and concluded that the proposals would both raise revenue and "at the same time distribute the tax burden more equitably" (U.S. Congress, House 1934, 7). One example of a representative taxpayer comparison, reproduced in table 11.4, shows the estimated effects of these proposals on a single man and on a married man with no dependents.

The representative taxpayer concept remains in use, as evidenced by table 11.5, which is from the *General Explanation* of the Economic Recovery Tax Act of 1981 (U.S. Congress, JCT 1981). Tax liabilities under prior law and under the act are compared for five categories of taxpayers in each of nine income levels.

11.3.5 Problems

The representative taxpayer approach has several limitations that were well-known by early researchers. Nothing inherent in the representative taxpayer approach ensures that the examples typify either all taxpayers or affected taxpayers rather than arbitrary choices. Supplemental data on the distribution of taxpayers by categories are needed to assess one dimension of representativeness. The representative taxpayer approach also cannot address questions of horizontal equity because variations in the income sources, consumption patterns, and tax burden of taxpayers within any category cannot be incorporated. In evaluating possible horizontal equity effects of variations in consumption patterns, Newcomer (1937b, 7–8) concluded that "there is no reason to suppose, however, that these expenditures will so successfully counterbalance one another that tax burden will be much the same for all, and no claim

Table 11.4 Comparison of Present and Proposed Tax Amount Paid in Taxes ($)

	If All Earned Income[a]		If Half Earned Income and Half Dividends[b]		All Dividends[b]	
Net income ($)	Present Law	Proposed	Present Law	Proposed	Present Law	Proposed
Single male:						
2,000	40	32	0	0	0	0
3,000	80	68	20	8	0	0
3,500	100	86	30	18	0	0
4,000	120	104	40	28	0	0
4,500	140	122	50	38	0	0
5,000	160	140	60	48	0	0
6,000	240	216	80	108	0	40
7,000	330	292	110	166	10	80
8,000	420	368	140	224	20	120
9,000	510	448	170	282	30	160
10,000	600	538	200	350	40	210
12,000	800	728	320	496	80	320
14,000	1,020	938	460	662	140	450
16,000	1,260	1,168	620	848	220	600
18,000	1,520	1,428	800	1,068	320	780
20,000	1,800	1,728	1,000	1,328	440	1,000
25,000	2,640	2,648	1,640	2,148	880	1,720
30,000	3,600	3,708	2,400	3,108	1,440	2,580
40,000	5,920	6,148	4,320	5,348	2,960	4,620
50,000	8,720	9,098	6,720	8,098	4,960	7,170
60,000	12,020	12,558	9,620	11,358	7,460	10,230
70,000	15,820	16,498	13,020	15,098	10,460	13,770
80,000	20,120	20,948	16,920	19,348	13,960	17,820
100,000	30,220	31,168	26,220	29,168	22,460	27,240
200,000	86,720	87,638	78,720	83,638	70,960	79,710
500,000	263,720	264,608	243,720	254,608	223,960	244,680
1,000,000	571,220	572,088	531,220	552,088	491,460	532,160

can be made that these detailed expenditures and the tax burden resulting from them are typical of the income group in question. These specific consumption taxes are not, however, a large part of the tax burden for any income group." In general, Newcomer states that, in addition to variations resulting from alternative incidence assumptions, (1937b, 10) "substantial variations [in estimated tax burdens] might be obtained by reasonable variations in the assumptions concerning the nature of income, expenditure, and property." A final problem is that the income measure against which tax burden is assessed, particularly in earlier studies, generally is a measure of income subject to tax. This income measure varies with tax law. In the absence of additional information about all income sources, taxpayers could change income classes

Table 11.4 (*Continued*)

Net income ($)	If All Earned Income[a]		If Half Earned Income and Half Dividends[b]		All Dividends[b]	
	Present Law	Proposed	Present Law	Proposed	Present Law	Proposed
Married male, no dependents:						
3,000	20	8	0	0	0	0
3,500	40	26	0	0	0	0
4,000	60	44	0	0	0	0
4,500	80	62	0	0	0	0
5,000	100	80	0	0	0	0
6,000	140	116	20	8	0	0
7,000	210	172	50	46	10	20
8,000	300	248	80	104	20	60
9,000	390	328	110	162	30	100
10,000	480	408	140	220	40	140
12,000	680	583	220	351	80	235
14,000	900	778	340	502	140	350
16,000	1,140	993	500	673	220	485
18,000	1,400	1,228	680	868	320	640
20,000	1,680	1,498	880	1,098	440	830
25,000	2,520	2,348	1,520	1,848	880	1,480
30,000	3,480	3,378	2,280	2,778	1,440	2,310
40,000	5,800	5,743	4,200	4,943	2,960	4,275
50,000	8,600	8,633	6,600	7,633	4,960	6,765
60,000	11,900	12,003	9,500	10,803	7,460	9,735
70,000	15,700	15,868	12,900	14,468	10,460	13,200
80,000	20,000	20,258	16,800	18,659	13,960	17,190
100,000	30,100	30,358	26,100	28,358	22,460	26,490
200,000	86,600	86,783	78,600	82,783	70,960	78,915
500,000	263,600	263,708	243,600	253,708	223,960	243,840
1,000,000	571,100	571,158	531,100	551,158	491,460	531,290

Source: Reproduced from U.S. Congress. House. 1934. Report of Mr. Doughton, 6–7. *The Revenue Bill of 1934*. 73rd Cong., 2d sess. H. Report no. 704, 6–7.

[a] Earned income means wages, salaries, professional fees, or other amounts received for personal services actually rendered.

[b] Dividends from stock of domestic corporations. Same treatment is accorded interest from partially tax-exempt government bonds.

when the tax law definition of income changed, without there being any change in their pretax ability to pay. Comparisons within income classes of the tax burdens of representative taxpayers under significant changes in the law would be inconsistent and misleading. Furthermore, if the proportion of total income subject to tax under a given tax law varies by income group, evaluations of progessivity would be incorrect.

Table 11.5 Comparisons of Federal Individual Income Tax Burdens Under Prior Law and under the Act for Tax Year 1984 (Tax Liability [$])[a]

	Single Person			One-earner Married Couple with No Dependents			One-earner Married Couple with Two Dependents			Two-earner Married Couple with No Dependents[c]			Two-earner Married Couple with Two Dependents[c]		
Income[b] ($)	Under Prior Law	Under the Act	Reduction	Under Prior Law	Under the Act	Reduction	Under Prior Law	Under the Act	Reduction	Under Prior Law	Under the Act	Reduction	Under Prior Law	Under the Act	Reduction
5,000	250	193	57	0	0	0	−500	−500	0	0	0	0	−500	−500	0
10,000	1,177	915	262	702	539	163	374	291	83	702	504	198	374	261	113
15,000	2,047	1,572	475	1,625	1,253	372	1,233	952	281	1,625	1,193	432	1,233	900	333
20,000	3,115	2,392	723	2,457	1,885	572	2,013	1,549	464	2,457	1,795	662	2,013	1,469	544
30,000	5,718	4,385	1,333	4,477	3,443	1,034	3,917	3,003	914	4,477	3,278	1,199	3,917	2,838	1,079
40,000	8,886	6,827	2,059	7,052	5,434	1,618	6,312	4,874	1,438	7,052	5,154	1,898	6,312	4,615	1,697
50,000	12,559	9,673	2,886	10,183	7,825	2,358	9,323	7,165	2,158	10,183	7,413	2,770	9,323	6,753	2,570
60,000	16,392	12,839	3,553	13,602	10,456	3,146	12,634	9,706	2,928	13,602	9,886	3,716	12,634	9,211	3,423
100,000	31,792	27,155	4,637	28,878	22,896	5,982	27,878	22,056	5,822	28,878	21,846	7,032	27,878	21,006	6,872

Source: Reproduced from U.S. Congress JCT (1981, 26), table IV-4.

[a]Includes the impact of the rate reductions and the deductions for two-earner married couples. Other individual income tax provisions not reflected here are indexing, the child care and dependent care credit, charitable contributions for nonitemizers, rollover period for sale of residence, and changes in the taxation of foreign earned income. Assumes that deductible expenses are 23% of income.

[b]Assumes that all income is wage and salary or self-employment income.

[c]Assumes lesser earning spouse earns 25% of combined income.

11.4 Aggregate Data Studies

11.4.1 Summary

Aggregate data measures of tax burden add two extensions to representative taxpayer analysis. The first extension uses estimates of the distribution of income and "allocators" of tax burden, such as consumption of taxed goods, by size class to calculate the distribution of total taxes paid by each income class. Comparisons of the distribution of taxes to the distribution of income allow evaluations of the overall progressivity or regressivity of the tax system. The second extension includes all federal, state, and local taxes through aggregated reports of taxes collected across the Nation rather than relying on a few illustrative (although carefully researched) states. (Pechman's 1951 comparison of federal income tax burdens in 1941 and 1947 is one of the few major aggregate data studies that examines only one tax source.)

Newly available income distribution data made aggregate data studies possible beginning in 1940. Aggregate data studies were used in setting tax policy throughout the 1940s and 1950s. These measures continued to be calculated through the 1960s (Bishop 1967; Herriot and Miller 1971a, 1971b) and continue to be used in making policy at the state level. In federal tax policy analysis, they have largely been replaced by microdata studies that allow more detailed analyses and estimates of horizontal equity.

11.4.2 Data

The unpublished Shere report (Shere 1934) calculated total national tax burdens as a proportion of income and wealth from 1899 to 1933 based on national income and wealth series developed by the National Industrial Conference Board. Distributions of income and wealth, and therefore of tax burden, were not calculated.

Pettengill (1940) extended Newcomer's study of the tax burden of representative taxpayers to develop a distribution of total tax burden across income classes. The extension depended heavily on a "fortunate coincidence" (1940, 62) in the years covered by Newcomer's study and by the National Resources Committee report on the distribution of consumer incomes in the United States, 1935–36 (Baird and Fine, 1939).

Colm and Tarasov (1941), another early aggregate data study, notes that actual statistics on the desired data rarely exist for the categories required for the analysis. Lacking these data, researchers use estimates based on other data sources to distribute estimates of total taxes and income across income groups, where the estimated totals themselves might be based on relatively small samples. "Yet it is frankly admitted that this is an experimental approach that requires further refinement. It is hoped that the 1940 Census of Population, in conjunction with a more detailed analysis of the 1939 income tax returns, will permit more accurate statistics on the distribution of incomes than the one used in the present report" (1941, 2).

Consider, for example, only the basic data sources listed by Colm and Tarasov (1941). (The lists of the supplementary general material and special topics—often specific state studies—are at least as long.) The National Resources Committee provided data on consumer incomes and expenditures and on the structure of the American economy. The Commerce Department provided data on state income payments and national income and other financial statistics of state and local governments, along with the wonderful miscellany of the statistical abstract. Estimates of federal, state, and local revenues were provided by the Treasury, along with data on individual and corporate income tax returns through the Statistics of Income. The Social Security Board provided information on median wages of covered workers. The BLS provided data on urban consumer purchases.

The creation of the Joint Committee on the Economic Report and its Subcommittee on Economic Statistics reflected widespread awareness of the fragmented state of data needed for policy-making. By 1949, when Musgrave et al. (1951) studied the distribution of tax burden in 1948, the situation was little improved, with the available evidence "discouragingly scarce" (1), and in some cases imposing "limitations [that] are appalling" (8). As Pechman noted in commenting on the debate about the Musgrave study, the available data were at best "recalcitrant," with "no officially recognized annual distributions of income and consumption by income classes, let alone tax distributions which depend on these basic data" (Pechman 1951, 204). Income data were taken from the 1949 Survey of Consumer Finances, with expenditure totals derived as residuals from reported income less income taxes and savings. Expenditure distributions, required for the distribution of sales and excise taxes, were derived from BLS budget studies for a limited number of cities.

Long-standing reconciliation problems among survey data (such as the Survey of Consumer Finances), administrative record data (such as the Statistics of Income), and national account estimates provided grounds for much of Tucker's (1951, 1952) criticism of the Musgrave study. The limitations of the available consumer budget studies, and an alternative proposal for dealing with them, were a second dimension of the criticism.

11.4.3 Assumptions and Results

Disagreements about appropriate statistical sources also reflected the lack of a consensus on the appropriate definition of income for tax burden measures. The Haig-Simons definition of income (consumption plus change in net worth) had not yet emerged as the standard definition in applied work, although the concept had long been accepted in theory. In practice, the considerable limitations of data on assets and imputed income (important for rural residents, homeowners, and for recipients of fringe benefits) made it difficult to implement this concept. An alternative income concept, proposed by Pechman (1951) and similar to that used by Musgrave et al. (1951), was the income concept used for tax purposes. Taxable income corresponded more closely to a money income concept, and had the advantage of being readily available from Statistics of Income.

The state of tax incidence theory was no more settled than that of income theory. It had long been understood that assumptions about the ultimate incidence of corporate, sales, payroll, and excise taxes clearly affected conclusions about the distribution of tax burden. But the theory provided mixed guidance on which taxpayers actually bear the burden of the various taxes. At the same time, it was recognized that tax burden could not be measured independent of incidence assumptions (see, e.g., Colm and Tarasov 1941, 2). The incidence of taxes remained undetermined in theory in part because the tasks of specifying the full workings of a general equilibrium solution were then near the frontiers of economic theory (see, e.g., Oakes 1942). Reflecting the ambiguous state of theory, tax burden studies presented conclusions based on a series of alternative incidence assumptions (see, e.g., Newcomer 1937b; Colm and Tarasov 1941; Pettengill 1940; Adler 1951; and Pechman 1951). Typically, differences among studies were attributable as much to fundamental differences in income concept and data sources as to differences in incidence assumptions. (See, e.g., the analysis by Musgrave et al. 1951 of differences among their results and those of Colm and Tarasov 1941 and Adler 1951.)

Although the studies vary in their specific burden measures, they tend to agree on the general shape of the tax burden distribution before and after World War II. That structure is roughly U-shaped: regressive at the lowest income levels, approximately proportional over middle incomes, and progressive at higher income levels.

The results of aggregate data studies are generally summarized in two sets of comparisons. The first comparison is between the percentage of total income received by each income class and the percentage of total taxes paid by that class (e.g., Colm and Tarasov 1941, 28; and Musgrave et al. 1951, 26). This information sometimes is used, together with data on the distribution of households across income classes, to evaluate the equity of the tax system through Lorenz curves or Gini coefficients (as do Pettengill 1940; Adler 1951; Pechman 1951). When such comparisons are made across tax regimes, their interpretation can be complicated if the income distributions change in ways that cause the Lorenz curves to cross (see, e.g., Pechman 1951). The second comparison is of taxes paid as a percentage of income across income classes. This comparison reveals the progressivity of the tax system. Both comparisons are contained in table 11.6, which reproduces the summary table from Musgrave et al. (1951).

11.4.4 Policy Uses

Federal tax policy, as it responded to the array of problems facing the nation from the 1930s through the 1950s, was shaped in part by the tax burden stud-

Table 11.6 **Distribution of Tax Payments by Income Groups: Summary**[a]

Item	Spending Unit Income Brackets (thousands of dollars)							
	Under 1	1–2	2–3	3–4	4–5	5–7.5	7.5 and over	Total
Amounts (in $ million):								
1. Federal	620	2,243	5,392	6,682	5,079	6,754	17,010	43,794
2. State and local	433	1,123	2,131	2,512	1,755	2,061	3,542	13,552
3. All levels	1,052	3,366	7,523	9,194	6,834	8,815	20,552	57,344
Percent of yield total:								
4. Federal	1.4	5.1	12.3	15.3	11.6	15.4	38.8	100.0
5. State and local	3.2	8.3	15.7	18.5	12.9	15.2	26.1	100.0
6. All levels	1.8	5.9	13.1	16.0	11.9	15.4	35.8	100.0
Percent of income:								
7. Federal	16.5	16.2	18.6	19.0	19.3	21.1	30.1	22.3
8. State and local	11.6	8.1	7.3	7.1	6.7	6.4	6.3	6.9
a. State	5.8	3.9	3.7	3.7	3.5	3.4	3.4	3.6
b. Local	5.8	4.2	3.7	3.5	3.2	3.0	2.8	3.3
9. All Levels	28.1	24.3	25.9	26.1	26.0	27.6	36.3	29.2
Addenda:								
10. Income received	3,747	13,850	29,037	35,207	26,283	31,953	56,542	196,619
11. Percent of income[b]	1.9	7.0	14.8	17.9	13.4	16.3	28.8	100.0
12. Percent of spending units	12.2	17.7	22.9	20.1	11.6	10.2	5.3	100.0

Source: Reproduced from Musgrave et al. (1951), 26.
Note: Details may not add to totals because of rounding.
[a]Standard assumptions throughout.
[b]Includes income imputed under standard corporation assumption.

ies. Aggregate data studies (except for Tucker 1951) tended to similar conclusions despite reliance on a diversity of data sources, time periods, assumptions, and methodologies. All concluded that the federal tax structure was highly progressive, primarily because corporate and personal income taxes and death taxes that applied to the upper end of the income distribution offset regressive federal excise and payroll taxes. The total tax burden, including state and local taxes, was found to be less progressive, with taxpayers in the lowest income brackets sometimes found to bear a higher ratio of taxes to income than middle-income taxpayers (see Adler 1951; Pettengill 1940; as well as Musgrave 1952, 1953; Colm and Wald 1952; and Pechman 1951 above). Increasing the progressivity of the tax structure, either by raising statutory income tax rates for upper-income brackets or raising their effective tax rates through base broadening, was a consistent goal of federal tax policy. The choice among alternative revenue sources to balance budget deficits, hold down inflation, and pay for wars was made not only on the basis of their relative yield and administrative feasibility, but also on the basis of their relative effects on equity.

World War II financing took account of the conclusions of early tax burden studies that the federal income tax was the most progressive of the federal government's tax instruments. Congress raised rates and lowered exemptions to the federal income tax, turning the income tax into a broad-based tax. In the early 1950s, policy recommendations in the Economic Report of the President (1951) addressed the growing tax burden and problems in measuring it when prices and incomes were growing rapidly. The Joint Committee on the Economic Report shared those concerns. It proposed quelling inflationary tendencies induced by financing the Korean War by selectively raising the excise taxes that would most affect middle- and upper-income taxpayers: "If tax burdens are so great as to shock the sense of justice or equality, some way is found to avoid them or to pass them on into higher prices," and therefore, specific tax proposals "should take cognizance of the fact that the people in the lower-income brackets . . . are already overburdened . . . by the increasing cost of living and the present level of taxes," and new taxes should be targeted "to absorb surplus purchasing power where it exists" (U.S. Congress, JCER 1951, 7–8).

11.4.5 Problems

The data available through the 1950s and the aggregate data approach did not allow measures of horizontal equity within income classes to be calculated. Horizontal equity was an issue because of the postwar growth in sources of untaxed income that would tend to increase the variability of tax burdens within an income class. Pechman (1958) noted this problem in a discussion of Goldsmith's conclusion that pre- and postwar income distributions were similar. The 1959 Tax Revision Compendium, a summary of congressional hearings (U.S. Congress, House Committee on Ways and Means 1959), also raised the question of horizontal equity. Despite the growing concern, however, there were few alternatives available for empirical work. Data on the taxes, income, and consumption of individuals and families, together with ways to link these data would have been required to construct the necessary tax burden measures. The income measure would need to be independent of the current tax law, as well. The unit of interest for equity comparisons, usually the household or family unit, was rarely the unit for which data was available. In particular, income tax data were presented on the basis of filing units, generally different from the family or household survey units underlying expenditure data and other income surveys.

Additional questions about the internal consistency of assumptions on the incidence and timing of taxes were raised by Prest (1955). Many of the inconsistencies reflected difficulties inherent in applying a theoretical framework that is essentially a long-run general equilibrium framework to the analysis of a single period.

11.5 Microdata Studies

11.5.1 Summary

Microdata studies represent one of the two major directions of current tax burden research. Microdata studies improve upon aggregate data models in their greater capability to model variations in tax burden across individuals within an income class (i.e., to address horizontal equity), their relative independence from the tax base defined in current law, and their ability to describe results by demographic and nontax economic characteristics of policy interest. The first tax microdata model, developed at Treasury in the early 1960s, was used to assess tax burden in constructing President Kennedy's 1963 reform proposals. Microdata models are widely used in current policy analysis by the Office of Tax Analysis (OTA) of the Treasury Department and the Joint Committee on Taxation, among others. The OTA simulation model and its relationship to new data developments and limitations are discussed in section 11.7 below.

11.5.2 Data and Technology

The need for data on individual economic units in order to measure the equity of tax burden among individuals with similar incomes but differential access to exclusions and differential patterns of consumption, income, and savings had been noted as early as 1951 (Pechman), but neither the data nor the means to analyze them became available until the early 1960s.

Data

The heavy data demands that tax burden studies make were partially met by the growing availability of tax and survey microdata. Serious gaps, however, persisted. A 1964 study conducted for the Subcommittee on Economic Statistics by T. Paul Schultz examined the statistics available on the size distribution of personal income in the United States and presented a series of recommended changes (U.S. Congress, JEC 1965a). A number of those recommendations were directly relevant for measuring the income component of tax burden. Several of those proposals addressed the lack of data on wealth and nonlabor income, a serious omission for any attempt to construct a comprehensive income measure. The upcoming 1970 census could be modified to collect net wealth data and also more finely detailed categories of personal income than before. The annual Survey of Consumer Finances also was an obvious potential vehicle for collecting data on net worth of consumer units, particularly in light of the panel character of the data collection in 1961–63. Finally, demographic and financial data could be collected from an expansion of the individual income tax form.

Subsequent hearings and collections of views by statistical agencies and users of federal statistics resulted in similar recommendations for more detailed and timely data (U.S. Congress, JEC 1965a, 1965b, 1966, 1967, 1969). Schultz's recommendation for using new computer technology to link data collected by various statistical agencies was repeated in the later hearings and emerged as a proposal for a central statistical service center. When the problem of maintaining personal privacy under such a center was raised, proponents were confident that stringent safeguards could enhance rather than reduce the confidentiality of government statistical records (U.S. Congress, JEC 1967). In an increasingly computerized era, however, public concern about privacy was growing as evidenced in the 1969 hearings before the Subcommittee on Economic Statistics. The perception that an Orwellian Big Brother was possible created a firestorm about the upcoming 1970 census, particularly when coupled with debates over proposals by the statistical agencies that citizens should be compelled, under threat of jail or fine, to respond. In the face of public opposition, the proposal for a central statistical service center fell by the wayside. Neither of the two remaining proposals bore fruit in their original form. Rather than being expanded, the Survey of Consumer Finances was soon discontinued. Concerns about respondent burden and privacy limited expansions of the federal income tax forms.

A new wave of detailed surveys on income, wealth, poverty, and movements among income classes was begun in the 1960s to address these data needs. Public-use versions of the Statistics of Income individual return data were available from the early 1960's. The 1967 Survey of Economic Opportunity collected information on assets and nonwage income from 30,000 households. Public-use microdata tapes for the monthly CPS were first made available for March 1968. The CPS collected demographic and income information on individuals and also on their households. Longitudinal surveys, such as the Panel Survey of Income Dynamics (PSID) and the series of National Longitudinal Surveys (NLS) of age cohorts of men and women, were begun.

Despite these new surveys, none collected income, consumption, and wealth in a single, nationally representative, large-scale statistical source. To the contrary, data availability in general worsened until recently. The 1963–64 Survey of the Financial Characteristics of Consumers remained the most recent source of wealth data on an individual basis until the Federal Reserve Board repeated the survey in 1983 and (on a limited basis) 1986. The current sample size is an order of magnitude below that of the CPS. The Survey of Income and Program Participation (SIPP) meets the need Schultz articulated in 1964 for detailed demographic and economic data over time in a broad-based national survey, and includes one-year-apart surveys of wealth in its longitudinal framework for 1983–84 (see McNeil and Lamas 1989). Needs for detailed data on the receipt and cost of fringe benefits by individual taxpayers, stated by Pechman (1951) and repeated periodically (see U.S. Congress, JEC 1965b; Triplett 1983) remained largely unmet. For example, although the May 1979 CPS collected data on the receipt of employer-provided retirement and health benefits and repeated similar questions in May 1983 and May 1988, it did not collect either the amount of employer contributions for these benefits or the incidence of other benefits. Consumption and expenditure data were provided at intervals of a decade (by the Survey of Consumer Expenditures conducted for the BLS in 1960–61 and 1971–73) until the current series of ongoing Consumer Expenditures Surveys began in 1980. Reliance on some method of record linking or of imputing data missing on the basic data source remains an essential component of current tax burden methodology.

Computing Technology

Developing a sample of tax returns that would permit detail and accuracy as well as speed and flexibility in modeling the burdens of alternative tax provisions required computer technology. The Internal Revenue Service had joined with the Census Bureau in 1955 to purchase a computer. The Statistics of Income samples were then put on computer tapes, but the format could not be readily adapted to different analytical uses outside specific Statistics of Income applications. Researchers, IRS advisory groups, and tax policymakers recommended creating a microdata file for tax policy research. The first microdata computer tape of a sample of individual tax returns for use in examining tax burdens was not produced until February 1962. The data were a 100,000-record subsample of the 429,000 tax returns used to produce the 1960 Statistics of Income tabulations. The subsample was produced and stored on computer tape at the request of the Office of Tax Analysis (OTA) of the U.S. Treasury. The computer technology available, while it made the project feasible at all, was costly and cumbersome. The data file required 50 reels of tape, the model required four to six weeks of programming time for each set of complex changes in tax provisions, and simulations consumed as much as eight hours of computer time, with total cost of a model run exceeding $1,000 (in 1962 dollars).

Computing cost was not the sole resource constraint. Techniques that made statistical matches among records from multiple surveys in attempts to fill gaps in the individual surveys typically required even greater programming and computing capabilities than analyses of single microdata files. Because of the resources required, microdata models tended either to rely on a sole data source (as did the OTA model) or to be long-term research products describing a period a year or more in the past. Research commissioned by the OTA in the mid-1970s dramatically reduced the computer time needed to produce a matched file that had desirable statistical properties. The standard optimal technique required five weeks for one of the six steps in the match; the new technique (Barr and Turner 1978) required six hours. Documenting all the matching, weighting, imputing, extrapolating, and tax calculating programs that produced the final tax model data base demanded commitment of scarce staff resources.

Continuing declines in quality-adjusted computing costs make the computing services that microsimulation require increasingly affordable. The microsimulation model has become an integral part of tax policy formation for both the OTA and the Joint Committee on Taxation, and remains a major evaluation tool for policy analysts outside the federal government.

Statistical Innovations

An important innovation for tax burden research was instituting efficient sampling techniques in the Statistics of Income program. When the wartime conversion of the income tax to a broad-based tax dramatically increased the number of tax returns, Statistics of Income's prewar practice of tabulating a relatively high proportion of returns (e.g., one out of four returns in 1926) quickly became cumbersome (Natrella 1966). Improved sampling produced a manageable number of returns for analysis, and the sample size continued to drop as sampling technique became increasingly sophisticated.

11.5.3 Studies Based on Microdata

Studies Based on One Microdata Source

Annual public-use versions of the Statistics of Income sample were made available to other researchers beginning with the 1962 sample (Natrella 1966). Pechman's 1965 study of the change in tax burdens under the Revenue Act of 1964, the earliest published study using microdata, was based on a sample of 100,000 federal tax returns. With access to the details of individual records, tax liability could be calculated from the individual records rather than from income class averages. Variations in definitions of income could also be explored.

The tax return sample increased modeling capabilities, but room for improvement remained. Returns were available only for individuals required to file tax returns under the current tax law, but information on those not required to file was needed to model the effects of tax proposals that made major modifications to the Internal Revenue Code. Modeling capabilities also were constrained by the limited information recorded on tax returns. Demographic data were not recorded on tax returns, although policy questions often asked about the equality of tax burdens across demographic groups. There was no way to join tax returns of related individuals to form real families, although the unit of policy interest was generally the family rather than the individual. Treasury testimony (in U.S. Congress, Senate, Committee on Finance 1962) and Pechman (1965) reflect these limitations. Treasury's adjusted gross income measure and Pechman's taxable income measure both depended on income items reported on the tax return, rather than on a broader Haig-Simons income measure.

A series of microdata models of tax burden followed these seminal studies in the 1960s and early 1970s. The new studies drew on technical innovations and new microdata sources. Bossons developed "A General Income Tax Analyzer" in 1966 for Canada, using 1964 tax return data (Bossons 1967). The introduction acknowledges the integral role of the computer in the development and practical use of that model. The raw data, 412,000 tax returns, initially were stored on 16 reels of tape before similar returns were aggregated into a more tractable 19,000 groups. Bossons's study describes its methodology and data sources clearly and provides the 200 pages of computer code required to convert the raw data into final printed tables. This documentation appears to be the first public offering of such material to other potential analysts. The pragmatic effect of the model on Canadian tax policy was to make it feasible to examine the effect of a series of alternative rate schedules and thereby to "obtain a significantly lower rate schedule that would raise sufficient revenue and which would come closer to meeting the commission's objectives" than the original, hand-calculated rate schedule (Bossons 1967, 2). Estimates of tax burden by income, age, occupation, and sex were calculated for alternative tax schedules.

Researchers interested in measuring U.S. tax burden applied similar methodologies to new data sources. A new National Survey of Consumer Expenditures and Income for 1960–61, conducted by the BLS, was the basic data source in an aggregate data study by Bishop (1967) comparing tax burdens in 1961 and 1965. Herriot and Miller (1971a, 1971b) relied on tabulations from the 1968 CPS as the basic data source in their aggregate study, supplemented by distributions of consumption, wealth, and taxes from the 1960–61 BLS Expenditure Survey, the 1960 Survey of Consumer Finances and the 1963 Survey of Financial Characteristics of Consumers, and the Statistics of Income.

A series of studies exploited the underlying microdata of new surveys. Browning and Johnson (1979) conducted a tax burden study using the 47,000-household CPS microdata from March 1975. Longitudinal data from the PSID for 1967–77 (including income and asset data, federal tax payments, and family and other demographic data) were used by Ott and Dittrich (1981) to examine changes in tax burden under the Revenue Acts of 1969 through 1978. Berliant and Strauss (1983, 1985) make use of an 11-year series of public-use Statistics of Income tax data files, with several hundred thousand observations in each year's file (about twice the size of the OTA's tax file). The computational resources required by the size of the data sets and the complexity of their burden calculations were large enough both for comment and discussion of methods for reducing the size of the computations. The NBER also maintains a microdata model based on Statistics of Income data (Feldstein 1987).

Tax burden models based on a single underlying microdata source share several limitations. Models based on tax records have little information on income from nontaxable sources and no information at all on those not required to file under current law. The taxpaying unit generally is not the family or spending unit whose relative welfare is being evaluated under alternative tax structures; demographic and other information needed to form family units are not collected on tax returns. The models based on nontax survey data are better able to combine data to form appropriate family units and to analyze the tax burden of alternative demographic groups, but typically have less precise information about the taxes actually paid by the surveyed units. Similar problems during the 1960's were encountered by researchers interested in developing size distributions of income to measure poverty and analyze its causes (Budd and Radner 1969).

Studies Based on Multiple Microdata Sources

Exact and statistical linkage of several microdata files were proposed as a method of providing the information missing from any single survey. The movement toward matching of data sets was partially motivated by the decreasing cost and increasing speed at which such tasks could be accomplished. Prices for second-generation computers had been declining since 1962, and the introduction of third-generation machines in the mid-1960s lowered the prices of older machines as well as providing new technology whose own quality-adjusted price also continued to decline over time (Triplett 1989). Exact-match experiments conducted in the 1970s produced, for example, the 1973 three-way exact match of the IRS, CPS, and Social Security Administration records. Confidentiality problems, however, made the resulting data difficult for most researchers to use whether outside government or within. Statistical linkage of tax return records from the Statistics of Income and the CPS was first accomplished not for calculating tax burden but for measuring poverty (Budd and Radner 1969), although the applicability of the technique to improved tax research was clearly stated. The importance of advances in computer technology to statistical linkages was also explicitly noted.

The first tax burden study to use statistically linked microdata was Pechman and Okner (1974), based on the 1967 Survey of Economic Opportunity and the 1966 Statistics of Income public-use sample. The Survey of Economic Opportunity had observations on about 30,000 households, and the Statistics of Income sample contained about 87,000 returns. Updated versions of the original Survey of Economic Opportunity–Statistics of Income data, with the CPS replacing the Survey of Economic Opportunity, continued to be used to analyze the distribution of tax burdens (Pechman 1985 and 1986). The OTA constructed statistically matched data for its tax model in 1976 and used that model in preparing tax reform proposals in 1977. Statistically linked microdata from the CPS and the Statistics of Income became its standard tax model data base.

11.5.4 Assumptions and Results

Tax burden measures based on microdata models generally show the overall tax structure from the 1960s through 1980s to be roughly proportional, despite differences among the models in data sources, theories of tax incidence, and estimation methodologies. The proportional tax structure contrasts with early representative taxpayer and aggregate data studies that showed a U-shaped structure.

An important advantage of microdata models over aggregate data models is that tax burden estimates can be calculated to assess horizontal equity. Such calculations, made by Ott and Ott (Commission to Revise the Tax Structure 1973), Pechman and Okner (1974), and Pechman (1985), show substantial variations in burden among households with similar incomes. Tables 11.7 and 11.8 reproduce tables from Pechman and Okner that use microdata to assess the degree of horizontal equity in the tax system. Means, standard deviations, medians, and quantile variations in effective tax rates are calculated for two alternative sets of incidence assumptions. The calculations are made separately for each population income decile. The degree of variability of effective tax rates varies by income class under both sets of incidence assumptions. Effective tax rates for demographic and economic subgroups, such as the aged and nonaged and homeowners and renters, are calculated in table 11.8 for a detailed series of taxes under the same two sets of incidence assumptions. Table 11.9 reproduces a table from the Commission to Revise the Tax Structure (1973) showing horizontal equity by income class based on frequency distributions of effective tax rates by income class.

Table 11.7 Mean and Median Effective Federal, State, and Local Tax Rates and Measures of Variability of Tax Rates under Incidence Variants 1c and 3b, by Population Decile, 1966 (in percentages)

	Variant 1c				Variant 3b			
Population Decile	Mean	Standard Deviation[a]	Median	Quartile Deviation[a]	Mean	Standard Deviation[a]	Median	Quartile Deviation[a]
First[b]	16.8	30.1	15.3	6.1	27.6	35.9	23.0	6.6
Second	18.6	14.6	17.8	5.3	24.8	16.3	23.6	4.9
Third	21.6	19.6	21.3	4.1	26.0	12.6	25.0	4.2
Fourth	22.6	8.8	22.1	3.8	25.9	10.5	25.2	3.7
Fifth	22.8	6.5	22.6	3.2	25.8	7.3	25.4	3.2
Sixth	22.7	5.5	22.6	2.8	25.6	5.8	25.6	2.6
Seventh	22.7	6.6	22.4	2.7	25.5	5.5	25.3	2.4
Eighth	23.1	5.9	22.7	2.5	25.5	5.2	25.4	2.2
Ninth	23.2	5.4	22.9	2.4	25.1	4.9	25.1	2.2
Tenth	26.2	10.2	24.5	3.9	25.0	8.6	24.6	2.5

Source: Computed from the 1966 MERGE data file. For an explanation of the incidence variants, see Table 3-1. Reproduced from Pechman and Olkner (1974), 67.
Note: Variant 1c is the most progressive and 3b the least progressive set of incidence assumptions used in this study.
[a]See text for the definition of the standard deviation and the quartile deviation.
[b]Includes only units in the sixth to tenth percentiles.

Table 11.8 **Effective Federal, State, and Local Tax Rates for Various Demographic and Economic Groups under Incidence Variants 1c and 3b, 1966 (in %)**

Group and Variant	Individual Income Tax	Corporation Income Tax	Property Tax	Sales and Excise Taxes	Payroll Taxes	Personal Property and Motor Vehicle Taxes	Total Taxes
Nonaged:							
Variant 1c	8.7	3.2	2.5	5.2	4.9	.3	24.8
Variant 3b	8.6	4.1	3.2	5.1	4.6	.3	25.9
Aged:							
Variant 1c	6.9	8.2	5.9	4.5	1.9	.2	27.6
Variant 3b	7.2	6.6	4.4	4.7	2.8	.2	25.9
Homeowners:							
Variant 1c	8.4	4.4	3.4	4.7	4.0	.3	25.2
Variant 3b	8.3	4.6	3.6	4.7	4.0	.3	25.6
Renters:							
Variant 1c	8.7	2.7	1.9	6.1	5.6	.2	25.3
Variant 3b	8.5	4.0	2.8	6.0	5.3	.2	26.9
Urban:							
Variant 1c	9.0	3.8	2.7	5.0	4.6	.3	25.4
Variant 3b	9.0	4.2	3.1	5.0	4.5	.3	26.0
Rural-Farm:							
Variant 1c	6.0	4.6	4.3	5.4	3.7	.3	24.3
Variant 3b	6.0	5.5	4.6	5.3	3.8	.3	25.5
Single persons:							
Variant 1c	11.1	6.5	3.7	5.7	4.3	.2	31.6
Variant 3b	11.5	5.0	3.0	5.9	4.6	.2	30.2
Married couples, no children:							
Variant 1c	9.0	5.9	4.3	4.7	3.7	.3	27.9
Variant 3b	9.2	5.2	3.6	4.8	3.8	.3	26.8
Married couples, two children:							
Variant 1c	8.7	2.7	2.2	5.0	4.8	.3	23.8
Variant 3b	8.5	3.8	3.1	4.9	4.6	.3	25.2

Source: Computed from the 1966 MERGE data file. For an explanation of the incidence variants, see table 3-1. Reproduced from Pechman and Okner (1974), 72.
Note: Variant 1c is the most progressive and 3b the least progressive set of incidence assumptions used in this study.

11.5.5 Policy Uses

Tax burden studies based on microdata models have generally concluded that the prevailing tax structure was roughly proportional to income for most of the population, with the Federal income tax the major progressive component. (Browning and Johnson [1979], who found the present system highly progressive, are exceptions.) Proportionality of taxes and progressivity of the

Table 11.9 Frequency Distribution of Effective Tax Rates for Selected Income Classes under Alternative B and Present Law, 1971 (households in thousands)

	3,000–4,999		5,000–6,999		10,000–11,999		50,000–99,999	
Rates	Present Law	Alternative B	Present Law	Alternative B	Present Law	Alternative B	Present Law	Alternative B
0–1	3183.55	2284.00	1750.92	60.10	120.89	14.17	2.53	.00
1–2	643.89	4359.29	661.78	643.49	54.85	1.14	.58	1.15
2–3	667.76	902.44	640.64	3811.53	196.81	53.33	1.38	.00
3–4	837.12	.00	712.51	3269.93	227.73	137.44	.12	.00
4–5	580.57	.00	694.13	248.60	437.12	245.24	.23	.00
5–6	621.13	.00	534.22	.00	703.06	2126.21	.23	2.30
6–7	688.97	.00	612.63	.00	722.58	3902.95	.35	.00
7–8	254.89	.00	579.72	.00	1008.46	1238.60	4.94	.00
8–9	49.94	.00	866.65	.00	839.72	18.03	8.14	4.59
9–10	18.03	.00	632.58	.00	1101.17	.00	6.32	.00
10–12	.00	.00	285.71	.00	889.72	.00	2.89	.00
12–14	.00	.00	57.77	.00	785.73	.00	28.49	5.98
14–16	.00	.00	.00	.00	472.01	.00	35.76	10.45
16–18	.00	.00	4.59	.00	4.59	.00	80.15	18.26
18–20	.00	.00	.00	.00	42.11	.00	78.16	19.20
20–22	.00	.00	.00	.00	117.59	.00	79.28	39.09
22–24	.00	.00	.00	.00	13.15	.00	79.80	61.98
24–26	.00	.00	.00	.00	.00	.00	85.65	145.45
26–28	.00	.00	.00	.00	.00	.00	64.40	134.71
28–30	.00	.00	.00	.00	.00	.00	44.81	111.90
30–34	.00	.00	.00	.00	.00	.00	32.21	77.83
34–38	.00	.00	.00	.00	.00	.00	41.72	59.94
38–42	.00	.00	.00	.00	.00	.00	12.37	.00
42–46	.00	.00	.00	.00	.00	.00	2.08	.00
46–50	.00	.00	.00	.00	.00	.00	.23	.00
50–54	.00	.00	.00	.00	.00	.00	.00	.00
54–58	.00	.00	.00	.00	.00	.00	.00	.00
58–62	.00	.00	.00	.00	.00	.00	.00	.00
62–66	.00	.00	.00	.00	.00	.00	.00	.00
66–70	.00	.00	.00	.00	.00	.00	.00	.00
Total Households	7,545.85	7,545.73	8,033.85	8,033.65	7,737.29	7,737.11	692.82	692.83

Source: Reproduced from Commission to Revise the Tax Structure (1973), 182–83.
Note: Total households in each class differ slightly due to rounding.

federal income tax remain relatively stable conclusions across studies and across alternative incidence assumptions within a study. Horizontal inequities are found within income classes, attributable to specific features of the Internal Revenue Code (additional exemptions or exclusions, for example) and to variations in income sources and consumption patterns.

The policy implications that follow from these conclusions are to broaden the tax base, lower tax rates (especially at lower incomes), and eliminate excise taxes, thereby increasing horizontal equity while achieving the desired vertical distribution of the tax burden. These conclusions are common to most of the microdata studies (Browning and Johnson 1979 again are an exception) as well as common to prior studies based on aggregate data (see the 1959 Tax Revision Compendium [U.S. Congress House Committee on Ways and Means 1959]; e.g., as well as Musgrave et al. 1951). Not surprisingly, the major tax reform proposals of the last decade have reflected these conclusions.

The first Treasury tax model was immediately put to use in preparing President Kennedy's 1963 Tax Message. That Message proposed, in "the most urgent task confronting the Congress in 1963," to reform the federal tax system to provide stimulus to the economy and to minimize "inequities and complexities that affect similarly suited taxpayers in wholly different ways," while making the largest proportionate reduction "to those at the bottom of the economic ladder" (U.S. Congress, House 1963, 154–55). Table 3 of that Message compares distributions of tax burden among income classes under then-current law and under the proposed law. Since 1963, tables produced from the OTA and the Joint Committee on Taxation microsimulation models have been used extensively in the consideration of all major tax bills.

11.5.6 Problems

Despite their advances over aggregate data models, microdata models still are limited with respect to data, economic theory, statistical theory and practice, and computer technology. The limitations reduce the models' abilities to address policy questions in ways that inform the debate rather than diverting the debate to the merits of the estimates they generate.

Theoretical problems, unresolved with respect to aggregate data models, persist in microdata models. Even in the definition of income, where consensus in principle on the Haig-Simons definition of income has a long history (see Musgrave 1985), differences in interpretation arise in practice. Thus, both Pechman and Okner (1974) and Browning and Johnson (1979) adopt Haig-Simons income definitions, but differ on, among other things, which transfer income items are included. The studies differ also in their assumptions on the shifting of taxes, an area where there is somewhat less consensus in the literature. The absence of a consensus on incidence complicates evaluations of the models. Whalley (1984) presents a series of calculations showing the sensitivity of tax burden measures to alternative incidence assumptions and income measures similar to Pechman and Okner (1974), on the one hand, and to those of Browning and Johnson (1979), on the other. A comparison of pairs of tax burden measures shows that the choice of shifting assumptions alone can determine whether the tax structure appears to be progressive or regressive. Similarly, the choice of income concept alone can determine progressivity or regressivity. Other assumptions, such as the choice of time period (single periods or lifetimes) over which tax burden ought to be measured, and the economic unit (e.g., families, households, or tax returns) also directly affects the conclusions.

The statistical matching of two microdata sets raises a host of unresolved statistical questions about the properties of the resulting matched data set. See, for example, the discussion about the Survey of Economic Opportunity and the CPS linkage underlying Pechman and Okner (1974) (Okner 1972a, 1972b; Sims 1972; Peck 1972; Budd 1972), and a parallel discussion of linkages between other microdata sets (Okner 1974; Sims 1974). Treasury sponsored further research on statistical problems with merged data files (Kadane 1978) and also sponsored new research on alternative linking techniques with better statistical properties (Barr and Turner 1978). Policy needs unmet by existing data sets outweighed criticism of matched data sets, however, and microsimulation models linking data from multiple sources rapidly became standard in tax policy and other policy settings (Barr and Turner 1978). Research has continued to improve the statistical properties of such data sets with missing data (see, e.g., Kalton 1983; Rodgers 1984; David et al. 1986; Rubin 1987; and Little and Rubin 1987).

Beyond the problems of statistical matching, microdata models encounter additional statistical problems. The subgroup of interest for a specific policy problem frequently is a subgroup for which the underlying sample is too small to make accurate estimates. For example, policies are frequently evaluated for their effect on the poor or the elderly, or on the recipients of one kind of income versus another, while the original sample was not designed to represent those subgroups. Another problem is that analyses are typically wanted for the current period or for a federal budget period, while data become available only with a lag (e.g., 1986 tax return data will become available in 1988). The data must be extrapolated to current and future dollar levels through implicit or explicit modeling of growth and change.

11.6 Applied General Equilibrium Studies

11.6.1 Summary

Applied general equilibrium models developed over the last 15 years into the second major tool for analyzing tax policy and its effects on the distribution of tax burden. Practical implementation of these models was spurred by formal proofs of the existence of competitive equilibrium under quite general conditions and the development of efficient computing algorithms, together with computer speed and capacity to make their solutions practical as well as possible. Applied general equilibrium models quickly added features of the tax system and grew increasingly disaggregated. The appeal of these models for analyzing tax policy is the appeal of general, rather than partial, equilibrium analysis itself. The general equilibrium approach provides a formal framework for examining the interaction among various taxes and transfer programs and their joint effect on economywide allocation, distribution, and growth questions. Tax burden analysis and the tax incidence literature both are generally couched in general equilibrium terms. Much of the empirical analysis used in the policy debate was nevertheless set in partial equilibrium terms (see, e.g., Musgrave et al. 1951; Pechman 1985; Cilke and Wyscarver 1987; U.S. Congress, Congressional Budget Office 1987).

The first relatively large-scale applied general equilibrium models were developed in the early 1970s (Shoven and Whalley 1972; Shoven 1976). The evolution of applied general equilibrium models is recounted elsewhere (Fullerton, Shoven, and Whalley 1978; Shoven and Whalley 1983; Piggott 1985). A disaggregated general equilibrium model of the United States was developed by Fullerton, Shoven and Whalley (1978) with support provided in part by the OTA. These models have been applied to a series of tax policy problems ranging from general distortions induced by taxation (Shoven and Whalley 1972; Fullerton and Gordon 1983) to the analysis of specific reform proposals such as switching to a consumption tax (Fullerton, Shoven, and Whalley 1983). A subgroup of general equilibrium models has been used to examine the dynamic properties of alternative tax policies such as the duration of the adjustment process and the distributions of tax burdens at intermediate stages during the process (Feldstein 1978; Auerbach and Kotlikoff 1983; Auerbach, Kotlikoff, and Skinner 1983). The general equilibrium models themselves have incorporated some dynamic elements (Ballard et al. 1985).

11.6.2 Data

The data demands of the general equilibrium models range more broadly, but require less detail than, those of microdata models. Income, consumption, and tax data for individuals are required, but generally are aggregated to income classes. Additional data not required by the aggregate and microdata models include an input-output matrix for producers and a transition matrix linking producer goods to consumer goods, as well as data on investment, government purchases, and foreign trade. The data are assembled for a single year or an average of years. Applied general equilibrium models share data reconciliation problems common to other approaches to measuring tax burden, including resolving differences among alternative sources of similar data and differences between theoretical concepts and actual measures.

The data gaps that limit microdata models also limit applied general equilibrium models. In particular, the lack of wealth data and of the income from it make it difficult to construct models of intertemporal choices between consumption and savings that accurately reflect particular time periods.

11.6.3 Assumptions and Conclusions

The existence of computable applied general equilibrium models coincided with a new wave of literature on theoretical tax incidence (Shoven 1976; Rosen 1978; Ballentine and Eris 1975; Vandendorpe and Friedlaender 1975;

Feldstein 1977; McLure and Thirsk 1975a, 1975b; McLure 1975). The applied framework provided an opportunity to quantify the tax burden resulting from existing incidence theories and also provided the means to calculate the consequences of alternative theories.

A long-run perspective on the process of adjusting to changes in tax laws can be constructed from sequences of equilibria that add current savings to the capital stock and income of future periods. This sequence also can be used to generate a sense of the length of the adjustment process to the final equilibrium and to calculate the incidence and size of the tax burden on various groups during the process. A parallel literature has developed on the dynamic properties of alternative reforms, such as switching from a consumption to an income tax, and vice versa (Eaton and Rosen 1980; Bernheim 1981; Summers 1981; Auerbach and Kotlikoff 1983; Auerbach, Kotlikoff, and Skinner 1983).

11.6.4 Policy Uses

Applied general equilibrium models make several significant contributions to tax burden measurement and tax policy formation. The structure of the models provides a formal mechanism for applying alternative tax incidence assumptions about the full range of taxes and for analyzing the effect of taxes on real income, economic efficiency, and growth. Applied general equilibrium models permit changes in tax revenues under alternative tax structures to be separated from the distortions in economic efficiency caused by taxation. Measures of excess burden under alternative tax structures and measurement concepts can be calculated and compared (Auerbach and Rosen 1980; Auerbach 1985; Diewert 1985).

Conclusions on the distribution of tax burden based on applied general equilibrium models have influenced tax policy in a more indirect way than have conclusions based on microdata models. General equilibrium results currently make their mark on policy by influencing economists' views, but generally are not a standard tool for analysis either in Congress or at the Treasury. The models have several problems that make them less suitable for day-to-day policy analysis than microdata models.

11.6.5 Problems

Computational requirements for the models, although dropping at the same time computing costs are falling, remain large enough that researchers still search for ways to reduce them (Ballard et al. 1985). Because consumption time is partially a function of the dimensionality of the model, the need to minimize time counterbalances the desire for more disaggregated models. The current version of the Ballard et al. model, for example, has 12 consumer categories, 15 consumer goods, and 19 producer goods, plus taxes, government, and exports. This is much more detailed than the two-by-two models of Harberger and Diamond, but remains below the level of disaggregation available in microdata models. Despite efforts to increase computational efficiency, general equilibrium models remain too cumbersome to be practical in policy analysis. Further, they lack the flexibility of microdata models in terms of examining the tax burden of specific population subgroups as need arises. Moreover, like representative taxpayer and aggregate data measures, they ignore variability in income, consumption, and taxation within subgroups.

The models also depend on strong assumptions about the specific forms of utility and production functions. The forms are chosen as much for their tractability as for their theoretical properties, with Cobb-Douglas, constant elasticity of substitution, and fixed coefficients forms common. (An alternative approach is based on econometric estimations of flexible functional forms for utility and production functions; see Jorgensen 1984.) Elasticities are chosen from the empirical literatures, which are themselves often in disagreement about appropriate theory, estimation methodology, and data (see, e.g., discussions of "the" elasticity of labor supply in Borjas and Heckman 1979; Hausman 1981; and Killingsworth 1983). Incidence theory plays as important a role in the conclusions reached in general equilibrium models as in microdata models, and is no more resolved. A final concern about applied general equilibrium models is that test statistics to assess their reliability have not been developed and sensitivity analyses of the effect of alternative assumptions remain relatively uncommon (Whalley 1984).

11.7 OTA Microsimulation Studies

The Office of Tax Analysis in the Department of the Treasury maintains a microsimulation model that it uses to estimate and evaluate distributional, revenue, and economic impacts of individual income taxes. A similar model is maintained by the staff of the Congressional Joint Committee on Taxation. During the recent tax reform process, the model was used to examine the effects of thousands of proposed changes to the Internal Revenue Code. The issues examined ranged from the effect of changes in a single provision to the interaction among sets of provisions and also included analyses of the distributional effects of proposed changes. Additional features of the model and its data base allowed these issues to be analyzed on a family as well as a tax return basis, provided distributional consequences based on several alternative income measures, and estimated the impact on the number of tax filers. Finally, the data base contained income and population measures independent of the current law, allowing comparisons of alternative proposals against a common measure and also allowing the modeling of provisions that applied to components of income not taxable (and therefore not reported on tax forms) under the prereform law. The simulation model, the data base developed and used during the tax reform process, and the construction of a Haig-Simons definition of income are described in detail in Cilke and Wyscarver (1987), Nunns (1987), and Nelson (1987). The model itself is documented in Wyscarver (1985).

The series of tax burden measures considered during the tax reform process included estimates of the proportion of families with tax increases and tax decreases, of percentage tax reductions for families by income category and itemizing status, as well as percentage tax reductions by income class (U.S. Treasury, Division of Tax Research 1985a, 1985b; U.S. Congress, JCT 1986). Additional tax burden considerations were shown in comparisons of the number of tax returns in each income class that would show selected income sources, adjustments, and deductions under then-current law and under reform proposals. The distribution of tax liability under prior law and under the Tax Reform Act of 1986 for these tax burden measures are given in tables 11.10–11.13 below.

The choice of income measure clearly affects both the estimated distribution of taxes by income class and the effect of reform proposals. Table 11.10 presents distributions based on three alternative income measures. Adjusted gross income (AGI), a somewhat expanded income measure (labeled MEI, for modified expanded income), and family economic income (FEI, a measure closer to the Haig-Simons concept than AGI or MEI) are considered in turn. The associated tax unit concepts also vary among the measures. AGI and MEI are calculated on a return basis, while FEI is calculated on a family basis. AGI is the measure readily available from tax returns, while MEI is a measure developed and used by the Joint Committee on Taxation and FEI is used by OTA.

Tables 11.11–11.13 demonstrate the variety of analytical tabulations the tax model makes possible. The distribution of family economic income and of

Table 11.10 Individual Tax Liabilities under 1988 Law, Before and After the Tax Reform Act of 1986, by Economic Income of Families, Modified Expanded Income of Returns Age 16 and over, and AGI of Returns (1983 levels of income)

Income Class ($1,000s)	AGI of Returns Prior Law	AGI of Returns TRA Law	AGI of Returns % Change	MEI of Returns Age 16+ Prior Law (%)	MEI of Returns Age 16+ TRA Law (%)	MEI of Returns Age 16+ % Change	Economic Income of Families Prior Law	Economic Income of Families TRA Law	Economic Income of Families % Change
0–10	1.9	1.7	−15.6	1.2	1.0	−17.7	.5	.4	−24.3
10–15	4.8	4.3	−14.6	3.6	2.8	−25.8	1.7	1.2	−34.1
15–20	6.5	6.4	−6.5	5.3	4.9	−13.0	3.2	2.7	−18.9
20–30	16.5	16.4	−4.9	14.1	13.8	−6.7	10.5	10.2	−7.1
30–50	29.5	29.8	−3.5	28.9	28.6	−5.9	26.3	26.3	−4.8
50–100	19.2	20.2	.2	22.5	23.7	.0	31.0	32.3	−.8
100–200	8.6	8.7	−3.7	8.9	9.3	−.1	10.6	11.2	.1
200+	12.9	11.9	−12.3	15.4	15.9	−1.8	16.1	15.5	−8.5
Total	100.0	100.0	−4.7	100.0	100.0	−4.7	100.0	100.0	−4.7
Addendum:									
Negative income	.1	.5	.1	.0	.0	.0	.1	.3	.1

Source: Reproduced from Nelson (1987), 96.

one of its components, corporate income, can be compared in terms independent of current tax law in table 11.11. In addition, the table shows distributions of individual income tax and individual and corporate tax liabilities that held before the Tax Reform Act of 1986. The major components of adjusted gross income and taxable income (including deductions, adjustments, and exemptions) under 1983 and 1988 law are shown for each AGI class in table 11.12. Both the number of returns and dollar amounts are given. Many of the same AGI and taxable income components under 1983 and 1988 law are given in table 11.13, but are distributed according to FEI rather than AGI. In addition, table 11.13 presents distributions of FEI components that are not included in AGI, such as food stamps, welfare benefits, health and medical insurance, and the net rental value of owner-occupied housing.

Two current policy concerns place new emphasis on the revenue and tax burden consequences of single tax provisions and sets of provisions, in addition to the overall tax burden consequences of current law. First, the process leading to the Tax Reform Act of 1986 involved evaluating the distributional consequences of alternative packages of rate reductions and base broadening proposals. The initial goal (U.S. Treasury 1984) of distributional and revenue neutrality evolved into a final goal of equitable distribution of the tax reductions that had been achieved (U.S. Congress, JCT 1987). To achieve these goals and maintain them through postreform proposals for changes in the law requires knowledge of the changes in the distribution of tax burden resulting from changes in individual provisions and from interactions among

Table 11.11 **Distributional Comparisons of Corporate and Family Economic Income, and Individual and Corporate Income Tax Liabilities (1983 levels, 1988 law)**

Family Economic Income ($1,000s)	FEI (%) (1)	Corporate Income (%) (2)	Distribution of 1988 Pre-TRA Law Tax Liabilities: Individual (%) (3)	Individual and Corporate (%)[a] (4)
<0	−.24	.23	.10	.12
0–10	3.23	1.24	.47	.58
10–15	5.28	2.29	1.67	1.77
15–20	6.85	3.76	3.22	3.30
20–30	16.08	10.65	10.51	10.53
30–50	29.88	23.26	26.29	25.83
50–100	26.85	31.89	30.98	31.12
100–200	6.15	12.70	10.63	10.94
200+	5.89	13.99	16.13	15.81
Total	100.00	100.00	100.00	100.00

Source: Reproduced from Nelson (1987), 88.

[a]Assumes corporate income taxes are distributed in proportion to corporate income in family economic income.

Table 11.12 **All Returns: Gross Income, Adjustments, Deductions, Exemptions, Taxable Income, and Taxes under 1983 and 1988 Law (1983 level and distribution of income; no. of returns in thousands, amounts in $ millions)**

		Wages and Salaries		Interest		Dividends in AGI		Business Income or Loss		Capital Gains in AGI		Pensions in AGI	
AGI Class* (000)	No. of Returns (1)	No. of Returns (2)	Amount (3)	No. of Returns (4)	Amount (5)	No. of Returns (6)	Amount (7)	No. of Returns (8)	Amount (9)	No. of Returns (10)	Amount (11)	No. of Returns (12)	Amount (13)
1983 law:													
Under 10	34,647	28,943	149,475	11,832	20,558	2,107	3,696	2,667	(286)	1,620	4,273	2,425	8,832
10–15	13,907	11,740	143,294	6,083	16,460	1,016	1,845	1,186	4,433	757	1,025	1,864	11,480
15–20	10,836	9,462	160,580	5,431	14,276	1,004	2,724	1,128	5,161	787	994	1,301	9,841
20–30	16,466	15,119	367,359	9,990	23,740	1,828	4,772	1,898	9,365	1,665	1,825	1,484	12,653
30–50	15,358	14,286	518,333	11,644	35,755	2,721	8,334	1,957	15,280	2,403	5,234	1,631	17,119
50–100	4,293	3,798	208,398	3,830	25,546	1,799	10,767	791	15,094	1,624	6,882	520	7,892
100–200	623	498	49,527	605	9,598	427	6,640	158	6,291	410	5,547	76	1,365
200 and over	161	130	34,781	159	7,871	130	8,427	45	9,937	126	18,595	17	632
Total	96,293	83,976	1,631,745	49,574	153,803	11,032	47,205	9,830	65,276	9,392	44,375	9,317	69,814
1988 law:													
Under 10	35,166	29,079	149,860	11,832	20,558	2,945	3,998	2,669	(285)	1,533	11,011	2,943	11,612
10–15	13,969	11,740	143,294	6,083	16,460	1,473	2,029	1,188	4,433	757	2,756	2,006	12,697
15–20	10,850	9,462	160,580	5,431	14,276	1,438	2,891	1,128	5,161	786	2,759	1,380	10,426
20–30	16,474	15,119	367,359	9,990	23,740	2,896	5,102	1,898	9,365	1,665	5,454	1,538	13,490
30–50	15,363	14,286	518,333	11,644	35,755	4,337	8,923	1,957	15,280	2,408	13,979	1,728	18,021
50–100	4,293	3,798	208,398	3,830	25,546	2,268	11,138	791	15,094	1,625	18,111	565	8,444
100–200	623	498	49,527	605	9,598	475	6,724	158	6,291	411	14,112	80	1,448
200 and over	161	130	34,781	159	7,871	139	8,452	45	9,937	126	46,414	18	712
Total	96,900	84,111	1,632,130	49,574	153,803	15,971	49,258	9,834	65,276	9,312	114,597	10,258	76,851

Table 11.12 *(Continued)*

AGI Class* (000)	Net Rents, Royalties, Partnership, etc., and Farm Income		Social Security Benefits in AGI		Other Gross Income		Total Gross Income		Moving Expense		Employee Business Expense		Two-Earner Deduction	
	No. of Returns (14)	Amount (15)	No. of Returns (16)	Amount (17)	No. of Returns (18)	Amount (19)	No. of Returns (20)	Amount (21)	No. of Returns (22)	Amount (23)	No. of Returns (24)	Amount (25)	No. of Returns (26)	Amount (27)
1983 law:														
Under 10	3,047	(28,006)			1,849	(9,186)	34,594	149,347	199	263	501	1,352	679	241
10–15	1,329	(529)			1,649	1,084	13,907	179,090	296	450	717	1,642	1,195	645
15–20	1,354	(490)			2,266	2,378	10,836	195,461	215	309	882	1,705	1,754	1,248
20–30	2,480	(362)			5,046	5,466	16,466	424,814	347	720	1,728	3,225	5,116	4,827
30–50	3,070	(16)			6,089	5,521	15,358	605,551	324	1,054	2,163	4,428	7,063	8,727
50–100	1,645	3,821			1,719	2,992	4,293	281,389	123	625	749	1,997	1,704	2,485
100–200	446	5,034			249	1,223	623	85,224	27	221	98	526	129	217
200 and over	137	7,407			75	991	161	88,639	3	31	19	157	27	56
Total	13,508	(13,141)			18,941	10,470	96,240	2,009,516	1,533	3,671	6,857	15,033	17,666	18,445
1988 law:														
Under 10	3,066	(18,193)	3	13	13,470	(9,491)	35,116	169,060						
10–15	1,331	74	15	19	7,568	1,021	13,969	182,763						
15–20	1,358	51	157	157	7,236	2,608	10,850	198,750						
20–30	2,480	608	1,482	2,418	13,112	8,563	16,474	433,676						
30–50	3,070	1,800	1,793	4,539	13,687	11,597	15,363	623,679						
50–100	1,644	7,421	615	1,637	4,144	5,916	4,293	300,065						
100–200	446	8,142	111	391	610	2,569	623	98,409						
200 and over	137	11,041	33	124	160	2,096	161	121,302						
Total	13,531	10,943	4,210	9,298	59,988	24,879	96,850	2,127,702						

continued

Table 11.12 *(Continued)*

AGI Class* (000)	IRAs: No. of Returns (28)	IRAs: Amount (29)	Other Adjustments: No. of Returns (30)	Other Adjustments: Amount (31)	Total Adjustments: No. of Returns (32)	Total Adjustments: Amount (33)	AGI: No. of Returns (34)	AGI: Amount (35)	No. of Non-itemizers (36)	Amount of Standard Deduction (37)	No. of Itemizers (38)	Amount of Excess Itemized Deductions (39)	Total No. of Exemptions (40)	Value of Exemptions (41)
1983 law:														
Under 10	608	1,021	1,226	2,556	2,464	5,434	34,593	143,914	32,105		2,542	7,968	60,620	60,620
10–15	977	1,996	1,213	1,082	3,194	5,814	13,907	173,276	10,931		2,977	11,211	32,113	32,113
15–20	1,250	2,638	1,242	663	3,679	6,563	10,836	188,899	6,965		3.872	12,830	27,992	27,992
20–30	2,892	6,567	2,402	1,335	8,233	16,674	16,466	408,141	7,137		9,330	38,021	47,960	47,960
30–50	4,960	12,336	2,950	2,286	10,605	28,804	15,358	576,749	3,021		12,338	71,075	50,175	50,175
50–100	2,496	6,288	1,161	2,185	3,364	13,573	4,293	267,816	318		3,975	41,388	14,525	14,525
100–200	361	953	190	991	462	2,890	623	82,333	33		590	13,224	2,147	2,147
200 and over	107	260	44	414	125	917	161	87,722	7		155	12,804	560	560
Total	13,649	32,060	10,427	11,512	32,126	80,668	96,239	1,928,850	60,516		35,778	208,521	236,092	236,092
1988 law:														
Under 10	339	496	956	1,185	1,252	1,682	35,116	167,538	33,379	98,483	1,788	12,914	56,279	70,576
10–15	502	914	1,117	648	1,556	1,562	13,969	181,395	11,594	38,765	2,376	16,018	29,100	46,038
15–20	614	1,138	1,210	578	1,741	1,716	10,850	197,236	8,143	28,197	2,707	17,706	25,992	41,859
20–30	1,437	2,769	2,402	1,335	3,615	4,104	16,474	429,954	9,378	34,644	7,096	50,746	45,953	74,304
30–50	1,847	2,435	2,950	2,286	4,431	4,721	15,363	619,479	5,047	20,133	10,317	88,521	48,440	78,557
50–100	380	434	1,161	2,185	1,442	2,619	4,293	297,682	630	2,578	3,663	46,839	13,746	22,282
100–200	44	62	190	991	222	1,053	623	97,416	46	192	577	13,614	1,941	3,148
200 and over	10	16	44	414	51	430	161	120,890	10	43	151	12,090	496	805
Total	5,173	8,265	10,029	9,621	14,308	17,886	96,850	2,111,590	68,226	223,036	28,675	258,443	221,948	337,569

Table 11.12 *(Continued)*

AGI Class* (000)	Taxable Income		Taxable Income Less ZBA		Tax Before Credits		Credits		Alternative Minimum Tax (AMT)		Earned Income Credit (EIC)		Net Income Tax Liability	
	No. of Returns (42)	Amount (43)	No. of Returns (44)	Amount (45)	No. of Returns (46)	Amount (47)	No. of Returns (48)	Amount (49)	No. of Returns (50)	Amount (51)	No. of Returns (52)	Amount (53)	No. of Returns (54)	Amount (55)
1983 law:														
Under 10	29,536	112,771	19,428	53,156	19,403	6,705	1,192	234	14	253	6,208	1,770	22,428	4,972
10–15	13,650	131,241	13,387	94,647	13,397	13,514	1,894	581	7	38	0	0	13,232	12,990
15–20	10,789	148,359	10,716	117,710	10,716	18,237	1,992	690	4	23	0	0	10,534	17,607
20–30	16,420	322,522	16,373	272,667	16,371	46,734	4,213	1,311	18	69	0	0	16,265	45,542
30–50	15,339	455,734	15,328	405,938	15,328	80,804	5,272	1,850	77	293	0	0	15,300	79,307
50–100	4,280	212,122	4,278	198,047	4,277	51,674	1,941	1,341	108	749	0	0	4,278	51,149
100–200	620	67,088	620	65,064	620	23,265	390	848	51	710	0	0	622	23,157
200 and over	160	74,522	160	74,001	160	34,360	123	975	20	1,251	0	0	161	34,674
Total	90,794	1,524,360	80,291	1,281,230	89,273	275,293	17,017	7,829	299	3,386	6,207	1,771	82,822	269,398
1988 law:														
Under 10	18,895	56,737			18,907	9,206	969	118	30	228	6,603	3,838	24,196	5,482
10–15	12,873	83,574			12,883	12,652	1,707	377	2	3	3,788	1,080	13,621	11,200
15–20	10,738	109,883			10,738	16,698	1,751	386	5	8	274	8	10,694	16,312
20–30	16,394	270,637			16,394	43,794	3,596	741	9	18	0	0	16,381	43,067
30–50	15,353	432,420			15,353	77,692	4,311	966	30	57	0	0	15,353	76,778
50–100	4,287	226,162			4,287	51,455	1,710	546	57	99	0	0	4,288	51,001
100–200	622	80,538			622	22,323	371	336	43	123	0	0	623	22,107
200 and over	161	108,052			161	30,421	121	314	18	208	0	0	161	30,312
Total	79,322	1,368,003			79,345	264,242	14,535	3,785	195	745	10,665	4,926	85,318	256,258

Source: Reproduced from Nunns (1987), 104–7.
[a]Adjusted gross income (AGI) as defined under 1983 law.

Table 11.13 **Tax Return Income, Additional Items in Economic Income, and Tax Items for Families in 1983 (1983 tax law, 1983 level and distribution of income; no. of families in thousands, amounts in $ millions)**

		Wages and Salaries		Interest		Dividends in AGI		Business Income or Loss		Capital Gains in AGI		Pensions in AGI	
Economic Income Class[a] (000)	No. of Families (1)	No. of Families (2)	Amount (3)	No. of Families (4)	Amount (5)	No. of Families (6)	Amount (7)	No. of Families (8)	Amount (9)	No. of Families (10)	Amount (11)	No. of Families (12)	Amount (13)
Under 10	14,531	5,628	24,678	2,841	6,510	371	721	784	(3,269)	484	2,521	1,057	7,989
10–15	12,067	7,625	62,478	4,006	11,387	666	693	940	2,102	534	933	1,424	8,982
15–20	11,177	8,329	98,678	4,373	12,178	734	1,202	994	2,779	594	946	1,215	7,675
20–30	18,498	15,211	269,529	8,934	23,357	1,573	3,250	1,932	6,335	1,423	2,208	1,922	12,926
30–50	21,745	19,426	559,272	13,752	36,823	2,730	6,319	2,709	12,183	2,431	4,470	2,095	15,383
50–100	11,653	10,609	478,760	9,421	38,842	3,457	12,975	1,869	19,604	2,733	7,144	1,293	12,965
100–200	1,326	1,103	81,758	1,263	13,498	869	9,316	384	11,839	765	5,740	197	2,862
200 and over	364	295	56,593	358	11,207	298	12,728	122	13,703	270	20,413	41	1,033
Total	91,361	68,227	1,631,746	44,948	153,802	10,697	47,205	9,735	65,275	9,233	44,375	9,244	69,814

Table 11.13 ***(Continued)***

Economic Income Class[a] (000)	Net Rents, Royalties, Partnership, etc., and Farm Income: No. of Families (14)	Amount (15)	Other Gross Income: No. of Families (16)	Amount (17)	Total Gross Income: No. of Families (18)	Amount (19)	Moving Expenses: No. of Families (20)	Amount (21)	Employee Business Expense: No. of Families (22)	Amount (23)	Two-earner Deduction: No. of Families (24)	Amount (25)	IRAs: No. of Families (26)	Amount (27)
Under 10	934	(15,902)	562	(3,836)	7,473	19,411	39	61	107	368	124	37	56	69
10–15	946	(1,172)	787	134	9,612	85,534	118	163	287	646	407	156	294	512
15–20	1,118	(903)	1,319	842	9,750	123,396	178	269	504	1,083	871	450	551	1,041
20–30	2,244	(946)	3,701	3,318	17,025	319,973	348	563	1,349	2,821	3,137	2,289	1,832	3,839
30–50	3,696	(1,339)	6,999	5,585	20,804	638,689	486	1,124	2,576	4,760	7,456	7,791	4,806	11,316
50–100	3,239	1,346	4,664	4,162	11,389	575,793	314	1,112	1,745	3,992	5,174	6,905	5,026	12,687
100–200	819	3,226	534	892	1,319	129,131	33	289	224	1,020	426	688	788	2,035
200 and over	302	2,549	165	(627)	364	117,597	9	89	46	342	70	130	220	562
Total	13,297	(13,141)	18,729	10,470	77,734	2,009,525	1,531	3,671	6,839	15,033	17,666	18,445	13,572	32,059

continued

Table 11.13 *(Continued)*

Economic Income Class[a] (000)	Other Adjustments: No. of Families (28)	Other Adjustments: Amount (29)	Total Adjustments: No. of Families (30)	Total Adjustments: Amount (31)	AGI: No. of Families (32)	AGI: Amount (33)	Adjustments to AGI under 1983 Law: No. of Families (34)	Adjustments to AGI under 1983 Law: Amount (35)	Amount of Unreported Income (36)	Total Social Security and RR Retirement: No. of Families (37)	Total Social Security and RR Retirement: Amount (38)	Addendum: Nontaxed SS and RR under 1988 Tax Law: No. of Families (39)	Addendum: Nontaxed SS and RR under 1988 Tax Law: Amount (40)
Under 10	301	567	486	1,103	7,473	18,309	873	621	20,127	7,107	31,861	7,101	31,686
10–15	623	646	1,285	2,124	9,612	83,410	1,749	1,245	18,196	4,717	28,791	4,715	28,200
15–20	820	706	2,103	3,549	9,750	119,847	2,466	2,137	21,889	3,691	23,985	3,689	23,190
20–30	1,988	1,505	6,096	11,013	17,025	308,961	6,713	7,329	43,189	5,280	34,291	5,279	32,328
30–50	3,487	2,093	11,957	27,081	20,804	611,610	12,893	20,646	62,100	4,985	33,652	4,982	28,150
50–100	2,569	2,872	8,439	27,548	11,389	548,247	9,280	21,985	51,212	2,589	17,129	2,588	11,992
100–200	448	1,884	1,041	5,909	1,319	123,223	1,229	4,252	14,657	332	2,314	332	1,360
200 and over	116	1,237	278	2,342	364	115,254	352	1,611	20,535	82	577	82	304
Total	10,353	11,512	31,684	80,668	77,734	1,928,862	35,554	59,827	251,903	28,782	172,601	28,768	157,210

Table 11.13 *(Continued)*

Economic Income Class[a] (000)	Unemployment Compensation No. of Families (41)	Amount (42)	Workmen's Compensation No. of Families (43)	Amount (44)	Veterans' Benefits No. of Families (45)	Amount (46)	Food Stamps No. of Families (47)	Amount (48)	Welfare Benefits No. of Families (49)	Amount (50)	Pension and Profit Sharing Plans No. of Families (51)	Amount (52)	Health and Medical Insurance No. of Families (53)	Amount (54)
Under 10	906	1,331	297	553	612	1,209	3,437	3,516	2,820	6,863	2,211	749	2,282	1,758
10–15	1,537	3,024	423	920	459	1,207	2,838	3,201	1,698	4,879	3,712	2,083	4,072	3,996
15–20	1,587	3,666	513	1,071	479	1,576	1,962	2,221	1,215	3,526	4,759	3,826	5,201	5,848
20–30	1,983	5,107	1,044	2,779	847	3,124	1,786	2,029	1,262	3,974	10,421	13,040	11,293	14,347
30–50	1,218	2,776	1,454	4,181	925	3,685	738	1,037	682	2,396	16,208	33,491	16,842	27,480
50–100	617	1,354	732	2,204	471	1,658	133	249	174	677	9,825	33,498	9,838	20,636
100–200	55	133	41	120	43	255	7	13	4	19	1,019	6,056	1,006	2,282
200 and over	5	8	14	39	4	18	0	0	0	0	274	4,377	266	613
Total	7,907	17,399	4,518	11,868	3,839	12,731	10,900	12,266	7,856	22,333	48,428	97,120	50,800	76,960

continued

Table 11.13 *(Continued)*

Economic Income Class[a] (000)	Military Benefits and Fringe Benefits		Other Untaxed Employer Contributions		Less: Taxable Pensions		Earnings on Pension Funds		Earnings on Life Insurance, IRAs and Keoghs		Real Pretax Corporate Economic Income		Less: Dividends before Exclusion	
	No. of Families (55)	Amount (56)	No. of Families (57)	Amount (58)	No. of Families (59)	Amount (60)	No. of Families (61)	Amount (62)	No. of Families (63)	Amount (64)	No. of Families (65)	Amount (66)	No. of Families (67)	Amount (68)
Under 10	2,134	467	2,959	78	2,215	(10,476)	2,478	791	2,027	213	6,066	3,269	806	(848)
10–15	2,916	1,278	5,007	250	1,986	(10,233)	4,126	2,757	3,300	469	7,340	5,111	1,048	(882)
15–20	3,325	1,866	6,195	440	1,539	(8,663)	5,177	4,320	4,054	803	8,057	8,411	1,131	(1,364)
20–30	6,321	4,211	12,849	1,377	2,331	(14,130)	11,102	13,032	8,798	2,432	15,385	23,807	2,457	(3,595)
30–50	9,237	7,035	18,288	3,358	2,485	(16,390)	16,801	27,732	13,721	6,769	20,394	52,013	4,483	(6,900)
50–100	5,670	5,423	10,328	3,204	1,478	(13,693)	10,124	31,261	9,376	8,274	11,442	71,310	4,698	(13,719)
100–200	644	942	1,055	473	209	(2,875)	1,057	6,147	1,209	2,667	1,319	28,408	969	(9,492)
200 and over	174	684	282	183	44	(1,036)	281	3,390	325	1,195	361	31,288	316	(12,788)
Total	30,421	21,908	56,963	9,364	12,287	(77,496)	51,146	89,430	42,809	22,822	70,365	223,617	15,908	(49,587)

Table 11.13 *(Continued)*

Economic Income Class[a] (000)	Less: Dividends of Pension and Insurance Funds		Less: Capital Gains in AGI		Real Net Capital Gains Except Securities		Inflation Adjustment for Interest Received		Inflation Adjustment for All Other Income		Excess Tax Depreciation		Tax Exempt Interest	
	No. of Families (69)	Amount (70)	No. of Families (71)	Amount (72)	No. of Families (73)	Amount (74)	No. of Families (75)	Amount (76)	No. of Families (77)	Amount (78)	No. of Families (79)	Amount (80)	No. of Families (81)	Amount (82)
Under 10	4,007	(175)	484	(2,521)	462	165	5,826	(2,762)	1,287	1,948	1,152	1,275	6	35
10–15	6,092	(595)	534	(933)	476	(71)	8,020	(5,160)	1,106	616	1,234	478	16	27
15–20	7,052	(932)	594	(946)	534	230	8,582	(5,897)	1,205	723	1,381	550	21	19
20–30	14,021	(2,809)	1,423	(2,208)	1,285	388	15,950	(12,639)	2,333	1,588	2,687	1,190	114	111
30–50	19,188	(6,004)	2,431	(4,470)	2,196	1,152	20,493	(22,214)	3,804	2,777	4,433	1,946	290	456
50–100	11,080	(6,782)	2,733	(7,144)	2,545	2,949	11,416	(24,348)	3,393	3,287	3,642	2,366	444	1,374
100–200	1,254	(1,362)	765	(5,740)	712	2,141	1,315	(8,003)	922	2,056	876	1,472	299	3,056
200 and over	337	(750)	270	(20,413)	261	14,712	364	(5,989)	317	2,975	307	2,103	178	5,927
Total	63,032	(19,410)	9,233	(44,375)	8,470	21,665	71,966	(88,012)	14,365	15,972	15,713	11,381	1,367	11,005

continued

Table 11.13 *(Continued)*

Economic Income Class[a] (000)	Real Net Rental Value of Owner Occupied Housing: No. of Families (83)	Real Net Rental Value of Owner Occupied Housing: Amount (84)	Other Economic Income: No. of Families (85)	Other Economic Income: Amount (86)	Total Adjustment from 1983 Law AGI to Economic Income: No. of Families (87)	Total Adjustment from 1983 Law AGI to Economic Income: Amount (88)	Economic Income of Families: No. of Families (89)	Economic Income of Families: Amount (90)	No. of Non-itemizers (91)	No. of Itemizers (92)	Amount of Excess Itemized Deductions (93)	Total No. of Exemptions (94)	Value of Exemptions (95)
Under 10	5,724	4,512	54	3,390	14,469	67,949	14,530	86,257	13,819	713	3,630	14,203	14,203
10–15	6,221	7,693	34	444	12,055	68,793	12,067	152,203	10,633	1,435	6,026	22,486	22,486
15–20	6,393	7,824	25	417	11,169	77,544	11,177	197,391	8,951	2,225	8,064	25,747	25,747
20–30	11,278	11,780	41	877	18,486	154,615	18,498	463,575	12,229	6,269	24,918	50,505	50,505
30–50	15,172	9,556	98	1,743	21,745	249,998	21,745	861,603	9,019	12,727	62,650	71,403	71,403
50–100	9,371	9,515	109	1,928	11,653	225,804	11,653	774,044	2,566	9,087	66,350	44,910	44,910
100–200	1,189	2,784	66	1,332	1,326	54,107	1,326	177,329	125	1,201	19,086	5,395	5,395
200 and over	326	1,694	70	4,478	364	54,432	364	169,684	24	341	17,796	1,447	1,447
Total	55,673	55,357	498	14,608	91,267	953,243	91,360	2,882,085	57,365	33,998	208,520	236,097	236,097

Table 11.13 *(Continued)*

Economic Income Class[a] (000)	Taxable Income		Tax before Credits		Credits		Alternative Minimum Tax (AMT)		Earned Income Credit (EIC)		Net Income Tax Liability	
	No. of Families (96)	Amount (97)	No. of Families (98)	Amount (99)	No. of Families (100)	Amount (101)	No. of Families (102)	Amount (103)	No. of Families (104)	Amount (105)	No. of Families (106)	Amount (107)
Under 10	5,325	22,561	3,441	1,642	348	88	11	228	1,307	407	4,343	1,383
10–15	8,784	58,210	7,318	5,140	817	174	6	22	2,331	655	8,259	4,336
15–20	9,351	87,944	8,468	9,236	1,204	368	4	17	1,297	351	8,967	8,544
20–30	16,715	236,079	16,114	29,356	3,047	912	12	41	863	237	16,213	28,280
30–50	20,658	480,334	20,469	72,609	5,862	1,834	45	244	340	99	20,445	70,967
50–100	11,343	439,812	11,316	85,049	4,516	2,014	105	498	65	21	11,294	83,607
100–200	1,306	100,049	1,304	29,145	770	1,007	72	601	2	1	1,307	28,791
200 and over	356	99,372	356	43,133	275	1,424	43	1,733	1	0	359	43,517
Total	73,838	1,524,361	68,787	275,311	16,838	7,822	299	3,384	6,206	1,771	71,187	269,425

Source: Reproduced from Nunns (1987), 125–28.

provisions. Second, the Gramm-Rudman-Hollings budget constraint imposes a search for revenue neutrality for expenditure proposals that the postreform era suggests should also be distributionally neutral. Consequently, the tax model is being called upon to aid in examining the changes in tax burden of proposed financing of expenditure provisions, such as extending Medicare to include catastrophic health care, that previously would have been unlikely to entail explicit tax policy concerns.

Data availability and frequency have improved markedly since the tax burden studies of the 1930s. But for some policy questions, the necessary data still do not exist, and for other questions, the data are available only from several separate surveys and not jointly. The series of tax burden measures that could be considered during the tax reform process depended on data availability. The OTA model uses statistical matching techniques to join information from several surveys together to form synthetic data files. For example, a statistical match joined similar records in the Statistics of Income and the CPS. Where data are available only through smaller surveys, such as consumption data from the Consumer Expenditure Survey, imputations are made to records in the larger surveys. The matching and imputation techniques themselves can introduce problems, as discussed in the context of microdata problems. Another problem is that those data that do exist rarely coincide in their reference periods and availability. One or more of the data sets usually must be extrapolated forward to a common base year, in addition to extrapolations needed to move the final tax model database forward to the current year and to the federal budget period, a period roughly five years into the future.

Several of the gaps are highlighted in the process of creating a Haig-Simons income concept. The process requires information on income, wealth, consumption, and taxes for each unit, family, or individual in the tax model database (Nelson 1987). Among the necessary data, wealth data are the most scarce both in frequency of collection and size of sample (see Lipsey and Tice 1989). In this, gaps in data for tax policy needs coincide with one of the major statistical gaps noted by the current American Economic Association report on U.S. economic statistics (Juster 1988). For example, in the 1983 Survey of Consumer Finances was the first national survey of the income, wealth, and financial behavior of households since the 1963 Survey of Financial Characteristics of Consumers. The 1983 Survey of Consumer Finances surveyed 5,400 households, a sample size sufficient to generate reliable national estimates of wealth components and distributions (Juster 1988; Avery, Elliehausen, and Kennickell 1988), but small compared to the 75,000-observation Statistics of Income and 120,000-observation CPS samples. Moreover, the Survey of Consumer Finances sample size for cross-classifications of interest for tax policy (e.g., specific income sources for households by age and income groups) quickly becomes very small. The CPS provides information on income and transfer payments for a very large sample but has well-known nonresponse patterns that reduce the usable sample, especially for high incomes (David et al. 1986). Furthermore, some taxed income may not be suitable for inclusion in a Haig-Simons income measure, such as nominal capital gains and pensions.

The SIPP data have many more observations than the Survey of Consumer Finances, but tend to show lower wealth totals, with the shortfalls occurring in sources (such as small business equity, closely held corporate equity, real estate other than own home, etc.) of considerable policy interest. Tax return data in the Statistics of Income provide fairly detailed data on income that is taxable under current law, but not on untaxed income. Moreover, tax returns lack the details on the composition of that income and the rates of return it reflects that are necessary components of indirect wealth calculations.

Another important gap is data on employee benefits. Federal tax policy excludes many employee benefits from taxable income in exchange for imposing regulations intended to extend those benefits to more, usually lower income, workers. Policymakers need to know whether the benefits accrue as intended and whether workers and employers trade them for other benefits or higher money wages. As papers presented at a previous conference have shown (Triplett 1983), such data are scant. Some data are available on benefit characteristics and costs together with information on the employer and employee (Wood 1988), but the level of aggregation is high (one-digit industry and three occupational classes) and neither financial characteristics of the employer nor other demographic and economic characteristics of the worker are available. Similarly, there are some household surveys that collect information on the incidence of fringe benefits (the CPS and SIPP occasionally do so), but usually lack employer expenditures and most characteristics of the employer.

For some current policy concerns, the Haig-Simons income concept yields disconcerting tax burden results. Consider, for example, comparing the tax burdens of the elderly and the nonelderly. Under the Haig-Simons accrual concept, pensions enter income of the worker as the employer contributes to the pension fund and as the fund earns a return on contributions and do not enter the income of the retiree when the pension benefit is received. Tabulations of income and tax burden for the elderly alone, as would be prepared, for example, for alternative proposals changing the personal exemption levels available to the elderly, produce theoretically correct but intuitively anomalous results. Retirees whose income sources are taxable pension income are shown as having tax liability but no current income.

Capital gains present the same problem. Gains are included in economic income when they accrue, but tax is paid when the gains are realized, which often occurs in a period different from the accruals. Taxpayers in any period who realize capital gains appear to have tax liabilities out of proportion to their measured income.

Changes in the underlying demographic structure of the population present challenges to tax policy as well as to social policy. The inadequacies of existing data for describing changes in forms of family units, work patterns over the life cycle, intrafamily resource allocations, and so forth, make the available measures of tax burden no better than any of the traditional measures of household income, wealth, or savings.

11.8 Conclusions

The course of tax legislation throughout the last 50 years consistently considered and was shaped by conclusions based on tax burden measures. Assessments of where the tax burden falls determined the form taken by tax increases or decreases (e.g., the choice between excise and income taxes) and influenced the structure of specific taxes (e.g., in linking personal exemptions and standard deductions to the poverty level in the federal income tax or in apportioning rate changes among tax brackets).

The history of empirical tax burden measurement reflects the broad outlines of developments in economics over the same period. Theoretical and methodological advances, new computing technologies, and new sources and kinds of data all produced new measures of tax burden. At the same time, tax burden measures have theoretical foundations only as firm as the economic theories and the corresponding structures of partial, general, and dynamic models that underlie them. In this theoretical arena, much remains open for further research, whether in terms of incidence theory (in microdata models, general equilibrium models, or dynamic models) or the choice among broader welfare measures (in general equilibrium models). Computational algorithms for solving general equilibrium models are becoming more efficient, and the introduction of duality theory to general equilibrium modeling reduces the number of required computations. Current computing technology makes microsimulation models of increasingly detailed analyses a standard feature of the policymakers' ordinary tool kit.

Pragmatic constraints to microsimulation models stem primarily from the limits of data availability and the reliability of imputation and statistical matching and extrapolation techniques employed to compensate for those limits. These constraints, shared with other economic and social policy applications, will apply for the near future. Improved tax burden measures for policy uses are more likely to come from advances in incidence and measurement theory that allow stronger inferences from a static supply of data.

References

Aaron, H. J. 1975. *Who Pays the Property Tax?* Washington, D.C.: Brookings.

Aaron, Henry J. and Michael J. Boskin. 1980. *The Economics of Taxation.* Washington, D.C.: Brookings.

Adler, J. H. 1951. The Fiscal System, the Distribution of Income, and Public Welfare. In *Fiscal Policies and the American Economy.* New York: Prentice Hall.

Atkinson, A. B. 1980. Horizontal Equity and the Distribution of the Tax Burden. In *The Economics of Taxation,* ed. H. Aaron and M. Boskin. Washington, D.C.: Brookings.

Auerbach, A. J. 1985. The Theory of Excess Burden and Optimal Taxation. In *Handbook of Public Economics,* vol. 1, ed. A. J. Auerbach and M. Feldstein. New York: North-Holland.

Auerbach, A. J., and L. J. Kotlikoff. 1983. National Savings, Economic Welfare, and the Structure of Taxation. In *Behavioral Simulation Methods in Tax Policy Analysis,* ed. M. Feldstein. Chicago: University of Chicago Press.

Auerbach, A. J., L. J. Kotlikoff, and J. Skinner. 1983. The Efficiency Gains from Dynamic Tax Reform. *International Economic Review* 24(1): 81–100.

Auerbach, A. J., and Harvey S. Rosen. 1980. Will the Real Excess Burden Please Stand Up? (or, Seven Measures in Search of a Concept). NBER Working Paper no. 495.

Avery, Robert B., Gregory E. Elliehausen, and Arthur B. Kennickell. 1988. Measuring Wealth with Survey Data: An Evaluation of the 1983 Survey of Consumer Finances. *Review of Income and Wealth* 34:339–69.

Baird, E., and S. Fine. 1939. The Use of Income Tax Data in the National Resources Committee Estimate of the Distribution of Income by Size. In *Studies in Income and Wealth,* vol. 3. New York: National Bureau of Economic Research.

Ballard, Charles L., D. Fullerton, J. B. Shoven, and J. Whalley. 1985. *A General Equilibrium Model for Tax Policy Evaluation.* Chicago: University of Chicago Press.

Ballentine, J. G. 1975. On the General Equilibrium Analysis of Tax Incidence. *Journal of Political Economy* 83:633–44.

Ballentine, J. G., and I. Eris. 1975. On the General Equilibrium Analysis of Tax Incidence. *Journal of Political Economy* 83:633–44.

Barr, R. S., and J. S. Turner. 1978. A New, Linear Programming Approach to Microdata File Merging. In *1978 Compendium of Tax Research.* Washington, D.C.: Department of the Treasury, Office of Tax Analysis.

Berliant, M. C., and R. P. Strauss. 1983. Measuring the Distribution of Personal Taxes. In *What Role for Government?* ed. R. J. Zeckhauser. Durham, N.C.: Duke University Press.

———. 1985. The Horizontal and Vertical Equity Characteristics of the Federal Individual Income Tax, 1966–1977. In *Horizontal Equity, Uncertainty, and Economic Well-Being,* ed. M. H. David and T. Smeeding. NBER Studies in Income and Wealth, vol. 50. Chicago: University of Chicago Press.

Bernheim, B. D. 1981. A Note on Dynamic Tax Incidence. *Quarterly Journal of Economics* 95:705–23.

Bishop, G. A. 1967. *Tax Burdens and Benefits of Government Expenditures by Income Class, 1961 and 1965.* New York: Tax Foundation.

Blough, R. 1937. Discussion on The Distinction between "Net" and "Gross" in Income Taxation. In *Studies in Income and Wealth,* vol. 1. Washington, D.C.: National Bureau of Economic Research.

———. 1952. *The Federal Taxing Process.* New York: Prentice-Hall.

Blough, R., and C. Shoup. 1937. *The Federal Revenue System.* Washington, D.C.: U.S. Department of the Treasury.

Blum, J. M. 1959. *From the Morganthau Diaries: Years of Crisis, 1929–1938.* Boston: Houghton Mifflin.

———. 1965. *From the Morganthau Diaries: Year of Urgency, 1938–1941.* Boston: Houghton Mifflin.

Borjas, G., and J. J. Heckman. 1979. Labor Supply Estimates for Public Policy Evaluation. *Proceedings of the Thirty-First Annual Meeting of the Industrial Relations Research Association,* 320–21. Madison, Wis.: Industrial Relations Research Association.

Bossons, J. 1967. *A General Income Tax Analyzer.* Studies of the Royal Commission on Taxation. Toronto: University of Toronto, Institute for Policy Analysis.

Bradford, D. F. 1976. Factor Prices May Be Constant but Factor Returns Are Not. *Economic Letters,* 199–203.

———. 1981. The Incidence and Allocation Effects of a Tax on Corporate Distributions. *Journal of Public Economics* 15.

Break, G. F. 1974. The Incidence and Economic Effects of Taxation. In *The Economics of Public Finance,* ed. Alan Blinder et al. Washington, D.C.: Brookings.

Bridges, B., Jr. 1975. The Harberger Incidence Model: A Comment. *National Tax Journal* 28(4): 462–66.

Brittain, J. A. 1972. *The Payroll Tax for Social Security.* Washington, D.C.: Brookings.

Browning, E. K. 1986. Pechman's Tax Incidence Study: A Note on the Data. *The American Economic Review* 76(5):1214–20.

Browning, E. K., and W. R. Johnson. 1979. *The Distribution of the Tax Burden.* Washington, D.C.: American Enterprise Institute for Public Policy Research.

Bruecker, J. K. 1981. Labor Mobility and the Incidence of the Residential Property Tax. *Journal of Urban Economics* 10:173–82.

Budd, E. C. 1972. Comment on Constructing a New Data Base from Existing Microdata Sets: The 1966 Merge File. *Annals of Economic and Social Measurement* 1(3):325–42.

Budd, E. C., and D. B. Radner. 1969. The OBE Size Distribution Series: Methods and Tentative results for 1964. *American Economic Review* 59(2):435–49.

Calvo, G., L. J. Kotlikoff, and C. A. Rodriguez. 1979. The Incidence of a Tax on Pure Rent: A New (?) Reason for an Old Answer. *Journal of Political Economy* 87:869–74.

Cilke, James M., and Roy A. Wyscarver. 1987. The Treasury Individual Income Tax Simulation Model. *Compendium of Tax Research 1987.* Washington, D.C.: Department of the Treasury, Office of Tax Analysis.

Colm, G. 1937. Public Revenue and Public Expenditure in National Income. *Studies in Income and Wealth,* vol. 1. Washington, D.C.: National Bureau of Economic Research.

Colm, G., and H. Tarasov. 1941. *Who Pays the Taxes?* Study for the Temporary National Economic Committee. Monograph no. 3. Investigation of Economic Power. 76th Cong., 3d sess.

Colm, G., and H. P. Wald. 1952. Some Comments on Tax Burden Comparisons. *National Tax Journal* 5(1):1–14.

Commission to Revise the Tax Structure. 1973. *Reforming the Federal Tax Structure.* Washington, D.C.: Fund for Public Policy Research.

Congressional Research Service. 1984. *Federal Statistics and National Needs.* 98th Cong., 1st sess., S. Rept. 98–191.

Council of Economic Advisers. See U. S. President.

Courant, P. N. 1977. A General Equilibrium Model of Heterogeneous Property Taxes. *Journal of Public Economics* 8:313–27.

Cragg, J. C., A. C. Harberger, and P. Mieszkowski. 1967. Empirical Evidence on the Incidence of the Corporation Income Tax. *Journal of Political Economy* 75:811–21.

———. 1970. Corporation Tax Shifting: A Rejoinder. *Journal of Political Economy* 78:747–77.

David, M., R. J. A. Little, M. E. Samuhel, and R. K. Triest. 1986. Alternative Methods for CPS Income Imputation. *Journal of the American Statistical Association* 81(393):29–41.

Debreu, G. 1959. *Theory of Value: An Axiomatic Analysis of Economic Equilibrium.* New Haven Conn.: Yale University Press.

Devarajan, Shantayanan, Don Fullerton, and Richard A. Musgrave, 1980. Estimating the Distribution of Tax Burdens. *Journal of Public Economics* 13:155–82.

Diamond, P. A. 1978. Tax Incidence in a Two Good Model. *Journal of Public Economics* 9:283–99.

Diewert, W. E. 1985. The Measurement of Waste and Welfare in Applied General Equilibrium Models. In *New Developments in Applied General Equilibrium Analysis,* ed. J. Piggott and J. Walley. New York: Cambridge University Press.

Dosser, D. 1961. Tax Incidence and Growth. *The Economic Journal* 71(283):572–91.

Driffil, E. F., and Harvey S. Rosen. 1981. Taxation and Excess Burden: A Life-Cycle Perspective. NBER Working Paper no. 698.

Eaton, J., and H. Rosen. 1980. Taxation, Human Capital, and Uncertainty. *American Economic Review* 70(4):705–15.

Engquist, E. J., Jr. 1961. Developments in Processing Statistics from Tax Returns. Paper presented at the American Statistical Association annual meeting, New York City.

Feldstein, M. 1974. Tax Incidence in a Growing Economy with Variable Factor Supply. *Quarterly Journal of Economics* 88(4):551–73.

———. 1977. The Surprising Incidence of a Tax on Pure Rent: A New Answer to an Old Question. *Journal of Political Economy* 85:349–60.

———. 1986. The Welfare Cost of Capital Income Taxation. *Journal of Political Economy* 86, no. 2, pt. 2: 29–50.

———. 1978. Imputing Corporate Tax Liabilities to Individual Taxpayers. NBER Working Paper no. 2349.

Fullerton, D. 1980. Estimating the Distribution of Tax Burdens. *Journal of Public Economics* 13.

———. 1983. Replacing the U. S. Income Tax with a Progressive Consumption Tax. *Journal of Public Economics* 20:3–23.

Fullerton, D. and R. Gordon. 1983. A Reexamination of Tax Distortions in General Equilibrium Models. In *Behavioral Simulation Methods in Tax Policy Analysis,* ed. M. Feldstein. Chicago: University of Chicago Press.

Fullerton, D., J. B. Shoven, and J. Whalley. 1978. General Equilibrium Analysis of U. S. Taxation Policy. *Compendium of Tax Research.* Washington, D.C.: Department of the Treasury, Office of Tax Analysis.

———. 1983. Replacing the U.S. Income Tax with a Progressive Consumption Tax. *Journal of Public Economics* 20:3–23.

Galper, H., and E. Toder. 1984. Transfer Elements in the Taxation of Income from Capital. In *Economic Transfers in the United States,* ed. M. Moon. NBER Studies in Income and Wealth, vol. 49. Chicago: University of Chicago Press.

Goldsmith, S., G. Jaszi, H. Kaitz, and M. Liebenberg. 1954. Size Distribution of Income since the Mid-Thirties. *Review of Economics and Statistics* 36(1):1–32.

Haig, R. M. 1921. The Concept of Income. *The Federal Income Tax.* New York: Columbia University Press.

Hall, R. E. 1968. Consumption Taxes versus Income Taxes: Implications for Economic Growth. *Proceedings of the Sixty-First National Tax Conference.* Columbus, Ohio: National Tax Association.

Harberger, A. C. 1962. The Incidence of the Corporation Income Tax. *Journal of Political Economy* 70(3):215–40.

———. 1978. On the Use of Distributional Weights in Social Cost-Benefit Analysis. *Journal of Political Economy* 86, no. 2, pt. 2: 87–120.

Hausman, J. 1981. Labor Supply. In *How Taxes Affect Economic Behavior,* ed. H. J. Aaron and J. A. Pechman. Washington, D.C.: Brookings.

Herriot, R. A., and H. P. Miller. 1971a. The Taxes We Pay. *Conference Board Record* 8(5):31–40.

———. 1971b. Who Paid the Taxes in 1968? Washington, D.C.: Bureau of the Census.

Johnson, J. A. 1967. *The Incidence of Government Revenues and Expenditures.* Report for the Ontario Committee on Taxation. Ottawa: Queen's Printer.

Jones, R. W. 1965. The Structure of Simple General Equilibrium Models. *Journal of Political Economy* 73: 557–72.

Jorgenson, Dale W. 1984. Econometric Methods for Applied General Equilibrium Analysis. In *Applied General Equilibrium Analysis,* ed. H. E. Scarf and J. B. Shoven. Cambridge: Cambridge University Press.

Juster, R. T. 1988. The State of U.S. Economic Statistics: Current and Prospective Quality, Policy Needs, and Resources. Paper presented at the fiftieth anniversary conference of the Conference on Research in Income and Wealth. Washington, D.C., May.

Kadane, J. B. 1978. Some Statistical Problems in Merging Data Files. In *1978 Compendium of Tax Research.* Washington, D.C.: Department of the Treasury, Office of Tax Analysis.

Kalton, G. 1983. *Compensating for Missing Survey Data.* Ann Arbor: Institute for Social Research, University of Michigan.

Kiefer, D. W. 1984. Distributional Tax Progressivity Indexes. *National Tax Journal* 37(4):497–513.

Kiefer, D. W., and S. Nelson. 1986. Distributional Effects of Federal Tax Reform. *Proceedings of the Seventy-ninth Annual Conference of the National Tax Association—Tax Institute of America.* Columbus, Ohio: National Tax Association.

Killingsworth, M. 1983. *Labor Supply.* Cambridge: Cambridge University Press.

Kotlikoff, L. J., and L. H. Summers. 1979. Tax Incidence in a Life Cycle Model with Variable Labor Supply. *Quarterly Journal of Economics* 93(4):705–18.

———. 1987. Tax Incidence. In *Handbook of Public Economics,* vol. 2, ed. A. Auerbach and M. Feldstein. Amsterdam: North Holland.

Krzyzaniak, M., ed. 1966. *Effects of Corporation Income Tax.* Detroit: Wayne State University Press.

Krzyzaniak, M., and R. A. Musgrave. 1970. Corporation Tax Shifting: A Response. *Journal of Political Economy* 78:768–73.

Leven, M., H. G. Moulton, and C. Warburton. 1934. *America's Capacity to Consume.* Washington, D.C.: Brookings.

Lipsey, R., and H. S. Tice, eds. 1989. *The Measurement of Saving, Investment, and Wealth.* NBER Studies in Income and Wealth, vol. 52. Chicago: University of Chicago Press.

Little, R. J. A. and D. B. Rubin. 1987. *Statistical Analysis with Missing Data.* New York: Wiley.

McLure, C. E., Jr. 1970. Tax Incidence, Macroeconomic Policy, and Absolute Prices. *Quarterly Journal of Economics* 84(2):254–67.

———. 1971. The Theory of Tax Incidence with Imperfect Factor Mobility. (in English). *Finanzarchiv* (Tübingen) 30(1).

———. 1975. General Equilibrium Incidence Analysis: The Harberger Model after Ten Years. *Journal of Public Economics* 4(2):125–61.

———. 1980. The State Corporate Income Tax: Lamb in Wolves' Clothing. *The Economics of Taxation,* ed. H. J. Aaron and M. J. Boskin. Washington, D.C.: Brookings.

———. ed. 1984. *The State Corporation Income Tax: Issues in Worldwide Unitary Combination.* Stanford, Calif.: Hoover Institution Press.

McLure, C. E., Jr., and W. R. Thirsk. 1975a. A Simplified Exposition of the Harberger Model, I: Tax Incidence. *National Tax Journal* 28(1):1–27.

McLure, C. E., Jr., with the assistance of R. Klein. 1975b. A Simplified Exposition of the Harberger Model, II: Expenditure Incidence. *National Tax Journal* 28(2):195–207.

———. 1975c. The Harberger Model: Reply, *National Tax Journal* 28(4):467–70.

McNeil, J., and E. Lamas. 1989. Year-Apart Estimates of Household Net Worth from the Survey of Income and Program Participation. In *The Measurement of Saving, Investment, and Wealth* ed. R. Lipsey and H. S. Tice, 431–62. NBER Studies in Income and Wealth, vol. 52. Chicago: University of Chicago Press.

Mieszkowski, P. M. 1969. Tax Incidence Theory: The Effects of Taxes on the Distribution of Income. *Journal of Economic Literature* 7:1103–24.

———. 1972. The Property Tax: An Excise Tax or a Profits Tax? *Journal of Public Economics* 1(1):73–96.

———. 1984. The National Effects of Differential State Corporate Income Taxes on Multistate Corporations. In *The State Corporation Income Tax: Issues in Worldwide Unitary Combination,* ed. C. McLure. Stanford, Calif.: Hoover Institution Press.

Mieszkowski, P. M., and G. R. Zodrow. 1984. The Incidence of the Local Property Tax: A Reevaluation. NBER Working Paper no. 1485.

Morgenstern, O. 1963. *On the Accuracy of Economic Observations,* 2d ed. Princeton, N. J.: Princeton University Press.

Musgrave, R. A. 1952. Distribution of Tax Payments by Income Groups: A Review. *Proceedings of the 4th Annual Conference on Taxation.* Columbus, Ohio: National Tax Association.

———. 1953. General Equilibrium Aspects of Incidence Theory. *American Economic Review* 42:504–17.

———. 1959. *The Theory of Public Finance.* New York: McGraw Hill.

———. 1985. A Brief History of Fiscal Doctrine. In *Handbooks of Public Economics,* vol. 1, ed. A. J. Auerbach and M. Feldstein. New York: North-Holland.

Musgrave, R. A., J. J. Carroll, L. D. Cook, and L. Frane. 1951. Distribution of Tax Payments by Income Groups: A Case Study For 1948. *National Tax Journal* 4(1):1–53.

Musgrave, R. A., K. E. Case, and H. Leonard. 1974. The Distribution of Fiscal Burdens and Benefits. *Public Finance Quarterly* 2(3):259–311.

Musgrave, R. A., and D. W. Daicoff. 1958. Who pays the Michigan Taxes? Michigan Tax Study, Staff Papers, Lansing.

Musgrave, R. A., and L. Frane. 1952a. Concluding Note. *National Tax Journal* 5(1):39.

———. 1952b. Rejoinder to Dr. Tucker. *National Tax Journal* 5(1):15–35.

Musgrave, R. A., and Tun Thin. 1948. Income Tax Progression, 1929–1948. *Journal of Political Economy.* 56:498–514.

National Bureau of Economic Research. 1937. *Studies in Income and Wealth,* vol. 1. New York: NBER.

———. 1943. *Income Size Distributions in the United States.* Studies in Income and Wealth, vol. 5. New York: NBER.

———. 1951. *Studies in Income and Wealth,* vol. 13. New York: NBER.

National Resources Committee. 1938. *Consumer Incomes in the United States: Their Distribution in 1935–36.* Washington, D.C.: National Resources Committee.

Natrella, Vito. 1966. Historical and Future Development of Statistics of Income. Paper delivered at the American Statistical Association, 126th annual meeting, Los Angeles, Calif., August 15–19.

Neisser, A. 1951. Study of Federal Tax Burdens at Pre-Korean and Post-Korean Rates. Washington, D.C.: U.S. Department of the Treasury, Office of Tax Analysis. Typescript.

Nelson, S. C. 1987. Family Economic Income and Other Income Concepts Used in Analyzing Tax Reform. In *Compendium of Tax Research 1987*. Washington, D.C.: U.S. Department of the Treasury, Office of Tax Analysis.

Netzer, D. 1966. *Economics of the Property Tax*. Washington, D.C.: Brookings.

Newcomer, M. 1937a. Discussion on Public Revenue and Public Expenditure in National Income. In *Studies in Income and Wealth,* vol. 1. Washington, D.C.: National Bureau of Economic Research.

———. 1937b. Estimate of the Tax Burden on Different Income Classes. *Studies in Current Tax Problems*. New York: Twentieth Century Fund.

Nunns, J. R. 1987. Tabulations from the Treasury Tax Reform Data Base. *Compendium of Tax Research 1987*. Washington, D.C.: U.S. Department of the Treasury, Office of Tax Analysis.

Oakes, E. E. 1942. The Incidence of a General Income Tax. *American Economic Review Proceedings*. 32:76–82.

Okner, B. 1972a. Reply and Comments to Constructing a New Data Base from Existing Microdata Sets: The 1966 Merge File. *Annals of Economic and Social Measurement* 1(3):325–42.

———. 1972b. Constructing a New Data Base from Existing Microdata Sets: The 1966 Merge File. *Annals of Economic and Social Measurement* 1(3):325–42.

———. 1974. Data Matching and Merging: An Overview. *Annals of Economic and Social Measurement* 3:347–52.

Ott, A., and L. Dittrich. 1981. *The Federal Tax Burden on Households*. Washington, D.C.: American Enterprise Institute for Public Policy Research.

Pechman, J. A. 1951. Distribution of Income: Before and After Federal Income Tax, 1941 and 1947. In *Studies in Income and Wealth,* vol. 13. New York: National Bureau of Economic Research.

———. 1953. Some Technical Problems in the Measurement of Tax Burdens. *1952 Proceedings of the 45th Annual Conference on Taxation*. Sacramento, Calif.: National Tax Association.

———. 1958. Comments on The Relation of Census Income Distribution Statistics to Other Income Data. In *An Appraisal of the 1950 Census Income Date*. NBER Studies in Income and Wealth, vol. 23. Princeton, N.J.: Princeton University Press.

———. 1965. *Individual Income Tax Provisions of the Revenue Act of 1964*. Washington, D.C.: Brookings.

———. 1985. *Who Paid the Taxes, 1966–85*. Washington, D.C.: Brookings.

———. 1986. Pechman's Tax Incidence Study: A Response. *American Economic Review* 76(5):1219–20.

Pechman, J. A., and B. A. Okner. 1974. Who Bears the Tax Burden? Washington, D.C.: Brookings.

Peck, J. K. 1972. Comments on Constructing a New Data Base from Existing Microdata Sets: The 1966 Merge File. *Annals of Economic and Social Measurement* 1(3):325–42.

Pettengill, R. B. 1940. Division of the Tax Burden Among Income Groups in the United States in 1936. *American Economic Review* 30(1):60–71.

Piggott, John R. 1985. Introduction to *New Developments in Applied General Equilibrium Analysis,* ed. J. Piggott and J. Whaley, New York: Cambridge University Press.

Piggott, J., and J. Whalley. 1985. Economic Effects of U.K. Tax-Subsidy Policies: A General Equilibrium Appraisal. In *New Developments in Applied General Equilibrium Analysis,* ed. J. Piggott and J. Whalley. New York: Cambridge University Press.

Prest, A. R. 1955. Statistical Calculations of Tax Burdens. *Economica* 22(87):234–45.

Price Statistics Review Committee. 1961. *The Price Statistics of the Federal Government.* New York: National Bureau of Economic Research.

Rodgers, W. L. 1984. An Evaluation of Statistical Matching. *Journal of Business and Economic Statistics* 2(1):91–102.

Rosen, H. S. 1978. The Measurement of Excess Burden with Explicit Utility Functions. *Journal of Political Economy* 86, no. 2, pt. 2: 121–35.

Rubin, D. B. 1987. *Multiple Imputation for Nonresponse in Surveys.* New York: Wiley.

Sato, R., and R. F. Hoffman. 1974. Tax Incidence in a Growing Economy. *Public Finance and Stabilization Policy,* ed. W. L. Smith and J. M. Culbertson. Amsterdam: North-Holland.

Scarf, H. E. 1967. On the Computation of Equilibrium Prices. *Ten Economic Studies in the Tradition of Irving Fisher,* ed. W. J. Fellner, New York: Wiley.

Shere, L. 1934. The Burden of Taxation. U.S. Department of the Treasury, Division of the Research and Taxation. Memorandum.

Shoup, C. 1937. The Distinction Between "Net" and "Gross" in Income Taxation. *Studies in Income and Wealth,* vol. 1. Washington, D.C.: National Bureau of Economic Research.

———. 1969. *Public Finance.* Chicago: Aldine.

———. 1972. Quantitative Research in Taxation and Government Expenditure. In *Public Expenditures and Taxation: Fiftieth Anniversary Colloquium IV.* NBER General Series no. 96. New York: Columbia University Press.

Shoup, C., R. Blough, and M. Newcomer. 1937. *Studies in Current Tax Problems.* New York: Twentieth Century Fund.

Shoven, J. B. 1976. The Incidence and Efficiency Effects of Taxes on Income from Capital. *Journal of Political Economy* 84:1261–84.

Shoven, J. B., and J. Whalley. 1972. A General Equilibrium Calculation of the Effects of Differential Taxation of Income from Capital in the U.S. *Journal of Public Economics* 1:281–321.

———. 1984. Applied General Equilibrium Models of Taxation and International Trade. *Journal of Economic Literature* 22(3):1007–51.

———. 1983. Applied General Equilibrium Tax Modeling. *Staff Papers, International Monetary Fund.* 30(2):394–420.

Sims, C. A. 1972. Comments on and Rejoinder to Constructing a New Data Base from Existing Microdata Sets: The 1966 Merge File. *Annals of Economic and Social Measurement* 1(3):325–42.

———. 1974. Comment. *Annals of Economic and Social Measurement,* 3:395–98.

Simons, H. C. 1938. *Personal Income Taxation.* Chicago: University of Chicago Press.

———. 1950. *Federal Tax Reform.* Chicago: University of Chicago Press.

Slemrod, J. 1983. A General Equilibrium Model of Taxation with Endogenous Financial Behavior. In *Behavioral Simulation Methods in Tax Policy Analysis,* ed. M. Feldstein. Chicago: University of Chicago Press.

Smith, J. D. 1975. *The Personal Distribution of Income and Wealth.* NBER Studies in Income and Wealth, vol. 39. New York: Columbia University Press.

Stiglitz, J. E. 1978. Notes on Estate Taxes, Redistribution, and the Concept of Balanced Growth Path Incidence. *Journal of Political Economy* 86, no. 2, pt. 2: S137-S150.

Summers, L. H. 1981. Capital Taxation and Accumulation in a Life Cycle Growth Model. *American Economic Review* 71(4):533–44.

Triplett, J. E., 1983. *The Measurement of Labor Cost.* NBER Studies in Income and Wealth, vol. 48. Chicago: University of Chicago Press.

———. 1989. Price and Technological Change in a Capital Good: A Survey of Research on Computers. In *Technology and Capital Formation,* ed. D. W. Jorgenson and R. Landau, Cambridge Mass.: MIT Press.

Tucker, R. S. 1951. Distribution of Tax Burdens in 1948. *National Tax Journal* 4(3):269–85.

———. 1952. Rebuttal. *National Tax Journal* 5(1):36–38.

Twentieth Century Fund, Inc. Committee on Taxation. 1937a. *Facing the Tax Problem: A Survey of Taxation in the United States and a Program for the Future.* New York: Twentieth Century Fund.

———. 1937b. *Studies in Current Tax Problems.* New York: Twentieth Century Fund.

U.K. Parliament. 1927. *Report of the Committee on National Debt and Taxation.* (Colwyn Commission Report). Cmd. 2800.

U.S. Congress. Congressional Budget Office (CBO). 1987. *The Changing Distribution of Federal Taxes: 1975–1990.* Washington, D.C.: CBO.

U.S. Congress. House. 1934. *The Revenue Bill of 1934.* 73rd cong., 2d sess. Report no. 704.

———. 1942. *The Revenue Bill of 1942.* 77th cong., 2d sess. Report no. 2333.

———. 1963. *Revision of Our Tax Structure: Message of the President of the United States.* 88th cong., 1st sess. Doc. 43.

U.S. Congress. House. Committee on Ways and Means. 1941. *Revenue Revision of 1941: Hearings* (rev.) vol. 1. 77th Cong., 1st sess. April and May 1941: Washington, D.C.: Government Printing Office.

———. 1942. *Revenue Revision of 1942: Hearings,* vol. 1. 77th Cong., 2d. sess. March 1942. Washington D.C.: Government Printing Office.

———. 1959. *Tax Revision Compendium: Compendium of Papers on Broadening the Tax Base.* Washington, D.C.: Government Printing Office.

———. 1963. *Hearings on the President's 1963 Tax Message.* 88th cong., 1st sess. Washington, D.C.: Government Printing Office.

———. 1966. *Legislative History of H.R. 8363, the Revenue Act of 1964,* ps. 1–4. 89th Cong., 2d sess. Public Law 88–272. Washington, D.C.: Government Printing Office.

———. 1985. *Hearings on Comprehensive Tax Reform,* pt. 1. 99th Cong., 1st sess., ser. 99–41. Washington, D.C.: Government Printing Office.

U.S. Congress. Joint Committee on the Economic Report. 1948. *Statistical Gaps.* 80th Cong., 2d sess. Washington, D.C.: Government Printing Office.

———. 1951. *Joint Economic Report on the 1951 Economic Report of the President.* Washington, D.C.: Government Printing Office.

———. 1954. *Report of the Joint Committee on the Economic Report.* 83d Cong., 2d sess. Washington, D.C.: Government Printing Office.

U.S. Congress. Joint Committee on the Economic Report and the Select Committee on Small Business (House). 1952. *Constitutional Limitation on Federal Income, Estate, and Gift Tax Rates.* 82d Cong. Washington, D.C.: Government Printing Office.

U.S. Congress. Joint Committee on Taxation. 1981. *General Explanation of the Economic Recovery Tax Act of 1981.* 97th Cong., 1st sess. Washington, D.C.: Government Printing Office.

———. 1986. Data on the Distribution by Income Class of the Tax Reform Act of 1986. Washington, D.C.: Government Printing Office.
———. 1987. *General Explanation of the Tax Reform Act of 1986 (H.R. 3838).* 99th Cong. Public Law 99–514. Washington, D.C.: Government Printing Office.
———. 1965a. *The Distribution of Personal Income.* 88th Cong., 2d sess. Washington, D.C.: Government Printing Office.
———. 1965b. *Improved Statistics for Economic Growth.* 89th Cong., 1st sess. Washington, D.C.: Government Printing Office.
———. 1966. *Improved Statistics for Economic Growth.* 89th cong., 2d sess. Washington, D.C.: Government Printing Office.
———. 1967. *The Coordination and Integration of Government Statistical Programs.* 90th Cong., 1st sess. Washington, D.C.: Government Printing Office.
———. 1969. *Review of Federal Statistical Programs.* 91st Cong., 1st sess. Washington, D.C.: Government Printing Office.
———. 1981. *Employment Act of 1946, as Amended with Related Laws.* 97th Cong., 1st sess. Washington, D.C.: Government Printing Office.
U.S. Congress. Senate. Committee on Finance. 1942. *Withholding Tax: Hearings.* 77th Cong., 2d sess. August 19, 1942.
———. 1951. *Revenue Act of 1951: Hearings, Part 1.* 82nd Cong., 1st sess., June and July 1951.
———. 1963. *Hearings on H. R. 8363, The Revenue Act of 1963.* 88th Cong., 1st sess. Washington, D.C.: Government Printing Office.
———. 1976. *Hearings on H. R. 10612, The Tax Reform Act of 1975.* Pt 5. 94th Cong., 2d sess. Washington, D.C.: Government Printing Office.
U.S. Department of Commerce. Bureau of Economic Analysis. 1986. *The National Income and Product Accounts of the United States, 1929–82. Statistical Tables.* Washington, D.C.: Government Printing Office.
U.S. Department of the Treasury. 1977. *Blueprints for Basic Tax Reform.* Washington, D.C.: U.S. Department of the Treasury.
———. 1978a. *The President's 1978 Tax Program.*
———. 1978b. Statement of the Honorable W. Michael Blumenthal, Secretary of the Treasury, before U.S. Congress. House, Committee on Ways and Means, January 30.
———. 1981. Statement of the Honorable John E. Chapoton, Assistant Secretary of the Treasury (Tax Policy)—Designate, before U.S. Congress. House, Committee on the Budget, Task Force on Tax Policy, March 13.
———. 1984. Report to the President. *Tax Reform for Fairness, Simplicity and Economic Growth.*
———. 1985a. *The President's Tax Proposals to the Congress for Fairness, Growth, and Simplicity.*
———. 1985b. Statement of the Honorable James A. Baker, III, Secretary of the Treasury, before the Senate Finance Committee, June 11.
U.S. Department of the Treasury. Division of Research and Statistics. 1937. *Tax Revision Studies, 1937: General Statement, Revenue Estimates, Summaries and Recommendations.* Washington, D.C.: U.S. Treasury.
———. 1938. *Statistics of Income Supplement: Compiled from Federal Income Tax Returns of Individuals for the Income Year 1934,* sec. 1. Washington, D.C.: U.S. Department of the Treasury.
———. 1940. *Statistics of Income supplement: Compiled from Federal Income Tax Returns for 1936,* secs. 1–4. Washington, D.C.: U.S. Department of the Treasury.
U.S. Department of the Treasury, Division of Tax Research. 1942. Allocation of the Tax Burden by Income Classes. Memorandum.

———. 1943. *Individual Base Book.* Washington, D.C.: U.S. Department of the Treasury.
———. 1947a. *Individual Income Tax Exemptions.* Washington, D.C.: U.S. Department of the Treasury.
———. 1947b. *The Tax Treatment of Earned Income.* Washington, D.C.: U.S. Department of the Treasury.
U.S. President. 1951. *Economic Report of the President.* Washington, D.C.: Government Printing Office.
University of Wisconsin Tax Study Committee. 1959. Distribution of State and Local Taxes In Wisconsin. *Wisconsin's State and Local Tax Burden.* Madison.
Vandendorpe, A. L., and A. F. Friedlaender. 1976. Differential Incidence in the Presence of Initial Distorting Taxes. *Journal of Public Economics* 6:205–29.
Wertz, K. L. 1978. A Method for Measuring the Relative Taxation of Families. *The Review of Economics and Statistics* 145–50.
Whalley, J. 1984. Regression or Progression: The Taxing Question of Incidence Analysis. *Canadian Journal of Economics* 17(4):654–82.
Wood, G. D. 1988. A New Measure of the Cost of Compensation Components. *Survey of Current Business* 68(11):38–43.
Wyscarver, R. A. 1985. The Treasury Individual Income Tax Simulation Model. U.S. Department of the Treasury, Office of Tax Analysis.

Comment Martin H. David

The Framework for Burden Studies

Atrostic and Nunns undertake an ambitious survey of the methodology and empirical basis for understanding the "burden of taxation." My remarks complement their review and focus on four topics: scope, evaluation, error, and new data requirements. Let me begin by reviewing their definitions and framework. Early in the discussion the authors state:

> A tax is a compulsory payment to the government from which the taxpayer recevies no direct benefit. . . . Payment of taxes, through lower factor incomes or higher product prices, reduces a taxpayer's real income. Tax burden measures attempt to quantify this decrease in utility and to evaluate the decrease against a measure of ability to pay. . . . Taxation also imposes administrative and compliance costs.

Table 11C.1 relates this definition to other kinds of payments and receipts that are relevant to understanding the welfare of individuals. The table considers both taxes and transfers. The distinction between coercive and voluntary payments is paralleled by a division of transfers into entitlements (automatic receipts) and means tested (or conditional receipts). The quid pro quo corresponding to payment or receipts is classified by the nature of the corresponding change utility that derives from change in consumption bundles available.

Martin H. David is a professor of economics at the University of Wisconsin at Madison.

Table 11C.1 Payments Relevant for "Burden" Analysis

Quid pro quo (Direct Benefit or Cost)	Nature of Transaction			
	Compulsory		Voluntary	
	Payment	Receipt	Payment	Receipt
None	1. "Pure" taxation			
Nonexclusive	2. Property taxes		Contributions	5. In-kind transfers
Exclusive	3. FICA	4. EITC	Consumption	Factor sales 6. Cash transfers

The case mentioned by Atrostic and Nunns, no change in real goods and services is what I will call category 1, one of three important cases. The others are cases in which the payment generates benefits for large numbers of persons, that is, nonexclusive benefits (category 2), and cases in which the payment generates a benefit that is specific to the individual making payment, or exclusive benefits (category 3).

It is important to note that a substantial part of government finance corresponds to entries other than category 1, which the authors use as their definition of taxes. Atrostic and Nunns point out that "tax burden" studies have generally been limited to a study of income, property, sales, and payroll taxes, numbered 1–4 in table 11C.1. They mention that property taxes and payroll taxes may be "benefit taxes" under some ideal system of equilibration in the marketplace that includes "voting with your feet" and complete certainty of lifetime endowments.

The separability of taxes, transfers, and expenditures in the analysis of "burden" does not really work: the existence of tax features such as EITC and personal exemptions make it clear that some aspects of the compulsory tax system have similar effects on the consumer's budget constraint to elements of the cash transfer system. A complete understanding of the vertical equity of the behavior of the fisc would clearly be incomplete without considering transfers. Problems of integrating tax and transfer systems are significant (and have occupied analysts in several of the major pieces of tax legislation over the past 20 years).

Some Features of the Tax System Substitute for Voluntary Expenditures

For example, tax deductibility of charitable contributions matches "tax expenditures" to the outlays of consumers in their voluntary budgeting of consumption. These points suggest a first difficulty in burden analysis:

Problem 1. "Pure" tax burden studies are too limited. The burden of revenue raising must account for the benefits (costs) of other kinds of taxes and transfers. Debate on the size of public sector requires an understanding of the burden of both financial and real consequences of government activity.

An accepted understanding of "burden" among economists today is welfare loss. Measures of welfare loss are based on three conceptual foundations. The most carefully articulated is that an analytic relationship exists between the raising of revenues by altering after-tax prices and the dead-weight loss (DWL) of the system. That is, the excess of the rise in the expenditure function over the yield of the tax system. Deriving burden in this framework requires an explicit measure of parameters of the utility function.

The second and third conceptual foundations of dead-weight loss were more prominent in discussions of political economy a generation ago, but deal with problems of public choice. A collective agreement must be reached on whose utility function is to be used in burden analysis. That is, some characteristics of taxpayers create heterogeneity of tastes. (For example, large families will consume more food and housing than small families with a given income. This difference in behavior has been considered relevant to taxation and is recognized in the existence of personal exemptions, tax rate schedules, and standard deductions.) Heterogeneity in tastes can be recognized by including relevant characteristics of taxpayers in the estimation of utility parameters. The converse is that characteristics that are not considered relevant for discrimination in the design of tax/transfer systems must be disregarded in estimating the parameters of the utility function (and ignored in policy making). Musgrave (1959) implicitly recognizes this idea in his definition of horizontal equity.

The third conceptual framework is related to the second. Vertical equity implies an understanding of the marginal utility of income (wealth of endowment) as income increases. Marginal utility must decline, and it must decline more than some critical rate to assure that the socially desired tax system is not regressive in relation to income (endowment).

Problem 2. Burden relates to utility and dead-weight loss. Measurement of burden reflects an implicit consensus on relevant heterogeneity, which becomes embedded in parameter estimates. Subsistence and satiation imply that the marginal utility of increases to the endowment must fall.

We note that none of the tables presented by Atrostic and Nunns shows burden in this utility sense. (Two difficulties have been critical: developing acceptable equivalence scales and modeling intertemporal choices of consumers.)

Implementation of these notions of burden measurement requires data on endowments, spending behaviors, and income-producing behaviors of the population (aggregated into decision units). This creates the third major problem for burden studies.

Problem 3. Empirical data on the joint distribution of endowment, leisure, consumption, and lifetime accumulation are needed to estimate utility functions and to determine the distribution of burden in the population.

The various methods used to estimate burden described by Atrostic and Nunns overcome the three problems of scope, utility, and data requirements in a variety of ways.

Representative Taxpayer Methods

The representative taxpayer approach ignores all three problems. It assumes values for the taxpayer's endowment and deductively applies a tax rule to demonstrate an outcome variable. The approach survives because it gives an intuitive understanding. It fails to be informative because (*a*) there are no measures of the importance of the cases simulated, (*b*) the method does not admit avoidance responses, and (*c*) no measure of compliance cost can be generated. It fails to be scientific because no understanding of the quantitative importance of examples can be generated. While the scientific value of this method is small, we need to learn from its effectiveness in communicating to policy makers. The tabulation of individual taxpayers with more than $1,000,000 of AGI who paid no taxes, beginning in the mid-seventies, and the subsequent tabulation of corporate taxpayers with no liabilities after 1981 strongly motivated the subsequent tax legislation.

Aggregative Data Studies

The methods used in aggregative data studies approach at least one of the three problems. The data problem is circumvented by aggregation. It is assumed that all data on households refer to the same universe, or decision makers. Second, shifts in the expectation of conditioning variables are assumed to "cause" shifts in the mean response of decision makers. Third, the universe of decision makers is exogenous to the policy experiments being carried out. Work by Reynolds and Smolensky (1977) and Gillepsie (1965) needs to be cited because they consciously attempt to deal with the burden of both transfers and public-good producing expenditures of government. Aaron and McGuire (1970) attempted, and their work is unusual, to account for the declining marginal utility of consumption, thereby tackling the second problem cited.

The aggregative studies give modest insight into reality including the effects of avoidance behaviors on the status quo. The scientific shortcomings of such studies are that they offer no basis for ascertaining error and they incorporate little or no behavioral response in calculating the tax burden under counterfactual conditions. Such studies are always limited by some principle for classifying the population. Once selected, no alternative perspective on the population is possible.

Microdata Studies

Microdata studies offer several orders of magnitude of improvement on the aggregative studies. They replace the concentration on means in the aggregative method with a procedure that permits nonzero covariance among variables assembled from different data sources. (In the language of survey specialists, a procedure akin to mean imputation is replaced by mean plus empirical error distribution for the statistically matched cases.)

The convenience of the microdata methods is flexibility. The statistically matched data set implicitly contains the information required to display burden calculations in a number of dimensions. Curiously, this flexibility has seldom been used to display the inherent variability of the population, as in tables 11.7 and 11.9. Furthermore, little has been done with analysis of heterogeneity in the population and a concern to understand the second problem more deeply.

The most neglected research on statistically matched data is the study of error. I repeat criticisms raised repeatedly, most recently by Smeeding (1980). We know almost nothing about the variance in the statistical matching process. While efforts have concentrated on minimizing the distance between two records for a match, almost nothing has been done on three easily studied questions. (*a*) We have knowledge of exact matched tax, income, and benefit data. Simulation of statistical matches on those data would give a clearer understanding of the error involved in the process used by the OTA to generate its individual income tax model. (*b*) As Kadane (1978) suggested, evidence on the missing partial correlations that is currently ignored in the statistical matching process should be gathered and incorporated into the procedure. (*c*) Rubin (1987) advocates multiple matching (multiple imputation) so that we can know the variance that is generated by the algorithm for matching and can calculate better measures of association that depend on the imputation. None of these ways of improving statistical matches is beyond our current capabilities and all would help us understand the robustness of the representation of the distribution of population characteristics that we use in microsimulation.

Other high priorities for the micromodel are to add estimates of compliance costs to allow us to compare tax systems that are correct but difficult to administer with tax systems that are pragmatic and consider real resource costs involved in compliance and administration. Ott and Ott (1969) and H & R Block (Roper Organization 1977) provide data that could be used for such measures.

I would urge that the classifier used in discriminating the effects of a tax system on vertical equity should relate to wealth, rather than income. The total of physical capital, financial capital, and human capital should be estimated for each economic decision unit, and burden should be tabulated in classes based on that total. This allows us to consider the effect of tax laws on the distribution of burden between generations and to incorporate an estimate of unrealized capital gains.

General Equilibrium Modeling

The Treasury's general equilibrium (GE) model is the most sophisticated and the most vulnerable basis for assessing burden. The GE makes use of parameters of the utility function. It integrates consumption, saving, and factor supply decisions within a household population. And it models the total response of the economy to a change in tax structure. (It is paradoxical that the GE models incorporate utility functions, yet have seldom been used to assess questions of vertical equity, while the microsimulation models that use no utility framework, have been relied upon for that purpose.) Over the past 20 years we have learned a number of critical facts about GE modeling.

Disaggregation of GE Models from Two Sectors and Two Factors Is Essential

Shoven (1976) demonstrated that variation in the tax system within the corporate manufacturing sector produced as much welfare loss as the distinctions between corporate and noncorporate enterprises. Mieszkowski (1972) demonstrated without a doubt that the land factor must be considered separately from reproducible capital and labor because of its relation to nontradable goods and immobile factors. Feldstein (1977) considered the importance of land as a vehicle for transferring wealth over time.

What we have not yet learned is how much disaggregation is informative. The greater the number of sectors, factors, and assets, the more complex the problem of "calibrating" the model and estimating underlying price data. At what point such disaggregation ceases to be informative because the errors in the data overwhelm the signal, we do not presently know. It seems essential to test the robustness of our present understandings to variations in the degree of disaggregation, a computational experiment that has been notably absent in the literature.

Variations in the Cost of Capital

We have learned that cost of capital varies widely by industry, asset type (Fullerton, Gillette, and Mackie 1988), legal organization, and financing arrangements (King 1977). We have not yet learned how to harness this price variation to an understanding of the economy. Fullerton and Henderson (1987) assume values for critical elasticities of substitution that determine the sensitivity of legal organization and asset composition to relative cost of capital. Needless to say, the results are not convincing as a description of real economic processes. A major effort must be made to develop behavioral models of these responses based on observational data.

Tax Law Asymmetries

We have learned that tax law asymmetries sharply differentiate the marginal consequences of investment between firms that carry forward losses and firms that do not (Altshuler and Auerbach 1987). GE models have not yet incorporated this critical fact.

Elasticities of Substitution in Energy and Labor

We have learned that the elasticities of substitution between energy and capital, and between energy and labor, are substantial (Berndt and Wood 1979). The modeling of "value added" by CES functions of labor and capital in combination with a Leontief fixed-coefficient matrix determining the demand for intermediate product is clearly a poor representation of this knowledge. More generally, the production sector is curiously flexible in substitutions between capital and labor and totally inflexible in the use of intermediate products. This weakness can and should be remedied.

The GE model makes no attempt to deal with behavioral responses to transfers and rules out problems in measuring burden that arise from public expenditures. The GE model incorporates a utility function that lacks the subsistence parameters that have been common in consumer demand systems and which would be critical for understanding relative burden of the poor and the rich. The model is not estimated, and no information is generated on the errors entailed in its policy simulation.

Scientific evaluation of the GE model calls for a variety of approaches. Reestimation of production and consumption submodels with state of the art functional forms is a beginning. Perhaps more important is to understand the appropriate degrees of aggregation in this undertaking. As with macromodeling in general, more sectors and more representative consumers do not necessarily add to our understanding of the economy. Just as in the field of scientific sample design, information gains must be balanced against costs—in this case costs of estimation and model solution.

Process of Research on Tax Burden

Up to now the government has been a monopolist with control of the major databases used in tax burden studies. It has limited access to information generated by its models, and it has attempted to control legislative processes by asserting point estimates for the effects of changes in tax legislation. In the future this process can and should be radically different. The capability already exists in the private sector to emulate the microsimulations carried on by the Treasury. What is lacking is an institution that allows access to the databases for scientific research by nonpartisan economists. Models for such access exist—and are described in Smeeding, Rainwater, and O'Higgins (1988) and McGuckin and Pascoe (1988). The technology exists to make this type of access inexpensive and within reach of solo researchers, as we have demonstrated with SIPP-ACCESS at the University of Wisconsin (National Research Council 1988; David 1985).

It will be important to coordinate the efforts of the Treasury, the Congressional Budget Office, and the Department of Health and Human Services to achieve the integration of tax and transfer considerations in a single microcomputer model. We know what to do. The potential to learn more than we have in the last 50 years is enormous.

References

Aaron, Henry, and Martin S. McGuire. 1970. Public goods and income distribution. *Econometrica* 38:907–20.

Altschuler, Rosanne, and Alan J. Auerbach. 1987. The significance of tax law asymmetries: An empirical investigation. NBER Working Paper no. 2279, August.

Auerbach, Alan J., and James M. Poterba. 1987. Tax asymmetries and corporate tax reform. In *The effects of taxation on capital accumulation,* ed. Martin Feldstein, 343–76. Chicago: University of Chicago Press.

Berndt, Ernst, and David O. Wood. 1979. Engineering and econometric interpretations of energy-capital complementarity. *American Economic Review* 69:342–54.

Cilke, James M., and Roy A. Wyscarver. 1988. The Treasury individual income tax simulation model. *Compendium of tax research: 1987,* 43–76. Washington, D.C.: Government Printing Office. 76.

David, Martin H. 1985. Designing a data center for SIPP: An observatory for the social sciences. *Proceedings of the social statistics section of the American Statistical Association.*

Feldstein, Martin S. 1977. The surprising incidence of a tax on pure rent. *Journal of Political Economy* 85:349–60.

Fullerton, Don, Robert Gillette, and James Mackie. 1988. Investment incentives under the Tax Reform Act of 1986. *Compendium of tax research: 1987,* 173–202. Washington, D.C.: Government Printing Office.

Fullerton, Don, and Yolanda Kodrzycki Henderson. 1987. The impact of fundamental tax reform on the allocation of resources. In *The effects of taxation on capital accumulation.* ed. Martin Feldstein, 401–44. Chicago: University of Chicago Press.

Gillespie, W. Irwin, 1965. Effect of public expenditures on distribution of income. In *Essays in fiscal federalism,* ed. Richard A. Musgrave. Washington, D.C.: Brookings.

Kadane, Jay. 1978. Some statistical problems in merging data files. In *Compendium of tax research: 1978,* 159–82. Washington D.C.: Government Printing Office.

King, Mervyn A. 1977. *Public policy and the corporation.* London: Chapman & Hall.

McGuckin, Robert H., and George A. Pascoe, Jr. 1988. The longitudinal research data base: Status and research possibilities. *Survey of Current* Business 68 (November): 30–37.

Mieszkowski, Peter. 1972. The property tax: An excise of a profits tax? *Journal of Public Economics* 1:73–96.

Musgrave, Richard. 1959. *The theory of public finance.* New York: McGraw-Hill.

National Research Council. 1988. *The behavioral and social sciences: Achievements and opportunities,* ed. Dean R. Gerstein, R. Duncan Luce, and Sonja Sperlich. Washington, D.C.: National Academy Press.

Ott, Attial F. and David J. Ott. 1969. Private Costs of Filing Individual Income Tax Returns. In *Studies in substantive tax reform,* ed. Arthur B. Willis 59–63. Chicago: American Bar Foundation and Southern Methodist University.

Reynolds, Morgan, and Eugene F. Smolensky. 1977. *Public expenditures, taxes, and the distribution of income: The United States, 1950, 1960, 1970.* New York: Academic Press.

Roper Organization, Inc. 1977. *The American public in the income tax system: A study of public attitudes toward the federal income tax system.* Storrs, Conn.: Roper Center for Public Opinion Research of the University of Connecticut.

Rubin, Donald B. 1987. *Multiple imputation for nonresponse in surveys.* New York: Wiley.

Shoven, John B. 1976. The incidence and efficiency effects of taxes on income from capital. *Journal of Political Economy* 84:1261–84.

Smeeding, Timothy M. 1980. Discussion of the MERGE 1973 data file. In *Microeconomic simulation models for public policy analysis,* ed. H. Havemen and Kevin Hollenbeck, 1:29–34.

Smeeding, Timothy, Lee Rainwater, and Michael O'Higgins. 1988. *Poverty, inequal-*

ity, and the distribution of income in an international context: Initial research from the Luxembourg Income Study (LIS). London: Wheatsheaf Books.

Comment Joseph A. Pechman

Atrostic and Nunns have prepared a comprehensive history of the development of measures of the distribution of tax burdens. I thought I might supplement their excellent account with some observations about the development of microdata files, with which I was closely associated. I would also like to suggest what might be done to improve the state of knowledge about the distribution of income and taxes.

My first encounter with microdata files occurred in the late 1930s, when I was assistant director of the Wisconsin Income Study. This study, which originated under the auspices of the Conference on Research in Income and Wealth, provided tabulations and, later, analyses of Wisconsin income tax returns for the years 1929–36 (Hanna, Lerner, and Pechman 1948). I believe that this was one of the first large-scale uses of computers in the analysis of the distribution of income and taxes. Because of the limitations of these early computers, the tabulations were generally of the Statistics of Income variety. We also had a longitudinal sample of returns for the years 1929–36 and were able to prepare income distributions for 2, 3, . . . , 7 years. I was aware of the potential use of computers for simulation exercises, but the computers were much too slow and primitive for this purpose.

The work on income distribution after World War II was carried forward mainly by Selma Goldsmith and her associates Maurice Liebenberg and Hyman Kaitz in the Department of Commerce (Office of Business Economics 1953; Goldsmith et al. 1954). Liebenberg and I had been members of a small staff at the Office of Price Administration, headed by Hildegarde Kneeland, which prepared estimates of the distribution of income for the purpose of estimating the taxes needed to reduce consumption to manageable levels during the war (Office of Price Administration 1943). We were all aware of the limitations of consumer expenditure surveys and tabulations of tax returns for income distribution purposes. These early efforts relied heavily on statistical (and even graphic) techniques to project earlier distributions (for example, the 1935–36 consumer income and expenditure survey of the National Resources Planning Board) to subsequent years and to estimate the upper tail of the distribution. Later, the Office of Business Economics (now the Bureau of Economic Analysis) began publishing annual distributions of income that were based on tax return data and the Census Bureau's Current Population Surveys

Joseph A. Pechman is the late director of Economic Studies and senior fellow at the Brookings Institution.

(CPS), but these estimates were suspended because of the cost of preparing them and concern about their accuracy.

The first use of a tax model or tax file was in 1961, when I persuaded Internal Revenue Service Commissioner Mortimor Caplin to make available to Brookings a sub sample from the Statistics of Income. Stanley Surrey, who was Assistant Secretary of the Treasury for Tax Policy at the time, supported my request to obtain the tax file for research purposes. The first file, which was for the year 1960, was used to make estimates of marginal and effective tax rates by income classes and to simulate the revenue and distributional consequences of structural changes in the tax system (Pechman 1965a). In those early days, the programming was done by Donald Tucker, then a young graduate student at MIT. When the Treasury began to realize the potential of the tax file, it soon organized a small staff to prepare its own estimates of the effects of administration and congressional tax legislative proposals. At Brookings, we have used the annual tax files almost continuously since those early days to analyze the distributional effects of changes in the tax law (see, e.g., Pechman 1965b).

The idea of merging the tax and CPS survey data to estimate a "correct" distribution of tax burdens occurred to me during the 1950s, when I was attempting to make estimates of the progressivity of the tax system. Colm and Tarasov in the late 1930s and Musgrave et al. (1951) in the late 1940s had used survey data to make such estimates, but I was acutely aware of the limitations of those data, particularly in the top income classes. Moreover, the use of microdata rather than grouped data to estimate tax liabilities would give us greater accuracy and more flexibility in the calculations that could be made, particularly for the top and bottom tails of the income distribution.

The first MERGE file was created at Brookings in the early 1970s. It was a statistical match between the 1966 tax file and the 1967 Survey of Economic Opportunity, which contained income and consumption data for 1966 (Pechman and Okner 1974). Later, we prepared MERGE files on the basis of the CPS surveys for the years 1970 and 1975. I was fortunate to have as my associates in this enterprise Ben Okner and Joe Minarik, who developed the computer techniques for matching large data sets. These files provided the basis for the preparation of detailed estimates of the distribution of tax burdens by income classes for 1966, 1970, 1975, 1980, and 1985 (Pechman 1985).

In principle, a MERGE file should provide accurate estimates of the distribution of tax burdens by the social and economic characteristics of the population. The most common breakdown is by income classes, but comparisons by size of family, home ownership vs. rental, age groups of family heads, and sources of income are also possible. In addition, estimates of the variability of tax burdens within various population groups can be calculated (see tables 11.7 and 11.8 of Atrostic and Nunns). Of course, all measures of tax burden depend on the incidence assumptions used and these are by no means settled by the public finance fraternity. I have presented eight different sets of incidence assumptions that span the range of opinion in the profession about tax incidence.

Several others have also prepared MERGE files, but the number is relatively small because of the time-consuming and costly nature of the operation. The Treasury has produced several files for its purposes, most recently to estimate the effects of the big tax reform that was finally enacted in 1986. The Congressional Budget Office has also prepared similar files to estimate changes in the distribution of tax burdens between 1975 and 1990. Peat, Marwick, and Main has a MERGE file for a recent year. There may be others in existence, but I am not aware of them.

There are two criticisms of the MERGE file technique, only one of which I agree with. The first is that statistical matching may not provide an accurate picture of the composition of income by income classes. I am not qualified to pass judgement on this criticism, but I have a hunch that the error, if any, is small.

The other criticism is one that I myself have expressed many times. The problem is that the top tail of the Consumer Population Surveys does not resemble the tail of the income distribution that we know exists from tax returns. My associates and I have simply spliced on the tax tail to the survey data and made corresponding reductions in the number of family units in the lower part of the distribution to arrive at an overall distribution of income. I am not sure what the others have done, but I suspect they make approximately similar adjustments. Considering the advanced state of our technology, it is criminal that we are forced to use such an unsophisticated technique for so important a purpose.

The remedy is to prepare an *exact* match between the Census CPS distributions, tax returns, and other administrative records, such as the Social Security records. An exact match would automatically provide accurate data on the composition of income of the sample units and would also tell us what correction needs to be made to the upper tail of the distribution. I will leave it to the statisticians to devise techniques for splicing the tax return data onto the CPS data in the top tail of the distribution.

An exact match has been completed by federal agencies at least twice in the past to my knowledge—for 1963 and 1973 (Social Security Administration 1980 and 1981). The procedures were very time-consuming, so that the results were ancient history when they were finally published. It seems to me that the time has come to plan for exact matches, say, once in every two or three years to provide the basis for accurate MERGE files, complete with breakdowns by income sources, demographic and employment data, and family status. Since there will be problems of confidentiality, this project must be undertaken by a federal agency, probably the Bureau of the Census, and should be released as promptly as possible.

In closing, I should like to urge the Bureau of Economic Analysis to resume its work on income distribution. The availability of the microdata from tax returns and the CPS surveys should make it easier to estimate the distribution of income. If BEA were to resume its income distribution work, it could help promote the idea of making periodic exact matches within government circles. It is time to emerge from the primitive stage and to enter the much more advanced stage that modern technology permits.

References

Colm, Gerhard, and Helen Tarasov. 1940. *Who Pays the Taxes?* Study for the Temporary National Economic Committee. Monograph 3. Investigation of Concentration of Economic Power. 76th Cong., 3d sess.

Goldsmith, Selma F. et al. 1954. Size Distribution of Income Since the Mid-thirties. *Review of Economics and Statistics* 36:1–32.

Hanna, Frank A., Sidney M. Lerner, and Joseph A. Pechman. 1948. *Analysis of Wisconsin Incomes*. NBER Studies in Income and Wealth, vol. 9. New York: National Bureau of Economic Research.

Musgrave, Richard A., et al. 1951. Distribution of Tax Payments by Income Groups: A Case Study for 1948. *National Tax Journal* 4:1–53.

National Resources Planning Board. 1938. *Consumer Incomes in the United States: Their Distribution in 1935–36*. Washington, D.C.: Government Printing Office.

———. 1938. *Family Expenditures in the United States: Statistical Tables and Appendixes*. Washington, D.C.: Government Printing Office.

Office of Business Economics, U.S. Department of Commerce. 1953. *Income Distribution in the United States by Size, 1944–1950*. Washington, D.C.: Government Printing Office.

Office of Price Administration. 1943. *Civilian Spending and Saving, 1941 and 1942*. Washington, D.C.

Pechman, Joseph A. 1965a. A New Tax Model for Revenue Extimating. *Government Finance and Economic Development,* ed. Alan T. Peacock and Gerald Hauser, 231–44. Paris: Organization for Economic Cooperation and Development.

———. 1965b. Individual Income Tax Provisions of the Revenue Act of 1964. *The Journal of Finance* 20:247–72.

———. 1985. *Who Paid the Taxes, 1966–85?* Washington, D.C.: Brookings.

Pechman, Joseph A. and Benjamin A. Okner. 1974. *Who Bears the Tax Burden?* Washington, D.C.: Brookings.

Social Security Administration, U.S. Department of Health and Human Services. 1980. *Matching Administrative and Survey Information: Procedures and Results of the 1963 Pilot Link Study.* Studies from Interagency Data Linkages. Report no. 3. Washington, D.C.

———. 1981. *Methods of Estimation for the 1973 Exact Match Study.* Report no. 10. Washington, D.C.

12 Policy Users' Panel

Charles L. Schultze, Rudolph G. Penner, Ian A. Stewart, and Roger B. Porter

A Note From the Volume Editors

Government data are vital for research and for many other private sector uses. However, in nearly all cases the budgetary and program justification for government data collection rests on the government's own needs for policy analysis.

How well do government statistical systems of the United States and Canada meet the need for policy-analytic data? What are the major requirements for improved or new data? Do the organizations of statistical systems, or the ways they function, have shortcomings whose correction would improve the responsiveness of statistical agencies to emerging data needs?

The panel of policy users were invited to share, in an informal discussion, thoughts on these and other questions, drawing on their extensive experiences in policy-analytic positions in the U.S. and Canadian governments. The following is an edited, shortened version of the discussion, based on the transcript of the session.

Roger B. Porter

For this panel we have three people who have consumed an enormous amount of economic statistics in a variety of policy-analytic positions in governments of two countries.

Charles L. Schultze is the director of Economic Studies at the Brookings Institution. Rudolph G. Penner is a senior fellow at the Urban Institute. Ian A. Stewart is the former deputy minister of Finance for Canada. At the time of the conference, Roger B. Porter was the IBM Professor of Business and Government at Harvard University. He subsequently became assistant to the president for economic and domestic policy in the Bush administration.

Charles L. Schultze is well known to all of us. Charlie's academic career began at the University of Maryland. During the Truman administration, he took his first government post as a staff member in the Council of Economic Advisers. He stayed on at the Council for most of the Eisenhower years, and then went to the Brookings Institution. In the 1960s he returned to government, serving as assistant director and subsequently director of the Bureau of the Budget during the Kennedy and Johnson administrations. He was chairman of the Council of Economic Advisers from 1977 to 1981, and he is now director of the Economic Studies program at Brookings.

Our second speaker, Rudolph G. Penner, hails originally from Canada, was educated at the University of Toronto, then came south to Johns Hopkins University where he received his Ph.D. He began his academic career at the University of Rochester. He came into the government in 1970 as a staff member of the Council of Economic Advisers, moved on to be the chief economist at the Department of Housing and Urban Development, then served as the chief economist at the Office of Management and Budget until 1977. He subsequently became a senior fellow at the American Enterprise Institute, is well known to many of you as the most recent director of the Congressional Budget Office, and is now at the Urban Institute.

Ian A. Stewart, the Canadian member of our panel, was educated at Queen's College, won a Rhodes scholarship, and went on to study at Trinity College, Oxford. He came to the United States to earn his Ph.D. at Cornell University. He taught at Dartmouth and then returned to Canada to spend eight years at the Bank of Canada, building econometric models. He was induced into the government in 1973 to do what he described to me as "long-term energy research." Shortly afterward the roof fell in and he became what he described as a "policy person." He served in the Privy Council, which is one of the central coordinating institutions in the Canadian government, became deputy minister of the Department of Energy, Mines and Resources (that is the number 2 position in the department, the senior position for a career civil servant), and then the deputy minister of the Ministry of Finance. He has held several advisory posts, retired from the civil service two years ago, and is now writing and advising and teaching.

This is a very distinguished group of people.

Charles L. Schultze

I suspect I am going to disappoint the organizers by arguing that if you want to set statistical priorities do not rely for your primary guidance on policy users. A lot of you may think the way policy users look at statistics is captured by a remark attributed to Winston Churchill: "When I call for statistics about the rate of infant mortality, what I want is proof that fewer babies died when I was prime minister than when anyone else was prime minister." I do not believe that policymakers really act that way. In fact, ever since the 1970s when Richard Nixon allegedly made several unsuccessful attempts to shape statistical reports according to political ends, the statistical establishment in the federal government has been exceedingly well insulated against political pressure. Nevertheless, there are several reasons why the policy use of statistics is not the best guide to statistical priorities.

There are two broad uses of economic statistics from the policymaker's standpoint. First, current economic indicators of various kinds keep the policymakers and their economic advisors informed about the current state of the economy—measures of output, income, employment, trade flows, prices, wages, and so forth, both in the aggregate and in detail. Sometimes the quality of indicators can slip for various reasons, external and internal, with consequences ranging from merely inconvenience and delay to serious error. The problem of invoice backlogs in the import trade statistics until very recently was a good case of the latter. I have nothing original to say on this aspect of the statistical system. If anything, a relatively casual judgment suggests that the resources allocated to that area of government statistics—that is, information about the current state of the economy—are quite substantial relative to the need.

The second, and I think the major, use of economic and social statistics for policy purposes lies in its "indirect" use. That is, to the extent that bodies of statistical data make it possible for researchers to provide a better understanding of how our economy or some segment of it works, then statistics will be useful for policymakers and their advisors in choosing appropriate actions and designing programs and policies. There are few policy decisions ever won or lost by the direct availability of some body of statistics. Only as the statistics feed in through the mediation of substantive research and help policymakers or their advisors to understand economic and social behavior will those statistics ultimately become useful in making better policy.

Indeed, I will go further. With some clear exceptions, bodies of statistical information will be useful not so much because they directly suggest answers to policy problems, but mainly indirectly as the research based on such information helps us better understand how society and the economy work. Accordingly, one should not look to the policymaker for determining where to set priorities for improving the statistical system. Rather, to set priorities one should identify key aspects of economic behavior about which policymakers are likely to be concerned in the medium-term future and where better understanding of that behavior can potentially be achieved by the provision of new or improved statistical data. To put it another way, if by using that new data researchers can improve our understanding of economic behavior, there is a reasonable chance that professional advisors can improve their advice to policymakers, and a small but still nonzero chance that policymakers will actually take the advice.

On the criterion I have suggested, I would give particularly high priority to two areas in allocating resources toward the improvement of the statistical system over the next decade. Since both of those areas, not surprisingly, are also emphasized in the report of the American Economic Association Committee on the Quality of Economic Statistics, I will be very brief.

In my mind, a terribly important area is improving our understanding of the determinants of productivity growth, which, as all of you know, has been proceeding at a very slow pace for the last 15 years. I emphasize one particular aspect of the problem, although I do not want to suggest that it is by any means the only one.

Macroeconomic growth accounting—that is, analysis at the aggregate level—while it has been extremely valuable, has come about as far as it can in helping us understand the causes of the productivity slowdown. We now need to devote much more effort to improving disaggregated measures for the analysis of productivity growth. Here I commend to you the suggestion of my colleague, Edward F. Denison, who argues that, in addition to working toward correcting the very obvious shortcomings in our industry measures, we should also turn attention to an alternative—disaggregated output per unit of input by end product categories, as distinguished from industry categories.

As the second specific objective, I would urge that the United States launch, or at least take the lead in launching, an international effort (and it would take an international effort) to construct an international flow of fund series, with its associated portfolio and balance sheet information. More than any other single statistical undertaking, this could help us improve our currently feeble ability to understand and forecast broad changes in international capital flows and exchange rates. This would be an ambitious undertaking, and, as I said, would require international cooperation, perhaps most appropriately led by the International Monetary Fund or the OECD. But the United States should try to convince other countries to support such a goal.

As a policy user and as a one-time budget director, the most important thing I could say about the U.S. statistical system from an institutional standpoint is that it is far too decentralized. I doubt that we need a Canadian or British degree of centralization. That is, we can keep the major statistical agencies separate. But we do need a chief U.S. statistical officer, not under the control of any operating department.

My own view of the functions to be performed by the chief statistical office is very close to option number 2 in James Bonnen's set of recommendations in 1981 (*Statistical Reporter* [February 1981]). This office would serve three main purposes.

First, it would carry out research and planning for long-term improvements in the statistical system. Many of the most important statistical improvements require substantial lead time and investment. They consume substantial resources. The chief statistical office, which I will call the CSO, working jointly with the statistical agencies and the research community, should evaluate long-term priorities and make recommendations with respect to the long-term allocation of resources.

Second, the CSO should have a continuing annual budget function. That office should negotiate with the OMB for an overall statistical budget and then have responsibility for acting like a little OMB in allocating that budget among the agencies. At the margin, the budget for the Bureau of Labor Statistics, the Census Bureau, the Bureau of Economic Analysis, and the Agricultural Statistical Agency should be evaluated against each other. It makes no sense whatsoever to trade off Census and BEA against tourism promotion in the Commerce Department and to evaluate the BLS statistical program against occupational safety inspection or the training programs of the Department of Labor. It would be too big a step politically, and probably unnecessary, to bring all the statistical agencies within one agency. There are some merits for operating a decentralized system, including providing a dollop of competition. But the budget allocation among major statistical programs ought to be centralized.

The third function of the CSO should be to take responsibility for a careful long-term program to create merged and matched microdata files from statistical and administrative records. I have more to say on this than time allows, but the essence of the problem in my judgment is political and not statistical. Although my current ignorance on these matters is fairly deep, there are statistical tools available to reduce the statistical problems. Politically, however, it is a dynamite problem and I think the appointment of a central statistical officer under conditions I will discuss in a moment might go a long way toward providing the kind of insulation and political neutrality that might help the process forward. My own experience at the old Budget Bureau was that data matching was an incredibly sensitive matter with the Congress. When one began to talk about merging files, particularly administrative files and any hint of tax records, you are immediately in trouble.

Where within government to locate this chief statistical office is a problem for which there is no best answer. It cannot be in any current cabinet department. The Secretary of Labor will not accept statistical budget allocation from the Secretary of Commerce, much less from a subordinate official of the Secretary of Commerce, and of course, vice versa.

You could locate the CSO as an independent office in the Executive Office of the president. But if it is independent, quite frankly, it will have little power. You can call a new office anything you want, but if the head of that office does not see the president frequently and participate with him in important decisions, the agency will have little power. So even though I would like to make the CSO independent and put it in the Executive Office of the president, I think it will have to be subordinated to some other official to give it any power.

Reluctantly, as a last resort, I would put it in the Office of Management and Budget, but with a director who is presidentially appointed and confirmed by

Congress. Simultaneously I would start a tradition—not a law—of having a consortium of the major professional societies present to the president a limited list of candidates for the job from which he selects a nominee. Now, if I were OMB Director, I would not favor this idea. But I am not budget director any more and this solution is the best way I can invent to get this tremendously important job done. If we could establish the position at a high level, and initially fill it with a person of great integrity, though politically aware, a lot of things might be doable that are now impossible. I stress particularly my third function listed above, which is getting around the political problem of creating merged, sophisticated, longitudinal data files that include use of administrative records.

Finally, a CSO director of high integrity and nonpartisan stature located in the Executive Office of the president might help prevent or rectify what I will label the occasional statistical disaster. I have two quite different examples of disasters. The first one has to do with the CPI.

Between 1977 and 1981, interest rates and house prices soared. The consumer price index at the time was constructed to treat owner-occupied housing as an investment good, not as an element in the cost of living with a stream of housing services. Consequently, it overstated the rise in the cost of living between 1977 and 1981 by some 10%, against the more appropriate "experimental" CPI X-1. In the four years 1977–81, a period with which I am painfully familiar, the overstatement in the inflation rate was 1.5% per year and the consequences were enormous. A significant fraction of wages were formally indexed, and another large fraction were informally indexed, so that this statistical anomaly had really serious economic effects. In addition, Social Security and other federal entitlement programs were vastly overindexed. Because the new CPI, when its homeowner component was finally converted to a flow-of-services pricing system, was linked into the old one at virtually the peak of the "distortion," we never got rid of the overstatement.

Making what, from hindsight, seems like the obvious and extremely desirable change to a flow-of-services concept turned out to be politically impossible. In the early 1970s the BLS had considered changing to a flow-of-services concept (and some staff members had been urging the change even earlier). There are two alternative ways of implementing a flow-of-services concept—the user-cost approach and a rental equivalence approach. Neither of them is free of conceptual and measurement problems. The BLS initially proposed a rental equivalence measure and put together an experimental index incorporating that technique, but user groups, especially the labor unions, registered strong opposition (not, presumably, because rental equivalence was inferior to the user-cost method, but because either method would have resulted in a lower growth of the CPI and less wage indexation). Later on, in 1977, the alternative technique was considered, but all sorts of technical objections were raised by a user agency panel within the administration as well as by BLS business and labor user groups.

In the mid-1970s, when the change might have been made, the overstatement of inflation in the existing index did not seem large enough to overcome user-group objections and the statistical imperfections of the two alternatives. Late in 1978 and 1979, when sharply rising interest rates and home prices made the overstatement in the index egregiously large, the normal scheduled revision of the CPI had already taken place; the Carter administration was afraid that any top-level decision to impose a subsequent change would be widely interpreted as a bald political move to downplay the extent of inflation. And so nothing happened, while month-by-month the CPI overstatement helped make the inflation problem and the budget problem worse.

This was a case where we literally needed to trade off statistical purity for political, in the "big" sense, purposes. We did not have a mechanism for doing it in a politically sanitized way. Ironically, the problem was not political interference in a substantive statistical decision, but the fact that a change highly justified on substantive grounds would have been interpreted as a purely political maneuver. Conceivably, a CSO director with an outstanding professional stature and the breadth of knowledge to understand, early on, the need to trade off statistical purity against economic requirements might have had the public reputation for independence sufficient to give the action the necessary political cover. On the other hand, I may be waxing romantic; history might have played out the same way even had a CSO then existed.

The second area is a different kind of statistical disaster—the whole issue of environmental pollution. As you know, the federal government has all kinds of environmental regulations. Although I may conceivably be operating on out-of-date evidence, it is my impression that the scientific information on which many environmental regulations are based is very poor. My view of this is strengthened by reading Russell and Smith (in this volume). I think it needs a huge input of additional resources in order to get better information. My position is neither pro nor antienvironment, because it will cut different ways at different times. The present situation is an ongoing statistical disgrace, and perhaps my proposed Chief Statistical Office could help a bit.

Rudolph G. Penner

Economists are a peculiar lot. Though assuming that the rest of the world is motivated by self-interest, we are unusually reticent as a profession in furthering our own interests legislatively. We do not appeal to the Congress to restrict entry into our profession or to restrict the import of foreign economic analysis produced at unfairly low wage rates. There is, however, one area in which we do perform more like the typical lobbyist: we sometimes do have a knee-jerk reaction to push for the production of more and better data almost regardless of cost.

But pressure an economist just a little bit and he or she will quickly revert to style and start doing cost-benefit analyses of more and better data. Moreover, we are trained to be sensitive to social costs as well, and in the data collection business the social costs are often very high when economic units have to devote much time and trouble to responding to complex questionnaires.

Prodded by the invitation to give this talk, I began to think of the problem in terms of cost-benefit analysis. As difficult as it might be to measure the costs of collecting better data, the benefits to policymakers are much more nebulous and impossible to analyze in the formal manner favored by economists. That does not prevent me from concluding, however—and here I do sound like a more typical lobbyist—that the nation does not spend enough on data gathering because of strong political and bureaucratic biases against such activity.

One serious problem arises just from the fact that we keep our nation's budget on a cash flow basis. When cash flow budgets get tight, investments are often the first thing cut, and information gathering is more in the nature of an investment. As a public manager, I did it myself. When hard pressed, the first thing I considered cutting at the Congressional Budget Office was our modest data collection effort, which seemed less immediately important than maintaining the quality of day-to-day operations.

The bias against spending on data is strengthened by the very fact that the benefits are so nebulous. Much of a policy analyst's work involves forecasting the effects of policy changes on the budget and the economy, and that usually implies forecasting the economic environment in which the policy will be implemented. As we all know, forecasting is more art than science. If forecasting is art, then very obviously forecasting the effect of better data on the accuracy of the forecast must be art squared! Rather than attempting a comprehensive scientific, or even an artistic, analysis of the problem, let me engage in some random musing about different unrelated aspects of data collection as seen by a policy analyst.

Can I really claim that devoting more resources to gathering and improving of statistics would reduce the artistic, and increase the scientific, component of forecasting and ultimately improve its accuracy? I actually believe that we could improve our very short-run forecasts a little bit, and that would help with the 21-month forecast that's necessary every calendar year to forecast the budget totals for the next fiscal year. But I do not want to claim that we will ever be accurate enough to satisfy the requirements of legislators who are constantly frustrated by changes in budget estimates, and who sometimes draft laws (such as Gramm-Rudman-Hollings) that require a level of pinpoint forecasting accuracy that will never be delivered.

Nevertheless, I do believe that a small improvement is possible. I say that because I think with the state of economic statistics today, we are not often very good at even forecasting the recent past. And if we cannot forecast the past, there is really little hope of improving the forecast of the future.

I think, moreover, that forecasting the past better may occasionally mean actually ceasing the production of data that do more to confuse than enlighten. That would give us more resources to focus on improving the data that are published where the marginal costs of such improvements are relatively low.

Most working policy analysts that I know are constantly frustrated by major revisions in preliminary data. It is partly their own fault, and here I plead guilty as well. As a group, I admit we suffer from a severe psychological deficiency. While we may warn our noneconomist bosses that preliminary data might be revised substantially, we nonetheless feel a need to provide a highly sophisticated analysis as to why a particular preliminary number came out the way it did. Several months later we find ourselves providing an equally sophisticated, but often totally contradictory, explanation of why the revised number came out the way it did. So I am suggesting that while we are searching for ways to spend more on data collection, there may also be cases where too much is published too soon. It may be possible to improve those preliminary numbers by spending money in a cost-effective way. In some cases, however, it may be more effective to spend money improving the quality of data that are produced with a *greater* time delay.

Economists have done some sophisticated work to determine whether preliminary numbers contain any systematic bias, and they have been ingenious at devising filters to remove such biases. This is very useful but it is only part of the story. A preliminary number may be totally unbiased but it can still do a great deal of mischief if it is changed a lot in revision—by changed a lot, I mean changed sufficiently to alter one's view of what has taken place. Let me be brave enough to suggest a very simple test for variables that are routinely forecast by macroeconomic forecasters. If it could be shown, for example, that the Blue Chip Survey, or some other average of the main large econometric models, typically forecasts that quarter's real GNP better than the preliminary number released the next month, I'd have a serious question as to whether the preliminary number adds any useful information, and whether it should continue to be published unless it can be improved significantly.[1] There are, however, a lot of numbers on which this test would not work very well because macroforecasters do not spend a lot of time in forecasting them—for example, things like retail sales, durable goods orders, monthly inventory numbers, and so on. Without having seen or done any analytic work on the issue it is my impression that those numbers are often revised by enormous amounts. Perhaps I just remember the times when they were revised that I found to be embarrassing.

We live in an era when inappropriate policies based on inappropriate numbers can do a great deal of harm, and I believe that our standards in judging those preliminary numbers should be quite stringent. We live in fact in a bud-

1. See Gregory N. Mankiw and Matthew D. Shapiro, "News or Noise: An Analysis of GNP Revisions," *Survey of Current Business* (May 1986); Knut Anton Mork, "Ain't Behavin': Forecast Errors and Measurement Errors in Early GNP Estimates," *Journal of Business and Economic Statistics* 5 (April 1987).

get era, when in theory a bad forecast can inspire a sequester of expenditures under Gramm-Rudman-Hollings, and that is serious business indeed.

Changing the subject in a more positive direction, I believe there are areas in which data can be improved greatly with fairly modest expenditures of resources. Being a budget person, I especially think of data generated by some of the operating agencies of the government. These numbers are usually generated as a result of the normal operations of an agency, but managers are often quite insensitive to the needs of forecasters and outside analysts. I think inexpensive modifications in the way the data are produced and organized could greatly enhance their value.

Given the policy importance of forecasting revenues and analyzing the revenue loss or gains associated with changes in the tax law, I used to be particularly frustrated while at the Congressional Budget Office by the nature of tax data produced by the Internal Revenue Service. Because of long time delays in producing the Statistics of Income, one does not know when withheld taxes come in whether they are payroll taxes or income taxes. Taxes withheld and, say, reported on the first quarter Form 941 for a corporation will not be posted by IRS to individual tax and social security accounts for a year to two years later. The nature of the data makes it difficult to estimate the effective tax rate applied to particular types of income, such as capital gains. There are many other problems.

I do not blame the IRS for this. They suffer from a lack of resources—and perhaps more important, their job is to collect taxes, not to be a data collection agency.

A similar affliction affects the customs service. Their job is to collect tariffs and to administer other elements of trade law, and yet Wall Street is obsessed by the trade data that they collect as a by-product of their main role. I think the customs service recently has become very much more sensitive to the importance of their data collection role, but it is probably safe to say the trade data are still of terribly low quality.

I could cite many more instances where administratively produced data could be improved greatly. The only way you can improve such data is to improve the incentives of the managers of those agencies. Obviously, the best way we can do that is to compensate them in their budgets for the resources that they devote to improving their data collection efforts. Within their appropriations, funds could be earmarked for data collection, but as a matter of principle I dislike that kind of micromanagement by the Congress. Besides, if it is done that way, agency mangers may still be unclear about exactly the type of data that would be useful.So I would much prefer that appropriations go to users, such as CBO and OMB, to allow them to contract with operating agencies for the required data. The nature of the collection effort could then be described precisely and tailored exactly to the needs of the users. This is already done to some degree, but I can speak from personal experience that it is often difficult to convince a congressional appropriation committee that a data effort is worthwhile. A lot of education and persuasion is needed, and it has to be admitted that the benefits of such statistical activities are quite nebulous.

So much for cheap ways to collect data. A particularly expensive way of collecting data involves social experimentation. I have become a fan of this approach over the years, but it is a tough case to argue. Some very expensive mistakes have been made. Experiments have sometimes been designed to ask questions that were misguided, and when more relevant questions were uncovered, the experimental design was ill-suited to answering them with precision. Moreover, the inherent temporary nature of an experiment may distort responses and provide misleading estimates of the economic effects of a more permanent transfer program. But I still believe that such experiments are tremendously valuable.

I managed the housing allowance experiment for two years at HUD and while I do not believe that it was designed well enough to provide the sort of data that economists might like to have about the effects of housing subsidies on housing markets, much was nevertheless learned about those markets. And more important, much was learned about how to run a particular kind of transfer program. That information proved extremely valuable in subsequently designing the "section 8" subsidies for existing housing. Though Congress did not accept all that we thought we had learned from the experiment, the efficiency of the housing program was greatly improved.

Perhaps I am arguing more for demonstration projects than for scientific experiments. The design does not have to be highly scientific for policy analysts to learn a lot about how particular programs work.

These ramblings have been random (much like a lot of the data that we produce about the economy). I do not have an overall conclusion, but I should not end a talk like this without praising the data collection efforts now undertaken and the highly devoted professional people who work in data collection agencies. Whatever our complaints, certainly our data are among the best in the world and I think the extent to which its collection has been shielded from political pressures is nothing short of remarkable. Finally, as a profession we economists do have an obligation to educate our policymakers as to the value of more and better numbers, while we also have the responsibility to remain sensitive to the costs of the effort.

Ian A. Stewart

I thought that in my contribution to this panel I would try to choose a niche—that is a popular expression in Canada today when we are feeling enormously trade threatened by a competitive world, and we are all being exhorted to choose niches. Rather than speak, as might have been anticipated, on the menu of issues that afflict the policy adviser, particularly in the macroeconomic management field, I thought that I would choose as my territory, not policy advising, but policy-making. I thought I might review the climate of intelligence that prevails in cabinet rooms as economic and social policy issues are discussed, and how data and analysis serve the resolution of policy discussions. Second, I would choose not macroeconomic policy-making but the making of socioeconomic policy.

However data and analysis flow through policy advisors into policy discussions, as one sits around policy-making tables one recognizes that the level of sophistication around that table is enormously variable. The level of economic and social literacy is also enormouly variable. Whatever the ideology, whether conservative, liberal, Whig, or Tory, players come to the table slaves of myths, historical myths of various dimensions. Some of these myths are data based, some are not. But together they form a mishmash of views and prejudice, and it is the task of the policy adviser to enlighten and assist in reaching some sort of policy conclusion.

Anyone who has watched these gatherings or participated in them will recognize one thing straight away, it seems to me. The creation of the System of National Accounts—whatever else it has done for the synthesizing of an enormous range of economic data for the support of the economic research process, for the enlightenment of economists themselves—perhaps its principal and major contribution has been to raise the degree of literacy in the population at large, and especially the degree of policy literacy in the semiliterate, semisophisticated circles of cabinet policymakers, none of whom come to the game of economic and social policy-making by profession, but by political occupancy. Though there have been frequent frustrations in that process, I do draw the conclusion that the making of macroeconomic policy, as errant as it may have been through the troublesome decades of the seventies and eighties, would have been prodigiously more difficult had there not been this synthesizing model of how the economy is put together. It permitted policymakers to talk together in ways that were several degrees, in fact I would argue considerable degrees, above ignorance.

The National Accounts, a system to which this conference has been almost totally dedicated since its founding, has not had a counterpart on the social side. One of the great tragedies, it has seemed to me, has been the lack of a similar coordinating apparatus for the organizing of social data and thought. Within statistical agencies, this lack has led to the gathering and organization of economic data dominating the task of social measurement. Though there have been abortive efforts—the net national accounting discussions of the seventies, and the birth of social indicators, and the dreams of systems of social indicators, objective and subjective—none of these movements has managed to produce a synthesis of social data that corresponds to the power of the system of national accounts.

If I would urge the conference in a new direction, it would be to work out a measurement agenda that relates to any number of policy issues coming down the pike—health policy, education policy, policy toward the aged, child care, the reform of the social security system, the relationship between tax reform and the transfer system generally (tax transfer integration as it is called). Particularly relevant in Canada is the reform of regional economic incentives (which frequently are essentially social transfers and have not much to do with economic policy) and unemployment insurance systems with large income transfer components. Perhaps the most critical of all (and here I agree with Charlie Schultze), environmental policy, with its national and international ramifications is a major issue. If that is not a long enough agenda to dominate research conferences for the next few years, it is also an agenda on which policy advisors have too little to say to cabinet members. The systematic factual foundations on which cabinet members have the capacity to consult and debate these issues amongst themselves is extraordinarily limited.

In one of my roles as a graduate of the public service of Canada, I sit on an advisory board to our central statistical agency, Statistics Canada, and offer that agency gratuitous advice. I have been attracted, since I began to know of it, by the work of Richard and the late Nancy Ruggles, on the notion of satellite accounting, of extending the system of national accounts through the welding of administrative data bases and demographic data into accounts that subject specific aggregates in the national accounts to more intense scrutiny. As subsequent discussion of these issues has taken place at Statistics Canada, it has become clear that there is also an opportunity to begin to blend into these boxes, these subsatellite boxes, if you like, measurements that are not necessarily economic in origin. I would take issue with the discussion this morning, in the position that some of you took, that economists should keep their hands away from and not be sullied by non-economic data. One might use these boxes to begin to portray aspects of society, and policy issues, such as the health system, the education system, the work system, all of which have aspects about them which are beyond the narrowly economic and whose policy discussion entails research issues that are certainly beyond the narrowly economic. Issues of institutional change, central to many social issues, play little part in strictly economic analysis.

One such issue that is being pursued at Statistics Canada at the moment is a health account. Now, obviously, the remedial system, whose transactions are reported on in the national accounts, is but a part, and a small part, of what we mean by the health system. Questions of healthful life-styles and questions of genetic contributions to health may be best addressed by following longitudinal populations through their lives and considering questions of where public policy ought to act on the larger system and where not. These questions include, of course, aged health care, which may make inappropriate demands on the remedial system as we know it and may involve the innovation of new institutions of palliative care, as well as of modest care not demanding the intense resources of the remedial system.

The attraction of such work, of course, is that though we Canadians pride ourselves on running one of the better public health systems in the world, it is under inexorable cost pressure. Health is an annual issue in both our provinces and in the federal government as the costs continually outstrip the rate of growth of GNP, and the rate of rise of government expenditure elsewhere. What is to be done about this inexorable rise, which may threaten the system itself? Solutions will depend on our capacity to create new quasi-medical institutions that provide some of the services of the current remedial system, but do so in ways that are vastly less costly and vastly less using of national resources. That is an example of the job to be done. One can portray to policymakers the opportunities for intervention if intervention is indeed to be recommended. But better data and analysis will also permit policymakers themselves to display to their publics the manner in which they think about the health system, to explain the manner in which their interventions are tailored and why, and to be judged by these policies. Data will permit them to explain why they believe the structures of policy they have adopted will deal with whatever they perceive to be the crises of the health system in ways superior to investing more national resources in existing institutions.

A similar set of considerations can be applied to the other major expenditure in our social sector, education. Canada, I think, leads the OECD countries in the total volume of federal, provincial, and local resources devoted to education as a proportion of GNP. Though we can add up the total aggregate amount, and do so in the national accounts, whether the allocation of those funds in primary, secondary, postsecondary, and technical institutions is the appropriate allocation, whether the outputs from that system have anything to do with the output demands of the Canadian economic or social or cultural system, whether there are alternatives to the structures of that system which would serve Canadian needs better are questions that are not easily answered with the data bases as we now array them. Hence, our quarrels about education policy are traditionally, within the cabinet circles I speak of, issues of more resources or less, not issues of institutional reform, institutional restructuring, or education rethinking. Again, I suspect this is so principally because the data bases and the synthesis of these data bases that we offer our decision makers simply do not invite these structures of thought to rise and do not throw light on these sorts of questions if they are asked.

Another paper at this conference demonstrated the blending of administrative data and survey data to greatly enhance our capacity to simulate alternate structures of social policy.

I may be wrong, but it struck me as an observer from the north that the U.S. tax reform process was enormously fertilized and facilitated by the appearance of legislators, executives, and policy analysts carrying the same sheaf of data printouts. Thus, data at least offered a first-order estimate of the consequences of changing parameters of the U.S. tax system and at least permitted the beginning of a discussion. For example, if municipal bonds are to remain tax free then the costs are x billion dollars, and if that x billions are to be put back into the system, then compensating changes must be made somewhere else. As simpleminded as it may seem, that is leagues beyond where most tax reform discussion begins in most principalities of the world. Without even bringing in analyses based on the behavioral consequences of redistributions of burden and incidence, it permits public policymakers to begin to argue their differences, and the differences in their behavioral assumptions, on a broad data base that starts the discussion some miles past the starting point.

I have frequently been asked: What is the probability that Western industrial countries will ever fundamentally reform their social security systems? From right, left, and center, from analysts, from government policymakers themselves, there is a broad general agreement that social security systems need reform. They are enormously resource using and awash with inefficiencies, the resources do not flow particularly to those in need, an enormous proportion flows to the middle and upper middle class, there are holes in the safety nets, and there are new and emerging problems—age, child care—but so deeply vested are the interests of the current recipients that change is difficult. Politicians are badly burned whenever they try a little piece of incremental reform. Unless something much more systematic can be done, the likelihood is that we shall plow on incrementalizing reform and incrementalizing new systems on top of old systems. As economists, we all recognize that within the structures of existing systems the perversities are economically damaging. They are not only heavily resource using, many of them involve taxback rates of over 100% and behavioral consequences that we do not begin to understand. It seems to me again that if we are to make progress, and this is perhaps a very radical notion, then we have to create, as we have with tax reform, the capacity to array first-order effects. We must be able to address the question of who wins and who loses by massive reform of the social security system. Like the incidence and burden of tax, who are the net payers and the net benefiters under a broad social security reform? If one can get that far and get the numbers that are, if not precise, at least acceptable to decision makers, one can then, it seems to me, disseminate them to the public at large and encourage a public debate that is vastly more informed than the pure prejudice, mythology, and fear that social security reform debates currently engender.

Well, those are a number of examples of the point that I wanted to make, that the creation of the national accounts was a heroic, synthetic exercise that had benefits well beyond the economics profession. It has been a sea change in the literacy not only of populations at large but of the character of public policy debate. Only such heroic syntheses can enable debate and policy formation to move forward in other areas that are likely to seem as intransigent as macroeconomic policy-making once did (and many aspects of which still do!). Let me just add a few more examples.

There is a growing myth in most western societies that we all face a rising level of dependency ratios, as the baby boom (which Canada had in a magnified way) moves through to old age. I have just had a demographic lesson that persuades me that this is not nearly the demographic threat that it is popularly believed to be. But as the aged do become absolutely more among us, institutional pressures will be exerted of a particular kind as we move expenditures from child care to aged care and have to choose the forms of aged care, the ratio of public support to private support, and so on. I should note that these seem more frequently public support decisions in Canada than they do in the United States. Within the aged-care issue, in turn, lie issues of who will do the caring and how it will be done: Is it a dominantly female occupation, an underwage occupation? And if there are not revolutions in social thought, are we not likely to go through a charade in which the same people take care of old people as always, with an explicit wage (and, hence, entering the national accounts), but a low wage, with all of the strains that that may invite. Again it seems to be an issue on which quite simpleminded arraying of systematic data on nationwide choices can inform the debate. Of course, economic and behavioral research is critical, but the arraying of the data itself is critical to the sophistication with which research and debate may take place.

Finally, to the environment. To join with Charlie Schultze, I find the issues here, as he does, intimidating. The UN report, The Commission on the Economy and the Environment (Mrs. Brunt, the Prime Minister of Norway, was the chair of that) has not, I believe, had as much currency in the U.S. as in other parts of the world. Elsewhere, it has launched a public debate and has launched the natural sciences, of which we spoke this morning, into a series of international conferences intent on assembling international and national data banks of environmental data and improving the science. This makes one optimistic that we may slowly but surely grow the capacity to array to decision makers models of economic–environmental interaction that provide productive leads on how to manage this problem, both domestically and in its interactions with the international institutions of trade and finance, and the worldwide allocations of resources.

So those are some thoughts as a contributor to the debate. They are born, as I have said, out of the radical view that some forms of reform can only be engineered in their totality, that partial reform invites too much resistance, misinformation, and misunderstanding to be brought off. If radical change is considered, then one has to be able to display alternative states in sufficient detail that policymakers and the electorates can make rational choices.

Roger B. Porter

We have been treated to three remarkably stimulating and provocative sets of opening remarks.

Charlie Schultze noted the highly decentralized nature of the statistical gathering, analysis, collection, and dissemination system in the United States and the virtues of bringing a little more order to this system. Rather than go all the way to a single centralized agency, as in Statistics Canada, his proposal, as I understand it, is to create an office of statistics and lodge it in the Office of Management and Budget to help coordinate the federal government's statistical activities.

I am very sympathetic to the problem he raises, and would simply note from my experience in the Ford administration how we dealt with this problem in a less ambitious, and possibly less successful, way. One of the working groups, or subcommittees, of the Economic Policy Board in that period was a Subcommittee on Economic Statistics. It was chaired by one of the members of the Council of Economic Advisers, Burton Malkiel. Its members included the directors of the Census Bureau, the Bureau of Labor Statistics, Bureau of Economic Analysis, and, if my recollection serves me correctly, eight or nine other officials from policy-making and statistical agencies. The subcommittee tried to undertake several of the roles that Charlie envisions for the central statistical officer. The subcommittee identified long-range planning priorities for expenditures on economic statistics. It served a crucial function in the annual budgeting process, preparing a detailed analysis for the director of the Office of Management and Budget, Jim Lynn, as to where changes ought to be made in the budgets of various statistical agencies and how resources ought to be directed. Jim Lynn indicated to me that he found the work of this subcommittee enormously valuable, and that he adopted their recommendations almost in whole.[2]

Charlie also mentioned, as a function of the CSO office, dealing with the long-term problem of merging and matching data files. In seven years in the government I have seen a fair amount of blood spilled and some ferocious debates, but I do not think I have seen anything to quite match the ferocity of the discussion when the IRS and Census Bureau debate the issue of matching and merging data files. The argument is a very compelling one by the group that is having their files merged: "These data were collected with a promise of confidentiality to the user and we believe that when data are matched and merged the confidentiality cannot be safeguarded. If that confidentiality is ever transgressed our ability to collect the data that we need will severely suffer." I would hope that whatever entity is created, whether it is a chief statistical officer or something else, that we could solve the merging and matching problem.

Rudy Penner, in his challenging and stimulating set of remarks, referred to the frustration that many policymakers have with the preliminary data that come their way. We live in an instant society, policymakers are anxious to take the pulse of what is going on. Most policymakers, in my experience, are des-

2. Volume editors' note: The subcommittee continued to function in much the same way during the Carter administration, where it was chaired by CEA member, Lyle Gramley.

perately worried about being behind the power curve, about finding out things too late. They want to discover a problem that needs correcting before the problem has gotten too serious. Accordingly, they reach to get all the data that they can as quickly as they can to take the economy's pulse. But as Rudy pointed out, very frequently the preliminary data that are being provided policymakers go through enormous revisions. In the meetings I participated in, frequently the preliminary data receive a great deal more attention than the subsequent revisions. I concur with Rudy's notion that perhaps some greater delay in releasing certain numbers is in order and that the compulsion we have to get a hold of preliminary data may need to be arrested.

Finally, Ian Stewart provided us with a very provocative set of remarks both commending the tremendous contribution the national income accounts have made to the structuring of economic policy discussions, and stressing the need for a similar type of synthetic accounting in dealing with a broad range of social issues. From my experience in attending policy discussions on both economic and social issues, I feel there is a lot to what he says with respect to the quality of those discussions and debates. The national income accounts have done a remarkable job in helping to structure discussions of economic policy. I am perhaps a little less confident than he is that a similar synthesis can be produced, that we can guarantee some comparably useful set of accounts, for many of the social problems that we face. His observations, however, certainly ring a true bell with me.

Panelists' Discussion and Responses to Questions from the Floor

Charles L. Schultze. You might handle Rudy's problem about the initial GNP releases by calling the first one a forecast. Do not do anything different, just call it forecasting one month ahead on all data and two months on some data.

Ian Stewart discusses the tremendous contribution that the invention of the national income accounts has made to the discussion of public policy, and I agree. It calls to mind, however, the old motto that the best is the enemy of the good. That is, the NIPA were put together only because we did not let all the theoretical types loose on the national income accountants. If you brought in a pure theorist who had never heard of the NIPA and described them, and told him that people sometimes used those accounts for describing what has happened to economic welfare, he would give you 85,000 reasons why this is a terrible series. So it may also be that in creating a unified framework of social statistics one of their requirements is going to have to be forgetting some of what they know.

Rudolph G. Penner. I might ask Charlie a question. First of all, I never found much of a problem in working in government arising from the fact that our statistical gathering is so decentralized. I may just have had the wrong experiences, but I think we do a fairly good job of coordinating the effort—probably as good a job as coordinating separate divisions of a centralized office.

But if you do believe centralization is important, I am not really clear as to why you did not go all the way and want a Statistics Canada–type centralized bureau. I'm very bothered by the notion of putting a statistical czar in some agency like OMB. While OMB is described as the center of neutral competence by political scientists, I have always thought that was a very bad description. Every agency has a role and OMB's role is to save money. Jim Lynn, a former director of OMB, used to call himself the "abominable no-man." I really think there is a conflict of interest between collecting and coordinating good data and saving money for the government, and I think you would run into that conflict wherever you put your czar. So why not have a big agency if you really think it is important to have central control?

Charles L. Schultze. (*a*) You won't get it; (*b*) I am much less ambitious than you are. You ask, If you don't centralize it, where do you put it? I have a fundamental problem with an independent central statistical office whose director would never see the president—he would have little influence when it really counted. That is my problem. If you look around at the relatively small independent agencies in the United States government, they have very little clout, except where they get it directly through Congress. So I do not think operational centralization is very important, but I think centralization of planning and budget it. I want a planning head, some sort of an overall supervisory head, and a budget allocation head, I don't want an operating head. The central problem here is not that you have to put a new CSO in OMB—you'd face the same problem if you had an independent agency.

Let me make one final point: I think there is a little bit of an advantage to having a very mild competition between the agencies in terms of the integrity of their statistics, and the imagination they can put into it. That competition is not very intense, and it should not be, but it is there and it is useful.

Ian A. Stewart. On the statistical agency organization issue, faraway fields look green. We are rather proud of our centralized agency. The question that always rises in our minds, however, is: If it were divided amongst the user agencies, would the motivation of the statistical arm of the user agency—whether it is treasury or finance or whatever—be stronger than the motivation it can sustain in an isolated centralized agency?

I am not sure our centralized organization solves the allocation of resources to statistics any better than you do. It is certainly a continuous problem to sustain interest in the adequacy of resources being applied to information gathering, whether there is a centralized agency or whether it is a series of diverse agencies spread amongst the agencies of government. I think Statistics Canada employees would generally agree that the most exciting period of that agency was during the birth of the national accounts. I think it is fair to say that virtually every economist with academic respectability in Canada spent a summer at some time or other working in Statistics Canada as part of that exercise. It was the era in which that agency participated in economic debate in town and in economic policy formation, in a formal and informal way, far more than it now does. It is now becoming an isolated statistical agency, and there is a price for that isolation.

Question from the floor. I wonder if it would not be the case that Charles Schultze's coordinating body would not be a very tempting target to those who would like to push the political levers rather quietly in order to achieve political objectives?

Charles L. Schultze. I see, on the one hand, no reason to believe it would be easier for the president (or the White House staff) to tromp on this chief statistical officer than it would be for the White House to tromp on the head of the Bureau of Labor Statistics. It obviously does depend on the kind of people you pick. You have to initiate the new office in the same spirit of integrity as we have already created in the major statistical agencies; you have got to build up a tradition of people who have a lot of integrity. And if you do not do that, you are in trouble. You would be in trouble if you had a hack as head of either the new CSO or the BLS. In fact, if I had to push this, it is probably a little harder to lean on a presidential appointee in the executive office of the president maybe, than it is on the head of an agency within one of the cabinet departments. And finally, I do want to have as CSO someone who has some ability occasionally to trade off a bit of statistical purity for nonstatistical policy purposes, but in an informed and prudent manner.

Rudolph G. Penner. The difficult political problem is knowing how to perfect the statistics that are used to distribute billions of dollars around the economy. For example, the poverty line is in so many formula grants, and there are numerous other statistics of this type. As our experience on the CPI showed, it is almost impossible to improve fund allocating statistics because the improvement involves the rearrangement of so many bucks. I do not think a czar can do it. I have given thought to the notion of outside commissions and all sorts of other things, but it is a very serious problem because it generally means that we are stuck with very bad numbers, because they cannot be improved for political reasons.

Robert Eisner (from the floor). It seems to me that policymakers are circumscribed in their framework for discussion and decision by the data that happen to be available and by the way that these data are formulated. I hope that the economics profession and the data collection agencies themselves will show some initiative in terms of trying to recast data and collect data in series that would be useful.

Consider all of the discussion we hear on investment, and whether enough of our resources are going to investment, and what our national saving rate is. Those discussions are oriented overwhelmingly around a very narrow measure of investment. With all due respect to Charlie's objections to the theorists, any economist knows that investment constitutes all economic activity that accumulates wealth or resources for future production. The gross investment of our domestic economic series constitutes perhaps about 15%–20% of what we ought to count as investment, which would include human capital, government capital accumulation, household capital accumulation, investment in the environment, and the like. I hear economist after economist bemoaning that the national saving rate has gotten so low and that we have to do something. But the national saving rate they are talking about, whether low or not, has almost nothing to do with the national saving that provides wealth for the future. Some of us have made efforts collecting data of this kind, and the Bureau of Economic Analysis even had a section working on this, but the budget costs were such that the section was cut out. I do not know where to start to try to persuade policymakers, or the profession, to push. I think these conceptual issues may have a much bigger payoff for policy determination than all of the questions we are discussing about whether to have one statistical agency or many, or how to put them together.

Thomas Juster (from the floor). On Charlie's notion about the czar, it seems to me that the problem is not that the present set of things is not reasonably well coordinated. The basic difficulty is that there are lots of occasions in which what is needed is some kind of increase in resources from somewhere to do something that is nontrivial.

Everybody agrees we need to understand something about productivity in the services. That is not a new problem, that problem has been around since at least the 1960s; this is now the 1980s, the problem has gotten worse because the services have gotten bigger. At no point along the last several decades has someone in a policy-making position come along and said: "This is a problem where (*a*) there is some data we could generate and (*b*) some analysis needs to be done that we're going to support." I guess if you had a czar, and the czar had enough foresight, something might have been done about *x* years ago. Certainly something needs to be done about it now. But the input comes from one agency, the output from another agency, the price index is from a third agency, god knows if they are consistent.

The reason for a czar is that you cannot handle certain kinds of local allocation problems of a major sort. I am very uneasy, however, about putting it in a place (OMB) that has two functions—that is, minimize paperwork burden and minimize budget. As soon as you put a czar in a place where, if you want to do something you have to *not* do something else, that is bad news.

On public access to merged files, the barrier is that the central location for that is the Census Bureau; they are, with some justification, worried about the flak that will appear if someone goes and does something foolish. An obvious solution to that is put some pretty stiff penalties on people who abuse access to merged files. Then people would understand that, though there is a nonzero risk of identifying people, there is a pretty stiff penalty if you get accused of revealing confidential data, and you have got to pay it out of your own salary.

Somehow or other, you have to get away from the notion that you can't use merged files unless there's a nonzero risk of identification, because nothing that you ever do will give you a nonzero risk, and if it is so small as to be approaching zero, but still nonzero, the Census folks are under pressure of law to say they cannot afford to take the risk.

Charles L. Schultze. On the second point you made, I know little about it but based on what little I know I agree with you. On the first point, you did make one comment on which I think you have things backward—that the problem of putting the czar in OMB is like putting the fox in charge of the chickens. There exists, for example, a science adviser to the president who is often terribly useful in helping allocate among various science budgets, but who is terribly greedy in trying to enlarge the overall budget for science. So in my estimation the problem would be almost the other way—I might have a real claimant right in the middle of OMB. I do not think I would worry too much about the chief statistical officer being penurious. I would worry more that the budget director has got himself a presidential appointee representing a vested interest.

Rudolph G. Penner. I guess I disagree with that. I really do think that you have grave difficulty serving more than one goal. The problem goes beyond the point of just the budget for data collection. There are some sorts of data that some people would rather not collect, because they may suggest very expensive programs to correct some problem you formerly did not know about. So I think there would be very severe biases at OMB—biases we need very badly in all sorts of other policy areas.

Unidentified questioner from the floor. In this discussion of possible political problems in OMB or within an administration, we lose sight of another political question, and that is the direct statistical policy-making role of Congress. It seems to be increasing—for example, in the trade bill there are a lot of provisions about statistics. Do the speakers regard that as a problem?

Charles L. Schultze. You are quite right. I have not paid that much attention to the trade bill, but every trade bill apparently does it. In order to get a large majority vote on the Tokyo round trade bill in 1980, the then Special Trade Representative agreed to let Senator Russell Long put in an amendment that prohibited the Census Bureau from reporting currently the f.o.b. value of imports. These issues are not terribly important to somebody who is trying to negotiate a trade bill, so some stupid statistical things come out. I do not know what you do about it. You face it all the time, and I hope the less of it the better, but I do not have any answer.

Addresses of Contributors

B. K. Atrostic
Office of Tax Analysis
Department of the Treasury
Washington, DC 20224

Ernst R. Berndt
Sloan School of Management, E52–452
Massachusetts Institute of Technology
50 Memorial Drive
Cambridge, MA 02139

Roy Blough
10450 Lottsford Road
Mitchellville, MD 20716

Michael J. Boskin
Department of Economics
Stanford University
Stanford, CA 94305

Carol S. Carson
Bureau of Economic Analysis
U.S. Department of Commerce
Washington, DC 20230

Martin H. David
Department of Economics
University of Wisconsin
1180 Observatory Drive
Madison, WI 53706

W. Erwin Diewert
Department of Economics
University of British Columbia
Vancouver, BC V6T 1Y2
Canada

Martin Feldstein
President and Chief Executive Officer
National Bureau of Economic Research
1050 Massachusetts Avenue
Cambridge, MA 02138

Milton Friedman
Hoover Institution
Stanford, CA 94305

Zvi Griliches
National Bureau of Economic Research
1050 Massachusetts Avenue
Cambridge, MA 02138

Daniel S. Hamermesh
Department of Economics
Michigan State University
East Lansing, MI 48824

Charles R. Hulten
Department of Economics
University of Maryland
College Park, MD 20742

Dale W. Jorgenson
Department of Economics
Littauer Center, Room 122
Harvard University
Cambridge, MA 02138

Robert E. Lipsey
National Bureau of Economic Research
269 Mercer Street, 8th Floor
New York, NY 10003

Robert R. Nathan
Robert R. Nathan Associates
1301 Pennsylvania Avenue, NW
Suite 900
Washington, DC 20004

James R. Nunns
Office of Tax Analysis
Department of the Treasury
Washington, DC 20224

Robert P. Parker
Bureau of Economic Analysis (BE-7)
U.S. Department of Commerce
Washington, DC 20230

Rudolph G. Penner
The Urban Institute
2100 M Street, NW
Washington, DC 20037

Paul E. Pieper
Department of Economics
University of Illinois
Box 4348
Chicago, IL 60680

Roger B. Porter
John F. Kennedy School of Government
Harvard University
Cambridge, MA 02138

Sherwin Rosen
Department of Economics
University of Chicago
1126 East 59th Street
Chicago, IL 60637

Clifford S. Russell
Director
Vanderbilt Institute for Public Policy Studies
1208 18th Avenue, South
Nashville, TN 37212

Charles L. Schultze
The Brookings Institution
1775 Massachusetts Avenue
Washington, DC 20036

Carl Sumner Shoup
RR1 Box 303
Center Sandwich, CT 03227

V. Kerry Smith
Department of Economics and Business
North Carolina State University
Box 8110
Raleigh, NC 27695–8110

Ian A. Stewart
141 Cameron Avenue
Ottawa, Ontario K1F OX2
Canada

Thomas H. Tietenberg
Department of Economics
Colby College
Waterville, ME 04901

Jack E. Triplett
Chief Economist (BE-3)
Bureau of Economic Analysis
U.S. Department of Commerce
Washington, DC 20230

Author Index

Subject Index